MATERIAL CULTURE
IN AMERICA

MATERIAL CULTURE IN AMERICA

UNDERSTANDING EVERYDAY LIFE

HELEN SHEUMAKER

and

SHIRLEY TERESA WAJDA,

Editors

A B C ● C L I O

Santa Barbara, California
Denver, Colorado
Oxford, England

Material culture in America : understanding everyday life / Helen Sheumaker and Shirley Teresa Wajda, editors.
    p. cm.
    Includes bibliographical references and index.
    ISBN 978-1-57607-647-7 (hard copy : alk. paper) — ISBN 978-1-57607-648-4 (ebook) 1. Material culture—United States—History—Encyclopedias. I. Sheumaker, Helen. II. Wajda, Shirley Teresa.
GN560.U6M37 2008
306.097303—dc22

2007025074

12 11 10 09 08   1 2 3 4 5 6 7 8 9 10

This book is also available on the World Wide Web as an ebook. Visit www.abc-clio.com for details.

ABC-CLIO, Inc.
130 Cremona Drive, P.O. Box 1911
Santa Barbara, California 93116–1911

Senior Production Editor: Cami Cacciatore
Editorial Assistant: Sara Springer
Production Manager: Don Schmidt
Media Manager: Caroline Price
Media Editor: Ellen Rasmussen
File Manager: Paula Gerard

This book is printed on acid-free paper. ∞

Manufactured in the United States of America

Contents

List of Contributors

Janet Abbate, *Virginia Polytechnic Institute and State University*

Alexis Antracoli, *St. Francis University*

Kelly J. Baker, *Florida State University*

Mary Anne Beecher, *University of Oregon*

Elizabeth Belanger, *Brown University*

Megan Benton, *Pacific Lutheran University*

Zara Anishanslin Bernhardt, *University of Delaware*

Jeffrey Blankenship, *Smith College*

David Brody, *Parsons School of Design*

H. Christian Carr, *Sweet Briar College and Sweet Briar Museum*

Kerry Dean Carso, *State University of New York, New Paltz*

Natasha Casey, *independent scholar*

Hsiao-Yun Chu, *San Francisco State University and Stanford University Libraries*

Elise Madeleine Ciregna, *University of Delaware*

Matthew David Cochran, *University College, London*

Tom Collins, *University of Texas*

Gary Collison, *Pennsylvania State University, York*

Netta Davis, *Boston University*

Pamela Dorazio Dean, *Western Reserve Historical Society*

Donna M. DeBlasio, *Youngstown State University*

Thomas Andrew Denenberg, *Portland Museum of Art*

Virginia Dressler, *independent scholar*

Meredith Eliassen, *San Francisco State University*

Victoria Estrada-Berg, *University of North Texas*

Sandra M. Falero, *California State University, Fullerton*

Rachel Farebrother, *Swansea University*

Daniel Farr, *independent scholar*

Lyles Forbes, *The Mariners' Museum*

Kathleen Franz, *American University*

Susan Garfinkel, *Library of Congress*

Ellen Gruber Garvey, *New Jersey City University*

Mohammad Gharipour, *Georgia Institute of Technology*

Emily Godbey, *Iowa State University*

Beverly Gordon, *University of Wisconsin*

Rebecca S. Graff, *University of Chicago*

Beverly K. Grindstaff, *San Jose State University*

Jurretta Jordan Heckscher, *Library of Congress*

Bryn Varley Hollenbeck, *University of Delaware*

Evie T. Joselow, *independent art historian*
Nicholas Katers, *independent writer*
Heidi Kenaga, *University of Memphis*
Susan A. Kern, *College of William and Mary*
Steven Lubar, *Brown University*
Laura A. Macaluso, *City University of New York, Graduate Center*
Kirin Makker, *Smith College*
Martin J. Manning, *U.S. Department of State*
Donald B. Marti, *Indiana University at South Bend*
Katherine Stebbins McCaffrey, *Boston University*
W. Douglas McCombs, *Albany Institute of History and Art*
Alexis McCrossen, *Southern Methodist University*
Karen McGarry, *Trent University*
Jay Mechling, *University of California, Davis*
Molly Merryman, *Kent State University*
Melinda Talbot Nasardinov, *Historic New England*
Rebecca R. Noel, *Plymouth State University*
Monica Obniski, *Art Institute of Chicago*
Michael O'Malley, *George Mason University*
J. Todd Ormsbee, *San Jose State University*
Katherine Ott, *National Museum of American History, Smithsonian Institution*
Krista M. Park, *University of Maryland*
Gabriella M. Petrick, *New York University*
Christine Photinos, *National University*
Linna F. Place, *University of Missouri, Kansas City*
William S. Pretzer, *Western Michigan University*
Jennifer Pustz, *Historic New England*
Elizabeth Redkey, *Siena College*
Tina Reuwsaat, *Southern Oregon Historical Society*

Jeffrey Reznick, *Institute for the Study of Health and Occupation, American Occupational Therapy Foundation*
Robert B. Ridinger, *University Libraries, Northern Illinois University*
Janet S. Rose, *University of Kansas*
Michael K. Rosenow, *University of Illinois at Urbana-Champaign*
Rachel Sailor, *University of North Texas*
Lynn Sally, *New York University*
Ann Schofield, *University of Kansas*
Ezra Shales, *Alfred University*
Aaris Sherin, *St. John's University*
Helen Sheumaker, *Miami University (Ohio)*
Ami Sommariva, *University of California, Davis*
Susan V. Spellman, *Carnegie Mellon University*
Matt Stefon, *Boston University*
Anne Stephenson, *University of Chicago*
Elizabeth Throop, *Eastern Kentucky University*
Katherine Leonard Turner, *University of Delaware*
Janet Tyson, *University of North Texas*
Terrence L. Uber, *Kent State University*
Shirley Teresa Wajda, *Kent State University*
Katherine Walker, *University of Richmond*
Jason Weems, *University of Michigan–Dearborn*
Jane Weiss, *State University of New York, Old Westbury*
Tamara Wilde, *University of Iowa*
Elizabeth A. Williams, *Nelson-Atkins Museum of Art*
Psyche Williams-Forson, *University of Maryland*
Wendy A. Woloson, *Library Company of Philadelphia*
James Yasko, *National Baseball Hall of Fame*

Introduction

As you drove, rode, or walked—or even bicycled—to the library in which you may be reading this introduction, you moved through a built environment planned and created by others to accommodate specific activities. Your trip to the library was constrained by street placement, traffic laws, and traffic lights. Once on the sidewalk, you may have had to navigate decorative sidewalk planters, benches, fountains, and steps. Once inside the library, you may have passed through a turnstile or metal detector and stored your backpack. All along the way, from your home to the library, you were moving within an environment that not only reflects what was deemed practical and sensible but also mirrors larger social, cultural, economic, and historical patterns: How theories of urban planning altered the way individuals interacted within cities. How the adaptation of electricity lengthened the day and made cities attractive. How the manufacture of materials such as concrete, glass, rubber, and plastic and their uses ease aspects of our lives but create problems of waste. How books work.

The fact is, at every moment of every day, you are surrounded by, interact with, and are defined by objects made or altered by humans. Whenever you touch things, you connect with other humans, past and present. Your grandmother's quilt warms you in the winter and reminds you of her tenderness. Do you recall how she made the quilt? The pattern she created? Did she fashion the quilt of scraps from her other sewing projects, or did she purchase the material as well as the pattern? Did she sew the coverlet by hand or with a machine? The bicycle you learned to ride when you were a child brings to mind memories of scraped knees and the thrill of speed. Perhaps your parents gave you the bike as a much-desired birthday present. You may not have considered, however, how the bike was designed and manufactured by persons unknown to you. You may not have understood how it came to be sold to your parents by retailers at a specialty bicycle store or a discount "big box" store.

Material culture encompasses those things that have physical form and presence, whether an object you can hold in your hand; an environment in which you live, work, worship, or play; or an image of the landscape you captured with your digital camera as you traversed a pond or a mountain range. Material culture is, then, culture made material—that is, it is the physical manifestations of human endeavor, of minds at work (and play), of social, economic, and political processes affecting all of us. The scholarly analysis of human made or altered environments and things is called *material culture studies*. It is an awkward phrase, to be sure. Yet its emphasis on the material to explore and understand the invisible systems of meaning that humans share—culture—makes it a worthy endeavor. Many people, from university scholars and museum curators to amateur collectors, explore the past and present not through documents but through objects and images, buildings and structures, and the human-altered environment.

This volume introduces readers to the types and forms of American material culture as embodied in the various approaches adopted by scholars, curators, and collectors. An important innovator in the field, art historian Jules David Prown (1982, 2) observed, "the term *material* culture . . . refers quite directly and efficiently, if not elegantly, both to the subject matter of the study, *material*, and to its purpose, the understanding of *culture*." Where objects are subjects, material culture specialists may be found. Individuals with training in art, aesthetics, materials conservation, history, anthropology and archaeology, technology, architecture, economics, sociology, museum studies, and library science bring a variety of perspectives, theories, and methodologies to the field. Included in this volume, then, are entries on the various academic disciplines that incorporate material culture in the study of American society and culture, past and present. Entries include discussions of theoretical issues, methodologies, and professional practice—that is, how material culture is organized for the purposes of analysis, interpretation, and exhibition. The majority of the entries engage Americans' material lives, from clothing to automobiles to houses to cities to junk.

The entries in this volume exemplify material culture studies as "centrifugal" or a "pattern," one that Kenneth L. Ames (1980, 295) described as moving "outward from small issues to larger, more encompassing, and more fundamental concerns." The promise of American material culture studies has been, and remains, to expand the understanding of human existence through attention to the relationships between objects and people in what anthropologist Mary Douglas (1979), speaking of consumption, has called the "world of goods." To that end, we endeavored to include entries that engage broadly specific forms of American material but also entries that reflect how a cultural phenomenon, such as aging or consumption or ethnicity, may be more fruitfully explored by including things in its study. In short, a consideration of the material culture of Americans' lives allows us to tell a richer, more complex story of the nation and its peoples. Indeed, such a consideration changes what we know and how we tell the nation's stories.

Material culture studies in the United States has found a professional home both in the museum and in the interdisciplinary field of American Studies. The alliance of material culture studies and American Studies is based on the necessity of employing the theories and methodologies of a variety of disciplines, as well as deriving new knowledge at disciplinary interstices. Both fields explore the geopolitical unit called the United States of America and the idea of America. American Studies programs across the nation feature training in material culture studies, and the American Studies Association hosts the Material Culture Caucus.

History of Material Culture Studies in the United States

The study of the material culture of the United States is a relatively recent academic field, but the collection and study of artifacts have taken place since before the nation's founding. Americans have always attempted to understand the world through things and in so doing preserved material culture, created collections, and undertook historical and cultural interpretation with tangible things. Men and women living in the seventeenth, eighteenth, and nineteenth centuries tended to collect "antiquities" of ancient (or at least very old) or extinct societies, relatively newer relics of historical places and persons, and, of course, family heirlooms. In 1786 Charles Willson Peale (1741–1827) created his museum in Philadelphia devoted to the exhibition of oddities and antiquities for the paying public. What gives Peale a claim to being an investigator of American material culture is that he was interested in codifying an "American type" through the unique specimens of natural history found only in North America. In addition, Peale, as an artist, created a portrait gallery of American revolutionary heroes in an effort to characterize an American type distinct from European national characters.

Thus, American material culture studies began in the hands of collectors, individuals intent on collecting not only fine art but also objects they believed represented an American type independent of—or at least different from—other cultures. In the face of the Industrial Revolution, Americans saved artifacts of Native Americans, "antique" hand tools, and relics of a past that seemed to be quickly slipping away. As the new nation involved itself in overseas trade, the souvenirs of distant places and peoples were also objects of curiosity and collecting. Americans enjoyed creating collections of their own. Children in particular were encouraged to create "cabinets of curiosities" filled with natural specimens, such as leaves, moss, minerals, and insects, or "found" objects of interest, such as pictures given as premiums for the purchase of household goods or souvenirs from visitors. Early historical societies were likewise cabinets of curiosities; Peale had employed Linnaean classification to his North American natural history specimens; the systems of classification that would order later library and museum collections were not developed until further along in the century.

In 1876, the United States held its centennial in Philadelphia, but interest in colonial-era American relics had been increasing in New England and the Great Lakes states since the Civil War (1861–1865), when women adopted historic dress costumes and created "New England kitchens" as part of United States Sanitary Commission fairs to raise funds for the care of soldiers. Even before the war southern women were "rescuing" the past; Ann Pamela Cunningham (1816–1875), for example, formed the Mount Vernon Ladies' Association in 1853 to acquire and restore the home of George and Martha Washington. Colonial-era household furnishings and decorative arts, Revolutionary War–era memorabilia and relics related to historic personages all became desired collectibles by individuals and museums, especially after the 1893 Columbian Exposition in Chicago, where the Liberty Bell, among many Revolutionary War–era artifacts, were displayed.

State historical societies began with the formation of the Massachusetts Historical Society in 1791. National, state, and local historical societies valued antiquarian material culture, collecting single items with historically valuable provenance. For example, the Smithsonian Institution, founded in 1846, has the uniform coat, waistcoat, and knee breeches of George Washington (1732–1799), the first president of the United States. In some ways, this era marks the beginning of material culture studies, since collectors, borrowing from the methods used by historians of art and architecture and archaeologists, were interpreting material culture to understand and narrate the nation's past.

That past seemed a simpler time after the devastation of the Civil War and the rampant industrialization of the Gilded Age. For native-born white Protestants, nostalgia for the past was a salve against the forces of modernization. Immigrants from southern and eastern Europe flocked to U.S. cities, presenting to some a threat to American traditions and democracy. The United States' entrance onto the world stage through war and trade led to the oversight of colonial populations that, with immigrants at home, brought issues of race, ethnicity, and equality to the fore. Subjugated peoples became subjects of study. By the 1890s, anthropologists were also paying sustained attention to Native American cultures, and systematically investigated the material culture traditions of different tribal groups through fieldwork and collection. Many scholars and curators involved with the collection activities acted from an impulse to preserve the cultures they believed to be dying out and thus in danger of being lost. Today, scholars and representatives of those various peoples point out that these same practices reinforced racial and cultural ideologies that had originally undermined and sometimes decimated Native American peoples as they were colonized. Current national and international efforts at repatriating cultural property recognizes these efforts as forms of looting or plundering; how modern law intersects with differing ideas of ownership, possession, and rights in the past is only beginning to be examined.

While interest in Native American material culture often stemmed from a belief that those cultures were essentially "dead" and not integral to the history of the United States, historians focused on the experiences of white European colonists in a belief that that past constituted a "real" American story. Though professional historians embraced the "scientific" method of historical analysis dependent on documentary sources, other individuals, especially women, focused on the artifacts of everyday life. Alice Morse Earle (1853–1911) wrote seventeen books on colonial life in British New England. Local and state historical societies, many of which were founded just after the Civil War, were restructured and began collecting artifacts as well as documents. National women's groups often concentrated on the collection of American relics; the Colonial Dames of America was founded in 1890, and the Daughters of the American Revolution had a national organization by 1896. Both organizations included in their activities the preservation of dwellings they deemed historically important. The emphasis on buildings as biography and history and the perceived preeminence of New England as the "birthplace" of American culture were also evident in the entrepreneurial activities of antiquarian Wallace Nutting (1861–1941) to promote historical tourism and reproduction furnishings and the establishment in 1910 of the Society for the Preservation of New England Antiquities (now Historic New England).

In the 1920s, the nation's wealthy underwrote private and public collections and historic preservation. Automaker Henry Ford (1863–1947) began collecting historic buildings and artifacts for his re-creation of American everyday life now called the Henry Ford Museum and Greenfield Village in Dearborn, Michigan. Wealthy collector-philanthropist John D. Rockefeller, Jr. (1874–1960) provided funds in 1927 to restore what is now Colonial Williamsburg in Virginia. Extant museums shifted collecting policies from the high arts and culture of Europe to American art, sculpture, and decorative arts. The Metropolitan Museum of Art in New York City added its American Wing in 1924 with the help of donor and collector Richard Townley Haines Halsey (1865–1942). There visitors could view period rooms—exhibit spaces furnished with period-correct interior architectural finishes, wall hangings, furniture, and other domestic decorative arts.

In addition, major periodicals promoting the interest in collecting were founded in this decade. *The Magazine Antiques*, for example, was first published in 1922. Leading collectors and curators lent their expertise through sensitive examination of not only the physical attributes of objects but also the historical circumstances of their manufacture, use, and circulation. Today, these individuals are called *antiquarians*. Their studies are characterized as overtly nostalgic; indeed, many antiquarians did yearn for a bygone era of supposedly greater virtue and republican mores. Nevertheless, their emphasis on the things of the past provided new avenues of historical research.

The study of American material culture was greatly enhanced and democratized through New Deal funding of President Franklin Delano Roosevelt (1882–1945). The Index of American Design, containing some 20,000 illustrations of American decorative and utilitarian objects, employed artists through the auspices of the Federal Art Project. Reflecting the quest to document the common folk as well as create a "usable past," the Index, along with the Historic Sites Survey, constituted the first comprehensive inventory of the nation's decorative arts and built environment. In addition, the Farm Security Administration's documentary photograph surveys chronicled the nation's everyday life. The Federal Writers' Project employed folklorists, anthropologists, and writers to compile oral histories and ex-slave narratives. The products of these efforts as well as state guides comprise a lasting record of the material culture of everyday life.

After World War II (1939–1945), material culture studies emerged as an academic field crossing several disciplines. The emergence of the United States as a world power and the perceived necessity of defining American culture as exceptional and apart from the Socialist and Communist nations during the cold war led to a flurry of studies promoting the somewhat celebratory idea of "American Exceptionalism." Although its roots may be traced to the 1930s, the interdisciplinary field of American Studies was expanded through the establishment of many university departments and programs. American Studies scholars embraced material culture studies in their examinations of American literature, the arts, and history.

Yet it was the social and political activism of the 1960s and 1970s that led to the permanent inclusion of American material culture studies in course offerings. The quest for civil rights by African Americans, women, and Native Americans, as well as efforts to achieve social justice for the poor, the uneducated, and the unemployed led scholars, particularly historians, to question traditional narratives of American history. Borrowing from the "pots and pans" history of early twentieth-century antiquarians as well as the insights of French scholars seeking to write "total history," these "New Social Historians" sought to recover the histories of those Americans who did not leave their own written records. The collections of museums and historical societies and historic houses became centers for such study, providing through collecting, exhibition, and interpretation innovative insights into the lives of almost all Americans, not only the elite. Aiding this investigation were expanded federal and state government programs in historic preservation, as well as the popular curiosity about the nation's past centering on the 1976 bicentennial.

Scholarly journals dedicated to American material culture studies were founded in this era as well and were distinct from earlier antiquarian or collectors' magazines. *Winterthur*

Portfolio, established by the Henry Francis du Pont Winterthur Museum in 1964 to publish scholarship in American decorative arts, expanded in 1979 to include all American material culture. *Pioneer America: The Journal of Historic American Material Culture*, the publication of the Pioneer America Society, was founded in 1978. The journal is now named *Material Culture*. Established more recently were scholarly journals dedicated to the international study of material culture: the *Journal of Material Culture* (1999) and *Home Cultures* (2004).

Objects embody power and thus serve to define relationships of individuals and groups. The conditions of an object's manufacture have historically concerned material culture scholars, but only as far as this knowledge accounts for the physical properties and specific history of the object. With the insights of cultural studies, material culture scholars are now interested in distribution systems—economic, technological, commercial—that allow the study of the allocation and circulation of power within a society. The shift from connoisseurship and artifact analysis to the analysis of objects as cultural commodities and as social relation is a dramatic and necessary one.

Representation, as another focus of cultural studies scholarship, has also proved influential. The "message" or "meaning" of an object was understood as stable over time. Reflecting the adaptation of art-historical formal analysis, material culture studies held to the assumption that objects worthy of collection and study should be beautiful and that that judgment was not historically contingent. In short, a thing of beauty in the eighteenth century would always be a thing of beauty. Today the field acknowledges through its scholarship that meaning not only shifts over time but also is dependent upon its audience. Objects do not possess fixed meanings. Individuals, whose responses are structured by an array of factors (social position, gender, economic background, educational level, race, ethnicity, etc.), "know" objects in different ways.

For example, an ornate silver service can connote wealth, high status, the mastery of elaborate etiquette, and leisure. For the house servant, though, the same set can represent hard, physical work; long hours of lifting, standing, walking, carrying, and attending to others; and a different form of mastery: that of exacting preparation and maintenance of domestic and serving skills. As another example, one of the overriding goals of advertisers is to "fix," or stabilize, the meaning of a product. "A motor scooter is fun!" advertisements exclaim. Woe to the motor scooter manufacturer, however, if teenagers simply reject that message and instead view motor scooters as nerdy, pitiful, ugly, and worst of all, uncool.

One drawback of cultural studies theory is that its practitioners often do not consider the physical, tactile "thing-ness" of material culture, emphasizing as it does critical theory and abstraction. Thus material culture studies offers a vital corrective to this tendency toward generalization. As Dick Hebdige (1981) asks: Is an image of a motor scooter *the* motor scooter? No. The elision of the material object for its visual representation ignores humans' other senses (touch, smell, taste, for example) as well as insights to be gained through the physical, and not virtual, inspection of design, manufacture, and use.

How to Use this Volume

This encyclopedia is not an antiquer's or collector's guide. The specificity of guides dedicated to one type or era of a given object or to a specific maker or type of fabrication furthers our knowledge of the object, enhances connoisseurship, and democratizes collection activities. As much as one purpose of American material culture studies is the encyclopedic survey of American things, it is not yet possible within the confines of one volume to account for, describe, and discuss the full wealth of material culture created, used, and altered by various groups in the American experience. What this volume attempts to provide, however, is a map of American material culture and its study. Maps outline and describe, providing instruction and necessary information for further knowledge. We conceptualized entries in three categories: The first category includes the scholarly disciplines and fields that emphasize or incorporate material culture as subjects or evidence, and the documentary evidence that scholars use to study material life. The second category contains entries defining and discussing various aspects of human experience within the boundaries of what is now the United States. The last category contains entries on classes, forms, and types of American material culture—the stuff itself. The volume reflects the field's historic emphasis on everyday life and domestic material culture but also includes entries that push beyond that emphasis.

The bibliography offers listings of journals, the seminal works of American material culture studies theory and methodology, useful research tools, selected studies on specific objects, and a general survey of works, categorized by the larger scholarly approaches to the field. We have attempted to include essays published in journals that remain unindexed in major journal databases now available on the World Wide Web.

Acknowledgments

We are indebted to many. Miriam Forman-Brunell initiated this project and remains a source of friendship and wise advice. Susan Garfinkel not only wrote important entries but generously offered much needed advice at all the right times. With her expertise as editor of *Winterthur Portfolio*, Lisa Lock suggested strategies and authors that were always perfect and welcome. Advisory board members Simon Bronner, Miriam Forman-Brunell, Susan Garfinkel, Beverly Gordon, Karal Ann Marling, and Charles McGovern contributed by writing entries or giving advice and by the example of their excellent work in the field. Early in the process editor James Ciment provided wise and timely counsel. At ABC-CLIO, Alex Mikaberidze, Craig Hunt, Cami Cacciatore, and Ellen Rasmussen were patient, good-humored, and always quick with replies and welcome guidance.

The scope of this project has changed greatly from our initial conception. We thank all the contributors who not only wrote engaging and informative entries but who, in their initial responses to our requests and calls, reminded us of what we had not yet or fully considered. The volume is much the better for all the discussions we have had with contributors. It is a bit poorer for the entries that went unwritten either for the lack of scholarship devoted to a certain subject or the unavailability of the appropriate scholar or expert.

We found in the course of our work that many individuals have widely varying ideas of what *material culture* means and what its study requires. Though one of the early goals of American material culture studies was to create a systematic approach to the study of all material things, the field remains divided among the imperatives of various disciplines and between university-affiliated scholars and museum professionals. We hope, however, that the work at hand helps to further the dialogue about the field, its shape, and its promise. We further hope that readers find this volume useful in their own study of Americans' material culture.

We dedicate this volume to the memory of Rodris Roth. Rodris, who joined the Smithsonian Institution as a curator in 1956, was an exemplary material culture studies scholar in and of the United States. Landmark articles such as her essay on the material universe and etiquette of eighteenth-century tea drinking contextualized the meanings and uses of the most everyday things of life. She not only served the discipline of history and expanded the study of American material culture but she also contributed to the nation's sense of self through her decades of work at the National Museum of American History and other institutions, her varied scholarship, and her activities in countless historical groups. That this volume exists at all is due in part to Rodris's gracious example of the worth and joy of illuminating the past for others.

References and Further Reading
Ames, Kenneth L. 1980. "Folk Art: The Challenge and the Promise." In *Perspectives on American Folk Art*, ed. Ian M. G. Quimby and Scott T. Swank, 293–324. New York: W. W. Norton.
Douglas, Mary, and Baron Isherwood. 1979. *The World of Goods: Toward an Anthropology of Consumption*. New York: Basic Books.
Hebdige, Dick, 1981. "Object as Image: The Italian Scooter Cycle." *Block* 5: 44–64.
Prown, Jules David. 1982. "Mind in Matter: An Introduction to Material Culture Theory and Method." *Winterthur Portfolio* 17 (1): 1–19.
Schlereth, Thomas J. 1982. *Material Culture Studies in America: An Anthology*. Nashville, TN: American Association for State and Local History.
St. George, Robert Blair, ed. 1988. *Material Life in America, 1600–1850*. Boston: Northeastern University Press.

Adolescence

The transitional period between childhood and adulthood is *adolescence*, also known as the *teenage* years. In the United States, this life stage is often perceived as a stressful phase marked by rebellious behavior, bodily changes (puberty), and the search for a sense of identity. While the term was used as early as the mid-1500s, it was in 1904, with the publication of psychologist G. Stanley Hall's *Adolescence*, that the life stage was generally recognized in American culture. Material culture plays a significant role in adolescent life, and it functions as a means of expressing a sense of individual and group identity.

Hairstyles, body piercings, tattoos, clothing, food, magazines, movies, video games, music, and increasingly, portable technology such as iPods and cell phones are markers of personal expression. Having the "right" hairstyle or brand of jeans is a way of both achieving acceptance in a desired group and communicating status. Individual choices about material culture also intersect with group identities to which adolescents wish to conform. Magazines devoted to teen culture flourished after World War II (1939–1945), and continue to be popular.

Adolescence is often marked by rebellion. Many teenagers try for the first time activities or substances proscribed by law or adults: sex, cigarettes, alcohol, and drugs. This rebellious trend is epitomized by the young 1950s movie star James Dean (1931–1955). With his cigarettes, slicked-back hair, and leather jacket, Dean effectively utilized material culture to serve as a poster boy for American teen rebellion.

Group activities are an important component of adolescent life. Many teenagers are involved in sports competitions, music, drama, academic clubs, or other social activities. Many undergo various life change rituals during adolescence. Religious rituals like Jewish bar/bat mitzvahs or Catholic confirmations, both occurring around age thirteen, represent symbolic steps toward adulthood. Between the ages of sixteen and eighteen, most American adolescents learn to drive and acquire a driver's license, begin to vote, and are eligible for military service. High school graduation, accompanied by a senior portrait photograph, a prom, and a commencement ceremony, signals the passage from adolescence to adulthood.

Karen McGarry

See also Adulthood; Body Modification; Childhood; Education and Schooling; Human Body; Rite, Ritual, and Ceremony

References and Further Reading

Hall, G. Stanley. 1904. *Adolescence: Its Psychology and Its Relation to Physiology, Anthropology, Sociology, Sex, Crime, Religion and Education.* New York: D. Appleton and Company.

Milner, Murray, Jr. 2004. *Freaks, Geeks, and Cool Kids: American Teenagers, Schools, and the Culture of Consumption.* New York: Routledge.

Vadeboncoeur, Jennifer A., and Lisa Patel Stevens, eds. 2005. *Re/Constructing "the Adolescent": Sign, Symbol, and the Body.* New York: Peter Lang.

Adulthood

Human *adulthood* covers the years from the late teens to the end of life and is often equated with sexual maturity. This life stage interfaces with a range of material culture in the United States whereby experience, class, gender, and ethnicity figure in historic and contemporary definitions of adulthood and expectations about behavior and responsibilities. These definitions are codified by law (evident in rules governing military service, marriage, and alcohol consumption), society (rites of passage such as debutante balls and high school graduation), and family and social custom. Adult humans overwhelmingly design, create, and use material culture; the "average" human (typically male) organizes the American built environment and the dimensions of the objects humans daily use. Material culture thus orders experience and defines status based on age and its attendant meanings and responsibilities.

Secular rituals of American adults employ distinct artifacts. Historically, adult lifespan changes were reflected in clothing (such as styles specific to courtship, marriage, widowhood, work, and leisure activities); accommodations (specific to disability, pregnancy, and the elderly, for example); and physical, legal, and social transitions (such as menopause, divorce, retirement, becoming a parent or grandparent, and burying a loved one). Young adults' material culture includes artifacts associated with coming of age, such as a driver's license or voting card, dating or getting engaged, and sexual initiation. The size and style of everyday objects delineate adulthood: Sports equipment and grooming devices are fitted to the body, for example. Often forms change in style to demarcate adulthood: Boys in the nineteenth and early twentieth centuries wore knee breeches ("short pants"), adopting long trousers upon achieving manhood. Age-specific music and magazines in the twentieth and twenty-first centuries reveal the use of life stages as marketing strategy as much as recognizing that each stage possesses its own consumer goods to shape identity.

The onset of biological maturity requires specific material culture in the care of the body, for example, shaving toiletries, cosmetics, and birth control medication and devices. Adult body modification includes permanent changes such as tattoos, piercings, and cosmetic surgery and temporary modification provided by such garments as girdles, brassieres, support hose, wigs, and toupees. Other adult activities employ various sexual aids and contraceptive devices and alcohol, drug, and tobacco accessories, such as shaving toiletries, cosmetics, birth control medication and devices, and clothing.

To cope with the temptations and exigencies of grown-up life, adults have gathered into groups such as the nineteenth-century men's secret societies, the anti-vice societies fueled by the Comstock laws, temperance groups, suffrage societies, book clubs, abolition and anti-lynching associations, unions, fraternities and sororities, and more recently, support groups such as Alcoholics Anonymous or the Cancer Survivors Network. Such groups use symbols, ritual artifacts, and print to secure goals or maintain and inform membership.

Katherine Ott

See also Adolescence; Human Aging and the Aged; Human Body; Rite, Ritual, and Ceremony; Sex and Sexuality

References and Further Reading

Featherstone, Mike, Mike Hepworth, and Bryan Turner, eds. 1995. *The Body: Social Process and Cultural Theory*. London: Sage.

Kidwell, Claudia Brush, and Valerie Steele. 1989. *Men and Women: Dressing the Part*. Washington, DC: Smithsonian Institution Press.

Advertisements and Advertising

To *advertise* is to make something publicly known. With the rise of trade in the nineteenth century, advertising was not only increasingly devoted to making the public aware of goods and services but to persuade the public to purchase them. Advertisements served to reflect the social world and cultural values and to orient individuals toward new and changing values through the attachment of values to things. In doing so, advertisements offer evidence of humans' attitudes toward and consumption of material objects. The history of advertisements is the history of changing social and cultural values, media technology, and business practice.

Colonial-Era Print Culture

Advertisements did not appear until the 1600s. These advertisements, at least in England and the American colonies, predominantly took the form of printed handbills and broadsides that publicized both social events, such as fairs, and items for purchase, such as coffee, tea, and other consumer goods.

Advertisements, which early on were in the form of descriptive lists presented in a single column without illustration and in the same typeface as the news, appeared in newspapers throughout the colonies as a means of support for printers to offset subscription rates. Advertisements announced the availability of coffee, tea, turtles, books, wigs, wine, and entertainment, as well as slaves and servants. Notices of lost possessions, including runaway slaves, servants, and wives, often appeared with the enticement of a monetary reward. Such items reveal much about the social relations of colonists as well as their material life.

Nineteenth-Century Industrialization

With increasing literacy and wealth, advertisements became more common in the nineteenth century. First appearing in the 1700s, "personal" advertisements became increasingly common. These notices or cards ranged from seeking jobs and workers to pursuing matrimony or declaring divorce. Advertisements began to appear on passenger vehicles and even on placards that were carried for display by a person. During the 1830s and 1840s improvements in printing such as lithography and steam-powered printing presses resulted in the proliferation of posters. Posters advertising performances and services, and to some degree products, were plastered on public and private buildings. Responding to criticism and legal action, bill posters resorted to working at night to avoid being caught by police officers. By the late 1830s billposter plastering had become so problematic that it was regulated in many cities.

The rise of mass industrialization introduced many changes in advertising practices.

Advertising space in newspapers was first sold in 1864, and in 1867 Lord & Taylor department store became the first to use double-column newspaper advertising. Nationally distributed monthly magazines began to carry advertising. The emergence of brand names and trademarks in the 1870s necessitated informative advertising to win customers' loyalty: Borden's Condensed Milk, Quaker Oats, Heinz sauces, Singer sewing machines, and Kodak cameras became household items. Vividly colored trade cards, popularized by lithographer Louis Prang (1824–1909), were mass produced to sell brand-name goods throughout the United States. The introduction of nationally distributed mail order catalogues in the 1870s brought advertising into more American homes. The 1884 invention of the Linotype composing machine increased efficiency and lowered costs of printing and permitted cheaper color printing. Color (or chromo) lithography enlivened posters and billboards. Advertisements were regarded by many as visual pollution but were embraced by others as art. Consumer products began to employ beauty and sex appeal in an attempt to attract a consumer audience. For example, beautiful women were incorporated into advertisements seeking to sell products as varied as bicycles and cigarettes. Celebrities such as minister Henry Ward Beecher (1813–1887) lent their reputations and words to sell goods—in Beecher's case, Waltham watches and Pear's soap.

Twentieth-Century Mass Culture and Mass Consumption

By the early 1900s, mass industrialization, new products, and increased market competition led advertisers to create not only new methods to encourage the consumption of goods but also to establish a profession dedicated to that endeavor. *Printer's Ink*, a magazine aimed at advertisers, was established in 1881. Although Philadelphian Volney B. Palmer (1799–1864) established the first American advertising agency in 1841 and such enterprises were found in major American cities in the Gilded Age, copywriters (those who wrote advertising text), illustrators, and designers formed a new professional class in the early twentieth century. Advertising agencies took advantage of new forms of cultural technology as well as studies of psychology, sampling, and lifestyle consumption to expose large numbers of potential consumers to their goods and services. Advertising in the 1920s began to integrate social identity and the consumption of goods—it was no longer about encouraging people to want things, but about enforcing a feeling of shame or embarrassment for not possessing certain goods.

Radio shows were advertisements, with entertainment interspersed with lengthy commercial appeals from the show's sponsors. (*Soap opera* is derived from radio broadcasts of daytime drama programs that were sponsored by laundry detergent manufacturers.) Airplanes were used to advertise products by flying over vacation and recreation destinations with banners.

Billboards and postings alongside roadways began to flourish as Americans embraced auto travel; estimates suggest that by 1908 1,610 miles of billboards were erected across the United States. Beginning in the 1920s, electrified signs and billboards appeared (the earliest, albeit rare, electric signs date back to the late 1870s). New York City became known for its electric displays; for example, in 1930 Times Square had an electric Wrigley's Gum advertisement eight stories high and a block long.

Television commercials, with their ability to employ moving action, appeared in the 1940s. As with radio, television shows were advertisements in themselves, with commercial sponsorship of each program. Typically, television shows opened with an announcement, "brought to you by . . ." While early television shows, often funded by businesses seeking to sell products or services, were built around product placement, today's television advertising is dominated by commercials that appear between programs. Some remnants of product placement, as a means of defraying production costs, persist as films and television shows feature product placement within their visual narratives.

In the 1980s advertisers began to take advantage of the World Wide Web. Advertisements continued to incorporate visually stimulating tactics, such as vivid colors and eye-catching pictorials. Advertising can now "pop up" and appear when one is online. Internet advertising as yet is subject to little regulation and is not constrained by geographic considerations. As Internet use of search engines has increased, advertisers have also exploited these Web sites by paying to position their companies or products at the top of search lists.

Advertising has evolved from simple statements of a product's availability or virtue to today's advertising that weds individual identity to products. Consumers often participate in this process, even displaying commerce on their bodies, usually through clothing emblazoned with logos, political slogans, and brand names. Consumers are, in essence, purchasing products and paying for the privilege to serve as advertisements for other potential consumers. Today, Americans are inundated with so many advertisements that it is difficult for any one ad to attract an audience.

Daniel Farr

See also Commercials; Consumerism and
   Consumption; Graphic Design; Mail Order

Catalogues; Patents, Trademarks, and
Brands; Political Ephemera; Popular Culture;
Print Culture; Trade Cards; Trade Catalogues

References and Further Reading
Ewen, Stuart. 1976. *Captains of Consciousness: Advertising and the Social Roots of Consumer Culture.* New York: McGraw-Hill.
Gudis, Catherine. 2004. *Buyways: Billboards, Automobiles, and the American Landscape.* New York: Routledge.
Henkin, David M. 1998. *City Reading: Written Words and Public Spaces in Antebellum New York.* New York: Columbia University Press.
Lears, T. J. Jackson. 1994. *Fables of Abundance: A Cultural History of Advertising in America.* New York: Basic Books.
Marchand, Roland. 1986. *Advertising the American Dream: Making Way for Modernity, 1920–1940.* Berkeley: University of California Press.

Aesthetic Movement

The American Aesthetic Movement was a short-lived (1870s–1880s), influential effort to incorporate the principles of art and beauty into everyday life. Spurred by the publication in the United States in 1872 of Charles Locke Eastlake's (1836–1908) *Hints on Household Taste* and inspired by the display of exotic art and artifacts at the United States Centennial Exhibition of 1876, men and especially women dedicated themselves to learning, creating, and purchasing well-made and beautiful things. Painting, architecture, and the decorative arts were the media of Aesthetic principles.

"Art for art's sake" has often been employed to describe the Aesthetic Movement's philosophy. Yet an examination of the many treatises and decorating manuals published by its adherents argues that the quest for the beautiful was a moral one. George Ward Nichols' (1837–1885) *Art Education Applied to Industry* (1877) called for art

Art pottery was but one product of the Aesthetic Movement. These examples from Maria Longworth Nichols Storer's Rookwood Pottery of Cincinnati, Ohio, were displayed at the 1904 St. Louis World's Fair. (Library of Congress)

teaching as an antidote to overmechanization and the loss of humanity, and Clarence Cook's (1828–1900) *The House Beautiful* (1878) served as a decorating bible. Middle- and upper-class Americans created societies and clubs dedicated to all or one of the decorative arts, and they established magazines such as *The Art Amateur: Devoted to the Cultivation of Art in the Household* (1879–1903) to promote their ideas.

The Aesthetic Movement fostered collective endeavors. Associated Artists, for example, was a decorative firm cofounded in 1879 by textile artist Candace Wheeler (1827–1923) and artist-designer Louis Comfort Tiffany (1848–1943). George Ward Nichols' wife, Maria Longworth Nichols Storer (1849–1932) founded Rookwood Pottery in 1880

after her experience in an amateur art pottery club in Cincinnati, Ohio, a center of arts activity in the era.

The domestic interior was the focus of the Aesthetic Movement. Interiors were harmonious in color and tone (browns, greens, and grays were popular), but elaborate and often geometric "surface ornaments" in contrasting vibrant colors covered walls, furniture, screens, window and door textiles, and other surfaces. Rejecting the dependency on historical style such as the then-popular Renaissance Revival, Aesthetic designers borrowed freely from the past as well as from distant cultures such as Japan, India, and Persia. Nature provided popular textile and silverware motifs such as lilies, sunflowers, peacocks, butterflies, and dragonflies. The emphasis on authenticity and faithful reproduction characteristic of other art movements was not at work here.

One defining feature of Aesthetic design was its practice of combining historical design with the exotic; the asymmetry of Japanese art influenced ceramic and silver designs. Americans could also display in their parlors their taste in *japonisme* through the purchase of objects increasingly available in Japanese novelty stores. Easels, bookcases, bric-a-brac shelves ("whatnots"), and other display furniture reflected the Aesthetic Movement's penchant for collecting *objets d' art* and other curios. Textiles draped mantels, pianos, and other furniture, and carpets from Turkey, Persia, and India, sometimes layered one upon the other, covered floors. In contrast to the earlier American middle-class practice of matched suites of furniture, proponents of Aesthetic design counseled a mix of styles and the arrangement of furniture in groups to facilitate various activities. Advertisements by manufacturers of "art furniture," such as that of Herter Brothers (1864–1906), "art glass," and "art wallpaper" easily signaled to consumers the fashionableness of these styles and designs.

The Aesthetic Movement was a democratic one in that the movement's willingness to embrace machine-made goods allowed many Americans to purchase artistic wares. The Arts and Crafts Movement that quickly followed rejected the machine and emphasized form, structure, and materials rather than surface ornament. The sensuous attenuation of natural forms that characterizes the Art Nouveau style would also replace the Aesthetics' love of geometry and symmetry.

The movement's legacy is more than its amazing output of fine and decorative arts. Aestheticism also offered women new possibilities for creativity and employment. Indeed, Aesthetic dress—long, loose gowns made of velvet, silk, or wool that freed women from corsets and bustles—seems a symbolic portent of women's increased political and economic power in the twentieth century. The establishment or enlargement of museums, museum schools, and schools of art and design in this era may be credited to the powerful ideology of the Aesthetic Movement.

Shirley Teresa Wajda

See also Art Nouveau; Arts and Crafts Movement; Eastlake Style; Interior Design; Renaissance Revival; Style

References and Further Reading

Blanchard, Mary Ward. 1998. *Oscar Wilde's America: Counterculture in the Gilded Age.* New Haven, CT: Yale University Press.

Burke, Doreen Bolger, et al. 1986. *In Pursuit of Beauty: Americans and the Aesthetic Movement.* New York: Metropolitan Museum of Art/Rizzoli.

Cook, Clarence. 1878. *The House Beautiful: Essays on Beds and Tables, Stools and Candlesticks.* New York: Scribner, Armstrong and Company.

Grier, Katherine C. 1988. *Culture & Comfort: People, Parlors, and Upholstery 1850–1930.* Rochester, NY: Strong Museum; Amherst: University of Massachusetts Press.

McClaugherty, Martha Crabill. 1983. "Household Art: Creating the Artistic Home, 1868–1893." *Winterthur Portfolio* 18 (1): 1–26.

African America

The study of the material culture of African Americans is complicated and enlivened by issues of race, class, and ethnicity over the almost 400-year history of Africans in what is now the United States. How much and what sort of African cultural traditions persist in African American practice? How did African Americans create their own cultural traditions using the objects of other, dominant cultures, despite or because of harsh conditions of slavery or racial subjection? What material objects and uses are based within an African American ethnic identity? How have people of African descent affected the material culture of the broader American society?

Africans' and African Americans' experiences depended on a wide range of variables: when they arrived in the Americas; to what degree they were part of a large or small, homogenous or heterogeneous cultural group; and their access to money and goods. Scholars have explored these issues through handicrafts, such as pots, quilts, and baskets; items of clothing and personal ornamentation; houses and yards; foodways; and the holiday Kwanzaa. Beyond the material objects that people make or own, scholars have explored the larger material world and its effect on African Americans through access to consumer goods, transportation systems, and patterns of work.

Scholars use a variety of methodologies to explore the African American past. Historical archaeology has opened the doors to a frustratingly silent documentary record about the lives of slaves and free blacks in early America. Artifacts from plantation sites often reveal that slaves had their own preferred patterns of use for the objects and spaces allotted to them by their owners. Archaeology has proven that the sparse legal descriptions of slave life were merely that, and slaves almost always had more material goods than documents would have us know. Anthropologists use tools of cultural analysis to trace patterns of language, religion, music, use of space, or ornamentation. Sociologists contribute aggregate statistics that help identify larger population movements and patterns, as well as what falls outside those larger patterns.

Whether by force or by choice, immigrants from various parts of Africa came to North America and created heterogeneous or homogeneous groups. Many people who suffered forced immigration came from West Africa, in the region stretching from Senegambia to Angola, and included many different cultures such as Yoruba, Kongo, Bakongo, Vodun, Mande, Ejagham, and Ibo. Immigrants also came from the interior and the eastern part of the African continent and from the West Indies, often by circuitous means. Later waves of African immigrants greatly affected how those groups sustained or adapted cultural practices in their new home. An early thesis held that African culture could not have survived the passage to the New World and the shock of forced labor. In 1941 anthropologist Melville Herskovits (1895–1963) asserted that Africanisms (African beliefs and practices retained in new cultural surroundings) indeed survived and influenced American culture during and after slavery.

The brief summaries of various material goods and methods of inquiry treated here are by no means comprehensive, but represent major trends in thinking about the complex subject of African American material culture. The experience of slaves differed in seventeenth-century Virginia, eighteenth-century Rhode Island, and nineteenth-century Louisiana. Some blacks were never enslaved and/or lived urban lifestyles very different from rural enslaved blacks whose first freedom was after emancipation.

Handicrafts

African American handicrafts are often utilitarian objects that display cultural preferences for form, design, decoration, or color. Slaves who made pots augmented their rationed cookware by adding the forms they needed for religious practice or for cooking methods they preferred. Some coarse earthenware *colono* pots from the colonial South display West African cosmograms (symbols for the universe, often a pair of crossed lines,

The open-fired, unglazed earthenware known as "colonoware" has been found through archaeological excavations of plantations in the Southeast United States. These shards, found at Drayton Hall in Charleston, South Carolina, were parts of vessels used by African American slaves for cooking and storage. The manufacture and forms of colonoware resemble West African pottery but also show adaptations to Euro-American forms. (Carter C. Hudgins/courtesy Drayton Hall, a site of the National Trust for Historic Preservation)

sometimes within a circle) and show evidence that ties them to healing rituals. Slaves in North Carolina made stoneware jugs with verses or applied faces that often had African features.

Nineteenth-century quilts are frequently treated as folk art. These quilts often reused fabric, buttons, ribbon, and other materials and sometimes contained messages in word or symbol about freedom or Christianity. Twentieth-century quilts from the small and long-isolated community of Gee's Bend, Alabama, are celebrated for their compositions of vibrant color, visual rhythm, and exciting patterns that rank them among important works of modern art. Sweetgrass baskets woven by women in the South Carolina low country echo forms from Africa and those used in rice cultivation in America in the eighteenth and nineteenth centuries. The basket weavers rediscovered many African forms during a craft renaissance

brought about by folk ethnographers who interviewed and photographed the weavers in the 1930s.

Clothing and Personal Adornment

Clothing and personal adornment were often the only means of individual expression available to enslaved people. Studies of slave clothing consider how slaves used the clothing masters provided, as well as how people often reused and refashioned rationed clothing and castoffs. Planters many times offered special articles of clothing such as jackets or suits as incentives for good work. Artifact assemblages from slave sites often include buckles, beads, buttons, and sewing paraphernalia that reflect activities of self-fashioning beyond the labors of laundering and mending. Slaves who had access to commercial stores frequently purchased small items for personal adornment, such as ribbons, buckles, fabric, and mirrors. Free African

Americans in northern cities held dress balls during the early National period. The white press often derided these balls, despite the similar dress and behaviors of the participants to those at balls attended by whites.

Between the Civil War (1861–1865) and the mid-twentieth century, blacks used clothing and personal ornamentation in two distinctly political and opposite ways. Elite blacks, who sought to distance themselves from the worst caricatures that whites had developed about blacks, adopted the etiquette of white middle-class Americans in their smoothed hair and conservative styles of dress—suits and ties for men and "polite" dresses for women. Their dress and activities signified that they did not perform menial labor, that they were educated, and that they identified with mainstream American values. In a radical affront, however, other blacks adopted flashier dress that proclaimed black identity as outside mainstream white culture. The zoot suit riots of the 1940s were the culmination of white resistance to a swaggering style of dress for men and women, as were nightclub behaviors popular with both young blacks and Mexicans, which seemed extravagant during wartime rationing and worrying. The 1960s and 1970s brought ethnic hair styles, such as the Afro and braids, and African-inspired clothing and ornamentation that simultaneously asserted African heritage and allegiance to the American Black Power movements. With new trends in fashion, black entrepreneurs developed special products for black hair and skin, as well as established millinery and dress shops that answered the needs of an African American consumer population.

Houses and Yards

While houses built for slaves tended to reflect the functional and design aesthetics of their white owners, the slaves' use of the buildings and the yard space around them reflected personal and cultural practices. Houses and yards show evidence of family groups, how men and women used yards differently for work and leisure activities, and the keeping of gardens and livestock pens. Following the Civil War, many rural blacks lived in small, government-built dwellings that came to be known as *freedman's houses*, where people found self-expression in the functional and ornamental use of yard areas. In the twentieth century, the houses of many poorer African Americans reflected regional building practices, and how those same people used and decorated their yards and gardens remains a topic of African American studies. The long, narrow, single-room-wide and three-or-four-room-deep "shotgun"-style house came to be associated with African Americans in many of the cities, where it supplied whole neighborhoods of worker housing. (The name comes from the idea that one could fire a shotgun through the front door and it would pass straight through each room and out the back door.) A shotgun house district in Wilson, North Carolina, is on the National Register of Historic Places.

Foodways

Enslaved Africans used many of the cooking techniques in America that they had known in Africa, including cooking stewed meals in a single pot over an open fire or hearth. While one-pot meals were not unknown to other cultures, African ingredients—watermelon, eggplant, field peas, benne (sesame), yams, and peanuts (carried first to Africa from South America by the Spanish)—filtered into the American diet. In plantation kitchens, with access to multiple pots and methods, black cooks fed generations of whites during and after slavery. Thus African tastes for flavor, texture, and ingredients were present in the everyday lives of many people. The migration that carried blacks from fields to factories in the first half of the twentieth century also brought barbecue (meat baked in a vinegar-, catsup-, or mustard-based sauce), ribs (pork spareribs cooked with sauce), greens (boiled leaves of collard, turnip, mustard, kale, or spinach, cooked with meat), cornbread, chitterlings (fried pork intestines), and other *soul food* to city restaurants that migrants opened in their neighborhoods.

Kwanzaa

The holiday of Kwanzaa (December 26 to January 1) is a modern celebration of family, community, and culture that uses a specific set of material objects combining a range of African concepts and cultures (including Ashanti and Zulu). Dr. Maulana Karenga, professor of black studies at California State University, Long Beach created Kwanzaa in 1966 as a way to unite the African American community. Each day of the seven-day celebration invokes one of the seven principles, such as *umoja* (unity) and *kujichagulia* (self-determination). The holiday is marked by the daily lighting of *mishumaa saba* (seven black, green, and red candles) held in a special candleholder called a *kinara*. The Kwanzaa set includes a *mkeka* (straw mat) that symbolizes the foundation. In addition to the *kinara*, celebrants place on the *mkeka* some *mazao* (fruit and vegetable crops) to symbolize the harvest and other items representing family. Through their design and use, the Kwanzaa objects commemorate African heritage and reinforce African American community and learning.

Consumer Goods, Transportation Systems, and Patterns of Work

The larger material world that includes access to production, distribution of goods, public transportation, and the social aspects of certain kinds of work has also affected the material culture of African America in pro-

found ways. In the early twentieth century black consumers preferred national brand-name goods when possible to avoid local store owners who tried to cheat black buyers with inferior or underweight goods. When southern whites hired black women as domestic workers, it was the female cooks, nurses, housekeepers, and laundresses who used buses and trolleys to get from their black neighborhoods to white ones. These same women were poised to boycott public transportation and challenge segregationist policies in the 1950s. African American men very often worked within their own neighborhood and did not make the same use of public transportation. Black women also carried on other tasks such as laundry or mending at their own homes, which had to be equipped for washing, drying, ironing, starching, sewing, and keeping clean someone else's clothing.

The architectural fittings of racial segregation affected African Americans' use of the material world. Segregation meant that many southern theaters, hotels, restaurants, courthouses, and bus and train stations had separate entrances, stairs, ticket windows, restrooms, water fountains, and seating areas. Some towns had two schools, two theaters, two shopping districts, and other mechanisms to separate people of different races. In many locales, concerned African Americans invested personally to build new and better school buildings and community centers that would serve their families. Many of these places are now landmarks and are becoming memorials to the civil rights movement in the United States.

Recent Scholarship

While much of African American material culture and fine arts was ignored during the nineteenth century and viewed as folk or outsider art during the early part of the twentieth century, the last part of that century saw the validation of African American cultural activity in its own right. African America in all its facets grew as a serious inquiry since the 1960s, when many colleges and universities added Black Studies (or African American studies) to their curricula. The 1980s saw both old and new historic sites, museums, and exhibitions generating the need for specific knowledge about African American material culture. Museums dedicated to founding fathers, such as George Washington's Mount Vernon (1754–1787), Thomas Jefferson's Monticello (1769–1809), both in Virginia, and the Hermitage (1819–1845) of Tennessean Andrew Jackson, which formerly celebrated a white, male past, engaged directly with the histories of the other people who lived and worked on such plantations and great houses. The National Park Service began its African American Heritage project, and many museums began archaeological and documentary investigations to tell about the slaves and free blacks who worked, lived, raised families, and died on historic sites. Museums reconstructed slave quarters, mounted exhibitions, held homecomings for black and white descendants of ancient families, or otherwise determined that their sites' African American history is significant to the history of all Americans. In addition, new museums and historic sites now mark the places and events of the Underground Railroad, the civil rights struggle, and other aspects of African American history.

Susan A. Kern

See also African American Foodways; Consumerism and Consumption; Ethnicity; Folklore and Folklife; Historic Preservation; Museums and Museum Practice; Race; Slavery

References and Further Reading

Ferguson, Leland. 1992. *Uncommon Ground: Archaeology and Early African America, 1650–1800*. Washington, DC: Smithsonian Institution Press.
Holloway, Joseph E., ed. 1990. *Africanisms in American Culture*. Bloomington: Indiana University Press.
Singleton, Theresa A., ed. 1985. *The Archaeology of Slavery and Plantation Life*. Orlando, FL: Academic Press.
Sobel, Mechal. 1987. *The World They Made Together: Black and White Values in Eighteenth-Century Virginia*. Princeton, NJ: Princeton University Press.
Vlach, John Michael. 1991. *By the Work of Their Hands: Studies in Afro-American Folklife*. Charlottesville: University Press of Virginia.
White, Shane, and Graham White. 1998. *Stylin': African American Expressive Culture from Its Beginnings to the Zoot Suit*. Ithaca, NY: Cornell University Press.

African American Foodways

Food meets a host of human needs—nutritional, communal, economic, and even political. It also has a role in power relations, stereotypes, and assumptions. *Foodways*—patterns of procurement, preparation, presentation, and consumption—are no different. Any discussion of African American foodways must include how, where, when, with whom, and why certain foods have and continue to be a part of the cultural patterns associated with many African Americans. Food is part of a cultural system that involves dietary behaviors, environmental conditions, cultural meanings associated with certain foods, and the historical factors that contribute to the persistence or change in food behaviors.

Most conversations of African American foodways begin with the evolution of African diets in the New World. These early diets were not singular in form. Rather they were the result of influences from many different areas over particular periods of time. Major changes and adjustments in the

African diet were due in no small part to the slave trade in the seventeenth, eighteenth, and early nineteenth centuries. Many enslaved people experienced malnutrition, vitamin deficiencies, and even death as a result of the treacherous, months-long journey across the Atlantic Ocean. Most were provided small portions of grains or African yams. After spending months in this condition, it would often take a very long time before they were able to resume eating foods that would strengthen their health.

Southern plantation diets varied, even though they were typically sparse. Much depended upon the provisions given by the plantation owner. According to slaves' narratives, planters' journals, and travelers' diaries, most slaves were allocated a small portion of meal, molasses, low cuts of pork, and maybe coffee. Depending upon slaves' geographical location, they might also have been able to supplement their diet with rice or fish. Some planters allowed their slaves to own gardens and have access to livestock, which provided vegetables and meat (usually chicken) to eat or to sell. Still other enslaved people were given permission to hunt in order to supplement their diets. These activities were few and far between, however, because many plantation owners felt these tasks took time away from work.

The diets of many blacks, no matter the region they reside in, resemble those of southerners because the majority of Africans entered the New World as slaves in the South. For this reason, the emphasis is often placed on African American foodways as part of a southern subsistence. Even more importance is given to black people consuming pork entrails and other low cuts of meat as a result of their enslaved status. These points notwithstanding, it should not be overlooked that there were free and escaped blacks living across the United States. While many black

people born in the United States are familiar with southern foods and cuisines, others have a greater affinity for diets influenced by regional foodways of the Southwest, Midwest, and New England. African American foodways are complex and varied, owing to myriad contributions of peoples and environments from Rhode Island to California and beyond.

Psyche Williams-Forson

See also African America; Food and Foodways; Race; Slavery

References and Further Reading
Moore, Stacy Gibbons. 1989. " 'Established and Well Cultivated': Afro-American Foodways in Early Virginia." *Virginia Cavalcade* 39: 70–83.
Paige, Howard. 1999. *Aspects of African American Foodways*. Southfield, MI: Aspects Publishing Company.
Spivey, Diane M. 1999. *The Peppers, Crackling, and Knots of Wool Cookbook: The Global Migration of African Cuisine*. Albany: State University of New York Press.
Titus, Mary. 1992. "Groaning Tables and Spit in the Kettles: Food and Race in the Nineteenth-Century South." *Southern Quarterly* 20 (2–3): 13–21.
Whitehead, Tony, and Psyche Williams-Forson. 2003. "African American Foodways." In *The Encyclopedia of Food and Culture*, ed. Jonathan Katz, 425–437. New York: Gale.

Agricultural Architecture

Agricultural architecture comprises many different structures that accommodate the functions of American farms and ranches and their human and animal occupants: residences, barns, stables, carriage houses, chicken houses, smokehouses, silos, icehouses, greenhouses, and other outbuildings. Farm structures take a wide variety of forms ranging from simple sheds to majestic New England barns to modern factory-farm buildings. Like all architecture, agricultural buildings reflect historical influences, cultural factors, geographical factors, and behavior patterns; farms are arranged in accordance with prevailing beliefs about class and gender and attitudes toward animals and land. In the United States, agricultural buildings became symbolic ingredients in the cultural myths celebrating the rural yeoman, individual land ownership, and the open spaces of the West. The characteristic structures and settings of ranches and farms pervade the iconography of American culture and have heavily influenced the forms of nonagricultural architecture and artifacts.

Ranches

The earliest extensive European settlements in North America were established in the Southwest, where Spanish colonists appropriated land that Native Americans had irrigated and cultivated for at least 2,500 years. The Spanish established ranches to raise cattle, goats, sheep, and horses, adapting techniques developed in North Africa and Spain. In contrast to the compact farms of the eastern English and Dutch colonies, ranch buildings usually sprawled over many acres. Spanish architectural motifs such as clay tile roofs, adobe or stucco walls, and rooms facing open courtyards were employed in the many houses built for owners and workers, stables, workshops, kitchens, and storage facilities located in several clusters scattered over the range.

Over the nineteenth century, the western ranch became a symbol resonant of a vast, untamed American frontier. Spreading beyond the original region of Spanish colonization to the Rocky Mountain region and northwest, ranch buildings were roughly constructed of local materials, often including split logs and stone. Buildings generally included a main house for the ranch owners,

one or more bunkhouses for hands, cook shacks, barns and other livestock shelters, storage sheds, corncribs, toolsheds, and workshops for blacksmiths and craftsmen, as well as still more temporary structures such as tents and lean-tos. The improvisational quality of the buildings underscored the sense that architecture was not the essence of the ranch; rather, the heart of the ranch was the almost immeasurable stretch of land over which the herds and cowhands ranged, a vast rugged space that reduced the intermittent clusters of makeshift buildings to insignificance. In late nineteenth-century western novels, the defining trait of ranching was its rejection of domesticity: The sprawling, dusty, rough-edged western ranch and, still more, the solitary cowhand who roved the endless acres on horseback and slept under the sky stood for a peculiarly American notion of masculinity, at once united with and at war with unconquered nature.

Family Farms

The small-scale farms established in the eastern seaboard colonies represented continuity with the colonists' cultural backgrounds, their aspirations to a new social order, and their adaptation to the new environment, including the climate, available materials, and techniques adopted from Native American construction. Early farms typically consisted of a modest house and barns constructed of logs or boards and were similar in form: one-story rectangles subdivided into two or more multipurpose rooms (hall-parlor plan) as necessary, sometimes with attics and shallow cellars for storage. Logs, woven plant fibers, and sod substituted for preferred stone, brick, and boards, depending on what was readily available and functional in a particular region.

Over the eighteenth and nineteenth centuries, farmers expanded or replaced the earlier buildings and added more specialized structures, including smokehouses, woodsheds, corncribs, and icehouses. Houses and barns reflected both the exigencies of American farm life and the emergence of distinctively American identities. The republican ideal, if not the reality, of the independent family farm headed by a citizen-farmer exerted a powerful influence on the development of characteristic New England and Middle Atlantic farmsteads through the eighteenth and early nineteenth centuries. The sense that the farmer was an autonomous individual, rather than one small component of an interdependent corporate entity, differentiated free Americans from European peasants in popular ideology, even where women, slaves, indentured laborers, and minors actually constituted most of the population. Conceptualized as self-sufficient entities through much of that period, individual farms not only produced crops and livestock but also grew the fodder for the animals, raised gardens for family meals, manufactured the tools for maintenance, and produced clothing and other domestic necessities. Often most of these activities took place within the two sometimes connected main buildings, the farmhouse and the barn, a convenient arrangement in the severe northeastern climate.

Farmhouse Design

Efficiency was not the sole factor shaping the form of farm buildings. The assertion of dignity and cultural capital was a driving force, even for relatively humble farm families. As early as the seventeenth century, American farmers incorporated elegant architectural motifs such as centrally placed doorways, symmetrical windows, and covered porches into their dwellings. The egalitarian ideology extending the idea of refinement and elegance to the working farm was still more influential in the eighteenth century: Imitating European manor houses, farmers expanded simple one- or two-celled structures into Georgian-style, multicelled houses with specialized spaces, delegating socializing, sleep, and manufacturing into distinct units.

In settled regions, the level of architectural sophistication grew steadily over the nineteenth century. Wood clapboard farmhouses sported Classical Revival motifs, including pillars, semicircular fanlights, and large, symmetrically placed windows; interiors often included several bedrooms, a "front parlor" for entertaining guests, an informal sitting room for family and close friends, a kitchen and pantry, and, at least in some plans published in agricultural periodicals, a library. While L-shaped or rectangular frame houses with gable roofs and clapboard siding remained popular throughout the century, upscale agricultural periodicals such as the *New England Farmer* (1822–1890) and *The Southern Agriculturalist* (1841–1846) disseminated plans for Italianate and Tudor-style farmhouses. The periodicals also published plans submitted by readers. Farm women often submitted plans that accommodated the work of child care, food preservation, and laundry in the layout of the house. As the industrialization of textile and tool production removed some tasks from the farmhouse to the factory, the house became a locus of education, morality, and emotional nurturing as well as a workplace. Rooms often progressed from more formal functions at the front, facing the road, to farm labor at the back of the house, facing the stable or barn: the parlor nearest the formal front door; an intermediate region of family rooms in the middle of the house; and a kitchen and pantry, mud room or sink room, woodshed, hay barn, and barn as the "back house."

Farmstead Design

Like the farmhouse, the barn testified to the multiple roles and dimensions of the family farm. Barns were typically placed within easy reach of the house, readily available to family members, since both men and women had tasks in the barn (although the distribution of tasks was usually gendered). A single large barn with several levels, subdivided into various spaces and including a hayloft and cellar, became increasingly common by the nineteenth century. Two basic barn types were the "English barn," with doorways at the center of each long side, and the "German barn," with an opening in the gable end. Corn and wood might be stored within the barn or in separate small structures; some tasks required separate structures, such as smokehouses for preserving meat and fish, sugar shacks for boiling down maple sap, and privies. The barn and outbuildings, like the house, were designed to meet or at least indicate high expectations for the farm family's convenience and comfort.

Didactic literature paid as much attention to barn improvement as to residential architecture. Barns were venues to display the farm family's cultivation; prominent landscape architect Andrew Jackson Downing's (1815–1852) *The Architecture of Country Houses* (1850) dedicated a forty-page section to "Hints for Cottage and Farm Stables," featuring plans for structures that combined decorative details like trimmed eaves with sensible arrangements for a cow barn, stables, carriage or wagon, grain storage, root cellar, threshing floor, and hayloft under a single roof. Small modifications of traditional barn designs, such as trapdoors for shoveling manure into a cellar or lower level, allowed progressive farmers to manure their fields more conveniently, thereby producing better fodder crops for their animals. Larger interior spaces improved ventilation for healthier animals. An innovation in the 1880s, cylindrical silos for fodder storage spread rapidly throughout dairy farms. Some adventurous farmers promoted polygonal barns as modern solutions. By the end of the nineteenth century, family farms had become a cultural icon symbolizing American domestic virtues: self-sufficiency and public-spiritedness, close-knit family and community ties, the compatibility of physical work and mental elevation, and the promise that effort and thrift would lead to abundance.

Plantations

While similar aspirations informed some small farms in the South, the region, which depended heavily on slave labor, clung more closely to the model of feudal European agriculture. Although yeoman farmers with few or no slaves outnumbered them, aristocratic planters dominated the cultural landscape. Grand-scale plantations represented less than one percent of all slaveholding family farms, but the elite estates and the hierarchical ideology they embodied exerted a formidable influence over southern farm arrangements. On large plantations, enslaved laborers frequently were housed in minimal one-cell shacks or cabins, while owners occupied larger buildings imitating as many elements of aristocratic English manor house architecture as the owners could afford. By the end of the seventeenth century the dwelling of a well-to-do "gentleman farmer" might have eight to ten rooms, including a parlor, and a variety of other structures for various purposes; over the eighteenth and nineteenth centuries, plantation owners' houses grew steadily more imposing and elaborate. Although on small farms slaves sometimes lived in their owners' houses, the estates of the elite were arranged to etch clear architectural distinctions between elegant main houses and the outbuildings, a category comprising the actual farmers' dwellings.

Far more than in the northern states, southern planters who aspired to refinement distanced themselves from the actual work of farming and the workers who performed it. The "big house" typically occupied an elevated spot toward the front of the property, often with kitchens and workrooms toward the back or in adjacent structures. Stables occupied an intermediate position between the house and the hog sheds, chicken sheds, cattle barns, crop storage, smokehouses, toolsheds, workshops, and other utilitarian sites for farm work, in which the slaves' quarters were included. Owners seldom provided sufficient means for slaves to approach European standards of elegance. Despite their marginal status and their poverty, the slaves who farmed plantations developed distinctive communities. Owners generally dictated that slave housing take the form of rectangular gabled cabins, but slaves sometimes arranged the quarters into close-clustered villages to facilitate visiting and easy transitions between indoor and outdoor living spaces. When permitted to design their own dwellings, some communities incorporated West African architectural elements, utilizing local materials to build dwellings with clay walls, dirt floors, and steep thatched roofs that were adaptable, easily maintained, and well insulated.

Modern Era

A *farm* is currently defined by the United States Census Bureau as any place that produces $1,000 or more of agricultural products. Thus, the term can include truck farms, orchards, vineyards, stables, and even feedlots and large domestic gardens. Nevertheless, the architecture of the American farm and ranch now reflects a dramatic shift toward large-scale factory farming and the demise of the family farm over the course of the twentieth century. Near metropolitan areas, farms and ranches have given way to suburban subdivisions and urban sprawl. In rural regions, many farms are enormous single-crop or single-animal operations owned by major international corporations. Like factories or warehouses, the structures on such farms are usually large sheet-metal or cinder block buildings meant to perform industrial-scale operations with maximum efficiency and minimal human labor. Hogs and chickens are for the most part raised entirely within buildings; feeding and waste disposal are mechanized using chutes and conveyor belts. Although dairy and beef cattle still sometimes range over pastures, cows are milked mechanically in barns, with milk conveyed through miles of plastic tubing, and beef cattle are concentrated into enclosed feed lots to be fattened on grain and assorted supplements before slaughter. Trailers, mobile homes, and comfortable modern houses that can be maintained and heated have superseded farmhouses. These realities, however, have not dislodged the nostalgic imagery of the American family farm. Advertisements and packaging depict red barns with cylindrical silos and split-rail fences rather than the modern reality; tourist bureaus display images evoking rolling acres. The housing developments and shopping malls that have replaced farms in urbanized areas often make architectural reference to their predecessors, through "ranch houses" and "colonials," split-rail fences, or wooden outbuildings. These nostalgic gestures do little to arrest the gradual disappearance of the traditional farm and ranch from the landscape.

Jane Weiss

See also Agricultural Work and Labor; Animals; Architectural History and American

Architecture; Domestic Architecture; House, Home, and Domesticity; Slavery; Work and Labor

References and Further Reading
Bushman, Richard L. 1992. *The Refinement of America: Persons, Houses, Cities*. New York: Alfred A. Knopf.
Carter, Thomas, ed. 1997. *Images of an American Land: Vernacular Architecture in the Western United States*. Albuquerque: University of New Mexico Press.
Ferguson, Leland. 1992. *Uncommon Ground: Archaeology and Early African America, 1650– 1800*. Washington, DC: Smithsonian Institution Press.
Hausladen, Gary J. 2003. *Western Places, American Myths: How We Think about the West*. Reno: University of Nevada Press.
Hubka, Thomas C. 1984. *Big House, Little House, Back House, Barn: The Connected Farm Buildings of New England*. Hanover, NH: University Press of New England.
McMurry, Sally. 1988. *Families and Farmhouses in Nineteenth-Century America*. New York: Oxford University Press.
Noble, Allen G., and Richard K. Cleek. 1995. *The Old Barn Book: A Field Guide to North American Barns and Other Farm Structures*. New Brunswick, NJ: Rutgers University Press.
Nylander, Jane C. 1993. *Our Own Snug Fireside: Images of the New England Home, 1760–1860*. New Haven, CT: Yale University Press.
Small, Nora Pat. 2003. *Beauty and Convenience: Architecture and Order in the New Republic*. Knoxville: University of Tennessee Press.
Vlach, John Michael. 1993. *Back of the Big House: The Architecture of Plantation Slavery*. Chapel Hill: University of North Carolina Press.
Wilson, Chris, and Paul Groth, eds. 2003. *Everyday America: Cultural Landscape Studies after J. B. Jackson*. Berkeley: University of California Press.

Agricultural Fairs and Expositions

The United States currently has slightly more than 2,600 agricultural fairs, occasionally called expositions. Most began as agricul-tural displays and competitions; all but a few still give much of their attention to agriculture, an emphasis that sets them apart from other big exhibitions, but most devote large shares of their space and their patrons' energy to a host of other subjects and entertainments. Fairs are and always have been enormously diverse and relatively inexpensive. Important state fairs, such as Minnesota's, entertain more than a million visitors each year, and popular county fairs, such as that in Elkhart County, Indiana, report more than a quarter of a million in attendance.

European Roots
Modern fairs trace their ancestry to commercial fairs, or festive markets, which flourished nearly everywhere in ancient and medieval times. At that time, in the *Oxford English Dictionary*'s words, a *fair* was almost universally understood to be "a periodical gathering of buyers and sellers, in a place and at a time ordained by statute or by ancient custom." By the 1700s those commercial fairs were supplanted by agricultural shows, such as the one that the Society of Improvers in the Knowledge of Agriculture began in 1723 in Edinburgh, Scotland. The new shows were not without buying and selling, but they focused on innovations, especially new breeds of sheep, and competitions among exhibitors for prizes, or premiums.

Early History of American Agricultural and State Fairs
Those new events, which would take the old name *fair* from the early nineteenth century onward, spread west of the Atlantic soon after the American Revolution. In 1809 a handful of leaders in the Federal District (the District of Columbia), Maryland, and Virginia organized the Columbia Agricultural Society, which began a short series of semi-

annual exhibits that included sheep shearings, other exhibits of livestock and wool, and demonstrations of new plows. The Columbia shows stopped during the War of 1812 just as similar events were proliferating in the North.

The northern fair tradition began with Elkanah Watson (1758–1842), a Massachusetts entrepreneur who organized the Berkshire (Massachusetts) Association for Promoting Agriculture and Manufactures, which staged its first livestock exhibition in 1811. The Berkshire County shows were quickly imitated by other county organizations, particularly in New England and New York. These shows, inspired by similar efforts in England, included, after the sponsoring society's private election of officers, a parade to church, prayer and oratory, and then judging of exhibits located on the town common. The best exhibits won premiums, usually cash prizes. In the early years, all of this activity could be done in one day, but the events soon grew in length.

The cost of premiums also rose. So the Berkshire society pursued a state subsidy and received $200 in 1817. When the Massachusetts, New Hampshire, and New York legislatures began to subsidize all of their states' agricultural societies two years later, fairs (as the shows were increasingly called) further developed in the region. State subsidies were unreliable; agricultural societies and fairs multiplied when funds were provided, and they became inactive, or died, when they were not. But in the long run growth was enormous.

Initially local, fairs broadened their messages and their audiences after 1838, when the New York State Agricultural Society attempted the nation's first state fair. State fairs proliferated from 1849, when Detroit hosted Michigan's first, until 1861, when Oregon, despite the Civil War beginning

back East, joined the parade. Only the "Great Fair of St. Louis," which began in 1856 and went bankrupt in 1894, seriously rivaled the state fairs' popularity. St. Louis drew huge crowds in the 1860s and even more in the next decade with beautiful landscape architecture; agricultural exhibits so impressive that farm journalist Norman Jay Colman (1827–1911) wrote that farmers really had to attend. When the great St. Louis fair collapsed, Colman blamed incompetent management. Surely the fair had been damaged, as were others in the Midwest, by competition from the Chicago World's Columbian Exposition of 1893 and an economic depression that lasted until 1897.

Criticism

As fairs grew and multiplied, agricultural journalists, whose business was also growing, reported that fairs had abandoned their original progressive purposes and become vulgar entertainments. In 1857 *The American Agriculturalist*'s editor wrote that he had attended few fairs that year; those offered little more than horse races, which discouraged him from attending others. Other journalists fretted specifically about women who competed in horse races at some fairs.

Despite criticism fairs prospered into the early twentieth century. Most of the nation's local and state agricultural societies (no fewer than 912) sponsored fairs by 1858. The number of societies rose to 1,367 in 1868 and 2,740 in 1913, hosting as many fairs as they do today. Relative to population, the states from Ohio to Nebraska had more than their share of agricultural societies and fairs in 1858, as they still do. Middle Atlantic and Pacific states had nearly their shares; New England had a few more. The South, except for the border states (notably Kentucky), had much less than its share. Fairs came to the South mostly after the Civil War, when

Yankee-influenced state legislatures began to subsidize them in the northern manner.

Race and Region

Southern fairs demonstrated the complexity of the region's race relations. For example, black and white North Carolinians enjoyed their state fair together until 1891, when North Carolina started to have a "colored day," which did not keep some black people from attending on other days as well. In 1890 South Carolinians started a "colored state fair," and then Booker T. Washington's Tuskegee Institute began to host shows that were widely imitated around the South. Segregation showed fresh energy in the 1920s, when Mississippi's "Negro State Fair" began, but it was far from absolute. In Neshoba County, Mississippi, for example, Choctaws, whites, and blacks attended their famous fair together through the first half of the twentieth century. In 1954, when the Supreme Court's decision in *Brown v. Board of Education of Topeka, Kansas* inspired a fresh civil rights crusade, some fairgoers observed that black people were absent. Despite awareness, segregation continued.

Racial diversity also made a mark in the West, where Indians organized some of their own fairs. The most important and earliest example was the Indian International Fair in Muskogee, Indian Territory, which Cherokee and Creek leaders started in 1874. Kiowa, Comanche, Arapaho, Cheyenne, and some of the "civilized" peoples from the territory's east participated in 1875. Federal officers approved the fair and its purpose, which clearly was acculturation. A Kiowa banner stating "We need Schools, Cows, and Ploughs," was typical of other slogans used at the event. But the fairs had widespread Indian support and continued until the Muskogee Fair, not distinctively Indian but an occasion for both Indians and whites to see horse races, took its place. In the twentieth century, probably starting in 1938 with the Navajo Nation Fair of Window Rock, Arizona, some fairs offered expressions of Native American culture along with other attractions that people expected at fairs. Cultural expressions, notably dance and rodeos, are also characteristic of powwows; the fairs' attention to agriculture and their early support of acculturation, however, set them apart from powwows.

Reform and American Fairs' "Golden Age"

In 1909 sociologist Kenyon Butterfield, describing "farmers' social organizations" in Liberty Hyde Bailey's authoritative *Cyclopedia of American Agriculture*, judged that fairs had experienced a "golden age" in the mid-nineteenth century. He also wrote that the fairs' critics had been, and still were, right to think that growth had brought trouble. Fairs were originally intended to improve agriculture. Desperate promotion had made them mere entertainments. If fairs were to be valuable again, they had to be called back to what critics believed was their original purpose.

In fact, revival efforts had begun not long after the Civil War, during the fairs' golden age. The Order of the Patrons of Husbandry (the "Grange") created exemplary fairs without horse races or alcohol soon after its founding in 1867 and well into the next century. Some Grange efforts quickly failed, but others continue to this day. Now the numerous Grange fairs in Massachusetts are chiefly small, brief, and without livestock, but Grangers also have exhibits at many big northeastern fairs, including the Eastern States Exhibition in West Springfield, Massachusetts, and conduct a few ambitious shows of their own, notably the Durham Fair in Connecticut, the Connecticut Agricultural Fair, the Grange Encampment and Centre County Fair in Pennsylvania, and the St. Joseph County, Michigan, Grange Fair.

The most important fair reform effort came from, and continues to be led by, 4-H. (The four Hs stand for hands, head, health, and heart.) Formally organized mostly after World War I, 4-H traces its origins back to the last few years of the nineteenth century, when agricultural college leaders made various efforts to overcome the discouragement with farming that they feared was spreading among rural children. Devoted to extension work (reaching beyond their campuses into the countryside), they helped to create clubs of farm youngsters that operated little instructional farms. The clubs spread all over the country. By the 1910s and 1920s juvenile farm clubs began to exhibit their products at fairs. Then the 4-H movement, which was the union of those clubs, seized control of many local fairs or, in some states, all of them. A fairly typical example of that seizure happened in Elkhart County, Indiana, where 4-H was vital to the fair from the 1920s onward. In the 1940s, when the financially troubled Fair Association turned the fair over to the American Legion, which refused to ban liquor from the fairgrounds, 4-H began to have its own separate fair.

Finally, in 1955, the new Fair Board, on which 4-H clubs were and are heavily represented, took charge of the fair system. The 4-H organization shares leadership, especially of the biggest fairs, with the people whom historian Wayne Caldwell Neely in 1935 called "professional fair managers." In 1891, during a brief period in which a great many professional organizations were founded, fair managers created the International Association of Fairs and Expositions, which is still at work. It keeps managers of about half the nation's fairs, and most of the big ones, aware of national trends. It also

subjects them to advertisements, notably of entertainers who would like to appear at their fairs, and keeps them in touch with midway companies that provide the types of amusements that most interest many fair visitors. Future Farmers of America, 4-H, the National Grange, and other earnest people have kept the fairs' progressive, educational tradition alive. But fairs, managers understand, are also popular shows.

Modern Visitors, Modern Changes

The fact that fairs have continued to draw throngs of visitors, even though the number of people who have experience in and knowledge of agriculture has precipitously dropped, has inspired some to suggest that fairs drop the pretense of being primarily agricultural. Ohio acted on that idea in 1961 when authority over its state fair passed from the state's venerable Board of Agriculture to the new Expositions Commission, which took a very broad view of the fair's purpose. The Farm Bureau staved off such change in neighboring Indiana. Then Indiana's state fair has lately attracted about three-quarters of a million visitors each year. Ohio's state fair counted almost a million attendees in 2000, which was down from its attendance in the mid-1980s.

Fairs have broadened their focus, but serious agricultural displays with instructional intentions continue. Some of that activity takes place at specialized agricultural events, such as the Vermont Farm Show, which invites farmers to display competitively their honey, eggs, maple produce, and other goods in Barre for a few days each January. Similarly, the Pennsylvania Farm Show, also held in January, is a purely agricultural and home economics spectacle. Other kinds of instruction are attempted at typical fairs, with all of their frivolity, where experts offer small agricultural lessons to people who are unlikely ever to see a cow milked or a sheep sheared anywhere else. The American Dairy Association draws crowds to watch a milking parlor at the Minnesota State Fair; many organizations and some government agencies offer instructional, or what they hope are persuasive, exhibits. Such efforts surely attract much less attention than do midways and musical performances, but they maintain continuity in the history of agricultural fairs and expositions in the United States.

Donald B. Marti

See also Animals; Consumerism and Consumption; Leisure, Recreation, and Amusements; Native America; Race; Tourism and Travel

References and Further Reading

Braudel, Fernand. 1982. *The Wheels of Commerce.* New York: Harper & Row.
Butterfield, Kenyon. 1909. "Farmers' Social Organizations." In *Cyclopedia of American Agriculture*, ed. Liberty Hyde Bailey, vol. 4, 289–296. New York: Macmillan.
Marti, Donald B. 1986. *Historical Directory of American Agricultural Fairs*. Westport, CT: Greenwood Press.
Neely, Wayne Caldwell. 1935. *The Agricultural Fair*. New York: Columbia University Press.
Wessel, Thomas, and Marilyn Wessel. 1982. *4-H: An American Idea 1900–1980*. Chevy Chase, MD: National 4-H Council.

Agricultural Work and Labor

Agricultural workers and laborers are instrumental in bringing domesticated plant and animal products to market. Most agricultural workers toil on farms and nurseries, while others handle farm and ranch animals, operate farm equipment, and sort and process raw agricultural products. Farmworkers and farm laborers are distinguished from *farmers*, who own and operate their agricultural enterprises.

American farms have always relied upon the use of paid or unpaid laborers. African slaves were forcibly imported into the colonies to labor on farms and plantations; indentured servants, usually Europeans, were also put to work on small family farms. Prior to the Great Depression, most farm laborers were unpaid family members, local residents ("hired hands"), or slaves. Temporary farm laborers reflected the diversity of the nation, especially the less privileged groups. African Americans (both before and after slavery); Mexicans and Mexican Americans in the Southwest; and Chinese, Japanese, and Filipino immigrants in California all found a bare subsistence working on farms and ranches. Children, whether family members, enslaved, or those of workers, have always been a source of farm labor. Family farms have periodically experienced economic crises, notably in the 1890s, 1920s–1930s, 1950s, and 1980s. These economic downturns pushed many farm owners into the roles of paid farm laborers. For example, the Dust Bowl of the 1930s created the exodus of farm families from Oklahoma to California, chronicled in novelist John Steinbeck's *The Grapes of Wrath* (1939) and in the documentary photographs of the federal government's Farm Security Administration. Many attempts to organize or unionize farm workers have been made; the most notable of these efforts is César Estrado Chávez's (1927–1993) and Dolores Huerta's National Farm Workers Association (now United Farm Workers).

The material culture of agricultural work and labor is twofold. First, the machinery and technology of farming has directly affected the work lives and economic fates of farm laborers. Mechanized farming literally put thousands of farm laborers out of work; the experiences of migrant farm workers during the Great Depression reflected weather conditions, general economic realities, and the introduction of tractors on farms. Fertilizers, improved farming techniques, and other technologies have also changed how agricultural work is performed. Farm work is one of the most dangerous occupations in the nation: chemicals, heavy air particulate matter (dust), machinery, repetitive motion, and taxing physical labor contribute to the threats to workers.

Second, farm laborers and workers have shared a unique material culture, embodied in the temporary housing they have traditionally inhabited. By the mid-1800s, many larger farms that relied upon migrant or temporary farm labor built houses for their workers. From the nineteenth century to the present, this housing has been remarkably consistent: simple rectangular boxes made of wood, with a front door and two windows, usually slightly elevated from the ground. These work camps, as they were known during the Great Depression, offered substandard living conditions. Today, temporary or migrant agricultural laborers find housing locally, take up residence in traditional work camps, or live in trailer housing provided by the farm owner.

Helen Sheumaker

See also Agricultural Architecture; Poverty; Slavery; Technology; Work and Labor

References and Further Reading
Griffith, David, Ed Kissam, et al. 1995. *Working Poor: Farmworkers in the United States.* Philadelphia, PA: Temple University Press.
Higbie, Tobias. 2003. *Indispensable Outcasts: Hobo Workers and Community in the American Midwest, 1880–1930.* Urbana: University of Illinois Press.
Schob, David E. 1975. *Hired Hands and Plowboys: Farm Labor in the Midwest, 1815–60.* Urbana: University of Illinois Press.
Sosnick, Stephen H. 1978. *Hired Hands: Seasonal Farm Workers in the United States.* Santa Barbara, CA: McNally & Loftin.

Air and Space Transportation

The history of the air and space transport of humans in the United States is often dated to 1903, with Orville (1871–1948) and Wilbur (1867–1912) Wright's sustained, mechanized flight of an airplane at Kitty Hawk, North Carolina, on December 17, 1903. Before that time, however, humans had been able to travel through the air via the lighter-than-air balloon and, to a lesser extent, the glider and early forms of the helicopter (ornithopter). Dirigibles—airships consisting of controllable balloons filled with hydrogen and later helium—date from the early 1900s. The Wright brothers had experimented with gliders and were inspired by European efforts to create steam-powered, heavier-than-air "aerials" or "air carriages." The Wright brothers' use of an internal combustion engine set off rapid development of machine-powered aviation in the United States.

Capital investment in this new technology was matched by popular fascination with manned flight in the next several decades, making heroes of those who set landmarks in flight, including Calbraith Perry Rodgers (1886–1955), Charles Lindbergh (1902–1974), and Amelia Earhart (1897–1937).

Commercial aviation began in the late 1920s. Unpressurized cabins, the inability to fly at night, constant refueling stops, and other impediments made air transportation uncomfortable and unattractive for nearly everyone but businessmen, adventurers, and pilots. In the 1930s, the introduction of comfort and flight attendants, as well as larger, more dependable airplanes, aided the ever-increasing numbers of (mostly upper-class) Americans who traveled by air. Not until the latter half of the twentieth century, however, was air travel democratized: technological improvements (including jet engines, metal alloys, fuels, and radar); the expansion of airports and increased competition to lower airfares; the promotion of safety; and the promise of comfort provided by pressurized passenger cabins, restroom facilities, media entertainment, and food services convinced many Americans that flight was an efficient and enjoyable travel choice.

The military utilized airplanes beginning with World War I. At first, early fighter planes were not equipped with weaponry, and pilots were given pistols to fire upon enemy planes and soldiers. Fixed weapons on airplane wings were used by the end of the war. The Air Corps was established in December 1941 to bolster defenses against German U-boats during World War II. During the Korean and Vietnam wars, the use of the helicopter was vital in difficult terrain for medical, supply, and troop transport purposes. Corporations such as McDonnell Douglas, formed in 1967, capitalized on the rising needs of military aviation, as well as the burgeoning space program and civilian airliners.

An important offshoot of aviation development has been the space program, beginning with the National Aeronautics and Space Administration in 1958. The space program used former stunt and Air Corps pilots in testing the possibilities of space travel. The success of the Soviet space program accelerated the American effort, and on July 20, 1969, American astronauts in *Apollo 11* landed on the moon. Many attempts at launching satellites and manned missions into space failed, but on April 10, 1981, the Space Shuttle *Columbia* successfully launched into an orbit around Earth. Recent space mission failures such as the *Challenger* explosion of January 1986 have cast doubt as to the efficacy of space travel, even as tourists have since traveled in space.

Nicholas Katers

See also Land Transportation; Technology; Tourism and Travel; Water Transportation

References and Further Reading
Bilstein, Roger E. 1984. *Flight in America, 1900–1983: From the Wrights to the Astronauts.* Baltimore, MD: Johns Hopkins University Press.
Dade, George C., and George Vecsey. 1979. *Getting Off the Ground: The Pioneers of Aviation Speak for Themselves.* New York: E. P. Dutton.

Alternative Foodways

Alternative foodways define different sets of material practices and foodstuffs than the foodways of the dominant culture. Through prescription or proscription they represent modifications to the hegemonic food system in order to attain some combination of improved physical health, greater economy of time or money, environmental sensibility, enhanced American identity, higher spiritual quality, or more virtuous character. Intertwined in the concept are the physical body, national body, spiritual being, and body of the land itself. Simply put, theorists and practitioners of alternative foodways aspire to create better modes of production and consumption than the foodways of the masses.

The history of alternative foodways is arguably as old as any other pattern of acquiring, preparing, and eating food. Whether owing more to folk wisdom, magical thinking, or the best and worst of contemporary scientific thought, alternative foodways and the healing arts and sciences have been, and remain, inextricable. The ancient Greek philosopher Hippocrates (ca. 460 BCE–380 BCE) echoed common human sensibility when he wrote, "Thy food shall be thy remedy."

Studies of native cultures reveal contending "American" foodways before the arrival of Europeans. Early explorers such as Bartolomé de las Casas (1484–1566) remarked, with variable accuracy, on Native American foodways, and subsequent arrivals characterized them as savage and uncivilized and native lands as untilled and unimproved. These attributes have been alternatively reviled and emulated, laying the foundation for an enduring conflict between the wild and the cultivated as reified in food, such as reformers' continuing debate between natural, or brown, and processed, or white, foods.

Thus begins a long tale of competing visions of American foodways, and of the adoption or avoidance of foodways to improve physical and mental well-being and perhaps to enhance spiritual aspirations. These alternative foodways were conceived and prescribed to achieve environmental ideals, set cultural boundaries, define identities, and maintain or subvert group associations. Alternative foodways may be categorized as (1) the foods themselves, including natural or organic foods but also processed foods such as graham flour, peanut butter, Corn Flakes, and Grape Nuts; (2) food additives; (3) food practices such as Horace Fletcher's (1849–1919) chewing protocol, fasting, or food combining; (4) food-related paraphernalia and establishments, from patent weight-loss devices to Sylvester Graham's (1794–1851) vegetarian boarding-houses and sanitaria such as that in Battle Creek, Michigan; and (5) marketing and packaging materials relating to the vending of alternative foodways, including countless tracts and publications, catalogues, and "expert" testimonials.

To the extent that the United States was founded as an ideal alternative nation and culture, its many and varied foodways have tended to be represented as ideally alternative. American foodways are notoriously hard to define, but there are certain central tenets. They are innovative, plentiful, portable, pure, simple, authentic, contradictory, and contrary. Many alternative foodways arose out of utopian or religious movements, such as the Seventh-Day Adventists and John Harvey Kellogg (1852–1943), who founded the Battle Creek Sanitarium; Shaker dietary precepts; and Eastern religious influences on the foodways of the 1960s counterculture. The American Revolution had a similar creedal influence on American foodways, as Thomas Jefferson (1743–1826) wrote extensively on ideal food habits and diet, as did Benjamin Franklin (1706–1790). Franklin may well represent the quintessential American relationship with alternative foodways, as he related that he adhered to the vegetarian philosophy of Thomas Tryon (1634–1703) until reflecting that fish eat other fish so why should he refrain from eating them: "So convenient a thing it is to be a reasonable creature," he wrote in his autobiography, "since it enables one to find or make a reason for everything one has a mind to do." This quixotic, malleable stance continues to characterize American alternative foodways.

Netta Davis

See also Food and Foodways; Utopian Communities

References and Further Reading
Belasco, Warren. 1989. *Appetite for Change: How the Counterculture Took On the Food Industry, 1966–1988.* New York: Pantheon Books.
Haber, Barbara. 2002. *From Hardtack to Home Fries: An Uncommon History of American Cooks and Meals.* New York: Free Press.
Levenstein, Harvey A. 1988. *Revolution at the Table: The Transformation of the American Diet.* New York: Oxford University Press.
Sack, Daniel. 2000. *Whitebread Protestants: Food and Religion in American Culture.* New York: St. Martin's Press.

Animals

Animals are living, sensate material beings with the legal status of property in the United States. Humans are animals, too, but the focus here is on nonhuman animals and their place in the material culture of humans. The nature of animal cognition, intelligence, and consciousness is still the subject of intense debate. Nonhuman mammals especially raise for humans many questions about the very nature of humanity. Human thought about nature and culture, about subject and object (the Cartesian dualism of Western philosophy), about the origins of our natural world, and about other large questions invariably include reflections on nonhuman animals.

People use animals in many of the same ways as and for many of the same reasons that they use other material objects—sometimes for instrumental purposes and sometimes for expressive, symbolic purposes. Instrumental purposes include work and the provision of food and shelter. Expressive, symbolic purposes range widely, from the custom of keeping pets to the role of animals in providing entertainment or education to the role of animals in our human religions and mythologies.

The Consumable Animal

Animals played a key role in human prehistory and history. Native Americans relied heavily on hunting and on domesticated animals (dogs and horses) for sustenance. Hunting and fishing provided animal flesh as food, but animals also provided hide and fur for clothing, shelter, and bedding. Other animal parts—such as bones, teeth, horns, and even the bear's penis bone—provided material for tools, for the decoration of bodies and of clothing, and for purely ritualistic or artistic creations. The holistic approach of Native American cultures does not distinguish between the instrumental and symbolic uses of animals; the hunting, fishing, killing, and consumption of an animal was both instrumental and symbolic. Native American creation myths and other traditional narratives (e.g., Navajo coyote stories) involve animals, which are represented in the art, song, and dance used to perform the narratives. Animals appear in the masks, costumes, and other ritual objects associated with native ceremonies.

European immigrants to North America, as well as Africans brought as slaves, carried with them new customs using animals, and these customs often blended into new forms. The Europeans brought hunting traditions, including the material culture associated with hunting, from firearms and knives to butchering traditions to duck decoys and duck calls. Traditions regarding the building of hunting blinds, platforms, and even the hunting camp cabin are part of the material world of hunting. Hunting dogs themselves could be considered material objects used in the hunt, as hunters breed and train the dogs to be extensions of the hunter.

Europeans, Africans, and other immigrants also brought foodways involving meat and fish. Throughout American history, some Americans have consumed wild game. Domestic cattle, pigs, sheep, goats, and fowl came to provide the bulk of animal protein in the American diet, and the variety of foodways involving meat and fish touches on issues of gender, ethnicity, region, religion (food taboos), and the urban/rural split. Certain cuts of meat have come to be so central to some ethnic identities that the eating of the meat in traditional ways (e.g., "soul food") constitutes an important performance of group identity. Traditional foods are among the last vestiges of ethnic identity to be lost in the Americanization of immigrant groups in the United States. The belief that the consumption of certain animal parts (powdered animal horn, bull testicles, oysters, and so on) bolsters male virility combines folk foodways with folk medical beliefs.

Humans also consume animal bodies for personal adornment. Animal skin, feathers, and fur are central to clothing. Animal feathers adorn hats (threatening bird species extinctions that led to strict governmental controls on hunting birds for feathers), bear claws and shark's teeth are worn as necklace charms, and exotic animal parts (e.g., alligator hides) are used as fashion accessories.

The Working Animal

Humans domesticated some species of animals for the work they could do. Horses, donkeys, mules, and oxen are in this category (Americans usually only eat the oxen), as are working dogs, from herding dogs to dogs that assist disabled people to police dogs to disaster rescue dogs. In some cities police ride horses for mobility and for physical intimidation when needed; elsewhere horses and mules pull buggies and carriages for carting tourists.

The Pet Animal

Sixty-three percent of United States households in 2005 had a pet. Pet animals occupy the important symbolic space between what is wild and what is tame. Unlike wild animals or those kept for labor or food (including milk and eggs), pets often occupy the domestic space of the humans. Americans name their pets, and in general Americans do not eat the animals they name. Not quite animal and not quite human, pets are for many Americans a primary mediator between nature and culture.

People keep pets for a variety of reasons. Pets provide companionship and protection; dogs can serve as the eyes, ears, and limbs of disabled people; dogs can accompany a hunter and can protect the home; and having pets can be the means for teaching children to take responsibility for a living thing. Pets are part of the material world for owners (or *guardians,* as they are sometimes called) in two important ways: as material displays of identity and as objects at the center of a system of consumption and display.

Pets that serve no utilitarian function may have use as part of a person's performance of individual or group identity. Many people see a similarity between their own personalities and the sort of pet they own, so the choice of pet (including the breed within the species) and the open display of that pet to others becomes an important element in the performance of identity. People who share the same taste in pets may feel they belong to a group that shares other attributes. Some sorts of rare or exotic pets can serve the status functions economist Thorstein Veblen (1857–1929) first described as "conspicuous consumption."

Veblen's insight suggests the second important aspect of the material world of pets—objects bought for pets. Americans spent $17 billion in 1994 on their pets, and that number increased to nearly $36 billion in 2005. The pet business is the seventh largest retail area in the nation, and the number of businesses selling pet-related commodities increases every year. The material culture of pet keeping parallels the material culture of humans—from food and shelter to clothing, jewelry, toys, and pet cemetery grave markers.

The Animal as Spectacle

Another category of animal that mediates between nature and culture, between the wild and the tame, is the animal that is the object of human gaze. Natural history museums began in the United States with Charles Willson Peale's (1741–1827) museum in Philadelphia (opened 1786). An artist and naturalist, Peale displayed stuffed animals in natural groupings. The Smithsonian Institution (founded 1846) had limited display of animals, but the American Museum of Natural History (founded 1868 in New York City) became the first great natural history museum in the United States, featuring scientifically accurate dioramas of animals and plants in natural groupings and poses. The California Academy of Sciences (1874) and other great natural history museums followed the model established by the American Museum. In these museums, animals are displayed as would be any other object thought worthy of a museum presentation, and the museum gift shop emphasizes the commodity value of the displayed animals in forms the visitor can take home as a souvenir of the visit. Historians note that the three great institutions of accumulation and display—the museum, the department store, and the world's fair—all emerged in the last three decades of the nineteenth century in Great Britain and the United States, and all were doing the same cultural work of creating consumer desire suitable to sustain the economy's transformation from a production-oriented economy to a consumption-oriented one.

Zoos and wild animal parks accumulate and display live animals. Zoos in Europe and the United States arose in the mid-nineteenth century as an institutional response to developments in natural history, including Darwinism (Charles Darwin, *The Origin of Species*, 1859). The first zoological gardens in Europe opened in the 1860s and 1870s, and the Philadelphia Zoological Garden opened in 1874 (in Fairmount Park, the site of the United States Centennial Exposition two years later). American zoos were created in the decades when increasingly urbanized Americans sensed a loss of the frontier and of wild nature. Zoos gradually evolved from displaying animals in small cages to large

natural habitats (always with scientific and educational purposes at the forefront), and some large wild animal parks let the animals roam freely while the visitors are confined to vehicles moving through the park. Animatronic animals at Disneyland and Disney World are essentially the mechanical versions of these wild animal parks.

Animals are also the object of the human gaze in performance. Some wild animal parks feature performances by animals—among the oldest of these are porpoise shows at tourist attractions like Marineland in Florida, but performing animals would also include rodeo animals, circus animals, and animals used in other entertainments (e.g., in magic acts). Animal rights activists and others launched a critique of all of these settings—zoos, circuses, wild animal theme parks, and rodeo—beginning in the 1980s, and they have at one time or another been at the center of controversy as communities debate how animals shall be treated.

Sport hunting rose in the late nineteenth century, in part as a romanticized performance of the self-reliance and masculinity thought to be threatened by modernity and by the feminization of American culture. As opposed to subsistence hunting, sport hunting should be treated as another setting where the animal is a spectacle, both during the hunt itself and as a trophy to be displayed in the hunter's home.

Toy Animals

Besides living pets, inanimate animals occupy many homes. Oral, written, and visual stories have used animals as characters and as moral actors. The rise of mass-mediated images continues this use of animals as the substitutes for humans in fables. Walt Disney (1901–1966) did not invent the genre of the natural history film, but he popularized the genre in film and on television. He also popularized storytelling with animal characters in animated films, and Disney marketed the animal characters in every way possible, including as dolls and miniaturized animals.

In America, some of the earliest playthings—from wooden hobbyhorses to stuffed bears—represent animals. Fitting the aims of the moral instruction of children, a hand-carved Noah's Ark with animals was a common child's toy. The machine manufacture of toys increased the sorts and numbers of animal representations, and some of these toys reveal gender preferences. Reflecting in part gendered toy marketing, girls collect "My Little Pony" and other horse-related figures far more than do boys, who might collect miniature dinosaurs, wild animals, or fantasy animals (e.g., dragons). Adults also collect material objects representing animals. It was not only children who fed the Beanie Baby (pellet-filled, bag-like small animal dolls) craze of the 1990s, and adults are the main market for collectable animal figurines in plastic, porcelain, ceramics, and glass.

The Souvenir Animal and the Market

Tourism is a primary economic resource for many American communities, and since the late nineteenth century animals have played an important role in marketing tourist sites. Alligators, for example, have helped market Florida for more than a hundred years, just as armadillos have helped market Texas, or lobsters Maine. Tourists can carry away from the experience a souvenir that often assumes the shape or image of the animal associated with the site. States designated official state animals (even more precisely, state mammals, reptiles, birds, etc.), and these animals appear on state license plates and other material objects advertising the state. Some state flags bear images of animals, such as

California's (a vestige of the brief "Bear Flag Republic" with its grizzly bear emblem). Visitors to zoos, animal theme parks, natural history museums, and other animal-based attractions carry away souvenirs with the likeness of animals, whose symbolic power (perhaps as totems) survives the modern touristic experience. Sometimes the consumer does not even need to enter the wild or visit a tourist site to collect the material object associated with wild animals. A trip to the shopping mall will suffice, where the shopper will find The Nature Store or another other retailer specializing in natural history merchandise.

Jay Mechling

See also Agricultural Fairs and Expositions; Children's Material Culture; Children's Toys; Consumerism and Consumption; Ethnicity; Folklore and Folklife; Food and Foodways; Native America; Popular Culture; Souvenirs; Sports; Tourism and Travel; Work and Labor

References and Further Reading

Gillespie, Angus K., and Jay Mechling, eds. 1987. *American Wildlife in Symbol and Story.* Knoxville: University of Tennessee Press.
Grier, Katherine C. 2006. *Pets in America: A History.* Chapel Hill: University of North Carolina Press.
Hanson, Elizabeth. 2002. *Animal Attractions: Nature on Display in American Zoos.* Princeton, NJ: Princeton University Press.
Herman, Daniel Justin. 2001. *Hunting and the American Imagination.* Washington, DC: Smithsonian Institution Press.
Price, Jennifer. 1999. *Flight Maps: Adventures with Nature in Modern America.* New York: Basic Books.

Anthropology and Archaeology

Anthropology is the holistic study of humanity, and as such concerns every aspect of human existence. Anthropology, especially the subfield of cultural anthropology, which explores symbolic behavior, has a long history of involvement with material culture, which serves both as a component of various theories of social analysis and interpretation and as objects produced in the human past retrieved by archaeological excavations submitted to systematic description and scientific analysis. Both prehistoric and historic archaeology as scientific and historical fields seek to recover (often through excavation), document, classify, and analyze material and human remains with other environmental data and other records to explain human culture and history.

Theoretical Beginnings

The interweaving of anthropology and American material culture studies began with the foundation of the first academic department of anthropology at Columbia University in 1895 under German immigrant professor Franz Boas (1858–1942). Boas brought with him experience working in the Royal Ethnological Museum in Berlin with physical anthropologist Rudolf Virchow (1821–1902) and ethnologist Adolf Bastian (1826–1905), scientific training in physics, and prior fieldwork studying the Inuit people of Baffin Island in the Canadian Arctic. His view of the cultural value and significance of material objects went beyond the mere gathering of exotic items as isolated and curious specimens of human creativity, an idea reflected in many museum collections in the nineteenth century when ethnographers began to view made objects as expressions of specific cultural behavior. Boas understood the necessity of analyzing not only objects' physical properties but also the clearly defined context of meanings and use given them by their makers. This emphasis on what Boas termed the *historical method* was in part a response to the sometimes insecure data used as the bases for other theoretical approaches to the study of human cultures and stressed obtaining as many specific bits of information about a society as possible, a transfer of the mind-set of the physical sciences to the new field of anthropology. This was in contrast to the approach to cultural study promoted by the Bureau of American Ethnology under the direction of explorer John Wesley Powell (1834–1902), who considered the evolution of cultures from one stage of development to a more complex successor to be illustrated by, among other things, the material objects fashioned by local technologies. The collection and description of artifacts from across the world contributed greatly to the growth and diversification of the holdings of the major museums of the United States and created a pool of potential data sources for later generations of material culture scholars.

Boas' view of material culture heavily influenced his students, one of whom was Margaret Mead (1901–1978). Within American anthropology, material culture was utilized as a source of information until the 1920s, when it became merely a part of anthropological description and was only treated as a special field as related to (what was then termed) primitive art, technology, and aesthetics. Its continuing use as a research component, however, made it necessary by the 1930s to place it within the language and theory of the field. The earliest formal definition of *material culture* appeared in 1937 in an essay written by Clellan S. Ford (1909–1972), which states that "the actions . . . of manufacture, use and nature of material objects constitute the data of material culture. . . . Artifacts themselves are not cultural data, although . . . they are often the concrete manifestations of human actions and cultural processes" (Ford 1937, 226). This focus on material culture as manufactured object held sway from the 1930s into the

1950s and became more limited still, center-ing on technologies used by a group of peo-ple to survive in a particular set of environ-mental conditions.

A second and widespread application of material culture was as the basis of culture areas, to illustrate cultural diversity and to establish categories of meaning and the dif-fusion of objects (most effectively when strict geographic and chronological limits had been set). An inventory of the material cul-ture of the group being studied also became a standard feature of any ethnography. The absence of a generic working definition did not seriously hamper the concept's applica-tion to field research in anthropology, and this approach remained an integral part of American cultural anthropology, with the precise interpretation of material culture varying according to each researcher's goals, until the appearance of the writings of Claude Lévi-Strauss in the 1970s. He con-sidered material culture to be a pattern expressing a deeper level of structure and meaning not directly accessible to conven-tional fieldwork, in effect recovering the complete mind-set of people distant in both space and time, taking the level of analysis one step beyond merely what the people called an object or for what it had been used.

Archaeological Applications

Paralleling the theoretical discussions within anthropology, archaeologists in the 1970s also discussed the potential of material cul-ture by expanding ideas first expressed by historical archaeologists. Material culture has the advantage for archaeologists of being the only form of culture that remains intact over time. A sharp contrast is made between *prehistoric archaeology*, where excavated material serves as the only source of infor-mation on a particular culture and its people, and *historic archaeology*, the sites of which

date from a time when the societies in ques-tion were literate and capable of recording their own pasts and internal affairs in a range of surviving and accessible documen-tary sources. In the American context, this field is concerned with the development of a distinctive national culture since the sev-enteenth century, its collisions with and bor-rowing from the Native American societies, and its relationship to European sources of manufacture. James Deetz (1930–2000), in his book *In Small Things Forgotten: The Archaeology of Early American Life*, noted that "since historical archaeology must deal with not only excavated material from the Amer-ican past but also all that has survived above ground . . . it is truly the study of American material culture in historic perspective" (Deetz 1977, 25). Four years later, William Rathje wrote "A Manifesto for Modern Material Culture Studies" in which he declared the defining characteristic of archaeology to be "a focus on the interaction between material culture and human behav-ior, regardless of time or space" (Rathje 1981, 52). Material culture was also regarded as a necessary element in the planning of histor-ical archaeological projects, both as back-ground and as one of the factors of any effective regional survey, although the ques-tion of how to make archaeologists and his-torians mutually aware of the potential benefits of interdisciplinary research contin-ues to be debated.

Archaeology (and the multiple types of data a controlled excavation can retrieve on the life of the people who inhabited a site) bases its methodology and analysis squarely on items of material culture that have sur-vived in various states of preservation. In some cases, such as the early architecture of the Plymouth colony in Massachusetts and the growth of Maryland's first capital, St. Mary's City, archaeological excavation provides the only source of data on settlements that either have no written records or have at best fragmentary ones. Artifacts can provide insights into the written data that have been preserved as well, offering new perspectives on subjects absent from the printed records, such as diet, social class, and medical care. The analysis of material culture offers a useful approach not only to a wide range of social questions, through its emphasis on the distribution of specific forms such as building types or pottery styles, but also to intangible aspects of the social systems that had caused them to be constructed or traded.

Perhaps the most unusual type of material culture accessible to archaeology is actual surviving structures, which can range from remnants of fortifications (as in Pittsburgh, Pennsylvania, where only the blockhouse of Fort Pitt remained above ground prior to excavation), to dwellings still in the possession of the original family, to places of worship. These buildings offer the excavator firsthand models of the time in which they were built, which can be used to interpret techniques of construction and clarify points mentioned in documentary records for a specific site where these exist. A few years before Ford defined *material culture*, one of the most ambitious projects of historical archaeology and restoration carried out in the United States was initiated by John D. Rockefeller, Jr. (1874–1960). His goal was the restoration of the colonial capital of Virginia, Williamsburg, where many eighteenth-century buildings had survived. Beginning with the restoration of Bruton Parish Church, a building in continuing use, the Williamsburg project swiftly grew into a long-term research effort where both aspects of material culture investigation were pursued, from analysis of public records to the conservation and typing of all sorts of colonial artifacts,

from bricks and window leads to ceramics, glassware, and textiles. Seventy years later, Williamsburg stands as one of the premier historical archaeological sites, where visitors are shown the importance of daily life as reconstructed on the basis of items recovered in whole or in fragments.

Museum Archaeological Collections

A museum collection of artifacts from any time period provides an additional source of information for the archaeologist, in the form of the documentation about the excavation of sites now lost to natural processes or destroyed by human agency, or sites that have been worked only intermittently over a period of decades. The sheer size of many of the object collections from various parts of a specific region such as New England may also serve to illustrate a variety of forms of a particular vessel type or its alteration over time, which can assist in the rough historical placement of a site that might have no other means of being dated. These collections, however, suffer from several flaws, particularly the tendency of collectors to look for the unusual and exotic specimens rather than the often dull and widespread tools and vessels in common use, making them illustrative of a partial range of what was present at a site, if not in daily use, rather than a complete picture of the possible forms of colonial pottery or glassware. Another difficulty with older collections, especially those gathered by amateur antiquarians in the late nineteenth century, is incomplete or absent documentation, which raises problems of identifying the exact location of the original finds and the distribution of specific artifact types. An aspect of material culture study within anthropology and archaeology receiving more public discussion in recent years is the question of ownership of excavated materials, in particular human skeletal remains, and the demands by Native

Americans identifiably descended from an archaeological population for the return (repatriation) and reburial of specimens acquired by either legal or illegal excavation.

The last two decades of the twentieth century were marked by an expansion of the use of material culture into new archaeological contexts beyond known historical sites and the recovery of lost colonial-era settlements such as Martin's Hundred in Virginia. Notable topics researched during this period in rural archaeology ranged from the recovery of the unwritten details of life in the slave quarters of Louisiana and Georgia and links to African cultural survivals to the impact of rural capitalism on farms in Appalachia and life on a colonial rice plantation in South Carolina. Urban archaeology (some of it the result of salvage projects) made use of the dense concentrations of artifacts in documented neighborhoods to study the past of the Chinese and African American communities of Sacramento, California; a general store site from gold rush–era San Francisco; and the saloons of Virginia City, Nevada. This western research was matched in the East by an archaeological consideration of the residential and commercial districts of Harper's Ferry, West Virginia, and a study of Baltimore's material culture from 1780 to 1904. State archaeological journals began to feature more interpretive pieces involving the use of material culture data on a wide range of subjects, among them African cultural survivals among both slaves and free people of color, pottery from the Spanish missions of Florida, and the working-class communities of nineteenth-century Minneapolis. The amorphous collections begun in the nineteenth century had come full circle, integrating and preserving the daily lives of their makers for the questions of new generations.

Robert B. Ridinger

See also Collecting and Collections; Community; Cultural Geography; Cultural History; Folklore and Folklife; Museums and Museum Practice; Social History; Vernacular

References and Further Reading

Crowell, Elizabeth A. 2000. "Walking in the Shadows of Archaeologists Past: Researching Museum Collections and Associated Records to Elucidate Past Lifeways." *North American Archaeologist* 21 (2): 97–106.

De Cunzo, Lu Ann, and John H. Jameson, Jr., eds. 2005. *Unlocking the Past: Celebrating Historical Archaeology in North America*. Gainesville: University Press of Florida.

Deetz, James. 1977. *In Small Things Forgotten: The Archaeology of Early American Life*. Garden City, NY: Anchor Books/Doubleday.

Ford, Clellan S. 1937. "A Sample Comparative Analysis of Material Culture." In *Studies in the Science of Society*, 225–246. New Haven, CT: Yale University Press.

Martin, Ann Smart, and J. Ritchie Garrison, eds. 1997. *American Material Culture: The Shape of the Field*. Winterthur, DE: Winterthur Museum.

Oswalt, Wendell H. 1982. "Material Culture in Anthropology." In *Culture and Ecology: Eclectic Perspectives*, ed. John Kennedy and Robert B. Edgerton, 56–64. Washington, DC: American Anthropological Association.

Quimby, Ian M. G., ed. 1978. *Material Culture and the Study of American Life*. New York: W. W. Norton.

Rathje, William L. 1981. "A Manifesto for Modern Material Culture Studies." In *Modern Material Culture: The Archaeology of Us*, ed. Richard A. Gould and Michael B. Schiffer, 51–66. New York: Academic Press.

Wilderson, Paul W. 1975. "Archaeology and the American Historian: An Interdisciplinary Challenge." *American Quarterly* 27 (2): 115–132.

Antiques

Antique historically qualifies an object or practice as "old fashioned" or "out of date." As a noun, *antique* refers to a sought-after relic. United States Customs and Border Protection regulations deem an imported object an antique if it is more than one hundred years old. Within the United States, *antique* is defined also by the market: auction houses, antique dealers, and collectors disagree about the required age of an object to be considered antique. Some concur with the United States Customs' definition; others argue that seventy-five years is the threshold between modern or vintage and antique. An antique may be anything from a bottle to a baseball card to a chair to an automobile.

Antiques, including those in museums or in use by private individuals, may be acquired in a number of ways. They are often passed as heirlooms from one generation to the next in families. They can also be purchased in antique stores, at auctions, at garage sales, or through newspaper, magazine, and Internet advertisements. The trade in antiques is chronicled and aided by periodicals such as *The Magazine Antiques, Maine Antique Digest,* and *Arts & Antiques* and by the steady publication of collectors' and price guides.

One mark of an antique is its *patina,* or apparent signs of age: wear marks, discoloration, stains, fading, chipping, paper foxing, and the like. Examples of patina include a worn corner on a desk, a layer of polish that has gradually built up on a table, or a slight discoloration on a mirror. For connoisseurs, there is a fine balance between the state of preservation in an antique and the patina that proves its age; an item in terrible condition, though it acquired this look through the years, may be too damaged to be collectible.

An antique is also characterized by and valued for its style. As tastes change over time, the styles of handcrafted and manufactured goods change. A bed made in the 1890s would most likely have been made in a different style and with different technology than a bed made today; thus, its look or style would mark the bed as old fashioned or out of style—an antique. Moreover, many items are particularly valued today as antiques because they are no longer made. Their very existence connects us to past and seemingly exotic—or at least different—lifeways. The complex sets of silverware manufactured in the United States during the Gilded Age, for example, feature utensils—sardine tongs, nut picks, and ice cream hatchets—that are no longer part of silver services.

Perhaps the most compelling markers of an antique are the stories associated with the object. Anthropologists Arjun Appadurai (1986) and Igor Kopytoff (1986) note that these "cultural biographies" or "life histories" accumulate as an object moves through many hands. With a fascinating story—for example, learning that an ax for sale at auction was once used by Abraham Lincoln (1809–1865)—even a seemingly mundane tool becomes more desirable and, indeed, a relic as well as an antique.

Provenance, a documented record of manufacture and ownership, is essential in proving an antique's authenticity and assigning value. Fakes appear on the antiques market; experts, curators, connoisseurs, and collectors are wary of the sophistication counterfeiters have achieved. The authenticity of an antique is not based only on style, patina, or provenance, but on all three characteristics.

For many, the antique appeals because of its durability and perceived authenticity—for example, handcrafted rather than mass produced; an exemplar of a perceived "pure" style; or a reminder of a past perceived as more truthful, honorable, simple, or artistic. The periodic revivals of historic styles in decorative arts and architecture are based on a perceived relevance to a society's conception of its self and purpose. For example, the Classical Revival of the late eighteenth and early nineteenth centuries reminded Americans creating their own nation of the political values of the ancient Greek and Roman civilizations.

In recent years, acquiring, appraising, and admiring antiques have become a large part of American popular culture. *Antiques Roadshow*, a television series that originated in Great Britain, has a large following on American public television. The number of antique "marts" and dealers has proliferated in the last twenty years, as has the availability of such businesses on the World Wide Web. So popular is this activity that the term has become a verb: *antiquing*.

Rebecca S. Graff

See also Auctions; Collecting and Collections; Consumerism and Consumption; Fakes; Heirlooms; Secondhand Goods and Shopping; Style; Yard Sales

References and Further Reading

Appadurai, Arjun. 1986. "Introduction: Commodities and the Politics of Value." In *The Social Life of Things: Commodities in Cultural Perspective*, ed. Arjun Appadurai, 3–63. Cambridge, UK: Cambridge University Press.
Department of Homeland Security, Bureau of Customs and Border Protection. 2006 (2001). *What Every Member of the Trade Community Should Know About: Works of Art, Collector's Pieces, Antiques, and Other Cultural Property.* http://www.cbp.gov/xp/cgov/toolbox/legal/informed_compliance_pubs/.
Kopytoff, Igor. 1986. "The Cultural Biography of Things: Commoditization as Process." In *The Social Life of Things: Commodities in Cultural Perspective*, ed. Arjun Appadurai, 64–91. Cambridge, UK: Cambridge University Press.
Rosenstein, Leon. 1987. "The Aesthetic of the Antique." *Journal of Aesthetics and Art Criticism* 45 (4): 393–402.
Thompson, Michael. 1979. *Rubbish Theory: The Creation and Destruction of Value.* Oxford, UK: Oxford University Press.

Apartments, Tenements, and Flats

Apartments are dwellings in multiunit buildings that developed in the mid-nineteenth century in France and quickly spread to the United States. In rapidly growing urban areas, apartment buildings provided an efficient way to house many people in a small or expensive area. Apartments are adaptable for housing all classes of persons. One notable example of a luxury apartment house is the Dakota (1884) located in New York City. Apartment buildings usually have more than one story; until the development of the elevator and steel frame construction, they often did not exceed five or six stories. The highrise apartment building became commonplace in densely inhabited cities. Some—for example, Chicago's Marina City (1964–1967) apartment buildings, which appear as two corncobs rising into the sky—make a distinctive impression on cities' skylines. Other forms of apartment buildings include dwellings more adapted to urban and suburban neighborhoods. Duplexes, fourplexes, and other small multifamily units are common throughout the United States. These structures can be of one or more stories.

Flats and *tenements* are specific types of apartments, usually applied to those that are in some way substandard and associated with working-class or poor neighborhoods. *Flat* is a term used more commonly in Great Britain than the United States, but in America it refers to an apartment of one floor, often with a separate entry, and few amenities such as hot water—hence the term *cold-water flats*. A *railroad flat* is one that is in a substandard building with the rooms arranged in a row, with one room acting as the corridor to the next, and windows only in the front and rear rooms. While *tenement* originally referred to property that is held by tenure, it has come to mean an apartment in the slums. Similar to the railroad flat is the *dumbbell tenement*, which was developed by James E. Ware (1846–1918) in 1879. This building form was so named because the middle part of the floor plan tapered in; the idea was to allow light and air into the central portion of the building through a shaft without reducing the width of the front and back of the building. The shaft was a health and safety hazard, acting as a convenient duct for flames to leap from one story to the next as well as a malodorous garbage dump that spread disease. Dumbbell tenements were eventually outlawed, though other forms of tenements continued to be constructed.

Donna M. DeBlasio

See also Architectural History and American Architecture; Cities and Towns; Domestic Architecture; House, Home, and Domesticity

References and Further Reading
Gelernter, Mark. 1999. *A History of American Architecture: Buildings in Their Cultural and Technological Context.* Hanover, NH: University Press of New England.
Kessner, Thomas. 1977. *The Golden Door: Italian and Jewish Immigrant Mobility in New York City, 1880–1915.* New York: Oxford University Press.
Kraut, Alan M. 2001. *The Huddled Masses: The Immigrant in American Society, 1880–1921,* 2nd ed. Wheeling, IL: Harlan Davidson.
Maddex, Diane, ed. 1985. *Built in the U.S.A.: American Buildings From Airports to Zoos.* Washington, DC: National Trust for Historic Preservation.
Rifkind, Carole. 1980. *A Field Guide to American Architecture.* New York: Penguin.

Architectural History and American Architecture

Architecture encompasses the built environment. Buildings provide researchers with a great deal of evidence about how people lived in the past. *High-style* architecture includes civic, public, commercial, and ecclesiastical buildings that have long been studied as symbols of a group's, community's, or nation's ideals, or as works of art, designed by professionals, that may be categorized as aesthetic masterpieces of a certain style or construction type. Domestic architecture, including vernacular structures created by anonymous builders as well as those designed by architects, has been of particular interest because houses provide clues to how ordinary people lived. Often, history revolves around a privileged few who leave diaries and correspondence to posterity. What about people of lesser means? Often their legacy is the buildings in which they lived. Architecture, while not always permanent, is less ephemeral than other types of historical records. Used in conjunction with drawings and photographs, such as letters and diaries, probate records, building and zoning codes, building manuals, architectural treatises, and popular literature, architecture is evidence of social, economic, and cultural change.

The Professionalization of Architecture and Architectural History in the United States

Though architecture as a profession of gentleman-scholars and men trained by practicing builder-architects had been recognized in the eighteenth century, architectural history in the United States began to develop at the same time that professional schools of architecture and landscape architecture emerged, in the second half of the nineteenth century. The Massachusetts Institute of Technology in Cambridge accepted students in its school of architecture in 1865. Even before schools dedicated to architecture were established, Americans could learn the profession's required skills and knowledge through a variety of institutions that offered drawing instruction, lectures, programs, and access to books. Many Americans went abroad to learn architecture and its history. The assemblage of buildings at world's fairs offered architects a means to display designs as well as explore the designs of structures of other nations and architects. The many illustrated publications of these expositions were readily available to the American public.

In 1933, the federal government implemented the Historic American Buildings Survey (HABS) to give unemployed architects work in documenting American buildings through measured drawings, photographs, and written descriptions. HABS is still in operation today and the vast collections of HABS and the Historic American Engineering Record, available online through the Library of Congress, chronicle the range of American buildings and regions, from New Mexico's Acoma Pueblo to the designs of Frank Lloyd Wright (1867–1959). Another watershed moment in American architectural history was the foundation of the Society of Architectural Historians in 1940 and the establishment of the *Journal of the Society of Architectural Historians* in 1941.

In the 1960s schools of architecture debated the role of architectural history in their curricula. For much of the previous century, architectural history had been treated as a specialty within the history of art. Little interaction occurred between architectural historians in departments of art history and historians within schools of architecture, and little discussion had taken place about the specific needs of architects-in-training. Schools of architecture have increasingly hired historians of architecture and the built environment, of landscape, and of design to teach professional-track students apart from students in the liberal arts.

A backlash against "traditional" histories of architecture based on style and design

purity and/or the prominence and success of the architect was in full swing in the 1970s. Historians of American architecture applied the theories and methodologies of anthropologists, folklorists, and social historians to explore the ordinary—*vernacular*—built environments of the nation. One of the challenges for this new breed of architectural historian is peeling away the layers of history in a building. Some architectural historians take an "archaeological" approach, in which the building becomes a treasure trove of information in much the same way excavated earth and its contents provide historical evidence of human life for the archaeologist. In the past, many architectural historians emphasized the formal aspects of style adopted by professional architects: historians simply studied building facades, often in relation to innovative materials and technology, or, as in art history, studied an architect's works in relation to that architect's life and ideas. Today, more in-depth studies of architecture include consideration of construction methods, the meaning and uses of interior spaces, and the role of the patron and community in the style and design of a building. Importantly, the many structures of anonymous builders are now included in architecture historians' studies.

Vernacular Architecture

The Vernacular Architecture Forum (VAF) was founded in 1980 to codify and expand the study of everyday buildings used by ordinary people. The VAF publishes annual collections of essays (originally in books but now in journal format) entitled *Perspectives in Vernacular Architecture*. Vernacular buildings are anonymous in that the builders or designers and the patrons or occupants are often unknown. The study of vernacular architecture is by necessity multidisciplinary. The methods of archaeology, social history, folklore, ethnography, art and architectural history, anthropology, cultural geography, sociology, geography, oral history, and literary criticism and theory all intersect with the study of vernacular architecture.

In recent years, some vernacular architecture specialists have applied their interpretive tools and approaches to high-style architecture. The building fabric and landscape of Thomas Jefferson's (1743–1826) Neoclassical Monticello (1796–1809), for instance, reveals how enslaved people circumvented traditional boundaries reserved for white visitors by moving through and around the plantation house in ways that undermined social hierarchies.

Such changes in interpretation question historic house preservation. James (1751–1836) and Dolley Madison's (1768–1849) Montpelier (ca. 1760) in Orange, Virginia, had undergone extensive remodeling over two centuries. In the current restoration, the house will be returned to its appearance in the 1820s, reducing a fifty-five-room mansion to a twenty-two-room house. To do so, the Montpelier Foundation demolished the wings of the building, built by the du Pont family in the early 1900s, a move that raised questions about preservation, restoration, and museum interpretation. What time period should a historic house museum display? Is it possible to preserve the layers and still present a cohesive historical narrative over time?

Regionalism and Ethnicity

Buildings do not usually move (although some do, as in the case of Sturbridge Village in Massachusetts or Greenfield Village in Dearborn, Michigan, which are collections of historic structures gathered together as open-air museums). Because of their relative immobility, buildings represent particular regional practices and cultures.

Historians of vernacular architecture are careful not to make generalizations about colonial American architecture as a whole because of regional variations in style, form, and construction techniques. Seventeenth-century colonial architecture in Massachusetts, primarily settled by English immigrants who brought their building methods with them from their particular regions within England, are different from the colonial buildings in the Hudson Valley in New York, originally a Dutch colony. A host of factors can play a role in determining building construction methods. For instance, southern colonists in the seventeenth century built earth-fast structures with light framing in response to social conditions, climate considerations, and the cash crop economy of tobacco.

To determine how people used particular rooms, architectural historians examine closely the building fabric and floor plans. American builders often responded to European developments in architectural design, striving in rural areas to imitate high-style buildings found in urban centers or in Europe. The development of the center hall plan in the eighteenth century represents the aspirations of the eastern seaboard mercantile house owners to emulate the Georgian houses of England, for example. The exteriors of American houses from the eighteenth century through the late nineteenth century may display a variety of outward forms, but the center hall remained consistent for many years. In the mid-nineteenth century, eight-sided house plans became popular after the publication of Orson Squire Fowler's (1809–1887) book *A Home for All: The Gravel Wall and Octagon Mode of Building* (1848). Octagon plans had been used in the past, most notably by Thomas Jefferson at Poplar Forest (1806–1812) near Lynchburg, Virginia, and by Dr. William Thornton (1758–1828) at the Octagon House (1799–1801) in Washington DC. In *A Home for All*, Fowler argued that octagon houses provided more window surfaces, natural light, and healthier ventilation than traditional house plans. Octagon houses enjoyed popularity for only a short time, but as artifacts, they can tell us about attitudes toward health and well-being and the importance of new building technologies. Perhaps the grandest octagon house was Longwood in Natchez, Mississippi, designed in 1861 by Samuel Sloan (1815–1884), but many more modest octagons appeared throughout the United States.

The Impact of Pattern Books

Regional variation diminished in the nineteenth century with the rise of professionalism in architecture. In 1797, Asher Benjamin (1773–1845) published the first American builder's handbook, *Country Builder's Assistant*, which was followed by *The American Builder's Companion* in 1806. Benjamin addressed carpenters, who could borrow the architectural details illustrated in Benjamin's books for their own projects. As the century wore on, builder's guides were replaced by architectural pattern books featuring house elevations and plans. Middle-class clients could choose from a dizzying array of architectural styles. The rampant eclecticism in architectural styles is a hallmark of nineteenth-century American architecture. Andrew Jackson Downing (1815–1852) was the key author of such pattern books, including *Cottage Residences* (1842) and *The Architecture of Country Houses* (1850). Downing promoted an aesthetic called the *picturesque* and encouraged people to build houses that blended into their natural environments. Reacting to rapid urbanization and industrialization, Downing and his readers idealized the country as an escape from the city, a counterbalance to refresh the soul.

The Impact of Modernization

After the Civil War (1861–1865), American architects continued to employ revival styles—such as the Renaissance Revival and Romanesque styles—dependent on European practices exemplified by the École des Beaux-Arts in Paris. The vibrant city has pushed architects to develop new designs in response to technological innovation in construction and materials, real estate values, patrons' desires, and new forms of working and living. In the 1880s, steel, for example, enabled American architects to imagine and design the skyscraper. The lighter, more pliable steel replaced the load-bearing stone masonry of large structures. Other innovations such as plate glass, elevators, plumbing, electricity, and reinforced concrete changed both the construction and style of buildings, heralded in the International style of the early twentieth century.

Urban and Suburban Living

With the increased population of cities (fueled by immigration), new forms of dwellings appeared in the United States in the mid-nineteenth century. Multiple-unit dwellings, including working-class tenements and middle-class apartments, became ubiquitous in American cities, where land values were increasing. Factory workers in industrial towns such as Lowell, Massachusetts, also found themselves living in boardinghouses, identical cottages, or tenements built by mill owners to house workers.

The balloon frame, an easily constructed and inexpensive method of timber framing created in 1833, contributed to the development of suburbs, now the dominant residential pattern in the United States. Suburban development was intimately linked with new transportation systems, from early omnibuses and ferries to commuter trains and automobiles in the twentieth century. In the nineteenth century, the notion of "separate spheres" was manifested in the detached, single-family homes for the middle class, in which women ruled a new "cult of domesticity" while men worked in the cities during the day and returned home in the evening. Houses became symbols of permanence in an American world that was in actuality transitory; in the suburbs, the popular Colonial Revival style expressed the ideal of the stable nuclear family at the turn of the twentieth century. Suburbs were considered an escape from the industrialization and urbanization of American cities, ironically made possible by the technology of transportation.

Levittown, on Long Island, New York, epitomized the post–World War II suburb made possible by the automobile. The conformity of the houses in the typical American suburbs spawned by Levittown and the increasing sprawl of urban centers has led to a movement known as *New Urbanism*, which began in the 1980s in Seaside, Florida. This anti-sprawl movement offers pedestrian-friendly, mixed-use developments with single-family and multiple-unit dwellings, parks, offices, and stores within close proximity along tree-lined streets. The houses often feature large front porches and rear garages, which suggest a simpler time when communities were close knit and families were not reliant on car travel. Just as nineteenth-century house owners could choose from an array of architectural styles, so too may residents of these new developments enjoy a great deal of choice among builders and house styles, all of which are familiar and nostalgic for an imagined past. For the environmentally conscious, the idea that New Urbanism encourages development on sites within metropolitan areas is appealing. Denver's Stapleton is a case in point; it is a vast tract formerly used as Denver's airport

that is now being filled with houses, schools, and commercial buildings. New Urbanism projects reveal a great deal about the larger cultural and social context of American life in the early twenty-first century.

Kerry Dean Carso

See also Agricultural Architecture; Cities and Towns; Civic Architecture; Classical Revival (Neoclassicism); Colonial Revival; Commercial Architecture; Cultural Geography; Domestic Architecture; Federal Style; Georgian Style; Gothic Revival; Historic Preservation; Homeless Residences; House, Home, and Domesticity; Houses of Worship (Ecclesiastical Architecture); International Style; Mill Towns; Modernism (Art Moderne); Penitentiaries and Prisons; Planned Communities; Postmodernism; Renaissance Revival; Suburbs and Suburbia; Utopian Communities; Vernacular

References and Further Reading

Anderson, Stanford. 1999. "Architectural History in Schools of Architecture." *Journal of the Society of Architectural Historians* 58 (3): 282–291.

Brunskill, Ronald W. 1970. *Illustrated Handbook of Vernacular Architecture.* New York: Universe Books.

Cohen, Jeffrey A. 1994. "Building a Discipline: Early Institutional Settings for Architectural Education in Philadelphia, 1804–1890." *Journal of the Society of Architectural Historians* 53 (2): 139–183.

Jackson, Kenneth. 1985. *Crabgrass Frontier: The Suburbanization of the United States.* New York: Oxford University Press.

MacDougall, Elisabeth Blair, ed. 1990. *The Architectural Historian in America.* Washington, DC: National Gallery of Art.

St. George, Robert Blair, ed. 1988. *Material Life in America 1600–1860.* Boston: Northeastern University Press.

Upton, Dell. 1998. *Architecture in the United States.* Oxford, UK: Oxford University Press.

Upton, Dell, and John Michael Vlach, eds. 1986. *Common Places: Readings in American Vernacular Architecture.* Athens: University of Georgia Press.

Art Deco

Art Deco, also known as Style Moderne, was a major decorative style of the 1920s and 1930s particularly in western Europe and the United States. The style was named after the Exposition Internationale des Arts Décoratifs et Industriels Modernes, a major exhibition of decorative arts held in Paris in 1925, where sleek, fashionable goods took center stage. Art Deco is characterized by elegance and sophistication and often uses geometric forms, stylized natural forms, repetition, and symmetry. Designers used modern materials such as chromed steel, Bakelite, and glass, as well as expensive natural materials like jade, marble, and ebony, often polished to a high shine. These gleaming, streamlined forms celebrated the technological progress of the machine age and attracted a wealthy clientele. Although mass production lowered the cost of some Art Deco furniture and consumer goods, many of its most notable pieces were rare or one-of-a-kind objects made for wealthy elites.

The Art Deco style celebrated the Machine Age by combining new manmade materials with streamlined design. This 1936 Kodak Bantam Special features the use of black and polished aluminum in a sleek repeating motif. Industrial designer Walter Dorwin Teague, apparatus designer Joseph Mihalyi, and electrical engineer Chester W. Crumrine share various patents in the design of this camera for the Eastman Kodak Company. (Condé Nast Archive/Corbis)

Like its predecessor, Art Nouveau, Art Deco rejected excessive historicism, aiming instead for a style to suit the modern age. It touched many fields, including but not limited to architecture, fashion, transportation, graphic design, and furniture design. Cubism and the German Bauhaus provided important influences toward abstraction, although unlike the former two movements, Art Deco was unabashedly consumer oriented. Art Deco practitioners frequently gave their work exotic touches by borrowing from the decorative styles of ancient Egypt, Mesoamerica, Africa, and the Far East.

Notable Art Deco monuments include New York City's Rockefeller Center (1929–1940); the Chrysler Building (1926–1930) by William Van Alen (1883–1954); and the Empire State Building (1931) by Shreve, Lamb, and Harmon (founded 1929), as well as numerous movie theaters in Hollywood, California.

Hsiao-Yun Chu

See also Art Nouveau; Design History and American Design; Industrial Design; Modernism (Art Moderne); Style

References and Further Reading

Benton, Charlotte, Tim Benton, and Ghislaine Wood, eds. 2003. *Art Deco: 1910–1939*. London: V & A Publications.
Duncan, Alastair. 1986. *American Art Deco*. London: Thames and Hudson.
Wood, Ghislaine. 2003. *Essential Art Deco*. London: V & A Publications.

Art History and American Art

Art history denotes an academic discipline that seeks to understand the visual arts and their objects, artists, and modes of production, reception, and circulation within historical frameworks. Traditionally, practitioners had conceptualized art's history tele-ologically, as a carefully selected chronology of great artists (predominantly painters and sculptors in the Western tradition) whose works built upon the formal innovations of prior artists in an unending progression toward representational "truth." In modern practice, this definition of art history as an insular "history of art" has diminished as art historians focus additional attention on the relationships that exist between works of art and their specific cultural and historical moments. In this more contextual approach, works of art are understood in several overlapping ways, including: (1) formally, as expressive objects that seek development of visual/aesthetic forms capable of representing specific engagements with the external world; (2) historically, as artifacts whose representational form and depicted content can be interpreted as evidence for understanding the social and historical context of their production; and (3) structurally, as constitutive components of larger, culturally embedded systems of experience, knowledge, and meaning making. Finally, as art historian David Carrier (2003, 176) notes, the practice of art history is shaped by the fact that viewers experience works of art *in the present*, beyond the historical context of their original production and circulation. Art history, therefore, is also an open-ended process and recognizes that artworks, as material objects existing across time and space, continue to engender new meanings and histories.

As a discipline that identifies the interpretation of material things (works of art) as its primary function, art history is deeply invested in many of the same issues as material culture studies, but especially the development of interpretive methods and determination of object typologies. In the case of the former, the kinds of object-centered visual analysis developed in art history provide an important groundwork for studies in material culture. Centered on the transformation of visual/sensorial experience into textual explanation, art history provides the analytical tools and critical lexicon for interrogating an object's material characteristics—from style and formal arrangement to iconography and semiotics—in order to discover the cultural patterns that underlie them. These visual-interpretive methods offer material culture studies more humanistic modes of object engagement than the predominantly quantitative, functionalist, and economically inscribed concerns of history and the social sciences. For instance, the cross-fertilization of methods between colonial American art and material culture has enabled scholars to perceive in everyday household items (furniture, teapots, etc.) articulations of aesthetic desire, metaphor, and other forms of cultural meaning normally reserved for high-art objects such as painting and sculpture.

The application of art historical analysis to non-art objects is not without complication, however, with the predominant concern being how to differentiate between types of objects, especially those of high and low culture, art and non-art. Art historians have long argued for the uniqueness of the visual arts as a mode of cultural discourse that retains a certain (if problematic) detachment from the world of everyday things. All works of art are material objects, but all objects are not works of art. Instead, art historians believe that art exists as a culture-specific subcategory of material culture that satisfies a specific set of culture needs (which in the Western tradition are often abstract, spiritual, and aesthetic, as opposed to real, concrete, and functional purposes of tools, clothing, etc.). The question of categorization, therefore, is more than a simple judgment of taste or quality (although it involves both) and requires recognition that although

objects may communicate across a range of cultural levels, their potential for meaning is also limited by the function assigned to them by culture. Thus, questions of quality (perhaps better understood as "richness of meaning") do matter, but not simply in terms of high/low culture or artistic/aesthetic merit. Furthermore, the boundaries between artifacts of art history and material culture gain fluidity through acts of appropriation, as when a tool such as a hammer or an automobile becomes a source of aesthetic fascination, or when an abstract painting becomes the pattern for an article of clothing.

The recent expansion and formalization of material culture studies has caused art historians (in both Western and non-Western fields) to reconsider the relationship between the two scholarly endeavors. The debate has focused largely on the hierarchy of objects, with art historians (particularly those in the Western tradition) arguing for the unique importance of art as such, while others (especially popular culture specialists and, ironically, non-Western art historians) seek to demonstrate the value of analyzing traditionally non-art objects. Embedded in this debate over objects is a contest of cultural venues. Fine art is often discussed in relation to "high" culture, while material objects are more commonly considered part of "the everyday world." The central role of museums in art history adds contention to this division, as objects' installations in museum collections can drain their original cultural purpose and recode them within a system based largely on Western codes of value, rarity, and aesthetics.

The American Context

As a field within the discipline of art history, American art has been defined traditionally as beginning with the European colonization of North America in the sixteenth century and ending with the emergence of the United States as an economic, a cultural, and an artistic superpower after World War II. In recent years, however, both of these points have come to be contested. At the front end of the field, where the traditional focus has been Anglophile art from the eastern seaboard, art historians have begun to explore a larger topographic and cultural footprint by expanding to other parts of the continent (such as the Gulf Coast and Mexico) and giving greater attention to the indigenous expression and its cross-fertilization with European colonial art. At the other end, some scholars assert that the ascendancy of American art (and culture) as a new, universal form of expression represents a break with the scholarly trajectory of American art history. Others reject this notion, arguing that this division instead reflects a biased art historical ideology—the attempt of a select group of scholars to canonize postwar art with a strict chronology of European artistic development that begins with the Italian Renaissance and stretches unbroken into contemporary practice.

With a period of study that stretches more than 400 years, American art history is conceived not through paradigms of stylistic development (as is the case with most European fields: Renaissance, Baroque, Modern, etc.), but rather by what is posited as a continuous and unique cultural heritage. In this respect, American art shares affinities with many non-Western fields, whose identities are also culturally, rather than stylistically, formulated. In some cases, this condensation of centuries of history into a single monolithic category of "American art" has had the problematic effect of constructing homogeneity and unification while downplaying difference. It implies, in essence, that all artworks created in the American con-

text embody components of an essential, and insular, American spirit. Frequently, these interpretations have been tied to the triumphal narratives of progress that long permeated American history. More recently, however, the recognition of multiculturalism has led many American art historians and museum curators to break down such monolithic historical narratives and to recognize the potential for polyvalence of artistic expression. In particular, the scope of study in American art has expanded to include ethnic subspecializations such as African American, Asian American, Native American, and Latino art. This shift toward more open-ended forms of interpretation and the recognition of difference, along with the field's traditional focus on art's social and historical functions, has made the field of American art a locus for development of new methods for exploring the complex, sometimes contradictory, ways that expressive objects function as interlocutors in the negotiation of cultural identity and belief. Art historians have proven especially adept at interpreting objects "against the grain"— in ways that call into question an object's overt meaning—in order to illuminate competing orders of knowledge that exist in a culture and its discourses. An example of the value of such an approach is art historian Kirk Savage's assertion that a post–Civil War statue of a standing Abraham Lincoln alongside a freed but kneeling slave does not simply celebrate the end of slavery but subtly reinscribes racial servitude through the sculpture's positioning of the figures.

American Art History and American Material Culture

The interplay between art history and material culture has been particularly active in this American context, where fewer art historians engage in the formal and ideological battles over the maintenance of object hierarchies and, by extension, disciplinary boundaries. The reasons for this relationship are threefold. First, because American art as such is a relatively recent development (the field emerged in the 1950s and 1960s), it lacks the long lineages of artists, styles, and tastes that serve as rigid boundaries in European art history. In the absence of such an institutionalized history, and amidst the more frequent multicultural encounters of the American experience, artists and historians alike have been more receptive to exploring different modes of cultural expression and objecthood. Second, because American art historians have had to overcome the denigration of American art as provincial and its artworks as derivative of European accomplishment, they are less apt to link cultural significance to judgments of aesthetic quality. Third, from its beginnings American art history has shared substantial overlaps in interests and methods with scholars in American history, and especially American Studies. As a result, the discipline was founded upon and maintains a belief that art's history is best understood when its objects are contextualized within their broader historical moment. In such an approach, non-art material objects act not merely as backdrops but also as coequal sources that can be comparatively analyzed alongside works of art as a means to perceive larger cultural practices and ideas.

A final factor in forging the relationship between American art history and material culture studies has been the emergence of visual studies (or visual culture) as a corollary to art historical practice, and as a field of study in its own right. Like material culture, visual studies departs from art history in its choice of objects, focusing on visual artifacts whose primary purposes lie outside the aesthetic and qualitative definitions of art history. Yet visual studies appears at first glance more easily assimilated into art history, as the ways that one experiences its objects are primarily sight based, like the majority of artworks. One may, for example, use a material object without stopping to consider its look. By contrast, even the most everyday advertisement, poster, or illustration declares its existence as an object *to be seen*. In this sense, visual studies might be seen as an intermediary between art history and material studies—one that has helped facilitate the transmission of methods and practices between the realm of the art historian and that of the materialist.

Jason Weems

See also Collecting and Collections; Design History and American Design; Land and Landscape; Museums and Museum Practice; Photography; Printmaking and American Prints; Style; Visual Culture Studies

References and Further Reading
Carrier, David. 2003. "Art History." In *Critical Terms for Art History*, 2nd ed., ed. Robert Nelson and Richard Shiff, 174–187. Chicago: University of Chicago Press.

Corn, Wanda. 1988. "Coming of Age: Historical Scholarship in American Art." *Art Bulletin* 70 (2): 188–207.

Davis, John. 2003. "The End of the American Century: Current Scholarship on the Art of the United States." *Art Bulletin* 85 (1): 544–580.

Gombrich, E. H. 1985. *Meditations on a Hobby Horse and Other Essays on the Theory of Art*. 4th ed. Chicago: University of Chicago Press.

Gombrich, E. H. 1995. *The Story of Art*. 16th ed. New York: Phaidon.

Macy, L., ed. 2005. "Art History." *Grove Art Online*. www.groveart.com.

Minor, Vernon Hyde. 2004. *Art History's History*. 2nd ed. Upper Saddle River, NJ: Prentice-Hall.

Nelson, Robert S., and Richard Shiff. 2003. *Critical Terms for Art History.* 2nd ed. Chicago: University of Chicago Press.

Preziosi, Donald, ed. 1998. *The Art of Art History: A Critical Anthology.* New York: Oxford University Press.

Prown, Jules. 2001. *Art as Evidence: Writings on Art and Material Culture.* New Haven, CT: Yale University Press.

Prown, Jules, and Kenneth Haltman. 2000. *American Artifacts: Essays in Material Culture.* East Lansing: Michigan State University Press.

Savage, Kirk. 1999. *Standing Soldiers, Kneeling Slaves: Race, War, and Monument in Nineteenth-Century America.* Princeton, NJ: Princeton University Press.

Art Nouveau

Art Nouveau as a style of decorative arts flourished in Europe during the late nineteenth and early twentieth centuries but did not achieve the same popularity in the United States. The style was characterized by flowing lines of ornament, often referred to as *whiplash curves*, which were seen in furniture, metalwork, porcelain, and the graphic arts. Although many of its design motifs were stylized from nature, including flowers such as lilies and roses, they were rendered in novel ways that set them apart from historicist styles. This search for novelty in decoration and material characterizes Art Nouveau.

The style takes its name from a gallery in Paris founded in 1895 by Siegfried Bing (1838–1905), called *L'Art Nouveau,* in which the works of many leading European designers incorporating stylized naturalistic design motifs were displayed. Included among these designers was Louis Comfort Tiffany (1848–1933), an American whose work was most often associated with the style. Art Nouveau was further disseminated internationally by

The use of free-flowing, naturalistic designs defines the Art Nouveau Movement. This "Pond Lily" table lamp, made of iridescent favrile glass and bronze base, was produced by Tiffany Studios in Corono, Queens, New York, in the first decade of the twentieth century. (Jacob Babchuk/iStockPhoto)

the 1900 Exposition Universelle held in Paris, in which Tiffany also participated.

Tiffany's designs were almost wholly inspired by nature and were also influenced by the asymmetrical design of Japanese decorative arts. Best known are his glass pieces, many produced using new techniques discovered through experimentation at the glassworks of Tiffany Studios, including stained glass windows, lamps, and vases. Typical decorative motifs include flowers, fruits, plants, and insects.

H. Christian Carr

See also Decorative Arts; Design History and American Design; Glass; Style

References and Further Reading

Burke, Doreen Bolger, Jonathan Freedman, and Alice Cooney Freylinghuysen. 1986. *In Pursuit of Beauty: Americans and the Aesthetic Movement*. New York: Metropolitan Museum of Art.

Duncan, Alastair. 1998. *Masterworks of Louis Comfort Tiffany*. New York: Harry N. Abrams.

Greenhalgh, Paul, ed. 2000. *Art Nouveau 1890–1914*. New York: Harry N. Abrams.

Arts and Crafts Movement

The Arts and Crafts Movement (1880–1920) was based on a set of principles and the pursuit of related ideals rather than the pursuit and creation of an aesthetic style. Nevertheless, the material culture of the Arts and Crafts Movement is distinctive. Artists, architects, critics, and social reformers sought remedies to what they saw as the dehumanizing forces of late nineteenth-century industrialization and mass production. The machine was considered both the cause and symbol of the degradation of labor in American culture; many American reformers saw in the writings of English craftsman William Morris (1834–1896) and English critic John Ruskin (1819–1900) a guiding philosophy. (Morris and other upper-class artists, craftsmen, and reformers created the Arts and Crafts Exhibition Society in London in the 1880s, which gave the movement its name.) The pursuit of art in every aspect of everyday life provided the means by which physical labor could be ennobled and mental labor and physical labor reintegrated. The Arts and Crafts Movement challenged industrial capitalism and the appearance, purpose, and meaning of the domestic decorative arts and architecture that Americans made, purchased, and used.

Ideals and Implementation

Decorative arts scholar Wendy Kaplan has observed that the Arts and Crafts philosophy incorporated in its reaction to modernization the following tenets: the joy in labor, the simple life, truth to materials, unity in design, honesty in construction, democratic design, and fidelity to place (Kaplan et al. 2004, 11).

To some adherents the Arts and Crafts ideal was best realized through the nostalgic embrace of the small communities and handicrafts of the Middle Ages. In the "simple life" offered by the artists' colonies and utopian communities such as Rose Valley Association (Moylan, Pennsylvania; 1901–1909), Roycroft (East Aurora, New York; 1895–1938), and Byrdcliffe (Woodstock, New York; 1902–1915), medieval, guild-controlled crafts were undertaken. The vernacular artisanry of medieval pottery and weaving, metal- and woodworking, and bookbinding represented the movement's scorn of superfluous or artificial ornamentation and idealization of natural materials and design inspiration. These colonies' artists and craftsmen took as their inspiration their local environments: Native flora provided the resource for the stylized ornamentation of furniture or naturalistic ceramic forms.

Still other Arts and Crafts proselytizers founded craft and design schools or facilitated home industries for women, industrial workers, and the poor. Women were particularly prominent in the movement; for example, Cincinnatian Maria Longworth Nichols Storer (1849–1932) founded the Rookwood Pottery Company in 1880, amidst the Aesthetic Movement. Although Storer would state that her purpose in founding the pottery was her own gratification, the company's wares adhered to several Arts and Crafts tenets: handmade, high quality, naturalistic styles and ornamentation, and adaptation of Oriental designs (*japonisme*). Interior designer Candace Wheeler (1827–1923) promoted careers for women not only by her example as a professional and creator of Associated Artists but also by her establishment with others of the Women's Exchange, an institution through which women's handmade objects (especially textiles, embroidery, lace, and pottery), no matter the quality, were sold. Hundreds of women's exchanges were founded in the United States between 1890 and 1910. Other women, such as reformer Jane Addams

(1860–1935), encouraged craft production in the nation's settlement houses and in "settlement schools" in poverty-stricken Appalachia, a region that was also considered an enclave of a simpler, folk past. Many reformers had to reintroduce "folk" crafts to Appalachia.

Reform and the Domestic Decorative Arts

Charles Locke Eastlake's (1836–1908) *Hints on Household Taste in Furniture, Upholstery, and Other Details*, published in the United States in 1872, along with the establishment

The design of this 1917 Oklahoma City, Oklahoma, bungalow interior contains several emphases of the Arts and Crafts Movement: simpler lines, natural forms, and unity of design from the built-in bookcase and fireplace to the chairs and lighting fixture. (Library of Congress)

of domestic periodicals in the succeeding five decades, emphasized the pursuit of art within the domestic sphere. American Arts and Crafts leaders traveled to learn the practices of their counterparts in England and Europe, but the Arts and Crafts movement remained local in character and somewhat nationalistic in purpose. The emphasis on the vernacular and human comfort impelled Arts and Crafts advocates to develop a design vocabulary centered on the home in the form of the popular bungalow. Architects such as Will Lightfoot Price (1861–1916) took inspiration from medieval or "Queen Anne" cottages, while brothers Charles Sumner Greene (1868–1957) and Henry Mather Greene (1870–1954) adapted stuccoed Spanish missions in their designs of California bungalows. American log cabins and Native American crafts provided the design source for vacation "Adirondack camps" and resort hotels, such as the Old Faithful Inn (1902–1903) in Yellowstone National Park. Architect Frank Lloyd Wright's (1867–1959) Prairie style made use of regional materials and simple, open floor plans.

Mission style, characterizing adobe Spanish colonial missions and introduced to easterners at the Chicago World's Fair in 1893, was applied by Gustav Stickley (1858–1942) through his periodical *The Craftsman* (1901–1916) to other products, but especially furniture. Usually manufactured of oak or ash, joined by the preindustrial method of mortise and tenon, rectilinear in form, and upholstered with leather or canvas, Mission furniture could easily be adapted to mass production and to the popularity of the do-it-yourself ethos inspired by the Arts and Crafts movement. Stickley created the "Homebuilder's Club" in the pages of *The Craftsman*, offering designs for living in the Arts and Crafts philosophy. In that vein several manufacturers offered house kits:

Aladdin and Sears Honorbilt Homes were but two companies to provide Americans with houses boasting open floor plans, inglenooks, built-in bookcases and cabinets, half-timbered design or shingles, and other increasingly recognizable forms of the Arts and Crafts aesthetic. Appealing to the nostalgic sensibility of the movement, the Charles B. Limbert Company (1902–1944) of Grand Rapids and Holland, Michigan, successfully manufactured quaint "Holland Dutch" furniture.

The Arts and Crafts Movement wished to integrate art and everyday life through the belief in art as regenerative and inspirational; through the use of natural, "honest" materials; and through the reorganization of the fundamental relationship of workmanship, work, and the individual creator. The wish to integrate all aspects of mental and physical activity through art created a characteristic style found in limited-edition books, textiles, dress, ceramics, glass, furniture, and architecture.

Shirley Teresa Wajda

See also Aesthetic Movement; Eastlake Style; Handicraft and Artisanship; Interior Design; Utopian Communities

References and Further Reading

Boris, Eileen. 1986. *Art and Labor: Ruskin, Morris, and the Craftsman Ideal in America.* Philadelphia, PA: Temple University Press.

Clark, Robert Judson, ed. 1972. *The Arts and Crafts Movement in America, 1876–1916.* Princeton, NJ: Princeton University Press.

Kaplan, Wendy, et al. 1987. *"The Art that is Life": The Arts & Crafts Movement in America, 1875–1920.* Boston: Museum of Fine Arts and Little, Brown.

Kaplan, Wendy, et al. 2004. *The Arts and Crafts Movement in Europe and America: Design for the Modern World.* New York: Thames & Hudson in association with the Los Angeles County Museum of Art.

Kardon, Janet, ed. 1993. *The Ideal Home 1900–1920: The History of Twentieth-Century Craft in*

America. New York: Harry N. Abrams for American Craft Museum.

Lears, T. J. Jackson. 1981. *No Place of Grace: Antimodernism and the Transformation of American Culture, 1880–1920*. New York: Pantheon Books.

Attics

The space found directly under a building's roof is called the *attic* (or *garret* or *loft*). The nostalgic image of "grandma's attic" or attics as treasuries of long-forgotten family heirlooms depends on attics' primary purpose as a storage space but overlooks the other purposes attics served. A building's temperature is regulated in part by the unmoving air in this space, and historically this space in American domestic dwellings has been used variably for storage, household production, sleeping, and play.

Loft spaces, though often dark, cramped, and cold and damp in winter, served many uses. Family members, servants, slaves, and at times guests climbed a ladder or small stairway to find straw pallets or mattresses on which to sleep amidst trunks, barrels, and baskets of foodstuffs, household tools, and other possessions. In larger, well-built buildings, attics aided household efficiency and cleanliness by providing a storage space for tools, possessions, and other materials. Children's furniture and clothing, out-of-season clothing, and household furnishings subject to seasonal use were put away for safekeeping and eventual retrieval.

Throughout the seventeenth, eighteenth, and nineteenth centuries, attics in the summer and fall provided optimal environments in which to dry and preserve herbs and flowers—even meat—and to store safely flour, oats, and other dried foods year-round. Laundry was often hung on clothesline strung across the space. Household production activities, such as spinning, weaving, and other handcrafts, were undertaken in the attic.

Servants in middle- and upper-class homes found their quarters in the attic, in the basement, or on the uppermost bedroom floor (but distanced from family members' bedrooms). By the twentieth century, the employment of technologically advanced heating and cooling systems allowed the attic environment to be regulated year-round; bungalow attics were created with built-in storage units and windows and could be used as a children's playroom or bedroom as well. Attics have served as potential useful spaces convertible to the specific needs of a household.

Shirley Teresa Wajda

See also Bedrooms; Cellars and Basements; Servants' Spaces

References and Further Reading

Clark, Clifford Edward, Jr. 1986. *The American Family Home, 1800–1960*. Chapel Hill: University of North Carolina Press.

Garrett, Elisabeth Donaghy. 1990. *At Home: The American Family, 1750–1870*. New York: Harry N. Abrams.

Nylander, Jane C. 1993. *Our Own Snug Fireside: Images of the New England Home, 1760–1860*. New York: Alfred A. Knopf.

Auctions

An *auction* is a public sale in which individuals (bidders) compete through offering money (bid) for a proffered item. The highest bidder wins the auction and is allowed to pay for and acquire the item. Through bidding the market value of certain types of goods—especially artworks and antiques—is established. While most people commonly associate auction houses with the sale of fine art, antiques, and other collectibles, auction activity varies greatly in the United States. Items commonly sold at auction include furniture and decorative objects, real estate, paperback book publishing rights, airline tickets, tobacco, and even fish. Perhaps the most highly charged type of auction in American history was the slave auction. Before the legal abolition of slavery in 1865, African and African American men, women, and children were displayed, examined, and auctioned off to the highest bidder, often in the public squares of America's major cities.

As public events, auctions are at times theatrical performances. The key performers may include the auction house, under whose auspices the auction takes place; the auctioneer, who recognizes the bids and maintains the event's pace; the seller, who has placed goods for sale through the auction house; and the bidder/buyer, who attends the auction on the hunt for bargains and treasure. And if the buyer cannot be at the auction in person, a dealer specializing in the type of commodity being sold can bid on the buyer's behalf.

Auctions have taken place since ancient Roman times. The major auction houses in the United States today include Sotheby's, Christie's, and most recently, eBay, an Internet auction site. Auction houses can employ a variety of methods in their transactions. The classic, most popular model is the *English auction*, where bids are given in ascending value and the person with the highest bid pays for the item. In the *Dutch* (or *reverse*) *auction* the bidding descends from a higher price—thus the person with the first bid is also the person with the last bid. The *Japanese simultaneous auction* involves many people giving different bids at the same time, and of these the highest bid is selected. The *silent auction*, frequently used as a fund-raiser for charities, allows participants to place bids on items by writing their names and bid amounts on lists; at the end of the event, the highest bid wins.

Besides the bidding itself, several elements make up an auction. The auction house may publish an auction catalogue containing photographs and descriptions of items for sale. The conditions of sale—the rules and regulations set by the auction house—are commonly found in the catalogues as well as being publicized before the auction. Prior viewings, usually at the auction site, allow potential bidders an opportunity to view items before the bidding begins.

Auctions are often held to resolve social, financial, and criminal situations where ownership is unclear, such as the problem of disposing of the estate of a relative, bankruptcy and foreclosures, or liquidating assets seized from felons. Because their prices are publicized as value is established, auctions can influence the prices of commodities at future sales.

Rebecca S. Graff

See also Antiques; Commodity; Consumerism and Consumption; Fakes; Money, Currency, and Value; Secondhand Goods and Shopping

References and Further Reading

Hamilton, Charles. 1981. *Auction Madness: An Uncensored Look Behind the Velvet Drapes of the Great Auction Houses*. New York: Everest House.
Learmount, Brian. 1985. *A History of the Auction*. London: Barnard and Learmount.
Smith, Charles W. 1989. *Auctions: The Social Construction of Value*. New York: Free Press.

Automobile Camping (Auto-Camping)

Recreational automobile camping began as a pastime for the wealthy but became more affordable, and thus more popular, during the early decades of the twentieth century. *Camping*, that is, the setting up of an outdoor domicile (whether permanent, in the form of a campsite, or temporary), is a leisure activity encouraged by the development of the automobile and of attendant travel.

Late nineteenth-century recreational campers had conducted their journeys in horse-drawn wagons. These affluent travelers were quick to embrace the automobile and the greater convenience it brought to their outdoor adventures. They were soon joined by upper-middle-class motorists, who shared their appreciation for independent wandering.

One of the main obstacles these early motor tourists faced was the poor condition of American roads. Most road-building efforts since the mid-1800s had focused on the railroads, and the nation's public road system remained limited and was poorly maintained. Yet early automobile enthusiasts saw themselves as latter-day frontier adventurers, and in the touring literature of the era they recounted with pride the challenges of early automobile travel, including mud traps, mechanical problems, inaccurate maps, and boulder-strewn roads. They also embraced the many difficulties involved in setting up makeshift camps on the side of the road each evening. The apparent pleasure they took in "roughing it" did not, however, prevent them from becoming enthusiastic consumers of a great range of automobile and camping accessories that American companies soon began to market to them.

By the 1920s, automobiles had become more affordable and automobile ownership more widespread. Recreational automobile camping also became more affordable and expanded in popularity during the early decades of the twentieth century. As the number of Americans on the road increased, so too did the demand for better roads and roadside accommodations. This demand resulted in ambitious road improvement projects as well as the development of municipal and, later, private campgrounds.

Motor camps came to be understood as an expression of American ideals. They offered a space in which people of different classes and regions could mingle freely, unhindered by ostentation and social hierarchies. The motoring heroine of Sinclair Lewis's (1885–1951) 1919 novel *Free Air*, an upper-class easterner named Claire Boltwood, delights in her journey west and the great variety of travelers she and her father encounter on the road. In the course of their journey, they meet mechanics, farmers, and professors. Sitting beside a camp bonfire with her new friend, a young mechanic named Milt, Claire exclaims, "There is an America! I'm glad I've found it" (140). A similar scene occurs in the 1934 road film *It Happened One Night*, in which society belle Ellie Andrews (actress Claudette Colbert), accompanied by newspaperman Peter Warne (actor Clark Gable), explores the democratic space of the motor camp. She is at first startled to learn that she must wait in line to take a shower, but from the end of the line she grins happily.

It would be a mistake, however, to take too literally such portrayals. Free camps quickly gave way to private pay camps, whose fee structures limited access for poorer guests or funneled them into the less desirable areas of the camp. Racial minorities were frequently excluded.

Between the 1920s and 1940s, auto camps offered increasingly comfortable accommodations, including cabins with beds and stoves, and eventually private showers and kitchenettes. These early "motor hotels" were the beginning of the American motel industry.

Christine Photinos

See also Automobiles and Automobility;
Highways and National Highway System;
Land Transportation; Service Stations;
Tourism and Travel

References and Further Reading
Belasco, Warren James. 1979. *Americans on the
Road: From Autocamp to Motel, 1910–1945.*
Cambridge, MA: MIT Press.
Franz, Kathleen. 2005. *Tinkering: Consumers
Reinvent the Early Automobile.* Philadelphia:
University of Pennsylvania Press.
It Happened One Night. 1934. Columbia Pictures.
Lewis, Sinclair. 1919. *Free Air.* Lincoln: Univer-
sity of Nebraska Press.
Patton, Phil. 1986. *Open Road: A Celebration of the
American Highway.* New York: Simon &
Schuster.

*Completed Model Ts roll off the Ford Motor Company
assembly line in Highland Park, Michigan, circa 1917.
The assembly line deskilled workers but also provided
American consumers with cheaper cars. (Library of
Congress)*

Automobiles and Automobility

The *automobile*, a motor-propelled, wheeled
vehicle operated by and carrying passengers, is a dynamic form of material culture.
Corporations, designers, engineers, and consumers all aided in the social construction of
the automobile, determining its design and
its cultural importance as a machine, consumer product, and form of mobility. The car
provided Americans with a new consumer
technology with which to practice their technological skills and display their cultural
agendas. As technological objects, automobiles have embodied machine politics, have
served as instruments of power, and have
provided the symbolic focal point for various political causes from suffrage to consumer rights. Cars have also provided fertile
ground for personal and community expression, and consumers used the automobile
to promote their own agendas, reshaping
the machine to fit their needs and desires.
Policymakers, planners, corporations, and
drivers used and continue to use the automobile to restructure the national landscape,
laying highways, building suburbs, and
developing new kinds of architecture to
accommodate the car. Automobiles, therefore, fulfill the call by material culture scholars to consider material objects as influential
in historical change.

The Automobile as Product
and Symbol of Mass Production
and Mass Consumption

On Thanksgiving Day in 1895, Americans
witnessed their first automobile race in
Chicago. Within a few days of the race,
inventor Thomas A. Edison (1847–1931) predicted that the horseless carriage would
soon take over American roads (Flink 1988,
23). The invention of the automobile had an
international lineage that included contributions from inventors in Germany, France,
and Great Britain. Innovators in the United
States, though, introduced critical changes in

production that made the automobile one of the most formidable mass-consumer products of the twentieth century. The first of these innovations was mass production, which changed the production of the automobile and its relationship to consumers.

Encouraged by races like the one in Chicago, American inventors, mechanics, carriage makers, and bicycle manufacturers entered the heady competition to create automobiles. Among these individuals was Henry Ford (1863–1947), who declared that he would "build a car for the great multitude." Ford did not invent the car, although he was among the many inventors in the United States experimenting with the internal combustion engine. Rather, Ford perfected the manufacturing process of assembly line production, or mass production, at his factory in Highland Park, Michigan, in 1913. Once built of component parts by skilled workers, cars now moved down an automated assembly line where semi-skilled workers added parts until a complete vehicle emerged at the end of the factory. The results of assembly line production were great: Ford could produce more vehicles, more quickly and less expensively than other manufacturers. Coupled with Ford's five-dollar day, a 1914 program to ensure worker regularity by paying over twice the daily rate, and vertical integration, a system in which the same company owns all the different aspects of making, selling, and delivering a product, mass production also became known as *Fordism*, a system of manufacturing that is often credited with the mass consumption of the automobile. Indeed, by World War I, Ford controlled nearly half the market for new cars in the United States.

The Model T democratized auto ownership and became an icon of American mobility and ingenuity. If American journalists had once worried about cars as elite objects and potential instigators of class division, the Model T and similar low-priced cars quelled such criticisms. Most middle-class Americans could own a Model T after 1913. In order to make the car more accessible to the multitudes, Ford's Model T had a democratic design. Built high above the ground with a light, flexible frame, it could withstand the rugged condition of American roads. Americans did not just drive their "Tin Lizzies" (another name for the Model T); they also tinkered with them, changing the bodies with after-market accessories. Farmers, for instance, used the Model T as a multipurpose technology by adding truck beds and adapting the engines to run a variety of farm equipment. Because of its affordability and adaptability, the Model T remained in production from 1908 until 1925.

The long life of the Model T might now seems exceptional because of a second major innovation in American auto production, the annual model change, or *planned obsolescence*. Credited to Alfred P. Sloan (1875–1966), president of General Motors in the 1920s, planned obsolescence, the idea that models would be phased out and replaced with new ones each year, changed not only the auto industry but also the way Americans thought about consumption. General Motors advertised the idea that there was a car for every purse, or income level, and every person in a family. After the mid-1920s, middle-class consumers were encouraged to buy a new car every year, and the annual automobile shows made viewing the new models into a cultural spectacle of progress. By the 1930s, annual automotive consumption was inextricably linked to the health of the American economy and promoted as a solution to the economic reversals of the Great Depression. Planned obsolescence was not enough to end the

Depression, however. It would not be until the postwar abundance of the 1950s and 1960s that Americans would again engage in the consumer revelry typified by the annual automobile shows.

Consumers and Auto Culture

After mass production, a wide swath of American consumers embraced the automobile as an object that would give them access to private transportation, make leisure travel less expensive, and give them a new form for personal expression. Although auto ownership was often circumscribed by class and race, the automobile and automobility—the association of personal mobility with the automobile and ideas of independence—became part of "the American Dream" through popular culture from advertising, popular music, and literature to auto races and pleasure travel. The automobile became almost synonymous with the family vacation by the 1920s. In addition, popular music, from songs like "My Merry Oldsmobile" (1905) to "Little Deuce Coupe" (1963), celebrated the automobile as a key to spatial and personal freedom. On the other hand, modern literature like F. Scott Fitzgerald's *The Great Gatsby* (1925) used the car as a symbol of the inequalities of modern life.

Automobility allowed consumers to express personal desires and group aspirations for social equality. Almost from the beginning, young Americans used the family automobile to change traditional patterns of courtship. Robert S. Lynd (1892–1970) and Helen Merrell Lynd's (1894–1982) sociological study of American culture, *Middletown: A Study in American Culture* (1929), revealed that American youth used the car to remove dating from the chaperoned confines of the house in the 1920s. In the same period, women demonstrated their equality with

men by driving and often repairing their own cars, and using them in parades advocating women's suffrage. Another group of drivers, middle-class African Americans, bought cars in the 1920s and 1930s to escape the humiliation of Jim Crow segregation on trains and created alternative landscapes of travel.

During the Great Depression, automobile ownership actually increased, despite economic hard times. During World War II, automobile manufacturers began producing materiel such as armaments for the war effort. It was not until 1942, however, that domestic automobile manufacture ceased and major automakers began aircraft production, in part due to federally mandated conversion. In addition, the Office of Price Administration rationed gasoline, not because of fuel shortages but to conserve the rubber used in automobile tires. After World War II, automobile production and sales rapidly regained ground and soon exceeded prewar levels, in part due to the development of new, car-dependent residential developments and shopping venues tailored for automobiles, such as shopping centers and drive-in restaurants.

Consumers also used the material culture of the automobile as a form of cultural expression and grassroots politics in the twentieth century. American travelers redesigned the automobile to underscore their sense of personal freedom on the open road; they remade their autos into private sleeping quarters to avoid urban hotels. In the 1930s, cars with travel equipment evolved into larger house trailers and provided a way for some Americans to avoid property taxes and move more freely during the Great Depression. In the 1950s, male subcultures turned used cars into *hot rods*, demonstrating their mechanical skills. Hot rods were met with concerns about youth rebellion and in some cases laws restricting street racing as well as the design of cars allowed on local roads. By the 1960s and 1970s, Latinos turned their cars into *low riders*—cars with low suspension, elaborate interiors, and mural-like artwork. Low riders became material forms of "outsider aesthetics" that challenged the dominant culture to recognize social and cultural difference. Automotive design also offered a platform for grassroots political action. As consumer advocate Ralph Nader wrote in his famous 1965 book, *Unsafe at Any Speed*, design could be deadly when manufacturers like General Motors spent more money on styling than on safety. In the 1960s, the battle over the rear suspension of General Motor's Corvair empowered consumers' advocates.

Changing the Built Environment

As Americans incorporated the automobile into daily patterns of travel and commuting, they changed the built environment. In the 1920s, Henry Ford called for the automobile to help Americans escape the city for the new "crabgrass frontier" of the suburb, which he and many of his contemporaries considered a healthier, more ideal space. Manufacturers developed an auto-centered vision of the future and aided in the replacement of older forms of public transportation such as trolleys. American drivers shared this vision and advocated for more and better roads. For better or worse, a growing reliance on the automobile created new spaces dedicated to a mobile life centered on the car. Roads became "buyways," new spaces for advertising and commerce. As Americans moved to the suburbs, especially after World War II, they changed the architecture of houses, stores, schools, and entertainment venues to accommodate the car. Architects rearranged private dwellings and commercial centers by adding parking spaces at the front of buildings. Indeed, parking would become one of the most vexing problems of automobility, with various architectural and regulatory solutions, such as parking meters, that marked the landscape. After World War II, drivers enjoyed the novelty and convenience of eating at drive-in restaurants and seeing movies at drive-in theaters, and cities and states, aided by federal funding, built highways that cut through and eventually bypassed cities, encouraging businesses to leave the city for the suburbs.

Although many saw these changes as progress, others did not. Scholars, environmentalists, and citizens' groups opposed highway projects and questioned the material effects of automobility. Despite an oil crisis in the 1970s and more recent efforts to revive public transit, the automobile has remained an important part of Americans' material experience, symbolized most recently in the growing popularity and recent politicization of NASCAR (National Association for Stock Car Auto Racing).

Kathleen Franz

See also Automobile Camping (Auto-Camping); Consumerism and Consumption; Highways and National Highway System; Land Transportation; Service Stations; Suburbs and Suburbia; Technology; Tourism and Travel

References and Further Reading
Flink. James J. 1988. *The Automobile Age*. Cambridge, MA: MIT Press.
Franz, Kathleen. 2005. *Tinkering: Consumers Reinvent the Early Automobile*. Philadelphia: University of Pennsylvania Press.
Gudis, Catherine. 2004. *Buyways: Billboards, Automobiles, and the American Landscape*. New York: Routledge.
Hounshell, David. 1985. *From the American System to Mass Production: 1800–1932: The Development of Manufacturing Technology in the United States*. Baltimore, MD: Johns Hopkins University Press.

National Museum of American History. n.d.
"Americans on the Move." National
Museum of American History, Smithsonian
Institution, http://americanhistory.si.edu/
onthemove.

Post, Robert C. 1996. *High Performance: The
Culture and Technology of Drag Racing, 1950–
1990*. Baltimore, MD: Johns Hopkins University Press.

B

Base Metalwork and Metalware

Base (or *parent*) *metals* are those metals defined as common and not precious; iron, lead, tin, copper, nickel, aluminum, and zinc, for example, are plentiful and mined throughout the world. Base metals corrode easily when in contact with oxygen (noble metals, such as gold, resist corrosion). Alloys created of base metals—brass, pewter, and Britannia—have been used widely in North America. Base metals are employed to create a wide variety of material culture, from iron I-beams in buildings and railroad tracks to the bodies of moving vehicles, weapons, and currency to house-, dining-, and kitchenware to decorative arts. This essay surveys the uses of common base metals in the domestic environment.

With fire, anvil, hammer, and tong, blacksmiths since the Middle Ages have created from iron many utilitarian and decorative features of buildings and streets, farms and townhouses, and kitchens and parlors. Base metals' malleability adapted well to fashionable styles. Blacksmiths were among the first European colonists in North America in the seventeenth century. As early as 1648, iron ore was mined and smelted in Saugus, Massachusetts. Early metalworkers applied their skills not only to iron but also to lead, tin, pewter, brass, and copper, often in response to custom orders. Smiths at their forges were integral to the viability of a village or town. By the American Revolution, the metal trades were specialized: locksmiths and coppersmith and gunsmiths, pewterers and nail makers, ax makers and razor grinders. Nevertheless, the colonists depended on England for many raw metals and finished products.

Iron

Iron was, and is, as fundamental to America's industry, transportation, and warfare as it was, and is, to daily life in the forms of cookware, stoves, and lighting devices. Iron ore must be processed through heat provided by coke in blast furnaces to be rendered usable as wrought and cast iron or steel. Iron foundries were established in the American colonies by the mid-eighteenth century. The discovery of the great iron ore deposits throughout what would become the United States ensured that ironwares would be widely available by the Civil War (1861–1865).

Wrought iron, which has little carbon, resists rust. In the American colonies wrought iron was used as architectural ornament in fences, stair railings, balconies, and gates, the styles of which were readily available in pattern books. The metal was also utilized decoratively in interiors through the creation of fireplace equipment, screens, and window and door hardware.

By the 1850s, iron processing and forges had begun to be industrialized, and the cost of wrought iron fell. In the 1850s, however, cast iron, more versatile in its production and application, became the more popular choice for the rest of the century. Formed in molds, cast iron was used widely, not only in housewares, heating and cooking stoves, and architectural and garden ornament but also in building and bridge construction, war materiel and transportation, and farm and industrial implements and machinery.

By the end of the nineteenth century, the introduction of color into the production spaces of the domestic dwelling was achieved in part due to the introduction of enameled cast iron in items from sinks to cookware. An application of a vitreous enamel glaze to cast iron pots and frypans rendered them rust-proof and required less maintenance as it provided for better cleaning in an era in which sanitary methods were applied more assiduously to the kitchen and bathroom.

Copper and Brass

Copper, reddish-brown in color, was mined in Connecticut, New Jersey, and Maryland in the early eighteenth century, but copper ore remained scarce until western mines were found in the nineteenth century. The metal was fashioned by Native Americans, espe-

cially in the East, for use as human adornment, as ceremonial objects, and as the material for tools. European colonists employed copper to make cookware and utensils, as well as drawer pulls and doorknobs. Copper was instrumental in the print revolution and in daguerreotypy in the first half of the nineteenth century.

Brass, an alloy of copper and zinc, is often used in lighting devices. Candlesticks in great numbers were imported from England until the American Revolution. Kettles, pans, pots, and even stills were the popular forms of brasswares in the domestic dwelling. Fire-dogs and fireplace implements were also cast in brass. The artisans of the Arts and Crafts Movement, such as the Roycrofters, employed both copper and brass in lamps and lampshades, bookends, desk sets, tablewares, and ornamental fixtures. These metals were often hammered by hand.

Tin

Before 1750, much of the tin in colonial America was exported from Germany to England to be fashioned into wares and sent to the American colonies. By the American Revolution, the English could produce tin-plate sheets to be sent to American tinsmiths for manufacturing utensils, vessels, lanterns, and other useful items. Rather than craft specific pieces, such as cooking utensils, tinsmiths in the early nineteenth century began producing wares in larger numbers for commercial trade. Tin peddlers served as links between small tinsmiths and factories and the consumers from the late eighteenth through the early twentieth century, though the rise of factory production after the Civil War and the rise of retail stores generally replaced the peddler. By the 1920s, aluminum had replaced tin in kitchenwares, and steel and stainless steel entered the market after

World War II (1939–1945). Plain and enameled tinware, for both kitchen use and domestic decoration, is still produced.

Painted tinwares (also called *toleware*), imitating Chinese lacquer imported from England, were popular in the late eighteenth-century United States. These items served as the impetus for a domestic industry for decorative painted tinwares in the nineteenth century.

Pewter

Pewter is a metal alloy of tin, antimony, copper, and in early America, lead. This malleable alloy has a low melting point and is often cast in brass or bronze molds, primarily for tablewares and decorative pieces. Pewter's softness allows it to be carved, punched, pressed, and turned on a lathe.

Pewter possesses a long history of wide use. England's pewterers' guilds were founded in the fourteenth century. "Touch marks" (trademarks) and quality marks were employed by pewterers to "sign" and advertise their wares and to guarantee the value of the metals used. Pewter's brightness and luster imitates silver, and by the sixteenth century pewterwares could be found in all households except those of the very poor. Pewter's luster required constant scouring, making its maintenance labor intensive. More importantly, pewter's lead content was toxic; modern pewterwares do not contain lead.

Pewterers in colonial America were undertaking their trade by the middle of the seventeenth century. Because raw materials were unavailable and England's mercantilist policies inhibited the pewter industry (unworked pewter and lead were periodically taxed and tin ore was forbidden to be exported to the colonies), American pewterers more often melted down old pieces to make new wares: dining utensils; plates, bowls, and other tablewares; candlesticks; and lamps. English pewterwares, especially tea and coffee services, were created specifically for the American market before the Revolution. Nevertheless, American pewterers did succeed in trade: these include Frederick Bassett (1740–1800) of New York City, William Will (1742–1798) of Philadelphia, Thomas Danforth II (1731–1782) and Thomas Danforth III (1756–1840) of Connecticut, and Nathaniel Austin (1763–1807) of Charlestown, Massachusetts. By 1800, cheaper, colorful, and relatively maintenance-free china and glassware were replacing pewter, as were newly created metals such as Britannia and silverplate.

Britannia

Close in composition to pewter, *Britannia*, a metal alloy of tin, copper, and antimony (with additions at times of bismuth, brass, or zinc), was developed by English craftsmen at the end of the eighteenth century. By the first decade of the nineteenth century, American craftsmen, especially in New England, had begun to produce Britannia housewares, creating an industry that thrived until the Civil War.

Unlike pewter, Britannia, originally known as "white metal," possesses a silvery luster and resists tarnishing. The more economical and hard Britannia could be molded, die cut (stamped), and spun (on a lathe) in a variety of shapes that could more easily incorporate changing decorative style. Various parts of a given object were cast (molded), turned (on a lathe), then soldered together. Due to the metal's versatility, craftsmen often imitated with it designs in silver or silverplate. Machine-made Britanniawares became a cheaper alternative to silver. Spoons, candlesticks, tea and coffee pots, cream cups, sugar bowls, mugs, tumblers, soup tureens and ladles, urns, salvers, vases, caster frames, covered boxes, shaving boxes, snuff boxes, inkstands, spittoons, lamps, and looking-glass frames were all made of Britannia.

Early manufacturers of Britannia in the United States include Thomas Danforth Boardman (1784–1873) of Boston, Massachusetts; Israel Trask (1786–1867) of Beverly, Massachusetts; George Richardson (1818–1848) of Cranston, Rhode Island; and Samuel Ely Hamlin (1774–1864) of Providence, Rhode Island. Other American manufactories of Britannia included Connecticut's Meriden Britannia Company, Massachusetts' Taunton Britannia Manufacturing Company (which would become Reed and Barton), and Ohio's Sellew and Company, which supplied city shops and rural peddlers along the eastern seaboard as well as the western frontier (made accessible by the Erie Canal, completed in 1825). English makers of Britannia also competed in the American market. James Dixon and Sons of Sheffield, for example, employed four American agents to market its wares, mostly tea and coffee services. The introduction of electroplating silver onto base metals (silverplate) in the 1830s led to the decline of Britannia by the Civil War.

Shirley Teresa Wajda

See also Ceramics; Decorative Arts; Design History and American Design; Glass; Silverwork and Silverware; Style; Technology; Tools, Implements, and Instruments

References and Further Reading
Fennimore, Donald L. 1975. "Metalwork." *American Art Journal* 7 (1): 93–106.
Goyne, Nancy A. 1965. "Britannia in America: The Introduction of a New Alloy and a New Industry." *Winterthur Portfolio* 2: 160–196.
Hale, Rosemary D. 1967. "Cookware: A Study in Vertical Integration." *Journal of Law and Economics* 10: 169–179.
Hyde, Charles K. 1998. *Copper for America: The United States Copper Industry from Colonial Times to the 1990s.* Tucson: University of Arizona Press.
Kauffman, Henry J. 1966. *Early American Ironwork: Cast and Wrought.* New York: C. E. Tuttle.
Kauffman, Henry J. 1968. *American Copper and Brass.* Camden, NJ: Thomas Nelson and Sons.
Laughlin, Ledlie I. 1940. *Pewter in America.* 2 vols. Cambridge, MA: Riverside Press.
Mulholland, James A. 1981. *A History of Metals in Colonial America.* Tuscaloosa: University of Alabama Press.
Snyder, Ellen Marie. 1985. "Victory over Nature: Victorian Cast-Iron Seating Furniture." *Winterthur Portfolio* 20 (4): 221–242.
Sonn, Albert H. 1979 (1928). *Early American Wrought Iron.* New York: Bonanza Books.

Bathrooms

With its definitive combination of sink, toilet, and tub and/or shower, the bathroom is found in almost every American house, thanks to a combination of technology, awareness of the effects of hygiene upon health, shifting attitudes toward privacy and convenience, and ultimately the setting of minimum legal housing standards. According to the 2000 United States Census, 99.5 percent of American dwellings had complete plumbing facilities (complete bathrooms), the highest percentage in the world.

Yet the American domestic bathroom has been commonplace only since the turn of the twentieth century. From the colonial era through much of the nineteenth century, human waste was deposited outdoors. Bathing, which was not a common activity by any means, took place in a portable tub in a multipurpose room that also was the site of cooking, eating, and household crafts in the colonial era, requiring privacy as bedchambers were adopted throughout the nineteenth century.

Human Elimination

Until the mid- to late-nineteenth century, most households used outhouses or chamber pots that were dumped out of doors at the earliest opportunity. Even if hygiene was not a concern, the smell of human waste was not welcome indoors and harsh words were reserved for those who would install new-fangled water closets indoors. By the late 1800s, advances in water closet design, coupled with urban public sewer and waste treatment systems, impelled the integration of private water closets into new houses—typically adjacent to a second-floor bedroom. By the middle of the twentieth century, 85 percent of American households had indoor toilets.

Bathing and Showering

Unlike elimination, bathing was an optional activity—one that many men, women, and children only minimally undertook. By the mid-1700s, bathing was starting to be perceived as virtuous, but even in the early 1800s, some municipalities prohibited regular bathing. More typically, one might repair to a bedchamber and make use of a basin and pitcher of water, a sponge, and, in the mid-1800s, soap. By the century's end, permanently installed, but not plumbed, bathtubs were part of a handful of wealthy households.

As piped-in public water became available and as awareness increased of connections between cleanliness and good health, the number of houses with tubs increased. Still, a modern bathroom—combining toilet, sink, and tub—was a sign of relative affluence into the twentieth century. By the mid-1900s, however, about 95 percent of houses had running water, 85 percent had indoor toilets, and 80 percent had fixed bathtubs or showers.

Since the mid-twentieth century, the basic requirements of the bathroom have been complicated by demands for greater privacy, convenience, and comfort. Air-jet and whirl-pool tubs, double sinks, exotic tile for the floors and walls, and other expensive amenities became common features. The number of bathrooms per house has increased, with new houses and apartments typically boasting full bathrooms adjoining most, if not every, bedroom.

Janet Tyson

See also Bodily Cleanliness and Hygiene; Technology

References and Further Reading
Hunter, Christine. 1999. *Ranches, Rowhouses & Railroad Flats: American Homes: How They Shape Our Landscapes and Neighborhoods*. New York: W. W. Norton.
Ierley, Merritt. 1999. *Open House: A Guided Tour of the American Home, 1637–Present*. New York: Henry Holt.
Ogle, Maureen. 1992. *All the Modern Conveniences: American Household Plumbing, 1840–1890*. Baltimore, MD: Johns Hopkins University Press.
Rogers, Kate Ellen. 1962. *The Modern House, U.S.A.: Its Design and Decoration*. New York: Harper & Brothers.

Bedrooms

The *bedroom* is a domestic space designated primarily for sleeping. As its name states, however, a bedroom is intended to hold a bed and bedstead, and it is this function, and not sleep, that signals the room's historic role as a symbolic and not merely a functional space.

Early American Sleeping Spaces

The British, Dutch, German, and Swedish colonists did not construct bedrooms in the first century of settlement in North America. In the typical hall-parlor house plan, the *parlor* (sometimes called the *best room*) held the householder's prized items, including the bed and bedstead. Domestic space was not democratic space. The heads of the household slept in the parlor, while other members of the household (family members, visitors, servants, and slaves) slept in the hall or in the unheated spaces under the roof. Beds were few and straw- and grass-filled ticks were common. Both were often shared by family members as well as servants, guests, and at times strangers.

By the mid-eighteenth century, some colonists were constructing houses with bedchambers. Separated by passageways and stairways from other household activities, the bedroom (whether heated or not) became dedicated to acts increasingly considered private: sleeping and dressing, of course, but also the entertainment of invited family members and friends. Bedchamber furniture could include trunks, chairs, chests of drawers, mirrors, desks, and side tables. Beds and bedsteads were hung with bed curtains and dressed with linen and were expensive and valuable possessions. A chamber pot was found beneath the bed or in a washstand. Illness and childbirth mandated isolated rest away from the household, and a parlor or master's bedchamber could be converted into a sick chamber. An "invalid chair" boasted wings with which to combat drafts and a comfortable down-filled cushion upon which to rest. The bedstead itself was wood with a rope or wood-slat bottom on which a straw-filled tick lay. On this sat the heavy (goose) feather bed, a bolster, sheets, pillows, blankets, and counterpane (bedspread). Bed hangings were to match curtains, asserting again the importance of the room. Difficult to clean, the bed was aired and usually replenished with straw and down in the spring.

Nineteenth-Century Privacy

Throughout the nineteenth century at least one bedroom could be found next to the parlor on the ground floor of many middle-class American dwellings; this was the *master bedroom* (although the room's accoutrements were often feminized). Like its colonial predecessor, this room allowed for privacy for conjugal relations; when necessary, this room served also for births and the mother's "lying in" afterward.

Bedrooms were generally segregated on the second floor, and access to each was controlled by the stairways (public and service or back) and by a single door linking each chamber to a common hallway. As with the downstairs parlor, bedroom furniture could be purchased in matched "suites" of various woods and styles. Washstands, in an era before indoor plumbing, and often costly wardrobes to hold clothing, before the inclusion of closet storage in bedrooms, were desirable items. Mass-produced, cheaper "cottage furniture" of painted pine or other softwood mimicked the fashion of coordinated sets of bedstead, chests of drawers, and chairs. Paint colors were soft: gray, pale blue or lavender, and white. Heating systems ensured cleanliness as well as warmth, and the introduction of these systems, along with the threat of fire to the yards of bed hangings and linen, led advice writers to admonish readers to do away with the bed drapery. Dependent on the house plan and the relationship to their employers, servants' sleeping quarters could be located in the attic, on the same floor as the family, next to the kitchen, or in the basement.

Twentieth-Century Individualism

The introduction in the twentieth century of fashionable single-story dwellings—such as the bungalow and the ranch house and their urban counterparts, the apartment, tenement, and three-decker buildings—offered a variety of floor plans locating bedrooms just off the social hub of the house or segregated in a "sleeping zone" apart from public spaces. Some bungalow plans included "sleeping porches," screened spaces that were purported to be healthier by maximizing access to fresh air. Mass-produced mattresses, box springs, and bedsteads, standardized by size, lowered the price of furnishing bedrooms.

Although the establishment of psychology in the early twentieth century would redefine what it was to be a male, a female, an adult, an adolescent, a child, and an infant, a century earlier advice writers counseled that a person's character was properly developed in the privacy and freedom allowed in having a bedroom of one's own. What is consistently found in nineteenth- and twentieth-century childrearing guides is the evolution of gender-specific advice, culminating in children of the same sex sharing rooms, if not beds—and only if the family could not afford a bedroom for each child. Decorating manuals, then and now, tend to espouse gender-specific colors and design themes for children. Bedrooms today for young and old are bedecked with a variety of themes related to fashion or to popular culture and are, in practice, personal living rooms, equipped with televisions, computers, telephones, refrigerators, games, and toys, signaling perhaps a democratization of domestic space and definitely a celebration of consumerism.

Shirley Teresa Wajda

See also Adolescence; Adulthood; Childhood; Parlors; Servants' Spaces; Sex and Sexuality

References and Further Reading

Clark, Clifford E., Jr. 1986. *The American Family Home, 1800–1960.* Chapel Hill: University of North Carolina Press.

Cromley, Elizabeth Collins. 1990. "Sleeping Around: A History of American Beds and Bedrooms. The Second Banham Memorial Lecture." *Journal of Design History* 3 (1): 1–17.

Garrett, Elisabeth Donaghy. 1989. "The Bedchambers." *At Home: The American Family, 1750–1870*, 109–139. New York: Harry N. Abrams.

Boardinghouses

A *boardinghouse* is a private domestic dwelling or multiple-use commercial facility in which individuals pay to reside and/or have meals provided. Boardinghouse living was a common practice throughout much of American history. Company houses were some of the first forms of privately operated boardinghouses to be established; they supported business enterprises in mill towns and on the frontier. Typical boardinghouses, establishments privately operated by families to earn income, became popular during the westward expansion of the mid-nineteenth century. Commercial boardinghouses, resembling small hotels, offered inexpensive housing options in cities, along with tenements and apartments. Some families chose to co-inhabit with other families as boarders, creating two-family households.

The difference between a private and a commercial boardinghouse was delineated in the number of boarders accommodated: establishments housing more than six boarders were zoned as commercial boardinghouses or small hotels. Single women were sometimes stigmatized if they resided in boardinghouses located outside respectable residential neighborhoods, since *boardinghouse* also euphemistically referred to *bordello*. Thomas Butler Gunn's (1826–1903) satire *The Physiology of New York Boarding-Houses* (1857) chronicled boardinghouse living during the antebellum era as families moved into industrializing cities. Filled with anecdotes about scheming landladies, carousing bachelors, slovenly housemaids, and an odd cast of fellow boarders, the book helped boardinghouse life emerge as an aspect of cosmopolitan American culture.

Women's histories reveal broader trends of female labor in boardinghouses. Women's work, including taking in boarders, was a crucial factor in the financial success of both urban and rural families during the early nineteenth century. Running a boardinghouse was a rigorous process: the weekly cycle of monotonous tasks included laundry; baking; mending; and daily cycles of cooking, cleaning, and serving. While husbands could leave the boardinghouse to work and run errands, wives and children kept the operation going even when they were ill, injured, or pregnant. Women recognized the economic value of their labor; the value of cash income as well as the value-added income produced by ordinary tasks and by taking in boarders constituted a means for women to bring cash into the household during the nineteenth century. Compared with taking in sewing, running a grocery, catering from their kitchens, or working as unpaid labor in their husband's trades, operating a boardinghouse brought dependable income that could be reinvested into businesses or supply family needs. Widows utilized the same skills to operate larger commercial boardinghouses as "sole traders." Married couples often set up boardinghouses on multipurpose properties so that a wife could earn income taking in boarders while her husband practiced his profession in proximity to home and family.

Boardinghouse living was attractive to new arrivals to the United States, supplying a surrogate family along with room and board. Immigrants clustered in boardinghouse communities or "quarters," including Latin and French quarters and Chinatowns. Kosher boardinghouses offered meals prepared in accordance to Jewish law. Immigrant groups generally included young men of similar professions. Mealtime became an opportunity to socialize and network for men who enjoyed similar foods and spoke the same language. Accustomed to living in urban areas, immigrants set up their own grocery and dry goods stores, liquor stores, and restaurants, in addition to boardinghouses.

Boardinghouse society was transient in nature, a testament to the cultural meaning of American mobility. Diaries and travel logs by ordinary Americans from colonial times to the early twentieth century record stays in boardinghouses, hotels, and lodging houses, lasting from a few weeks to several months. Soldiers, sailors, and traveling salesmen boarded with families between jobs, where meals and maid service were provided for a small price. As boardinghouse culture matured, adjunct businesses including music education and distribution of materials for cottage industries emerged as boardinghouse operators hired professionals to provide services in their establishments. Medical practitioners offered boarding to patients who needed extra care while being treated. Boardinghouse living waned during the early twentieth century as urban planners focused on creating apartment communities to accommodate the emerging American sensibility that single-person habitation was acceptable.

Meredith Eliassen

See also Cities and Towns; Commercial Food Venues; Homeless Residences; House, Home, and Domesticity; Service Industry Work and Labor

References and Further Reading
Boydston, Jeanne. 1990. *Home and Work: Housework, Wages, and the Ideology of Labor in the Early Republic*. New York: Oxford University Press.

Gamber, Wendy. 2002. "Tarnished Labor: The Home, the Market, and the Boardinghouse in Antebellum America." *Journal of the Early Republic* 22 (2): 177–204.

Groth, Paul Erling. 1994. *Living Downtown: The History of Residential Hotels in the United States.* Berkeley: University of California Press.

Jensen, Joan M. 1980. "Cloth, Butter and Boarders: Women's Household Production for the Market." *Review of Radical Political Economics* 12 (2): 14–24.

Bodily Cleanliness and Hygiene

Concerns about bodily cleanliness and hygiene have historically fueled a growing market of goods for the proper care and appearance of the body and the environment in the United States. Until the mid-nineteenth century bathing was an uncommon daily practice among all social classes; the best hygienic practices of the time were primarily sponge baths without soap. On the other hand, social bathing, such as visiting spas and public baths, was a popular leisure activity for the upper classes. Over the course of the 1800s bathing tubs, showers, and bathing facilities became more readily available, and by 1850 regular personal washing was common practice among the middle and upper classes, with the use of soap to wash the body becoming common by the Civil War (1861–1864). Manuals devoted to human physiology, bodily cleanliness, and healthy buildings became required textbooks for school and home in the 1830s, marking the systematic introduction of hygiene as a body of knowledge devoted to the understanding of the human body and the maintenance of health. In addition, etiquette guides counseled cleanliness as fundamental to sociability.

As adequate water and sewer systems became more available in cities and towns in the early 1900s, the invention and manufacture of flush toilets and bathing facilities for the home transformed hygiene practices. Bombarded by persuasive advertising, Americans increasingly consumed soaps and toiletries to clean their bodies. Inventions of the early twentieth century, such as mass-produced toilet paper in roll form (1907), the disposable razor (1901), and the modern toothbrush (1938), all furthered hygienic standards. The disposable sanitary napkin and the tampon (1929) transformed conceptions of menstrual hygiene. The adhesive bandage, invented in the 1920s, and the use of antibiotics, begun in the 1940s, changed the American understanding of bodily health and disease. The washing machine, first appearing in rudimentary form in the 1800s but mechanized, electrified, and mass produced in the twentieth century, heightened standards of clothing cleanliness.

In recent years, hygienic concerns have shifted beyond the constraints of smell and visible cleanliness to the microbial world. By the 2000s antibacterial soaps and sanitizers, as well as air and water filtration systems, had become common hygienic products in the American domestic dwelling.

Daniel Farr

See also Advertisements and Advertising; Bathrooms; Cosmetics, Toiletries, Perfumes, and Colognes; Etiquette and Manners; Human Body

References and Further Reading

Bushman, Richard L., and Claudia M. Bushman. 1988. "The Early History of Cleanliness in America." *Journal of American History* 74 (4): 1213–1238.

Hoy, Suellen. 1995. *Chasing Dirt: The American Pursuit of Cleanliness.* New York: Oxford University Press.

Vinikas, Vincent. 1992. *Soft Soap, Hard Sell: American Hygiene in an Age of Advertisement.* Ames: Iowa State University Press.

Body Modification

Body modification is the deliberate, permanent alteration of the human body for decorative, ritualistic, religious, or cultural reasons. For the purposes of this essay, self-chosen body modification in the form of body piercing and tattooing is discussed. Cosmetic surgery, though elective in many cases, is not treated here.

Body Piercing

In its simplest form, *body piercing* is the practice of creating a hole on the surface of the soft tissues of the body for the purpose of inserting or wearing some type of adornment. Body piercing is an ancient, worldwide practice. Body piercing typically includes the wearing of an adornment in the openings made by piercing. The adornments or jewelry inserted in a body piercing vary according to the cultural traditions of the wearer. Likewise, certain types of piercings reflect particular kinds of cultures, cultural groups, or trends. Body piercing, while often generalized incorrectly within what has traditionally been the broader subject of tattooing, is a distinct and unique form of bodily art and adornment that involves different skills, tools, and resulting bodily visual forms.

In contemporary Western cultures, body piercing is most commonly known in the form of simple ear piercings, worn primarily by women but also now by some men throughout the Western world. Body piercing in the form of unusual piercings, or *nonmainstream body modification* as anthropologist James Myers labeled it in 1992, has grown in popularity in Western cultures over the past twenty years. Nonmainstream body modification typically refers to piercing, branding, and scarring, although body piercing is the most commonly practiced of these three. All of these forms typically involve the placement of bodily marks or holes on places other than the ears, or, if on the ears, either with abundant holes in the ears and ear cartilage or with very large holes, sometimes of an inch or more in width (as opposed to the tiny, almost invisible hole of the common ear piercing).

Other unusual piercings are those of the tongue; of the eyebrow, lip, nose, or other facial tissues including the labret (the lower lip); and of the navel, nipple, and genitalia (the penis and scrotum in males or the labia and clitoris in females). In this context, body piercings typically are marked by a variety of adornments that have unique material forms constructed of nonprecious metals such as stainless steel formed into steel balls, bolts, or rings of various sizes. For example, a common tongue piercing adornment is a simple stainless steel shaft through the tongue with a round stainless steel screw ball that appears to lie on the top of the tongue. Facial and navel piercings are typically stainless steel rings or straight shafts of various sizes that look like barbells.

Specific types of piercings have been associated with specific subcultural styles or trends such as those known under the rubrics of "modern primitives" or "neotribalism," or are simply associated with some forms of popular or alternative music. With its adoption of a nihilistic style that featured torn t-shirts, dirty clothing, and safety pins sometimes worn through holes on the body, punk rock brought body piercing to popular attention in the mid-1970s in Great Britain and the United States. By the mid-1990s, body piercing booths were featured routinely along with music groups at such popular alternative music festivals as Lollapalooza (founded in 1991). More significantly, the practice and material effects of body piercing grew out of various sexual subcultures that often experimented with notions of power, pain, and pleasure. Today, body piercing studios are found throughout the world.

Tattooing

Tattooing—the insertion with a sharp needle or instrument of inks or other pigments under the epidermis—is an ancient form of permanent body decoration. The word *tattoo* is derived from the Polynesian *tatu* or *tatau*, meaning "mark" or "strike." Captain James Cook (1728–1779) saw these "marks" on the inhabitants of the South Pacific islands he visited in 1769, and members of his crew adopted the practice. Tattooing is not, as many critics assert, a "primitive" magical or religious practice. The practice has existed in the West since the Neolithic era.

Now primarily a popular form of self-expression and group identity, tattooing had been utilized in American history for purposes of control. For example, Euro-Americans employed tattoos to brand criminals and slaves throughout the seventeenth, eighteenth, and nineteenth centuries. Heavily tattooed bodies of members of non-Western societies, including Native Americans and Hawaiians, were displayed in Phineas T. Barnum's (1810–1891) New York City museum and traveling circuses throughout the nineteenth and twentieth centuries, leading Americans to equate exoticism and even criminality with the practice. Thus defined, tattooing became symbolic of "otherness" and defined civilization against such "primitive" customs.

Sailors, by virtue of their travels to cultures that more openly embraced tattooing, helped to spread the practice to Western seaports. They employed tattoos as commemorative markers of sea voyages. During the American Civil War (1861–1865) and the two world wars, soldiers, marines, and seamen acquired tattoos to signal membership in a specific unit or regiment, to commemorate battles, to define their masculinity through tattoos objectifying women, or to declare their bonds of affection to others through the marking of names, images, or symbols on their bodies.

Commercial but unregulated tattoo parlors appeared in the United States during the 1920s. The employment of *flash sheets*—charts of tattoo designs—standardized tattoo decorations and iconography. State laws regulating or forbidding tattooing were passed to control the spread of disease, including syphilis. Fear of disease and the advent of the Great Depression led to a decline in tattoo parlors. The practice was revived in the 1960s, with the interest in Asian cultures brought about by the Vietnam conflict, counterculture politics and aesthetics, and the rise of leisure. Men constituted the primary consumers of tattoos; today, the gendered connotations of tattoos, bravery and masculinity, have been challenged by the increasing numbers of women who choose to express their individuality with tattoos. Medical doctors have adapted tattooing to offer permanent cosmetics (eyeliner and lip color, for example) to women. Temporary tattoos and henna tattoos are increasingly popular.

Since the 1960s tattoo artists have sought distinction by ignoring conventional tattoo designs and creating their own unique expressions. These appeal to a youth culture invested in this newly acceptable form of commercially available, seemingly noncomformist social identification. Various social groups have adopted tattoos as identification, including rock groupies, punk rockers, and Goths as well as members of street and prison gangs and racist organizations. Tattooing as a ritual and commercial practice and tattoos as a form of visual culture and self-expression in the United States require more study.

Janet S. Rose

See also Adolescence; Human Body; Penitentiaries and Prisons; Popular Culture; Rite, Ritual, and Ceremony; Sex and Sexuality

References and Further Reading
DeMello, Margo. 2000. *Bodies of Inscription: A Cultural History of the Modern Tattoo Community*. Durham, NC: Duke University Press.
Myers, James. 1992. "Non-mainstream Radical Body Modification: Genital Piercing, Branding, Burning and Cutting." *Journal of Contemporary Ethnography* 21 (6): 267–307.
Rose, Janet. 2001. "And Ears Don't Count: Body Piercing in America and Other Variations on the Theme of Belonging." Ph.D. diss., University of Kansas.
Rubin, Arnold, ed. 1988. *Marks of Civilization: Artistic Transformations of the Human Body*. Los Angeles: University of California, Los Angeles.
Vale, V., and Andrea Juno. 1989. *Modern Primitives: An Investigation of the Contemporary Adornment and Ritual*. Eugene, OR: RE/Search Publications.

Books

The book is an ancient cultural entity whose material form has long embodied its social and cultural significance. Books historically have been accorded nearly sacred status, both as emblems of the religious texts they often held and as reifying vessels of preserved human imagination, experience, and knowledge. With the advent of print technology in the fifteenth century, the book also became one of the first material objects to be produced on a large scale and sold for profit in a commercial marketplace. In the United States books continue to sit squarely, if often paradoxically, at that intersection of culture and commerce.

Printed books have long been a powerful agent of two often intertwined forces. On one hand, they have helped to clarify and preserve diversity within societies, fixing and sustaining communities formed by a shared language, religious or political belief, or ethnic heritage. Books' material forms often help to articulate those distinctions among cultural communities, just as they have long functioned as markers of social class, signaling wealth, education, family lineage, and "taste." On the other hand, books are often credited with enabling a broader, more democratic access to a common, uniform fund of information and ideas. By creating and disseminating multiples of identical texts, printed books helped to establish a widely accessible body of standardized knowledge and to ensure that diverse minority communities of belief and expression survive and cohere.

The Colonial Era
The first printing press in North America arrived in Mexico in 1539, a scant seventy years after medieval entrepreneurs began to carry Johannes Gutenberg's (ca. 1398–1468) invention beyond Germany. Although a printing press did not reach British North America until 1638, its purpose was in part the same as its arrival in Mexico: Just as early Franciscan missionaries in Mexico exploited the iconic power of print to awe and subdue the indigenous peoples, so too was the aim of John Eliot's (ca. 1604–1690) translation of the Bible into the Algonkian language in 1663, *Up-Biblum God*, the most ambitious book produced in the early Harvard College print shop. In seventeenth-century America the book often served as a tool for conversion and conquest as well as devotion and worship.

Early printers were closely monitored and their work restricted to ecclesiastical, civil, and educational materials sanctioned by state and church authorities. As controls eased in the eighteenth century, many colonial printers soon developed a brisk, profitable trade in ephemera—handbills, broadsides, pamphlets, and especially newspapers—but relatively few books. Most of the books owned and read by colonial Americans were either brought personally from Europe or imported. American book authors and readers were eager to retain a cosmopolitan link to those European hubs of intellectual and publishing activity. Reliance on imports was also materially mandated, since the colonies' fledgling paper mills and type foundries were unable to obtain in sufficient quantities the better-quality raw materials needed for books. The crude typography, lack of craftsmanship, and relatively poor material quality of most American publications—broken and mismatched type, inferior paper, unskilled typography, and so on—highlighted their provincialism and reinforced a deep sense that "real" books were those whose form and content reflected venerable European bookmaking traditions.

Two printers played influential roles in asserting new standards for American book design and production that were informed by European traditions. Philadelphia statesman and printer Benjamin Franklin (1706–1790) was among the first to pay serious attention to the material aspects of print, tacitly invoking professional (that is, European) standards of quality as a barometer of cultural seriousness and maturity. Franklin emulated the leading typographic innovators of the day in Great Britain and France, and he ambitiously sought to model exemplary design for his American colleagues with his own best work. Like all skilled and knowledgeable printers, Franklin was implicitly savvy about the subtle ways that the typographic and material dimensions of a printed text, or what critic Jerome McGann (1991) calls its "bibliographic codes," shape its cultural import and meanings.

Similarly, Massachusetts printer Isaiah Thomas (1749–1831) worked tirelessly to develop, promote, and dignify the quality of American printing. His remarkable career spanned nearly fifty years, beginning with his founding in 1770 of the revolutionary *Massachusetts Spy*, soon the most read newspaper in New England. After the war he imported large quantities of the best types and ornaments from Britain; ordered presses from new American manufacturers; and quickly established a printing, publishing, and bookselling empire. His activities helped to make print seem pervasive in the new republic; many Americans encountered the fruits of his labor at nearly every turn of their reading lives, from primers, newspapers, and novels to almanacs, hymnals, and Bibles.

Nineteenth-Century Industrialization

For more than three hundred years, books had been produced in roughly the same way: compositors set type by hand, combining individual pieces of metal type to create forms of text pages that were positioned securely on the bed of a wooden press. The raised surface of the type was then inked by hand with large leather balls, damp paper was positioned carefully over the inked type, and pressure was applied to transfer the ink from the type to the paper. Working steadily at top speed, a skilled team of pressmen could thus produce about 250 impressions an hour—that is, they could print one side of 250 sheets.

In the nineteenth century new steam-powered presses soon performed the entire operation in a fraction of the time required for hand operation. By mid-century, machines working at top speed could produce between 1,600 and 2,400 impressions an hour, a rate that eclipsed handpress production roughly eightfold. At about the same time a breakthrough in papermaking technology—the replacement of cotton and linen pulps with those made from chemically processed and cooked wood fibers—dramatically increased the supply of paper that could be produced, at strikingly lower prices, by the new papermaking machinery.

Along with steady population growth; an emphasis on education and literacy; and emerging national transportation, financial, and communication systems, industrialized printing methods helped to fuel a widespread boom in book production and consumption. For the first time it seemed appropriate to use the term *mass production*. Although books remained the most elite form of print—usually regarded as more substantial, expensive, and "serious" than newspapers, pamphlets, and other ephemera—the abundance of machine-printed editions, their relatively inexpensive prices, and the growing numbers of Americans both able and motivated to read them led to a striking popularization of the book in the United States. While traditional trade publishing took root during this period, it was dwarfed by more focused religious, educational, and institutional publishing activity. School textbooks were (and remain) one of the largest categories of books produced; Noah Webster's (1758–1843) *Blue Back Speller* alone sold some seventy million copies in the hundred years following its publication in 1783. Not-for-profit organizations and evangelical publishers like the American Tract Society issued millions of volumes addressed to common readers. Many relatively small ethnic, religious, and political communities sustained energetic publishing programs throughout the century, their identities distilled through print.

Mass production enabled a new kind of visible "branding" that both underscored the commercial or ideological nature of many books and visually articulated the many emerging niche communities of readers. Series of older, "classic" titles reprinted in identical format and often sold in sets or "libraries" grew popular, especially among those anxious to equip their houses with books that mimicked in content and form the collections of prosperous genteel families. Books intended for entertainment rather than edification thrived in distinctive new material forms as well; the popularity of so-called dime novels (which mostly sold for a nickel), marked by bold yellow paper covers and dramatic, even lurid, woodcut cover illustrations, signaled an avid appetite for fiction whose sensational formulaic content was shrewdly mirrored in their uniform material forms.

By the 1890s the final technological breakthrough toward fully mechanized book production occurred when Ottmar Mergenthaler (1854–1899) and Tolbert Lanston (1844–1914) developed rival systems (Linotype and Monotype, respectively) for mechanical type casting and composition, eliminating the last element of handcraft in the production process. In the ensuing decades savvy publishers used a new proliferation of design variables—typefaces, papers, formats, cover and jacket decorations—to attract particular audiences. More than ever, books' material form became a tool for registering, or defining, the cultural character of both content and reader, of both product and consumer.

The Return of Handcraft

Even as important new technological and commercial changes in the 1890s fully modernized book production, a growing number of critics lamented that such changes achieved economy and plenitude at the expense of material and aesthetic integrity. Inspired by the passionate arguments of William Morris (1834–1896) and other leaders of the Arts and Crafts Movement urging a return to craft-based preindustrial production standards, the preeminent American printer of the era, Theodore Low De Vinne (1828–1914), led the way toward improving the material quality of printed books. De Vinne championed the use of sturdier, darker typefaces and pioneered new processes of finishing machine-made paper so that its surface was more receptive to ink. While Morris and his followers felt that mechanization intrinsically cheapened the material and hence spiritual dignity of printed books, De Vinne sought more commercially pragmatic ways to ensure that mechanized processes might better approach the production ideals of handcraft.

In the 1920s and 1930s, the goal of higher standards of book production took on a new, seemingly urgent cultural dimension. As the United States emerged from World War I in a position of international political, economic, and industrial leadership, many feared that American culture was ill suited for a comparable preeminence. Readily deemed emblematic of "culture" itself, the shoddy manufacture and careless design of most American books seemed to signal a disturbing poverty of their intellectual substance and significance. Many critics loosely but widely blamed this debasement less on the limitations of machinery than on publishers' capitulation to popular demands for cheap, plentiful, and ever-changing books. The interests of commerce, they feared, had outpaced those of culture.

Efforts to improve the material quality of books, and thus to honor better the cultural traditions they represented, subtly addressed both physical and symbolic concerns. The American Institute of Graphic Arts was founded in 1923 to raise bookmaking standards in the nation's printing industry. Simultaneously, a veritable boom in "fine" bookmaking—ostensibly without concern for cost or popular taste—occurred. Although their producers contended that high-quality materials and craft necessarily, if regrettably, restricted the number of such better-made books, the limited edition sizes underscored fine books' role in demarcating cultural status. Even as the new term *middlebrow* was surfacing to describe popular-but-respectable cultural tastes, exemplified by the debut of the Book of the Month Club in 1926, fine editions tacitly registered an elite, "highbrow" position of cultural hierarchy, invoking the familiar notion that books' materiality reveal their owner's character and cultural authenticity.

The Paperback Revolution of the Twentieth Century

Following the lead of Great Britain's innovative Penguin Books, in 1939 Robert Fair De Graff (1895–1981) initiated Pocket Books, inexpensive, paperbound reprints of well-known and respected titles. The initial ten books published included *Five Great Tragedies* of Shakespeare, two recent hardcover bestsellers, an Agatha Christie mystery, two "tie-ins" to the Hollywood films *Topper* and *Wuthering Heights*, the 1928 Pulitzer Prize–winning *Bridge of San Luis Rey*, and the children's classic *Bambi*. What was revolutionary about these books was not their bright red endpapers and plastic-laminated soft bindings (paper covers had long been common for "cheap" books) but the mainstream respectability of their content and the radically new marketing and distribution networks through which they were sold. Pocket

Books were the first mainstream books sold not only in bookstores but in unconventional retail outlets: variety stores, train stations, magazine stalls—wherever magazines were sold. This brought "real" books into thousands of new locations, where their modest price (initially twenty-five cents, comparable to the price of a magazine) and ready availability made them instantly popular. Although the deeply ingrained association of paper covers with ephemeral, inferior content continues (largely fueled by formulaic genre publishing), these modern paperbacks forever challenged the notion that cheap form meant cheap content. Above all, the new format enabled literally millions of Americans to read and own mainstream book titles for the first time.

The Digital Revolution

The closing decades of the twentieth century witnessed the most profound change in the material nature of books since Gutenberg: a rise of electronic methods of creating, storing, and distributing texts that may portend the end of the book as a printed, physical object. Many herald this watershed technological development as nothing less than revolutionary in its social, economic, and cultural impacts, altering forever the ways humans encounter—and hence how humans read, understand, and value—the written word. Others fear those changes, anxious that device-dependent digital technology will never become as transparent as that of print, never allowing the imaginative and intellectual absorption that seems foundational to the experience of reading itself.

It seems most likely, however, that digital books will not entirely replace printed ones, just as print did not render handwriting obsolete. In fact, digital technology may well divide the world of books into two classes. Books used largely for information may become predominantly digital, well served by electronic media's advantages of instant revision, nonlinear search and retrieval, and massive storage capacity. Those books read for experience, whether for intellectual engagement or for pleasure, may remain largely printed. Regardless, as a book's materiality becomes in a sense optional, it will only grow in significance, seen more than ever as a manifestation of cultural expression and meaning.

Megan Benton

See also Education and Schooling; Ephemera; Fanzines; Graphic Design; Handicraft and Artisanship; Literary Studies and American Literature; Popular Culture; Print Culture; Scrapbooks; Technology

References and Further Reading
Amory, Hugh, and David D. Hall, eds. 2000. *The Colonial Book in America*, vol. 1 of *A History of the Book in America*, 5 vols, ed. David D. Hall. Cambridge: Cambridge University Press.
Benton, Megan. 2000. *Beauty and the Book: Fine Editions and Cultural Distinction in America.* New Haven, CT: Yale University Press.
Blumenthal, Joseph. 1977. *The Printed Book in America.* Boston: David R. Godine.
Davis, Kenneth C. 1984. *Two-Bit Culture: The Paperbacking of America.* Boston: Houghton Mifflin.
Gaskell, Philip. 1972. *A New Introduction to Bibliography.* New York: Oxford University Press.
McGann, Jerome J. 1991. *The Textual Condition.* Princeton, NJ: Princeton University Press.
Moylan, Michele, and Lane Stiles, eds. 1996. *Reading Books: Essays on the Material Text and Literature in America.* Amherst: University of Massachusetts Press.
Rubin, Joan Shelley. 1992. *The Making of Middlebrow Culture.* Chapel Hill: University of North Carolina Press.
Tebbel, John. 1987. *Between Covers: The Rise and Transformation of Book Publishing in America.* New York: R. R. Bowker.
Thompson, Susan Otis. 1996. *American Book Design and William Morris*, 2nd ed. New Castle, DE: Oak Knoll Books.

Burial Grounds, Cemeteries, and Grave Markers

Burial grounds and cemeteries in the United States contain a uniquely accessible collection of many millions of grave markers spanning the history of European contact with the New World. Native American burial grounds extend the time frame thousands of years into the past. Burial grounds and cemeteries are sites of memory where families and communities have created, shaped, and tended their histories and identities. Race, class and social status, gender, religion, and ethnicity are among the many aspects of culture reflected in burial grounds, cemeteries, and grave markers. Moreover, because grave markers are usually dated, because they tend to remain in place long after being erected, and because they are usually made of durable materials, they offer students of material culture unique control over the three dimensions of any object—time, space, and form. In addition, grave markers' dual nature as both texts and artifacts offers a wealth of precise information about the spread and evolution of cultural ideas and values.

Colonial- and Early National-Era Burial Grounds

Colonial- and early National-era burial grounds tell a story of local and regional cultures. Burial grounds in old New England towns contain tens of thousands of decorated grave markers ranging from folk art to sophisticated baroque styles. The typical early imagery of skulls, hourglasses, crossed bones, and other reflections of mortality unflinchingly announced the finality of earthly existence. Epitaphs such as a common pair of lines that advised, "As I am now, so you shall be,/ Prepare for death and follow me" frequently underscored the message of mortal-

ity. By contrast, early grave markers in German Lutheran and Reformed churchyards in the Mid-Atlantic colonies were typically decorated with stylized suns, moons, hearts, tulips, compass stars, and other Germanic-derived folk decorations. Scots-Irish Presbyterian grave markers decorated with a variety of images including thistles, coffins, Scottish crosses, and coats of arms illustrate a third major strain of colonial-era mortuary art.

Beginning in the eighteenth century, grave marker styles were influenced by a developing national culture as the international Georgian style increasingly supplied a standardized set of neoclassical images of urns, willows, and architecture. In the early nineteenth century, further cultural consolidation was evident in the rapidity with which marble displaced local sandstone, schist, and slate as the principal material for grave markers and monuments. By mid-century, the religious sentimentality sweeping the nation appeared in cemeteries as images of clasped hands, angels, Bibles, fingers pointing heavenward, and lambs to indicate children's graves. Epitaphs referring to mortality practically disappeared, replaced by sentimental phrases such as, "Asleep in Jesus," "Just Sleeping," and "Gone Home" that echoed popular hymn lyrics.

Nineteenth-Century Cemeteries

The growing industrialization and urbanization of the first half of the nineteenth century resulted in the creation of many new municipal institutions including hospitals, asylums, model prisons, and public libraries. With the founding of Mount Auburn Cemetery on the outskirts of Boston in 1831, municipal burial grounds became part of this civic revolution. Mount Auburn, a nondenominational, nonprofit burial ground, displayed its stylish monuments and tombs amidst a sweeping landscape of ponds, lakes, hills, curving roads and paths, and plantings that expressed the Romantic Movement's adoration of nature. By 1860, one or more "rural" cemeteries could be found in or near most major American cities, and modest versions had sprung up in lesser cities and in towns. As the first large public parks, Mount Auburn and its major imitators annually drew visitors from around the country and abroad by the tens of thousands.

At first, the rural cemeteries that replaced old, overcrowded, unsanitary urban graveyards were self-consciously didactic. In presenting visitors with an idealized landscape in which to encounter timeless art, noble sentiments, and shrines to local heroes, cemetery founders hoped to teach the refined tastes and civic virtues that could counteract the disruptions caused by urbanization, immigration, and industrialization. Once cemeteries were removed from the direct oversight of the church, however, they lost much of their original didactic purpose as they increasingly came to reflect the acquisitive values of the Gilded Age commercial world. Thousands of wealthy businessmen and industrialists created shrines to themselves by turning their large family plots into miniature estates with extravagant grave markers; tombs; templelike family mausoleums with stained-glass windows; and statuary of marble, granite, or bronze—all in stylish Gothic, Egyptian, or Classical revival forms.

The rural cemetery style, with its wide roads and houses of the dead, were laid out much like the suburbs emerging on the outskirts of larger cities in the late nineteenth century. Established in 1836, Philadelphia's Laurel Hill Cemetery, pictured here in 1979, attracted tens of thousands of visitors annually. (Library of Congress)

Changes in American cemeteries reflected not only cultural and market forces but also technological changes and the reorganization of work. The craft tradition of independent stone carvers and small-shop production of the nineteenth century was increasingly supplanted by large-scale monument businesses. Improved transportation, the increasing use of power tools, and the growing professionalization of the monument and cemetery industries allowed a few large marble and granite quarry operations to supply a network of local monument businesses across the nation. Increasing standardization was the inevitable result.

Twentieth-Century Memorial Parks

In the early twentieth century, the cemetery was again changing, as rural cemeteries created by a paternalistic civic culture gave way to explicitly commercial enterprises. The lawn mower, the automobile, suburbanization, and other changes fueled this shift toward the minimalist memorial park cemetery with its uniform bronze or granite markers placed flush to the ground for easy maintenance. High-end memorial park cemeteries such as Forest Lawn in Glendale, California, near Los Angeles, combined all aspects of the mortuary business, from funerals to cremations and burials.

Other important modern developments include the creation of national military cemeteries in the wake of the Civil War; the growth of pet cemeteries after World War II; and more recently, the increasing personalization of grave markers, the rediscovery or invention of memorial traditions such as leaving sentimental objects at grave sites, and the creation of "virtual" cemeteries on the Internet.

National trends never obliterated ethnic, regional, and local traditions, however. Major nineteenth- and early twentieth-century regional styles include the iron crosses of the German and Russian-German Great Plains; the above-ground tombs of Louisiana, particularly in New Orleans; and the Upland South folk cemetery complex. African American cemetery and grave marker traditions have been identified and studied. Chinese, Japanese, Vietnamese, Gypsies, Ukranians, Italians, Poles, Mexicans, Cubans, and peoples of many other nationalities, religions, and cultural backgrounds have been continuously adding to the stock of distinctive cemetery and grave marker traditions in the United States. "Folk" or amateur-made markers continue to be used, sometimes alongside permanent markers, sometimes as the only markers. The recuperation of the identities of disabled individuals who died while institutionalized in asylums and prisons is ongoing; their grave markers, once inscribed only with numbers, are being replaced with names and life dates. Although the growing popularity of cremation may be diminishing the cultural importance of cemeteries, many indications confirm that cemeteries will continue to be places that reflect a rapidly evolving popular culture in tension with innumerable ethnic, religious, local, and regional traditions.

Gary Collison

See also City Parks; Folklore and Folklife; Funerals; Funerary (Sepulchral) Monuments; Memory and Memorabilia; Mourning; Mourning and Ethnicity; Public Monuments and Popular Commemoration

References and Further Reading
Jackson, Kenneth T., and Camilo José Vergara. 1989. *Silent Cities: The Evolution of the American Cemetery*. New York: Princeton Architectural Press.
Jordon, Terry G. 1982. *Texas Graveyards: A Cultural Legacy*. Austin: University of Texas Press.
Linden-Ward, Blanche. 1989. *Silent City on a Hill: Landscapes of Memory and Boston's Mount*

Auburn Cemetery. Columbus: Ohio State University Press.

Ludwig, Allan I. 1966. *Graven Images: New England Stonecarving and Its Symbols, 1650–1815*. Hanover, NH: University Press of New England.

McDowell, Peggy, and Richard E. Meyer. 1994. *The Revival Styles in American Memorial Art*. Bowling Green, OH: Bowling Green State University Popular Press.

Meyer, Richard E., ed. 1992. *Cemeteries and Gravemarkers: Voices of American Culture*. Logan: Utah State University Press.

Meyer, Richard E., ed. 1993. *Ethnicity and the American Cemetery*. Bowling Green, OH: Bowling Green State University Popular Press.

Morris, Richard. 1997. *Sinners, Lovers, and Heroes: An Essay on Memorializing in Three American Cultures*. Albany: State University of New York Press.

Sears, John F. 1989. "Prisons, Asylums, Cemeteries, Parks." In *Sacred Places: American Tourist Attractions in the Nineteenth Century*, 87–121. Amherst: University of Massachusetts Press.

Sloane, David Charles. 1991. *The Last Great Necessity: Cemeteries in American History*. Baltimore, MD: Johns Hopkins University Press.

C

Cellars and Basements

Cellar and *basement* are considered synonyms in American usage; however, each refers to a space that possesses distinct qualities. The interchangeable use of the two terms probably evolved from the fact that cellars are frequently located in basements in a variety of buildings.

In domestic dwellings, a *cellar* is a subterranean room or group of rooms generally used for storing perishable items such as wine, beer, fruit, vegetables, or other foodstuffs. The cool and relatively constant temperature of the space makes it ideal for this purpose, but cellars have also been used to store coal or other fuels or to provide temporary protective shelter, as in a storm cellar. Not all cellars are located within or underneath a building. Most are windowless. If located within a building's foundation, the cellar is accessed through a doorway in the basement. If located elsewhere, entry is through a surface-level doorway.

A *basement*, the lowest part of a building that is completely or partially underground, may extend under the entire structure or a portion of it. The majority are built with enough height for the average person to stand upright in it; some are merely crawl spaces. Basements are accessed via stairways that connect to the interior of the house and may also have an outdoor entrance.

Nineteenth-century American house plans reveal that basements contained cellars for storage of food and fuel and, toward the latter part of the century, furnaces. Some plans show servants' quarters, the kitchen, and the scullery in the basement. Keeping the kitchen and servants below the main floor hid the productive activities of the household, as was middle- and upper-class practice. Some architects advised avoiding placement of these rooms in the basement because of dampness, poor lighting, and generally unpleasant conditions.

Kitchens disappeared from basement plans over the course of the twentieth century. The number of domestic servants declined, so servants' quarters decreased in size or were removed. Storage, laundry facilities, and utility systems remained located under the foundation. Two early twentieth-century additions were a workshop and, depending on the grade of the property, a garage.

In the 1920s and 1930s, the recreation room began appearing in basement plans. Improved heating systems, decreased in size, significantly influenced this new use of basements by increasing open space. Additionally, the new systems functioned on gas or oil. These fuels were much cleaner than coal and eliminated the need for coal storage. Better waterproofing and the use of casement windows that provided more light and better ventilation also contributed to making the space more comfortable. Recreation rooms reached the height of popularity in the 1950s, but many families today continue to refinish basements for recreational and living space.

Pamela Dorazio Dean

See also Attics; Kitchens and Pantries; Recreation Rooms; Servants' Spaces

References and Further Reading

Clark, Clifford E., Jr. 1986. *The American Family Home, 1800–1960*. Chapel Hill: University of North Carolina Press.
Snodgrass, Mary Ellen. 2004. *Encyclopedia of Kitchen History*. New York: Fitzroy Dearborn.

Ceramics

Ceramics are objects created of clay fired at a high temperature and frequently coated with *glaze,* an oxide mixture applied to a surface to impart an impermeable and ornamental coating. Ceramics, including stoneware, earthenware, and porcelain, comprise utilitarian food processing and storage vessels, everyday and formal diningwares, and decorative objects. The study of ceramic design, manufacture, and use reveals consumption patterns, technological changes, shifts in taste, and cultural trends.

Colonial-Era Ceramics

Seventeenth-century settlers in North America made utilitarian bricks and vessels from native regional clay, as soil and wood for kilns were abundant. Drawing upon diverse European traditions, simple, lead-glazed ceramics were made from Virginia to Maine. These earthenware objects frequently had incised decoration.

Potters advanced the ornamentation of redware by decorating pottery with *slip,* thinned liquid clay used to embellish the surface of a vessel, and the process of *sgrafito,* whereby the surface is incised to reveal the clay body underneath. Elaborately decorated and colorful sgrafito vessels were part of the Pennsylvania German tradition. *Stoneware,* a durable utilitarian medium that was fired at a higher temperature than earthenware (thus becoming vitrified and nonporous), was crafted in the early eighteenth through nineteenth centuries from Virginia to Vermont. Stoneware's dull color was enriched by cobalt blue decoration that was painted or incised. Stoneware could also be decorated by slip, impressed clay, and salt glaze.

Americans of considerable means relied on imported Chinese, French, or other European porcelain, which was composed of kaolin and petuntse (feldspar that cements a vessel and seals pores) and characterized by its translucent appearance, hard body, and pure white color. In 1770 Gousse Bonnin (1741–1779) and George Anthony Morris (1742 or 1745–1773) founded the first American porcelain factory in Philadelphia. Bonnin and Morris evoked the then-current European Rococo style and taste for *chinoiserie.* The company succumbed to economic pressures two years later, mostly due to competition by less expensive foreign porcelain.

Nineteenth-Century American Innovations

The early nineteenth-century vogue in French taste translated to classically shaped vessels, overglaze decoration in a polychromatic color palette, and gilded ornamentation. The foremost proponent of this taste in the United States was Philadelphian William Ellis Tucker (1800–1832), whose porcelain competed with imported varieties and utilized European design motifs. American manufacturers desired to capitalize on American consumers who continued to purchase foreign luxury goods. Charles Cartlidge & Co. (later Union Porcelain Works, established 1848, Greenpoint, Brooklyn, New York) produced goods that focused on the burgeoning middle-class consumer market and developed new products and innovative American motifs instead of replicating foreign models.

The mid-nineteenth century was a period of great experimentation for American ceramic manufacturers. Many firms employed mold making and slip casting as a method of mass production that also provided integral decoration. In 1828, brothers David and Joseph Henderson pioneered the nation's first commercially successful earthenware and stoneware company in Jersey City, New Jersey. Using English prototypes and practices, the firm renamed in 1833 the American Pottery Manufacturing Company, provided modestly priced ceramics for the growing middle class by casting stoneware and yellowware in molds. *Rockingham*, purportedly named for eighteenth-century English porcelain made on the estate of the Marquis of Rockingham, was created using complex relief molds and distinguished by its mottled glaze resembling tortoise shell. *Parian*, an unglazed porcelain biscuit that provided a sculptural ceramic medium, was introduced in England in the mid-nineteenth century and named for the island of Paros in the Aegean Sea, which was noted for its marble. Molds were employed for most ceramics, but parian was refined by hand, providing affordable sculpture and table-

ware for the growing middle class. Pottery was considered a hallmark manufacture: stoneware producers Norton Pottery and the United States Pottery Company, both of Bennington, Vermont, exhibited decorative pieces and technically inventive ceramics at the 1853 New York Crystal Palace Exposition.

The 1876 United States International Centennial Exhibition in Philadelphia was a landmark exhibition in the history of ceramics. The fair boasted important ceramic displays which included English Doultonware, French Haviland, and Japanese pottery. American potteries were desperate to compete and therefore hired foreign-trained potters. German-born Karl L. H. Müller (1820–1887) designed for the Union Porcelain Works its iconic Century Vase, which featured elaborately decorated bands of American motifs including bison heads, gold eagles, a relief of George Washington, and six biscuit panels illustrating events in American history.

At the Centennial Exhibition, Americans surveyed European and Japanese pottery, providing an impetus for china painting that led to the Art Pottery Movement. The movement's goals of elevating public taste and improving American design spread to cities such as Boston, New Orleans, and Chicago, where art potteries and art societies formed. Important china painters and potters visited the Exhibition, including M. Louise McLaughlin (1847–1939), Maria Longworth Nichols Storer (1849–1932), Hugh Cornwall Robertson (1845–1908), and Charles Volkmar (1841–1914). McLaughlin's major contribution to American ceramics was the pioneering of underglaze painting. Storer's art pottery firm, Rookwood Pottery in Cincinnati, Ohio, the largest and most influential operation, initiated innovative glazes and new decorative treatments focusing on American, japanesque, and nature motifs. During this period numerous commercial art pottery ventures, such as Van Briggle (Colorado Springs, Colorado), Teco (Terra Cotta, Illinois), and Grueby (Boston, Massachusetts). It was this last pottery that introduced the popular matte glaze "Grueby green." Other potteries promoted social agendas, including Marblehead (Massachusetts), Paul Revere Pottery (Boston, Massachusetts), and Newcomb, a New Orleans pottery with a mission to educate young women for arts employment.

Twentieth-Century Dichotomy: Mass Production and Studio Potters

A proliferation of ceramic schools and ceramic publications (such as Adelaide Alsop Robineau's [1865–1929] *Keramic Studio*), commercial collaboration between artists and industry (including the organic dinnerware of Russel Wright [1904–1976]), and a growing relationship between ceramics and sculpture characterize twentieth-century ceramics practice. English potter Charles Fergus Binns (1857–1934) became the first director of the New York College of Clayworking and Ceramics at Alfred University in 1900. Binns influenced a generation of American studio potters (including Robineau) with his instructive methods of treating clay with exacting precision to produce classic shapes and textured glazes.

Modernism of the 1920s and 1930s was punctuated by a search for national identity. American Viktor Schreckengost, who studied in Vienna before working for Cowan Pottery Studio in Rocky River, Ohio, designed Jazz Bowls, a comment on American culture and the Jazz Age. The postwar period witnessed the rise of studio potters. Finnish-born potter Maija Grotell (1899–1973), known for her intense colors, and later cratered, uneven glazes, directed the ceramics department at Cranbrook Academy of Art in Bloomfield Hills, Michigan. In a

similar aesthetic, émigrés Otto Natzler and Gertrud Natzler (1924–2005) created pottery with textured surfaces that were painted or incised. The prolific and influential Peter Voulkos (1924–2002), influenced by Japanese pottery and Zen beauty, embraced process and blurred the lines between deconstructed sculpture and expressive ceramics.

Monica Obniski

See also Aesthetic Movement; Decorative Arts; Design History and American Design; Modernism (Art Moderne)

References and Further Reading
Barber, Edwin Atlee. 1979 (1909). *The Pottery and Porcelain of the United States: An Historical Review of American Ceramic Art from the Earliest Times to the Present Day*. New York: Feingold & Lewis.
Clark, Garth. 1987. *American Ceramics, 1876 to the Present*. New York: Abbeville Press.
Denker, Ellen, and Bert Denker. 1985. *The Main Street Pocket Guide to North American Pottery and Porcelain*. Pittstown, NJ: Main Street Press.
Frelinghuysen, Alice Cooney. 1989. *American Porcelain, 1770–1920*. New York: Metropolitan Museum of Art.
Stradling, Diana, and G. Garrison Stradling, eds. 1977. *The Art of the Potter: Redware and Stoneware*. New York: Main Street Press and Universe Books.

Childhood

Developmental psychology—the study of behavior through all life stages from the fetus to old age—defines *child* as a person from the time of birth to the stage of physical maturity. Nevertheless, concepts of *childhood*—the period or condition of being a child—have evolved over time.

Adults have shaped, and continue to shape, the environments and experiences of childhood through the dominant values they establish and maintain. Extant historical artifacts of the different phases of childhood in what has become the United States reflect education and preparation for entering adult society. These artifacts—books, toys, clothing—wore out through use or were discarded when children moved toward the next phase of development. Theoretically, as soon as a child learns a new skill, he or she toys with this new ability, practicing and testing the skill until it is mastered. Through habituation, the child acquires values, preferences, and a worldview within the social contexts.

The material culture of childhood has often mirrored aspects of *childness*, that quality of curiosity about the larger world and the spirit or exploration that makes the familiar a place of wonder and amusement while providing glimpses into a broader cultural sensibility that combines innocence, imagination, and ingenuity. Child's play without practical purpose has made parents nervous that their children might learn idleness, mischief, and self-indulgence. During the nineteenth century the prevailing philosophy was that the more material wealth given to a child, the less chance the child might develop his or her inner resources. Maintaining a sense of play became an important aspect of early education. Following French philosopher Jean-Jacques Rousseau's (1712–1778) ideas on childrearing (most notably in his 1762 novel, *Emile, or On Education*), play in particular was fostered to help form basic attitudes and behaviors in a child in regard to people in his or her immediate surroundings—first family, and then society.

Childhood as a Historically Contingent State

The financial and emotional stability of many families is shattered during and after periods of war. Women historically were left to support families when husbands, brothers, or fathers were killed or disabled. During the early months of the Civil War (1861–1865), children traveled to battle sites and viewed skirmishes, and boys served as drummers and mascots during the war. Despite economic hardship, children were drawn into the dominant consumer-driven culture, and some became entrepreneurs as well as patriots. Girls became active fundraisers for specific units, hospitals, and soldiers aid societies for both sides of the war. In Philadelphia a flurry of "children's fairs" occurred during 1862 to raise cash and supplies for local companies and army hospitals. Schools gathered wagons of food and linens. Institutions, including asylums for the disabled, industrial and missionary schools, orphanages, houses of refuge, the "colored homes" for African American children, and public schools, donated handmade items sold to benefit the war effort. Children held their own "sanitary fairs" in backyards, on front porches, and in homes where they sold lemonade and baked goods. Schoolgirls gathered on Saturdays to sew, knit, and complete fancy needlework projects to sell.

Privacy

Historically, privacy has been the privilege of the powerful and wealthy, but by the nineteenth century the idea that freedom from the attention of others was critical to character development was evident in childrearing manuals. Seen as a "need," privacy was ensured by separate bedrooms or by the backyard clubhouse or secret hideout where adults were not allowed. In the novel *What Katy Did* (1872) by Susan Chancey Woolsey (1835–1905), protagonist Katy Carr and her friends hiked to a secluded marshy thicket at the bottom of a field near their house called "Paradise." In Booth Tarkington's (1869–1946) book *Penrod* (1910), a boy named Penrod Schofield placed a large box in an unused horse stall (as the family transitioned from their horse-and-buggy transportation to an automobile) to create his fortress stronghold. In Gene Stratton-Porter's (1863–1924) novel *A Girl of the Limberlost* (1909), Elnora, the unloved daughter of a poor but independent widow, managed to pay for her high school education by selling moths she collected in the Limberlost swamps in Indiana. Likewise, Scout and Jem in Harper Lee's novel *To Kill a Mockingbird* (1962) stashed their prized treasures in a secret tree nook.

Childhood as Preparation for Capitalist Society

Children were the first collectors, and adult collectors can often trace their interests to childhood passions. During the twentieth century, children began to manage small sums of money when they received *allowances*, small amounts of money used to purchase school supplies or lunches given at regular intervals. Children quickly learned to manage this resource to indulge in candy or to collect specific items. They were also, unintentionally, recyclers of ordinary household items, often transforming something old and discarded into something new. As early as the 1840s, authors of child-rearing advice books encouraged parents to teach children about re-using household fragments so that precious resources would not be lost or wasted.

Schoolboys were encouraged to pursue the American dream for material success in an increasingly industrialized society. Horatio J. Alger (1832–1899), the author of rags-to-riches stories for boys, instilled a sensibility that poor boys could raise themselves to great success through hard work, thrift, and moral fortitude. His first book, *Ragged Dick,*

or Street Life in New York (1868), launched his prolific career as a writer and crusader against child labor.

Children historically have worked to contribute to family economy. Children in slavery, like their parents, were bonded to masters. Family bonds were often broken when members were sold, brutality was often witnessed by slave children, and childhood itself under slavery was greatly shortened. The end of slavery in 1865 did not necessarily bring relief; rather, for many free black children in the South, poverty and the institution of Jim Crow segregation constructed a different kind of childhood. For immigrant children, especially in industrial urban centers in the late nineteenth and early twentieth centuries, hard and dangerous work was no stranger. Their labor, as well as injuries sustained while working on family farms or in factories, shaped their lives in adulthood. The material culture of these groups' childhoods has not been adequately explored.

A national draft instituted in 1917 revealed a high incidence of ailments in men that could have been prevented during childhood, so the federal government instituted the Children's Year to examine health and welfare issues affecting children in the United States. Research showed that the length of childhood diminished with industrialization, and social scientists recognized adolescence as a distinct period of emotional development at the end of the nineteenth century. In modern American society, what it is to be a child is an open-ended question, subject to legal, psychological, biological, social, political, and cultural definitions and debates.

Meredith Eliassen

See also Adolescence; Children's Dress; Children's Material Culture; Children's Toys; Child's Body

References and Further Reading
Calvert, Karin. 1992. *Children in the House: The Material Culture of Children, 1600–1900.* Boston: Northeastern University Press.
Fass, Paula S., and Mary Ann Mason, eds. 2000. *Childhood in America.* New York: New York University Press.
King, Wilma. 1998. *Stolen Childhood: Slave Youth in Nineteenth-Century America.* Bloomington: Indiana University Press.
Marten, James. 1998. *The Children's Civil War.* Chapel Hill: University of North Carolina Press.

Children's Dress

The evolution of *children's dress* in what would become the United States is directly linked to society's changing conceptions of childhood. In the seventeenth and eighteenth centuries, parents attempted to push their children to maturity as quickly as possible and dressed their offspring in constricting adult dress. In the nineteenth century, American society's preoccupation with ostentation and show led parents to adorn their children in elaborate and often uncomfortable, but more "childish," costume. In the twentieth and twenty-first centuries, parents and clothing designers have considered a child's physical comfort and mobility as the most important dictates of children's dress.

Colonial and Early National Eras
In colonial Anglo-America, children's dress closely paralleled that of their parents. Dressing children as "miniature adults" restricted their physical movement and reinforced cultural ideas that childhood was a dangerous, sinful time. Young boys and girls wore long gowns similar to those worn by women, along with *stays*, a type of boned corset intended to support a growing child's abdomen and encourage good posture. When a young boy reached approximately five years (and / or when toilet training had been successfully completed), he was *breeched*, which meant he traded his nongendered dress and stays for clothing similar to that of grown men.

In his 1762 novel *Emile, or On Education,* philosopher Jean-Jacques Rousseau (1712–1778) described childhood as a time of innocence and playfulness. New philosophies of this sort romanticized the idea of childhood and convinced parents that their offspring should not be rushed to adulthood, but cherished as children. At the turn of the nineteenth century, dress created specially for children began to emerge: Girls wore loose, high-waisted dresses, and boys were fit in *skeleton suits*, slim-fitting, high-waisted trousers that buttoned to a waistcoat.

Mid- to Late Nineteenth-Century Styles
The nineteenth-century Industrial Revolution created a middle class defined by proper consumption of status goods. A child's clothing indicated the family's social status. Boys wore various suits and military costumes, popularized by English royalty, and girls wore stockings, petticoats, and dresses, which shortened over the course of the century. Many middle-class adults considered display to be more important than comfort when choosing clothing for children. Often children's fashion involved stiff fabrics, lace, crinolines, bustles, and hats—what some critics called *frippery*. By dressing children in elaborate or romantic costumes parents showed that they could afford to indulge and enjoy their children's immaturity. Working-class parents curtailed their offspring's childhood by putting their children, dressed in plainly made clothes of cheap fabric, into the labor force at a young age.

The use of shoes as playthings rather than as footwear in this lithograph advertising poster reflects adults' defini-tion of childhood in the mid- to late nineteenth century. The various costumes worn by these children were criticized as frippery that reflected more social status than useful, age-appropriate dress. S. D. Sollers & Co., Philadelphia, Pennsylvania, 1874. (Library of Congress)

Twentieth-Century Reform

Children were a major focus of reform move-ments during the Progressive Era of the early twentieth century. Dress reformers focused on the health and comfort of the young and encouraged the relaxation and simplifica-tion of children's fashion. American society as a whole experienced a relaxation of social norms and manners. A new interest in sports and the outdoors made simple playclothes the standard for children. In a complete reversal of eighteenth-century fashion, chil-dren's clothing began influencing adult fash-ion, as grown men and women relaxed their dress styles.

Infant dress followed the same basic trend toward relaxation and comfort. In colonial America, babies were *swaddled*, wrapped tightly in bands of fabric in order to keep arms and legs immobile. As the practice of swaddling waned, parents dressed infants in long gowns that reached well below the children's feet and inhibited crawling. When a child was ready to walk, parents put their children into shorter dresses and petticoats. In the early twentieth century, rompers be-came popular for both boys and girls, as they allowed for early crawling and physical freedom.

The practice of dressing a young child in nongendered clothing for his or her first few years gave way in the early twentieth century to more immediate sex distinction in cloth-ing. A boy's breeching was slowly abandoned as parents distinguished their sons from their daughters in infancy and put toddler sons directly into rompers, short pants, or trousers. In the 1920s, the color coding of dress to represent gender, boys in blue and girls in pink, took hold. Before this, blue was thought to be a more feminine color, and pink, a derivative of red, was thought to be more masculine.

The gendered nature of blue and pink became deeply embedded in the mid-twentieth-century American psyche. The divide between boys' and girls' dress for older children diminished as girls began wearing pants, however. From the 1950s onward, children of both sexes and all economic levels began to wear denim jeans and sneakers. Although children's dress remained a display of their parents' social status, children's fashions focused on comfort, flexibility, and youthfulness.

Bryn Varley Hollenbeck

See also Childhood; Child's Body; Dress, Accessories, and Fashion

References and Further Reading
Calvert, Karin. 1992. *Children in the House: The Material Culture of Early Childhood, 1600–1900.* Boston: Northeastern University Press.
Ewing, Elizabeth. 1977. *History of Children's Costume.* London: B. T. Batsford Ltd.
Kidwell, Claudia Brush, and Valerie Steele, eds. 1989. *Men and Women: Dressing the Part.* Washington, DC: Smithsonian Institution Press.
Worrell, Estelle Ansley. 1980. *Children's Costume in America, 1607–1910.* New York: Charles Scribner's Sons.

Children's Material Culture

Children and youth (up to age 18 in present American society) use material objects to mark their identities and to communicate with others. Children are born without verbal language, so they live for a while in a world where meanings and activities are primarily physical and material. Developmental psychologists emphasize crucial moments when the child can distinguish between his or her own body and other objects, can understand cause and effect in the behavior of objects, and can understand how the mastery of objects provides important tools for satisfying needs and reaching goals. Evolutionary neurobiologists now understand the important coevolution of the human hand and the brain, such that the manipulation of physical objects with the hands is an important precursor to complex brain functions, including speech. Children denied access to a rich world of material objects for their manipulation and play do not develop their cognitive powers as well as those children nurtured with objects. Some children have what psychologists call *transitional objects*— a favorite blanket or stuffed animal the child needs for comfort during anxious times. Even when the child acquires language, material objects continue to provide means for communicating with others and for acquiring power in everyday life.

Once the infant can sit up and grasp objects within reach he or she usually begins to play with objects, testing his or her qualities and acquiring skills in using the objects. Infants play with food and other readily available material as part of their exploration of their worlds. Play with objects usually becomes more social (often with hard lessons about possession, ownership, and sharing), but children also retain and hone the skills of imaginary play, with material objects as the "props" in play scenarios. A found object can be enlisted in this imaginary play, as when a child holds a banana as a pretend baby or points a stick and informs his or her playmates that it is a gun. This "making do" with found objects is common in childhood and seems not to disappear when the child has access to machine-made, commercial objects created for and given to children by adults.

Children's play with material objects tends to follow a folk aesthetic, which is to say that the child creates the meaning of the object through accretion (adding with no logical ending point) and repetition. The folk aesthetic also favors process over product, so that the eventual destruction of the created object does not threaten the pleasure and meaning of its creation. Children's play in sand at a beach or in a sandbox nicely illustrates this folk aesthetic, as children will constantly add to their castles, holes, and the like until the player runs out of time or interest. Snow provides a similar play material for children, as does water.

In addition to putting found objects in the service of imaginary play, children also fashion their own toys. String figure games (e.g., "cat's cradle"), toys carved or assembled from wood or cardboard, and folded paper toys like "cootie catchers" are common. Toys like blocks and Legos™ are meant to spark creativity, but children also can employ toys for less approved uses, as when children play "dirty games" with Barbie dolls, assemble Legos as forbidden guns, or play dangerously with a bicycle. In these cases and more, children have converted a machine-made toy into a folk toy.

The world of manufactured toys is linked to a commercial world of mass-mediated narratives meant to create consumer desire in the child or adult. Television shows, films, and video games and the advertising associated with those media provide fantasy narratives demonstrating for youth the pleasures of having a game, toy, or item of clothing. The mass media provide some "scripts" directing the child how to use the material objects, as do older children when they teach younger children how to play with objects in approved and disapproved ways.

The pet is a living artifact in the child's world. Mammalian pets are interactive playthings, but even the least interactive pet (e.g., a goldfish in a bowl) can involve a host of material objects around the pet keeping. For some young people, such as those who live on a farm or are involved in 4-H, other domestic animals are often important parts of the child's material world.

The Material Child and History

Social and cultural historians attempting to write the history of childhood have found material culture to be rich evidence in the absence of more conventional evidence, like written documents. Material culture, for example, demonstrates the increasing individualism of the child during the eighteenth century, reflecting Enlightenment ideas about the nature of the child. Changes in children's clothing, the manufacture of special dishes and cups for children, and the use of separate bedrooms for children in middle-class families are among the material clues that Americans were coming to see childhood as a distinct period of life.

Once children were accorded their own rooms (even if shared with siblings) in the house, those rooms became the folk museums of children's material culture. Within limitations of resources and parental tolerance, children and youth can personalize their bedrooms with decorations and other objects that can be seen as part of the performance of individual identity.

The material culture of childhood also helps historians speculate on other important aspects of the changing lives of children. The change from buttons to zippers and then to Velcro™ fasteners in children's clothing, for example, suggests the increasing independence of children as marked by the ability to undress and dress oneself, and this also has implications for the toilet training of young children. Bicycles and skateboards signal mobility and independence, and American historians would have to consider the automobile as one of the most important material objects in the lives of middle-class American teenagers. Riding around the automobile is a whole customary culture of twentieth-century adolescence, including dating and dangerous play.

Crafts

Children move through a number of formal and informal organizations outside the home, and in many cases these organizations aim to introduce children to craft skills in making objects. Schools have craft projects, including the creation of gifts for parents, and the schooling of adolescents may include more formal training, such as shop classes (woodworking, metalworking, etc., usually for boys) and home economics classes (sewing, cooking, etc., usually for girls).

Equally interesting are the crafts projects common in youth organizations and summer camps. These organizations began in the late nineteenth century out of specific concerns that modern life was separating children from the more natural lives social Darwinism suggested was so important to their psychological and social development. The Arts and Crafts Movement in the United States and England responded to the increased presence of machine-made goods in everyday life with an ideology of the benefits of a return to handmade goods and a recovery of the social, moral, and even religious values of that more authentic relationship to the material world. The Arts and Crafts Movement entered children's lives through school programs and through the crafts programs of organizations like the Boy Scouts of America and the Camp Fire Girls

(both founded 1910). Boys and girls learned crafts (such as basket weaving and wood-carving) thought to be disappearing, and they also learned a range of craft skills associated with camping and cooking outdoors.

Arts and crafts for children helped spark a twentieth-century idea that middle-class children and adolescents needed "hobbies" to fill their spare time, in part for the youth's mental and social growth but also to occupy youth who might find trouble in their idle hours. Several commercial companies rose to produce the craft supplies that would serve some hobbies, and the rise of molded plastics helped stimulate a mid-century boom in plastic models assembled with glue and painted.

Hobbies often involve collecting and displaying objects. The Boy Scouts and similar youth organizations stimulated natural history collecting, and the Great Depression era saw a campaign for children to collect stamps, just like President Franklin Delano Roosevelt (1882–1945) did. The baby boom generation (those born between 1946 and 1964) born in the wake of World War II became a great hobby generation, and children continue collecting both manufactured goods and found objects. Manufacturers target the collecting and display tendencies among youth, sometimes creating goods (e.g., My Little Pony, Beanie Babies, and media-themed action figures) with direct instructions to "collect them all." Along with collecting came the impulse to display the collections, so that the young person's bedroom sometimes served a museumlike function.

Electronic Objects

One of the most recent developments in the material culture used by children and teenagers is the rapidly changing world of electronic objects. Analogic and then digital technologies entered bedrooms in the waning decades of the twentieth century, and in the new century the average middle-class young person has daily access to cell phones, computers, portable digital music players, instant messaging technologies, and hand-held video game players (increasingly capable of playing digital films and television shows). Far from isolating youth, the new technologies actually make it easier for young people to interact, even communicating in settings (e.g., school classrooms) where most social communications are suppressed. Cell phones doubling as digital cameras contain digital photo books of their youthful owners and their friends.

Jay Mechling

See also Animals; Bedrooms; Childhood; Children's Dress; Children's Toys; Child's Body; Collecting and Collections; Education and Schooling; Folklore and Folklife; Games; Technology

References and Further Reading

Bronner, Simon J. 1999. "Material Folk Culture of Children." In *Children's Folklore: A Sourcebook*, ed. Brian Sutton-Smith et al., 251–271. Logan: Utah State University Press.

Cross, Gary. 1997. *Kids' Stuff: Toys and the Changing World of American Childhood*. Cambridge, MA: Harvard University Press.

Gelber, Steven M. 1999. *Hobbies: Leisure and the Culture of Work in America*. New York: Columbia University Press.

Mechling, Jay. 1986. "Children's Folklore." In *Folk Groups and Folklore Genres*, ed. Elliott Oring, 91–120. Logan: Utah State University Press.

Sutton-Smith, Brian. 1986. *Toys as Culture*. New York: Gardner Press.

Children's Toys

Toys are the physical objects with which primarily children play. Toys have been the products of imagination (such as children using old boots to represent horses) and of parents' and children's own creations (such as folding cloth to form a baby doll). Children traditionally played a variety of games, but they did not have many toys. One toy that did exist in Native American culture was used in a variation of *diabolo*, a toy game of skill in which a spool was tossed on a string suspended between two sticks. Throughout American history, parents have preferred toys they believed fostered manliness in sons and femininity in daughters, and purchased or constructed toys that conformed to distinct gender roles for men and women.

In the eighteenth and early nineteenth centuries, American parents were influenced by the writings of John Locke (1632–1704) and Jean-Jacques Rousseau (1712–1778), who argued that the child was, in Locke's terms, a *tabula rasa*—a blank slate upon which character is written. As families migrated from the countryside to industrializing towns and cities, play became more purposeful and focused to inculcate specific gender-related skills. Androgynous toys, including baby rattles and teething rings, play hoops, the boat and animals of Noah's Ark, marbles, and jacks, have traditionally been popular with American children. "Pretending" toys that encourage children to imitate adult behavior such as miniature tools and certain dolls with accessories were considered to be educational. Parents throughout the nineteenth century wanted to raise children who could successfully function autonomously in an increasingly consumer-driven society.

The mid- to late nineteenth-century nursery developed as a result of increasing affluence of a growing middle class in the United States. Besides playing in a garden, a park, or a dwelling's yard, the middle-class white child might spend most of his or her time within the confines of the children's nursery or bedroom. Toys expanded the child's world in these spaces, where a child would not be exposed to the many dangers that might be found in other parts of the household.

The earliest manufactured toys were produced during the early 1840s by Francis, Fields & Francis in Connecticut and the Tin Toy Manufactory in Pennsylvania. Toys that reflected mid-century changes in technology including toy trains, complex building-block sets, and kits for making toys or models. Fantasy toys emerged during the twentieth century as new materials and mass production were introduced and adopted. New Jersey's Bergen Toy & Novelty Co., originally a tin soldier manufacturer, in 1938 started making plastic toys that were distributed in "five and ten" stores.

Mass-produced toys were and are geared to sell to mainstream culture; the history of toys in the nineteenth- and twentieth-century United States includes many examples of derogatory stereotyping of immigrant groups, Native Americans, and African Americans. In 1952 Hasbro introduced Mr. Potato Head, the features of which recall Italian produce vendors. In contrast, the popular Barbie doll, introduced in 1959, equates fashionable consumption and comfortable lifestyle with whiteness and beauty. G.I. Joe, introduced in mass production in 1965, was also white; a black G.I. Joe created at the same time was criticized as having stereotypical features. The complexities of race and ethnicity challenge toy manufacturers to appeal to a variety of consumer desires and demands and, increasingly, teach children to buy more toys. That lesson is abetted by film and television campaigns that offer toys as advertising and incentives.

Meredith Eliassen

See also Childhood; Children's Material Culture; Games; Technology

References and Further Reading

Calvert, Karin. 1992. *Children in the House: The Material Culture of Children, 1600–1900.* Boston: Northeastern University Press.

Cross, Gary. 1997. *Kid's Stuff: Toys and the Changing World of American Childhood.* Cambridge, MA: Harvard University Press.

O'Brien, Richard. 1993. *The Story of American Toys from the Puritans to the Present.* London: New Cavendish Books.

Child's Body

Adults have long treated the *child's body* as a physical object to be molded. White parents of the American colonial era expected the midwife to shape a newborn by straightening limbs, cupping the head to remove the conical effect of birth, and pulling skull bones together across the soft spot. As the child grew, he or she was wrapped in swaddling cloths to keep limbs growing straight, while gowns that exceeded the infant's length suggested the dignity of an older stature. Devices such as toddler corsets, standing stools, and walking carts, as well as long gowns, favored erect habits and early walking over crawling (which many believed degraded the child because it resembled an animal posture). By the second half of the eighteenth century, the freer ideas of such thinkers as John Locke (1632–1704) and Jean-Jacques Rousseau (1712–1778) had encouraged parents to surrender most of these implements and instead to form children by "hardening" them in the open air. Girls continued to receive active sculpting as mothers laced them into tight corsets at adolescence, seeking the prized "tenuous" and willowy physique.

Unfree children, including slaves, indentured servants, and apprentices, were treated in a still more objectified manner. Enslaved children in particular endured whatever their white masters desired, from being branded to serving as all-night nursemaids or as non-consensual sexual partners. Parents of slaves preferred their own shaping traditions—some left over from Africa or the West Indies, others developed on American soil—and raised their children with these goals in mind, as did free people of color.

Native American parents trained their children in keeping with tribal norms, varying by climate, diet, material culture, and religious practices. Many tribes, for instance, kept infants in cradleboards to help children's limbs grow straight, and the scanty clothing often worn by Eastern Woodlands children was partly intended to help harden them to their environment. Beginning in the late 1800s, the United States government undertook re-education of Native American children at boarding schools. Barbers cut hair, Caucasian-style clothing replaced blankets, and moccasins gave way to hard shoes. These material changes were often as traumatic as homesickness and new food.

In the late nineteenth century, especially among whites, the muscular Christianity movement encouraged teenage boys and young men to develop visible muscles through weight lifting and calisthenics, while team sports became a new craze. Girls gained freedom of movement as bicycling, tennis, and other sports became popular, but the corseted figure remained the ideal until the 1920s. Then, once the corset trend passed, drop-waist dresses and the flat-chested flapper look triggered a new diet craze; in the 1950s, hourglass figures and "bullet" bras changed the goal again. Through all these eras, adults have assumed the child's body was malleable and have handled children differently according to gender, race, and social class.

Rebecca R. Noel

See also Adolescence; Childhood; Children's Dress; Human Body; Native America; Slavery

References and Further Reading

Brumberg, Joan Jacobs. 1997. *The Body Project: An Intimate History of American Girls*. New York: Random House.
Calvert, Karin. 1994. *Children in the House: The Material Culture of Early Childhood, 1600–1900*. Boston: Northeastern University Press.
Mintz, Steven. 2004. *Huck's Raft: A History of American Childhood*. Cambridge, MA: Belknap Press.
Utley, Robert M. 2003. *The Indian Frontier, 1846–1890*. Albuquerque: University of New Mexico Press.

Chippendale Style

Chippendale, a style of American decorative arts, derived its name from the English cabinetmaker Thomas Chippendale's (1718–1779) *The Gentleman & Cabinet-Maker's Director*, a pattern book published in 1754 and reprinted in 1755, 1756, and 1762 in London. Copies of this book influenced furniture design in colonial cities with sophisticated patrons eager for the latest fashions, especially Charleston, South Carolina; Boston; New York City; Newport, Rhode Island; and Philadelphia.

Most Chippendale furniture is made of mahogany, which was sometimes gilded or painted. Pieces in this style include armchairs, side chairs, easy chairs, sofas, chests of drawers, dressing tables, high chests, occasional tables, frames and looking glasses, and decorative display brackets. The style also appears on porcelain, silver, and other metalwork made in America between 1755 and 1790.

Known as the "Modern" style when the pattern book was published, features of

The English cabinetmaker Thomas Chippendale's The Gentleman & Cabinet-Maker's Director *influenced American design after its publication in London in 1754. Plate 12 depicts three chairs that show the style's characteristic pierced backsplat, cabriole leg, and naturalistic carving. (Library of Congress)*

Chippendale design include standard decorative elements associated with the Rococo period such as serpentine S-scrolls and C-scrolls, stylized shell motifs, ribbons, foliage and flowers, and acanthus leaves. Cabriole legs are common.

Chippendale's pattern book also included furniture with Chinese elements such as fretwork, pagodas, and cranelike birds. The claw-and-ball feet often regarded as typical of the style are thought to be based on the Chinese design motif of the imperial dragon clutching a pearl in its talons. Gothic elements such as arches and quatrefoils are also incorporated, and the overall effect of Chippendale design can be characterized as one of lightness, elegance, and graceful motion.

H. Christian Carr

See also Decorative Arts; Design History and American Design; Furniture; Interior Design; Style

References and Further Reading

Chippendale, Thomas. 1966 (1762). *The Gentleman & Cabinet-Maker's Director*. New York: Dover.

Heckscher, Morrison H., and Leslie Greene Bowman. 1992. *American Rococo, 1750–1775: Elegance in Ornament*. New York: Harry N. Abrams.

Richards, Nancy E., and Nancy Goyne Evans. 1997. *New England Furniture at Wintherthur: Queen Anne and Chippendale Periods*. Winterthur, DE: Winterthur Museum and University Press of New England.

Cities and Towns

City and *town*, often interchangeable in usage, describe political entities defined in the United States by state law and measured by various government agencies and civic organizations in terms of population and geographic area. A *city* is defined in various

ways: as a state-chartered municipal corporation, a major hub of a region, or a center of
economic activity. Smaller in population and
size than cities, a *town* is a central place in
which goods and services are provided to a
populace residing within its boundaries or
in its immediate hinterlands. In some states,
however, *township* defines an administrative
area that is not necessarily urban in character. In addition, *city* is included in place
names, describing at times places that may
only be a small number of dwellings housing
a few dozen inhabitants. Cities and towns
are generally defined as urban areas apart
from but historically dependent on hinter-
land agricultural production. Material culture scholars have studied the physical
aspects of cities and towns—buildings, architectural style, and space; street plans and
signage; parks, playgrounds, and cemeteries;
and urban planning and its results.

Early American Towns, Townships, Townscapes, and Cities

European colonists brought with them to
the New World practical and utopian tem-
plates for the cities and towns they would
establish. Medieval cities were the sites of
cathedrals and seats of government. Quite
apart from the feudal system, walled market towns were distinct political units of free
men (called *citizens*, *burghers*, or *bourgeois*) who
elected their councils and enjoyed the protection of the king who had chartered the
towns. Though many American towns and
cities were built as seaports similar to and
named after those the colonists had left, Virginia's colonial capital of Williamsburg (1699)
was laid out to commemorate the reigning
monarchs William and Mary through a street
pattern laid out in a "W" and "M." Quaker
William Penn (1644–1718) remembered the
problems of overpopulation and poor administration of London and worked to avoid

them. His 1683 plan for Philadelphia allowed for city parks and large home lots
across a two-square-mile grid and sought
to remedy the ills of urbanization in the
aftermath of the Black Death of 1665 and
the London Fire of 1666. His plan failed.
Colonists long resisted building beyond the
sight of the Delaware River. Savannah, Georgia; Annapolis, Maryland; and New York
City are also examples of planned cities in
the wilderness.

The New England model of land settlement provided the basis of subsequent land
distribution methods in the United States.
New England towns were administrative
units dispensing land to farming families.
The New England town was also a community based on church membership and is the
birthplace of the town meeting as a form of
political participation. The western federal
lands ordered by the Northwest Ordinance
(1789), as well as the Connecticut Western
Reserve of Ohio, were surveyed and administered on the New England model of
townships.

By the end of the eighteenth century,
American towns and cities were small but
densely populated. Although contemporary visual depictions of these cities show
ordered streets and inviting parks that
reminded viewers of villages, census numbers and other evidence point to dangerously crowded conditions. New York and
Philadelphia counted more than 25,000 inhabitants in the nation's first census in 1790;
in 1800 Boston and Baltimore could be added
to that roll. As historian Carole Shammas
(1990, 506) has found, the average number of
persons per square mile in the United States
in 1800 was 6, whereas in Philadelphia and
New York City it was 40,000. Without city
services, with the necessity of fire to warm
and feed bodies, and with the keeping of
livestock in pens and backyards, urban life in

the early republic was noisy, odorous, and for those without means, difficult.

Throughout the nineteenth century and well into the twentieth, the greater number of Americans lived in small towns. In 1850, eighty-five cities counted populations more than 8,000, yet together they counted for only 13 percent of the nation's population. Towns, like cities, were established to facilitate trade. Towns often began as crossroads settlements of lean-tos and log dwellings, to be replaced by wood frame houses and, later, public and civic buildings such as town halls, libraries, and schools. Some states created towns as county seats, designing the towns on the central edifice of a courthouse, courthouse square, and attendant buildings. The symbolism of government and the philosophy upon which it is based are reflected in these plans and the architectural styles of the buildings. The nation's capital, designed by Pierre Charles L'Enfant (1754–1825) in the federal District of Columbia, employed Neoclassical design, radiating avenues, and open spaces upon a grid pattern in establishing the legitimacy and majesty of the new nation.

Industrialization and the Rise of the Cities

The new nation's population moved westward in the late eighteenth and early nineteenth centuries. At the same time, the population moved to cities, both old and new. The movement of capital from agriculture to industrial manufacturing led to many Americans' relocation to new mill towns built along river waterfalls. Port cities connected to the interior became centers of communication, transportation, commerce, and capital. The Erie Canal, completed in 1825, linked the Great Lakes region to New York City via the canal and the Hudson River. New York's location made it an economic capital by the Civil War (1861–1865).

Industrial factories changed the nature of cities, expanding over the course of the nineteenth century the "walking city," in which business could be conducted easily within the city's or town's compact borders. Suburbanization rose with industrialization, necessitating public transportation systems such as horse-drawn omnibuses, trolleys, and, by the end of the century, subways. Urban housing changed, as elites and the growing middle class removed to the suburbs. City apartments and tenements, not necessarily "up to code," were constructed and rented to wave after wave of employment seekers, including both native-born Americans and European immigrants.

Social Reform, the City Beautiful Movement, and the Rise of City Planning

What these new city dwellers found were bustling cities with little supervision by municipal government. Air pollution, poor sanitation systems, noise, and other health woes beset urbanites. In turn, political "machines," such as that controlled by the Democrats in New York City's Tammany Hall, provided services to those who could not afford them in return for their votes. By the end of the century reformers such as Jane Addams (1860–1935), at Chicago's Hull House, and New Yorker Jacob Riis (1849–1914), in his photographic exposé *How the Other Half Lives* (1890), would call attention to these problems that plagued especially immigrants. Artists such as Robert Henri (1865–1929) and his colleagues of the Ash Can school celebrated urban life, especially of the poor, in their paintings in the first two decades of the twentieth century. At the same time, capital was celebrated in the nation's cities in the construction of high-style apartment buildings and townhouses near city parks and museum districts, and of skyscrapers, the new "cathedrals of commerce" rising in cities' business districts.

The problems of the industrial city—filth and lack of sanitation, overcrowding and slum districts, transportation and government—elicited not only social and political reform but aesthetic reform as well. The World's Columbian Exposition of 1893 in Chicago employed European Beaux-Arts architecture in its idealized "White City" and sparked a movement to beautify the nation's cities. Led by architects such as Daniel Burnham (1846–1912), landscape designers such as Frederick Law Olmsted (1822–1903), and prominent citizens, the City Beautiful Movement advocated city planning, park systems, monumental government buildings, and wide boulevards to enhance city living and attract wealth. The movement's best-known spokesman was Charles Mulford Robinson (1869–1917), who wrote *Modern Civic Art or the City Made Beautiful* (1903).

The tenets of the movement were adopted by many towns and cities throughout the nation, but not without debate. Progressive social reformers saw in the City Beautiful Movement the use of beautiful facades to hide urban problems. In response, Progressive architects, settlement-house workers, real estate agents, and advocates of good housing assembled at the first National Conference on City Planning in 1909. Planned cities had been evident since the very beginning of colonization. City planning as a profession was the result of Progressives' concerns and actions.

Main Streets and Downtowns

Whether called High Street, Market Street, State Street, or some other name, many towns and cities boast a *main street*, a central corridor through a commercial district in which consumers and retailers united to create a healthy "bustle" that measured not only the economic vitality of the municipality but symbolized its moral and civic values as well. Regulated public markets were found on the main thoroughfares in colonial cities, increasingly surrounded by private shops; in the nineteenth century, department stores anchored these districts, such as New York City's Ladies' Mile. Photographic parlors, hotels, and other commercial leisure venues appeared as well. In the twentieth century these businesses were joined by chain stores, movie theaters, and business towers. Civic pride has always been joined to commercial success of main streets; city directories and tourist guides tout such sights and experiences in these downtown districts. The centrality of Main Street to American culture was also codified in Walt Disney's construction of an early twentieth-century streetscape based on his home town of Marceline, Missouri, at Disneyland in 1955. Today, many Disney theme parks throughout the world include "Main Street USA." The decline of central business districts and other commercial districts—signaled by vacant storefronts, shuttered shops, and empty streets—has elicited a variety of studies and remedies by municipal, state, and federal government; civic organizations; and corporations. Since the late 1980s many cities and towns have sought to revive commercial districts by creating nostalgic "quaintscapes" of streetlights, benches, plantings, and other amenities to lure tourists and inhabitants alike back to downtown.

Metropolises and the New Urbanism

The Great Depression of the 1930s and World War II (1939–1945) stymied, but did not stall, urban development. After the war, new ideas of urban planning, based on the popularity of the automobile and the preference for the International style in architecture, drastically changed the American cityscape.

With federal laws and programs encouraging home ownership and highway construction, "suburban sprawl" became a reality, leaving city centers and neighborhoods empty. In the 1950s and 1960s critics such as Lewis Mumford (1895–1990) and Jane Jacobs (1916–2006) challenged urban planners to rethink the city, in Jacobs' case in response to urban renewal programs that destroyed communities. By the 1980s New Urbanists were calling for new thinking as well. Based on the neighborhood with a discernible center, with a variety of dwellings in near proximity, New Urbanism counters the monumental scale of the International style and seeks in its place a human-scale, walkable city.

Shirley Teresa Wajda

See also City Parks; Civic Architecture; Commercial Architecture; Commercial Food Venues; Company Towns; Consumerism and Consumption; Cultural Geography; Department Stores; Homeless Residences; Leisure, Recreation, and Amusements; Mill Towns; Office Work and Labor; Public and Commercial Leisure, Recreation, and Amusement Venues; Public Markets; Suburbs and Suburbia

References and Further Reading

Bridenbaugh, Carl. 1938. *Cities in the Wilderness: The First Century of Urban Life in America, 1625–1742.* New York: Oxford University Press.

Bridenbaugh, Carl. 1955. *Cities in Revolt: Urban Life in America, 1743–1776.* New York: Oxford University Press.

Isenberg, Alison. 2004. *Downtown America: A History of the Place and the People Who Made It.* Chicago: University of Chicago Press.

Jacobs, Jane. 1993 (1961). *The Death and Life of Great American Cities.* New York: Random House.

Mumford, Lewis. 1961. *The City in History: Its Origins, Its Transformations, and Its Prospects.* New York: Harcourt, Brace & World.

Reps, John. 1998. *Bird's Eye Views: Historic Lithographs of North American Cities.* New York: Princeton Architectural Press.

Shammas, Carole. 1990. *The Pre-Industrial Consumer in England and America.* Oxford, UK: Oxford University Press.

Tolbert, Lisa C. 1999. *Constructing Townscapes: Space and Society in Antebellum Tennessee.* Chapel Hill: University of North Carolina Press.

Wood, Joseph S. 1997. *The New England Village.* Baltimore, MD: Johns Hopkins University Press.

City Parks

City parks in the United States have roots in the central squares of the seventeenth and eighteenth centuries and in the rural cemetery movement of the nineteenth century. Since then, city parks have been created to provide a green respite from the pressures of the modern city and embody American notions about the city and the country.

Early American settlements often featured a central green space that could be used for grazing livestock, drilling troops, and punishing criminals. Extant examples include the Boston Common in Massachusetts and the New Haven Green in Connecticut. Early city planners often included town squares, as featured in Philadelphia, Pennsylvania, and Savannah, Georgia. In the Southwest, Spanish town plans featured central plazas, as found in Santa Fe and Albuquerque, New Mexico. Although not specifically created for recreation, these central squares represent the first civic spaces open to all.

With nineteenth-century industrialization, American life was divided into work and leisure. Americans migrated to cities to find work in industry, and planners responded by attempting to provide outdoor respite for them. In 1831 botanist Jacob Bigelow (1787–1879) designed Mount Auburn Cemetery, the first American burial ground to incorporate a garden. This Cambridge, Massachusetts, cemetery set the standard for "rural cemeteries." Woodlands (circa 1789), once a Philadelphia mansion and estate of William Hamilton (1745–1813), himself a collector of plants and a landscape gardener, was converted in 1840 to a rural garden cemetery. Mid-nineteenth-century Americans used these graceful spaces as places of leisure, enjoying picnics, strolling, and riding in the cemetery: The rural cemetery was a place to see and be seen. Mount Auburn featured gently curving pathways that hugged manicured lawns dotted with clusters of trees. The rural cemetery incorporated ideas of European Romanticism as well as elements of American Transcendentalism, for both schools of thought believed in nature's restorative powers on the human psyche.

In 1857 New York City held a design competition for a central open space, and the winning design for Central Park influenced later city park design. Frederick Law Olmsted's (1822–1903) and Calvert Vaux's (1824–1895) Greensward Plan was largely informal and *picturesque*, a term that refers to landscapes that fall between the sublime wilderness and the beautiful geometric formal gardens like those of Versailles. The new design created a landscape with curvilinear paths tracing different use areas of the park, while vehicular traffic was kept at bay by sunken roads. Although the architects wanted Central Park to be a green emblem of democratic ideals, almost 2,000 subsistence farmers and squatters living in the area were driven out under eminent domain for the park's creation.

Philadelphia's Fairmount Park (1865), San Francisco's Golden Gate Park (1870), and St. Louis' Forest Park (1876) followed Central Park's lead in creating a bit of nature in the metropolis' midst. Ambitious projects like Olmsted's Emerald Necklace in Boston (1878–1895) created long parkways that connected the city's heart to the country with a green ribbon of landscape.

Although city parks had always offered space for horseback riding, strolling, and ice skating, in the latter half of the nineteenth century they became urban playgrounds with facilities designed for specific sports. Urban parks established in the twentieth century have followed suit. Skateboard facilities now dot some city parks, and pocket-sized parks are occasionally created from reclaimed parcels of urban real estate. Recently completed large projects include Chicago's Millennium Park.

Emily Godbey

See also Burial Grounds, Cemeteries, and Grave Markers; Cities and Towns; Land and Landscape

References and Further Reading

Cranz, Galen. 1982. *The Politics of Park Design: A History of Urban Parks in America*. Cambridge, MA: MIT Press.
Heckscher, August, and Phyllis C. Robinson. 1977. *Open Spaces: The Life of American Cities*. New York: Harper and Row.
Rosenzweig, Roy, and Elizabeth Blackmar. 1992. *The Park and the People: A History of Central Park*. Ithaca, NY: Cornell University Press.
Schuyler, David Paul. 1986. *The New Urban Landscape: The Redefinition of City Form in Nineteenth-Century America*. Baltimore, MD: Johns Hopkins University Press.
Tishler, William H. 1989. *American Landscape Architecture: Designers and Places*. Washington, DC: Preservation Press.

Civic Architecture

Civic architecture is defined as a class of structures that exist for the good of the people, from those buildings that house governmental functions to those that serve the public good: symphony halls, baths and recreational facilities, libraries and museums, and public memorials.

Early American Civic Buildings

The earliest examples of civic architecture in what would become the United States were of simple wood frame construction, echoing the medieval style of the mother country—England, France, the Netherlands, and Spain. After seeing to the immediate need of shelter, the New England meetinghouse was often the first structure erected and served not only as a church but also as the town hall. By the early eighteenth century, civic architecture reflected the styles imported from England, particularly the Georgian, with its emphasis on symmetry, classicism, and elegant simplicity. New civic buildings were often of masonry construction, conveying a sense of importance and permanence—as well as being fire resistant. The brick courthouse (1770) in Williamsburg, Virginia, one of the surviving examples of Georgian architecture, has a symmetrical facade, a classical pediment over the entrance, and a graceful steeple. One of Williamsburg's other important civic buildings, the brick capitol, is a reconstruction of the structure's 1705–1747 incarnation, which is believed to be the first time *capitol* was used for an American building.

Civic Structures in the Early American Republic

After independence, civic buildings continued to contain elements of classicism through the new nation's vogue for the Federal and Greek Revival styles. Americans saw the nation as a modern expression of republican Rome and democratic Greece, thus architectural elements inspired by those two ancient civilizations were deemed appropriate for American civic architecture. The Massachusetts State House (1795–1798) in Boston, designed by Charles Bulfinch (1763–1844), is an important example of a Federal-style civic structure. The Ohio Statehouse (1830–1860)

in Columbus is an excellent surviving example of a Greek Revival capitol building. Other civic buildings such as town halls and courthouses also reflected the popularity of classicism in the early nineteenth century. Much of Washington DC's civic architecture, from the White House to the United States Capitol to the Lincoln and Jefferson memorials, are expressions of Neoclassicism.

While never totally out of favor, Neoclassicism was superseded by other styles in the later nineteenth century. The Gothic Revival, which was used in Great Britain's Houses of Parliament (1860–1870), was popular for churches and even domiciles in the United States; however, it never became as popular for civic structures. The romantic French Second Empire, with its mansard roof, asymmetry, square towers, and exuberant decoration, was popular for civic buildings in communities large and small. One of the best surviving examples is the Philadelphia City Hall (1871–1901); the small community of Napoleon in Henry County, Ohio, boasts a Second Empire combination sheriff's residence and jail.

Gilded Age Revivalism

One of the most influential styles for civic architecture in the later nineteenth century was developed by Henry Hobson Richardson (1838–1886) and bears his name—Richardsonian Romanesque. Richardson took his inspiration from the mid-nineteenth century Germanic-influenced Romanesque Revival, but his buildings looked more to French and Spanish sources. Richardson's buildings were also much more massive than the earlier Romanesque Revival, retaining the rounded arches but using rougher finishes and polychrome decoration to add texture to his designs. One of his most influential public buildings was the Allegheny County Courthouse and Jail (1884–1888) in Pittsburgh,

Pennsylvania. Many communities large and small found this style attractive and believed it suggested a majesty and strength that people should expect from their government. Warren, a small community in northeastern Ohio, boasts as a landmark its Richardsonian Romanesque–style courthouse designed by La Belle & French in 1895; another excellent example is the Wayne County Courthouse in Richmond, Indiana, designed by James W. McLaughlin (1834–1923).

The late nineteenth and early twentieth centuries saw a revival of interest in classical architectural forms. Many American architects began studying at the École des Beaux-Arts in Paris, which greatly influenced their designs for years to come. The École's emphasis on Greek and Roman models was particularly influential in the design of civic buildings and structures. The World's Columbian Exposition held in Chicago in 1893 further solidified the hold classicism had on architects. The "White City" section of the fair, with its monumental classical buildings designed by important architects like Daniel Burnham (1846–1912), was an inspiration for architects and clients alike. New civic buildings at the end of the nineteenth and beginning of the twentieth centuries not only directly copied elements from Greek and Roman examples but often adapted features from the Renaissance, which in turn had also found inspiration in ancient civilizations. McKim, Mead, and White (est. 1879), one of the nation's foremost architectural firms, also greatly enhanced the interest in classicism with important buildings like the Boston Public Library (1888–1895), which is in the Second Renaissance Revival style.

Twentieth-Century Experiments in Civic Design

Classicism remained in vogue as the appropriate style for schools, libraries, art museums, city halls, courthouses, and other civic buildings and monuments until the mid twentieth century. There are some notable exceptions such as the Art Deco Kansas City, Missouri, City Hall (1936–1937) and the Buffalo, New York, City Hall (1929–1931). In the last half of the twentieth century, more experimentation was introduced in the design of American civic buildings. Postmodernist architects, who rejected the sterility of the International style in favor of a modern interpretation of older architectural forms, designed a number of civic buildings. Michael Graves, for example, designed the Portland, Oregon, Public Service Administration Building (1981–1982), which flaunted a huge keystone on the upper stories and an extensive use of polychrome (blues, browns, and deep reds). While the keystone harkens back to classical architecture, the colors suggest an anticlassicism and instead owe much more to Art Deco than anything else. Even newer monuments such as Maya Lin's Vietnam Veterans Memorial (1982) and the Franklin Delano Roosevelt Memorial (1997), both in Washington DC, are of distinctly contemporary design with little or no reference to classical sources.

Donna M. DeBlasio

See also Architectural History and American Architecture; Art Deco; Cities and Towns; Classical Revival (Neoclassicism); Federal Style; Georgian Style; Gothic Revival; Postmodernism; Public Monuments and Popular Commemoration; Renaissance Revival

References and Further Reading

Gelertner, Mark. 1999. *A History of American Architecture: Buildings in Their Cultural and Technological Context.* Hanover, NH: University Press of New England.

Handlin, David P. 2004. *American Architecture,* 2nd ed. London: Thames and Hudson.

Maddex, Diane, ed. 1985. *Built in the U.S.A.: American Buildings From Airports to Zoos.*

Washington, DC: National Trust for Historic Preservation.

Poppeliers, John, and S. Allen Chambers, Jr. 2003. *What Style Is It? A Guide to American Architecture*, rev. ed. Hoboken, NJ: John Wiley and Sons.

Rifkind, Carole. 1980. *A Field Guide to American Architecture*. New York: Penguin.

Roth, Leland M. 1979. *A Concise History of American Architecture*. New York: Harper & Row.

Classical Revival (Neoclassicism)

Also called *Neoclassicism*, the *Classical Revival* was a mid-eighteenth-century international cultural movement that heralded a reawakened interest in the ancient Greco-Roman world. From the 1740s onward, archaeological discoveries at Pompeii and Herculaneum (Roman cities buried during the eruption of Mt. Vesuvius in 79 CE) caught the imagination of Europeans, among them the German Johann Joachim Winckelmann (1717–1768), who wrote *Thoughts on the Imitation of Greek Works in Painting and Sculpture* in 1750, the first text to recognize Greece as the source of classical art. The ideas spread from Italy across the Continent and to England. Englishmen James Stuart (1713–1788) and Nicholas Revett (1720–1804) produced their illustrated and thereby influential work, *The Antiquities of Athens*, between 1762 and 1830. Printing presses in London and North America produced a variety of architectural and art treatises, drawing books, prints, speeches, and plays influenced by Neoclassicism. Architect Asher Benjamin's (1773–1845) popular pattern books, especially the oft-printed *The American Builder's Companion* (1806), explained what has come to be termed the Federal style for public and domestic buildings and, in the post-1820 editions of the publication, etched for Americans the Greek Revival style. Architect Minard Lafever

(1797–1854) also promoted the Greek Revival as the contemporary fashion in *The Modern Builder's Guide* (1833) and *The Beauties of Modern Architecture* (1839). The Greek Revival was so widely adopted it was often called the Modern or National style.

Americans found in Greek and Roman architecture the fullest expression of democratic and republican values and thus adopted the Classical Revival style in their first major government buildings in the new federal capital of Washington DC. The Classical Revival style in architecture is based on the orders of Greek architecture (Doric, Ionic, and Corinthian) with American structures often imitating marble in wood painted white. Building plans and proportions closely copied Greek examples.

Americans chose this style for its direct associations with the ancient world and the beginnings of democracy over the Rococo style, which had developed out of the French monarchy and which Americans considered frivolous—a reminder of the luxury that was antithetical to republicanism. The symmetrical and solid Classical Revival style thus affected every aspect of American material culture. Domestic rural dwellings such as Thomas Jefferson's (1743–1826) Monticello (1793–1809), the Greek Revival "end houses" and templelike town halls on the Ohio frontier, and government buildings such as the United States Capitol (ca. 1793–1815) shared the same principles reified in form, proportion, and ornament. Decorative arts, such as the shield-back chairs of architect and artisan Samuel McIntyre (1757–1811), were ornamented with the Classical Revival motifs of swags, urns, garlands, medallions, and silhouettes. The employment of chiaroscuro and bold color, as well as the adaptation of Neoclassical dress, ornament, and scenes to modern subjects in the works of painters such as Benjamin West (1738–1820), Gilbert

After the revolution, Americans turned to the material culture of ancient Greek and Roman civilizations to express the new nation's commitment to democratic and republican values. Begun in 1793, the nation's Capitol in Washington DC exemplifies this Classical Revival, or Neoclassical, style. (Intell Photo Collection)

Stuart (1755–1828), and John Trumbull (1756–1843) and sculptors Horatio Greenough (1805–1852) and Hiram Powers (1805–1873) also testify to the influence of what many note as the first "American" style.

Laura A. Macaluso

See also Civic Architecture; Commercial Architecture; Decorative Arts; Domestic Architecture; Federal Style; Georgian Style; Style

References and Further Reading
Boyd, Sterling. 1985. *The Adam Style in America, 1770–1820.* New York: Garland.
Cooper, Wendy A. 1993. *Classical Taste in America, 1800–1840.* Baltimore, MD: Baltimore Museum of Art; New York: Abbeville.
Maynard, W. Barksdale. 2002. *Architecture in the United States, 1800–1850.* New Haven, CT: Yale University Press.

Collecting and Collections

To *collect* means to gather together. This definition implies that a collection need not be devoted to one type or form of material culture (or people, animals, plants, or ideas); food-bespattered breakfast dishes piled in the kitchen sink could be considered a collection. A *collection*, then, is defined by and is meaningful to its originator and in relation to other objects within it; it may be temporary or permanent, utilitarian or aesthetic, historical or contemporary. What Americans have historically understood as a collection, however, is the result of dedicated study and discriminating accumulation by amateurs, historical societies, libraries, and museums. At times, though, collecting is purely a business venture, meant to increase the worth of objects and the collector's wealth.

Since the second half of the nineteenth century when collecting itself became a widespread practice in the consumer societies of the United States and western Europe, various terms have been used to define purposely collected things. *Objets d'art* qualifies decorative or aesthetic works regarded, or created, as collectibles. Other terms describe collections that do not have any discernible order or value. *Bric-à-brac* refers to antique odds and ends or curiosities, harkening back to the late Renaissance practice of creating cabinets of curiosities rather than the modern system of classification and ordered exhibition. The English *knickknack* characterizes ornamental curiosities that please but are not *objets d'art*. A *gimcrack* seems to be a grade below *knickknack*, being a useless, unsubstantial, showy thing. Knickknacks and gimcracks, often used to characterize objects made for and accumulated by the American middle class, are just as often employed pejoratively to define useless and nonsensical clutter. A collection, on the other hand, possesses a discernible system of meaning: classification and order.

Collecting as Human Behavior

"To collect one's self" is a phrase that implies a person's selfhood is constituted of emotional "parts" that are gathered into a disciplined whole for appropriate social presentation. Psychologist Werner Muensterberger (1994), however, argues that collecting is "an unruly passion." He sees collecting as a compensatory activity; the collector is saddened or frustrated by some past disappointment or worried about the future. The acquisition of objects is only momentarily satisfying; in this theory the collector, considered narcissistic or obsessive, cannot be "healed" because what he or she collects

reminds him or her of those past disappointments. Muensterberger does not distinguish the dedicated, informed collector from the hoarder, whose activity is defined more accurately as repetitive acquisition and storage for future use. Certainly some individuals are addicted to collecting; surely more collect for enjoyment, for the acquisition of knowledge, and for the common good.

Business and marketing scholar Russell Belk (1995) argues that collectors have many motivations for their actions. He sees the history of collecting as intertwined with the history of consumption in the Western world. Collecting, then, removes objects from daily or general circulation to form a set of objects that acquires a new meaning. (For example, teapots acquired as collectibles are no longer used for brewing and serving tea; in relation to other collected teapots these objects are endowed with new meaning, whether as beautiful things, sentimental mementoes, or historical artifacts.) To Belk, collecting in a consumer society is a competitive, individualistic activity in which participants strive for mastery, whether of knowledge or of the market for a desired object. For critics of Americans' consumer society, collecting, as a specialized form of consumption, abets possessiveness and commodity fetishism; for others, collecting provides a pleasurable, satisfying, and creative activity because it offers constant novelty and variety.

Collecting and Collections in the United States

Much is known about individual, often wealthy, collectors, especially if the collections they created have been institutionalized as or in a museum. Such individuals include Wallace Nutting (1861–1941), Henry Francis du Pont (1880–1969), Electra Havemeyer Webb (1888–1960), Francis P. Garvan (1875–1937), and Abby Aldrich Rockefeller

(1874–1948), to name those who have been important to American material culture studies. Much is also known about art and anthropology collections created by American universities. Fewer systematic histories of collecting by non-elites exist, though; what we know of collecting practices has been offered through historians' forays into the diaries, letters, and records of specific middle-class Americans and sociologists' explorations of self-definition, consumption and class, and art and class in twentieth-century and contemporary American society.

Charles Willson Peale (1741–1820) is credited with the establishment of the first American museum (1786). Located in Philadelphia, Peale's museum offered natural history specimens classified according to Linnaean nomenclature. Peale also created and displayed a gallery of American Revolutionary heroes. Peale's efforts occurred amid a society well versed in collecting. Before the Revolution, Philadelphian John Bartram (1699–1777) (and later his son William [1739–1823]) created a botanical garden from which American and European collectors gained examples of plants. They and others traveled the eastern seaboard, gathering a variety of indigenous plants. Commonplace books, in which a person's reading was excerpted and categorized, was in fact commonplace among the literate. Benjamin Franklin (1706–1790) had already introduced in 1731 the idea of a social library to Philadelphia, and other notable townspeople created and enjoyed sizable private libraries.

Collecting was (and is) considered a useful habit to instill in children as a means through which children could learn about the world and about God. Throughout the late eighteenth and nineteenth centuries, children were encouraged through juvenile periodicals and novels and by their parents to create cabinets of curiosities or "museums." These cabinets were filled with things children found on their nature walks or around the house. Children also were given objects for their collections, and they sometimes purchased specific items for their cabinets. In the early twentieth century, Progressive educators advised schools to organize learning around "nature cabinets" filled with the specimens found by students.

With the rise of industrialization, collection of stamps, spoons, and famous individuals' signatures (made known through print) increased. Throughout the nineteenth century, American middle-class families displayed collections in their parlors. Wealthy individuals dedicated rooms in their houses to their collecting activities. Many upper-class Americans traveled in Europe in the Gilded Age and returned with fine art, sculpture, and decorative arts of Italy, France, Belgium, the Netherlands, and Germany. Middle-class families emulated this practice, collecting chromolithographs, photographs, and art prints into portfolios and displaying them on easels; purchasing bookcases to show matched sets of encyclopedias or an author's works; and arranging their travel souvenirs and art on tabletops and etageres. Art and antique dealers brokered taste through their enterprises. Hundreds of natural history specimen dealers supplied Americans with stuffed animals and birds, minerals and shells, fossils and insects. A collection indicated the availability and enjoyment of leisure time—an important sign of class status—as well as good taste. This activity paralleled the establishment or expansion of public libraries and museums throughout the nation. Boston's Museum of Fine Arts opened its doors in 1876, the nation's centennial. Local historical societies and libraries were established in great numbers in this era.

As conservation and anti–animal cruelty societies persuaded Americans against the killing of animals for decorative purposes, and as proponents of the Arts and Crafts Movement argued against the clutter of the Gilded Age parlor, Americans' collections did not necessarily change—they were moved to bedrooms and attics. From the 1880s onward, collecting mass-produced ephemera— photographs, trade cards, premiums—was ordered in albums and scrapbooks rather than displayed. Changes in the United States postal policies promoted in the first decade of the twentieth century a fad for postcard collection—"postal carditis." Professional baseball was promoted through card portraits of players offered by tobacco companies beginning in the 1880s; in the 1930s chewing gum manufacturers began offering baseball cards intended for collecting and timed to coincide with the professional baseball season, thus effecting anticipation and desire. Collecting as a hobby was promoted as "productive leisure" in the 1930s as an antidote to the mass unemployment of the Depression era.

Mass-Produced Collectibles

Since the 1950s, collecting has become work as well as a hobby for many Americans. Perpetrated by local and state amateur clubs and national professional associations dedicated to the study and promotion of a wide range of aesthetic, historic, and just plain curious forms of collectible material culture, Americans now collect via organized shows and swap meets, eBay, and other online venues, sometimes for pleasure and sometimes for profit.

The recognition of collecting as a special form of consumption has also spurred manufacturers to create "collectibles." Commemorative medals; ceramic figurines; and special editions of books, magazines, and newspapers are all created with the idea that, as a "collector's edition" or "limited edition," a given consumer good appears to have, or will have in the future, more value. The design, production, and sale of holiday-related goods, such as Hallmark's annual Christmas Keepsake Ornaments, unite sentiment and collection in the act of consumption.

The prospects of a collection's value led many manufacturers to offer goods and premiums as "one of a series," thus encouraging purchase and brand loyalty. This strategy has backfired in several instances—baseball cards, for example, were sold in the late 1980s in complete sets for "investment." Today, the overproduction of those cards has greatly decreased their market value. Purchased as complete sets rather than as individual cards to be irregularly acquired and traded, Topps baseball cards are an example of consumer desire trumping the pleasures of collecting.

Other consumer goods have inspired collection frenzies. Beanie Babies, a line of small, colorful, soft-pellet-filled sewn cloth animal dolls created by Ty Inc., propelled in 1996 a collecting mania. The company fed consumer desire by "retiring" dolls. Seeking to "corner the market," some individuals purchased great numbers of specific dolls. Like baseball cards in the 1980s, the "bubble" burst. World Wide Web sites devoted to Beanie Babies now list ways of "liquidating" one's collection, at "flea market" prices.

Property, Cultural Patrimony, and Repatriation

The debate between private collections of art and artifacts that are kept from public view and scholarly investigation is one of long standing. So, too, is the dilemma of retaining for the public's pleasure and education a given work of art or historical artifact. As institutions struggle to maintain collections in light of rising costs and diminished philanthropic and public support, works of art and other artifacts are deaccessioned to raise funds. In several cases, such as the 2005 sale by the New York Public Library of *Kindred Spirits* (1849), painted by native son Asher B. Durnd (1796–1886), the loss of what is considered a "public" possession is decried.

Increased attention has been given to the collection of materials with possible provenances of unlawful ownership. In 1998, the Association of Art Museum Directors issued guidelines with which the nation's art museums would conduct provenance research to ensure that their holdings of paintings and sculpture do not include works looted or seized by the Nazi regime between 1933 and 1945. The claims of Holocaust victims and their descendants have been a priority in these investigations. Governments of nations across the globe are now investigating the historical theft of personal and cultural property that has found its way to the international arts and antiques market. International agreements about cultural property have been strengthened.

Anthropologists and archaeologists since the 1980s have reexamined the ethics of past collecting practices. How have the meanings of artifacts of "primitive" societies been transformed when displayed in a museum of art or natural history? Related to these examinations is the question of *repatriation*— the return of artifacts, as cultural patrimony, to the descendants of societies from which the artifacts were taken. In answer to that question, the United States in 1990 passed the National American Graves Protection and Repatriation Act. This law recognizes the rights of Native Americans to their cultural property, defined by the law as human remains, funerary and sacred objects, and other artifacts. The repatriation movement acknowledges the destructive treatment of peoples by a government while it embraces the same peoples' rights to research, under-

stand, and write their respective histories and control their cultural identities. The movement further considers offensive the acts of plunder in the name of research as well as in the name of war and political domination.

Some American groups also find offensive the collection by individuals of materials that demean and symbolize historic subjugation and mistreatment. African American memorabilia, for example, has elicited scholarly and popular discussions. Does the collection, by African Americans and others, of mass-produced objects that exaggerate "blackness" to the point of stereotype and insult increase historical knowledge, or does the practice further discrimination? Does ownership of racist memorabilia change the original intent of these artifacts and images? Civil rights activist Julian Bond (2003, 59) argues that such collection by African Americans can serve as "acts of exorcism," or as politic acts of empowerment. In this sense African American collectors of such memorabilia are not undertaking for themselves repatriation; these objects were created by whites. Rather, African Americans are, through such collections, proclaiming the right to self identity.

Shirley Teresa Wajda

See also Anthropology and Archaeology; Childhood; Children's Material Culture; Consumerism and Consumption; Ephemera; Leisure, Recreation, and Amusements; Memory and Memorabilia; Museums and Museum Practice; Music Ephemera; Nostalgia; Political Ephemera; Scrapbooks; Souvenirs; Trade Cards

References and Further Reading
Barrow, Mark V. 2000. "The Specimen Dealer: Entrepreneurial Natural History in the Gilded Age." *Journal of the History of Biology* 33 (3): 493–534.
Belk, Russell W. 1995. *Collecting in a Consumer Society*. London: Routledge.
Bond, Julian. 2003. "Julian Bond Responds." *Southern Cultures* 9 (1): 59.

Casmier-Paz, Lynn. 2003. "Heritage, not Hate?: Collecting Black Memorabilia." *Southern Cultures* 9 (1): 43–58, 60–61.

Clifford, James. 1988. "On Collecting Art and Culture." In *The Predicament of Culture: Twentieth-Century Ethnography, Literature and Art*, 215–251. Cambridge, MA: Harvard University Press.

Conn, Steven. 1998. *Museums and American Intellectual Life, 1876–1926*. Chicago: University of Chicago Press.

Dilworth, Leah, ed. *Acts of Possession: Essays on Collecting in America*. New Brunswick, NJ: Rutgers University Press.

Elsner, John, and Roger Cardinal, eds. 1994. *The Cultures of Collecting*. Cambridge, MA: Harvard University Press.

Gelber, Steven M. 1999. *Hobbies: Leisure and the Culture of Work in America*. New York: Columbia University Press.

Jamieson, Dave. 2006. "Requiem for a Rookie Card: How Baseball Cards Lost Their Luster." *Slate Magazine*, http://www.slate.com/id/2146218.

Messenger, Phyllis Mauch, ed. 1989. *The Ethics of Collecting Cultural Property: Whose Culture? Whose Property?* Albuquerque: University of New Mexico Press.

Muensterberger, Werner. 1994. *Collecting, an Unruly Passion: Psychological Perspectives*. New York: Harcourt, Brace & Company.

Stewart, Susan. 1994. *On Longing: Narratives of the Miniature, the Gigantic, the Souvenir, the Collection*. Durham, NC: Duke University Press.

Colonial Revival

Often viewed as a historically informed aesthetic style that gained popularity in the wake of the United States' centennial celebrations in 1876, the *Colonial Revival* is better understood as a complex and long-lived movement with a profound impact on American culture. Ironically, this look to the past has its roots in modernity. While strains of filial piety and politically motivated nostalgia can be identified throughout American history, the need for an idealized past increased dramatically in the nineteenth century as the forces of industrialization, immigration, and urbanization transformed the United States into a geographically diverse and socially heterogeneous nation. By celebrating historical design in literature, the arts, and architecture, the Colonial Revival provided cohesive national symbols for the modern era and dramatically shaped the material world.

Literary Background

Although popular biographies chronicled the passing of the revolutionary generation and historical societies and museums cropped up during the early National period, interest in colonial artifacts was unusual in the antebellum era. Eyebrows rose, for instance, when Henry Wadsworth Longfellow (1807–1882) accepted a hoary eighteenth-century Cambridge, Massachusetts, mansion as a wedding present in the early 1830s. When Longfellow began to collect Queen Anne furniture for the venerable house, he was teased by a visiting British critic for filling his home with "trumpery antiquities" (Catalano 1983, 21). The very word *antique* still referred to the classical past in popular usage and was only humorously applied to American material culture.

Touring the Past

A growing tourist economy fueled interest in historical relics after the Civil War (1861–1865). Traveling to quaint villages, visiting romantic old houses, and collecting antiques became a popular upper-class pastime stoked by the widespread dissemination of writings by Longfellow, Harriet Beecher Stowe (1811–1896), and John Greenleaf Whittier (1807–1892) that animated historic places and objects in poems and prose. Great public displays of artifacts such as the "New England

Farmer's Home" at the 1876 International Centennial Exposition in Philadelphia captured the popular imagination and further fanned national interest in colonial furniture, silver, and objects from everyday life.

Decorating with antiques, considered eccentric behavior before the Civil War, became fashionable among the expanding middle class. In 1881 the art critic Clarence Cook (1828–1900) recommended that persons of taste include real or imagined ancestral objects in the home. Cook acknowledged the increasingly heterogeneous nature of modern American society when he noted that "everybody can't have a grandfather, nor things that came over on the *Mayflower* and those of us who have not drawn the prizes in life's lottery must do the best we can under the circumstances" (Cook 1881, 162).

Manufactured Nostalgia

The demand for symbolic reminders of colonial virtue not only created a ready market for antiques but also sparked an industry in suggestive reproductions. While a handful of cabinetmakers specialized in accurate copies of historical forms, early manufacturers concentrated upon creative, even fanciful, interpretations of period objects. Hybrid forms such as spinning-wheel chairs became popular additions to the domestic interior in the 1880s. Constructed of obsolete spinning-wheel parts, such objects were designed to trigger a set of ideas and associations about the past, rather than reproduce any one specific historical moment or style. Richly symbolic, the spinning-wheel chair developed just as textile production moved from the middle-class home to the factory and served as a reminder of traditional female roles in a time a great social change.

The Commodification of the Colonial

Widespread desire for a sense of authenticity in the face of the uncertainties of modern life not only brought specificity to colonial aesthetic at the turn of the century but also brought maturity to the market. Accurate reproduction furniture replaced fanciful spinning-wheel chairs. The mythic sweep of poets such as Longfellow and Whittier gave way to the targeted marketing of the ad man. Where once it had been acceptable to display an antique chair in the parlor, by the early twentieth century the entire decorative program of the house needed to be historically referential to be *au courant*. Furniture companies in Gardiner, Massachusetts, and Grand Rapids, Michigan, offered reproduction colonial furniture for every room of the house. Flatware manufacturers such as Rogers Brothers and Towle Silver provided eighteenth-century-style flatware. Large corporations employed colonial motifs to sell everything from mattresses to foodstuffs. The Colonial Revival offered a style to fit every ideology, from the rugged individualism of the so-called Pilgrim Century to the refined elegance of the Federal era at a price point affordable to all.

Principal Voices

The Colonial Revival attracted colporteurs in the form of tastemakers such as Wallace Nutting (1861–1941) and Royal Barry Wills (1895–1962). Nutting, a minister turned antimodern entrepreneur, offered books, hand-colored photographs—even a line of reproduction colonial furniture during the 1920s and 1930s. Through his popular writings and successful promotion of the Cape Cod–style house, Boston-based architect and author Wills helped to define suburbia as an idealized colonial village after World War II. As the United States moved from city to suburb in the mid-twentieth century, the ideals of the Colonial Revival provided a home for the American dream.

From the domestic interior to the built environment, the Colonial Revival remains one of the most persistent and pervasive organizing myths in American history. The idealization of colonial styles and forms provided a nation of immigrants with object lessons in group identity over the course of two centuries and remains a profound influence today. From spoons to chairs, houses to towns, the Colonial Revival is a distinct and dominant American idiom.

Thomas Andrew Denenberg

See also Antiques; Heirlooms; Historic Preservation; House, Home, and Domesticity; Interior Design; Nostalgia; Style

References and Further Reading
Axelrod, Alan, ed. 1985. *The Colonial Revival in America*. New York: W. W. Norton.
Catalano, Kathleen M. 1983. "The Longfellows and Their 'Trumpery Antiquities.'" *American Art Journal* 15 (2): 21–31.
Cook, Clarence. 1881 (1878). *The House Beautiful: Essays on Beds and Tables, Stools and Candlesticks*. New York: Scribner, Armstrong and Company.
Denenberg, Thomas Andrew. 2003. *Wallace Nutting and the Invention of Old America*. New Haven, CT: Yale University Press.
Kardon, Janet, ed. 1994. *Revivals: Diverse Traditions, 1920–1945*. New York: Harry N. Abrams.
Marling, Karal Ann. 1988. *George Washington Slept Here: Colonial Revivals and American Culture, 1876–1986*. Cambridge, MA: Harvard University Press.
Meyer, Marilee B., ed. 1997. *Inspiring Reform: Boston's Arts and Crafts Movement*. Wellesley, MA: Wellesley College Museum.
Monkhouse, Christopher P. 1982. "The Spinning Wheel as Artifact, Symbol, and Source of Design." *Nineteenth Century* 8 (3–4): 154–172.
Roth, Rodris. 1964. "The Colonial Revival and Centennial Furniture." *Art Quarterly* 27 (1): 57–81.
Wilson, Richard Guy, Shaun Eyring, and Kenny Marotta, eds. 2006. *Re-Creating the American Past*. Charlottesville: University Press of Virginia.

Commercial Architecture

Commercial architecture in what has become the United States varies greatly, from the Italianate blocks of late nineteenth-century main streets of towns and cities to contemporary suburban shopping malls. Generally, commercial buildings are places where businesses, usually retail, conduct their affairs. Besides places to buy goods, commercial structures include restaurants, lodgings, bars, and other sites where services are provided. The evolution of commercial architecture from the colonial period to the contemporary United States can tell us much about the expansion of cities and suburbs, changes in working and shopping habits, the rise of the consumer culture, the development of a service economy, and other important trends.

Colonial and Frontier Structures

In early and frontier America, commercial buildings were relatively small and usually simply constructed with local materials. With the abundance of wood, especially on the eastern seaboard, these buildings were usually of frame construction, much like other types of structures. Some commercial buildings—taverns, for example—were nearly indistinguishable (at least externally) from domestic dwellings. Other kinds of commercial enterprises included specialty shops such as those of milliners, silversmiths, and other similar trades. Proprietors often lived in the same building as their businesses; the shop was located on the ground floor while the residence was located either on the second floor or in the rear of the building. In sparsely settled areas, the buildings often had little decoration or design elements.

The growth of cities, even by the early eighteenth century, led to more sophisticated commercial building types reflecting current architectural trends. For much of the later colonial and early National periods, the predominant architectural styles, such as the Georgian, Federal, and Greek Revival, all contained elements derived from classical architecture such as symmetry, the use of pediments and columns, and graceful decorations such as swags and key patterns. Banks, for example, often used classicism to impart a feeling of grandeur and stability to their customers. Other commercial buildings, such as shops and taverns, frequently exhibited in vernacular form elements of contemporary architectural styles.

Urban Buildings in the Nineteenth Century

New construction techniques were eagerly adopted by architects for commercial buildings, especially in urban areas. The ever-present concern over fires led to more and more commercial buildings constructed of brick rather than wood. Also, with a growing population came the need for larger commercial buildings; in tightly packed New York, the only way to go was up. James Bogardus (1800–1874) pioneered the use of cast iron for facades as well as supporting members for new buildings. The iron frame took up much of the load bearing, as opposed to all-masonry buildings, where the walls bear most of the weight of the building. Masonry load-bearing buildings need ever-expanding bases in order to support the weight of taller structures. The use of the iron frame allowed for a smaller footprint, thus using less valuable ground space to erect taller buildings.

The use of the iron frame never became as widespread as did the use of the steel frame. Chicago architects Louis Sullivan (1856–1924) and Daniel Burnham (1846–1912) popularized the use of the steel frame in the late nineteenth and early twentieth centuries. Steel framing proved to be even more durable than iron and its use became even more widespread. Tall buildings, or skyscrapers,

appeared not only in major metropolitan areas like New York City and Chicago but even in small to mid-sized communities. Skyscrapers became status symbols as emerging cities sought the trappings of larger urban areas. While steel frame construction was very modern, these new buildings reflected whatever architectural styles were popular at the time of their construction, be it Beaux-Arts classicism, Richardsonian Romanesque, or other revival styles. As commercial structures, skyscrapers normally housed some kind of retail operation on the street level with offices on the upper floors. In the continuing search for better ways to fireproof buildings, concrete came into vogue as a building material. New methods of improving concrete, such as adding steel rebar, became a standard method of construction for all types of buildings, including commercial structures.

In the late nineteenth century, not only did the structure of commercial buildings take on new forms but a new type of retail store also appeared. Merchant Alexander T. Stewart (1802?–1876) opened one of the first department stores in the United States in New York City in 1846. Stewart's innovation, housing many retail departments in a lavish setting under one roof, inspired others to follow suit, including John Wanamaker (1838–1922) in Philadelphia and Marshall Field (1835–1906) in Chicago, as well as entrepreneurs in cities large and small. The department store responded to the needs of the expanding consumer culture and even took advantage of growing leisure time, especially among the middle class. Window shopping, facilitated by plate glass and electric lighting, became a popular outing for Americans everywhere. Other kinds of department stores, such as the five and dime, also appeared in the nineteenth century, making many products affordable for working-class people.

Although department stores quickly became a part of the American landscape by the turn of the twentieth century, Main Street shops, often of three or four stories, still maintained a presence in many smaller communities. Businesses like florists, specialty stores, restaurants, and other commercial enterprises were housed in smaller structures, which often had residences on upper floors.

Twentieth-Century Suburbanization and Change

Commercial architecture changed significantly in the late twentieth century, reflecting increased suburbanization in the United States. The supermarket began to replace "mom and pop" grocery stores as places where Americans bought their food and other necessities. The one-story shopping plaza with an enormous parking lot spread throughout the nation by the early 1950s. Taking the one-stop shopping idea one step further, the enclosed shopping mall pioneered by Austrian immigrant Victor Gruen (1903–1980) became the new center of much commercial activity in the latter half of the twentieth century. As a consequence, the appearance of these new types of structures contributed to the demise of downtowns nearly everywhere, as large department stores and smaller concerns pulled up stakes and moved to the suburbs. Urban developers in some cities built enclosed downtown malls to compete with the suburban counterparts, with mixed success. While malls continue to proliferate into the new century, in a weird turnabout, replica main streets began appearing in suburban areas, usually near or adjacent to an enclosed mall. Chain stores and restaurants found at malls are also found on these ersatz main streets, but access to each store is from the outside and the architecture often mimics late nineteenth- and early twentieth-century styles like Italianate and Colonial Revival.

"Big box" retail, epitomized by Wal-Mart (1961) and Sam's Club (1983), are ubiquitous on the American landscape and represent another important trend in commercial architecture—bargain shopping in suburbia, replacing five and dime stores. Where Main Street and downtown dominated most American communities, today's commercial area is represented by miles and miles of suburban shopping malls and strip plazas, chain stores and restaurants, Holiday Inns and Marriott Hotels, giving a sameness to the landscape.

Donna M. DeBlasio

See also Architectural History and American Architecture; Cities and Towns; Commercial Food Venues; Consumerism and Consumption; Department Stores; General (Country) Stores; Grocery Stores; Public and Commercial Leisure, Recreation, and Amusement Venues; Public Markets; Shopping Centers and Shopping Malls; Suburbs and Suburbia; Supermarkets

References and Further Reading

Fogelson, Robert M. 2001. *Downtown: Its Rise and Fall.* New Haven, CT: Yale University Press.

Gelertner, Mark. 1999. *A History of American Architecture: Buildings in Their Cultural and Technological Context.* Hanover, NH: University Press of New England.

Hayden, Dolores. 2003. *Building Suburbia: Green Fields and Urban Growth, 1820–2000.* New York: Pantheon Books.

Isenberg, Alison. 2004. *Downtown America: A History of the Place and the People Who Made It.* Chicago: University of Chicago Press.

Longstreth, Richard W. 2000. *The Buildings of Main Street: A Guide to American Commercial Architecture.* Walnut Creek, CA: AltaMira Press.

Maddex, Diane, ed. 1985. *Built in the U.S.A.: American Buildings From Airports to Zoos.* Washington, DC: National Trust for Historic Preservation.

Rifkind, Carole. 1980. *A Field Guide to American Architecture*. New York: Penguin.

Roth, Leland M. 1979. *A Concise History of American Architecture*. New York: Harper & Row.

Commercial Food Venues

A *commercial food venue* is any establishment that sells cooked food ready to eat, from pushcarts to taverns to hotels to restaurants. Until at least the late nineteenth century, the vast majority of meals in the United States were prepared and eaten in family dwellings. Only travelers and people without recourse to family support needed to buy prepared meals. As the nation industrialized, both ordinary and wealthy people started to buy cooked meals for convenience or enjoyment.

Colonial- and Early National–Era Taverns

In the colonial and early National periods, taverns or ordinaries offered drinks, food, and overnight accommodations. Depending on the size of the tavern, its location, and its usual clientele, it could be a busy city restaurant where merchants conducted business, a sleepy inn catering to travelers, or just a private house where a traveler could eat and sleep. Likewise, the food offered could range from complex city tavern specialties like turtle soup and syllabub (a dessert, either a drink or dish, of sugar, whipped cream, white wine, and lemon) to the "ordinary," meaning that guests at a humble tavern would simply join the tavern-keeper's family in whatever they were eating, most often stewed meat and corn bread.

Nineteenth-Century Eating and Dining

The rapid growth of American cities in the nineteenth century brought more opportunities to buy a cooked meal. In eastern cities, oyster cellars or oyster saloons were inexpensive and popular with all classes through the century. Hot corn, fruit, candy, pastries, sandwiches, drinks, soup, and even ice cream were sold from pushcarts on the street. In boardinghouses and hotels, meals were served at set hours and were included in the price of the room (known as the "American Plan"); guests were known to push, shove, and rush through the meal in order to get their money's worth.

The well-to-do considered dining in any public place inferior to dining in a private dwelling. This began to change when European-style, fine dining restaurants developed in eastern cities in the second half of the nineteenth century. These restaurants offered luxurious interiors, fine wines, and a self-consciously Continental cuisine, with menus written in French. Owned by a Swiss family, the famous Delmonico's was a series of restaurants in different locations around New York. From the 1840s well into the twentieth century, Delmonico's symbolized fashionable dining, attracting epicures as well as celebrities. Other restaurants, such as the Waldorf-Astoria Hotel's dining rooms, followed in the same vein. Large cities also boasted more casual restaurants, especially German restaurants, which offered a popular environment of live music, plentiful food, and lager beer. Toward the end of the century, middle-class Americans, emulating social elites, dined out more often at modest restaurants. The practice of fine dining gradually lost some of its male-oriented and extravagant connotations and became more open to unaccompanied upper-class and middle-class women and to family dining.

Twentieth-Century Variety

The surge of immigration in the late nineteenth century brought an influx of largely single men from Europe. Some stayed in boardinghouses run by fellow countrymen so that they could enjoy familiar foodways. Others provided a market for new restaurants. Tiny ethnic restaurants, delicatessens, bakeries, saloons, and pushcarts served "home cooking" to Greek or Italian or Russian or Jewish men and women.

At the same time, increasing numbers of white-collar workers commuted to work from outlying suburbs. Restaurants sprang up to serve quick lunches to these city workers. Some continued the practices of taverns or chophouses, serving heavy, substantial food to businessmen in a clubby atmosphere. Other new styles of restaurants catered to women (tea rooms) or to workers in a hurry and on a budget ("quick lunches," cafeterias, and Automats). Until Prohibition (1920–1933), most working men (and many businessmen) took the "free lunch" at saloons. For the price of a beer, usually a nickel, men could enjoy a meal ranging from a meager spread of pickles, crackers, or cheese to a bountiful buffet of hot and cold meats, soups, beans, and salads.

The greatest change in commercial food venues came with the automobile. Americans began to eat out more often at roadside or "fast" restaurants, on vacation or right in their home towns. Early chains, such as the Fred Harvey (1875) and Childs' (1889) restaurants, offered simple menus (steaks, chops, sandwiches, eggs) at moderate prices in sparkling-clean environments. Howard Deering Johnson (1896–1972) began expanding his chain of distinctive, orange-roofed roadside restaurants in the 1930s and 1940s. In small towns, drugstores opened lunch counters to serve sandwiches and sodas to residents; diners served more substantial hot meals (meatloaf, roasts, biscuits and gravy).

After the end of World War II in 1945, Americans began to eat out more often, at all types of restaurants: fine restaurants, fast-food restaurants like hamburger chains and pizza parlors, and mid-priced casual dining chains. Prewar fast-food chains like White Castle (1921) gave way to McDonald's (1954), Kentucky Fried Chicken (1956), and other competitors, where customers could drive in and quickly pick up hamburgers or fried chicken. Changes in the food-processing industry made both takeout and sit-down restaurant meals less expensive. The use of frozen, precooked ingredients and entrees beginning in the 1960s allowed restaurants to eliminate much of their trained staff; the food could be defrosted by unskilled workers. Pizzerias proliferated after it was discovered that dough could be prepared and frozen, shortening the preparation time for each pizza. Sophisticated Americans ate at fine restaurants catering to the latest trends: "gourmet" Continental food in the 1950s and 1960s; "nouvelle" or "California" cuisine restaurants in the 1970s and 1980s; and "authentic" ethnic or international "fusion" food in the 1980s and 1990s. By the end of the twentieth century, at least one-third of all American meals were eaten outside the home. Some Americans blame the national increase in obesity and heart disease on too many large-portioned, unhealthy restaurant meals.

Katherine Leonard Turner

See also Automobiles and Automobility; Boardinghouses; Cities and Towns; Ethnicity; Food and Foodways; Service Industry Work and Labor; Suburbs and Suburbia; Tourism and Travel

References and Further Reading
Gabaccia, Donna. 1998. *We Are What We Eat: Ethnic Food and the Making of Americans.* Cambridge, MA: Harvard University Press.
Hooker, Richard J. 1981. *Food and Drink in America: A History.* Indianapolis, IN: Bobbs-Merrill Company.

Levenstein, Harvey. 1988. *Revolution at the Table: The Transformation of the American Diet.* New York: Oxford University Press.

Levenstein, Harvey. 1993. *Paradox of Plenty: A Social History of Eating in Modern America.* New York: Oxford University Press.

Rice, Kym S. 1983. *Early American Taverns: For the Entertainment of Friends and Strangers.* New York: Regnery.

Schlosser, Eric. 2002. *Fast Food Nation: The Dark Side of the All-American Meal.* Boston: Houghton Mifflin.

Commercials

Commercials are advertisements created for radio and television. Broadcasting (whether radio or television) in the United States has been a corporate-sponsored industry since its inception in the early twentieth century. Commercials help to define and transmit information about many forms of material culture Americans purchase and use.

Radio advertisements emerged as early as 1922 when American Telephone & Telegraph's fledgling radio station proposed what it called *toll broadcasting*, or selling airtime to advertisers to cover new licensing and copyright costs. Despite criticism from public officials, commercials became part of the structure of broadcast radio.

Television heavily borrowed from radio's format and set commercials into the viewing structure. Single corporations paid for programs such as Texaco's *Texaco Star Theatre* (1948–1955) or Carnation Milk's *The George Burns and Gracie Allen Show* (1950–1958). In television's early days, the boundary between commercial and program was difficult to discern. For example, in the *Burns & Allen Show*, George Burns (1896–1996), Gracie Allen (1906–1964), and other characters would discuss the benefits of Carnation Milk within an episode's dialogue. Federal government reg-

ulation from the 1950s to the 1980s phased out this kind of direct sponsorship.

Various types of commercials populate the airwaves. *Commercials for products* vary in style, meaning, and narrative structure, but all of them are aimed at convincing the viewer to purchase a service or product. *Political advertisements* attempt to convince viewers to vote for or against a candidate or proposed law. *Infomercials* are lengthy advertisements that use extensive descriptions, testimonials from consumers, and product demonstrations. *Promotional advertisements* aim to sell television or radio programs to viewers or listeners. These advertisements are created by a network or station and promote an upcoming broadcast program. *Advertorials*, in print or as a televised program, appear as editorials providing objective information about goods, especially those goods affected by governmental policy and regulation. The most recent form of advertising specific to film and television is *product placement*, or the conspicuous placement of a product in a television program. All these types of advertising now appear on the World Wide Web, the newest form of commercial communication.

Sandra M. Falero

See also Advertisements and Advertising; Consumerism and Consumption; Patents, Trademarks, and Brands; Political Ephemera; Popular Culture; Trade Cards

References and Further Reading

Berger, Arthur Asa. 2000. *Ads, Fads, and Consumer Culture: Advertising's Impact on American Character and Society.* Lanham, MD: Rowman & Littlefield.

Schudson, Michael. 1984. *Advertising, the Uneasy Persuasion: Its Dubious Impact on American Society.* New York: Basic Books.

Schulberg, Pete. 1996. *Radio Advertising: The Authoritative Handbook,* 2nd ed. Lincolnwood, IL: NTC Business Books.

Commodity

A *commodity* is an object produced expressly for exchange within a matrix of overlapping social relations for the commodity's production and consumption. In material culture studies, many scholars have resisted focusing on the commodity, as it implies a mass-produced, popular object exchanged in a market. Instead, much work in material culture studies has focused on the handmade, which has been seen as the "traditional" material manifestations of an "authentic" experience. For the purposes of this essay, *handmade* denotes objects created outside industrialized production and distribution networks. Objects as varied as folk rocking chairs to high-art paintings have maintained a perceived value within the field of material culture studies by virtue of their perceived authenticity defined within the nature of the objects' creation. Yet when scholars study the material culture of the nineteenth and twentieth centuries, they find that consumer markets expanded exponentially in scope and size, which necessitates a turn toward theories of the commodity to explain how and why human beings relate to the commodified objects with which they surround themselves. Historically, the cultural meanings and social roles of objects were increasingly fulfilled by mass-produced commodities as Western culture moved from a preindustrial to a capitalist mode of production. Thus the distinction between high and folk and mass or popular culture becomes blurry, as objects and the materials used to make them have been, to ever-increasing degrees, caught up in the markets of mass production.

Production and Consumption

Bringing the commodity to the fore of material culture studies complicates the boundaries between art, folk, and mass, and of the role of the authentic in scholarly discussions of culture and experience. The consumption of commodities in a mass market is a constitutive feature of the industrialized world. Any examination of the circulation and meaning of objects within the historical period of production for consumption must be considered as it relates to the circulation of goods, desires, identities, and cultures in a consumer market of commodities and through a mass-mediated culture. Even objects that appear to be art and folk in contemporary culture are implicated in the social organizations of mass production. The commodity as a category of analysis focuses inquiry on the complexity of material objects: how they are produced, by whom, out of what materials, and within which culture they circulate to lend meaning to the lives of those who consume them.

The circulation of commodities, then, functions in a dialectic of production and consumption. Human beings have always had relationships with objects found or made, so let us make a distinction between the simple consumption of objects and *consumerism*, which can be said to be the particular social mode within which individuals consume commodities in the mass markets of capitalism. At a theoretical level, the production of commodities functions according to rationalized modes of capitalist production, whereas consumerism functions according to the consummation of nonrational desires, aesthetics, and cultural imperatives. Both the capitalist modes of production and consumerism are linked in mutually constitutive ways, making it impossible to talk about one without talking about the other. It is thus crucial to see how the rational ends of capitalist production are in a constant relationship to the nonrational desires to consume.

Theories of Value and the Commodity

Both classical liberal-economic theory and political-economic theory offer views of the production of commodities as a process of capitalist production. *Capitalism* is an economic market in which capital is invested in production for the sole purpose of generating more capital; capitalist production implies the modes of production that will most effectively generate more capital. Karl Marx's (1818–1883) political-economic theories of capitalism, and by extension consumerism, assume that capitalism is a cultural phenomenon of human relationships and that the values attributed to those relationships and their product—the commodity—are socially constituted. As early as *The German Ideology*, completed in 1847, Marx argued that although human beings need material objects to survive, the particular manifestations and fulfilling of those needs are constituted in a particular society of individuals and are historically and culturally specific.

In the purchasing relationship, Marx distinguishes between the use value of an object and the exchange value of an object. *Use value* is the value of the object relative to its socially and culturally constituted use. *Exchange value* is the value of the object relative to relationships of exchange. The social and cultural significance of a given commodity can be seen as a dialectical tension between the use value and exchange value.

In the exchange relationship, all commodities are exchangeable and therefore interchangeable where there is an equivalence of value. Equivalency allows dissimilar objects to be exchanged for each other or to be seen as having equal value (e.g., a ski parka may be equivalent in value to ten academic books). The exchange of commodities by definition requires the development of equivalencies, and therefore relative values, thereby reducing the qualitative distinction of commodities to their quantifiable forms (e.g., price or monetary equivalence). In the world of exchange, it is the exchange value of a commodity that has primacy through the equivalency of value such that use value fades away. In the social relationship of exchange, then, use value is necessarily subsumed by exchange value. That is not to say that use value no longer exists, but rather that in relations of exchange, the use value plays a secondary role in determining value. As equivalency stabilizes in a given market, the value of a given commodity seems to become natural, appearing to inhere in the object. This misrecognition of the naturalness of a commodity's value is *commodity fetishism*, or the relationship consumers have to commodities wherein the commodity is perceived to have value in and of itself, eclipsing the social relationships of its production.

Following in the footsteps of philosopher Adam Smith (1723–1790), among others, Marx posits the labor theory of value to explain the source of value. The theory states that the exchange value of a commodity derives from the labor necessary to produce the object. Thus the commodity is itself an objectification of the labor that produced it. Here, labor is understood to have two aspects: On one hand, there is the physical and material effort and the effect of labor, or labor itself; on the other hand, in the capitalist mode of production, labor exists as an abstraction, or the possibility of labor. Abstract labor, or labor power, is socially necessary for the relations of production to occur, for it is the labor power that the worker sells as his or her commodity in exchange for wages (another commodity form). In turn, the capitalist must pay the worker in wages high enough to reproduce that labor power in each subsequent working day.

Capitalism in its simplest form is the investment of capital in two areas, constant capital (the means of production such as tools and materials) and variable capital (labor) for the production of a commodity laden with surplus value, or an exchange greater than the cost of producing the commodity, thereby generating more capital. Marx assumes that the constant capital side is at a fixed value that cannot be manipulated in and of itself (but subject to the market); thus, surplus value must come from a labor that is of variable, or manipulable, value. The variation in labor's value comes from the socially necessary labor time, or the socially determined minimum labor time required to produce the value sufficient to reproduce labor power the following day. *Surplus value* is the difference between the socially necessary labor time and the actual labor time spent in production.

Circulation, Meaning, and Desire

Marx's project targeted the social inequalities of the relationships of production and was aimed at producing a social theory; it thus focused almost exclusively on production. For those concerned with the cultural value and roles of objects, this begs numerous questions about consumption: Why do consumers buy things in the first place? Does understanding the production and subsequent exchange value of a commodity explain why people purchase the commodity? Where does Marx's socially constituted significance (i.e., use value) of commodities come from, and how does it function in consumption? Consumerism scholar Martyn J. Lee (1993) notes that commodity fetishism separates the consumer from the production of the commodity (and by extension, the scholars of commodities from the production of the commodities they study) such that the commodity enters the market "empty of meaning," and that meaning must be "filled" in the marketplace. So clearly,

the filling of the commodity with a meaning is a social process in the circulation of commodities.

Material culture studies would thus demand a careful examination of use value in relationship to exchange value and the social forces of production and consumption. To begin a discussion of use value, or the socially constructed meaning ascribed to commodities, there must be an examination at the basic level of the relationship between needs and wants as they are manifested in particular historical moments as the structure of the desires and meanings that define use value for individuals and societies. Lee (1993, 26) offers a brief synopsis of the anthropological and psychological thinking behind the relationship of desire to individuals' needs and wants in cultural contexts, describing the general tendency "for people to invest a certain amount of their self into material objects as a way of managing their sense of place, social position and identity." Further, Lee argues that consumption patterns derive from specific conscious efforts at the level of individuals and groups to negotiate meaning and power through the signs associated with a particular good. Consumption occurs, then, not in a vacuum, but in a full-blown cultural sign system wherein the occupants have knowledge of the system. In this conception of commodities, the consumption of goods must not be separated from the consumption of the cultural meanings ascribed to the goods.

Furthermore, sociologist Colin Campbell (1987) suggests that *needs* indicate desire for objects that affect the quality of being, whereas *wants* indicate desire for objects that affect the quality of experience. Material culture studies covers the continuum between and among needs and wants, and in consumerism any given commodity may fulfill the role of consummating needs, wants, or both in varying degrees. In addition, for Campbell, *desire* is generally the consumer's psychoemotional understanding (conscious or otherwise) that a given object will fulfill its intended need or want, according to the pre-formed knowledge that the object will indeed fulfill the individual's need or want. Campbell's theory is helpful in distinguishing the social role of both desire and the consummation of desire. To meet a need is to satisfy the self through the utility of the commodity. To meet a want is to please the self through conscious attention to the experience of consumption.

The Commodity and Material Culture Studies

In sum, a turn to the commodity as a category of analysis pushes material culture studies toward a more complex understanding of the relationship between people and physical things, as those relationships are constituted to varying degrees in mass markets. The commodity demands that scholars ask questions not merely about the meaning or cultural function of an object but also about the social relations of production and consumption. A material culture analysis that takes into consideration the consumption of commodities will consider the relationship of labor and capital to an object's production, the source and location of the materials necessary for its production, the means of exchange of the object, and the socially constituted use values that may drive consumerism. Such analyses might also include a discussion of the degree to which a given commodity fulfills both needs and wants in the object's abilities to consummate the desires, both in qualities of being and qualities of experience, of individuals.

J. *Todd Ormsbee*

See also Consumerism and Consumption; Handicraft and Artisanship; Money,

Currency, and Value; Patents, Trademarks, and Brands; Work and Labor

References and Further Reading
Agnew, Jean-Christophe. 1990. "Coming Up for Air: Consumer Culture in Historical Perspective." *Intellectual History Newsletter* 12: 3–21.
Campbell, Colin. 1987. *The Romantic Ethic and the Spirit of Modern Consumerism*. Oxford, UK: Basil Blackwell.
Denning, Michael. 1990. "The End of Mass Culture." *International Labor and Working-Class History* 37 (Spring): 4–18.
Lee, Martyn J. 1993. *Consumer Culture Reborn: The Cultural Politics of Consumption*. New York: Routledge.
Martin, Ann Smart. 1993. "Makers, Buyers, and Users: Consumerism as Material Culture Framework." *Winterthur Portfolio* 28 (2/3): 141–157.
Marx, Karl. 1977. *Capital*, vols. I and II, trans. Ben Fowkes. New York: Vintage.
Marx, Karl, and Frederick Engels. 1970 (1846–1847). *The German Ideology*. New York: International.
Schlereth, Thomas J. 1995 (1982). *Material Culture Studies in America: An Anthology*. Walnut Creek, CA: AltaMira Press.
Stallybrass, Peter. 1998. "Marx's Coat." In *Border Fetishisms: Material Objects in Unstable Places*, ed. Patricia Spyer, 183–207. New York: Routledge.

Community

Since the late nineteenth century, sociologists, anthropologists, and folklorists have wrestled with the definition of human community. Originally a quality describing shared ownership or responsibility (as in goods held in common), *community* has been also employed to describe shared traits, beliefs, or practices of a group of people; the fellowship between persons; or a body of people organized into a political or social unity. Whatever the definition, there is a general agreement that *community* connotes a common sense of self and group identity or identification—even the "virtual communities" created by the World Wide Web. Community studies are many in number and approach; all are concerned with social relations.

Community Studies

At the heart of late nineteenth-century thinking about community is the belief that the forces of industrialization and urbanization characteristic of modern Western nation-states had created complex societies to replace the "traditional" bonds that characterized community: kinship, a finite place, and the sense of belonging, according to sociologist Ferdinand Tönnies (1855–1936). Tönnies' models of *gemeinschaft* and *gesellschaft* defined this dichotomy: *Gemeinschaft* described the model, small-scale traditional community as preindustrial, stable over long periods of time, and based on face-to-face contact, while *gesellschaft* described the impermanent, utilitarian, and at times abrupt relationships of people in a complex, urban industrial society. In some ways Tönnies and his peers mourned the loss of certain values and closeness in the face of modernization, displacing these values to the ideal of community. Sociologists in particular have wrestled with this legacy.

For example, Robert E. Park (1864–1944) understood this shift from traditional community to modern society as an evolutionary process. Park headed the first department of sociology in the United States, established at the University of Chicago in 1892. For nearly half a century department members influenced the practice of sociology throughout the nation. Park, his colleagues, and his students explored various methodologies to study society, from participant observation and fieldwork to surveys and statistical analysis. They used Chicago as their laboratory to answer questions about urban society, including race and ethnicity, occupation and class, and social problems such as poverty and crime. Park (1967, 1) defined *city* as "a state of mind, a body of customs and traditions, and of organized attitudes and sentiments that inhere in this tradition. The city is not, in other words, merely a physical mechanism and an artificial construction. It is involved in the vital processes of the people who compose it, it is a product of nature and particularly of human nature."

The emphasis on studying a geographically limited area, such as a rural town or an urban neighborhood, has consequences for the types of questions asked and conclusions drawn. Many sociologists and anthropologists study the social interactions within the community; others examine communities as a means to understand the impact of large social forces and structures. This is true of the best-known pair of American community studies authored by Robert S. Lynd (1892–1970) and Helen Merrell Lynd (1894–1982). *Middletown: A Study in American Culture* (1929) sought to comprehend the community on its own terms. As the authors wrote, "The aim . . . was to study synchronously the interwoven trends that are the life of a small American city. A typical city, strictly speaking, does not exist, but the city studied was selected as having many features common to a wide group of communities. Neither fieldwork nor report has attempted to prove any thesis; the aim has been, rather, to record observed phenomena, thereby raising questions and suggesting possible fresh points of departure in the study of group behavior" (Lynd and Lynd 1929, 3). In 1937 the Lynds published *Middletown in Transition*, seeking to understand the effects of the Great Depression on the inhabitants of what was in actuality Muncie, Indiana. The Lynds were one of the first research teams to employ the method of cultural anthropology commonly called ethnography, such as interviews, participant observation, and "objective" or "scientific" description, but they also used survey questionnaires, researched historical evidence, and undertook demographic study. The Lynds and their contemporaries were criticized by certain sectors of the American public who were insulted by the application of ethnography in studying foreign, "primitive" societies in comparison with modern American society. *Community studies* became a preferred designation for these research projects.

The New Social Historians of the 1970s applied the methods of ethnography and demography to studies of historic towns and villages. Though some historians claimed that their studies represented larger processes affecting the American people, too many of these studies offer conflicting interpretations. Nevertheless, historical community studies collectively offer a welcome corrective to those narrative national histories that ignore the common people and their worldview.

Community Studies and American Material Culture

Many sociological and historical American community studies, dependent on census records, diaries and letters, newspapers, and other documentation, ignore the material life of community members as evidence and as a category of analysis. Historian John Demos' *A Little Commonwealth: Family Life in Plymouth Colony* (1970), however, did employ probate inventories and did consider the use of domestic space in analyzing the relation of Puritan belief to everyday life through the basic social unit of the family. Nevertheless, while community studies often explore the impact and rise of consumer culture by surveying attitudes and measuring wealth, they rarely include analyses of artifacts in their research models.

Scholars of material culture have explored the creation and dissemination of objects through the study of a community or several communities defined by geographic or political boundaries. In *Making Furniture in Preindustrial America*, Edward S. Cooke, Jr., for example, compares furniture-making practices in two western Connecticut farming towns in the late eighteenth and early nineteenth centuries. By including an analysis of furniture and its manufacture, he finds a wealth of evidence about the shifting nature of labor in the tumultuous years between 1760 and 1820. Historical archaeologists, by virtue of their field, are limited to small-scale studies of neighborhoods, villages, and home sites, but they too explore social relations through the physical evidence of postholes and potsherds, the pipes and paraphernalia left in the ground by previous generations. Folklorists, interested in documenting and preserving traditional cultures, employ ethnographic methods as well as material culture analysis to reconstitute historic cultures and to trace folk forms—speech as well as artifacts—as a means of understanding a given community over time.

Communities of Objects

More recently, and in contradistinction to studies such as Cooke's that rely on individual makers and what they make, archaeologist Chris Gosden has placed emphasis more squarely on "communities of objects" that are longer lived than the humans who use them. Gosden (2006, 438) sees this approach, of "setting objects free from immediate human influence and control," as allowing the creation of "long-term histories" with which to understand how objects obey "logics of their own" (425) such as form, style, and decoration. In this way Gosden shifts the focus from the supposed or stated intent of the objects' makers to the objects' "biographies," which relate how those objects shape human thought and sensibility over time and from place to place. As Gosden (2006, 440) states, "material culture is vital to the notion of embodied or distributed intelligence." Such an approach conceptualizes anew objects as powerful agents of culture and history: Because objects "educate people's senses, and thus their basic appreciation of the world, they help shape and determine sequences of actions in making, using and exchanging things, and they also give rise to thought, then a very different notion of the relationship between people and things comes about, throwing into question many of our assumptions about the relations between people" (Gosden 2006, 440).

The Nation-State as an Imagined Community

Political theorist Benedict Anderson's concept of the modern nation-state as a socially constructed "imagined community," borrowed from anthropology, has influenced a number of disciplines in the humanities and social sciences. Anderson (1991, 6–7) defines *nation* as an "imagined political community": "imagined because the members of even the smallest nation will never know most of their fellow-members, meet them, or even hear of them, yet in the minds of each lives the image of their communion. . . . [The nation] is imagined as a community, because, regardless of the actual inequality and exploitation that may prevail in each, the nation is always conceived as a deep, horizontal comradeship." This concept considers the nation as a historical construct of modernity; since the Enlightenment, nations have held to the idea of popular sovereignty as the means of freedom rather than loyalty to a ruling family or a sacred belief. Anderson

points to the rise of vernacular languages (Latin had been the language of court and church) and the concomitant rise of print culture due to the printing press and the spread of capitalism (what Anderson terms *print-capitalism*) as factors in this historical transformation.

Anderson's theory has been adapted by literary historians and material culture scholars to apprehend how an artifact creates a community through purchase, readership, inscription, or use (marginalia in a book; marking or altering an object). Anderson himself later added to his 1983 work a chapter on the roles of censuses, maps, and museums as tools with which the communion of citizens of and in a nation takes place. Maps oriented readers to the delineated boundaries of a nation's sovereignty without reference to actual border markers (fences, stones, or posts). Indeed, in Anderson's argument, historically the map created a sociopolitical reality before there was a spatial reality, rather than the assumed reverse, that maps represent existing physical or geopolitical circumstances. Through the museum, a new nation claims its antiquity and thus legitimacy through a specific ideological frame with which to see—and imagine with others—what is displayed.

Shirley Teresa Wajda

See also Anthropology and Archaeology; Cities and Towns; Ethnicity; Folklore and Folklife; Planned Communities; Print Culture; Religion, Spirituality, and Belief; Rite, Ritual, and Ceremony; Social History; Tradition; Utopian Communities

References and Further Reading
Anderson, Benedict. 1991 (1983). *Imagined Communities: Reflections on the Origin and Spread of Nationalism*, rev. ed. London: Verso.
Cooke, Edward S., Jr. 1996. *Making Furniture in Preindustrial America: The Social Economy of Newtown and Woodbury, Connecticut.*

Baltimore, MD: Johns Hopkins University Press.

Gosden, Chris. 2006. "Material Culture and Long-term Change." In *Handbook of Material Culture*, ed. Christopher Tilley, Webb Keane, Susanne Küchler, Michael Rowlands, and Patricia Spyer, 425–442. Thousand Oaks, CA: Sage.

Lynd, Robert S., and Helen Merrell Lynd. 1929. *Middletown: A Study in American Culture*. New York: Harcourt, Brace and Company.

Lynd, Robert S., and Helen Merrell Lynd. 1937. *Middletown in Transition: A Study in Cultural Conflicts*. New York: Harcourt, Brace and Company.

Park, Robert E. 1967 (1925). "The City: Suggestions for Investigation of Human Behavior in the Urban Environment." In *The City*, ed. Robert E. Park and Ernest W. Burgess, 1–46. Chicago: University of Chicago Press.

Putnam, R. 2000. *Bowling Alone: The Collapse and Revival of American Community*. New York: Simon & Schuster.

Redfield, Robert. 1960. *The Little Community and Peasant Society and Culture*. Chicago: University of Chicago Press.

Company Towns

A *company town* is an entity created by a corporation for the purpose of encapsulating the work and leisure of employees into one environment, with residential and commercial ownership in the hands of the company. The development of such towns in the seventeenth and eighteenth centuries was haphazard and concerned with economic benefits to the company over employee well-being. The company towns of the late nineteenth and twentieth centuries were far more organized, adopting strict planning standards as well as employee benefits. The first documented company town in what would become the United States was the Braintree Iron Works in 1675, located in New England.

Competing visions of the new nation were realized in early model towns. In 1792, Alexander Hamilton (1757–1804) assisted in creating the first template for model towns in the United States in the form of Paterson, New Jersey, which embodied his vision of a nation based on manufacturing and commerce, while Humphreysville, Connecticut, evolved from the agrarianism of Thomas Jefferson (1743–1826). Mining towns emerged after the Civil War (1861–1865), along with lumber harvesting towns in the Pacific Northwest and agricultural towns in the South.

Chicago industrialist George Pullman (1833–1897) created Pullman, Illinois, in 1883. He wanted more control over workers, so his town had organized thoroughfares and a strict grid system. The factory was separated from the housing by an artificial lake. To ensure efficient housing development the town did not include parks or green space. The new town design failed to discourage riots, however, and a violent strike of Pullman workers occurred in 1894. President Grover Cleveland (1837–1908) formed the Strike Commission the same year, which placed the blame for the riot on inequity in town governance and on George Pullman's dominant role as both employer and city planner.

With the turn of the twentieth century came the advent of welfare capitalism, or the adoption of worker benefits in company towns, as an effort to placate labor unions and ensure hard work. The Kohler Company in Wisconsin is a prime example of these attempts at welfare capitalism. The village of Kohler, completed in 1925, provided recreational and scholastic activities for employees of the company. These activities included gun clubs, women's groups, and a company band. One distinct feature of the village was the wide streets lined

The company town of Pullman, Illinois, captured an idealized vision of industrial workers linked seamlessly as a unified work force. Workers' houses in Pullman, photographed here in the late twentieth century, provided shelter but also provided the means for the company to exert further control over its labor force. (Historic American Buildings Survey/Library of Congress)

with bushes and trees, an effort at beautification. The company attempted to separate itself from village affairs, but strikes in 1935 and 1954 challenged the Kohler family's endeavor.

The world wars required the creation of new military bases and civilian factories, which made company town development a necessity. United States Bureau of Labor statistics revealed that in 1930 just over two million people lived in company towns, and this number increased through 1945. Company towns began to disappear at the end of World War II, however, with the expansion of suburbs, improvements in national transportation systems, and the rise of a service economy in place of a manufacturing economy.

Nicholas Katers

See also Cities and Towns; Factory and Industrial Work and Labor; Mill Towns; Planned Communities; Work and Labor

References and Further Reading

Alanen, Arnold R. 1978. *Kohler, Wisconsin: Planning and Paternalism in a Model Industrial Village.* Cambridge, MA: American Institute of Planners.
Allen, James B. 1966. *The Company Town in the American West.* Norman: University of Oklahoma Press.

Crawford, Margaret. 1995. *Building the Working-man's Paradise: The Design of American Company Towns*. New York: Verso.

Computers and Information Technology

The area of *computers and information technology* (CIT) includes computing machines, software, and networks. From ancient origins in mechanical calculating devices, CIT has become a pervasive part of the United States' material, economic, and cultural landscape. It poses special problems for material culture studies because of its technical complexity and the seemingly "immaterial" nature of software and electronic communications. Most studies that take the materiality of computers seriously have been done by historians of technology, with little reference to the material culture literature. More recently, scholars focusing on "cyberculture" have explored the aesthetics and culture of virtual environments, which straddle the boundaries between material and imagined reality.

Technological Evolution

Hand-operated mechanical calculators were commonly used in business in the nineteenth-century United States. In 1889 Herman Hollerith (1860–1929) patented an automatic tabulating machine that was used for the 1890 U.S. Census; his company became the basis for International Business Machines (IBM) Corporation. During the first half of the twentieth century, tabulators were used in business while scientists used a different type of computer, the differential analyzer, for mathematical calculations. The first electronic digital computer, the Electronic Numerical Integrator and Computer (ENIAC), was built at the University of Pennsylvania during World War II (1939–1945) to calculate missile trajectories. What set this new type of computer apart from earlier special-purpose machines was that it could be programmed to perform different tasks, so that its applications were limited only by the user's imagination.

Technical advances in the postwar years led to a steady miniaturization of computers, from room-filling mainframes to refrigerator-sized minicomputers to today's desktop, laptop, and palm devices. New types of software and new hardware designs also transformed the experience of interacting with a computer. The earliest machines were large, noisy, and prone to frequent breakdowns. They were operated by setting switches and plugboards directly on the machine or punching binary or decimal codes onto strips of paper tape. Early programmers relied on training in applied mathematics, knowledge of the hardware design, and a willingness to troubleshoot unknown "bugs" in the system. The hardware in early machines was exposed, allowing skilled users to look at the physical state of the components and see how the program was progressing and what numerical values it had stored.

As computers became commercialized in the 1950s, manufacturers began to focus on making them easier for non-experts to use. Software improvements included the development of programming languages in the 1950s and the introduction in the 1960s of time-sharing operating systems, which allowed users to interact directly with the computer. Cathode-ray tube terminals, introduced in the 1950s, gave users visual feedback from a screen rather than a printout and allowed moving images to be displayed. The mouse, invented in 1965, allowed users to point to objects on the screen. The first large-scale networks were built in the late 1960s, including the military-funded Advanced Research Projects Agency Network (ARPANET),

The first electronic digital computer was created at the University of Pennsylvania in Philadelphia. Unveiled on February 14, 1946, the thirty-ton ENIAC (Electronic Numerical Integrator and Computer), shown in this undated photograph, could be programmed to perform different tasks, distinguishing it from earlier, special-purpose computers. (National Archives and Records Administration)

which would become the basis for the Internet. Software applications for business, education, and entertainment multiplied in the late 1970s with the introduction of personal computers and video games.

In the mid-1970s the Xerox Palo Alto Research Center in California developed a graphical user interface that combined icons, windows, menus, and a mouse, features that became standard in the 1980s. Graphical user interfaces incorporate assumptions about how people interact best with computers: that pictures are more intuitive than text; that the user will want to perform multiple activities in different parts of the screen; and that it is easier to control the computer using movements (with a mouse, trackball, or joystick) than to type commands. At the dawn of the twenty-first century, users no longer need to know how to program or understand the machine's internal workings; instead, they must be familiar with interface conventions and particular software products.

As computers became packaged for the mass market, the machines' operations were hidden from view. The almost aggressively plain beige boxes for sale to consumers reinforce the message that the magic of the computer lies *inside*. Its anonymous facade reflects a decentralized mode of production, with components manufactured by different companies, assembled by low-wage labor, and packaged by a third party. The heart of the computer, its processor, lies inside, invisible to the ordinary user. The networks that connect computers are equally invisible, encouraging the view that online interactions take place in an immaterial "cyberspace."

Material Aspects of CIT

While information technology has received little direct attention from material culture scholars, a number of disciplines and fields, including sociology and psychology, the history of technology, and cultural theory, have touched on this subject. Historians of technology have focused mainly on the design of computers rather than their use. They have documented the evolving science of building computers and identifying technical challenges and their solutions. Recent scholarship often takes a constructionist view, arguing that design choices reflect not merely rational technical criteria but also the beliefs, goals, culture, and resources of the designers. Some historians, such as Martin Campbell-Kelly and William Aspray (1996), stress the economic forces shaping the computing industry and the contrasting demands of scientific and business users. Others, such as Janet Abbate (1999) in her history of the Internet, analyze military influences on CIT, reflecting the fact that many computing innovations in the United States arose from defense projects.

The relative lack of historical or material culture studies focused on the use of computers may reflect the fact that computers do not fit easily into familiar categories of objects, such as industrial machinery or household appliances. As general-purpose, rapidly evolving machines, computers are used in a wide range of contexts and for a vast array of purposes. As the physical embodiment of the most abstract intellectual realm—mathematics—the computer also straddles the border between material and immaterial. Even its hardware is perceived in terms of numbers (kilobauds, megabits, gigahertz), while the term *information* suggests a free-floating knowledge independent of physical media or social contexts. The computer seems immaterial not only because its workings are hidden but also because they are complex and often mysterious to people not trained in mathematics or engineering. Some images of the computer have equated it with a "giant brain," an entity whose powers seem to transcend its material basis, while in popular culture, computers are often portrayed as menacing, yet oddly human, for example, HAL in *2001: A Space Odyssey* (1968) or Emmy in *Desk Set* (1954). Computers blur the boundaries between the mental and the material, the inanimate and the living.

Social Aspects of CIT

Social scientists have begun to explore some of the social and psychological implications of information technology use. Social scientist Sherry Turkle's *The Second Self* (1984) analyzes the psychology of interacting with a computer, arguing that people, especially children, tend to treat the machine as if it were another person. Using the computer leads children to question what it means to be alive, explore the boundaries between self and other, and develop different styles of expertise. Other researchers have looked at the visual imagery of computing, particularly in the subculture of video gaming, where violent and racial- and gender-stereotyped images are common.

Sociologist Manuel Castells (1996), among others, has noted the power of information technology to alter humans' experience of time and space. Since computer networks connect people across time zones, we become used to living in a world where time is relative—our morning is someone else's night—and where personal interactions are often asynchronous. Computers emphasize smaller units of time with which humans would otherwise deal: The imperceptible nanosecond becomes a measurable and valuable commodity, while a few seconds' pause to load a program seems interminable. Space becomes similarly compressed. The components that once filled a room now fit on a tiny silicon chip, their integrated circuits too small for the eye to see. Distance is no longer an obstacle to controlling machinery, conducting business, gathering information, broadcasting news, or interacting with other individuals.

Cultural studies theorists have explored three aspects of the materiality of information technology: space, community, and embodiment. The notion that computers create a simulated yet subjectively real "space" grew out of early computer games such as *Adventure* and the visions of science fiction authors such as Vernor Vinge and William Gibson, who coined the term *cyberspace*. The technical term *virtual*, originally meaning the simulation of a piece of hardware not actually present, as in *virtual memory*, was taken up in popular culture to designate the simulation of human experience: virtual reality. While virtual reality research has spawned some novel material objects, such as goggles and gloves that physically immerse users in a simulated environment, most people experience virtual spaces using ordinary interfaces and their imagination.

Information technology seems to be unique in creating this illusion of place: We speak of "cyberspace," but not "telephone space" or "television space." To explain this, cultural theorists have focused on two aspects of computer use: interactivity and creative participation. Unlike other media, computer programs respond to users' actions with feedback, just as real-world objects do. Also unlike most media, ordinary computer users have the opportunity to be designers, creating "rooms" in role-playing environments called multiuser domains (MUDs), characters in games, and home pages and Weblogs (blogs) on the Internet.

With virtual spaces come virtual communities, communications theorist Howard Rheingold has argued. These challenge the traditional notion of community as tied to place, which has been central to material culture studies of the built environment. Instead, online chat rooms allow users to form "communities of interest" regardless of their geographical location. Internet enthusiasts have hailed the virtual community as a bastion of democracy and freedom. Legal scholar Lawrence Lessig's *Code: and Other Laws of Cyberspace* (1999) responds to these utopian visions by arguing that the online environment will ultimately be shaped by those (mainly big corporations) who control the hardware and software infrastructure. Others have pointed to a "digital divide" between rich and poor as an obstacle to equal participation. These critiques are reminders that the material underpinnings of cyberspace, while invisible, impose important constraints on users.

The ability to create new identities online, studied by Turkle and others, questions the assumption that identity is based on embodiment. Much attention has been given to the use of online personae to explore alternative gender, racial, and sexual identities. Some celebrate virtual embodiment as a postmodern form of identity, while others question whether the physically embodied personality can ever be left behind. Few scholars have explored questions concerning the body as the site of interaction with the material world. Does interaction with virtual objects differ in culturally important ways from interaction with physical objects? How do our virtual depictions of clothing, objects, and built environments use cultural codes drawn from real artifacts? Much more attention has been directed toward the (mostly fictional) merging of physical bodies with computer technology to produce "cyborgs." Scholar-critic Donna Haraway (1991) and others have made the cyborg a metaphor for the human condition in an age of high technology. The cyborg blurs the boundary between artifact and human user, opening a potentially rich vein of material culture analysis.

Janet Abbate

See also Games; Human Body; Office Work and Labor; Space and Place; Technology

References and Further Reading
Abbate, Janet. 1999. *Inventing the Internet.* Cambridge, MA: MIT Press.
Bell, David, et al., eds. 2004. *Cyberculture: The Key Concepts.* New York: Routledge.
Campbell-Kelly, Martin, and William Aspray. 1996. *Computer: A History of the Information Machine.* New York: Basic Books.
Castells, Manuel. 1996. *The Rise of the Network Society.* Oxford, UK: Blackwell.
Haraway, Donna. 1991. "A Cyborg Manifesto: Science, Technology, and Socialist-Feminism in the Late Twentieth Century." In *Simians, Cyborgs and Women: The Reinvention of Nature*, 149–181. New York: Routledge.
Lessig, Lawrence. 1999. *Code and Other Laws of Cyberspace.* New York: Basic Books.
Rheingold, Howard. 1993. *The Virtual Community: Homesteading on the Electronic Frontier.* Reading, MA: Addison-Wesley.
Turkle, Sherry. 1984. *The Second Self: Computers and the Human Spirit.* New York: Simon & Schuster.

Consumerism and Consumption

Consumerism and *consumption* in the United States constitute not only participation in marketplace transactions to acquire goods but also an acceptance of membership in a society in which material goods occupy a central role. For most of the nation's history, the ability to *consume*—to purchase goods and services—has marked the degree of one's individual empowerment within American society. Scholars have disagreed about the significance of consumption, positing that material goods purchased in the marketplace offer freedom and modes of self-expression, and conversely that the reliance on the products of commodity capitalism indicate cultural and economic impoverishment.

Colonial Consumption Patterns

That the European colonists brought with them the early seeds of a consumption ethic is a certainty, though Native Americans engaged in acts of consumption, such as trading the pelts of indigenous animals for new supplies of guns, cloth, and alcohol, well before their arrival. Of the colonists, the Quakers were the most austere, eschewing all obvious luxuries in the belief that indulgence in material goods was an affront to God. Successful merchants, they did purchase sumptuous goods but displayed them with a characteristic simplicity. Politically conscious consumers, the Quakers often boycotted commodities produced by slave labor or those whose taxes financed war efforts, as in the case of the American Revolution.

The New England Puritans similarly circumscribed their material world. Believing that preoccupation with material goods diminished the glory of God, they enacted biblically based sumptuary laws prohibiting the manufacture and sale of fancy clothing. They chose household items and dress of modest design and color and permitted only small extravagances like lace trim on bonnets and handkerchiefs. Other settlers, such as those who settled in the South, were unfettered by strict religious doctrine and embraced extravagance. Their material choices, often of imported goods and fashions, maintained their close alliance and identification with their homeland.

Geography also prescribed material circumstance. Living in the hinterlands isolated people from port cities, key destinations of and sources for imported goods; only people living in these urban areas had any reliable access to a selection of commodities for sale. Middling sorts, possessing very little hard currency, employed the barter system well into the nineteenth century. Few could afford possessions beyond basic necessities. Although farmers did participate in broader market economies by selling their produce in towns and cities, they primarily relied on rural exchange economies.

In the mid-eighteenth century, market economies started to encroach on exchange economies even in more isolated regions. Farmers' increasing economic empowerment coupled with the loosening of religious strictures heightened both the desire for and availability of newer consumer goods. The nascent market ethos in the countryside stimulated the expansion of American society and culture: A new demand for goods created a need for more sophisticated and far-reaching trade networks. The traveling peddler not only improved the physical quality of people's lives by selling nonessentials like tinware and clocks but also expanded their cultural capital with works of literary fiction and nonfiction. A liminal figure, the traveling peddler simultaneously represented danger and seduction, personifying people's contradictory feelings about consumption itself.

Toward the end of the century, Americans in the city and the country had become more physically and psychologically comfortable with the presence of goods in their lives. Consumption was becoming an integral aspect of life and culture. Indeed, some have argued that the Revolution itself was motivated more by consumption than politics. Avid tea drinkers, colonists resented the heavy taxation on one of their primary consumer goods.

The Market Revolution

During the Jacksonian era (Andrew Jackson served as president from 1829 to 1837), membership in the newly emerging middle class was signified by people's ability to consume. Those who moved to port cities, lured in part by their material promise, found opportunities in a number of occupations providing them with disposable income. Internal improvements such as railroads, canals, and turnpikes facilitated the movement of goods and resources. Concurrently, application of water and steam power to manufacturing technologies increased exponentially domestic production of goods. Consumers, possessing both money and wherewithal, purchased a wider array of goods to make their lives more comfortable and to better their social positions.

The anxious middle classes of the 1840s and 1850s used material goods as a vocabulary with which to express their refinement. The pursuit of refinement through domestic consumption constituted a middle-class woman's job and established her position as the primary household consumer. Women who did not work spent their time and their husband's money making beautiful homes as necessary sanctuaries from the harsh public sphere of the marketplace. Such residences, paradoxically furnished with goods from that marketplace, also expressed a family's moral rectitude—an inversion of the eighteenth-century religious piety that rejected the emphasis on material goods. Free of familial obligations, single men in white-collar occupations were also active consumers; these "dandies," intent on impressing their cohorts and attracting women, often spent lavishly on fancy clothing and all-night revelry.

Increasing circulation of marketplace goods and their presence in the domestic sphere brought some anxiety. Cheap imitations of status objects abounded, blurring class and social boundaries. In highly populated areas filled with relative strangers, outward appearances provided crucial information about one's identity. Yet it became increasingly facile to manipulate that identity with the appropriate purchases, especially with help from the prolific advice literature.

Consumption during the Civil War (1861–1865) was limited for those in the South; Northerners' ability to maintain access to goods and commercial networks merely underscored their economic supremacy. Postwar events hastened the maturation of America's market economy and its citizens' acceptance of the resulting culture of consumption. The Centennial Exposition of 1876 in Philadelphia introduced the nation's manufacturing capabilities to the rest of the world. The World's Columbian Exposition of 1893, held in Chicago, subsequently celebrated the preeminence of American material might over that of other nations: Its industrial prowess and attendant consuming ethos became synonymous with national power and pride.

Mass Consumption

Government initiatives on the eve of the twentieth century facilitated consumption and included completing major railroad trunk lines, developing and using telegraphs and telephones, and implementing rural free delivery and parcel post. An expanding print culture, including newspapers, magazines, popular fiction, and almanacs, heightened consumer consciousness and desire. Montgomery Ward published the first mass mail order catalogue in 1872, and the partnership of Richad W. Sears (1863–1914) and Alvah C. Roebuck (1864–1948) followed suit in 1886. These "farmers' bibles" standardized American language and tastes by giving commodities specific names and presenting an array of aesthetically acceptable goods. Schoolteachers used the books for reading and geography lessons, inculcating a generation of future loyal consumers.

Waves of immigration coupled with better-paying jobs in manufacturing resulted in the proliferation of new goods—high and low quality alike—and more people who could afford to purchase them. Replacing specialty and dry goods stores were new urban institutions, department stores, offering an array of items under one roof. For the less economically empowered, "five and dime" stores, such as Woolworth's, sold cheaper items like notions and candies. Department stores, such as Macy's in New York City and Marshall Field's in Chicago, presented a selection of higher-end goods such as ready-made clothing and pianos. Containing tea rooms and spacious lounges, department stores became leisure venues for genteel women and made shopping no longer solely an expedient to obtain goods and status but a legitimate activity unto itself.

John Wanamaker (1838–1922) established his first department store in Philadelphia in 1876. A devout Presbyterian, Wanamaker believed that the new relationship between religion and consumption was one of coexistence—as private and public facets of the new American standard of living. Other religious men and women remained opposed to the rising tide of consumerism but ultimately had to accommodate it. Progressive Era reformers, themselves often motivated by religion, used immigrants' consumption decisions to gauge their degree of assimilation, seeing the desire for personal property as an internalization of American values and tastes.

Mid-nineteenth-century anxiety about the suspected duplicity of manufactured appearances gave way to the belief that one's material world accurately reflected one's personality. People's collective acceptance of what commodities signified about self and others had become so endemic, and to some, so pernicious, as to elicit biting social commentary. (Even sentimental holidays such as Mother's Day and Valentine's Day had been manufactured by the floral, greeting card, and candy industries of the late nineteenth century.) Sociologist Thorstein Veblen (1857–1929) wrote his critique, *The Theory of the Leisure Class*, in 1899. Veblen was one of the first to consider the significance of consumption activity based on social rather than economic or religious theory. Unlike Karl Marx (1818–1883), who remained preoccupied with production's alienating effect on the human condition, Veblen targeted consumption, arguing that its chief purpose was to help the nouveau riche rise in the social hierarchy, at the expense of others, through "pecuniary emulation." While subsequent writers have found fault with Veblen's absolute condemnation of consumption, his treatise has remained a seminal work, and his phrase *conspicuous consumption*—displaying one's possessions to others to demonstrate social and economic success—describes the primary motivations of twentieth- and twenty-first-century Americans.

By 1900 advertising was becoming an institution, promoting the idea that buying products meant engaging in modernity. Trademarks and brand names stood in as surrogates for anonymous and distant producers, fostering confidence and loyalty in purchasers who no longer maintained face-to-face relationships with the makers of their goods. Advertisements for products as varied as apple peelers and costume jewelry (products absent from the market even fifty years earlier) appeared everywhere as sandwich boards, posters, trade cards, packaging, window displays, and novelties. Advertising's proliferation even in rural areas transformed America's landscape; aided by radio, its total volume increased more than fourfold between 1914 and 1929.

Consumers began seeing themselves as a distinct group, bolstered by the work of such muckraking journalists as Upton Sinclair (1878–1968) and Ida Tarbell (1857–1944) and by government regulations such as the Pure Food and Drug Act of 1906. Consumers Research and Consumers Union (publishers of *Consumer Reports* starting in 1936) dedicated themselves, as part of the consumerism movement, to providing objective information about products to counterbalance the saturation and bias of promotional literature. The stock market crash of 1929 and the subsequent Great Depression only confirmed to skeptics the dire results of rampant spending, shaking people's faith that they could find salvation through pursuit of material goods.

The coming war similarly constricted consumer life. Industrial retooling to meet the demands of World War II (1939–1945) shifted production priorities from domestic consumer goods to war machines and materiel. Appliance companies made tanks and bombs. Clothing companies produced parachutes and uniforms. Rationing and recycling for the war effort, considered acts of patriotism, constituted consumers' domestic efforts to aid the Allied forces.

Post–World War II Boom

Following the war, Americans engaged in the largest production and consumption rates of all time. Companies returned to making formerly scarce consumer goods, which people used to fill their new suburban houses made affordable by the 1944 Servicemen's Readjustment Act (the "GI Bill of Rights"). The construction of Levittown, New York, a planned suburban development of small, very similar houses, began in 1947. Critiqued for their homogeneity, Levittown houses nevertheless exemplified suburban living. Home ownership and growing families gave people new opportunities to consume, and women remained the chief domestic consumers.

Postwar consumer goods not only provided nascent families with the commodities they needed but also expressed aesthetically an optimism in American culture and faith in the future symbolized in automobile tailfins, stiletto heels, and TV dinners. Even the eternally fecund Barbie doll, introduced in 1959, embodied a far-ranging faith in the American economy because its sole purpose was to acquire more clothing and accessories. Writers such as sociologist David Riesman (1909–2002), journalist Vance Packard (1914–1996), and feminist Betty Friedan (1921–2006) vocalized the postwar backlash against what they saw as the endless pursuit of material goods and the psychological toll it levied on men and women. Consumerism, rather than meaning the protection of consumers' interests, was increasingly employed to characterize the belief that increasing the consumption of goods was basic for a strong national economy.

New institutions making special accommodations for requisite automobile traffic, such as shopping malls and grocery stores,

developed to support suburban life. The largest shopping center boom, from the early 1960s to the early 1970s, coincided with and partially caused the decline of downtowns, formerly the main locale for community marketplaces. Afforded more leisure time and fortified by credit cards, more people frequented shopping malls. Worlds in themselves, they contained movie theaters, restaurants, conference centers, and health spas. The mall boom culminated in the Mall of America, located in Bloomington, Minnesota, which celebrated shopping as entertainment for the entire family, even boasting a full-size amusement park.

Americans in the late twentieth century could not escape their role as consumers. Facilitated by the Internet and cable television, commercial pleas entered places formerly inviolate, such as schools, museums, churches, libraries, and doctors' offices. Forms of leisure merely constituted reasons to spend, and travel offered the opportunity to spend someplace else. Rather than defining themselves through commodities, as they once had, Americans had become commodities themselves, their identities little more than the sum of their brand loyalty. Indeed, even personal service, formerly unquantifiable, had been broken down into discrete components and offered for sale via the "service industry." American consumption by the end of the twentieth century was characterized by a rampant materialism valuing surface over substance. In addition, American culture, manifest in its products (paradoxically made overseas), was exported internationally, as producers came to see other cultures as potential consumers of *America* as well. Americans had completely overcome geographic, religious, and economic limitations to consumption and expected the rest of the world to do the same.

Wendy A. Woloson

See also Advertisements and Advertising;
Auctions; Commercials; Commodity;
Department Stores; Fakes; Flea Markets; Gay
Consumerism; General (Country) Stores;
Grocery Stores; Holidays and Commemora-
tions; Mail Order Catalogues; Patents,
Trademarks, and Brands; Plainness
(Quakers); Public Markets; Secondhand
Goods and Shopping; Shopping Centers and
Shopping Malls; Supermarkets; Trade Cards;
Trade Catalogues; Yard Sales

References and Further Reading
Bronner, Simon, ed. 1989. *Consuming Visions:
    Accumulation and Display of Goods in America,
    1880–1920*. New York: W. W. Norton.
Campbell, Colin. 1987. *The Romantic Ethic and
    the Spirit of Modern Consumerism*. Oxford, UK:
    Blackwell.
Glickman, Lawrence B., ed. 1999. *Consumer
    Society in American History: A Reader*. Ithaca,
    NY: Cornell University Press.
Leach, William R. 1994. *Land of Desire:
    Merchants, Power and the Rise of a New
    American Culture*. New York: Vintage.
Lears, T. J. Jackson. 1994. *Fables of Abundance:
    A Cultural History of Advertising in America*.
    New York: Basic Books.
Lury, Celia. 1996. *Consumer Culture*. New
    Brunswick, NJ: Rutgers University Press.
Marchand, Roland. 1985. *Advertising the
    American Dream: Making Way for Modernity,
    1920–1940*. Berkeley: University of California
    Press.
Schor, Juliet B., and Douglas B. Holt, eds. 2000.
    The Consumer Society Reader. New York: New
    Press.
Veblen, Thorstein. 1952 (1899). *The Theory of the
    Leisure Class, an Economic Study of Institutions*.
    New York: New American Library.

Cosmetics, Toiletries, Perfumes, and Colognes

Since ancient times, humans have sought
to transform their faces and bodies through
the use of cosmetics, toiletries, perfumes, and
colognes. *Cosmetics* are preparations (creams,
oils, powders, and applications) that are
applied to the skin, and primarily to the face,
to enhance or improve appearance. *Toiletries*
are preparations such as soaps, washes, and
shampoos that are used to cleanse or treat
the body. *Perfumes*, liquids created of essential oils derived from plants or spices and
blended with fixatives derived from animals
(musk, for example), provide pleasing scents
to the body or clothing. *Colognes*, more appropriately called *eaux de cologne* and historically referred to as *toilet waters*, on the other
hand, are alcohol-based scents. Perfumes
and colognes are often, if erroneously, categorized as cosmetics or toiletries.

The American cosmetics and toiletries
industry was not strongly established until
the late 1800s. In part this was due to the
social dictates against cosmetics; "painted
women" were often considered lower class
or prostitutes. Throughout the 1800s beauty
products to improve complexions or whiten
skin were primarily created within the home
using "receipts" (recipes) from household
manuals and cookbooks. Cosmetics were
commercially produced during this period,
but sometimes included dangerous ingredients such as lead or mercury that could cause
disease or even death. By the end of the nineteenth century women's magazines began to
tout the use of cosmetics as appropriate enhancement of natural beauty or as a means
to hide physical imperfections.

In the early 1900s the market for cosmetics
and toiletries grew; the demand for these
products was filled by entrepreneurial
women such as African American Madame
C. J. Walker (1867–1919), immigrant Helena
Rubenstein (1885–1956), and working-class-
born Estee Lauder (1906–2004), each of
whom created successful commercial beauty
product lines. Products such as colored lip-
sticks, face powders, rouges, eyeliners and
eye shadows, nail enamels, hair shampoos

and setters, and perfumes became readily available by the 1930s. The rise of the film industry in Hollywood legitimated and augmented the growing acceptance of cosmetics use as a means of enhancing sexual allure. The particular requirements of lighting and filming compelled the development of cosmetics by film makeup specialists such as Max Factor (1877–1938). While products for women flourished in the first half of the twentieth century, comparatively few products, such as shaving creams, deodorants, hair creams, and colognes, were available to men.

Styles of women's makeup have changed in every decade of the twentieth century reflecting fashion trends. Hair styles have also been fostered by changing toiletry technology: commercially prepared hair dyes (1910s), hair spray (1940–1950s), hair mousses and gels, and hair regrowth treatments, especially for men, such as Rogaine (minoxidil) (1998). A growing market for men's products developed in the late 1990s. Perfumes and colognes proliferate, not only for the body but for automobiles, rooms, and moods. Today, a multitude of products, with attractive packaging and branded with names from Avon (founded 1886) to performer-celebrity Jennifer Lopez, are available to care for one's skin and hair, to mask body odors, and to enhance through makeup one's physical appearance.

Daniel Farr

See also Bodily Cleanliness and Hygiene; Consumerism and Consumption; Human Body

References and Further Reading

Angeloglou, Maggie. 1970. *A History of Make-Up*. New York: Macmillan.
Brumberg, Joan Jacobs. 1997. *The Body Project: An Intimate History of American Girls*. New York: Random House.
Halttunen, Karin. 1986. *Confidence Men and Painted Women: A Study of Middle-Class Culture in America, 1830–1870*. New Haven, CT: Yale University Press.
Peiss, Kathy. 1998. *Hope in a Jar: The Making of America's Beauty Culture*. New York: Metropolitan Books.
Vinikas, Vincent. 1992. *Soft Soap, Hard Sell: American Hygiene in an Age of Advertisement*. Ames: Iowa State University Press.

Cultural Geography

Cultural geography (also called *human geography*) examines, through the focus on the interaction of humans with the natural environment, the characteristics of regions and the origins and movements of cultures. Cultural geography's primary emphasis is human modifications to the natural environment. The emphasis placed on physical environments, as opposed to the systems and patterns of human movement, has varied through the discipline's history and across different schools of thought at different times.

Approaches and Evidence

Currently, there are two approaches to cultural geography. The first, older school focuses primarily on the interactions between people and the natural features of the landscape in specific locations. Typically, this research examines rural areas, underdeveloped regions, and the environmental impact of human civilization. Necessarily, physical landscapes and human habitation (the built environment) predominate.

The second, newer school emerged in the mid-1980s as a result of the "cultural turn" in geography as historical materialism (the view that economic development is the driving force of historical change and that humans' social existence determines their consciousness) and as the Birmingham school of cultural studies (so called because the scholars who founded cultural studies were located at the University of Birmingham, England) influenced the field of social geography. With the turn toward Marxist analysis promoted by the Birmingham school, the interest in larger systems of economic interaction, previously confined primarily to social geography, became dominant across cultural geography. Typically, these studies examine diversity and identity formation within urban or suburban communities while also studying the influence and interplay of global cultural systems.

Although the first approach is more frequently applied to rural areas and the second to urban and suburban areas, both frameworks can and are applied to the entire spectrum of human society. In either case, geography, along with other social and physical sciences, increasingly employs reflexive methodologies, considering the privileges and disadvantages researchers face due to their own race, class, ethnicity, gender, sexuality, or location on the rural-urban continuum. This interest in identity construction and diversity frequently requires the examination of material culture for the presence of different communities, since textual forms of evidence heavily favor members of dominant groups. Traditionally, cultural geographers rely on land surveys, demographic studies, and large-scale ethnography. In the quest to include a greater variety of voices, however, cultural geographers now also use novels, films, television programs, and other types of both fictional and nonfiction creative works, as well as material culture.

In addition, Geographical Information System—a satellite-linked, location-based database management system—has allowed the exact location and movement of people, objects, and landscape features to be marked and recorded through time. Consequently, larger volumes of data about the interactions of a greater variety of features can now be traced, allowing new types of research.

History

Place-based anthropological research of the late nineteenth century formed the foundation of early cultural geography. This is *Environmental determinism*—the idea that the physical landscape is the primary determiner of the shape of a culture. Further, adherents of this approach argued that certain cultures were intrinsically superior to other cultures; to these scholars, European imperialism was the result of the natural superiority of its environment and its peoples.

American scholars began to focus in the mid-1950s on identifying and describing distinct zones of correlated cultural and physical patterns—the study of *culture areas*. Concurrently, quantitative approaches, such as censuses and other demographic studies, began to supplant ethnographic methods. With the increased importance of systems and quantitative methods, interest in the material aspects of the environment lessened.

In order to counter the limitations of quantitative methods and the restrictions of the culture area approach's disdain for generalizing theories, various philosophical influences began to direct cultural geography once again toward ethnographic sources and broader theories in the 1970s. In the 1980s economic geographer David Harvey brought the power of economic forces to the center of cultural geography via British cultural studies. Consequently, the examination of the material again fell in importance as the systems of interaction became the focus of the field.

Increasingly, the central issue for all studies of people and geography has become identity:

Who has the power to determine how space is used? Who has the right to claim to belong to a space? For example, on the small scale, who has the power to determine what constitutes proper behavior in a public park or, on a larger scale, who has the right to claim citizenship of a nation? The landscape and built environment provide evidence for the symbolic and ideological structures, such as public propriety or citizenship, at the center of research on identity and power.

Although such forms of power are necessarily intangible, they do leave material evidence, or as power relations shift, material evidence of domination or subjugation is modified. In the United States, the success of the civil rights movement that began in the 1960s is evident in the gradual disappearance of separate facilities for African Americans and for whites. More recently, wheelchair-accessible bathrooms, texture tracks on the sides of subway platforms to provide warning for people using canes or guide dogs, and public buses accessible for people unable to climb stairs demonstrate the increased inclusion of people with disabilities in the public sector of American urban society.

Cultural Landscape

Like cultural geography, the interdisciplinary field of *cultural landscape studies* is concerned with the interaction of people and both natural and human-created landscapes. Where cultural geography may focus entirely on intangible patterns of movement and exchange, however, cultural landscape studies foregrounds the physical objects and spaces. Some cultural landscape scholars envision the landscape as a sort of text that stores ideologies and symbolic systems over time. Current theoretical approaches explore the actions of both individuals and groups acting with and against each other.

Cultural landscape studies grew out of the convergence of the study of fine art landscape paintings by art historians and the work of material culture scholars, especially those focusing on vernacular culture. As a result, vernacular landscapes and individuals' adaptations of formal landscapes serve as the focus for much of this type of work. Cultural geography, on the other hand, more frequently examines formal landscapes or officially endorsed spaces.

Historic Preservation

Building on the belief that a cultural landscape both embodies and shapes the cultural practices of the landscape's users, historic preservationists seek to document and, when possible, preserve historically important public and private built environments. Since economically disadvantaged and oppressed people are less likely to leave written records, landscapes are often the only records of some communities and cultures. Consequently, the move to study and preserve the historic built environment reflects the increased interest among scholars in general to study people from all segments of society.

The Historic American Buildings Survey and the Historic American Engineering Record, administered since 1933 by the National Park Service, the Library of Congress, and the American Institute of Architects, record and archive prominent historic spaces. The National Trust for Historic Preservation (founded in 1949), a private organization, works nationwide to preserve physically historically important spaces. Other projects, such as architect/activist Dolores Hayden's documentation and preservation project in Los Angeles, work with spaces officially recorded as less significant (according to official institutions). Hayden's project, described in *The Power of Place* (1999), uses both physical preservation and, when that is not feasible, public art installations to memorialize past uses for future generations.

The central interests of cultural geographers in historic preservation are the structures of power and the subsequent empowerment of different peoples: The landscapes serve as evidence of the larger social forces at work at specific times and over time.

Gentrification

A central issue for many contemporary cultural geographers is *gentrification*, the revitalization of older urban neighborhoods. Typically, nonwhite and lower-income people are gradually forced out of older neighborhoods while the older properties are either restored, often under the rubric of "historic preservation," or demolished and replaced. The new residents are more likely to be white and are usually of a higher social class. Notable sites of gentrification include Baltimore's Inner Harbor; Dupont Circle and the U Street Corridor in Washington DC; and New York City's Greenwich Village loft area and Harlem.

While cultural landscape scholars focus on the aesthetic and immediate cultural impact of historic preservation, cultural geographers focus more on the larger impact and structures surrounding the physical changes. Typically, historic preservation codes pick one moment in the neighborhood's history and require buildings to conform architecturally to that specific time period. By freezing the look of a neighborhood at a specific moment, these city codes necessarily erase any remaining evidence of other periods of history. Frequently, evidence of flourishing nonwhite, immigrant, or otherwise disenfranchised communities is lost through the gentrification process since these communities are deemed historically insignificant by policymakers and new inhabitants.

In addition to issues of historic preservation, such as which time period and uses are deemed the most important to protect and which time periods and uses are to be culled through demolition, scholars focusing on gentrification examine issues of social justice: who are displaced, the legal mechanisms used to execute redevelopment plans, and the public financing of projects—especially sports arenas and shopping districts—that often serve as the focal point for gentrification projects. For example, city regulations and patterns of enforcement for occupancy rates, as reported in census records, are typical form of evidence for cultural geographers.

Cultural Ecology, New Urbanism, and Urban Planning

A central issue of cultural geographers studying undeveloped regions has long been *cultural ecology*: the explicit examination of humans' interactions with natural resources. Initially defined by anthropologist Julian Steward (1902–1972) and emphasizing cultural determinism, current approaches such as political ecology explore the power relationships among different stakeholders and the use of common property resources. In the United States, the projects of cultural ecologists continue to include the allocation of resources from national forests and fisheries, the study of ecological disaster areas such as the sinking city of New Orleans, Louisiana, and the placement of green areas within housing developments.

More recently, cultural ecologists' attention has turned to the urban areas of developed nations. The New Urbanism movement promotes pro-environment, anti-sprawl, and anti–oil economy urban development as a solution for an impending social crisis caused by the decreased availability of fossil fuels. Intersecting with more traditional urban planning and the study of gentrification, New Urbanists suggest city planners return to the multiuse neighborhood models seen in older European and American cities. Thus, people would have little or no commutes and would live and recreate within the same community.

In addition to examining who has the right and power to shape a city, the ecologically focused arm of geography turns its attention toward how those people should shape cities, towns, and other aspects of the natural environment. In the long run, the stability of communities is highly dependent on the stability of the natural infrastructure underlying them.

Krista M. Park

See also Cities and Towns; Cultural Studies; Historic Preservation; Land and Landscape; Poverty; Space and Place; Suburbs and Suburbia

References and Further Reading
Harvey, David. 1989 (1985). *The Urban Experience*. Baltimore, MD: Johns Hopkins University Press.
Harvey, David. 1990. *The Condition of Postmodernity: An Enquiry into the Origins of Cultural Change*. Cambridge, MA: Blackwell.
Hayden, Dolores. 1999. *The Power of Place: Urban Landscapes as Public History*. Cambridge, MA: MIT Press.
Korr, Jeremy. 1997. "A Proposed Model for Cultural Landscape Study." *Material Culture* 29 (3): 1–18.
Lowes, Mark Douglas. 2002. *Indy Dreams and Urban Nightmares: Speed Merchants, Spectacle, and the Struggle over Public Space in the World-Class City*. Toronto: University of Toronto Press.
Meinig, Donald. 1979. *The Interpretation of Ordinary Landscapes*. New Haven, CT: Yale University Press.
Netting, Robert M. 1986 (1977). *Cultural Ecology*, 2nd ed. Prospect Heights, IL: Waveland Press.
Sandercock, Leonie, ed. 1998. *Making the Invisible Visible: A Multicultural Planning History*. Berkeley: University of California Press.
Tuan, Yi-Fu. 1977. *Space and Place: The Perspective of Experience*. Minneapolis: University of Minnesota Press.
Zukin, Sharon. 1995. *The Cultures of Cities*. Malden, MA: Blackwell.

Cultural History

The academic field of cultural history in the United States has two strands: The first, older strand is the engagement with the "high" or "elite" products deemed timeless, beautiful, and representative, such as art and sculpture, literature, theater, *belles lettres*; music and opera; and certain decorative arts. The second, more recent strand incorporates an anthropological definition of *culture* as the totality of a society, including popular and folk as well as high culture; the ideas of the philosopher and the intellectual as well as the laborer and the housewife; and the means by which experience is produced and understood. Since the 1970s this second, more encompassing definition has held sway as the New Cultural History, especially among historians who have been influenced by the French *Annales* school's theory of *mentalité*: a group's mode of thought.

Cultural history and social history have been intertwined for much of the twentieth and twenty-first centuries, though each field has emphasized different methods and topics. The New Social Historians of the 1970s were criticized for overlooking the experiences of the ordinary people they studied; the demographic methods these historians adopted produced numbers and charts that "normalized" social behavior of specific groups or communities rather than explored the variances of experience of individuals. In their quest to counter this tendency, the New Cultural Historians (or New Historicists) since the 1980s have embraced a fuller exploration of human experience by emphasizing how experience is articulated in behavior, language, and material culture, especially through the examination of a single person or family. Though one could make the case that Americans in the past do not fashion themselves in ways they do today, the concepts of the self and self-consciousness have proved fundamental to the work of these historians. In addition, the work of anthropologist Clifford Geertz (1926–2006) has been extremely influential. His concepts of *ethnography* as "thick description" and *culture* as semiotic revise investigation as interpretation. As Geertz (1973, 5) writes, "Believing, with Max Weber, that man is an animal suspended in webs of significance he himself has spun, I take culture to be those webs, and the analysis of it to be therefore not an experimental science in search of law but an interpretative one in search of meaning. It is explication I am after, construing social expression on their surface enigmatical."

The focus on uniqueness and the individual also led to an interest in the experience of persons at the margins or in transition. These studies do not follow the mold of "great man" biography; rather, they seek to explore how individuals shaped and changed their own identities within systems of power. The subfield of *microhistory*, the minutely detailed, intimate analysis of a person or an event, has been devoted to such inquiry. Yet, as historian Paula S. Fass (2003) has observed, a tendency exists to focus too much on practices at the margins of society rather than most people's experiences.

The New Cultural Historians have consciously interrogated narrative—how history is told—in response to criticisms of steril-

ity in social historians' graphs, charts, and descriptions. *Portrayal*, which implies fashioning and thus interpretation, rather than *description*, a form of transcription, may appropriately define the approach of the New Cultural Historians. More so than other forms of history, except perhaps biography, the New Cultural History allows for the free play of historians' creativity within the traditional limits of the discipline. Thus, New Cultural Historians are often self-reflexive in their works, signaling to readers when interpretation turns to speculation.

The New Cultural History and Material Culture

Historians after this "cultural turn" have embraced the idea of *cultural production* (the creation, enactment, and preservation of cultural life) in their study of the popular and the public as well as the private. For cultural historians, the rituals and performances of parades, festivals, and carnivals on the one hand, and dining, literacy, and intimacy on the other, are equally useful in delineating cultural life. Yet the emphasis on "reading" documentary evidence as performance at times truncates thorough interpretation and underestimates the evidentiery possibilities of material culture. The meanings of a given physical object may be many, conflicted, and contested in a historical place and time, yet those multiple meanings may be neglected by historians seeking to interpret in an event a specific mind-set or static performance. The "world of goods" from which a historical performer may fashion an identity is not thoroughly explored. Historian Richard Grassby (2005, 597) offers an example: "Clothes in a drawer have no meaning, but when worn they become a uniform with social and moral implications."

Yet clothes in a drawer are evidence—of wealth, consumer choice, personal hygiene, and the like. The clothes may have been inherited, unfashionable, or unworn but kept for sentimental reasons; they simply may have not fit. Nevertheless, in their keeping is evidence of choice and of culture. Material culture is rich with symbolism and subjectivity. How objects symbolize is based on physical properties that, for their makers and their users, were (and are) fundamental to the creation, fluidity, and power of meaning in a given place and time. At times, the use of material culture by cultural historians has been at odds with the argument within New Cultural History that social categories (such as identity, race, class, and ethnicity) are necessarily unstable. But material culture in the hands of some cultural historians has sometimes been used to prove their claims based on documentary evidence, rather than be considered as constitutive elements in self-fashioning and power relations based on political, economic, and social contexts. Following Geertz, material culture as a form of social expression must be construed as "enigmatical" and not self-evident.

Shirley Teresa Wajda

See also Anthropology and Archaeology; Cultural Studies; Ethnicity; Gender; Race; Social Class and Social Status; Social History

References and Further Reading

Burke, Peter. 2004. *What Is Cultural History?* Cambridge, UK: Polity Press.
Fass, Paula S. 2003. "Cultural History/Social History: Some Reflections on a Continuing Dialogue." *Journal of Social History* 37 (1): 39–46.
Geertz, Clifford. 1973. "Thick Description: Toward an Interpretive Theory of Culture." In *The Interpretation of Cultures: Selected Essays*, 3–30. New York: Basic Books.
Grassby, Richard. 2005. "Material Culture and Cultural History." *Journal of Interdisciplinary History* 35 (4): 591–603.
Hunt, Lynn, ed. 1989. *The New Cultural History*. Berkeley: University of California Press.

Cultural Studies

Cultural studies examines contemporary culture, from television shows and celebrities to cars and fashion, in an effort to understand its function and significance in relation to a particular society. Cultural studies scholars explore how meaning is generated in a culture and examine the motivations behind those meanings and the relationships of power involved in constructing them.

Origins

The Centre for Contemporary Cultural Studies (CCCS), established at the University of Birmingham in England in 1964, gave cultural studies its name. The writings of Richard Hoggart (the first CCCS director), Raymond Williams (1921–1988), E. P. Thompson (1924–1993) and Stuart Hall established cultural studies as an area with academia. Unlike traditional university disciplines, however, cultural studies was chartered as something of an "antidiscipline" for two primary reasons. First, the CCCS and in particular the work of Stuart Hall stressed the importance of cultural studies as a political act. Hall believed that cultural studies must always include an examination of relationships of power in its analysis of culture, and that cultural theory without its application in the "real world" (that is, outside academia) was meaningless. Second, all four scholars mentioned above undertook research on the working class and/or popular culture, areas previously undervalued and largely ignored by traditional university disciplines.

Critical Theory

As originally conceived within the context of the CCCS, cultural studies was primarily concerned with issues of class (especially the working classes). The influence of Karl

Marx (1818–1883), and later noted Marxists Antonio Gramsci (1891–1937) and Louis Althusser (1918–1990), in this regard is significant. As this "antidiscipline" grew, critical investigations of gender, race, and sexual orientation and representations of these identities in mainstream media were examined. Stuart Hall, for example, was especially interested in how racist ideology maintained its presence in modern societies through television programming. Hall's larger purpose was to consider how racist and other hierarchical ideologies could be challenged and dismantled.

Cultural studies disrupts academic disciplinary boundaries. Cultural studies differs from traditional academic inquiry in its interdisciplinarity, as it utilizes theories and methodologies from a wide variety of academic disciplines, including sociology, anthropology, psychology, literary theory, history, philosophy, film studies, political economy, art history, and communications.

Cultural studies was quickly exported from England around the world. It is important to note that as each nation or region adopted the approaches and politics of cultural studies, it also modified the practice. For example, Canadian cultural studies emphasizes issues of national identity and the concomitant impact on its culture by its southern neighbor, the United States, while Indian cultural studies attempt to make the discipline a completely indigenous field of study, disregarding the Western cultural studies canon as irrelevant within the context of the Indian experience.

Cultural Studies in the United States

Cultural studies took hold in American universities in the mid-1980s. The main difference between the British and American versions is that Hall's concept of cultural studies as a political endeavor was largely omitted in the American variant. The lack of political content of American cultural studies has genuinely shocked many of its British practitioners, who founded the discipline on the basis of overt political applications.

The introduction of cultural studies into the American academy clashed with the quantitative traditions of mass communications scholars with their emphasis on "hard evidence," as opposed to the perceived "soft theory" approach adopted by other scholars of society and culture. Cultural studies theorists have argued that studying, for example, the pop star Madonna Ciccone Ritchie constitutes one way in which individuals understand both their own identities and those of others around them. Furthermore, popular media texts are in essence cultural documents with the potential to reveal much about the culture in which they were produced.

Cultural Studies and Material Culture Studies

Similar to cultural studies, material culture studies is methodologically interdisciplinary in nature (borrowing from history and archaeology in particular) and also seeks to examine critically artifacts and other phenomena generally ignored by more mainstream academic traditions. Studies in material culture acknowledge that objects, even those some might consider banal or trivial, have meaning. Furthermore, such objects can reveal something about the culture in which they were produced. Both cultural and material culture studies often examine the issue of personal, subcultural, and wider cultural identities and the ways in which objects or texts are utilized to construct such identities. Dick Hebdige's 1981 groundbreaking article, "Object as Image: The Italian Scooter Cycle," is a prime example of this type of study. In this work Hebdige examines how the scooter was the focus of various ideas; the "meaning" of the scooter changes depending on the time, place, and individuals involved.

Popular culture studies that focus on manufactured, material goods have been strong, with studies on *Star Trek*, reality television, and other media. Other studies have used a physical object to explore issues of identity and consumerism. One scholar, Steve Waksman (2001), examined racial and gender ideologies through the development of the electric guitar, while the Barbie doll becomes a tool of sexual subversion in Erica Rand's (1995) study. The concreteness of material culture renders ideological content as a tangible entity, and thus allows for discussion of the ways ideology and identity are neither stable nor fixed.

Despite these similarities there are also some important points of tension and disagreement between the two fields. With its roots in archaeology and history, material culture studies is typically historical in nature. On the other hand, cultural studies tends to concentrate on contemporary phenomena and is often criticized for its lack of attention to historical context. Also, many note that cultural studies is a form of inquiry based on theory shaped by highly specific cultural conditions (e.g., 1960s English working-class culture) and then used to discuss other very different cultural phenomena.

Notwithstanding these disagreements, material culture studies and cultural studies continue to intersect in significant ways.

Today the most cursory glance at journals from both disciplines reveals the advantages of employing both schools in studies of culture.

Natasha Casey

See also Cultural History; Ethnicity; Fanzines; Gender; Popular Culture; Race; Social Class and Social Status

References and Further Reading

Dant, Tim. 1999. *Material Culture in the Social World: Values, Activities, Lifestyles*. Philadelphia, PA: Open University Press.

Grossberg, Lawrence, Cary Nelson, and Paula A. Treichler, eds. 1992. *Cultural Studies*. New York: Routledge.

Hall, Stuart. 1981. "The Whites of Their Eyes, Racist Ideologies and the Media." In *Silver Linings: Some Strategies for the Eighties*, ed. George Bridges and Rosalind Brunt, 28–52. London: Lawrence and Wishart.

Hebdige, Dick. 1981. "Object as Image: The Italian Scooter Cycle." *Block* 5: 44–64.

Lury, Celia. 1996. *Consumer Culture*. New Brunswick, NJ: Rutgers University Press.

Miller, Daniel. 1998. *Material Cultures: Why Some Things Matter*. Chicago: University of Chicago Press.

Rand, Erica. 1995. *Barbie's Queer Accessories*. Durham, NC: Duke University Press.

Sardar, Ziauddin, and Borin Van Loon. 1998. *Introducing Cultural Studies*, ed. Richard Appignanesi. New York: Totem Books.

Turner, Graeme. 1990. *British Cultural Studies: An Introduction*. Boston: Unwin Hyman.

Waksman, Steve. 2001. *Instruments of Desire: The Electric Guitar and the Shaping of Musical Experience*. New ed. Cambridge, MA: Harvard University Press.

D

Decorative Arts

An older, more discriminating category than the inclusive material culture, American *decorative arts* include historical furnishings of aesthetic interest, generally adaptations of western European conventions. Products of carpentry, masonry, metalwork, cabinetwork, ceramic and glass manufacture, weaving, leatherwork, and clock and instrument making, from large interior furnishings to small jewelry, have been classified as the *minor arts, applied arts, crafts, industrial arts*, and *decorative arts* to distinguish them from *architecture* and the so-called *fine arts*. The decorative arts have historically been defined through their exclusion from the fine arts of architecture, painting, and sculpture and as lacking the autonomy of those arts, but to some eyes, labeling household goods as "decorative" has obscured their functional and practical purposes. Students of material culture who seek to distinguish their focus on utility and everyday life from the art historian's interest in the fine arts often prefer the term *applied arts*, while the term *decorative arts* often is reserved to refer to expensive commodities.

Interpretation of Decorative Arts

Interpretations of the decorative arts differ according to periodization, method of fabrication, and type of material. Decorative arts have been characterized as artisan-based in the eighteenth century, as intellectually oriented within the Arts and Crafts Movement of the late nineteenth, as a designer art in the twentieth, and as upscale luxuries offered through mail order catalogues (e.g., retailers such as Pottery Barn and Crate and Barrel) in the twenty-first century. Some scholars work within the traditional definition of decorative arts, prizing only preindustrial handcraftsmanship, but many others now conduct research in a wide range of household furnishings in the nineteenth and twentieth centuries. Recently, scholars have expanded the field of decorative arts by including in their analyses less exclusive and less "beautiful" artifacts. They have also become more independent of the restraints imposed by the scopes of extant collections and the influences of collectors.

The investigation of American decorative arts developed first as an antiques trade in the late nineteenth century. Then, most museum departments collected only European furnishings. In their studies, the first enthusiasts for American decorative arts responded to changes wrought by the Industrial Revolution. Art historian Joseph Butler (1969, 287) explained these enthusiasts' romanticization of preindustrial workmanship and valuable materials: "While it was once the year 1800 at which scholarly interest waned, of late 1830 has become the date; the reason given is that quality declined with the Industrial Revolution and the resultant cessation of the handcraft system." Aesthetic appreciation for the decorative arts as a whole remains influenced by the Arts and Crafts Movement and writings of English art critic and designer William Morris (1834–1896).

The motivations of the first connoisseurs to collect American antiques—historical association, aesthetics, and antiquarianism—continue, but for the most part contemporary scholars focus on building precise attributions and investigating changes in style in addition to regional production methods and consumption habits. Increased access to public collections facilitated the maturation of comparative studies, especially via photography, print catalogues, and databases, and fostered greater precision in the year and place of origin, maker, ownership, form, style, and material of artifacts. The Society of Decorative Arts developed in the 1970s, a sign that within academia art historians were increasingly focusing on furniture, silver, and ceramics as meaningful topics of research.

Centers for the Study of American Decorative Arts

Connoisseurship in American decorative arts became an academic field at the Winterthur Museum, a collection of Americana and study center developed by Henry Francis du Pont (1880–1969) in the 1920s. Open to the public after 1951, it remains an influential institution because of its size, scope, and quality of artifacts and the Winterthur Program in Early American Culture established in 1952. Winterthur scholars and curators pursued the scientific study of antiques, researching details such as thumbpieces on eighteenth-century silver tankards and measuring ornament as a system of patterning and form as an expression of order. Henry Ford's (1863–1947) Greenfield Village (1929) and John D. Rockefeller, Jr.'s (1874–1960) Colonial Williamsburg (1926) were similar philanthropic projects that made decorative arts central to narratives of United States history.

In recent years, the application of x-radiography, cross-sectional microscopy, x-ray fluorescence, and scanning electron microscopy and spectroscopy has increased the precision of connoisseurship, and Colonial Williamsburg and Winterthur have been instrumental in applying these tools to American antiques.

Connoisseurship and Interpretation

A vital figure at Winterthur was Charles F. Montgomery (1910–1978), whose guide of fourteen points of analysis (overall appearance, form, ornament, color, analysis of materials, techniques employed by the craftsman, trade practices, function, style, date, attribution, provenance, condition, and evaluation) has been maintained by the field of study for more than forty years as a fundamental step toward literacy in the decorative arts.

Montgomery taught connoisseurship as a "science" with "principles." From a material culture studies perspective, "scientific connoisseurship" of American furnishings that results in numerical data or aesthetic celebration adheres too closely to art historical methods used by Giovanni Morelli (1816–1891) and Bernard Berenson (1865–1959). Montgomery did not intend his fourteen points to be applied as a schematic mode of data collection, however. His research on pewter and Federal-era furniture was based in a formalist method of cultural criticism popular in the 1950s, but he established conceptual connections between human behavior and formal issues. Montgomery looked at contexts, interpreting materials in relation to technical inventions, and he examined marks on silver in relation to tariff laws. The field of American decorative arts depends on this tension between the analysis of isolated portable artifacts as records of human thoughts on the one hand, and their contextualization within the knowledge of object types and human use over specific durations and in particular regions on the other.

Furnishings are essential to unlock the environmental psychology of domestic interiors. The examination of architecture has increasingly relied upon the decorative arts to understand the emotional and practical differentiation of rooms in the house in addition to its aesthetics. The classification of decorative arts remains useful because it is empathetic to a contemporary pluralist criterion. It defines its scope within relational meanings. Contemporary decorative arts scholarship at its best follows the contours of material belongings in a specific domestic or institutional context, not facts about a lone object or a narrow predisposition to one definition of culture or function.

Ezra Shales

See also Architectural History and American Architecture; Art History and American Art; Arts and Crafts Movement; Base Metalwork and Metalware; Ceramics; Design History and American Design; Furniture; Glass; Handicraft and Artisanship; Industrial Design; Silverwork and Silverware; Style; Textiles

References and Further Reading
Ames, Kenneth L. 1985. "The Stuff of Everyday Life: American Decorative Arts and Household Furnishings." In *Material Culture: A Research Guide*, ed. Thomas J. Schlereth, 79–112. Lawrence: University Press of Kansas.
Ames, Kenneth L., and Gerald W. R. Ward, eds. 1989. *Decorative Arts and Household Furnishings in America, 1650–1920*. Winterthur, DE: Winterthur Museum.
Butler, Joseph T. 1969. "The Decorative Arts." In *The Arts in America: The Nineteenth Century*, ed. Wendell D. Garrett et al., 285–382. New York: Charles Scribner's Sons.
Fleming, E. McClung. 1982 (1974). "Artifact Study: A Proposed Model." Reprinted in *Material Culture Studies in America*, ed. Thomas J. Schlereth, 162–173. Nashville, TN: American Association for State and Local History.
Fleming, John, and Hugh Honour. 1977. *Dictionary of the Decorative Arts*. New York: Harper and Row.
Frank, Isabelle. 2000. *The Theory of Decorative Art: An Anthology of European and American Writings, 1750–1940*. New Haven, CT: Yale University Press.
Gowans, Alan. 1976. *Images of American Living: Four Centuries of Architecture and Furniture as Cultural Expression*, 2nd ed. New York: Harper and Row.
Montgomery, Charles. 1982 (1961). "Some Remarks on the Science and Principles of Connoisseurship," reprinted as "The Connoisseurship of Artifacts." In *Material Culture Studies in America*, ed. Thomas J. Schlereth, 143–152. Nashville, TN: American Association for State and Local History.
Quimby, Ian M. G., and Polly Anne Earl, eds. 1973. *Technological Innovation and the Decorative Arts*. Charlottesville: University Press of Virginia.
Zimmerman, Philip D. 1981. "Workmanship as Evidence: A Model for Object Study." *Winterthur Portfolio* 16 (4): 283–307.

Department Stores

From the mid-nineteenth through the late twentieth centuries *department stores* played important roles as centers for material goods and hallmarks of the American urban built environment. Department stores arose in response to new technological developments and cultural trends that ushered in an age of mass production and mass consumption. The department stores that appeared in cities throughout the United States were larger and more diverse than their predecessors, general and crossroad stores. Stores like Macy's in New York City (1858), Marshall Field's in Chicago (1852), and Wanamaker's in Philadelphia (1876) dazzled customers with an array of clothes, accessories, home goods, and food items, each sold in their own "department." By the turn of the twentieth century, department stores had come to define city centers and symbolize one of America's favorite pastimes—shopping.

Department stores introduced a new system of retailing to the nation. Where previously stores had specialized in selling a specific type of goods, department stores contained a large diversity of products, catering to the every need of a customer. The size of the stores was a function of the growing market for ready-made goods. As new factories churned out inexpensive products, retailers created modern environments designed to transform everyone who entered into an impulse buyer.

Like the goods inside, the department store became a symbol of fashion and wealth in the city. Built with an attention to beauty and ornament, early department store architecture looked to Italian palaces for inspiration, using classically inspired columns, coffered ceilings, and delicate archways to create an atmosphere of luxury. New construction technologies allowed for the replacement of buildings' heavy masonry walls with cast iron frames and plate-glass windows. Plate-glass display windows brought the world of the department store out into the street, inviting pedestrians to gaze longingly

at interior treasures. Stores' lofty designs also helped to assuage middle-class fears about the morality of the new consumer-oriented culture by emphasizing shopping as a cultural activity.

Retailers found a customer base in women, who by 1915 purchased more than 80 percent of the goods sold in the nation. Department stores catered to their female shoppers by creating opulent interiors with such services and amenities as tea rooms, post offices, ladies' lounges, and daycares. Inside the stores, women could socialize, relax, and browse. The new industries of fashion and advertising also encouraged women's purchases and, correspondingly, their routine visits to the downtown stores by suggesting that material possessions served as indicators of a family's wealth.

The grand era of the urban department store came to a close in the 1950s. As middle-class Americans began to move into the suburbs, department stores followed suit, establishing themselves in suburban shopping centers. The rise of discount chain stores like K-Mart (1962) and Wal-Mart (1962) in the 1970s also decreased department stores' percentage of the retail market. Recently, however, department stores have played a central role in many urban revitalization projects, suggesting that while the grand emporiums of the past no longer exist, the age of the department store is far from over.

Elizabeth Belanger

See also Cities and Towns; Commercial Architecture; Consumerism and Consumption; General (Country) Stores; Shopping Centers and Shopping Malls; Suburbs and Suburbia

References and Further Reading
Abelson, Elaine S. 1989. *When Ladies Go A-Thieving: Middle-Class Shoplifters in the Victorian Department Store.* New York: Oxford University Press.

Benson, Susan Porter. 1986. *Counter Cultures: Saleswomen, Managers and Customers in American Department Stores, 1890–1940.* Urbana: University of Illinois Press.

Leach, William R. 1994. *Land of Desire: Merchants, Power and the Rise of a New American Culture.* New York: Vintage.

Design History and American Design

American Studies scholar Jeffrey L. Meikle (1995, 75) has written, "it is hardly surprising that few cultural historians can escape an involvement with design. Nor is it surprising that a coherent discipline or field of design history proves to be an elusive goal." Scholars variously situate the origins of *design* somewhere between the prehistoric invention of tools and the second flourishing of the Industrial Revolution, while others periodize according to the advent of specific technologies or terminologies such as William Addison Dwiggins' (1880–1956) coinage of *graphic design* in 1922 in professional recognition of its practitioners.

Nor is *design history* a monolithic narrative. The chronologically overlapping products of industrial, interior, and graphic designers have generated distinct histories supported by levels of theoretical complexity ranging from formalism directed to practicing graphic designers to advanced psychoanalytical readings offered by architectural theorists (Bush 1997). Others vary according to whether the designed object is regarded as the subject of inquiry or as a document through which analysis is conducted (Riccini 1998). For those engaged in material culture studies, the anonymous drafting and industrialized mass production that characterizes most designed goods complicate the traditional disciplinary focus on decorative arts directly reflecting the maker's hand.

International Origins of Design Studies

Most design histories begin with the technological innovations of eighteenth-century Europe and trace design professions arising from the practical demands of the first Industrial Revolution and its economic shift to consumerism, capitalism, and middle-class entrepreneurialism. As architectural and design historian Adrian Forty (1986, 29) points out, design becomes necessary as a separate production activity once a craftsman can no longer be responsible for every step from conception through manufacturing. Mid-eighteenth-century French and English proto-designers supplanted but benefited from guild workers and academy-trained artisans. In France, the tastes of the Bourbon kings fed the near-insatiable demand for domestically produced Rococo porcelains. In England, it was the Neoclassical style that signaled privileged knowledge born of the Grand Tour and English opposition to France, which spurred Josiah Wedgwood's (1730–1792) successful merger of technology, art, and commerce at his Etruria factory complex. The hallmarks of early industrially produced decorative arts are all present in Wedgwood's "Queen's ware" and still-distinctive blue and white Jasperware, from their close adherence to aesthetic taste secured by classical antiquity to their direct connection to royalty to the careful consideration given the efficient division of labor and packaging, transporting, and marketing of final products to the emerging middle class.

Rigid aesthetic principles over the applied arts gradually gave way to practical requirements. Nikolaus Pevsner (1902–1983), founder of design history as an academic field, acknowledged the international comparisons of manufactures and technologies showcased at London's Great Exhibition of 1851 constituted a watershed between nineteenth- and twentieth-century design. Products presented in direct comparison with one another allowed for a potent demonstration of beauty drawn on technological lines. That the exhibition was held in Joseph Paxton's (1803–1865) unprecedented iron and glass Crystal Palace further heralded a new type of cultural production with possibilities beyond mere industrial capability. Here art critic John Ruskin's (1819–1900) traditionalist outcry against ornament and "deception" found equal footing with artist/craftsman William Morris' (1834–1896) claim that "the more mechanical the process, the less direct should be the imitation of natural forms" (Sparke 1986, 41, n. 13). And if, as Pevsner wryly notes, figures such as Henry Cole (1808–1882), Owen Jones (1809–1874), Richard Redgrave (1804–1888), Matthew Digby Wyatt (1820–1877), and others responsible for preparing and staging the exhibition were those who most vociferously criticized many of its shoddy exhibits, these same figures ultimately saw their guidelines made standard practice. Subsequent English design reform under Prince Albert (1819–1861) required that every object "to afford perfect pleasure must be fit for the purpose and true in its construction," and in the process defined a national aesthetic based on new materials and the techniques which gave form to them (Pevsner 1985, 9–11). By the late nineteenth century, beauty defined by utility allowed figures such as French lithographer Jules Chéret (1836–1932) to claim fine arts status for his four-color lithographic posters. It was against this backdrop that the significant schools and movements of twentieth-century European design emerged.

Design and Design History in the United States

The situation in America was different. Design historian Arthur Pulos (1983, 3) notes that "The United States was in all likelihood the first nation to be designed—to come into being as a deliberate consequence of the actions of men who recognized a problem and resolved it with the greatest benefit to the whole. America did not just happen; it was designed." Moreover, American design practice emerged largely free of academic restrictions that governed its European counterpart. In the nineteenth century, the absence of aristocratic values expressed as taste and training and the new symbolic needs of the thriving capitalist consumer base equally informed mechanized production in the United States. The design tendency that arose to meet this need, however, was first expressed by a classically trained artist. In the first half of the nineteenth century, sculptor Horatio Greenough (1805–1852) wrote essays (published in 1948 as *Form and Function*) which outlined the principle of Functionalism as allowing the essential structure to determine the form and external appearance of a building. Functionalism separated the appearance of buildings and designed objects from historical precedents and royal dictates to establish not so much a unifying aesthetic per se but the appearance of pragmatic usefulness. Greenough's writings permitted architect Louis Sullivan (1856–1924), whose "The Tall Office Building Artistically Considered" (1896) gave rise to the influential, if oft-misused, dictum "form follows function," to view architecture and hence design as a logical and coherent process of problem solving based on the specifics of a given problem. Sullivan and the so-called Chicago School sought pragmatic solutions that combined function, structure, aesthetics, and meaning into a single organic unity. The operative idea that "beauty in useful objects is defined by their utility and honesty to materials and structure" led Functionalism to become the dominant American design philosophy during the first half of the twentieth century (Heisinger and Marcus 1983, 55). The emphasis on individualism in what also is called the Modernist aesthetic distinguished it from the similar pursuit of utopian-tinged rationality that characterized Germany's Deutscher Werkbund.

American Design in the Twentieth Century

World War I (1914–1918) occasioned enormous expansion of productive capacity and subsequent postwar growth of consumerism. The initial flourishing of designed goods was driven not by theories of aesthetics but by rationalization, standardization, new materials, and improved production techniques. While Functionalism continued to be important, it was increasingly augmented by heightened attention to surface appearance that created an immediate, even visceral visual impact. Against austere interwar ideals exemplified by the German Bauhaus traveling exhibit *Form Ohne Ornament* ("Form without Ornament") of 1924, American industrial designers emerged from the ranks of such diverse—and distinctly ornamented—occupations as set design, advertising, and illustration. Chief among those enshrined in histories of American design is Harley Earl (1893–1969), who prompted fundamental change in assembly line production through his work in the General Motors (GM) Art and Color Section. Recruited in 1926 to bolster sales of the newly released LaSalle, Earl assessed the problem as consumer fatigue brought about by the mechanically superior but unchanging Ford Model T, whose sales were then faltering after thirteen years of market dominance. Earl's solution was to bring a holistic re-envisioning of the automobile through integrated Art Deco–inspired sculptural body components and chromed steel "brightwork" intended to stimulate con-

sumer interest. His opinion that "People like something new and entertaining in an automobile as well as in a Broadway show" was embraced by GM president Alfred P. Sloan, Jr., (1875–1966) as the potent lure of "continuous, eternal change" (Gartman 1994, 8). No longer was ornament "criminal," as Austrian architect Adolf Loos (1870–1933) would have it, or morally suspect as it had been in the heyday of the American Arts and Crafts Movement, but rather it stood as a "visual entertainment" that became an essential American expectation of design.

By the late 1930s, American design was differentiated from its European counterparts by technology cloaked in fashion. Commensurate with the triumph of ephemerality in design came an emphasis on the designer's charisma and on products viewed less as accomplishments of design acumen than of his (the male pronoun is consciously chosen) forceful personality. Noted designers of the era included Raymond Loewy (1893–1958), Norman Bel Geddes (1893–1958), and Henry Dreyfuss (1904–1972), all of whom supplemented advertising campaigns for products created for major corporate clients with their own carefully groomed public images. For example, Loewy extended the informal call for entertainment in design with the promotion of a nearly mythic image of himself, as in the prominent venue afforded by the 1949 *Time* cover depicting the designer in a nimbus of streamlined locomotives and household consumer goods that emanated in creative profusion from his Brylcremed head.

Consumer demand slackened during the Great Depression and World War II (1939–1945), but postwar prosperity gave rise to a florescence of consumer goods whose exuberance of form and material comfort were at odds with the stylish reductive necessity of designers such as Italian Rationalist Achille

Castiglione (1918–2002). As a new super-power, the United States found its initial visual identity in the deeply individualistic Abstract Expressionist paintings of Mark Rothko (1903–1970), Jackson Pollock (1912–1956), and Franz Kline (1910–1962). Just as rapidly graphic designers such as Alvin Lustig (1915–1955), Paul Rand (1914–1996), Saul Bass (1920–1996), and others associated with the New York school laid claim to bold primary color and abstracted form. Lustig's 1945–1952 dust jackets for the New Directions "New Classics" series demonstrated designers' emerging eagerness to embrace inventive approaches that abandoned type-case compositions and accepted commercial styles in favor of symbolic "marks" indebted to modern art. His design "hit a fresh eye, unencumbered by any ideas of what art was or should be, and found an immediate sympathetic response," Lustig wrote in 1953 (Heller 1994). Similarly, Saul Bass' animated title sequences for *The Man with a Golden Arm* (1955) redefined the territory of design and, much like Chéret before him, blurred the disciplinary and professional boundaries between popular art forms. That Bass secured his reputation creating enduring logos for American Telephone & Telegraph, Quaker Oats, Warner Communication, among others, spoke to the flexibility of newly imagined design possibilities generated by commerce.

Changing Design, Changing Design History

Design histories changed correspondingly. Designed objects and graphics were no longer seen as derivatives of architecture, as Pevsner had it, but as constantly changing fashion. What mattered in design "was not its intellectual content, integrity and *zeitgeist* credentials; but its visual impact and appropriateness to particular—and temporary—circumstances" (Whiteley 1995, 38). Ac-cordingly the formal narratives of a Nikolaus Pevsner gave way to the equally painstaking but frequently irreverent observations of a Reyner Banham (1922–1988). A typical Banham essay mixes ruminations on the contradiction between the pastoral ideal and urban productivity with the complex of design rules for what he termed the American gizmo, "the small, self-contained unit of high performance . . . whose function is to transform some undifferentiated set of circumstances to a condition nearer human desires" (Banham 1996, 109–110, 113). Banham neatly encapsulated the material exuberance that characterized post-1920 American design, from Frank Lloyd Wright's (1867–1959) conflation of design and architecture to the fantasy, glitter, and swagger of 1950s automobiles and the commonplace stuff that constitutes the built environment of popular culture.

Where Banham marked the beginning of all-inclusive design history, Victor Margolin offers a comprehensive record of the current state of themes and directions in contemporary design history. In "Design History in the United States, 1977–2000," Margolin (2002) calls for comprehensive design histories, and his conclusion offers a succinct directive. It is evident, he writes, "that design is the subject of historical investigation from many quarters. . . . The volume of crossover work we are seeing between design history, material culture, American Studies, popular culture, decorative arts and the history of technology continues to grow. Particularly with the strong emphasis on the social context for understanding objects, there is likely to be more confluence among scholars in different research communities as the social dimension of an object overtakes the distinctions between its mechanical and aesthetic aspects" (Margolin 2002, 168).

Beverly K. Grindstaff

See also Architectural History and American Architecture; Art Deco; Art History and American Art; Arts and Crafts Movement; Decorative Arts; Disability and Disability Studies; Graphic Design; Industrial Design; Interior Design; Modernism (Art Moderne); Style

References and Further Reading
Banham, Reyner. 1960. *Theory and Design in the First Machine Age*. London: Architectural Press; New York: Praeger.
Banham, Reyner. 1996. *A Critic Writes: Essays by Reyner Banham*, ed. Mary Banham et al. Berkeley, Los Angeles: University of California Press.
Boime, Albert. 1987. *Art in an Age of Revolution, 1750–1800*. Chicago: University of Chicago Press.
Bush, Anne. 1997. "Criticism and the Discerning Eye." *Design Issues* 13 (2): 16–23.
Collins, Bradford R. 1985. "The Poster as Art: Jules Chéret and the Struggle for the Equality of the Arts in Late Nineteenth-Century France." *Design Issues* 2 (1): 41–50.
Forty, Adrian. 1986. *Objects of Desire: Design and Society, 1750–1980*. New York: Pantheon Books.
Gartman, David. 1994. "Harley Earl and the Art and Color Section: The Birth of Styling at General Motors." *Design Issues* 10 (2): 3–26.
Heisinger, Kathryn B., and George H. Marcus, eds. 1983. *Design since 1945*. Philadelphia, PA: Philadelphia Museum of Art.
Heller, Steven. 1994. "Born Modern." American Institute of Graphic Arts, http://www.aiga.org/content.cfm?contentalias=alvinlustig.
Loos, Adolf. 1970 (1908). "Ornament and Crime." Reprinted in *Programs and Manifestoes on 20th-Century Architecture*, ed. Ulrich Conrads, trans. Michael Bullock, 19–24. Cambridge, MA: MIT Press.
Margolin, Victor. 2002. *The Politics of the Artificial: Essays on Design and Design Studies*. Chicago: University of Chicago Press.
Meikle. Jeffrey L. 1995. "Design History for What? Reflections on an Elusive Goal." *Design Issues* 11 (1): 71–75.
Pevsner, Nikolaus. 1949 (1936). *Pioneers of Modern Design: From William Morris to Walter Gropius*. New York: Museum of Modern Art.
Pevsner, Nikolaus. 1985 (1968). *The Sources of Modern Architecture and Design*. New York: Thames and Hudson.
Pulos, Arthur J. 1983. *American Design Ethic: A History of Industrial Design to 1940*. Cambridge, MA: MIT Press.
Riccini, Raimonda. 1998. "History from Things: Notes on the History of Industrial Design." *Design Issues* 14 (3): 43–64.
Small, Harold A., ed. 1948. *Form and Function: Remarks on Art by Horatio Greenough*. Berkeley: University of California Press.
Sparke, Penny. 1986. *An Introduction to Design and Culture in the Twentieth Century*. New York: Harper & Row.
Sullivan, Louis. 1896. "The Tall Office Building Artistically Considered." *Lippincott's Magazine* (March): 403–410.
Thomson, Ellen Mazur. 1997. *The Origins of Graphic Design in America, 1870–1920*. New Haven, CT: Yale University Press.
Whiteley, Nigel. 1995. "Design History or Design Studies?" *Design Issues* 11 (1): 38–42.

Dining Rooms

The popularity of the *dining room* in American domestic dwellings waxes and wanes in relation to socioeconomic circumstances and attitudes about home life that favor more or less formality. In any given house today, the space for eating can be an extension of the living room or kitchen, the kitchen itself, or a separate dining room.

In the earliest colonial houses, families ate in the same hall or great room in which they cooked and worked. Starting in the late seventeenth century, larger houses in New England comprised additional rooms, including a front room furnished for dining and, in a frequent extension of earlier conventions, sleeping as well.

In the early nineteenth century, as the house, as "home," increasingly became perceived as a symbol of civilized order, rooms in even modest middle-class houses became more specialized in terms of use—and their use was recognized by their furnishings. The dining room, for example, typically contained a suite of a table with extra leaves, at least eight chairs, a china cabinet, and one or two sideboards laden with equally specialized linens, dishes, and utensils. Etiquette guides and household decorating and management manuals prescribed proper behavior in the ritual of dining through complicated explanations of the uses of tablewares.

Early twentieth-century disenchantment with the high economic and social costs of Gilded Age values encouraged less formal attitudes toward dining. In the late nineteenth century, house designs such as the bungalow featured alternative eating spaces and such alternative furnishings as the built-in table flanked by built-in benches. The 1950s ranch style house continued this trend toward a relaxed attitude about sociability, often merging the kitchen, dining, and living spaces. Comfort, convenience, and realistic cost continued to modify concerns about propriety: today informal dining spaces are popular across a broad spectrum of social classes.

Janet Tyson

See also Halls; House, Home, and Domesticity; Kitchens and Pantries; Living Rooms; Parlors

References and Further Reading

Carron, Christian G., et al. 1998. *Grand Rapids Furniture: The Story of America's Furniture City.* Grand Rapids, MI: Public Museum of Grand Rapids.

Clifford, Edward Clark, Jr. 1986. *The American Family Home, 1800–1960.* Chapel Hill: University of North Carolina Press.

Hunter, Christine. 1999. *Ranches, Rowhouses & Railroad Flats: American Homes: How They Shape Our Landscapes and Neighborhoods.* New York: W. W. Norton.

Ierley, Merritt. 1999. *Open House: A Guided Tour of the American Home, 1637–Present.* New York: Henry Holt.

Williams, Susan. 1985. *Savory Suppers and Fashionable Feasts: Dining in Victorian America.* New York: Pantheon Books.

Disability and Disability Studies

Disability refers to bodily difference, both physical and cognitive, including impairment and behavior or bodily states that mark people as atypical. Stigmatizing language, including words and phrases such as *handicapped*, *freak*, *physically challenged*, *moron*, and *cripple*, though still sometimes used, is grounded in an outmoded normative framework based on denominating people by one aspect of their existence (similar to racist, sexist, and other systems of bias) rather than seeing the whole person, as well as defining whole groups of people as deficient.

Disability is one of the most complicated areas of material culture and its study. Part of the difficulty in assessing the topic is that no comprehensive method of organization has been developed. Overarching artifact categories must take into consideration several perspectives, from that of the user and the maker to that of the person the artifact is used upon, in addition to all of the usual elements such as geographic region, economic status, ethnicity, gender, and materials. Large frameworks, like health and medicine, exclude too many social and political artifacts as well as cast the topic as medical, a position that has been successfully critiqued by disability studies scholars since the 1980s.

Disability can be temporary or permanent, hidden or visible, stigmatizing or valorous. In material terms, those nuances are illustrated by the difference between a neck brace and a leg brace, between the artwork of a person with bipolar disorder and of a person of short stature, between a Jerry Lewis–type "spaz" cartoon and a war veteran's pinned-up shirt sleeve. Differences among kinds of disability and the artifacts associated with them also carry different valences. For example, a cane used by a returning veteran, an elderly person, a person who suffered polio myelitis, or a person with low vision exhibits different designs, purposes, and meanings. Interpretation of disability shifts across impairments and eras as well. An industrial accident in 1870 might relegate a person to economic and social oblivion, but a motorcycle crash in 2000 might produce a paraolympic athlete.

Much of the history of disability has been characterized by paternalism and discrimination, so that the politics surrounding the existence of any particular artifact requires careful analysis. For example, the terms *patient*, *inmate*, *person*, *resident*, and *sinner* might all attach to one object, but each term carries a political point of view.

The Medical Model

The influence of the medical model of disability is perhaps the most intricate intellectual hurdle in working with the material culture of disability. The *medical model* is an umbrella term that describes approaching disability as a flaw or deficiency that requires cure or fixing, according to the system of diagnosis and treatment current in any particular era. In this framework, artifacts are assumed to be strategies for treatment, overcoming a defect, or altering a person's ability to meet a cultural norm or concept of appropriate performance. Needless to say, power inequities, stereotyping, and misunderstanding critically affect the identification and interpretation of objects.

Health-related artifacts with a direct disability association fall into several groups: rehabilitation (including physical and occupational therapy and shelter workshops), prosthetics, assistive devices, and sick room

and invalid supplies (fumigators, inhalers, walkers, spas, baths). The idea of rehabilitation originated in the early twentieth century on the heels of World War I, and by midcentury it had become a consumer-oriented movement that advocated for health care as a right. Devices to transport invalids or for mobility support have existed since early history, but their use and design underwent significant change following World War II, with the advent of new materials, computers, and the disability rights movement. Power wheelchairs, with airplane joy-stick controls, became practical in the 1950s and 1960s, followed by the lightweight-frame manual chairs that fueled wheelchair sports in the 1980s. The significant cultural aspect of power and lightweight chairs was that they provided independence by doing away with assistance (that is, pushers). Crutches and canes have been in use since biblical times but have remained largely unchanged in design, except for the switch from homemade to commercial manufacture and the use of lighter-weight materials. The polio epidemics of the first half of the twentieth century resulted in increased crutch production as well as attention to other assistive equipment, such as iron lungs (tank respirators) and rocking beds, orthotic devices (leg braces, splints) and strength amplifiers (grabbers, levered door handles, automatic door openers).

Prosthesis design also benefited from the postwar boom in new materials, especially in plastics and, more recently, microprocessors. Methyl-methacrylic, polytetrafluoroethylene (PTFT, a version of Teflon and Gore-Tex), and medical-grade silicon helped to foster such items as contact lenses, lens implants after cataract removal, artificial blood vessels and heart valves, shunts, artificial ears and noses, and limbs with a wider range of function and aesthetic appeal. These changes contributed to improved recovery rates, independence, self-esteem, health, and length of life for people who had disabilities that formerly would have resulted in hardship or limited amelioration.

Many people with disabilities reside in special-purpose institutions. Institutionalization entails a range of artifacts for feeding, clothing, and instructing people as well as surveillance and enforcing discipline. In asylums, people wore uniforms and might be placed in straightjackets and given lobotomies, electric shock therapy, or water treatment and a range of medications. Institutions housed people but also trained them in job skills such as basketry, broom making, piano tuning, and printing and Linotype work. Residential facilities had game rooms, social activities, and printed newsletters. Shelter workshops produced a range of commercial products. Many such facilities were closed or converted to other purposes over the past forty years. Nursing homes and group homes remain, and as with earlier institutions for people with disabilities, they are scrutinized for their social, moral, legal, and economic utility, all of which are reflected in the material record.

The Social Model
Critique of the medical model led to a *social model of disability*. This approach grew out of the work of sociologists in England in the 1970s and 1980s. The social model assumes that disability is constructed by cultural forces and is contingent upon such factors as economic status; religious mores; geographic location; and the shifting definitions of civil rights, community, health, independence, beauty, and human worth. The push for disability rights, grounded in a social model, reached full force in the United States following World War II, as disabled veterans, people who had had polio, and their families

and friends worked for inclusion and civil rights. The disability rights movement has produced a diverse material record. The difference between the medical and the social models is illustrated by comparing an early twentieth-century wicker invalid chair, meant for protected use inside a hospital environment with an early twenty-first-century electric-powered scooter with cushioned wheels and seat, back-up warning signal, and high-stress steel frame.

The political sea change in understanding disability is reflected in the slogans on buttons, posters, ephemera, and T-shirts, such as "Piss on Pity," "Deaf Pride," "Fry Rice, Not Brains," "Fight AIDS, Act Up," and "Attitudes Are the Real Disability." The universal access symbol of a wheelchair, first used in the late 1970s, has become a familiar icon. Several other access symbols have since been added, such as those indicating a telephone typewriter (TTY), assistive listening, and audio description (AD).

This change is also documented in the marketing materials produced by parent advocacy groups over the years, such as Easter Seals (founded in 1934 as the National Society for Crippled Children; renamed in 1967), The Arc (founded in 1950 as the National Association of Parents and Friends of Mentally Retarded Children; renamed several times until 1981, when the organization became the Association for Retarded Citizens of the United States, and in 1992, The Arc of the United States), United Cerebral Palsy (1949), and Muscular Dystrophy Foundation (1950). The March of Dimes (established as the National Foundation for Infantile Paralysis in 1938; renamed in 1979) initially focused on research on poliomyelitis and the care of people who had had it, and later focused on complications related to premature birth. It has produced a diverse artifactual record, such as posters, donation

Curb cuts to facilitate wheelchairs are but one aspect of the reconceptualization of the built environment to facilitate mobility and access for the disabled. Such changes are the result of the disability rights movement since World War II. (iStockPhoto)

containers, clothing, wristbands, ball caps, patches and stickers, and commemorative plates.

The Americans with Disabilities Act (ADA), passed in 1990, accelerated architectural change, especially removal of environmental barriers through the addition of ramps, railings and grab bars, and lowered water fountains and counters in public facilities. The ADA built upon the 1968 Architectural Barriers Act, the 1973 Rehabilitation Act, and Individuals with Disabilities Education Act of 1975.

The legal steps toward inclusion gave a creative and intellectual boost to the concept of universal design (UD). Also called *transgenerational design, design for all,* and *life span design, universal design* is associated with a loose-knit group of disability activists, designers, architects, and educators who shared a common belief in the right of all persons to access public space and participate in civic life. It focused on adapting the environment or providing tools rather than forcing the individual to change. Universal design emerged as a hybrid design system in the late 1960s and 1970s. Ron Mace (1941–1998), often credited as the father of universal design, and architect Ruth Lusher, both of whom had had polio, worked with U.S. Department of Justice staff in crafting ADA compliance guidelines for physical access. The "access" politics of universal design quickly spread from architecture to interior and office design and then into commercial product development and later into computer and software design and information technology. This all happened at the same time disability activists espoused access politics through grassroots organizing and demonstrations around the United States. Other historical influences, such as Frederick Winslow Taylor's (1856–1915) ideas on scientific management, ergonomics, and the rise of human factors research, contributed to development of seven basic principles of UD and their application to both the built environment and product design. Other environmental elements associated with UD and the ADA are public elevators with visible and audible signals, tactile colored strips along the edge of train platforms, automatic door openers, kneeling buses, and curb cuts (although curb cuts date from the 1940s).

Technology

The use of technology sets people with disabilities apart from other marginalized minority groups (although disability cuts across all groups). People with disabilities rely upon assistive devices to care for children, cook, eat, study, travel, read, bathe, and communicate. Most of the technology is for the activities of daily life: a shoe horn extender, a jar opener, a watch with Braille numbers, utensils with built-up handles, pill crushers (to assist swallowing), a lifting toilet seat, exercise equipment. Technological aids are often vernacular, homemade versions of commercial products (such as transfer boards to assist a person from a car seat to a wheelchair or from one chair to another) or adapted items such as toys with added handles or large switches for use by children with mobility impairments.

In addition to the technological aids already discussed, communication devices comprise another significant area of material culture. These include hearing aids, cochlear implants, TTYs, alarm clocks that light up,

computers with screen enlargement, mouth sticks for keyboards, puff and suck technology, voice recognition software, voice synthesizers, talking books, and Braille and Speak note takers. Communication technology has been especially crucial in the workplace.

Katherine Ott

See also Human Aging and the Aged; Human Body; Technology

References and Further Reading
Center for Universal Design. 1998. *The Universal Design File, Designing for People of All Ages and Abilities.* Raleigh: North Carolina State University, Center for Universal Design.
Linton, Simi. 1998. *Claiming Disability: Knowledge and Identity.* New York: New York University Press.
Longmore, Paul, and Lauri Umansky, eds. 2001. *The New Disability History: American Perspectives.* New York: New York University Press.
Ott, Katherine, David Serlin, and Stephen Mihm. 2002. *Artificial Parts, Practical Lives: Modern Histories of Prosthetics.* New York: New York University Press.
Pelka, Fred. 1997. *The ABC-CLIO Companion to the Disability Rights Movement.* Santa Barbara, CA: ABC-CLIO.

Domestic Architecture

The history of domestic architecture in the United States is marked by the conviction that the design of the private dwelling can mold or influence family life and individual character and, in turn, society at large. With every generation, the conception of the ideal American home changed, and the physical environment of previous generations was altered to suit contemporary needs. What remained constant was, and is, the idealization of the detached dwelling in the country or suburbs and the importance of historic architectural precedents, even as these precedents were disassembled and rearranged to suit anew the landscape and American society.

Colonial Architecture

The first domestic structures built by seventeenth- and eighteenth-century European colonists in North America adapted Native American housing forms. While these housing types differed regionally in style and material, they shared a common architectural philosophy: practical, simple dwellings constructed of abundant local resources. Permanence and increased migration from Europe led to the readoption of the colonists' domestic styles of their homelands. This approach continued the regional distinctiveness of colonial architecture because settlers were clustered by ethnic origin. This inherent regionalism of early American architecture, evident in choices of building elements and materials, has subsequently shaped the study of American domestic architectural history in this period.

The early eighteenth century brought a greater homogeneity in style on the eastern seaboard. This style has since come to be called *Georgian*, after the Hanoverian kings who ruled Great Britain for much of the century. Based on British classicism—often with elements such as columns, pilasters, and pediments—Georgian buildings were typically more symmetrical than their earlier colonial counterparts and were wholly different in scale, with more and larger windows.

Federal and European Revival Styles

A more refined Classical style influenced by the work of British architect Robert Adam (1728–1792) succeeded the Georgian style in the early decades of the new republic and is called *Federal* in the United States. At the same time, the Land Ordinance of 1785 sped the expansion of the country westward by requiring a systematic survey of the national domain. The use of a rectangular grid system in the survey was paralleled by a concomitant subdivision of cities and the development of the row house building type that exploited long, narrow city lots. Yet far from facilitating the egalitarian allotment of land, the grid system made land's commodity value explicit and class divisions became an unmistakable aspect of the built environment.

Invention of the cotton gin in 1793 and the subsequent increase in cotton production meant that slave quarters and large plantation estates became a significant part of landscape of the rural South. Many of the "big houses" were built in the Neoclassical or Greek Revival style, endowing plantation owners with architectural authority over the slave housing, typically small wooden cottages of similar, unadorned style. Although similar to the Federal style, Greek Revival architecture drew from Greek rather than British antecedents; houses were frequently built with the narrow end of the building and the gable ends of the pitched roof turned toward the street to make the second story of the house look like a pediment. In time, the burgeoning American middle class built simpler and smaller homes in this style. Still, through the nineteenth century, home ownership was in reality the privilege of the few, as witnessed by the proliferation of new domestic building types such as the boardinghouses of industrialists' company towns to house their many workers.

The ideal American dwelling was the detached cottage, which by the 1840s was no longer built in the Greek Revival style. Instead, social theorists and architectural pattern book authors such as Andrew Jackson Downing (1815–1852) and Alexander Jackson Davis (1803–1892) argued that Romantic and Gothic styles were in fact better suited as an indigenous American style. Greek Revival was cast as deceitfully decorative

Lyndhurst, a house designed in 1838 and expanded in 1864 by Alexander Jackson Davis, is a Gothic Revival building. With its asymmetrical turrets and picturesque setting overlooking the Hudson River, Lyndhurst offered its inhabitants a life that embodied the architectural styling and romantic outlook of a specific stylistic movement. (Library of Congress)

and formalistic. Stylistic change happened quickly, as pattern book and domestic advice manuals were very popular and influential: For many the home and the family were inseparable, and the power of the home to shape family life was incalculable. The nineteenth-century Gothic and Italianate styles were more informal and picturesque; their irregular footprints and rooflines brought the inside outside and the outside in. This freedom in design permitting asymmetry was further fueled by the material possibilities of the wood- and labor-saving balloon frame introduced in 1833. In cities, this romanticism manifested itself in row houses with cast-iron balconies and homes built of darker stone, with projecting bays adding texture and rhythm to facades. Later archi-

tectural historians such as Vincent Scully would view this period as the beginning of a true American "stick" style: The asymmetrical and picturesque domestic designs during this period would lay the foundation for modern experiments in domestic architectural planning.

Post–Civil War Eclecticism

The period after the Civil War (1861–1865) marked a great diversification of the American built environment due to the social and environmental consequences of greater industrialism. The middle class flocked to the suburbs and to individual dwellings surrounded by nature. These were built in a diversity of styles and colors, some with the elaborate details of the highly textured and asymmetrical Queen Anne style, but all owed a debt to technological innovations in transportation and building materials for their bucolic settings, affording urbanites the opportunity to quit rapidly growing cities. The last decades of the nineteenth century were a time of great immigration to the northern United States both from abroad and among freed slaves from the South. Many of these newcomers were housed in large tenement apartment buildings, most with unsanitary conditions. Urban multifamily living happened at the other end of the economic spectrum too, with much of the upper class clustering in palatial apartment buildings offering numerous amenities, among them units that safeguarded tenant privacy.

Early Twentieth-Century Reform

Social and architectural reformers decried Gilded Age excesses in interior decoration and exterior ornamentation, and the Progressive Era ushered in a period of austere, simple domestic design best exemplified by the bungalow. The bungalow took on regional characteristics and drew not only from the local vernacular but also from the architectural innovations of Prairie school architects such as Frank Lloyd Wright (1867–1959), who opened up house interiors in flowing spaces. Design advances increased the rationalization of the kitchen and bathroom, and more domestic resources were dedicated to sanitation technologies. Many of these simpler houses were built according to kits, domestic manuals, or designs published in magazines like *Craftsman* or the *Ladies' Home Journal*. These structures were built in increasing numbers as many working-class, second-generation European immigrants became able to purchase them.

Post-1945 Housing Boom

Federal government programs constructed large public housing developments in the 1950s and 1960s, providing housing for many inner-city residents displaced by slum clearance and urban renewal schemes. Private suburban housing received even more federal dollars, financing thousands of one-story ranch houses in developer-organized neighborhoods. Still, other modern architecture remained the purview of the very wealthy, in urban apartment buildings and exurban villas, and the very poor in federally financed high-rise buildings. The same period, too, saw a proliferation of alternative housing types, such as the mobile home.

Since the postwar building boom that produced modest-sized house developments like Levittown, New York, contractor-built homes have evolved to the ostentatious "mini mansions" or "McMansions," often incorporating eclectic combinations of historical building elements and complicated rooflines with multiple dormers. What remains constant is the strong attraction of historical building styles and building elements, often simply applied to the facade, and the symbolic importance of the American home. The ideal home remains the middle-class detached dwelling.

Anne Stephenson

See also Apartments, Tenements, and Flats; Architectural History and American Architecture; Boardinghouses; House, Home, and Domesticity; Mobile Homes and Trailer Parks; Planned Communities; Suburbs and Suburbia; Utopian Communities

References and Further Reading

Baxandall, Rosalyn, and Elizabeth Ewen. 2000. *Picture Windows: How the Suburbs Happened.* New York: Basic Books.

Blackmar, Elizabeth. 1989. *Manhattan for Rent, 1785–1850.* Ithaca, NY: Cornell University Press.

Bushman, Richard L. 1992. *The Refinement of America: Persons, Houses, Cities.* New York: Alfred A. Knopf.

Clark, Clifford E., Jr. 1986. *The American Family Home, 1800–1960.* Chapel Hill: University of North Carolina Press.

Cromley, Elizabeth. 1990. *Alone Together: A History of New York's Early Apartments*. Ithaca, NY: Cornell University Press.

Glassie, Henry. 1968. *Pattern in the Material Folk Culture of the Eastern United States*. Philadelphia: University of Pennsylvania Press.

Noble, Allen G. 1984. *Wood, Brick, and Stone: The North American Settlement Landscape*. Amherst: University of Massachusetts Press.

Scully, Vincent. 1971. *The Shingle Style and the Stick Style: Architectural Theory and Design from Richardson to the Origins of Wright*. New Haven, CT: Yale University Press.

Stickley, Gustav. 1979. *The Best of Craftsman Homes*. Santa Barbara, CA: Peregrine Smith.

Vlach, John Michael. 1993. *Back of the Big House: The Architecture of Plantation Slavery*. Chapel Hill: University of North Carolina Press.

Wallis, Allan D. 1991. *Wheel Estate: The Rise and Decline of Mobile Homes*. New York: Oxford University Press.

Wright, Gwendolyn. 1980. *Moralism and the Model Home: Domestic Architecture and Cultural Conflict in Chicago, 1873–1913*. Chicago: University of Chicago Press.

Wright, Gwendolyn. 1981. *Building the Dream: A Social History of Housing in America*. Cambridge, MA: MIT Press.

Dower Right

Known also as the "widow's portion" or "widow's third," a widow's *right of dower* was based in English common law and was a legal practice in the Anglo-American colonies and the United States into the first half of the nineteenth century. A husband could will to his wife any or all of his estate. A widow could invoke her right of dower to contest a will. If a husband died intestate (without a will), however, dower right guaranteed a woman financial support for herself and her minor children. This legal practice allowed a widow the uncontested right to one-third of her deceased husband's real property held during their marriage if there were children, and one-half if there were no children. In cases when the husband died insolvent, the widow's claim to dower held precedent over other creditor obligations.

A widow did not own outright the real property and/or goods assigned to her dower. Married women in early America only very rarely owned permanent title to lands or houses or other "immovables," tools, and farm animals. They owned only personal property such as clothing. Dower extended only for the life of the widow. After her death, the property reverted to her husband's children or creditors.

Documentation of dower right provides fascinating evidence of the historic use of material culture. Not only may historic gender roles be traced but the use of goods, daily living practices, and family relations are also chronicled in these documents. Dower rights were in many instances explicit. Some husbands detailed property and rights of access in terms of goods and space usage for their surviving family members. A widow would not inherit her husband's house, for example; often the eldest son would become the owner, and the house could be occupied by his family as well as the widow. She could be allowed a room or rooms of a house, with access to the cooking hearth and supplies of water, firewood, and food. Living space could be defined so that widows had the right to use certain stairs and passageways, truck a certain garden, and use specific pieces of household furniture. Though such explicit details were likely intended to forestall conflict and confusion, the new arrangements could just as easily extend or exacerbate familial discord.

Dower right as a legal precept declined as states adopted married women's property laws in the first half of the nineteenth century, when property rights generally underwent redefinition as the United States shifted from an agrarian economy based on landed wealth to an industrial economy based on wages and personal property. In 1945 the United States abolished the dower right.

Shirley Teresa Wajda

See also Gender; Heirlooms; Probate Records, Probate Inventories, and Wills

References and Further Reading
Main, Gloria L. 1989. "Widows in Rural Massachusetts on the Eve of Revolution." In *Women in the Age of the American Revolution*, ed. Ronald Hoffman and Peter J. Albert, 67–90. Charlottesville: University Press of Virginia for the United States Capitol Historical Society.
Salmon, Marylynn. 1986. *Women and the Law of Property*. Chapel Hill: University of North Carolina Press.
Ward, Barbara McLean. 1989. "Women's Property and Family Continuity in Eighteenth-Century Connecticut." In *Early American Probate Inventories: The Dublin Seminar for New England Folklife Annual Proceedings, July 11 and 12, 1987*, 74–85. Boston: Boston University.
Wortman, Marlene Stein. 1985. *Women in American Law. Volume I: From Colonial Times to the New Deal*. New York: Holmes & Meier.

Dress, Accessories, and Fashion

Dress, accessories, and *fashion* refer collectively to objects used to cover and adorn the human body and the stylea in which they are made —what might be termed the *material culture of personal apparel*. Other terms include *clothing, garments,* and *raiment. Accessories* are optional items that provide protection or aesthetically enhance clothing: hats, gloves, shoes and boots, fine and costume jewelry, belts, scarves, and ties. *Fashion* is the image created when many people choose to wear clothing in the same aesthetic style or taste. People create this desired appearance with specific clothing and accessories, announc-

ing to the world whether they are "in" or "out" of fashion.

American clothing is most commonly made from textiles. The materials from which textiles (or *fabric*, meaning originally a product of skilled workmanship or manufactured material and now interchangeable with *textile*) are made include natural fibers such as cotton, silk, wool, or leather, and man-made materials (often called *synthetics*) such as rayon, spandex, or nylon. Clothes cover the human body in various ways: the torso and arms (shirts, blouses, and tunics); the lower torso and legs (pants, breeches, and skirts); and upper and lower torso, arms and legs (dresses and robes).

Clothing and accessories provide visual keys to a wearer's identity. Every American, past and present, young and old, rich and poor, wore and still wears clothes. Fashion and clothing thus constitute key evidence of American society and how it changed over time, offering insight not just into personal preference about what people choose to wear each day but also the collective American experience.

History of Dress and Fashion in America

Despite the great diversity of clothing styles used by the many types of indigenous and immigrant peoples of North America, no folk or national costume per se exists in the United States. In the seventeenth and eighteenth centuries, European colonists in North America wore the clothing styles of their native lands, and few European-Americans adopted Native American dress, except for explorers and fur trappers. Native Americans, on the other hand, incorporated European clothing and textiles, in the forms of shirts or blankets, into costume repertoire.

In the eighteenth century, when textiles were expensive and difficult to obtain, clothing immediately marked a person's socioeconomic status. The American colonies, tied to Great Britain through the mercantile system, looked largely to London as the source of fashion. Portraits and prints, created by artists who kept abreast of the latest trends, disseminated new costume styles. Fully dressed fashion dolls were employed by tailors and dressmakers to display and create the latest styles. After Independence, American clothing still relied upon European models, but it also reflected the patriotic search for purely national political values. Americans adopted the "Empire" style popular in Napoleonic France, finding its classical simplicity, in which women wore high-waisted, slender gowns in imitation of Greek robes and men cut their hair like ancient Romans, particularly suitable to their classical democratic principles. At the same time, Americans sentimentalized the hunting shirt, a loose fitting work shirt worn first by American pioneers, then by backwoods Revolutionary War soldiers who wore it as their uniform, as symbolic of American patriotism and pioneer values.

Beginning in the late eighteenth century, but gaining momentum in the second half of the nineteenth century, mechanized textile and clothing production, a large immigrant workforce, the rise of mail order catalogues, the expansion of national transportation systems, and the establishment of department stores in urban centers allowed most Americans, whether living in the city or the country, whether rich or poor, to look more the same than ever before. When it came to fashionable dress, American men continued to look to London for guidance, but women began to look to Paris. The House of Worth was one influential design house that spread its designs in fashion plates. Popular magazines like *Godey's Lady's Book* (1830–1898) published such fashion plates, making them available to a wide range of American consumers.

As the nation expanded and industrialized, its citizens created the world's largest, most quickly expanding ready-to-wear clothing industry. The ready-to-wear clothing industry guaranteed that such ubiquitous clothing staples as the men's tailored business suit and women's wear like shirts and dresses, tweaked stylistically to reflect the latest fashion trends and available in a wide range of prices and fabrics, became readily available for easy purchase to nearly all American consumers. A distinctly American fashion industry arose in the twentieth century, establishing New York City and Los Angeles (particularly Hollywood) as new fashion centers coexisting with London and Paris. Blue jeans, manufactured in the nineteenth century as utilitarian garments created of sturdy denim for Western workmen, in the twentieth century symbolized a glamorized idea of a rugged, relaxed American lifestyle, while fashion magazines and Hollywood movies spread an American cultural aesthetic. Despite this increased communication about fashion trends, Americans in the latter half of the twentieth century sought indivdualized freedom in their sartorial choices. By century's end, the accessibility of the fashion industry and more relaxed social codes allowed for multiple ideas about appropriate, stylish clothing. In the current century, there seem to be more options than ever for wearing clothing and accessories that are "in fashion."

The Fashion System
Fashion may also be defined as a system in which design, style, and taste all play roles in creating sartorial codes designating status. Fashion ranges from expensive *haute couture* (high style) clothing created by designers, shown seasonally on runways, and criticized

by style experts, to street style, clothing ensembles created by ordinary people and displayed daily on urban streets. Scholars debate the history and theory of fashion but generally agree that what characterizes all fashion is constant change. Fashion offers a visual way, through collective clothing patterns, of understanding how people defined their social roles as well as themselves at a particular time and place.

For centuries, fashion has been dismissed as an irrational, frivolous social phenomenon. Yet fashion provides clues to cultural behavior on multiple levels. Many different ideas of what is fashionable can exist simultaneously within the same society, from the individual who uses fashion as a personal statement to the social group that uses fashion to express shared allegiance. Yet over time, fashion, through its sequence of design styles, reveals how behaviors change. Fashion, historically and currently, is of great economic importance. The mass production, distribution, and consumption of fashion, and communication about it, make it an essential means by which to study values through material culture.

Recent studies challenge the view that fashion is a peculiarly Western, modern phenomenon, debating whether it did in fact begin in Europe in the fifteenth-century Burgundian court of Philip the Good (1397–1467). Nevertheless, what is considered fashionable has always been considered innovative or modern, and as such fashion is consistently linked to the modern and urban, distinct from relatively unchanging clothing styles worn in more "traditional" and supposedly rural or preindustrial societies. The fashion system embraces an obsession with change and the new. Fashion can thus be controversial, igniting flashpoint issues for groups from religious fundamentalists (who believe women should hide their bodies with clothing to evince modesty and to avoid tempting men) to feminists (who see fashion as objectifying and eroticizing women and decry it as perpetuating the myth of "feminine" frivolity).

The fashion industry, including textile and clothing manufacturers, designers, shops, advertisers, and magazines, whose profits are fueled by quick changes in style and consumers' willingness to discard clothing before it is worn out, is often associated with Western capitalism. Scholars argue that, since the fashion industry relies on ever-increasing sales to make a profit, it changes dress style to force consumers into a cycle of constant spending. In other words, consumers wear what the fashion industry creates and dictates. Other scholars argue that there is an aesthetic, personal dimension to fashion that economics does not explain, and that the fashion industry does not always originate trends. Indeed, what often starts as counterculture street style (fashion that ordinary people create to make a statement) can become fashionable. The 1990s "grunge" mode, a slovenly, impoverished look of ripped jeans, flannel shirts, big boots, used dresses, and crocheted accessories, originally appeared on teenagers on Seattle's streets. Made visible in mass popular culture by the band Nirvana, grunge style soon appeared on fashion runways.

Interpreting Dress and Accessories

Dress serves many functions, from utilitarian to fashionable, and embodies many meanings, from personal aesthetic to group identity. Clothing both conceals and reveals the body and is capable of providing either modest coverage or erotic display. Clothing provides immediate clues about the wearer. People use clothing to project an image of their selves and how they want others to view them. Often accessories serve as theatrical props to enhance this projected image. Clothing allows people to adopt temporary identities (*disguise*). Among the social identities clothing can reveal are socioeconomic class (through status markers like designer labels and costly textiles); occupation (particularly with those in uniform, like nuns or police officers); politics (as with 1960s hippies, whose jeans, long hair, and fringed vests announced their leftist politics); social agendas (for example, people wearing the inverted red "V" AIDS ribbons); religion (from the dark, "old-fashioned" clothes of the Amish to the veiled robes of Muslim women); ethnicity (through folk costume, in particular); and nationality (through military uniforms or wearing a T-shirt with an American flag).

Dress and accessories also announce whether an individual conforms to or resists social standards for behavior. In the contemporary United States, clothing is more androgynous than ever before, with both men and women commonly wearing jeans, for example. Yet the United States, like most societies, has a history of using clothing to distinguish the sexes, and despite current androgynous fashions, American society still uses clothing to mark the wearer as male or female. American men who dress "in drag," wearing clothing and accessories traditionally reserved for women, like dresses and high heels, announce their defiance of social conventions about gender-appropriate fashion.

Zara Anishanslin Bernhardt

See also African America; Children's Dress; Child's Body; Etiquette and Manners; Gender; Human Body; Military Dress; Mourning; Mourning and Ethnicity; Native America; Religious Dress; Social Class and Social Status; Style; Textiles

References and Further Reading

Baumgarten, Linda. 2002. *What Clothes Reveal: The Language of Clothing in Colonial and Federal America: The Colonial Williamsburg Collection.* Williamsburg, VA: Colonial Williamsburg Foundation.

Cunningham, Patricia A., and Susan Voso Lab, eds. 1993. *Dress in American Culture.* Bowling Green, OH: Bowling Green State University Popular Press.

Davis, Fred. 1992. *Fashion, Culture, and Identity.* Chicago: University of Chicago Press.

De La Haye, Amy, and Elizabeth Wilson, eds. 1999. *Defining Dress: Dress as Object, Meaning, and Identity.* Manchester, UK: Manchester University Press.

De Marly, Diana. 1990. *Dress in North America.* New York: Holmes & Meier.

Kidwell, Claudia Brush, and Margaret C. Christman. 1974. *Suiting Everyone: The Democratization of Clothing in America.* Washington, DC: Smithsonian Institution Press.

Kidwell, Claudia Brush, and Valerie Steele. 1989. *Men and Women: Dressing the Part.* Washington, DC: Smithsonian Institution Press.

Rubinstein, Ruth P. 2001. *Dress Codes: Meanings and Messages in American Culture.* Boulder, CO: Westview Press.

Simmel, Georg. 1904. "Fashion." *International Quarterly* 10 (October): 130–155.

Wilson, Elizabeth. 2003. *Adorned in Dreams: Fashion and Modernity.* New Brunswick, NJ: Rutgers University Press.

E

Eastlake Style

The writings of English architect Charles Locke Eastlake (1836–1908) are credited with the introduction into the United States of a reform aesthetic in interior and architectural design. Known as the *Eastlake* style as well as the *Modern Gothic* style, this popular style rejected what Eastlake, following the aesthetic principles of English art critics and theorists William Morris (1834–1896) and John Ruskin (1819–1900), considered overwrought design, especially evident in heavily carved, machine-made furniture. In his widely influential treatise, *Hints on Household Taste in Furniture, Upholstery and Other Details*, published first in England in 1868 and then in the United States in 1872, Eastlake argued for the adaptation of medieval and Japanese designs to domestic material culture. Flat surfaces, incised motifs, geometric shapes, and fretwork (all easily created and duplicated by machine), Eastlake reasoned, created healthier environments by creating furniture that was more easily cleaned than the ornate furnishings favored by Americans. Eastlake also counseled against the overuse of textiles, especially in heavy furniture upholstery,

window treatments, and doorway drapery (*portiéres*). Last, he asserted that such "artistic" environments uplifted their inhabitants and honored the labor (whether handcrafted or machine made) that produced such environments. This statement reflected the philosophy of the later Arts and Crafts Movement.

Eastlake's treatise was but one of a great number of "household art manuals" that appeared in the United States in the last third of the nineteenth century. Rising living standards, especially for the American middle classes, created more leisure time for American families to pursue refinement in art and culture. The American middle-class dwelling was redefined as an art palace, one in which the family displayed its good taste and dedication to aesthetic pursuits through collections of art, sculpture, and books. Women's embroidery and other handicrafts symbolized aesthetic self-expression, though it was machine-made goods easily and abundantly available through department stores, mail order catalogues, and other retailers that filled American houses. To his dismay, Eastlake noted that his advice about simplicity and elegance was ignored by American

Charles Locke Eastlake's Hints on Household Taste in Furniture, Upholstery and Other Details, *published in the United States in 1872, popularized the new "Eastlake style." This marble and walnut Eastlake table, based on Japanese and medieval motifs, featured machine-made flat surfaces, incised motifs, geometric shapes and fretwork. (Illinois State Museum)*

manufacturers, who adapted his name to their lines of elaborately decorated "art furniture" and home furnishings.

Shirley Teresa Wajda

See also Aesthetic Movement, Arts and Crafts Movement; Interior Design; Style

References and Further Reading
Eastlake, Charles L. 1984 (1868). *Hints on Household Taste in Furniture, Upholstery and Other Details*, rpt. ed. Salem, NH: Ayer.
Madigan, Mary Jean Smith. 1975. "The Influence of Charles Locke Eastlake on American Furniture Manufacture, 1870–1890." *Winterthur Portfolio* 10 (1): 1–22.
McClaugherty, Martha Crabill. 1983. "Household Art: Creating the Artistic Home, 1868–1893." *Winterthur Portfolio* 18 (1): 1–26.

Education and Schooling

Americans have historically been educated in a variety of physical settings and with an even wider variety of tools for learning. *School* refers to a place of formal teaching and learning, as opposed to the many casual occasions and places in which knowledge is imparted and gained. School buildings are the most recognizable of the public structures in the nation's cities, towns, and villages. Many communities boast the survival of an iconic "one-room schoolhouse," linking individual communities with the past through the collective memory of shared learning experiences. American artists such as New York's Ezra Ames (1768–1836) portrayed in single and family portraits children's roles as students, as in *The Fondey Family* (1803). In the late nineteenth century, Winslow Homer (1836–1910) depicted the classroom in *The Country School* (1871) and *The Blackboard* (1877), replete with chalkboard drawing method. Homer's *Snap the Whip* (1872) memorializes childhood play in the yards of one-room red schoolhouses. The consistent linkage of the local elementary or high school with citizenship and national identity is maintained through the building's educative purpose and its use as a public meeting place, community center, emergency shelter, and sports arena.

The material aspects of the nation's efforts in education, from buildings, furniture, and books to playground equipment, reveal much about the nature and practice of schooling. As Richard McClintock and Jean McClintock (1968, 60) observe, "Designs for classrooms not only tell us much about the didactic means that were used therein; they also reveal the essence of the pedagogy that directed the educative efforts of past times." The establishment of schools separated education from the family dwelling and from the workplace and required trained professionals. By the first decade of the twentieth century, education administration was a profession, itself the result not of experience in the classroom but a college degree.

Colonial Efforts

Efforts to educate children were varied and sporadic in the colonial era. Very young children (some as young as three) attended private dame schools run by women in their homes, in which students learned the basics of reading, considered critical to religious practice through access to the Bible. Students learned their lessons by using a hornbook (a single page tacked to a wood paddle and covered by a thin, transparent sheet of horn) on which the alphabet and the Lord's Prayer were printed. Hornbooks were imported from England.

Primers were imported and published in the colonies, providing instruction in reading and religion. The best-known primer, the *New England Primer*, first published in the late seventeenth century, was still being printed into the 1830s. The Psalter (Book of Psalms), the New Testament, and the Bible were other texts to be mastered by colonial students. Other basic books of instruction included spellers (becoming Americanized by Noah Webster's 1783 *Blue Back Speller*), and in the eighteenth century, penmanship manuals. Rote instruction, recitation, and copying were the means of learning.

Through the rest of the century, schools were founded throughout the thirteen original colonies, often through Protestant denominations and through colonial law, led by Massachusetts Bay's reading law in 1642

and the colony's schooling law of 1647, which required townships of fifty families or more to provide a schoolmaster to teach children to read and write. Those townships populated by a hundred or more families were required to provide a Latin grammar school. Latin grammar schools were established to teach boys as young as six classical languages such as Latin, Greek, and Hebrew through which to interpret the Bible as well as prepare for admission to colleges and for professional and public service. Boston Latin School was opened in 1635, followed by similar schools in other port towns.

New grammar schools, writing schools, and private academies throughout the eighteenth century were established to teach subjects and skills useful to the growing mercantile economy: penmanship (shifting to "running hand" to facilitate quick copying by clerks), arithmetic and trigonometry, geography and natural sciences, history and philosophy, and modern languages. In the southern colonies, private tutors (often college students on vacation) taught in schoolhouses located on plantations.

Schooling in the Early Republic

Education was considered a primary means by which the ideals of the American Revolution could be passed from one generation to the next. The constitutions of the first thirteen states provided for public schools. The townships laid out in the five states that would be carved from the Northwest Territory would also set aside land on which to construct a public (known also as *district*, *grammar*, or *common*) school.

Private academies for boys had been established in the eighteenth century throughout New England and the Middle Colonies. Private female seminaries were founded in remarkable numbers in the fifty years after the American Revolution, symbolizing and enacting the more egalitarian philosophy of the nation's founders. These schools, at which students often boarded, were private, and they were prized by the towns in which they were located. Often run by women, female seminaries such as Miss (Sarah) Porter's School (Farmington, Connecticut) or Emma Willard's Troy Female Seminary (Troy, New York) offered courses in botany, arithmetic, and French. Feminine gentility was not overlooked: Female seminarians also learned drawing, needlework, and music. Schoolgirls' needlework in the forms of samplers, mourning pictures, maps, and globes exemplify this purpose. Cities with rising populations, such as New York and Philadelphia, adopted the ideas of Englishman Joseph Lancaster (1778–1838). Schoolrooms in Lancastrian schools accommodated up to 250 students. This "monitorial" method required that students leave their desks and move around the room to recite their lessons in front of chalk boards at which monitors heard their recitations.

Public schoolhouses were not only sites of learning; they were sites of protest as well. Boys in rural districts, for example, invoked Revolutionary rhetoric when they seized the schoolhouse from the schoolmaster. Arriving early for instruction, boys barred windows and doors to prevent the schoolmaster (and others) from entering the building. Demands for more recess, less schoolwork, and less use of corporal punishment for infractions were often the reasons for such actions. (Discipline had been enforced by ferrule or rod.) If the schoolmaster could not regain control of the schoolhouse in a timely fashion, he was usually dismissed by the community, which paid his salary and often provided room and board. Frequently schoolmasters were college students; by the end of the nineteenth century the nation's teachers were primarily women.

In the 1820s and 1830s, the common school was a topic of great interest throughout the nation. Educational reformers such as Horace Mann (1796–1859) and Catharine E. Beecher (1800–1878) argued for smaller rooms dividing students by age or achievement (thus *classrooms*) and better building design (often imitating private dwellings) to promote learning. Henry Barnard's (1811–1900) oft-published and updated *School Architecture* (1838), for example, included discussion of schoolhouse design as well as of the classroom equipment necessary for proper instruction and the inculcation of citizenship and moral virtue. Another educational reformer, A. Bronson Alcott (1799–1888), included in his classroom sculptured busts of Socrates, William Shakespeare, John Milton, and Walter Scott. Alcott and others argued against the use of the rod or other forms of physical punishment. The care of the child's body, as well as the education of his or her mind, was considered by these reformers. Proper spaces for education, including appropriately sized desks instead of benches (forms); child-sized tools; and well-lit, -ventilated, and -heated buildings were discussed. Gymnastics and other exercises were considered critical to the curriculum. School grounds were to be parklike, with trees and beautiful plants.

Barnard chronicled contemporary conditions of school buildings in his attempt to remedy what he saw as an inadequate environment. Villages and towns across the new nation were using dilapidated structures intended for other uses: An abandoned log cabin and a pig sty were used in several communities in Ohio's Western Reserve. Barnard counseled ventilation, heating, and sanitation systems, appropriate furniture and light, teacher's aids and libraries, as well as the employment of the Greek Revival style as proper to these "temples" of education. Windows were built at a level above the seated child's sight line to reinforce his or her focus on the lesson. Schoolchildren learned from the physical environment as much as they learned from their books and their teachers. Barnard's pattern book influenced much of the nation's public school building before the Civil War (1861–1865).

Late Nineteenth-Century Change

By the 1850s school buildings in many American cities were altered from large study halls with adjoining recitation rooms to smaller classrooms that divided students by grade (based on age and achievement) and facilitated more specialized instruction. This was a response to rising immigration from foreign nations and from the countryside. Architect Samuel Sloan's (1815–1884) "Philadelphia Plan" departed from Barnard's design of a large classroom connected to smaller rooms. Sloan proposed classrooms of equal size, each with movable partitions to create one large space. Despite the arguments of rationality and efficiency, such designs were often changed to accommodate costs—American taxpayers possess a history of endorsing public education through local boards of education but resisting its high price in taxation. Many rural communities resisted these reordered spaces. In 1920, the nation still counted nearly 200,000 one-room schoolhouses. (Religious sects such as the Amish use one-room schoolhouses today.) Still, the placement of schoolhouses and the extension of the school year into the planting and harvesting seasons reveal the importance of education to Americans.

Alternately designed as domestic dwellings or factories in the first half of the nineteenth century, schoolhouses in the latter half of the nineteenth century were constructed in many architectural styles and adorned with

meaningful sculptures. Protestant boarding schools adopted the Gothic Revival style, indicative of these schools' mission to prepare their students for college but also testifying through style notions of tradition. Public secondary (high) schools were often the largest buildings in a town, indicating the importance of democratic values—at least for white students. The number of schools established by the Freedman's Bureau for ex-slaves in the Reconstruction South spoke to the widespread belief in education as a tool of democracy and social and economic advancement. Nevertheless, Jim Crow legislation in the South segregated African Americans and whites into separate schools, while Northern communities often had racially segregated schools as well. Despite federal legislation and Supreme Court decisions such as *Brown v. The Board of Education of Topeka, Kansas* (1954), residential restrictions and patterns throughout the nation continue to reinforce historic segregation of schools.

Twentieth-Century Consolidation

By the beginning of the twentieth century, Progressive educators and individual communities fought over the proper environment for schooling as they agreed that schoolhouses should serve as a primary site of community life. New York City reformer Jacob Riis (1849–1914), for example, argued that proper school structures and adjacent playgrounds would eradicate the slum and its ills. Child labor laws and compulsory education statutes required more years of schooling as well as more subjects. High schools, for both boys and girls, had been established by the 1840s. Standardization of school buildings accompanied consolidation of separate one-room schoolhouses into districts in which new elementary and high schools were built. City school buildings were enlarged. Building codes were observed to ensure health and safety, and by the 1930s these structures had indoor plumbing and electricity. Architectural design incorporated sculpture and other artwork to instill morality, aesthetic sensibilities, and civic ideals.

The size of both elementary and high school buildings grew dramatically in the twentieth century, accommodating more students and services. Science laboratories, home economics kitchens, industrial shops, libraries, art studios, gymnasiums and locker rooms, music rooms and auditoriums, cafeterias, and playgrounds accommodated the many curricular and extracurricular activities of students, teachers, and community members. In urban and rural schools students created cabinets of natural specimens (leaves, insects, rocks, and shells), art galleries, and other collections through which to learn the lessons increasingly supplied by specialized textbooks and teachers. This "social efficiency" pleased reformer John Dewey (1859–1952), who argued that the schoolhouse should reflect the diverse society outside its walls. Educators called for flexible spaces to accommodate continuously the changes modern society demanded of student and citizen alike. Classroom specialization allowed self-directed individual and group activities. By the 1960s, the "open classroom," especially in kindergarten and elementary grades, was adopted to facilitate children's curiosity and self-development.

As symbolic centers for democracy, the nation's schools have always been sites of contest for equal rights for African Americans, women, Native Americans, and immigrants. Nevertheless, dilapidated school buildings, outdated books, and a lack of services and learning tools continue to give evidence of institutionalized racial discrimination in the nation. Some social critics, such as Jonathan Kozol, argue that the broken desks and windows and other material signs of social neglect he saw in his teaching days in one of Boston's inner-city schools signal a failure of American democracy.

Schoolyards and Playgrounds
"Recess," for many students, was the best time of the day. Away from the discipline imposed by the teacher and by the schoolroom, children could enjoy the freedom of running and shouting, visiting, and talking with each other. The rules of informal games and sports were passed along from older students to younger students. Still, adults understood that learning took place in play; early twentieth-century Progressive reformers instituted the "play movement" to build suitable areas in which children could exercise and enjoy games and sports in safe areas. Baseball diamonds; football fields; volleyball and tennis courts; and sandboxes, swings, merry-go-rounds, and climbing apparatus became standard equipment of the majority of schools in the United States.

Colleges and Universities
The English colonists of North America established colleges primarily for the preparation of ministers. The first, Harvard College, was founded in 1636 (though none of the original buildings remain). The founders of colleges and universities sought to create campuses (instead of yards) conducive to education and the specific missions of their institutions. Thomas Jefferson's (1743–1826) design for the University of Virginia (1825), for example, gathered faculty and students into a Neoclassical "academical village" around a lawn and facing the library, which he termed the "temple of knowledge." The New England town concept was applied to campuses of colleges founded in the 1860s: Frederick Law Olmsted (1822–1903) employed

this concept for his designs for Amherst College (Massachusetts) and the University of Maine at Orono, but also for Gallaudet University in Washington DC and the University of California, Berkeley. Gothicism and other revival styles mark the form of academic buildings in the latter half of the nineteenth century. The rise of architecture as a profession taught by universities facilitated the trend for architect-designed campus buildings for administration, galleries, classrooms, faculty offices, laboratories, libraries, and student dormitories by the end of the century. The phenomenal growth of the nation's institutions of higher education led to extraordinary, if at times haphazard, building throughout the twentieth century. For example, temporary housing such as Quonset huts was used by the returning soldiers who had enrolled in college under the 1944 Servicemen's Readjustment Act (GI Bill of Rights). The baby boom of the 1950s and 1960s also led to massive construction projects on numerous campuses. By the end of the twentieth century, many universities and colleges had become outdoor museums of clashing architectural styles, at times mirroring the debates about learning that are taking place inside campus classrooms and dormitories.

Shirley Teresa Wajda

See also Adolescence; African America; Architectural History and American Architecture; Books; Childhood; Children's Material Culture; Children's Toys; Civic Architecture; Classical Revival (Neoclassicism); Gothic Revival; Native America

References and Further Reading
Baker, Jean. 1985. "From Belief into Culture: Republicanism in the Antebellum North." *American Quarterly* 37 (4): 532–550.
Cavallo, Dominic. 1981. *Muscles and Morals: Organized Playgrounds and Urban Reform, 1880–1920*. Philadelphia: University of Pennsylvania Press.
Cooledge, Harold N. 1964. "Samuel Sloan and the 'Philadelphia Plan.'" *Journal of the Society of Architectural Historians* 23 (2): 151–154.
Cutler, William W., III. 1989. "Cathedral of Culture: The Schoolhouse in American Educational Thought and Practice since 1820." *History of Education Quarterly* 29 (1): 1–40.
Horowitz, Helen Lefkowitz. 1984. *Alma Mater: Design and Experience in the Women's Colleges from their Nineteenth Century Beginnings to the 1930s*. New York: Alfred A. Knopf.
Kaestle, Carl F. 1973. *The Evolution of an Urban School System: New York City, 1750–1850*. Cambridge, MA: Harvard University Press.
McClintock, Robert, and Jean McClintock. 1968. "Architecture and Pedagogy." *Journal of Aesthetic Education* 2 (4): 59–77.
Monaghan, E. Jennifer. 1988. "Literacy Instruction and Gender in Colonial New England." *American Quarterly* 40 (1): 18–41.
Ring, Betty. 1993. *Girlhood Embroidery: American Samplers and Pictorial Needlework, 1650–1850*. New York: Alfred A. Knopf.
Turner, Paul Venable. 1984. *Campus: An American Planning Tradition*. Cambridge, MA: MIT Press.

Empire Style

The American *Empire style* (1815–1840) derives from the French Empire style (1804–1814), which, under the rubric of Neoclassicism, originated with Napoleon I (1769–1821) as he established a national style to reinforce his image as emperor and draw parallels between the power and grandeur of France and the ancient Roman Empire. American Empire was not a replication but rather an adaptation of European influences with a clear American character. While the style served to link the United States' developing national identity with the traditions of classic Greek and Roman cultures, prosperous Americans adopted the style as an expression of their wealth and taste; early industrialization of the furniture trade created affordable versions for the expanding, increasingly affluent middle class.

This carved mahogany settee, attributed to New York City furniture maker Duncan Phyfe, exemplifies the early-to-mid-nineteenth-century Empire style in the United States. Empire style furniture featured massive forms, bold profiles, simplified shapes, and sculptural ornament, often with scroll or animal feet, saber or splayed legs, and scrolled arms. (Christie's Images/Corbis)

The two main exponents of the Empire style in the United States were Duncan Phyfe (1768–1854) and Charles-Honoré Lannuier (1779–1819). Scottish-born Phyfe produced high-quality furniture influenced by both English and French Neoclassical designs, and French-born Lannuier introduced a mix of Louis XVI style and early Empire styles, tailored to American tastes. The Empire style emboldened the delicate forms of Neoclassical style with massive, overscale forms, reliant on bold profiles, simplified shapes, and sculptural ornament. Furniture characteristics included highly polished rosewood and mahogany, gilded-bronze mounts, pillared supports, marble tops, scroll or animal feet, saber or splayed legs, scrolled arms, gilt-stenciling and lyre-shaped back splats; seating furniture was inspired by ancient Greek *klismos* and Roman *curule* chairs. Interiors featured classically inspired architectural elements, festooned silk draperies, and decorative objects ornamented with classical motifs including acanthus leaves, cornucopias, dolphins, anthemion, palmettes, and rosettes.

Elizabeth A. Williams

See also Classical Revival (Neoclassicism); Decorative Arts; Style

References and Further Reading
Cooper, Wendy A. 1980. *In Praise of America: American Decorative Arts, 1650–1830: Fifty Years of Discovery since the 1929 Girl Scouts Loan Exhibition.* New York: Alfred A. Knopf.
Cooper, Wendy A. 1993. *Classical Taste in America, 1800–1840.* Baltimore, MD: Baltimore Museum of Art; New York: Abbeville.
Fairbanks, Jonathan L., and Elizabeth Bidwell Bates. 1981. *American Furniture, 1620 to the Present.* New York: R. Marek.
Kirk, John T. 2000. *American Furniture: Understanding Styles, Construction, and Quality.* New York: Harry N. Abrams.

Ephemera

The definition of *ephemera* is as wide ranging as the material culture it describes.

Derived from the Greek word *ephemeron*, meaning short lived or transitory, the plural form *ephemera* most often refers to printed matter that is produced for a specific purpose, then discarded when that purpose is achieved. According to ephemera expert Maurice Rickards (1970, 9), "the word, ephemera, is used to denote the transient everyday items of paper . . . vital when they are needed, wastepaper immediately after. They flourish for a moment and are done."

Given this definition, the collection and study of ephemera may appear to many to be an eccentric and unnecessary undertaking. Yet an article of ephemera serves not only its immediate use. "Above and beyond its immediate purpose it expresses a fragment of social history . . ." (Rickards 1970, 10). The wide variety of printed matter—bookplates and bookmarks, paper currency and tax stamps, trade cards, business cards, mourning cards, visiting cards, business stationery, posters, reward notices, almanacs and calendars, broadsides and broadsheets, advertisements, bookplates, campaign buttons; event programs, playbills, leaflets and pamphlets, greeting cards, postcards, certificates of merit, labels, election ballots, brochures, paper dolls and soldiers, photographs, menus, sheet music, tickets, fanzines, political campaign signs, and more—constitutes an undercollected and understudied body of historical evidence of the everyday life, concerns, and interests of Americans.

Ephemera itself is a product of technology and represents the rise of industrial capitalism in what would become the United States. Broadsides—single sheets of paper printed only on one side—were produced by printers in the colonies of North America. Broadsides communicated official proclamations, news, advertisements, and public notices in public squares and markets, on buildings, and in taverns. Other broadsides of verses and ballads were sold by traveling "chapmen" (*chap* meaning cheap) for popular entertainment. The introduction of a display typeface in the first decade of the nineteenth century, accompanied by the innovations of steel engraving, lithography, and printing presses by mid-century, guaranteed Americans' continued attention to the increasing number of broadsides, broadsheets, advertisements, and posters around them. The use of wood pulp rather than textiles to create paper expanded exponentially the availability and usages of printed matter. Throughout the nineteenth century and into the twentieth, print technology ensured the rise of business through the ability to reproduce uniformly and in quantity logos, brands, trademarks, and other information of commerce, from a corporation's letterhead to the trade cards that that corporation offered storeowners to sell its goods to the use of media other than paper (metals, plastics, even T-shirts) to convey a corporation's identity and message.

These scraps of paper, the "stuff" of daily life, have enchanted Americans. In the latter half of the nineteenth century the collecting phenomenon was abetted by the production of "scraps" intentionally created for inclusion in scrapbooks. "Postal carditis" was a humorous "mania" affecting many Americans from about 1890 until the 1920s. Changes in federal policy and inexpensive photography and reproduction methods allowed Americans to indulge cheaply in the trade and collection of postcards. The rise of professional sports in the twentieth century led to the introduction and continuing popularity of trading cards of sports figures. The continuing fascination with the mundane and the incidental has been humorously captured in the creation and popularity of *Found* magazine (http://www.foundmagazine .com), though the editors have extended the definition of ephemera to include the hand-written as well as altered printed matter in their exploration of "someone else's life." Melancholy, rather than humor, is the leitmotif of the 2004 documentary film *Other People's Pictures* (directed by Cabot Philbrick and Lorca Shepperd), which explores collectors who "rescue" the memory of those anonymous individuals depicted in photographs at New York City's Chelsea Flea Market. Scholars have also turned to *vernacular photography* to include amateur work as well as commercial photography that has been traditionally neglected. "Scrapbooking" has experienced a renaissance in the early twenty-first century.

Anyone who has traded baseball cards, saved birthday cards, or created albums of printed matter dedicated to an event or a life has been a collector of ephemera. Collectors of ephemera range from hobbyists to amateurs to archivists and librarians. Indeed, it is the fact of the collection itself that lends value to these scraps by allowing for the sustained study of what was once deemed trivial, mundane, or incidental. Collectors often specialize in one form of ephemera, and this is reflected in the large collections donated to major archives, museums, and libraries that in turn have expanded collection policies to include the acquisition and care of ephemera.

Shirley Teresa Wajda

See also Advertisements and Advertising; Collecting and Collections; Fanzines; Graphic Design; Mail Order Catalogues; Music Ephemera; Political Ephemera; Popular Culture; Print Culture; Printmaking and American Prints; Scrapbooks; Souvenirs; Trade Cards; Trade Catalogues

References and Further Reading
Garvey, Ellen Gruber. 1996. *The Adman in the Parlor: Magazines and the Gendering of Consumer Culture, 1880s–1910s*. New York: Oxford University Press.

Rickards, Maurice. 1970. *This Is Ephemera: Collecting Printed Throwaways*. Brattleboro, VT: Gossamer Press.
Rickards, Maurice, and Michael Twyman, eds. 2000. *The Encyclopedia of Ephemera: A Guide to the Fragmentary Documents of Everyday Life for the Collector, Curator, and Historian*. London: British Library; New York: Routledge.
Roylance, Dale. 1992. *Graphic Americana: The Art and Technique of Printed Ephemera from Abecedaires to Zoetropes*. Princeton, NJ: Princeton University Library.

Ethnicity

Ethnicity, a concept applied to groups or communities who share or are perceived to share a common identity, often shapes material culture. Ethnicity is notoriously difficult to define, not least because ethnic cultural practices are always evolving and changing. The basis for such groupings can be varied, including common ancestry, history, cultural practices, language, and place of birth. Ethnicity has been a central concern for scholars of American material culture, who analyze artifacts produced in a society marked by immigration, slavery, and colonization. Early work on the subject in sociology and anthropology tended to focus on acculturation and assimilation: It was assumed that contact between groups would eventually result in a lessening of cultural distinctions. More recently, scholars of American material culture have specialized in one ethnic group's creation of and engagement with material culture. In particular, they have sought to identify specific groups with distinctive cultural traditions, considering the signs and symbols that act as markers of ethnic identity.

Historical Usage of the Term

The first recorded use of *ethnicity* to refer to a variety of social practices that identify a community and group is in sociologist

W. Lloyd Warner's (1898–1970) *Yankee City Series* (1941). This term is derived from *ethnic*, which derives from the Greek *ethnos*, referring to a people or a nation. Sociologist Max Weber (1864–1920) observed in 1922 that ethnic groups are often based upon a subjective interpretation of difference: Individuals identify with others as a result of perceived common interests or ancestry not necessarily grounded in objective fact. Weber suggests that ethnic groups often act as interest groups rather than simply as communities united by a shared history or culture. During the 1940s and 1950s, when assimilation was the dominant paradigm for exploring ethnicity, the term was used to refer to European immigrants and their descendants: for example, Jewish Americans, Irish Americans, and Italian Americans. Since the 1960s, *ethnicity* has also been deployed more broadly: It is now regularly used with reference to Native Americans and African Americans, albeit with the caveat that these groups be analyzed in the context of their specific histories of colonization and enslavement.

To complicate matters, *ethnicity* has been defined differently in various disciplines that bear on American material culture. In sociology, discussions of ethnicity have pivoted on an opposition between ethnicity and assimilation: The persistence of ethnic identities and cultural practices has been set against an assumption that ethnic groups will gradually blend into "mainstream" American culture. The tenor of this debate is perhaps most vividly illustrated by a comparison between two Jewish American writers: Israel Zangwill (1864–1926) and Horace M. Kallen (1882–1974). In his play *The Melting-Pot* (1909), Zangwill foresees a future of cultural unity, where distinct ethnic identities and ethnic tensions will dissolve in the crucible of America, while Kallen's cultural pluralism, in his essay "Democracy versus the Melting-Pot: A Study of American Nationality" (1915), makes room for an element of cultural and racial diversity. Kallen tackles the issue of how to create a national identity out of assorted individuals who possess very different cultural, ancestral, geographical, and linguistic backgrounds. Posing the question of how to balance the need to avoid a "cacophony" with the demands of democracy, he rethinks American identity to represent the nation as an orchestra divided into sections, "a multiplicity in a unity" (Kallen 1996, 92).

Sociologist Robert E. Park (1864–1944) believed assimilation was an inevitable process. He argued that all interethnic relations follow a four-stage pattern of contact, competition, accommodation, and assimilation. This concern with assimilation cast a long shadow on the discipline. When sociologists of the 1960s studied the "ethnic revival" of that period, their discussions were often inflected by the earlier debate. Nathan Glazer and Daniel Patrick Moynihan (1927–2003) famously declared that the melting pot "did not happen" (Glazer and Moynihan 1963, xcvii). They were not suggesting that the African Americans, Puerto Ricans, Jews, Italians, and Irish of New York had retained static or eternal identities unaffected by their experiences in the American city; rather, they argued that ethnic identities persisted in new forms.

In anthropology, more emphasis has been placed on the processes of group formation and the maintenance of ethnic identities. In *Old Societies and New States* (1963), Clifford Geertz (1926–2006) claims that certain kinds of bonds, such as family, ethnicity, and race, are primordial. By this he means that ethnicity is not primarily determined by external circumstances; instead, such ties have their roots in an emotional sense of belonging that is taken to be a fundamental and unquestioned part of individual and collective identity. Geertz's suggestion that ethnicity is something static and eternal could be contrasted with the more fluid and malleable definition of the term that emerges in Fredrik Barth's *Ethnic Groups and Boundaries: The Social Organization of Cultural Difference* (1969). Crucially, Barth challenges the notion that an ethnic group can be defined as possessing a distinctive and identifiable culture. Instead, he argues that the most important aspect of ethnicity is the construction of cultural, mental, and social boundaries that mark distinct groups. From such a perspective, the ethnic boundary, the sense of us versus them, defines the group, not the cultural attributes it encloses. Indeed, for Barth, contact between ethnic groups serves to sharpen ethnic distinctions as groups define themselves one against the other.

Contemporary definitions of ethnicity have also been heavily influenced by the political activism of marginalized ethnic groups in the 1960s. Particularly as a result of African American protest, a new understanding of ethnicity emerged, which recognized the extent to which cultural practices could be mobilized to articulate resistance to the dominant political system. The Black Power movement, with its slogans such as "black is beautiful," was not only a militant political group but it also placed cultural revival at the heart of its agenda. Explicitly attacking the logic of assimilation and white cultural supremacy, African Americans manipulated distinctive markers of their cultural identity, such as the Afro and dress, rethinking the relationship between material culture and politics. This notion of cultural resistance reverberated beyond the African American community. For example, the control of cultural artifacts in museums was central to the Native American Red Power

movement. In the wake of these campaigns, material culture could no longer be viewed as a static marker of identity; rather, it became an expressive resource that could be mobilized to signify resistance or alternative allegiance.

Scholars of American material culture have drawn on these key theories, among others, to define ethnicity according to the needs of their particular disciplines. For example, because it is difficult to draw conclusions about affective ties and self-identity from archaeological finds, archaeologists have often focused upon structural markers of ethnicity, such as geographical location. In folklore studies, theorists have incorporated ethnicity into studies of groups defined by linguistics and region. No matter how individual scholars define ethnicity, the problem of its relation to race has been a central concern.

Ethnicity and Race

In the 1940s, *ethnicity* was conceived as a more neutral substitute for the word *race*, a term tainted by its association with fascism. Race has often been seen in contradistinction to ethnicity: Whereas concepts of race stem from perceptions of physiological or biological difference, *ethnicity* is usually defined with reference to cultural parameters. It is important to point out that race has been discredited as an ideological construction, and this means that it is now more often defined in social and political terms. That said, despite the intellectual deconstruction of race as a term based in biological fact, racial categorizations endure.

Michael Omi and Howard Winant, in their *Racial Formation in the United States from the 1960s to the 1980s* (1986), argue that race is a powerful concept of social organization in the United States: While ethnicity is a marker of cultural identification, race offers a theoretical vocabulary through which to grapple with the structural features of racial oppression. Moreover, Omi and Winant raise concerns about the way ethnicity elides the roles of groups that have faced entrenched racism, such as Asian Americans, with immigrants of European origin and their descendants. Indeed, some critics have felt compelled to coin new terms to distinguish between the "voluntary" ethnicity of whites, who can choose whether to identify with their heritage, and groups such as African Americans, Asian Americans, and Native Americans, who have what sociologist Joane Nagel has called "mandatory ethnicity" imposed upon them, an ethnicity that not only ties them to their particular group but also incurs a level of social and political disadvantage.

Ethnicity and Material Culture

Any survey of literature on the theory of ethnicity demonstrates that the relationship between ethnicity and material culture is far from straightforward. A brief overview of one aspect of the study of ethnic groups' consumption of material culture, ethnic foodways, offers a snapshot of recent theorizations of the term.

Studies of African American food have revealed that a diet shaped by experiences of marginalization and poverty came to symbolize resistance to the dominant culture. Bessie Smith's blues song "Gimme a Pigfoot and a Bottle of Beer" is only one example of the way in which African Americans celebrated foods deigned to be inferior by whites (Warnes 2004, 161). If food was often bound up with cultural resistance for African Americans, the development of a distinctive Italian American cuisine cannot be understood without reference to class dynamics. Food had been scarce for peasants in Italy, but once in the United States, they imitated the styles of the rich who had dominated their

lives, converting the food of the elite into a marker of ethnic pride. By contrast, despite rich cultural traditions in music, dance, theater, and storytelling, food did not play a significant role in the construction of Irish American identity. To some extent, this can be explained by the association of foods such as the potato with famine and colonial oppression, but it also exposes an important relationship between ethnic traditions and gender roles. Women often act as transmitters of culture or carriers of cultural tradition. It could be argued that the high proportion of Irish American women in domestic service worked to dissociate food from ethnicity: Women learned American styles of cookery that altered their cooking habits at home, interfering with their role in preserving and maintaining a distinctive ethnic cuisine. Finally, in his study of Jewish American material culture, *Adapting to Abundance* (1990), Andrew Heinze adds a different inflection to the discussion: He shows the extent to which Jewish Americans gained acceptance in America as consumers of both food products and other material goods. Yet Heinze does not simply align consumption with assimilation; instead, he shows how Jewish Americans transformed consumer culture, giving prominence to cultural habits derived from eastern Europe.

Such a summary underscores that there are no hard and fast rules when it comes to studying the relation between ethnicity and material culture. As Heinze's work shows, while ethnic groups must be studied in the light of their own distinctive histories and cultural situations, it is also important to assess the group's place in the larger culture. Furthermore, as the history of Irish American and Italian American foodways suggests, ethnicity often interacts with other categories of identity, such as gender and class.

Rachel Farebrother

See also African America; African American
Foodways; Folklore and Folklife; Food and
Foodways; Gender; Mourning; Mourning
and Ethnicity; Native America; Race; Social
Class and Social Status

References and Further Reading
Barth, Fredrik. 1969. *Ethnic Groups and
Boundaries: The Social Organization of Culture
and Difference.* Boston: Little, Brown.
Geertz, Clifford, ed. 1963. *Old Societies and New
States: The Quest for Modernity in Asia and
Africa.* New York: Free Press of Glencoe.
Glazer, Nathan, and Daniel Patrick Moynihan.
1963. *Beyond the Melting Pot: The Negroes,
Puerto Ricans, Jews, Italians, and Irish of New
York City.* Cambridge, MA: MIT Press.
Glazer, Nathan, and Daniel Patrick Moynihan.
1975. *Ethnicity: Theory and Experience.*
Cambridge, MA: Harvard University Press.
Heinze, Andrew R. 1990. *Adapting to Abundance:
Jewish Immigrants, Mass Consumption, and the
Search for American Identity.* New York:
Columbia University Press.
Hollinger, David A. 1995. *Postethnic America:
Beyond Multiculturalism.* New York: Basic
Books.
Kallen, Horace M. 1996. "Democracy versus the
Melting-Pot: A Study of American National-
ity." In *Theories of Ethnicity: A Classical Reader*,
ed. Werner Sollors, 67–92. New York: New
York University Press.
Nagel, Joane. 1996. *American Indian Ethnic
Renewal: Red Power and the Resurgence of
Identity and Culture.* New York: Oxford
University Press.
Omi, Michael, and Howard Winant. 1986. *Racial
Formation in the United States: From the 1960s
to the 1980s.* London: Routledge.
Sollors, Werner, ed. 1996. *Theories of Ethnicity:
A Classical Reader.* New York: New York
University Press.
Warner, W. Lloyd. 1941. *The Social Life of a
Modern Community.* New Haven, CT: Yale
University Press.
Warnes, Andrew. 2004. *Hunger Overcome? Food
and Resistance in Twentieth-Century African
American Literature.* Athens: University of
Georgia Press.
Weber, Max. 1997. "What is an Ethnic Group?"
In *The Ethnicity Reader: Nationalism, Multi-
culturalism, and Migration*, ed. Montserrat
Guibernau and John Rex, 15–26. Cambridge,
UK: Polity Press.
Zangwill, Israel. 1909. *The Melting-Pot: Drama in
Four Acts.* New York: Ayer.

Etiquette and Manners

How Americans behave has long fascinated
foreign visitors and Americans themselves.
Etiquette, derived from European court ceremony, defines the formalities observed in
polite society. Where *etiquette* is used to
describe the set of rules governing social
behavior, *manners* is employed to describe
a person's social behavior, often judged in
relation to those rules of etiquette and the
standard they represent. Sociologists and
anthropologists have theorized that the purpose of etiquette and manners is to regulate
social behavior, to offer the means by which
people express their feelings, and to facilitate
communication not only between individuals but also to display one's place in the
social order (Hemphill 1999, 3–4).

American society has had a contradictory
relationship with etiquette. Etiquette is often
an exclusionary tool used to create and maintain social barriers impervious to groups
defined at the time as "lower sorts." Yet etiquette, in its promulgation of a widely
accepted behavioral code, also offers the
possibility of a classless society in which
higher social positions are theoretically
open to those who master the etiquette
code. Most historians have concluded that
these "established codes of behavior have
often served in unacknowledged ways as
checks against a fully democratic order and
in support of special interests, institutions
of privilege, and structures of domination"
(Kasson 1990, 3).

Without politeness, there is no rudeness.
Mind one's manners is an injunction to be

polite. Although everyone has manners, when one is accused of *not* having manners they are being indicted for not following or acknowledging appropriate social behavior. For those ascending the social ladder, the challenge is to learn a constantly evolving code of elite behavior, all the while risking condemnation of being rude and rustic in those instances of poor performance. Rudeness and poor manners indicate a society in danger; historically, such arguments are made nearly every generation against the young, against new immigrants, or, if social class is defined as a set of associated behaviors, against *parvenus* (recently wealthy or prominent persons) and the working classes. Appropriate manners earn an individual his or her membership in polite society; it is a sign that the civic order is intact.

A consideration of etiquette books reveals this social fluidity. The standard set of social rules changed over time, at times in response to foreign visitors' judgments of the manners of the Americans. One notes, for example, criticism of Americans' manners in a published traveler's account only to find, within the next decade, a "correction" or rebuttal in an etiquette book. Americans were enraged by English writer Frances Trollope's (1780–1863) *Domestic Manners of the Americans* (1832) as well as English novelist Charles Dickens' (1812–1870) *American Notes for General Circulation* (1842). Both authors condemned Americans for their provincialism.)

Scholars argue about the nature of conduct literature. Is etiquette prescriptive or descriptive? To what extent were these politeness guides followed? How, then, may such guides serve as historical evidence? Many guides in library collections contain inscriptions that reveal that such books were gifts. For what occasions might these books have been appropriate, and hopefully welcome, presents?

Colonial Deference and Gentility

Deference governed the British colonists' conduct in the nearly two centuries of settlement before the American Revolution. Puritan Massachusetts Bay and Quaker Pennsylvania incorporated Mosaic law (the biblical Ten Commandments) into their respective legal codes, thus enjoining colonists to adhere both to the centuries-old social hierarchy of king, nobility, and householders and, especially in these sects dissenting from the Church of England, to renewed biblical injunctions governing personal behavior. Their own actions had propelled a historical shift from the fixed social order of the Middle Ages to a more fluctuating world of "sorts" or "classes" of people.

The colonial elite constituted the sort who had leisure and access to expensive books. Courtesy books had traveled with the colonists to the New World. These works were translations of courtesy books developed in the late Renaissance in Italy and France, such as Baldasarre Castiglione's (1478–1529) *Book of the Courtier* (1528). The middling and lesser sorts learned and understood their social place and roles through the law, the Bible, ministers' sermons, and such rituals as "dignifying the seats" (assigning places according to social rank and age) in New England meetinghouses. Sumptuary laws that restricted the consumption of certain goods to elites reveal how material culture, especially dress, served to differentiate and distinguish the social order. Wigs and rings, lace and robes, silks rather than wool: All provided evidence of who should bow or curtsy to whom. The court system reinforced social hierarchy by penalizing the flouting of authority. Parents over children, masters and mistresses over servants, the governing over the governed: This reinforcement of authority and inequality was the primary focus of sermons and conduct literature for colonists in the seventeenth and early eighteenth centuries.

By the mid-eighteenth century, however, this system of deference was giving way to a new system of politeness based on relationships between equals—in the northern colonies at least. The southern colonies' widespread use of chattel slavery required adherence to traditional authority. Nevertheless, gentility reigned throughout the colonies. Once used to refer to the gentry or the well born, *genteel* now characterized people who practiced self-control in their emotions, in their bodies, and in their speech, all the while showing regard for other persons and their feelings. This was the system described in one of the first American guides, Boston schoolmaster Eleazar Moody's *The School of Good Manners* (1715). As an adolescent, George Washington (1732–1799) copied from a seventeenth-century English courtesy book a set of "Rules of Civility and Decent Behaviour in Company and Conversation." By the Revolution, Americans enjoyed the increased availability of conduct guides (including Lord Chesterfield's widely read *Letters of Advice to His Son*). Dancing masters, writing masters, and portrait artists provided advice and tutelage in bodily deportment to their patrons.

Conversation, as an indication of cosmopolitanism, was essential to social status, and nowhere else was conversation practiced and improved than at tea. Exotic for its importation from the Far East yet a popular beverage, tea was elevated symbolically by the rituals elites performed with it to further claims to cosmopolitanism. Beginning in the mid-eighteenth century, a new form of portraiture, the conversation piece, captured scenes of family members, guests, and servants performing their roles in the tea ceremony. Teas required appropriate equipment, from tables and chairs to silver or ceramic teapots, sugar and creamers, slop bowls, teacups and saucers, and silver spoons. Holding properly one's cup, silently sipping one's tea, balancing a piece of cake on one plate while holding a teacup in another: Successful execution of these acts, in combination with interesting conversation on a wide variety of topics in literature, arts, politics, and, at times, musical ability, was the performance required of ladies and gentlemen.

The Boston Tea Party of 1773 and the American Revolution did not stop tea ceremonies even though tea itself became a maligned symbol of British authority. Some Americans switched to herb teas and other drink, but the code of conduct based on the assumption and treatment of equals that had been active for a half-century before the events of the Revolution no doubt influenced its generation. The political order that was created after 1776 was the result of a longer historical process that is revealed in the changing definitions of social relations encoded in courtesy books based not on court but on class.

Nineteenth-Century "Parlor People"

The increase and consolidation of economic, not political, power were the primary forces girding social ritual after 1820. The rise of the middle class was reflected in the rapid publication of more than a hundred etiquette guides before 1860. These books were written by or borrowed heavily from English authors, and at times plagiarized each other. Technological developments in printing reduced the price of such books and raised the number of copies available for purchase. Historian C. Dallett Hemphill has argued that these books were considered "self-help" guides in this era of rapid urbanization and geographic and economic mobility. Interestingly, the books were full of more exacting directions for dress and deportment, public behavior, dining and conversing, and interactions with servants than previous generations' guides. This may have been because the middle class itself was in a liminal state—that is, in the process of fashioning itself, and needing sharper, definite rules with which to create and apprehend the emerging social order. Women, for example, were instructed often with the same advice to men, evidence of women's increased integration into social and public life. Indeed, in the latter half of the nineteenth century, more women authored etiquette guides as they also helped to define what came to be called "Society," a group in which membership was based on what was termed "good breeding" but relied overwhelmingly on wealth and family lines.

From the 1830s onward, American conduct book writers sought to curb the excesses of American democracy—defined as rudeness —with what appears to twenty-first-century readers as dictates rather than principles. Many authors prefaced their compendia with a discussion that all etiquette was based on the Golden Rule ("do unto others as you would have them do unto you"), but the same authors felt no compulsion for omitting or disparaging the poor, country folk, immigrants, and servants as incapable of the improvement implied by right behavior and adherence to the rules of etiquette.

The family dwelling for much of the nineteenth century was designed to accommodate a variety of social activities. Visiting, family and holiday celebrations, wedding ceremonies and receptions, and funerals took place in the front parlor and dining room. Within these rooms were specialized furniture forms, objects, and tools with which to carry out social ceremonies. Dining in particular was fraught with anxiety in the correct use of tableware and proper bodily performance. Etiquette guides as well as household manuals provide much evidence for the decoration and purposes of these rooms. By the end of the century, etiquette had become thoroughly ritualized, the principles behind its rituals perhaps lost to many Americans.

Twentieth-Century "Informality"

The rise of mass leisure and the firm establishment of consumer culture in the late nineteenth- and early twentieth-century United States reshaped etiquette. The increasing choice available in the marketplace of goods to fulfill desires was mirrored in the variety of choices available to readers of etiquette guides. Emily Post's *Etiquette: The Blue Book of Social Usage* (1922) represents this shift. For example, young women had several options in making their social debuts, including not to make a debut at all. Book authors were joined by newspaper columnists and radio and television advisers. Etiquette writers throughout the twentieth century have had, in historian John F. Kasson's (1990, 259) words, to balance "democratic pieties and the desire for social distinction and protection of class privilege." The early advertising industry at the end of the nineteenth century adopted the tone and strategies of etiquette manuals to teach consumers how to adapt new goods to proper social performance. Advertising, with its emphasis on market sectors, lifestyles, and claims to social status through the proper acquisition and use of things, also taught American consumers how to behave—and that behavior was linked to desire and satisfaction and not necessarily to civic duty. All goods, it seems, may be considered evidence of politeness and rudeness.

Shirley Teresa Wajda

See also Bodily Cleanliness and Hygiene; Community; Cultural History; Dress,

Accessories, and Fashion; Funerals; Human Body; Mourning; Mourning and Ethnicity; Parlors; Rite, Ritual, and Ceremony; Social Class and Social Status

References and Further Reading

Ames, Kenneth L. 1978. "Meaning in Artifacts: Hall Furnishings in Victorian America." *Journal of Interdisciplinary History* 9 (1): 19–46.

Aresty, Esther B. 1970. *The Best Behavior*. New York: Simon & Schuster.

Bushman, Richard L. 1992. *The Refinement of America: Persons, Houses, Cities*. New York: Alfred A. Knopf.

Goffman, Erving. 1959. *The Presentation of Self in Everyday Life*. New York: Doubleday.

Grover, Kathryn, ed. 1987. *Dining in America, 1850–1900*. Amherst: University of Massachusetts Press and Margaret Woodbury Strong Museum.

Halttunen, Karen. 1982. *Confidence Men and Painted Women: A Study of Middle-Class Culture in America, 1830–1870*. New Haven, CT: Yale University Press.

Hemphill, C. Dallett. 1999. *Bowing to Necessities: A History of Manners in America, 1620–1860*. New York: Oxford University Press.

Kasson, John F. 1990. *Rudeness & Civility: Manners in Nineteenth-Century America*. New York: Hill and Wang.

Roth, Rodris. 1961. "Tea Drinking in 18th Century America: Its Etiquette and Equipage." Paper 14, Contributions from Museum of History and Technology. *United States National Museum Bulletin* 225: 61–91.

Schlesinger, Arthur, Sr. 1968. *Learning How to Behave*. New York: Cooper Square.

Shields, David S. 1997. *Civil Tongues and Polite Letters in British America*. Chapel Hill: University of North Carolina Press.

F

Factory and Industrial Work and Labor

The material culture of factory and industrial workers helps explain the United States' evolution to an industrial society. The buildings, tools, machines, and industrial products themselves provided the terrain upon which workers and owners battled for control over work processes. Although technology and machinery varied radically across industries, issues of working for wages, time discipline, mass production strategies, and the assembly line mark the most important aspects of the material culture of factory and industrial work and labor.

The Factory System

After the introduction of the first factory by Samuel Slater (1768–1835) in 1790, factories spread slowly and unevenly in the North through the 1880s. In New England, textile entrepreneurs consolidated work processes under one roof, drawing young women and children to operate the looms. Work environments proved dark, dank, and dangerous as owners located factories near rivers to utilize water to power the machinery. Early textile factories regulated work by being reg-

ular: Though the mill buildings did vary, on the whole they were four to six floors in height, with each floor dedicated to one process of textile manufacture. A central mill building housing administrative offices was designated by a bell tower whose bell regimented the workday. By 1850 textile mills in New England clothed the nation. In factory centers such as Lowell, Massachusetts, working for wages represented a culture shock in a nation that prized republicanism, self-employment, and economic independence.

As factory workers adjusted to collecting wages, owners enforced new forms of discipline. Before the Civil War (1861–1865) most factories outside the textile industry remained groups of semiautonomous craftsmen's shops. Workers at a federal armory at Harpers Ferry, in one extreme example, came and went as they pleased, working just enough to produce a fixed quantity of goods ("stints"). Factory owners attempted to use clocks to regulate work schedules, which along with prohibitions against drinking on the job, rankled a workforce accustomed to setting its own time and workplace habits. By the 1890s the time clock, patented by Willard L. Bundy (1846–1916), was a standard fixture in factories. The time clock symbolized that control over time had largely shifted from employees to employers. Factory owners also attempted to quash other habits that they deemed noxious, especially workers' propensity to drink on the job.

Mass Production

Factory work changed radically in both scale and intensity in the last quarter of the nineteenth and first half of the twentieth centuries. In 1870 only a handful of factories employed more than 500 workers; in 1900 1,500 factories employed that number. Technological innovations, such as electricity, combined with managerial and architectural strategies to fuel the industrial ascendancy of the United States. The meat-packing industry developed the most sophisticated production process before the turn of the twentieth century by subdividing tasks and relying on a largely deskilled workforce who butchered animals in a highly efficient manner. Throughout the period, workers continued to work long hours, with ten hours a day serving as the norm but many working twelve-hour shifts.

Utilizing techniques of mass production and Frederick Winslow Taylor's (1856–1915) ideas of scientific management, factory work transformed from an arena ruled by workers' knowledge and skill to one defined by company overseers, or foremen. Specialists instructed and guided each worker's every move. Employers increasingly tied wages to piecework rather than timework. This form of remuneration meant that employers prized speed and efficiency above all else, including workers' health and safety. As Charlie Chaplin's (1889–1977) movie *Modern Times* (1936) depicts, the rise of the mass production industries and the assembly line represented the apex of deskilling and disciplining of the workforce, but also brought surging gains in production. These twin effects made the assembly line the most enduring symbol of industrial work in the twentieth century.

Michael K. Rosenow

See also Agricultural Work and Labor; Company Towns; Handicraft and Artisanship; Mill Towns; Technology; Time, Timekeeping, and Timepieces; Work and Labor

References and Further Reading
Biggs, Lindy. 1996. *The Rational Factory: Architecture, Technology, and Work in America's Age of Mass Production.* Baltimore, MD: Johns Hopkins University Press.
Nelson, Daniel. 1975. *Managers and Workers: Origins of the New Factory System in the United States, 1880–1920.* Madison: University of Wisconsin Press.
Roediger, David R., and Philip S. Foner. 1989. *Our Own Time: A History of American Labor and the Working Day.* Westport, CT: Greenwood Press.

Fakes

Fake qualifies objects that are intentionally created or altered to be presented as genuine but are not. A *forgery* is most often understood as a faked text meant to deceive and to have actually deceived, though the term also defines illegitimate or unauthorized copies of works of art. *Counterfeit* is used most often to refer to fraudulent goods of trade or to false currency. In common parlance, *fake*, *forgery*, and *counterfeit* differ from *replica* or *reproduction*. These types of documents and objects may not necessarily be fraudulent or illegal duplicates of an original. A reproduction may also be created in other media than the original. *Imitation* is most often used to describe a copy that does not replicate totally its original; that is, it offers the sense of the original but does not necessarily incorporate the same materials or methods of manufacture. Fake objects, as a class of material culture, provide evidence for inquiries about manufacturing and trade, desire, taste, and social status; the social practices of honesty and deception; and the cultural meanings of value and ownership, authenticity, and imitation in capitalist societies.

Scholarship, as well as museum, library, and archives collections policy, rests on the authenticity of a given artifact or document. *Authenticity* may be defined as being true in substance (a silver coin is silver and not a base metal), as being original as professed, or as related to the hand of a creator. An object's physical attributes and condition, provenance (history of ownership), and other pertinent evidence are considered in ascertaining whether that object is, as many Americans say, "the real thing" or, when that object is a market good, "the genuine article." Forensic scientific examination can discover fakery but not necessarily prove authenticity.

Document Forgeries

The British jurist William Blackstone (1723–1780) in 1769 defined *forgery* as "the fraudulent making or alteration of a writing to the prejudice of another man's right." Fake letters and official records such as birth certificates, passports, driver's licenses, wills, land records, and other documents endow falsely a right or property to a person while stealing that right or property from another or from the common good. Watermarked papers, inks, seals, stamps, and impressions have historically been employed or altered to create these spurious documents; printing presses, typewriters, photocopiers, and computer hardware and printers have also been employed in this endeavor. The same materials and machines, however, may be tested forensically to ascertain the authenticity of a document. Signs of wear and age, such as staining, yellowing, and foxing, are considered, as are handwriting implements and

styles. Other factors, such as the relationship of words or phrases to known practice in a given place and time, the internal stylistic consistency of the document, or the validation of information in the document's text in relation to known genuine documents, are also employed to determine the validity of the document.

Historians depend on the authenticity of evidence to ensure accuracy of interpretation. The value of historical evidence and literary works is not necessarily monetary; rather, such documents are invested with cultural meaning, more often than not as part of a nation's priceless heritage. Forgeries such as the W. T. Horn Papers, a collection of maps, diaries, and other materials sold by a Kansas man to the Greene County (Pennsylvania) Historical Society for $20,000 and published in 1945, provided new details about American leaders and the common folk. Professional historians questioned the collection and through both laboratory and historical analysis found the papers false. More recently, the death warrant of accused Salem witch Sarah Good was found to be forged. Both the Horn papers and the Good warrant, along with other forgeries, were created in the 1930s, testifying both to the nation's interest in Americana and the financial exigencies of the Great Depression. Works of poetry and literature are also imitated with the intent to defraud either by sale or by challenging authorial originality and reputation. As the market for collectible historical materials grows in scope and popularity, the creation and circulation of false documents will no doubt increase.

Fakes and the Art, Antiquities, and Collectibles Markets

Fake art and artifacts are created in several ways. A given forgery may be a new object that is presented as old or made by another individual, or it may be the result of piecing together historically authentic materials to create an object that simulates a known and likely desirable original. An object may also be enhanced—repainted, for example—so that its originality is impaired. Ironically, the forger must know as much as, if not more than, experts to be successful in his or her deception.

The art of the forger depends on Western culture's adherence to notions of originality, authorship, and property, as well as the changing definition of art dating to the European Renaissance. Once artworks and other objects became desirable for their uniqueness, novelty, or inventiveness, copying became the practice of learning and not originality. Such copying, however, could and did prove profitable in the increasing market for artworks and relics.

The lack of historical evidence and the subjectivity in aesthetic judgment and connoisseurship together create the conditions in which fake artworks, antiquities, and collectibles appear. Experts, auction houses, curators, librarians, and collectors employ their best judgment when considering the authenticity of an object. In lieu of strong historical evidence, subjective decisions based on style, manufacture, aesthetics, and other pertinent factors are made and are accepted if the experts making those decisions are acknowledged as such and if they possess a strong record of accurate attribution. The necessity of maintaining professional reputations of integrity and expertise has led individuals, auction houses, and museums to conceal errors. For museums this is especially problematic. Dependent on donors, a museum must not embarrass a donor who has given a fake object nor make it known that it has erred in such judgments so as to lose public trust and future donations. At the same time, a museum's credibility rests

upon the demonstration of expertise and honesty in ascertaining the authenticity of its holdings.

Counterfeit Consumer Goods
Counterfeit consumer goods are objects copied from originals, often with their trademarks and packaging, with the intent to defraud or deceive buyers. These goods are also called *pirated goods*. Economists point out that in the United States the traffic in counterfeit consumer goods weakens the national economy by lessening tax revenues, challenging consumer confidence, and lessening the value of a legitimate brand or good. It may also be argued that counterfeiters have satisfied consumer demand for certain goods. Since the 1980s American manufacturers have fought foreign and domestic counterfeiters, arguing that the traffic in these illegal goods impairs the United States economy, leads to domestic job loss, and even may aid in funding organized crime and terrorism. The United States Customs Service (now in the Department of Homeland Security) is charged with preventing illegal trade practices and with inspecting incoming shipments of merchandise for counterfeits as varied as compact discs, auto parts, designer shoes, and ceramics.

Americans have, in certain instances, embraced counterfeit goods as a means to protest what some see as the unfair prices and "snob appeal" of luxury goods. Other consumers see in these goods a means to display prestige or represent themselves as members of a higher socioeconomic status than they actually have. Imitative status goods are evident throughout the course of American history. Pinchbeck, for example, was often used to imitate gold but was actually an alloy of zinc and copper. Since the 1980s "knockoffs" of designer clothing (jeans in particular) and fashion accessories, especially when consumer demand is high and supply is thus limited or delayed, have been readily available through street vendors. Knockoffs represent consumers' familiarity with fashion trends and allow them to make claims to social status, especially through clothing and accessories. Popular jokes about tourists buying cheap Rolex watches or Gucci purses from New York City street vendors, only to discover that the watches are empty of their works or the Gucci logo is inaccurately rendered, are legion. Still other Americans, especially teenagers and young adults, see a counterfeit good, especially if comparable in design, utility, and price, as just another attractive consumer choice.

Genuine Fakes

Theorists argue that forgery, whatever the intent of the forger, possesses a democratic, subversive purpose in that it mocks and undermines elite pretensions and accepted definitions of value. Fake artworks, decorative arts, and other forms of material culture are, by virtue of their manufacture, original objects in and of themselves and thus "genuine" or "authentic" fakes and now prize collectibles as well. The rise of "appropriation art," in which artists such as Sherrie Levine admit to copying other artists' works, brings into question the definitions of *artist* and *forger*, the power of law, and the role of the market to define commodity, property, and value at a time when authenticity itself is being redefined in Western culture.

Shirley Teresa Wajda

See also Antiques; Collecting and Collections; Commodity; Consumerism and Consumption; Money, Currency, and Value; Patents, Trademarks, and Brands

References and Further Reading
Cohon, Robert. 1996. *Discovery and Deceit: Archaeology & the Forger's Craft*. Kansas City, MO: Nelson-Atkins Museum of Art.
Grafton, Anthony. 1990. *Forgers and Critics: Creativity and Duplicity in Western Scholarship*. Princeton, NJ: Princeton University Press.
Higgins, Richard S., and Paul H. Rubin. 1986. "Counterfeit Goods." *Journal of Law & Economics* 29: 211–230.
Middleton, Arthur Pierce, and Douglass Adair. 1947. "The Mystery of the Horn Papers." *William and Mary Quarterly* 3rd ser., 4 (4): 409–443.
Nickell, Joe. 1996. *Detecting Forgery: Forensic Investigation of Documents*. Lexington: University Press of Kentucky.
Pracht, Carl. 2002. "Sarah Good's First Death Warrant Resurfaces, or We Thought." *Collection Building* 21(2): 71–73.
Radnóti, Sándor. 1999. *The Fake: Forgery and its Place in Art*, trans. Ervin Dunai. Lanham, MD: Rowman & Littlefield.
Tom, Gail, Barbara Garibaldo, Yvette Zeng, and Julie Pilcher. 1998. "Consumer Demand for Counterfeit Goods." *Psychology & Marketing* 15 (5): 405–421.

Fanzines

Fanzines ("*zines*") are noncommercial, handmade, amateur publications with limited distribution. Zines offer an alternative to the mainstream press as well as an expressive venue for those marginalized in society. Most zine makers handle the production, publication, and distribution themselves. The common fanzine consists of photocopied text and images stapled together at the seam in the form of a booklet, usually "quarter size" (8½" × 11" paper sheet folded in half twice) or "half-standard size" (8½" × 11" paper sheet folded in half). Other zines are small enough to fit in a pocket, and some fold out into large posters. Most fanzines are assembled by hand, and some are modified after photocopying. Glitter, stickers, colored pencil drawing, and other handcrafted additions make the publication a somewhat individual piece of art.

Rarely seeking profit, zine makers often trade their zine for another in lieu of payment. Some give them away. Zine makers' motivation lies in distributing their thoughts, writing, and artwork. Zines broach a very broad range of topics: television and film, music (the largest genre in the United States), politics, local cultural scenes, sex, health, art, religion, personal diaries, and much more. Zine makers tend to privilege personal thought and revelation; little is taboo.

Some scholars find precedents for zines as far back as American Revolutionary Thomas Paine's (1737–1809) political pamphlets in the eighteenth century, but most point to the science fiction fan community in the early twentieth century as the beginning of zine production. *Fanzine* itself implies a connection to fan communities. The modern history of zines began in 1930 with the publication of *The Comet*, an amateur publication of science fiction stories by fans of the genre. According to R. Seth Friedman, author of *Factsheet Five* (a zine that critically reviews other zines), the advent of the mimeograph machine fueled zine production and from the 1930s to the 1950s (the golden age of science fiction), fanzines proliferated. Women and men were creating zines about other literary genres as well, and a sort of underground literary community was born.

By the 1960s, the availability of offset printing coincided with political upheaval and an alternative press emerged. Zine writers and scholars have several terms for small presses up to the 1990s: *underground press*, *alternative press*, and *small press*. Though some glossy magazines and newspapers fall under these terms, self-published fanzines were also circulated as part of the counterculture movement. In the 1960s and 1970s, with the innovations of the Xerox™ xerographic copy machine and punk music, zines acquired an aesthetic that emphasized handmade art and personal expression. Zine writers have formed networks and created communities around different identities, interests, and media texts.

The proliferation of zine writing in the 1990s led to attention from mainstream media, and several books consisting of collected zines were published. This has led to the yearly publication of *The Zine Yearbook*, which reprints the "best" zines of the year, and several how-to books that offer instructions on how to create one's own zine.

Sandra M. Falero

See also Books; Ephemera; Graphic Design; Literary Studies and American Literature; Popular Culture; Print Culture; Printmaking and American Prints

References and Further Reading
Block, Francesca Lia, and Hillary Carlip. 1998. *Zine Scene: The Do It Yourself Guide to Zines.* New York: Girl Press.
Duncombe, Stephen. 1997. *Notes from Underground: Zines and the Politics of Alternative Culture.* London: Verso.
Friedman, R. Seth. 1997. *The Factsheet Five Zine Reader.* New York: Three Rivers Press.
Robins, Trina. 1999. *From Girls to Grrrlz: A History of Women's Comics from Teens to Zines.* New York: Chronicle Books.

Federal Style

The writing of the United States Constitution in 1787 and the establishment of a new federal government in 1789 were accompanied by the adoption of a new style of architecture and decorative arts called the *Federal style*. In architecture this American Neoclassical style favored smooth facades, symmetry, columns, and detailing such as fanlights, dentils, and Palladian windows. American Federal style first evolved from British Neoclassicism, particularly through the architectural works of Robert Adam (1728–1792).

Interiors sometimes featured oval, round, or octagonal rooms; interior finishes included decorative, low-relief carved woodwork or plasterwork (which could be purchased as composition ornament), especially in fireplace surrounds. Adam's work, inspired by his Grand Tour travels in Europe and based on ancient Roman examples excavated at Herculaneum and Pompeii, arrived in the United States via pattern books beginning in the mid-1780s. Examples of this influence include Gore Place (1797–1804) in Waltham, Massachusetts, and the Nathaniel Russell House (1809) in Charleston, South Carolina.

The early nation's best-known practitioner of Federal style was Charles Bulfinch (1763–1844) of Massachusetts. Bulfinch's own European Grand Tour and time spent studying Adam's books at Harvard eventually led this public servant to become an architect. Extant Bulfinch designs include the Massachusetts State House (1795–1798) and the Harrison Gray Otis House (1795–1796), both in Boston. Due to the enormous popularity of the style and its associations with the Greco-Roman heritage of democracy, President George Washington (1732–1799) and Congress chose Federal-style plans by Frenchman Pierre Charles L'Enfant (1754–1852) for the new seat of the nation in Washington DC. The United States Capitol and the White House are only two of the many buildings, structures, and city planning ideas translated from European sources into American ones.

The symmetry and linearity of Federal architecture is also mirrored in the decorative arts. Furniture forms feature plain surfaces, often veneered and composed of architectural framing elements such as reeded or fluted moldings with understated ornamentation—inlay, brasses, and mirrors. Shield-back, or urn-back, or vase-back chairs, based on George Hepplewhite's (1727?–1786) *The Cabinet-Maker and Upholsterer's*

This circa 1790 to 1820 mahogany Pembroke table, attributed to New York City furniture maker William Whitehead, features many aspects of the Federal style: plain or veneered surfaces with flat, inlaid designs, fluted or reeded legs, and understated brass drawer pulls. (Christie's Images/Corbis)

Guide (1788), and specialized furniture for women's use, such as writing desks and sewing tables, were created in Philadelphia, Boston, and New York City. Silver and ceramic vessels offered through surface design commemoration of the Americans' victory in the Revolutionary War: Celebratory punch bowls carry images of American ships or leaders embellished by swags; the urn shape and restrained design are also found in silver and ceramic tea sets.

Laura A. Macaluso

See also Civic Architecture; Classical Revival (Neoclassicism); Decorative Arts; Domestic Architecture; Style

References and Further Reading
Cooper, Wendy A. 1993. *Classical Taste in America, 1800–1840.* New York: Abbeville Press.

Garrett, Wendell D. 1992. *Classic America: The Federal Style and Beyond*. New York: Rizzoli.

Garvan, Beatrice B. 1987. *Federal Philadelphia, 1785–1825: The Athens of the Western World*. Philadelphia, PA: Philadelphia Museum of Art.

Flea Markets

Flea markets are public venues, open on certain days or at certain times of the year (especially summer), in which new and secondhand goods and food are sold. Also called *swap meets* (especially in the western United States), *farmers' markets*, or *street markets* and *open-air markets* in cities, flea markets are distinguished by an informal economy based on wholesale and resale, bargaining and bartering, their casual design, and their locations on sites that have fallen into disuse or are utilized for different purposes at other times. Farmers' fields, drive-in theaters, parking lots, city streets, parks, and more recently, the buildings of closed factories and out-of-business retail stores are converted to temporary or permanent flea markets. Portrayed popularly as sites in which one may find "treasure" from another's "junk" or engage in thrifty shopping, some flea markets, especially those that are held annually or seasonally, have focused on antiques and collectibles and are now considered major events within the national antiques trade.

Perhaps due to their informal nature, flea markets have escaped the attention of professional historians. Popular histories trace the phenomenon to the 1860s *marches aux puces* (translated as "flea market") of Paris or to the 1880s Saint-Ouen market, located just outside Paris's city gates and amidst "rag and bone" men who set up market stalls against the walls. In 1885 Saint-Ouen's informal Sunday scrap metal auction was subjected to municipal authorities, who set days for market activities and improved the area. Street markets, market days, and other sorts of informal marketing (especially of secondhand goods) have an ancient past, and how these practices came with the European colonists to North America has yet to be fully traced and analyzed.

Many flea markets in the East and Midwest owe their establishment to seasonal farm and livestock auctions. In the 1920s and especially in the 1930s Depression, auction attendees brought with them secondhand household goods and agricultural equipment, homemade foodstuffs, and other items to sell to other attendees. Auction barn owners in turn built sheds for this activity; as livestock and dairy auctions declined in the 1950s, those buildings were converted to permanent flea market spaces. In the late 1970s flea markets such as New York City's The Annex Antiques Fair & Flea Market (commonly called the Chelsea Flea Market, and now combined with the Hell's Kitchen Flea Market) heralded a new era of counter-consumerism, as artists, college students, environmentalists, simple-lifers, and others sought alternative venues for consumption.

Due to their temporary, informal, and legally unregulated nature, flea markets historically have been associated with illegal activities, such as the sale of counterfeit or stolen goods. In the last fifty years, flea markets have succumbed to privatization, business organization, and government oversight. At many flea markets vendors pay a small fee for a space, stall, or booth from which to sell. The National Flea Market Association (NFMA), founded in 1997, exists to raise public trust in flea markets and to influence flea market activities through a professional code of ethics as well as lobby for legislation promoting these businesses. Published price lists now rationalize this once informal sec-ondhand market. Many "how to" books on selling secondhand goods aimed at Ameri-cans seeking new avenues of income have been published since the 1980s, a telling sign of the shift from the nation's industrial econ-omy to a service economy.

Now a multibillion-dollar industry, flea markets have grown in number, size, and popularity. The NFMA estimates that there are now more than 5,000 flea markets in the United States. Many markets now boast restrooms, snack bars, restaurants, and even hotels to accommodate the growing influx of visitors, and tourists, because flea market shopping in the early twenty-first century has become, like other forms of shopping, a popular leisure activity. Magazines such as *Better Homes and Gardens*, *Good Housekeeping*, and *Country Home* feature columns on deco-rating with "flea market finds."

Shirley Teresa Wajda

See also Antiques; Consumerism and Consumption; Junk, Scrap, and Salvage; Secondhand Goods and Shopping

References and Further Reading
Grover, Jill Williams. 2001. *Dime Store Decorat-ing: Using Flea Market Finds with Style*. New York: Sterling Publications.
LaFarge, Albert. 2000. *The U.S. Flea Market Directory: The Complete Guide to America's Best Flea Markets*, 3rd ed. New York: St. Martin's Press.
McClurg, R. S. 1995. *The Rummager's Handbook: Finding, Buying, Cleaning, Fixing, Using, and Selling Secondhand Treasures*. Pownal, VT: Storey Communications.
National Flea Market Association. n.d. Home page, http://www.fleamarkets.org/.
Naton, Leslie. 2005. *That Might Be Useful: Explor-ing America's Secondhand Culture*. Guilford, CT: Lyons Press.
Strasser, Susan. 1999. *Waste and Want: A Social History of Trash*. New York: Metropolitan Books.

Floor Coverings

Underfoot everyday in the United States is a variety of *floor coverings* that are used to guard against dirt brought from outside, withstand foot traffic, and complement the overall interior design of a room, hall, or public thoroughfare. Historically, rugs and carpets were costly movables that often were listed as possessions in wills and probate inventories. A *rug* originally defined a rough, often woolen piece of material used as a wrap to protect one's body during travel or as a coverlet. "As snug as a bug in a rug" de-rives from this meaning. *Rug* also was used, as it is today, to define a floor mat. *Carpet* originally referred to a thick woolen fabric, but its use was to drape tables and beds. Since the fifteenth century, *carpet* has been defined as a patterned fabric of many colors intended for use on floors and for the pur-poses of kneeling (at prayer, at court), stand-ing, and sitting. Interestingly, *carpet* was often associated with a lady's chamber, and as such carried at times some connotation of luxury and effeminacy. Nevertheless, a point of discussion in a council or public meeting was said to be *on the carpet*—that is, on the table covered with the carpet; to be *called on the carpet* was—and is—to be reprimanded.

Floor Coverings in Preindustrial America

Dirt was a more familiar, if unwelcome, guest in American domestic dwellings in the seventeenth and eighteenth centuries. Floors could be the packed bare earth, or layers of straw or grass, even stone; unfinished and painted wood planks were the most common surface by the eighteenth century, although on the frontier and among the poor, shelter overhead was the primary concern rather than protection underfoot. Still, medical and popular opinion held that dampness was a cause of illness, and colonial housekeepers used straw and sand (swept into patterns with twig-and-stick brooms) to absorb moisture as well as to sweep more easily the household's detritus out the door.

As Georgian style houses gained popularity in the eighteenth century, the ceremonial front or center hall could boast a painted and oiled canvas floor cloth or be left bare in the hot weather months. Floor cloths were at first imported from England. A popular pattern imitated in black and white the checked marble then fashionable in the houses of the wealthy. (Tile and brick were other forms of flooring used by wealthier Americans.) Floor cloths helped limit the tracking of dirt, dust, and mud throughout the house; these were more water-repellant surfaces than wood or sand and easily cleaned. Straw matting ("India mats"), which could be washed, replaced floor cloths in the summer from the late eighteenth century through much of the nineteenth century. Wool carpets were used in halls and on stairs at the end of the eighteenth century.

What rugs and carpets were available to Americans in the seventeenth and eighteenth centuries were either expensive, handmade, and often imported productions or were inexpensive and homemade. They were rarely trod upon with shoes and boots. Hand-knotted "Turkey work" rugs, imitating the fine work being found in Persia, Turkey, and India, were in the houses of the very wealthy. Rag rugs, made of scraps, adorned the hearths and hallways of even the poor. It was the use of the textiles on the floor—whatever the textile, whatever the floor—that marked a significant shift in the way Americans understood the relationship between dirt and domesticity.

As historian Richard L. Bushman (1992, 265) observes, by the 1830s, as the nation's

carpet manufacturers increased in numbers and output, Americans laid carpets in their houses: "A carpeted floor was a fitting surface for a gentleman's fine shoe, not for a farmer's boots." The feel of a carpet underfoot signaled silently the appropriate dress and behavior of a potential entrant into a house or a room. Carpets became a sign of respectable behavior, even in public places: Hotel parlors, photography parlors, and other commercial establishments in which decorum was decreed boasted softness underfoot.

Nineteenth-Century Mass Production and Fashionable Furnishings

In 1791, the first woven carpet mill in the United States was established in Philadelphia by William Sprague. Sprague's mill, and others like it in New Jersey, New York, and New England, used hand looms that could be powered by hand or foot by skilled carpet weavers. The carpet industry was revolutionized in 1839 by the invention of a carpet-weaving power loom by Erastus Bigelow (1814–1879), a Massachusetts inventor of a textile-making family. By 1850 the nation's carpet production had tripled, reducing prices, and the American middle class could enjoy in their parlors, dining rooms, and bedrooms a variety of carpets. Still, English ingrain carpets (made of pre-dyed fibers), with names after companies such as Kidderminster and carpetmaking centers such as Axminster and Wilton, remained prized possessions. These had been imported to the United States as early as the 1790s. Carpet was manufactured in 27" widths (Kidderminster, an ingrain carpet, in 36" width) and sewn together on site.

Americans tacked down their parlor carpets after stretching them from wall to wall. Bright colors and large patterns dwarfed a room's other furnishings; paintings and portraits show that in the first four decades of the nineteenth century restraint in other room furnishings displayed its carpet to best advantage. By mid-century, in country and in city, parlors, sitting rooms, and dining rooms were ablaze with color and pattern from ceiling to floor. Solid-color crumb cloths were found under dining room tables and over wall-to-wall carpets. Bedrooms were adorned by smaller bedside rugs; kitchens sported wood floors in most of the nation but tile floors were common in the South. Carpet use was seasonal; in the summer months carpets would be removed, cleaned, and replaced with bare wood floors and sand. While in place, a carpet was kept sweet by strewing damp tea leaves on its surface to gather up dust as one swept it. Carpets were turned and rotated to ensure even wear and moved from room to room to prolong their use. Melville Bissell's (1843–1889) invention of the carpet sweeper in 1876 made it possible to use carpets year round and to end the practice of taking up the carpet, dragging it outdoors, and subjecting it to a good beating to remove dust, dirt, and vermin. The first electric suction cleaner was patented in 1907; Herbert William Hoover's (1877–1954) version with a rotating brush was patented the following year. New worries about germs and cleanliness focused on the carpet as a haven of pests and disease were alleviated by these new "household servants." The new emphasis on the kitchen led to the use of linoleum after its introduction in 1890.

Mechanization also revolutionized handmade rugs. Hooked rugs, made by hand, imitated yarn-sewn colonial and early nineteenth-century rugs that were meant to adorn tabletops and beds (*bed ruggs*). Ebenezer Ross in 1886 created the "Novelty Rug Machine" that replaced rag strips with yarn. Essentially a punch hook, this "machine" hooked yarn through a jute-burlap fabric to make a pile surface carpet. Mass-produced patterns also guided the makers' hands. The fad for such rugs faded by century's end, although hooked rugs with new patterns and lighter-weight yarns were viewed by settlement house workers as a means by which the poor and the needy could make a living.

Twentieth-Century Revivals and Innovations

In 1928 Karastan rugs were sold in the United States, the first type of machine-made rug to reproduce "Oriental" rugs—that is, to weave through the back of the rug. The Chicago retailer Marshall Field & Co. had initiated this innovation by having an Axminster loom altered to create the very intricate designs of exotic, expensive carpets. The early twentieth-century quest for folk traditions and Americana also affected the nation's carpet industry. Tufted carpets, made from looms adapted from those used to make candlewick (chenille) bedspreads in Georgia, were produced with less material and labor. In addition, the very modern inventions of nylon, polyester, and polypropylene in the 1930s and 1940s led to their use as synthetic fibers in these machines after World War II restrictions ended. Tufted carpets are the most popular machine-manufactured carpets in the United States today. Vinyl flooring, introduced in the 1950s, is also popular in bathrooms, kitchens, recreation rooms, and other areas that experience constant wear.

Shirley Teresa Wajda

See also Decorative Arts; Technology; Textiles

References and Recommended Reading
Bushman, Richard L. 1992. *The Refinement of America: Persons, Houses, Cities*. New York: Alfred A. Knopf.
Garrett, Elisabeth Donaghy. 1990. *At Home: The American Family, 1750–1870*. New York: Harry N. Abrams.
Strasser, Susan. 1982. *Never Done: A History of American Housework*. New York: Pantheon Books.

Von Rosenstiel, Helene. 1978. *American Rugs and Carpets from the Seventeenth Century to Modern Times*. New York: William Morrow.

Folklore and Folklife

Folklore, or *folk culture*, is both the common expressive patterns, often rooted in tradition, by which people give meaning to their lives, and the particular forms that emerge from those expressions, such as stories, proverbs, songs, or baskets. *Folklore* is also the intellectual discipline that documents, analyzes, and works to preserve these cultural patterns and their forms, and to present them informatively outside their communities of origin. Because folklore is such a pervasive presence in human life, its boundaries have always been porous both as a discipline and as a mode of human culture. Material forms are a significant subset of folkloric expression, which is sometimes labeled separately as *material folk culture*, *folk art*, or *folk craft*. Material forms are also especially significant to the area of folklife studies, which seeks to bring a holistic approach to the understanding of folk communities.

Defining Folklore

The practices of folklore are artful, participatory, rooted in community, grounded in tradition, contextually specific, and often informally learned and communicated in face-to-face settings. In North America, folklore includes Blue Ridge Mountain quilts and Pueblo pottery, cowboy poetry and New Mexican wedding dances, Prince Edward Island fiddle tunes, Pennsylvania bank barns, and playing the dozens, but it can also be fifth graders sleeping in inside-out pajamas to make it snow, the slang that medical students learn to describe hospital patients, Vietnamese immigrants using supermarket foods in old family recipes, teddy bear shrines placed on interstate medians, and the use of emoticons in e-mails.

Definitions of folklore are complicated by the widespread misuse of the term. *Folk* and *folklore* have been wrongly taken to mean quaint, old-fashioned, or obsolete customs, or beliefs that are untrue or unreliable. *Folk art* is often incorrectly used to refer to art with a characteristically simplified appearance, either because it is produced by self-taught amateurs or it comes from a time when early American professional painters were insufficiently trained.

What folklore *is* can be clarified by differentiating it from two other modes of culture: popular, mass-media, or commercial culture on the one hand and academic, or elite, culture on the other. "In general," as the folklorist Henry Glassie (1968, 33) put it, "folk material exhibits major variation over space and minor variation through time, while the products of popular or academic culture exhibit minor variations over space and major variations through time." Unlike folklore, popular culture tends to originate in the productions of mass media and is based in the creation of commodities; often, it comes from outside into many communities at once. Elite culture typically depends on highly specialized institutional training and tends to emphasize individual talent and innovation over community; it may be associated with economic and political power as well. Folklore is typically learned in less formal settings by example and imitation, and its creativity typically flows from the interplay between a community's traditions and the subtle variations devised in individual mastery. Yet these contrasts have never been firmly fixed: when the nineteenth-century owner of the Robert Jenkins house in Talladega, Alabama, added a Tuscan-columned portico to his dogtrot dwelling, he appended an academic feature to a fundamentally folk housing form.

The Early Study of Folklore

The academic study of folklore first emerged in eighteenth-century Germany, as Romantic nationalists such as Johann Gottfried von Herder (1744–1803) sought to ground an emergent ideology of national identity in the language and oral traditions of the peasantry. In 1846, the English antiquarian William John Thoms (1803–1885) invented "folklore" as a rough translation of the German *Volkskunde*. Thoms defined *folklore* as "the Lore of the People," appealing for the documentation of the "manners, customs, observances, superstitions, ballads, proverbs, etc., of the olden time" now imperiled by the advances of modernity (quoted in Emrich 1946, 361). A similar impulse grounded the birth of academic folklore in North America. The year 1888 saw the founding of the American Folklore Society (AFS) as an organization dedicated to studying "Old English Folk-Lore," "lore of Negroes in the Southern States," the "lore of the Indian Tribes" and other longstanding American groups because these traditions were "fast . . . vanishing" (Newell 1888, 3).

As this repeated use of *lore* suggests, American folklorists' preoccupation with oral traditions persisted, laying a foundation of theoretical and methodological concerns within the field. From Finnish philologists, folklorists borrowed the so-called historic-geographic method of study, plotting the distribution of known variants of an item to identify its origins and paths of cultural diffusion. By studying Balkan singers of epics, folklorists came to understand how apparent improvisation involved combining repertoires of set phrases within established metrical and thematic structures. From the work of European scholars, American folklorists learned to analyze a wide range of oral traditions for shared motifs and elements that could be related to one another according to detailed taxonomies.

By the early twentieth century the discipline of folklore had also begun its long association with its sister discipline of anthropology, particularly because influential anthropologist Franz Boas (1858–1942)—a founder of the AFS and long the editor of the *Journal of American Folklore*—placed great emphasis on the importance of expressive culture to both disciplines. While this alliance with anthropology constantly risked a confusion of intellectual boundaries and disciplinary identities—the AFS and the American Anthropological Society held joint meetings until the 1960s—it also opened to folklorists the theoretical and methodological tools of ethnography. *Ethnography*, a method for comprehending a particular culture from the insider's view through direct, situated observation and engagement over time, has become a central practice in the study of folklore as well as in anthropology.

Public Folklore

The basic project of folklore was accelerated in the 1930s by an infusion of support from New Deal projects intended to document and preserve the nation's vernacular cultural heritage. Among the most important were the establishment of the Archive of American Folk Song (now the Archive of Folk Culture) at the Library of Congress in 1928; the launching of the Historic American Buildings Survey through the National Park Service in 1933; and the collecting of oral histories, including the stories of ex-slaves, through the Federal Writers' Project.

New Deal programs anticipated what has become since the 1960s the most important development in the discipline: the rise of "public folklore"; that is, the documentation, study, support, and presentation of folk culture in and through public institutions. From federal projects such as the National Heritage Fellowships and the Smithsonian's Festival of American Folklife to performances, exhibitions, publications, and apprenticeships at the state and local levels, the practice of public folklore has expanded both the discipline of folklore and public awareness of folk culture. It is estimated that by 2006 at least half of all American folklorists worked in the public sphere at least part time (Wells 2006, 7)—a significant dedication of resources to the preservation and sustenance of cultural heritage. Yet their roles as advocates and cultural mediators challenge public folklorists to work in tension between the communities whose cultures they document and present and the needs and expectations of their employers and the public.

Contemporary Folklore Studies

Folklorists have continued to expand and solidify their discipline through increasing attention to folk traditions in global perspective and through the integration of new approaches from fields such as sociolinguistics and performance studies. Since the 1960s, the central concerns of their research have moved away from a focus on the items of folklore (such as the proverb, the dance form, the chair) to the ways that elements of folk tradition reflect, negotiate, and sustain meanings and relationships within community. Such investigations would hardly be possible had folklorists not long since abandoned some of the alternately nostalgic and pejorative assumptions that attended the founding of the discipline: the erroneous beliefs that folklore is the product of a preindustrial past, disappearing under the pressures of modernity, and the related supposition that folklore is a mode of culture restricted to certain groups. As folklorist

Alan Dundes wrote in 1965 (2), "[t]he term 'folk' can refer to *any group of people whatsoever* who share at least one common factor. It does not matter what the linking factor is— it could be a common occupation, language or religion—but what is important is that a group formed for whatever reason will have some traditions which it calls its own." Folklorists now recognize that individual folk expressions will always change and may indeed disappear, but that folklore itself is a fundamental way of being human.

Material Culture and Folklife Studies

While material culture has always been seen as an important component of folklore studies, it received special emphasis during two periods of the twentieth century. Early in the century, a widespread interest in early American artifacts led not only to the rise of the Colonial Revival style but also to the amassing of large collections of historic artifacts now available for study. Noted collections from this period featuring large holdings of material folk culture include Henry Francis du Pont's (1880–1969) Winterthur Museum in Delaware, Abby Aldrich Rockefeller's (1874–1948) collection that became the Folk Art Museum at Colonial Williamsburg, and Electra Havemeyer (1888– 1960) Webb's Shelburne Museum in Vermont.

Folklife entered American usage in the 1960s through the work of folklorist Don Yoder, who adapted a Scandinavian term meant to emphasize the broadest panorama of traditional culture, including material forms, as parts within the larger whole. Material culture is central to folklife studies, as it encompasses the visible, physical aspects of traditional culture, providing a context for its more ephemeral expressions. Important work in material folk culture from this period includes folklorist Henry Glassie's *Pattern in the Material Folk Culture of the East-*

ern United States (1968) and the collection *Forms upon the Frontier* (1969) edited by Glassie and folklorists Austin and Alta Fife. Yoder published the edited collection *American Folklife* in 1976, which is also the year the American Folklife Center was chartered by Congress.

Folklore studies have especially influenced the larger material culture field in the area of methodology—how best to study material artifacts. Early scholars created formal typologies of artifacts, analyzing as well the relationships between form (the underlying structure of the artifact), material, and ornamental motif in the creation of shared genres of material expression. Works in the historic-geographic method, including Glassie's, focused especially on the relationship of location to the development and diffusion of genres. More recent ethnographic approaches have invited central attention to the issue of process, using fieldwork strategies to document the often-traditional practices used by folk artisans to achieve their final results. An important study that successfully incorporates all these influences is folklorist John Michael Vlach's *The Afro-American Tradition in Decorative Arts* (1978). In it, Vlach shows how traditional African forms have survived in contemporary African American folk artifacts, including shotgun houses and quilts, and documents the traditional African processes employed in the ongoing creation of coastal South Carolina sweetgrass baskets.

Folklorists studying material culture have most recently devoted new attention to the interchange among folk, popular, and elite modes of cultures through the processes of cultural appropriation, which can transcend analytic boundaries. Item-based examples include the adoption of traditional forms by new communities through mass manufacture, or the ways that mass-produced com-

modities become integrated into traditional cultures. At a broader ethical level, scholars have explored the complex and ambiguous effects of tourism on material culture in its traditional contexts, revealing how appropriation of traditional expressions for economic gain simultaneously redefines local communities in terms acceptable to an outside elite and provides those communities with the financial power to survive. Folklore studies will continue to offer unique insights into the dynamics of material culture in an ever more global world.

Jurretta Jordan Heckscher and Susan Garfinkel

See also Anthropology and Archaeology; Art History and American Art; Consumerism and Consumption; Popular Culture; Tradition; Vernacular

References and Further Reading

Bartis, Peter. 2002. *Folklife and Fieldwork: A Layman's Introduction to Field Techniques,* 3rd ed. Washington, DC: Library of Congress. http://www.loc.gov/folklife/fieldwork/index.html.

Bauman, Richard, ed. 1992. *Folklore, Cultural Performances, and Popular Entertainments: A Communications-Centered Handbook.* New York: Oxford University Press.

Bronner, Simon, ed. 1985. *American Material Culture and Folklife: A Prologue and Dialogue.* Ann Arbor, MI: UMI Research Press.

Bronner, Simon, ed. 1986 (2004). *Grasping Things: Folk Material Culture and Mass Society in America.* Lexington: University Press of Kentucky.

Dundes, Alan. 1965. *The Study of Folklore.* Englewood Cliffs, NJ: Prentice-Hall.

Emrich, Duncan. 1946. "'Folk-Lore': William John Thoms." *California Folklore Quarterly* 5: 4 (October): 355–374.

Fife, Austin, Alta Fife, and Henry H. Glassie, eds. 1969. *Forms Upon the Frontier: Folklife and Folk Arts in the United States.* Logan: Utah State University Press.

Glassie, Henry H. 1968. *Pattern in the Material Folk Culture of the Eastern United States.* Philadelphia: University of Pennsylvania Press.

Newell, William Wells. 1888. "On the Field and Work of a Journal of American Folk-Lore." *Journal of American Folklore* 1: 1 (April–June): 3–7.

Sims, Martha C., and Martine Stephens. 2005. *Living Folklore: An Introduction to the Study of People and Their Traditions.* Logan: Utah State University Press.

Vlach, John Michael. 1978. *The Afro-American Tradition in Decorative Arts.* Cleveland, OH: Cleveland Museum of Art.

Wells, Patricia Atkinson. 2006. "Public Folklore in the Twenty-first Century: New Challenges for the Discipline." *Journal of American Folklore* 119 (471) (January): 5–18.

Yoder, Don. 2001. *Discovering American Folklife: Essays on Folk Culture and the Pennsylvania Dutch.* Mechanicsburg, PA: Stackpole Books.

Food and Foodways

Food is the source of nutrients necessary for energy, growth, and life of organisms. The wide-ranging cultural practices associated with food that sustain and demarcate human societies are called *foodways*. Food has become a field of inquiry in its own right, with academic departments and scholarly societies devoted to its study. Food studies has its roots in anthropology. Structuralist anthropologists Claude Lévi-Strauss and Mary Douglas (1921–2007) examined the ritual aspects of food to elucidate how the form of food (raw, cooked, or plated) created and conveyed meaning. Architectural historian and social theorist Sigfried Giedion (1888–1968) saw the materiality of food as a way to examine how societies have controlled nature and to explore "forgotten" everyday objects. Recently, scholars across a range of disciplines—history, philosophy, sociology, literature, and cultural studies—have employed material and sensory perspectives in the study of food by considering the qualities or taste of particular foods.

Historical American Abundance

One of the more intriguing characteristics researchers observe in studying the food and foodways of the United States is that, overall, the population has been extremely well fed. Even in the colonial period, most Americans ate meat on a regular basis. With the expansion of ranching in the West and the emergence of large slaughterhouses in Chicago and St. Louis after the Civil War (1861–1865), railroads shipped ever-larger quantities of meat to urbanizing Eastern markets. Meat consumption after the Civil War through the early twentieth century became an important way for immigrants to distance themselves from the poverty they escaped in Europe while simultaneously embracing their ethnic heritage through culinary practice in the United States. Beyond meat, most foodstuffs were inexpensive and plentiful when compared to food in Europe. Before the twentieth century, American agricultural abundance was largely based on bringing broad expanses of western lands into cultivation and transporting these goods to growing eastern markets. By the first decades of the twentieth century, however, increased agricultural productivity relied on more intensive cultivation practices using established agricultural lands. Hybridization, diffusion of the tractor, and chemical fertilizers facilitated this growth after World War I.

Technology and Changing Foodways: The Twentieth Century

As the United States population shifted from a rural to an urban society in the 1920s, American food and food habits became increasingly industrial. Although ethnic foodways continued, many of the ingredients that made up these dishes were produced in distant factories or grown in fields far from urban centers rather than in local gardens. Generational changes also influenced the foods Americans ate. Second-generation immigrant women were more likely to use processed foods than their mothers or mothers-in-law, especially after World War II. The social calculus for this change is complex and includes factors such as class, workforce participation, gender ideals, regionalism, education, and modernity. Industrialization made available a wider array of food, particularly fresh and canned fruits and vegetables. The effect of this change was to dampen some regional and seasonal aspects of food habits across the nation. While Americans increasingly ate similar foods, there was no monolithic American diet. Rather, American food has always been a synthesis of available ingredients and cultural practice that reflected regional and ethnic differences.

The availability of food in the postwar period was largely predicated on new technologies and leveraging an industrial infrastructure to supply increasingly urban/ suburban markets. The suburban supermarket, which by the 1960s became the primary source for food, offered a much wider variety of products than urban groceries had. Consumers now needed an automobile to get to these distant stores. The development of the interstate highway system and long-haul trucking reduced delivery times for fresh produce and milk, often lengthening the shelf life, if not the quality, of these products. Refrigerators and freezers in both supermarkets and homes enabled stores to stock and consumers to purchase larger quantities of perishable foods. With the emergence of large domestic refrigerators in the mid-1950s, women could shop on a weekly rather than a daily basis. While frozen foods constituted a very small proportion of the American diet into the 1970s, mass production techniques and large freezer compartments in postwar home refrigerators allowed more people to consume these new foods.

Frozen orange juice also became a staple in many households because of concentrating and freezing technologies developed during World War II (1939–1945), which vastly improved the flavor of processed orange juice.

Health Costs and Class

The shift to industrial foods has not been without costs. As early as the mid-1950s, some food processors foresaw that obesity was becoming a problem. As food scientists and technologists developed and consumers ate more industrial foods, doctors and nutritionists began to realize that cheap, highly processed foods were causing health problems and that Americans were becoming fat. The new problem of an overnourished society required a dramatic change in eating habits that has proved difficult to effect. Ironically, the same groups—the poor and working class—who suffered from malnutrition in the early part of the century were also more likely to suffer from overnourishment at the end of the century.

The Racial Politics of Food

Although the general history of food in the United States is a story of abundance, when considering race, food could be equally oppressive. Whether it was Carolina rice cultivation in the eighteenth and nineteenth centuries or California fruit and vegetable cultivation in the twentieth, back-breaking fieldwork was racialized. In producing these crops, African American (in the case of rice) and Filipino, Chinese, Japanese, and later Mexican (in the case of fresh produce) field laborers could barely feed themselves on the rations or pay provided. The labor that kept most Americans well fed marginalized these workers.

Another form of oppression was based on access to food. A southern diet composed primarily of cornmeal and salt pork resulted in pellagra in poor black communities due to vitamin B deficiencies. It was also not uncommon for African American or Chinese cooks who took leftovers home to be accused of stealing, although cooks believed that "pan totting" was part of their compensation for spending long hours cooking for white families rather than their own.

Gabriella M. Petrick

See also African America; African American Foodways; Agricultural Work and Labor; Alternative Foodways; Commercial Food Venues; Ethnicity; Grocery Stores; Supermarkets; Technology

References and Further Reading
Belasco, Warren, and Philip Scranton, eds. 2002. *Food Nations: Selling Taste in Consumer Societies.* New York: Routledge.
Carney, Judith A. 2001. *Black Rice: The African Origins of Rice Cultivation in the Americas.* Cambridge, MA: Harvard University Press.
Diner, Hasia R. 2001. *Hungering for America: Italian, Irish, and Jewish Foodways in the Age of Migration.* Cambridge, MA: Harvard University Press.
DuPuis, E. Melanie. 2002. *Nature's Perfect Food: How Milk Became America's Drink.* New York: New York University Press.
Giedion, Sigfried. 1948. *Mechanization Takes Command: A Contribution to Anonymous History.* New York: Oxford University Press.
Horowitz, Roger. 2006. *Putting Meat on the American Table: Taste, Technology, Transformation.* Baltimore, MD: Johns Hopkins University Press.
Inness, Sherrie A., ed. 2001. *Kitchen Culture in America: Popular Representations of Food, Gender, and Race.* Philadelphia: University of Pennsylvania Press.
Korsmeyer, Carolyn. 1999. *Making Sense of Taste: Food and Philosophy.* Ithaca, NY: Cornell University Press.

Funerals

A *funeral* is a special religious or secular ceremony performed after a person dies. The funeral provides a way for mourners to express grief and to honor the deceased. For many people, a funeral also represents a passage from one life to another, rather than the end of a person's existence.

History

In seventeenth- and eighteenth-century America, the preparation of the body prior to burial was performed by family members, usually women, who washed the body and wrapped it in a shroud. A local carpenter or cabinet maker provided a simple pine coffin. The funeral procession proceeded from the home of the deceased to the stark burial ground where the body was given a final blessing. After the burial, mourners gathered to feast and celebrate the deceased's life. Tokens such as gloves and rings were sometimes given to mourners.

By the mid-nineteenth century, urbanization, the increased availability of consumer goods, the development of beautifully landscaped cemeteries, and a spiritual shift away from Puritan gloom to Christian uplift led to elaborate mourning and funeral practices. Coffins made of expensive woods and outfitted with decorative hardware became common. The use of the word *casket*, defining an elaborate box for jewels, began to replace the older term *coffin*. A specialized vehicle, the hearse, was designed to transport the casket to the cemetery. Caskets as well as hearses were lined with sumptuous silk, wool, or velvet upholstery. Custom-printed memorial cards, either black or white, edged in gilt, and containing a prayer, were given out at the funeral.

Rise of the Funeral Industry

The funeral industry professionalized in the 1860s with the adoption of sophisticated embalming techniques developed during the American Civil War (1861–1865). Professional organizations and trade papers for funeral directors, embalmers, and cremation professionals set standards and defined the training required for certification. The responsibility for the preparation of the body, the funeral service, and the burial or cremation arrangements were gradually taken away from family members and increasingly dominated by funeral, hospital, and medical professionals.

As the processes of dying and death took place in clinical surroundings such as hospitals, elaborate nineteenth-century mourning rituals receded, although some customs remain. Today, somber clothes are still usually worn at a funeral. Prayer cards are still disseminated. The horse-drawn hearse is now an elegant, specialized automobile. Some religions adhere to strict procedures; Judaism forbids embalming, for example, and requires a simple funeral and a wood coffin.

Traditions and the Modern Funeral

The most elaborate funerals in American history have been those of military, political, and religious leaders. These retain much of the same pomp and finery associated with major nineteenth-century funerals. Funerals can reflect unique local traditions, such as the New Orleans jazz funeral, which draws on ancient African rituals and African American slave traditions of music and dance. Contemporary variants on the basic funeral reflect individuality or ethnic diversity, such as hip-hop funerals, which incorporate black urban culture, rap music, and Afro-Caribbean musical, oral, visual, and dance forms; Hispanic funerals, which draw on Mexican, Cuban, or Spanish traditions; or funerals that blend traditional Native American Navajo beliefs with modern American Christian practice.

Elise Madeleine Ciregna

See also Burial Grounds, Cemeteries, and Grave Markers; Etiquette and Manners; Funerary (Sepulchral) Monuments; Mourning; Mourning and Ethnicity; Rite, Ritual, and Ceremony; Tradition

References and Further Reading
Habenstein, Robert W., and William M. Lamers. 1962. *The History of American Funeral Directing*, rev. ed. Milwaukee, WI: National Funeral Directors Association of the United States, Inc.
Laderman, Gary. 2003. *Rest in Peace: A Cultural History of Death and the Funeral Home in Twentieth-Century America*. Oxford, UK: Oxford University Press.

Funerary (Sepulchral) Monuments

Funerary (sepulchral) monuments provide information about a person, family, community, or society. A gravestone can reveal information about the person or persons buried at the site, as well as the craftsmanship and techniques used to make the stone, prevailing religious beliefs, popular taste, fashion, attitudes toward children, gender, domestic and family life, ideology and symbology, and death and burial. Another advantage of studying stone artifacts is that these degrade less readily than other materials.

From the seventeenth century through the first third of the nineteenth century, the material, shape, and design of gravestones usually followed a well-established pattern. Stonecutters often worked seasonally or as an adjunct to other or full-time trades. The stone, most often slate, was quarried locally and shaped into a slab with round or square "shoulders." Carved designs in low relief vary regionally, but in general motifs of the earliest period, such as winged skulls and hourglasses, emphasized death, man's sinful nature, and the passage of time. Toward the late eighteenth century and into the early

Nineteenth-century cemeteries in America were often landscaped like picturesque parks. Sculptures of angels, as in this example, were extremely popular, especially carved in white marble. Such monuments were meant to enhance the grounds and provide viewing interest for visitors. (Courtesy of Forest Hills Cemetery, Boston, Massachusetts)

nineteenth century, new motifs emphasized spiritual uplift and sentimental mourning of the departed; cherubs' heads and the Neo-classically inspired urn-and-willow design are two of the most predominant designs of this period.

The professionalization of the stonecutting industry, the emergence of American academic sculpture, and the rural cemetery movement in the first half of the nineteenth century combined to shift dramatically the types of gravestones and monuments erected. Gravestones in the nineteenth century were often white marble, either quarried in Ver-

mont or imported from Italy. Markers exhibit a wide variety of sizes, types, and motifs throughout the country, and represent a radical shift from the more sober slate stones of previous centuries. Typically, these emphasize the relationship of the deceased to the bereaved (for example "My Husband"); the piety, innocence, or virtue of the deceased; or sentimental themes such as the hope of a reunion in the afterlife. Children's graves are often marked with small doves, lambs, or sleeping children, while the graves of mature persons often exhibit harvested sheaves of wheat, lilies, ivy, oak, or laurel. A heightened awareness and appreciation of Greek, Roman, and European sculpture is also evident in the popularity of allegorical figures such as Hope and Faith and in the figures of angels. Occasionally, cemetery patrons commissioned works in bronze.

In the late nineteenth century, improvements in the machines to carve granite, as well as the relative solidity of the material compared to marble and slate, caused granite to become the material of choice in cemeteries, as it still is today. Gravestones and monuments continue to exhibit a wide variety of styles, although these tend to be simpler and plainer than nineteenth-century stones.

In addition to gravestones, funerary monuments were, and continue to be, made of other long-lasting materials, such as zinc and other metals, concrete or cement, and wood. Zinc, for example, is highly malleable and can take on ornate embellishment at less expense than hand-carved stone; concrete or cement was readily available by the mid-twentieth century, and is formed easily and embellished with rocks, shells, and other ornaments. Wood deteriorates relatively rapidly, but its use satisfied ethnic and regional preferences (such as in the Southwest) and was readily available to mourners.

Elise Madeleine Ciregna

See also Burial Grounds, Cemeteries, and Grave Markers; Funerals; Mourning; Mourning and Ethnicity

References and Further Reading

Deetz, James. 1996. *In Small Things Forgotten: An Archaeology of Early American Life*, rev. ed. New York: Anchor Books/Doubleday.

Ludwig, Allan I. 1966. *Graven Images: New England Stonecarving and Its Symbols, 1650–1815*, 3rd ed. Hanover, NH: University Press of New England.

Pike, Martha V., and Janice Gray Armstrong, eds. 1980. *A Time to Mourn: Expressions of Grief in Nineteenth-Century America*. Stony Brook, NY: Museums at Stony Brook.

Furniture

Furniture is defined as movable utilitarian or aesthetic objects that characterize a building's interior. Furniture is made in a range of materials, by various processes, and differs in decoration by region, time period, and intended user/consumer. Furniture marks social rituals and cultural progress, defines status and taste trends, and reflects mobility and innovations in technology.

Colonial-Era Forms and Manufacture

Seventeenth-century settlers in North America employed furniture manufacturing practices of their home countries' small towns from which they emigrated. Objects were weighty and rectilinear, continuing and elaborating specific provincial styles due to the difficulties of communication with rising European centers of culture such as London. British-trained craftsmen, foreign imports, and design books were the means of transferring styles and methods to the colonies. The three dominant technologies utilized for furniture making were medieval practices of turning, carving, and joining. Standard furniture forms, usually made of oak and other native woods, were cupboards, turned chairs, and six-board chests.

A change in furniture occurred at the turn of the eighteenth century as new technology, craftsmen, and materials were initiated. The William and Mary style, at its height around this time, was characterized by Baroque ornament, verticality, light appearance, decorative turnings, and double C-curves. More woods were available and new furniture forms were developed, including tea tables, dressing tables, easy chairs, high chests, and japanned (painted to appear as Asian lacquer) decoration. Queen Anne furniture, fashionable during the second quarter of the eighteenth century, exemplified artist William

Hogarth's (1697–1764) "line of beauty" through elegant forms, cabriole (S-curve) legs, vase-shaped backsplats, and high chests with scrolling pediments. Pieces such as the bedchamber dressing table suggested status and mobility because they indicated an increase in rooms of a house and a more refined life. During the eighteenth century, form became ornament as veneer (a thin layer of wood with an attractive grain pattern glued to the exterior of a less expensive wood) and grains of wood fashioned surface decoration. As a socioeconomic contrast, Windsor chairs, first made in Philadelphia in 1740 and based on English prototypes, were available to many Americans and were popular because they were light, standardized, and inexpensive. Windsor chairs were made in a variety of woods, including hickory, poplar, ash, pine, and maple, which were applied to different parts of the chair. They were frequently painted for decoration and to conceal the use of different woods in a chair's construction.

Philadelphia surpassed Boston in the late eighteenth century as the American center of mercantile wealth and trade and produced furniture in a luxurious Rococo taste. Thomas Chippendale's (1718–1779) *The Gentleman & Cabinet-Maker's Director* of 1754 provided design impetus for the mid- to late eighteenth century. Chippendale chair characteristics include ball-and-claw feet, brightly carved backsplats, square shoulders, cabriole or Marlboro legs, foliate and scrolling motifs, and mahogany wood. The use of imported mahogany indicated sophistication. Regional differences in eighteenth-century furniture style and technique materialized in major cabinetmaking centers, including Boston, Philadelphia, and Newport.

Nineteenth-Century Forms and Styles

After the Revolutionary War (1775–1783), Americans embraced the Neoclassical style, revealing a taste for English, and later French, furniture. Archaeological discovery of Pompeii and Herculaneum encouraged inquiry into classical antiquity. Based on designs by George Hepplewhite (1727?–1786) and Thomas Sheraton (1751–1806), the period's furniture exhibits symmetry, control, and rationality. Federal-style furniture is characterized by decorative treatments of fluted and reeded legs, swags, paterae, husks, and bellflowers. Standard New England Federal chairs were visually light with shallow carving, attenuated and rectilinear in design, and tighter and more compact than eighteenth-century examples. The port city of Baltimore, Maryland, enjoyed a period of wealth and prosperity around the turn of the nineteenth century and was a temporary rival to New York. Baltimore developed painted or "fancy" furniture that possessed bold patterns and colorful forms.

With the completion of the Erie Canal in 1825, New York City, now connected commercially to the American interior, became the style and economic center of the nation. The late Neoclassical or American Empire style applied a more archaeologically correct style, as exhibited by *klismos* forms and Grecian couches. Well-known cabinetmaker Duncan Phyfe (1768?–1854) and his shop produced outstanding furniture in excellent proportions, elegant lines, and luxurious woods. The furniture of Charles-Honoré Lannuier (1779–1819) promoted the French vogue for gilded ornament, which originated with Napoleon's architects Percier and Fontaine and their 1801 style guide, *Recueil de décorations intérieures*. Thomas Hope's (1769–1831) *Household Furniture and Interior Decoration* (1807) introduced English influences to the American Empire style. Some furniture forms of the period include pier tables, sideboards, and center pedestal tables.

Rococo, Gothic, and Renaissance revival styles were adopted for various interiors throughout the nineteenth century. European craftsmen, particularly from Germany, dominated the furniture trade. Rococo Revival, a playful reinterpretation of French Rococo, furnished parlors, while the Gothic taste, an international phenomenon popular in England and reinvigorated by A. W. N. Pugin (1812–1852), was suitable for libraries. In the United States, important figures include Gothic Revival architect Alexander Jackson Davis (1803–1892) and Andrew Jackson Downing (1815–1852), who influenced American architecture, furniture, taste, and landscape through his popular books *Cottage Residences* (1842) and *The Architecture of Country Houses* (1850). Some key pieces of this period are the etagere (for the display of decorative objects), hall stands, and parlor cabinets.

Technology continually altered furniture form and manufacture throughout the nineteenth century. Samuel Gragg (1772–1855) developed a patent in 1808 for steam-bending wood, a forerunner of the technique used to create bentwood chairs. Lambert Hitchcock (1795–1852) instituted mass production of chairs through the distribution of his factory-made, unassembled pieces throughout the states. John Henry Belter (1804–1863), whose factory employed German woodworking technology for bending wood, held patents for laminating and steaming processes. New materials were also utilized to construct furniture, including papier-mâché and cast iron. Mid-nineteenth-century inventions such as spring coils for seats and button-tufted upholstery produced comfortable furniture. The furniture industry was further transformed by mass-produced, inexpensive furniture manufactured in centers such as Grand Rapids, Michigan, and Cincinnati, Ohio.

World's fairs, forums to exchange goods, ideas, and technology, disseminated furniture designs. A paradigmatic shift occurred in the early 1870s as focus moved from elaborate French furniture to simple English furnishings. Important texts, such as Charles Locke Eastlake's (1836–1908) *Hints on Household Taste*, a middle-class moralizing text published in London in 1868 and in Boston in 1872, expounded the idea of hominess and sought to improve taste and design through Eastlake or "art furniture." British reform ideals ushered in a period known as the Aesthetic Movement, which was concerned with beauty and was influenced by foreign cultures. While many consumers purchased goods directly from retailers, high-end furniture was available from furniture and decorating firms, such as New York City's Herter Brothers, for wealthier patrons.

Twentieth-Century Trends

The Arts and Crafts Movement encouraged craftsmen, including Gustav Stickley (1858–1942) with his Mission furniture, to create simple furniture using "honest" construction. Frank Lloyd Wright (1867–1959) demonstrated an interest in Japanese aesthetic, which was sympathetic to Arts and Crafts ideals, through his furniture and interiors. Colonial Revival and other historicist styles were popular after World War I. Alternatively, American modern design, initially inspired by European progress, established an identity through the efforts of designers, such as Paul Frankl (1886–1958) and Donald Deskey (1894–1989), working in industrial materials. Bauhaus émigrés, including Ludwig Mies van der Rohe (1886–1969) and Walter Gropius (1883–1969), influenced furniture and interiors through the lens of Modern European architecture.

After World War II (1939–1945) Americans designed furniture of innovative materials, including molded plywood, various metals, fiberglass, and plastics. Many designers, such as Isamu Noguchi (1904–1988), Charles (1907–1978) and Ray Eames (1912–1988), and Harry Bertoia (1915–1978), created furniture for manufacturers Herman Miller and Knoll to furnish the modern interior. Concurrently, studio craft designers reacted against industrialization through hand production and traditional materials.

Current Furniture Studies

Furniture can be studied in terms of material, technique, style, usage, and its movement in the marketplace. There are numerous approaches to studying furniture, including maker-focused, regional, connoisseurship, cultural and social history, and socioeconomic investigation. Material culture studies have also begun to incorporate theoretical models from various disciplines, fields, and approaches, such as ethnography, historical archaeology, gender studies, and consumption analysis, which can be applied to the furniture field.

Monica Obniski

See also Aesthetic Movement; Arts and Crafts Movement; Colonial Revival; Decorative Arts; Design History and American Design; Gothic Revival; Handicraft and Artisanship; Industrial Design; Renaissance Revival; Rococo Revival

References and Further Reading
Ames, Kenneth L., ed. 1983. *Victorian Furniture: Essays from a Victorian Society Autumn Symposium*. Philadelphia, PA: Victorian Society in America.
Bates, Elizabeth Bidwell, and Jonathan L. Fairbanks. 1981. *American Furniture, 1620 to the Present*. New York: R. Marek.
Fairbanks, Jonathan L., and Robert F. Trent. 1982. *New England Begins: The Seventeenth Century*. Boston: Museum of Fine Arts.
Fitzgerald, Oscar P. 1982. *Three Centuries of American Furniture*. Englewood Cliffs, NJ: Prentice-Hall.
Heckscher, Morrison H. 1985. *American Furniture in the Metropolitan Museum of Art, Late Colonial Period: The Queen Anne and Chippendale Styles*. New York: The Museum and Random House.
Hurst, Ronald L., and Jonathan Prown. 1997. *Southern Furniture, 1680–1830: The Colonial Williamsburg Collections*. Williamsburg, VA: Colonial Williamsburg Foundation.
Montgomery, Charles F. 1978 (1966). *American Furniture, the Federal Period*. New York: Bonanza Books.

G

Games

Games include indoor and outdoor amateur and professional activities. Activities requiring physical prowess are called, colloquially, *sports*, and other activities are referred to as *games*, though the terms are often used interchangeably (as in the Olympic Games). Games—activities bound by rules and limited by time and space—may be competitive or may serve as a pastime or amusement. Outdoor games are demarcated by specialized equipment and playing fields and venues, distinctive uniforms or adornment, and particular sets of rules. Indoor games are categorized by either their material culture (for example, card games, dice games, or board games) or their focus (for example, skill, strategy, or chance). Games may be played by professionals or amateurs, children or adults.

Older games, dating back to ancient cultures and including checkers, Go, chess, mahjongg, pocket billiards, darts, and numerous card games, arrived in the United States with various waves of immigrants. New York City was the early center of the board game industry, an offshoot of the city's rise as a commercial and print capital. The first commercially produced board game in the United States, though, was manufactured in Salem, Massachusetts. *The Mansion of Happiness*, issued by the W. and S. B. Ives Company in 1843, taught moralistic values to its players. Its descendants include Springfield, Massachusetts, lithographer Milton Bradley's (1836–1911) *The Checkered Game of Life* (1860), now known as *Life*. Other nineteenth-century board games initiated Americans into modern society by imitating new activities such as department store shopping and political campaigning. As the growing middle class accumulated leisure time and surplus income in the early twentieth century, the classic American board games, many of which model different aspects of industrial and global society, reached the market: the commodities trading game *Pit* (1904), the real estate game *Monopoly* (1935), the who-dunnit game *Clue* (1949), and the war game *Risk* (1959).

The development of computer and video technology has increased the ways in which games are packaged and played. The video-game *Pong* (1958), the fantasy role-playing game *Dungeons and Dragons* (1973), the card trading game *Magic: The Gathering* (1993), and the imported German strategy game *Settlers of Catan* (1995) mark three new stages in the development of the heavily commercial contemporary game industry: game specialty stores, conventions, and media tie-ins such as game-based movies and books. In 1994, the Game Show Network (GSN) debuted on cable television, airing old and new game shows (television shows that pit contestants against each other for prizes).

As widespread media forms modeling society, games receive criticism for promoting undesirable behaviors. For example, first-person-shooter video games were blamed for the 1999 massacre at Columbine High School in Jefferson County, Colorado. More recently, violent and criminal aspects of the video game series *Grand Theft Auto* led to industry and distributor self-censorship and the rating of games. Elaborations of mainstream games, such as *Ghettopoly* (2003) receive criticism for explicit racism. Games historically have reflected and engaged social and cultural values, both beneficial and detrimental: They have served to instruct and inform Americans of all ages, but they have also abetted gambling.

Krista M. Park

See also Children's Material Culture; Children's Toys; Computers and Information Technology; Leisure, Recreation, and Amusements; Popular Culture; Recreation Rooms; Sports

References and Further Reading
Burnham, Van. 2001. *Supercade: A Visual History of the Videogame Age, 1971–1984.* Cambridge, MA: MIT Press.
Hofer, Margaret K. 2003. *The Games We Played: The Golden Age of Board and Table Games.* New York: Princeton Architectural Press.
Murray, Harold James Ruthven. 1952. *A History of Board-Games Other than Chess.* Oxford, UK: Clarendon Press.
Parlett, David. 1999. *Oxford History of Board Games.* Oxford, UK: Oxford University Press.

Gay Consumerism

Gay consumerism describes three overlapping material practices, ranging from gay men and lesbians (and to a lesser extent bisexual and transgendered people) consuming ordinary goods in transgressive ways to their influencing corporate behavior through spending power to defining gay people in terms of what they consume. Each of these strains of gay consumerism has influenced society as a whole. Throughout the twentieth century, for example, Americans drew on gay subcultural styles to refresh stale fashions. This had not made homosexual culture more mainstream but transformed straight society into the "cooler," ironic postmodern world of today. American corporations have changed hiring, benefits, and advertising practices in response to gay customer loyalty and boycotts of unfriendly companies. Many gay people have felt socially validated by their new status as a niche market. The combined effects of these practices are complex, especially when observed against the accelerating consumerism of society at large.

Consumption and Coding

The suppression of homosexuality through most periods of history has provoked coded displays of material goods. For instance, gay men in the early twentieth century were reputed to wear red neckties. Such practices were important not only in building social networks but also in establishing a sense of selfhood within a larger society that tried to make homosexuality invisible. Many material markers of gayness have been fashioned against cultural norms of femininity and masculinity, and dressing contrary to one's sex (commonly referred to as *cross-dressing*) has been a common form of resistant consumption. Gay life has been distinguished by *camp*, which both celebrates and parodies vulgar elements of culture. Anyone may own a shell-encrusted souvenir of Florida, but owning a hundred such items, carefully arranged by motif, is "camping it up." Consumption itself has been considered a feminine trait, so gay men are extraordinarily marked.

Gay Consumerism as Activism

Gay people cannot live by shell-encrusted souvenirs alone, and gays and lesbians have been able to assert power by spending money with gay-friendly businesses, from neighborhood delis to multinational corporations. Boycotts of the Florida Citrus Commission (due to their retention of Anita Bryant, a militant anti–gay rights activist, as their spokesperson in the 1970s) and other institutions viewed as insensitive or discriminatory toward gay people have also brought visibility to gay consumer power. Gay activists have pressured the media, through their viewing and purchasing behavior, to portray homosexuals in a sympathetic manner, and gay publications have offered enticing demographic data about their readerships. Now advertisements are as likely to flatter gay viewers as to make jokes at their expense, because companies hope to turn a profit from this newly discovered niche market.

Gays can hope to improve their lot by acting as citizen consumers, but such efforts may be only partially successful because of the complexity of determining what is best for gay people. For instance, gay organizations are divided about receiving donations from the Molson Coors Brewing Company, which has changed its discriminatory hiring practices but still has ties to the ultra-conservative Coors family.

Visibility and Advertising

Gay activism now encompasses loyalty to gay-friendly companies, and activities as easy as turning to the Logo Channel (a cable network providing gay-themed content) or purchasing specific brands of shoes are seen by many gays as "making a contribution" to gay visibility. Nonnegative portrayals of gay men and lesbians in movies, television, and advertisements have seemed to confer legitimacy on gay people. Some people debate whether visibility alone can bring substantive political changes, especially because niche advertising is compromised by advertisers becoming adept at producing ads that are "gay vague." Such ads communicate gay content to gay people in coded ways that straight people miss.

Corporate advertising has become an important funding base for gay media, yet many companies have pressured publications to reduce or eliminate potent sexual and political material, reducing important forums to innocuous lifestyle showcases. Not every gay person can dress like the actors in gay-themed movies, buy an automobile advertised in gay magazines, watch gay-themed shows on premium cable, or otherwise purchase their way into the gay community. Critics also worry that those buying a Mitchell Gold + Bob Williams sofa (formerly the Mitchell Gold Company; Mitchell Gold himself is a visible gay entrepreneur and activist) does not make one authentically gay any more than buying Kraft Macaroni and Cheese Dinner makes one authentically American.

No phenomenon illustrates the contradictions of gay consumerism better than the television show, "Queer Eye for the Straight Guy" (2003–2007), which appeared on the cable television network Bravo. While the popular program contains sexually inflected banter, the point of the show is that gay men can share their supposed superior powers of discrimination as consumers with apparently helpless straight people. Queerness in the show is defined by one's competency in using grooming products, cooking gadgets, glassware, and so forth. The show's unspoken and underlying drama hinges on whether straight men can take consuming advice from "queers" without becoming queer themselves. In defining gayness in terms of consumption practices, substantive engagement of gender and power issues are neatly avoided even as sponsors are served.

Elizabeth Throop

See also Advertisements and Advertising; Consumerism and Consumption; Gender; Sex and Sexuality

References and Further Reading

Chasin, Alexandra. 2000. *Selling Out: The Gay and Lesbian Movement Goes to Market.* New York: St. Martin's Press.
King Shey, Bruce. 2005. "Queering the Universal Rhetoric of Objects: Myth, Industrial Design, and the Politics of Difference." Master's thesis, California College of the Arts, http://sites.cca.edu/sightlines/2005/bkingshey_bio.html.
Sender, Katherine. 2004. *Business, Not Politics: The Making of the Gay Market.* New York: Columbia University Press.
Sontag, Susan. 2001 (1964). "Notes on Camp." Reprinted in *Against Interpretation, and Other Essays*, 275–292. New York: Picador.

Gender

Gender has been defined in a variety of ways, ranging from an equation of *sex* with *gender* to understandings of the economic, social, and cultural relationships among the sexes to issues of identity. *Gender* was originally defined as "innate" or "biological" attributes of men and women. The women's movement of the 1960s questioned this notion. Feminists pointed out that gender as a political ideology defined the organization of the relationships between men and women. These

relationships were thus socially constructed, not natural; *sex* could refer to a human's physical characteristics, while *gender* defined expected, often stereotyped social and cultural roles or attributes ascribed to those physical characteristics. These feminists highlighted the social nature of sex distinctions to counter biological determinism. *Gender* began to be understood as a society's ideas about men and women. Feminist scholars used this definition of gender to uncover and analyze historic constructions of "sex" roles. The inclusion of gender as a category of scholarly analysis demonstrates how sexual distinctions organize societies as well as how gender signifies power relationships.

Gender as an Analytical Category

In 1986, historian Joan Wallach Scott proposed that *gender* was more than a descriptor. Rather, the idea could be used to challenge previous historical paradigms. For Scott, previous approaches to gender as a category of analysis relied on physical difference between men and women without exploring how gender affects other areas of life, treated gender as a by-product of economic structures without understanding gender as an analytical tool, or reified the binary opposition between male and female without examining the constructed nature of this opposition. Scott thus proposed a two-part definition of gender. First, gender should be considered a creative force behind social relationships, which is based on supposed differences among the sexes. This would mean that gender is represented in cultural symbols and in the concepts that define these symbols. Additionally, Scott noted that gender is constructed through the relationships between institutions, organizations, and politics. Gender, then, is created in a variety of activities, interactions, historical periods, and places. Gender is subjective and articulates power relations; it legitimates and constructs social relationships, and it legitimates political power as well as criticizes it. For instance, power is coded as masculine, and enemies are characterized as effeminate. What Scott wanted to make clear was that the binary opposition between male/masculinity and female/femininity was not a given but that this opposition was contextual and constructed.

Gender as Performance

Cultural studies scholar Judith Butler complicated the study of gender further by suggesting that sex was gender all along. The binary of male/female cannot explain the gendered variation of humans. In *Gender Trouble* (1990), Butler argues that gender was a performance in which the body is repetitively trained to seem like a man or a woman, a "natural" being. Gender is trouble, then: As soon as one is assigned an identity based on gender, gender can be questioned if one does not conform to—perform—the role.

In 1959, Erving Goffman (1922–1992) pointed to the use of props and the body to present a self, and Butler reiterates this insight. In the performance of gender, props are required to make the performance "work." These props are often objects that signal the gender status of the person using them. Gender, as Butler noted, is an embodied process in which ideology is applied to bodies and to the artifacts used by these bodies. Gender is a process by which people create identities by using cultural ideals, other people, and objects.

Gender and Material Culture Studies

Written documents are often the primary sources for historical scholarship; those who did not leave written documentation are often omitted in the study of the past. Proponents of women's history and gender history have often used visual and material culture to understand the experiences of women as well as the experiences of men who were denied or did not have access to the tools of literacy.

The study of material culture often makes a society's gender assumptions visible, sometimes countering textual evidence. According to scholar Michael S. Kimmel (Martinez and Ames, 1997), the material culture of gender allows for at least four different analytical approaches. First, one can approach the gender of things: how objects, from cars to clothes, are defined as masculine, feminine, or neuter. Second, how things are valued might signal gender differentials. Objects created by women have historically been devalued or derogatorily labeled. For instance, women's arts have been understood as crafts, which are valued less than the fine arts. Third, the gender assumptions of individuals who produce things reproduce engendered things. Male doll makers, for example, often made their dolls work like machines with gears, wheels, and springs rather than think about who played with the dolls. Fourth, the material culture of gender helps create gendered beings. How men and women use these objects may reveal how they accept, reject, or mediate gender roles.

Clothing often reifies cultural constructions of gender. Since the Middle Ages, gender distinctions in dress have been visible in Western culture in that men overwhelmingly have worn pants and women have worn gowns. Wearing pants was almost taboo for women because pants were associated with masculine power. Until the nineteenth century, dress marked gender difference, but two changes in dress complicated gender roles: drawers (underwear) and bloomers. Women began wearing drawers with two leg tubes, which resembled men's trousers. Divided garments had been associated with masculinity, and undivided garments had been associated with femininity. These drawers blurred the boundaries, but they also affirmed feminine modesty in that they added another layer of clothing to women's bodies. These drawers were also open at the crotch and this openness signaled women's sexuality. These garments, despite their divided nature, still constructed women as different from men. Nineteenth-century dress reformers promoted bloomers and the short dress as better for women's health than corsets and long skirts. The outfit, dubbed "the American Dress," was highly controversial because the bloomers were visible underneath the skirt, and bloomers were basically pants. Bloomers blurred the sartorial distinction between men and women, and they were highly criticized by both men and women. "The American Dress" was never very popular, but utopian movements, like the Oneida Community, believed the costume reflected feminine modesty rather than an attempt to gain masculine power.

Men's dress has also changed, moving from the more ornate and complicated to the simple. In the eighteenth century, men dressed extravagantly to suggest their power and wealth, but by the nineteenth century, men adopted a plain clothing style to signal power. Men's fashions of previous generations were then coded as effeminate. By the end of the nineteenth century, women's clothing became more like men's clothing because of its practical nature, and men's clothing became more uniform. By the 1960s, unisex clothing (jeans, T-shirts, and intentionally "ungendered" fashions) made it more difficult to distinguish gender by dress.

Other forms of material culture and processes are also associated with gender: For example, cars and technology are often considered masculine enterprises. Gender also problematizes analyses of material culture. For instance, scholars have found that some studies of American material culture have assumed only male subjects. Historian Karin Calvert (1992) noted that before the 1980s, all the scholarship on children assumed a male child.

Gender as a category of scholarly analysis complicates presentations of race and class. Scholars have recognized the role gender plays in expressing ethnic, racial, religious, or class identities. Women are often the bearers of ethnic identities through conventions of dress. In yard art, gender highlights portrayals of race through yard figurines of black children—all male—who fish, eat watermelon, or serve. According to folklorist Jeannie Banks Thomas, the gender differential might reflect anxiety over black males in society and, perhaps, the desire to own black

This circa 1900 Singer Sewing Machine advertisement uses idealized images of women, the prominent display of a brand name and the assurance of quality to persuade customers to purchase the product. (Library of Congress)

males—but not black females. Social class as a category of analysis presents an interesting problem for material culture studies because the material culture of the wealthy is more readily available. Studies of material culture often reflect the experiences of middle- and upper-class men and women but not of working-class men and women. Pants, as a uniform of work on farms or in factories, may have symbolized power differently in working-class culture.

Objects often highlight the complexity of gendering. For instance, Jeannie Banks Thomas (2003) studied the gender characteristics of cemetery statues, yard art, and the Barbie doll. What she uncovered is that, taken alone, these objects often conform to gender roles, but *how* people use these objects complicates understandings of gender. Barbie might reflect stereotypes of women, but in play, children—girls and boys—use her in ways that resist gender norms. In play, Barbie wears Ken's clothes, fights G.I. Joes in combat, or hacks into computers. This play demonstrates the malleability of gender.

Kelly J. Baker

See also Cultural History; Cultural Studies; Dower Right; Dress, Accessories, and Fashion; Ethnicity; House, Home, and Domesticity; Race; Sex and Sexuality; Social Class and Social Status; Social History

References and Further Reading
Burman, Barbara, and Carole Turbin, eds. 2003. *Material Strategies: Dress and Gender in Historical Perspective*. Oxford, UK: Blackwell.
Butler, Judith. 1990. *Gender Trouble: Feminism and the Subversion of Identity*. New York: Routledge.
Calvert, Karin. 1992. *Children in the House: The Material Culture of Early Childhood, 1600–1900*. Boston: Northeastern University Press.
Goffman, Erving. 1959. *The Presentation of Self in Everyday Life*. New York: Anchor Books Doubleday.
Martinez, Katherine, and Kenneth L. Ames, eds. 1997. *The Material Culture of Gender, the*
Gender of Material Culture. Winterthur, DE: Winterthur Museum.
Scott, Joan Wallach. 1986. "Gender: A Useful Category of Analysis." *American Historical Review* 91 (4): 1053–1075.
Thomas, Jeannie Banks. 2003. *Naked Barbies, Warrior Joes, and Other Forms of Visible Gender*. Urbana: University of Illinois Press.

General (Country) Stores

Though still extant in the United States, the *general*, or *country*, *store* is considered a quaint remnant of the past. A rocking-chair-filled front porch, a cracker barrel, a pot-bellied wood stove, and cluttered shelves of goods characterize this important retail institution. This nostalgic image reflects popular and scholarly writings produced in the early twentieth century, when the impact of department stores, mail order catalogues, automobiles, and roads decreased dependence on local markets.

From the very first years of European settlement in North America, general stores were often the first businesses established in an area open to settlement, first along rivers and then, once roads were built, at crossroads and village and town centers. Shire towns in New England and county seats elsewhere in the colonies and later nation boasted public markets and a variety of commercial establishments to cater to increased trade due to government business, especially on court days. General stores in towns other than county seats provided a convenient means of acquiring goods in an era when traveling was difficult and expensive.

General store proprietors were entrepreneurs and often town leaders. Many general stores doubled as the local post office; the proprietor as postmaster was, through the nineteenth century, affiliated in local party politics because the postmaster was a political appointment. Social gatherings in general stores were peppered with local gossip but equally enlivened with political debate.

First and foremost, though, the general store's basic role was to acquire and redistribute a wide variety of foodstuffs; dry goods; building, farming, and household supplies; books; and other materials. A true barter system was not utilized; store proprietors often provided credit for customers in return for fresh produce (especially milk, butter, and eggs) and for services and labor to which a cash value was assigned. In some communities credit was extended to farmers until crops were harvested and sold. Farmers were allowed to pay their farmhands with a store credit (*self-order*). When money was in short supply due to the Panics of 1873 and 1893, general store proprietors' extending credit to customers helped maintain the well-being of small-town and rural families.

General stores were housed in small buildings similar to residential dwellings. Windows were small, so display was limited, and interiors were dark. Documentary and photographic evidence reveals that order and efficiency were evident in stock neatly arranged on wood counters and shelves. Store ledgers (*daybooks*) provide evidence of small-scale business, community and rural history, and the rise of consumerism in the twentieth century. Today, the convenience store (often affiliated with a gas station) has overwhelmingly replaced the general store, which had already fallen victim to national brands, department stores, mail order catalogues, suburbanization, and the automobile. Surviving general stores have now attained the status of tourist destinations, whether as historical sites or as nostalgia-inflected businesses.

Shirley Teresa Wajda

See also Consumerism and Consumption; Department Stores; Mail Order Catalogues

References and Further Reading

Atherton, Lewis E. 1949. *The Southern Country Store, 1800–1860*. Baton Rouge: Louisiana State University Press.

Carson, Gerald. 1965. *The Old Country Store*. New York: E. P. Dutton.

Schlereth, Thomas J. 1989. "Country Stores, County Fairs, and Mail-Order Catalogs: Consumerism in Rural America." In *The Consumer Culture and the American Home, 1890–1930*, ed. Glenda Dyer and Martha Reed, 27–45. Beaumont, TX: McFaddin-Ward House Museum.

Stofle, Richard W. 1972. "Whither the Country Store?" *Ethnohistory* 19 (1): 63–72.

Georgian Style

Georgian defines the fashionable shift of architectural and decorative design throughout the American colonies and England for much of the eighteenth century. Coinciding with the reigns of George I, II, and III (collectively 1714–1820), this style incorporated symmetry and geometric proportions in building forms with central axes; Neoclassical details such as Palladian windows and entranceways with columns, pilasters, and broken pediments; and hipped or side-gabled roofs. The Georgian style was the British component of the wider Neoclassical style sweeping through the Western world in the eighteenth and early nineteenth centuries.

Early American public buildings incorporating this style's updating of classical architecture include the Wren Building (ca. 1695) at the College of William and Mary designed by English architect Christopher Wren (1632–1723); the Governor's Palace (1706–1714) in Williamsburg, Virginia; Philadelphia's Pennsylvania State House (1732–1753), now known as Independence Hall; and Boston's Old State House (rebuilt 1711; redesigned 1747). American colonists copied this popular building form through British pattern books. Especially influential were the ideas of Andrea Palladio (1508–1580), which were conveyed through several works published in London and available in the colonies. Several editions of Palladio's *Four Books of Architecture* (1570) were owned by Thomas Jefferson (1743–1826), whose designs for Monticello (1769–1809) and the University of Virginia (1825) show Palladio's influence.

In domestic dwellings, the central-hall plan characteristic of this new building style replaced the hall-parlor house plan. Formerly, visitors entered directly into the house and were met by a family as they worked, slept, ate, and played. In a larger Georgian house visitors entered into a central stairway that ordered their passage through and experiences in the house. Visitors were guided to social spaces and away from the private and productive spaces located on upper floors and at the rear of the house.

The Georgian style heralded a new formality in social relations. The front, public spaces of the house—parlors and dining rooms—were now a sort of stage for proper social interaction. "Backstage" areas were those dedicated to bodies at rest or at labor in preparation for public display. Thus this style is also associated with a widespread change in social behavior based in part on the rising wealth of the nonaristocratic wealthy (the gentry) in the colonies. The gentry's wealth, as well as its cosmopolitanism, was displayed through the choices of brick and sometimes stone as a building material, elaborate windows (including sash windows and fanlights), interior finishes in plaster and wood carvings such as egg-and-dart moldings, and the application of ornamental designs such as swags.

Houses in the Georgian style include Stratford Hall (1730s) and Westover (1750s) in Virginia; Cliveden (1760s), near Philadelphia, Pennsylvania; and the many eighteenth-

Westover, the house built by planter William Byrd II in the mid-eighteenth century, commands a view of Virginia's James River. The brick building's symmetry, entranceway pediment, and hipped roof are features of the Georgian style. (Library of Congress)

century town houses of Annapolis, Maryland, and Charleston, South Carolina. Farmhouses and other vernacular dwellings as well feature the Neoclassical proportions, symmetry, and stylistic details of this popular building style.

Shirley Teresa Wajda

See also Agricultural Architecture; Civic Architecture; Classical Revival (Neoclassicism); Domestic Architecture; Social Class and Social Status; Style

References and Further Reading
Bushman, Richard L. 1992. *The Refinement of America: Persons, Houses, Cities.* New York: Alfred A. Knopf.
Herman, Bernard L. 2005. *Town House: Architecture and Material Life in the Early American City, 1780–1830.* Chapel Hill: University of North Carolina Press for the Omohundro Institute of Early American History and Culture.
Roth, Leland M. 2001. *American Architecture: A History.* Boulder, CO: Westview Press.

Upton, Dell. 1998. *Architecture in the United States*. New York: Oxford University Press.

Gifts and Gift Giving

A *gift* is most commonly understood as something material or immaterial given voluntarily without expectation of compensation. This popular understanding of gifts and giving influenced political philosopher Thomas Hobbes (1588–1679) who, in *Leviathan* (1651), defined a gift as something transferred outside the purview of a contract. Philosopher Karl Marx (1818–1883), writing in *Capital, Volume 1* (1867), defined a *gift* as something given for free and that was the opposite of a *commodity* (which is something given with the expectation of monetary compensation). Many twentieth-century anthropologists, sociologists, historians, and philosophers, however, note a tension between the popular understanding of gifts as free offerings and the actual practice of giving, which they see as a self-interested act that demands reciprocity from the recipient.

Theories of Gifts and Giving

Drawing from ethnographies conducted by others in societies throughout the world, anthropologist Marcel Mauss (1872–1950) developed a theory of the gift wherein the practice of giving, rather than embodying disinterested generosity, involves the expectation of reciprocity and the spirit of competition. Mauss considered gift exchange to be a phenomenon in which all social institutions were involved. He viewed gift economies (that is, economies based on gift exchanges) as predecessors to commodity economies (economies based on monetary exchanges), while noting that aspects of gift exchange continued in modern European life. Gift exchange, according to Mauss, depends on three obligations—to give, to receive, and to reciprocate. The obligations to give and receive are predicated on what Mauss saw as a universal need for people to enter into social exchange, which enables the parties to avoid war with one another. The obligation to reciprocate is predicated on the gift's spirit. To give a gift is to make a present of oneself, a mode of exchange radically opposed to the economy of commodity capitalism in which the relations of production that generate the exchanged object are obscured by exchange value.

Whether or not gifts generate profit for their givers, gift exchange and commodity exchange do differ in how they produce social relations. Gift transactions link the people involved in them. The gift continues to be identified with the giver and the transaction itself. Thus, gift relations bring people together while commodity relations pull them apart.

Anthroplogist Claude Lévi-Strauss argued that giving, receiving, and reciprocating are different modes of one phenomenon that underlies all aspects of social life: exchange. Lévi-Strauss elaborated this idea in *Elementary Structures of Kinship* (1969), placing the exogamous exchange of women by men in marriage at the origin of culture and society.

While the idea that cycles of exchange form the basis of society continues to be influential, it has not gone unchallenged. Feminist theorists, in particular, have levied a number of critiques against it. For one, this approach has been seen to obscure the economics and politics of sex/gender systems that produce the very categories of people (i.e., women and men) involved in the exchange. Others have pointed out that the whole gift cycle depends on a need to return, to regenerate, to recycle. In other words, systems of exchange are built on scarcity. What if, instead of scarcity, there is excess? Scholars following approaches to gifts and giving that address excess have pointed to mothering and writing as examples of giving without return.

The system of exchange theorized by Lévi-Strauss has also been critiqued for reducing social agents (i.e., people) to automata that mechanically follow the rules. Yet the cycle of exchange is often broken; gifts often do go unreciprocated. Giving may be theorized linearly, as a process embedded in time. This theoretical approach accounts for the uncertainty of reception and reciprocity that follow the initial offering. It also suggests that the time lag between gift and counter-gift is what enables individuals to believe that their gifts are given freely even though hindsight reveals that gifts tend to produce reciprocity.

Other scholars have argued that exchange does not dominate social life. Some objects cannot be given away. These "inalienable possessions" are fundamental to the creation of social hierarchy because they authenticate particular narratives about familial origin, narratives that draw on cosmological authority to legitimize social rank. Since women play important roles in the production, preservation, and control of these special objects, they have access to significant political power.

Histories of Gifts and Giving in America

Although gift giving took place on the North American continent long before European colonization, exchanges between European colonizers and indigenous peoples are some of the earliest analyzed by historians of the region now called the United States. European dealings with Native Americans are examples of gift relations that do not fit the model of reciprocity described by Mauss.

The French understanding of Indians not just as non-Christian strangers but as savages disqualified their dealings from the realm of gifts. Even though the French recognized that Indians referred to what they gave as gifts, the French did not feel grateful or obliged to indigenous gift givers because they saw them as unenlightened about the "true" value of things. Furthermore, although European missionaries attempted to impose Christianity onto Indians as a "gift," they intended it as a one-way transaction. For Native Americans, receiving such unilateral gifts was problematic, for they believed that violations of reciprocity were expressions of magic. Still, both parties used the rhetoric of giving in their exchanges because they viewed the power to give as the expression of sovereignty.

Nineteenth- and twentieth-century gift exchanges in the United States were complicated less by contact between European and Indian cultures than by the intrusion of the commercial market in producing and governing exchanges of gifts. Gift relations are an important part of life under capitalism. Capitalism tends to alienate relationships by placing a monetary value on nearly every interaction (for example, it is common to see media articles about the current cost of raising a child). This has affected how gifts are used to establish and maintain personal relations, since commodities are considered too impersonal for this use. Individuals use shopping to convert commodities into meaningful possessions that can be exchanged in personal relationships. Marketers capitalize on this practice by using the rhetoric of gifts and giving to promote their commodities. Homemade gifts, while generally associated with childhood, are perceived as separate from the market and, thus, are seen as more representative of the giver's identity than are commodities.

Many scholars have linked the growth of industrialization in the United States to the development of the nation's most spectacular gift-giving occasion: Christmas. During the colonial period, Puritan New Englanders suppressed Christmas, while southerners continued the European, seasonal practice of giving feasts and presents to laborers, including slaves. In 1865, Christmas was established as a national holiday in which first handmade and then inexpensive manufactured goods were exchanged among wide circles of acquaintants. Through the nineteenth century, industrialization and a focus on the home as a sanctuary that protected family from the perils of the modern public life transformed the holiday from a season of charity into a celebration of family. By 1910, the exchange of gifts was concentrated within the family, while friends and associates exchanged Christmas cards. In the late twentieth century, complaints about the unpleasantness of Christmas shopping as an activity that detracts from the "true" meaning of the holiday reflect the cultural distinctions between home and market that contributed to the development of Christmas giving.

Ami Sommariva

See also Commodity; Consumerism and Consumption; Heirlooms; Holidays and Commemorations; Native America

References and Further Reading
Carrier, James. 1995. *Gifts and Commodities: Exchange and Western Capitalism since 1700.* London: Routledge.
Lévi-Strauss, Claude. 1969. *The Elementary Structures of Kinship.* Boston: Beacon Press.
Mauss, Marcel. 1990. *The Gift: The Form and Reason for Exchange in Archaic Societies,* trans. W. D. Halls. New York: W. W. Norton.
Murray, David. 2000. *Indian Giving: Economies of Power in Indian-White Exchanges.* Amherst: University of Massachusetts Press.
Vaughn, Genevieve. 1997. *For-Giving: A Feminist Criticism of Exchange.* Austin, TX: Plain View Press.

Glass

Glass is a supercooled liquid consisting of silica (sand), an alkaline flux of potash or soda ash, and a stabilizer of lime or lead. Additives of metallic oxides impart color variations. When this mixture is heated to 1300–1500 degrees Celsius it forms "metal" (molten glass), which is then worked into various forms. Additional decoration can then be applied while hot or after annealing (cooling).

Early American Glassmaking
Functional and decorative articles of glass have always been an integral part of Anglo-America life. Glassmaking was the very first American industry, beginning in 1608 in Jamestown, Virginia. The earliest attempts at financially successful glass houses were numerous and short lived. Local houses struggled with inexperience, imperfections in raw materials, intense competition from foreign imports, inadequate distribution systems and consumers' preference for a finer quality of tablewares. Glass items imported from Great Britain and Europe far surpassed domestic attempts in color, quality, and form. Utilitarian items in nonleaded glass for storage, transport, and windows were the staple of the local production, but the established domestic houses failed to meet the growing demands of the expanding colonies. Only the elite could afford fine foreign glasswares.

Extant examples of early American glass show a distinct preference for mimicking English and European forms, but with an inherent difference in color and weight due to the limitations of local raw materials. Even so, various stylistic anomalies in tableware began to emerge as distinctly American, with particular emphasis on hot-work decoration using threading, lily-pad and raspberry-shaped appliqués, and tooled finials.

The first lead glass production in what would become the United States is credited to Henry Steigel's (1729–1785) American Flint Glass Works (1764–1774) of Manheim, Pennsylvania. Steigel's products set a precedent for a finer quality of ware able to compete with the English imports. Among the decorative techniques employed were pattern molding for pocket bottles, tableware, and engraved presentation pieces. Not until the foreign import embargoes, blockades, and the end of the War of 1812 did American glass production begin to flourish. During this period the better-known houses such as Pittsburgh's Bakewell, New England Glass, and Boston and Sandwich thrived.

Nineteenth-Century Technological Advances

As in other industries across the nation, the great advancements in technology in the nineteenth century directly influenced the availability, affordability, quality, and appearance of glass. The process of machine pressing glass was fully developed by 1827, permanently changing glass production. Patents for various mechanical glass presses and molds and new developments in glass chemistry led to unprecedented styles. Lacy pressed glass (1827–1850), particularly popular in a cup plate and tableware forms, became a middle-class alternative to expensive hand-cut glass. The invention of soda-lime glass in 1864 produced pressed items that looked like leaded glass but were lighter and a third of the cost. The bottle industry gave birth to another purely American style: the full-sized, mold-blown figural flask. With alcohol consumption per person approximately eight times greater than today, spirit flasks were in great demand. Combined with a growing sense of nationalism, Americans became enamored of these forms, which commemorated events and personages of cultural importance. Popular between 1815 and 1870, more than 750 known spirit flask patterns exist.

Flint (or leaded) glass lent itself particularly well to cutting. This decorative technique was augmented by the development of the steam engine to power the cutting wheels. First introduced in Philadelphia at the 1876 Centennial Exposition, elaborately cut geometric patterns in diamonds, pinwheels, rosettes, stars, and fans became known as rich or brilliant cut glass. The Corning, New York, area was so prolific in its production of these pieces that it was dubbed "the Crystal City." The brilliant period lasted until the advent of World War I in 1914.

The same companies producing brilliant cut glass also made cased and engraved glass. New casing technology encouraged the cold decoration of glass by means of cutting and engraving through several colored layers in the Bohemian style. Next to pressed wares, the Bohemian style became the most popular form of glassware through the 1880s.

Art Glass

International expositions, beginning with the London Crystal Palace Exposition in 1851, introduced the consumer and glass artist alike to ancient and new decorative styles from around the world. In the 1850s and 1860s further developments in chemical and mechanical processes led to new decorative techniques in cutting, etching, engraving, casing, cameos, silvered glass, machine threading, pull-up and crimping machines, and a variety of glass manufactured with special effects. This was the beginning of the American art glass movement that set the standard for the world for the next fifty years. Glass artists experimented with new forms, colors, and techniques in hot and cold decoration, and even developed glass mimicking ceramics, metals, and stone. Color technology reached its peak in the last quarter of the nineteenth century, resulting in a wide range of new hues, textures, layering, and heat-struck shading. Some of the better known houses were Hobbs, Brockunier in Wheeling, West Virginia, and Mount Washington and New England Glass, both in Massachusetts.

The late nineteenth-century Aesthetic Movement in England also inspired American glass artists to look to the past for design motifs, but with an innovative difference. Artist John LaFarge (1880–1963) struggled for years perfecting opalescent glass for use in his decorative windows. He also was the first to use molded and textured glass, multi-layered glass for depth, and free-form leading. Decorative arts innovator Louis Comfort Tiffany (1848–1933), in an attempt to replicate ancient Roman glass, developed his iridized glass method in 1892. Soon afterward he patented and began production of his Favrile glass vases. In 1903 Frederick Carder (1863–1963) founded Steuben Glass in Corning, New York. He soon patented his own version of iridized glass known as Aurene.

All these artists used the aesthetic properties of the glass itself to represent texture and dimensionality in the items produced in their studios. Specific combinations of multicolored glass were hand selected to represent the folds of garments; structure of leaves and flowers; and subtle shadings of earth, water, and sky. Various methods were also used to manipulate the hot glass, giving it an actual dimensionality and texture, to represent drapery, water, clouds, and more. These painstaking methods made the price of art glass unaffordable to all but the wealthy class. High-end art glass quickly was imitated by cheaper methods of manufacture, resulting in a degeneration of quality. Some of these examples are seen in the pressed and iridized carnival glass of the early 1900s. World War I would bring an end to many art glass houses in Europe and the United States.

Twentieth-Century Trends

The 1925 Exposition Internationale des Arts Décoratifs et Industriels Modernes held in Paris ushered in the Art Deco and Modernist movements, inspiring American artists such as Frederick Carder of Steuben Glass. Many of Steuben's most accomplished engraved presentation pieces date from this period, but the United States fell behind France, Italy, and Sweden in the production of luxury glass. The middle-class American glass market was dominated from the 1940s into the 1960s by the mass production of pressed or cut table and decorative ware manufactured by Libbey Glass Company (founded as New England Glass Company, 1818; renamed in 1892), Fenton Art Glass Company (founded 1905), and other long-established companies. Glass chemists in Corning continued to develop innovative products such as Pyrex for home, science, and industry. Glass also became an integral part of building materials for the modernistic steel-frame skyscrapers.

The modern Studio Art Glass Movement also had its beginnings in Corning. Harvey Littleton (1919–2006), an apprentice at Corning, worked with research chemist Dominic Labino (1910–1987) in 1962 at the Toledo Museum of Art to develop new formulas for lower temperature glass not requiring an industrial setting. New developments in glass manipulation in the forms of flame-working, fusing, sandblasting and kiln-formed work offered artists the opportunity to use the media as free-form artistic expression. The high visibility of the glass art of Littleton's student Dale Chihuly and the establishment of studio schools such as Pilchuck (established 1971) in Stanwood, Washington, and Corning Museum of Glass have marked a second renaissance in art glass production in the United States continuing to this day.

Tina Reuwsaat

See also Aesthetic Movement; Art Deco; Decorative Arts; Design History and American Design; Handicraft and Artisanship; Industrial Design; Modernism (Art Moderne)

References and Further Reading
McKearin, George S., and Helen McKearin. 1989. *American Glass*. New York: Crescent Books.
Miller, Bonnie J. 1991. *Out of the Fire: Contemporary Glass Artists and Their Work*. San Francisco: Chronicle Books.
Newman, Harold. 1977. *An Illustrated Dictionary of Glass*. London: Thames and Hudson.
Palmer, Arlene. 1993. *Glass in Early America: Selections from the Henry Frances du Pont Winterthur Museum*. Winterthur, DE: Winterthur Museum.
Papert, Emma. 1972. *The Illustrated Guide to American Glass*. New York: Hawthorn Books.
Revi, Albert. 1967. *Nineteenth Century Glass: Its Genesis and Development*, rev. ed. New York: Galahad Books.
Spillman, Jane Shadel, and Suzanne K. Frantz. 1990. *Masterpieces of American Glass*. New York: Crown Publishers.
Taylor, Gay LeCleire. 1990. *Out of the Mold*. Millville, NJ: American Glass Museum at Wheaton Village.
Wilson, Kenneth. 1994. *American Glass*. 2 vols. New York: Hudson Hills Press.

Gothic Revival

The Gothic Revival (also called *Romantic Revival*) is best known in architecture, but the style was manifested also in art, the decorative arts, and literature in the United States from the mid-nineteenth century into the twentieth. Its adherents in Great Britain and the United States emphasized building forms and styles of the Middle Ages, and later, handcraftsmanship and natural materials. As a movement based on the Romantic sensibilities of originality, sincerity, imagination, and direct experience, the Gothic Revival is characterized by a sense of nostalgia (for childhood or the past), horror, emotionalism (especially melancholy), and sentimentality. The architectural stone "ruin," ghost stories, folk tales, the picturesque or sublime landscape all evince an aspect of the Gothic Revival.

Dating its inception to Horace Walpole's (1717–1797) "gothick" house, Strawberry Hill, in England, the style traveled to the United States via books in the early to mid-nineteenth century. The American Gothic Revival appeared in domestic structures, but most often took form in church building, as in Richard Upjohn's (1802–1878) Trinity Church, New York City (1839–1846) or James Renwick's (1818–1895) St. Patrick's Cathedral, also in New York City (1853–1858). The major example of English Gothic Revival architecture is A. W. N. Pugin's (1812–1852) designs for the rebuilding of the Houses of Parliament, London, between 1840 and 1860. This structure brought forth associations of English medieval history and learning via English Gothic cathedrals. The style was later adapted to university campuses in the United States, such as the original buildings of the University of Chicago (after 1891) and the Cathedral of Learning at the University of Pittsburgh (1936). Unlike the more ubiquitous Federal style, with its disciplined application of Greco-Roman forms, Gothic Revival style presented Americans with a building mode that was attractive to the creative Romantic temperament but also to the scholarly and ecclesiastical mind. Educator Catharine E. Beecher (1800–1878) and her sister, the novelist Harriet Beecher Stowe (1811–1896), embraced the Gothic Revival in their (1869) advice manual, *The American Woman's Home*, suggesting that that moral, Christian home could be "a small church, a school-house, and a comfortable family dwelling . . . all be united in one building."

The Romantic mind-set was a sensibility first cultivated in Europe in the eighteenth century that crossed the Atlantic through the popular medieval novels of Scotsman Walter Scott (1771–1832). American authors such as James Fenimore Cooper (1789–1851) and Washington Irving (1783–1859) employed their skills in creating historical romances of the American past. The novels of Americans translated the Romantic sensibility into architectural form with the use of the *picturesque*, a style composed of castlelike crenellation, asymmetry, natural materials, decorated spires, and Gothic decoration. Two American architects of the Gothic Revival sometimes worked together: the architect Alexander Jackson Davis (1803–1892) and the landscape architect Andrew Jackson Downing (1815–1852). Important Gothic Revival houses in the United States include Davis' Lyndhurst (begun 1838, enlarged 1865–1867) in Tarrytown, New York, and Irving's Sunnyside (1832), also in Tarrytown designed by Downing. Downing likely collaborated with Davis to produce *Cottage Residences* (1842), a pattern book championing the picturesque style, called "Carpenter Gothic" in New England and "Hudson River Bracketed" in New York. Downing's popular *The Architecture of Country Houses* (1850) offers a treatise on the ideals of Romanticism as applied to architecture and morality, as well as a pattern book for the Gothic Revival style.

Laura A. Macaluso

See also Decorative Arts; Domestic Architecture; House, Home, and Domesticity; Houses of Worship (Ecclesiastical Architecture); Literary Studies and American Literature; Nostalgia; Style

References and Further Reading

Clark, Clifford E., Jr. 1976. "Domestic Architecture as an Index to Social History: The Romantic Revival and the Cult of Domesticity in America, 1840–1870." *Journal of Interdisciplinary History* 7: 35–56.
Howe, Katherine S., and David B. Warren. 1976. *The Gothic Revival Style in America, 1830–1870*. Houston: Museum of Fine Arts.
Loth, Calder, and Julius Trousdale Sadler, Jr. 1975. *The Only Proper Style: Gothic Architecture in America*. Boston: New York Graphic Society.
Stanton, Phoebe B. 1968. *The Gothic Revival and American Church Architecture: An Episode in Taste, 1840–1856*. Baltimore, MD: Johns Hopkins University Press.

Graphic Design

Historically rooted in printing and book arts, *graphic design* is an applied art in which a practitioner uses printing type and visuals (including photographs, illustrations, and charts) to communicate a message or an idea to a given audience. The profession originated in the latter half of the nineteenth century when innovations in printing and mass production led to increased demand for advertisements and printed materials. Influenced by movements such as Dadaism, Futurism, and De Stijl, the German Bauhaus (founded 1919) pioneered Modernist principles of pure form and the unification of art and craft to create products that were designed to be manufactured by or serve industry. The Bauhaus became a major international influence in design when many of its faculty and students were forced to flee the Nazi regime after 1933. Some of these designers, artists, and architects settled in the United States, where they influenced the conceptual thinking of American designers.

Paul Rand (1914–1996) led a graphics design revolution based on European Modernists' emphasis on pure form and simplicity rather than traditional formula and ornament. This "New Advertising" began in the late 1940s and continued into the 1960s. In addition to his creative output, Rand was a vocal spokesperson for design. He was one of the first practitioners to suggest the use of the term *graphic designer* rather than *commercial artist* or *art director*, and he championed Modernist principles in his work—especially

Graphic designer Paul Rand created this well-known logo for International Business Machines Corporation (IBM) in 1972, based on earlier designs he had also created for the company. Rand stressed Modernist ideas of pure form and simplicity. (Naljah Feanny/Corbis)

logos—for large American corporations. By the late 1960s many multinational companies used graphic design to create market identities through visual expression. Not all designers were interested in overtly commercial clients, however. As underground and protest movements began to influence popular culture, individual designers embraced grittier visions by making work for "psychedelic" rock groups and protest organizations.

The introduction of the personal computer and desktop publishing in the 1980s radically changed graphic design practice. Work that had previously taken hours to cut and paste up on boards could, with the click of a mouse, be done in minutes. While some designers used the computer as a labor-saving device, others were drawn to the new visual language made by pixels and dots. California, the birthplace of Adobe Software and the Macintosh, was also where designers

first experimented with this new visual vocabulary. April Greiman, a pioneer of a style referred to as California "new wave," embraced the restrictions of low-resolution output to create expressive combinations of type and image. Equally influential were typographer Zuzana Licko and her husband and partner, the Dutch-born graphic designer Rudy VanderLans. The couple published the underground design/culture magazine *Emigre*, which used typefaces (designed by Licko) that were specifically made for the coarse resolution printers of the 1980s.

The Internet and multimedia software in the 1990s created an entirely new arena for graphic designers. The discipline is continuously evolving, and contemporary graphic design includes street signage, posters, typography, print design, and Web and multimedia applications. Materials produced under the heading of *graphic design* are varied. There are as many personal styles and ways of interpreting a project as there are designers working today.

Aaris Sherin

See also Advertisements and Advertising; Books; Design History and American Design; Fanzines; Industrial Design; Print Culture; Printmaking and American Prints; Technology

References and Further Reading

Ashwin, Clive. 1984. *History of Graphic Design and Communication: A Sourcebook.* London: Pembridge Press.
Hollis, Richard. 2000. *Graphic Design: A Concise History,* rev. and exp. ed. New York: Thames and Hudson.
Meggs, Philip, and Alston W. Purvis. 2000. *Meggs' History of Graphic Design,* 4th ed. Hoboken, NJ: John Wiley.

Grocery Stores

Public markets dominated much of the American grocery trade from the colonial era through the mid-nineteenth century. There shoppers could find a range of items from produce, fish, meat, and bakery goods to shoes, clothing, household items, and livestock. By the 1850s, concerns over sanitation, combined with changing economic, settlement, and transportation patterns shifted food retailing to stores that carried only foodstuffs. These early *grocery stores* generally were small, independently owned, and managed ventures located both in town centers and rural communities. Grocers traded mainly on book credit, allowing customers to run a tab, payable on a monthly basis. Often located in urban ethnic enclaves, these stores best served the interests of the local community. Shopkeepers shared and retained intimate knowledge of customer needs and preferences, along with their economic status and social reputation. Clerks assisted customers on an individual basis, choosing and wrapping goods stored behind counter fronts or in bulk barrels. Many grocers employed delivery wagons and trucks to transport groceries, often ordered by telephone, directly to their customers.

Grocery production, distribution, and marketing underwent great changes at the turn of the twentieth century. Stores grew in size to accommodate the mass of brand-named canned goods and prepackaged items that came to dominate trade. Chain stores such as the Great Atlantic and Pacific Tea Company (A&P Economy Store) (1912) and Piggly Wiggly (1916) employed cash-and-carry shopping, a system of self-service, along with volume buying, to lower their operating costs and retail prices. In the 1930s, supermarkets took hold in suburban areas, making one-stop shopping the industry standard.

Susan V. Spellman

See also Cities and Towns; Commercial Architecture; Consumerism and Consumption; Food and Foodways; General (Country) Stores; Public Markets; Supermarkets

References and Further Reading

Atherton, Lewis E. 1939. *The Frontier Merchant in Mid-America.* Columbia: University of Missouri Press.
Mayo, James. 1993. *The American Grocery Store: The Business Evolution of an Architectural Space.* Westport, CT: Greenwood Press.
Strasser, Susan. 1989. *Satisfaction Guaranteed: The Making of the American Mass Market.* New York: Pantheon Books.
Tedlow, Richard S. 1990. *New and Improved: The Story of Mass Marketing in America.* Boston: Harvard Business School Press.

H

Halls

The *hall* in American houses has taken various forms, has been known by different names, and has served different purposes. In the earliest Anglo-American houses, the hall was one of two ground-level rooms, sometimes linked by a short corridor, off which opened the front door. Also called the *dwelling room* or *great room*, the hall was used for cooking, eating, indoor work, and amusements.

In the early nineteenth century, as work shifted to industrial and commercial sites, the domestic dwelling lost its identity as a center of productivity. Reconceived as the symbolic center for the family as a consumer group, the house was divided into numerous, specialized rooms that included the dining room, the parlor, and the entry hall.

From the 1870s to the end of the century, the entry hall of the middle- and upper-class family dwelling symbolized and facilitated the expected public and private performances of the dwelling's inhabitants and visitors. The hall's fashionable furnishings showcased cultural status. It also afforded access to the ceremonial front staircase and to individual rooms at the front of the house that often were no larger than the entry hall while the humble corridor served the rear service spaces.

At the turn of the twentieth century, a backlash against high-maintenance specialization and showiness led to the nearly universal embrace of bungalows and other less-formal house designs. Front doors opened directly into multipurpose living rooms, while short corridors led to and linked bedrooms and bathrooms. This informal plan has remained popular for houses, as well as apartments, although a late twentieth-century return to traditional status symbols inspired a resurgence of domestic interiors featuring ceremonial entry halls.

Janet Tyson

See also Dining Rooms; Kitchens and Pantries; Living Rooms; Parlors

References and Further Reading

Ames, Kenneth L. 1992. "First Impressions." In *Death in the Dining Room and Other Tales of Victorian Culture*, 7–43. Philadelphia, PA: Temple University Press.

Carron, Christian G., et al. 1998. *Grand Rapids Furniture: The Story of America's Furniture City*. Grand Rapids, MI: Public Museum of Grand Rapids.

Clifford, Edward Clark, Jr. 1986. *The American Family Home, 1800–1960.* Chapel Hill: University of North Carolina Press.

Hunter, Christine. 1999. *Ranches, Rowhouses and Railroad Flats.* New York: W. W. Norton.

Handicraft and Artisanship

The manual production of material objects—*handicraft and artisanship*—has been viewed both positively and negatively throughout the history of the United States. In the seventeenth century, making objects by hand was the prevailing method of production; by the mid-nineteenth century, it was an outmoded and ridiculed system of making things, and by the late nineteenth century, it was redefined as a revered tradition ripe for revival. Today, artisanship connotes an almost-quaint production mode and market that includes American small producers and foreign sweatshops. The historical process that informed these transitions is the Industrial Revolution, the era from the early nineteenth century to the early twentieth century when steam and electricity replaced muscle power, machine tools supplanted hand tools, the small shop was joined by large factories, and the social relations of work were transformed by entrepreneurial and, later, corporate capitalism.

In the seventeenth century, colonists brought their trades, tools, and craft techniques from their British or European homelands but quickly found that they had to adapt to different environmental and social conditions in North America. While tools and techniques remained traditional, craft traditions such as guild regulations and formal apprenticeship were never uniformly adopted on this side of the Atlantic Ocean.

Yet by the late eighteenth century a well-defined system of craft production was in place that supplied local needs, included re-invigorated workplace traditions, and displayed nascent forms of organization for employers and laborers. In the first third of the nineteenth century, these organizations became part of a developing labor union movement, as handcraft production and the traditional organization of artisan shops came under pressure from the technological and organizational changes associated with the Industrial Revolution.

As machines were increasingly substituted for handwork in many trades, the virtues of machine-made objects were promoted to the detriment of the image of things handmade. Craft products tended to be irregular in detail, quality was often suspect, and quantities were limited. By contrast, nineteenth-century factories produced great numbers of increasingly uniform objects of standard quality.

In the years 1875–1920, the Arts and Crafts Movement asserted the value of the "authentic" handmade object, the high-quality handicraft shop, and the artisan tradition of self-directed work over machine-produced products. Inspired by John Ruskin (1819–1900), William Morris (1834–1896), and others in Great Britain, this response to industrialism was more concerned with aesthetics but in some ways paralleled the social-political critiques of Karl Marx (1818–1883) and the Fabian Socialists. In the United States, the movement was identified with the Mission furniture of Gustav Stickley (1857–1942), the stained glass works of Louis Comfort Tiffany (1848–1933), the ceramics of the Rookwood (1880–1967) and Pewabic (1903–) potteries, the book trade products of papermaker Dard Hunter (1883–1966), and the architecture of the Craftsman and Prairie styles associated with Frank Lloyd Wright (1869–1959) and others.

In the middle decades of the nineteenth century, the interest in handwork persisted, sometimes associated with religious sects such as the Shakers or the Amish, or with producers of "folk art," whether or not they were aesthetically, socially, or economically "naïve." Still, mass production and mass consumerism characterized twentieth-century culture. With the rise of the antimaterialist counterculture of the 1960s, interest in handmade goods revived on a massive scale involving numerous individual craftsmen, artisan cooperatives, and even the mass marketing of handcrafted, foreign-made goods. By the end of the century, the terms *handicraft* and *artisanship* had been transformed into generic terms indicating goods (regardless of their method of production) that present themselves to consumers with an aura of individuality—a usage far removed from original definition of these words.

William S. Pretzer

See also Arts and Crafts Movement; Books; Commodity; Consumerism and Consumption; Decorative Arts; Factory and Industrial Work and Labor; Folklore and Folklife; Technology; Tools, Implements, and Instruments; Vernacular; Work and Labor

References and Further Reading

Jones, Michael Owen. 1975. *The Hand Made Object and Its Maker*. Berkeley: University of California Press.
Kaplan, Wendy. 1987. *"The Art that is Life": The Arts and Crafts Movement in America, 1875–1920*. Boston: Little, Brown for the Museum of Fine Arts, Boston.
Laurie, Bruce. 1989. *Artisans into Workers: Labor in Nineteenth-Century America*. New York: Hill and Wang.

Heirlooms

An *heirloom* is a material possession that has passed from generation to generation within a family. Historically, an heirloom is chattel, or personal property (apart from real estate), that is informally or legally inherited. Existing research, which intersects with the study of gifts, memorials, bereavement, nostalgia, law, kinship, and domestic culture, finds that heirlooms are intimately associated with familial and individual identities. This intimate relationship is connected to the length of time an heirloom has been kept within a family and the occasions at which it is transferred from one family member to another.

Anthropologist Annette B. Weiner has observed that heirlooms are simultaneously given and kept. Through their retention within the family over generations, these "inalienable possessions" accrue value and meaning while attempting to preserve social hierarchies by authenticating origins, kinship, and histories. Heirlooms are passed on at rites of passage, such as upon a giver's death or a recipient's graduation, in which subjectivities are reshaped.

The practice of passing objects from one generation to the next is highly gendered. Weiner observed that women are commonly the producers and controllers of these objects, revealing their agency in cultural reproduction. Furthermore, sociologist Rémi Clignet notes that men and women treat differently male and female heirs. Clignet argues that inheritance laws in the West have become less restrictive since the Enlightenment, enabling testators (those who have made legal, valid wills before death) to follow sentiment rather than economics in distributing property. This increasing freedom of testators is linked to a shift from mechanical to interpretive reproduction, in which the cultural identity that is reproduced from one generation to the next is equivalent to, but not identical to, its previous form.

Ami Sommariva

See also Antiques; Dower Right; Gender; Gifts and Gift Giving; Probate Records, Probate

Inventories, and Wills; Rite, Ritual, and
Ceremony

References and Further Reading

Clignet, Rémi. 1992. *Death, Deeds, and Descendants: Inheritance in Modern America*. New York: Aldine de Gruyter.

Hallam, Elizabeth, and Jennifer Lorna Hockey. 2001. *Death, Memory, and Material Culture*. Oxford, UK: Berg.

Ulrich, Laurel Thatcher. 1997. "Hannah Barnard's Cupboard: Female Property and Identity in Eighteenth-Century New England." In *Through a Glass Darkly: Reflections on Personal Identity in Early America*, ed. Ronald Hoffman, Mechal Sobel, and Fredrika J. Teute, 238–273. Chapel Hill: University of North Carolina Press.

Weiner, Annette B. 1992. *Inalienable Possessions: The Paradox of Keeping-while-Giving*. Berkeley: University of California Press.

Highways and National Highway System

Highways are public roads designed for automobile and truck traffic that connect major metropolitan areas. Also termed *freeways*, *expressways*, or *motorways*, highways are the principal or main (hence, *high*) roads forming the 160,000-mile *Interstate Highway System*. The interstate system was created by President Dwight D. Eisenhower (1890–1969) when he signed into law the Federal-Aid Highway Act of 1956. This law, also known as the National Interstate and Defense Highways Act, was the culmination of several attempts to modernize and systematize the nation's transportation routes.

History

Beginning in the 1890s, the Good Roads Movement advocated for better roads through its *Good Roads Magazine*, informational meetings, and political campaigns. In 1893, the Office of Road Inquiry (later, Office of Public Roads) was established in the Department of Agriculture. This was the first federal agency responsible for assessing the nation's roadways, and it undertook studies of existing roads, experimented with road-building materials, and studied methods of road maintenance. The Federal-Aid Road Act of 1916 (also known as the Good Roads Act) was the first federal highway policy and systematized road construction and funding, especially of rural post roads. The Federal-Aid Highway Act of 1921, the first to mandate and fund roads that were "interstate in character," increased aid to the states through a gasoline tax. During the Great Depression of the 1930s, highway construction slowed as states could not meet the matching requirements of the law. The Federal Highway Act of 1940 rededicated existing federal highway funds to planning and building highways for defense. In 1941, the 78,000-mile Strategic Highway Network was established for the nation's defense, by providing a network of highways on which military materiel and troops could efficiently travel. The Federal-Aid Highway Act of 1956 was the result: Not only did it create the Federal Highway Administration but it also was the largest public works program in American history.

Impact

Vanishing highway roadside attractions, such as billboards, car advertisements, and highway marker designs, tell as much about the lifestyles of the motoring public of yesteryear as the cars themselves. In the 1920s to 1940s, trailer courts and trailer "camps" had few amenities but provided an alternative for those who wanted a cheaper way to travel. Consumers increasingly demanded more uniformity and comfort in overnight accommodations, however, and trailer camps and courts were replaced after World War II with newly constructed motels. Several of the surviving motels are preserved as historical sites, as are the bridges and toll booths that were erected during the era. The expanding interstate system encouraged the growth of motel chains, gas stations, fast food restaurants, shopping malls, travel plazas, and truck stops that catered to the growing number of travelers. These new motels, restaurants, and gas stations were often located next to the interstate "cloverleaf" of entrance and exit ramps, on the edge of cities, and away from the older service buildings located in the center of cities.

Popular Culture and Iconology

The most well-known highway opened in 1926: U.S. Highway 66, "America's Main Street," which stretches 2,400 miles from Chicago to Los Angeles. It has inspired scores of novelists, poets, artists, moviemakers, and songwriters. A staple of American popular culture are the road movies that highlighted the popularity of automobiles, often with a high-speed car chase over highways and back roads. Highway and car travel was portrayed as a source of freedom and excitement (and ultimately, of doom).

The nostalgia for the experience of motoring on slower, narrower, and scenic highways of the past has resulted in the profitable hobby and business of highway travel-related collectibles. Authentic and replica automotive toys, mascots, ornaments, license plates, highway signs, postcards, and even automotive art recall the American experience of the open road.

Martin J. Manning

See also Automobile Camping (Auto-Camping); Automobiles and Automobility; Commercial Food Venues; Land Transportation; Mobile Homes and Trailer Parks; Service Stations; Souvenirs; Tourism and Travel

References and Further Reading
Kaszynski, William. 2000. *The American Highway: The History and Culture of Roads in the United States.* Jefferson, NC: McFarland and Company.
Ling, Peter J. 1990. *America and the Automobile: Technology, Reform, and Social Change.* New York: St. Martin's Press.

Historic Preservation

The practice of *historic preservation* in the United States ranges from local efforts to protect and maintain a historic structure, site, district, or landscape to federal policy governing the historic national domain. Individuals, groups, and governments preserve what is deemed valuable for many reasons: to ensure that a historically significant site, often of a famous person or of an event, serves as a lasting memorial, shrine, or lesson for future generations; to stimulate economic growth of a neighborhood, town, or city; to protect architecturally significant structures from the forces of change; or, especially in the twentieth century, to stimulate tourism. The historic preservation movement in the United States has elicited at times heated debates about the American people's shared past.

Preservationists range widely in expertise, from the dedicated citizen volunteer to the professional trained in law, engineering, history, architecture, and decorative arts. Graduate programs in historic preservation are offered by many American universities.

Nineteenth-Century Veneration of Great Men

The historic preservation movement in the United States is usually dated to 1853, when southern socialite Ann Pamela Cunningham (1816–1875) began a grassroots effort to save George Washington's (1732–1799) Mount

Vernon (built 1741–1742) for future generations. While not the nation's first successful preservation effort, Cunningham and her organization, the Mt. Vernon Ladies Association, set the tone for subsequent preservation efforts. The nascent preservation movement focused on saving properties associated with "great men" (in these years, always white) in American history. Sites like Mt. Vernon were deemed important in teaching American history as hero worship; such preservation activities were often spearheaded by women.

The Impact of the Nation's Centennial

The Philadelphia Centennial Exposition in 1876 helped to expand the focus of preservation efforts. With its celebration of the American Revolution, the Centennial Exposition piqued a renewed interest in all things colonial, including architecture. Preservationists started looking at saving structures that were examples of "quaint" architectural styles and forms. As with Cunningham's organization, these were largely private efforts. For example, in 1898, the Ipswich (Massachusetts) Historical Society restored the seventeenth-century John Whipple House—not because of Whipple (1596–1669), but because the house was the only surviving example of the type of Jacobean frame house with an overhanging second story. The same was true of the Paul Revere House (ca. 1680), which was restored more for its value as the oldest frame house in Boston rather than the association with Revere (1735–1818). In fact, the house's restorers took the structure back to its seventeenth-century appearance rather than how it might have looked in Revere's time. The preservation of the Revere House inspired William Sumner Appleton (1874–1947) to found the Society for the Preservation of New England Antiquities (SPNEA, now called Historic New England) in 1910. Appleton and SPNEA saw value in preserving buildings for their intrinsic value and were not concerned with exhibiting for inspirational or any other purposes. This notion of keeping buildings in current use as part of continuing American life, rather than isolating them as objects for veneration, has had consequences for historic preservation in the United States. While many structures are preserved for museum purposes, historic preservationists often seek to save historic properties for continuing use.

Historic Districts and Environments

Until the early twentieth century, preservationists tended to look more at saving individual structures rather than properties in relationship to their surroundings. The concept of the *historic district* dates from the 1920s and 1930s, when Charleston, South Carolina, established one of the first such districts in the United States. The establishment of the Society for the Preservation of Dwelling Houses was led by Charleston real estate agent Susan Pringle Frost (1873–1960). The organization supported zoning ordinances to save historic structures. By creating historic districts, Charleston preservationists supported the concept that it did not do much good if only one or two buildings escaped the wrecking ball. The sense of the past, or historical context, is rendered meaningful through the preservation of an area's built environment. New Orleans, Louisiana, also developed historic districts in this era. In 1936, a preservation commission was established with broad police powers to protect the city's historic resources, especially the French Quarter.

Almost concurrently with the development of the historic district was the establishment of Colonial Williamsburg. The Reverend Dr. W. A. R. Goodwin (1869–1939) and John D. Rockefeller, Jr., (1874–1960) led the effort to save the historic buildings of Virginia's colonial capital. Reverend Goodwin was long interested in preserving Williamsburg's past; he restored Bruton Parish Church and secured the neighboring George Wythe House (ca. 1755) as a parish house. He was able to convince Rockefeller to fund the restoration of the town, beginning with the 1926 purchase of the Ludwell-Paradise House (ca. 1755). Williamsburg is now a mix of restored original structures and reconstructions, setting a new standard for open-air museums. While highly successful, the interpretation in Colonial Williamsburg is very much a reflection of the time; for example, the colors of buildings and layout of gardens were more indicative of the 1930s Colonial Revival taste rather than eighteenth-century forms and fashions.

Federal and Private Support for Historic Preservation

The work of privately funded groups played no small part in historic preservation, especially in the nineteenth and early twentieth centuries. Like Cunningham's efforts, early preservationists could expect little or no help from government at any level; the only reason the federal government confiscated Arlington House (the Custis-Lee Mansion, built 1802–1818 in what is now Arlington Cemetery) was because it was a spoil of the Civil War, having been Robert E. Lee's (1807–1870) estate. The federal government did enact preservation-related legislation: The 1906 Antiquities Act authorized the president to proclaim as national monuments any landmarks, structures, and objects of historical or scientific interest that were on federally owned or controlled land. In 1916, Congress created the National Park Service (NPS), which would become the leader in the nation's preservation efforts. Other important legislation included the 1935 Historic Sites Act, which reauthorized the Historic

American Buildings Survey (created in 1933) and empowered the NPS to purchase privately owned sites and buildings, execute agreements with private owners to protect historic properties, maintain and operate such sites and buildings, and establish school programs.

The 1966 National Historic Preservation Act (NHPA) gave preservationists a boost from the federal government. The NHPA authorized the creation of the National Register of Historic Places, the establishment of the Advisory Council on Historic Preservation (ACHP), and the development of a system of state historic preservation offices (SHPOs) to carry out the functions laid out in the NHPA. The most significant part of NHPA is Section 106, which is the process by which all federal undertakings are reviewed by the SHPO and, if necessary, the ACHP to determine the effects of such undertakings on historic properties. The NHPA has been amended to strengthen Section 106, protecting Native American properties through the 1990 Native American Graves Protection and Repatriation Act, and even maritime properties with the 1987 Abandoned Shipwrecks Act. The effectiveness of the legislation is debatable; many properties have been lost, but doubtless many have been protected that might otherwise have faced the wrecking ball.

Private preservation efforts are evident throughout the nation; the privately funded National Trust for Historic Preservation works on the national level. Founded in 1947, the National Trust acts as an advocate for preservation issues, educates the public about the need for preservation, and assists in the training of new professionals in the field. The National Trust also owns and maintains a number of properties, including Montpelier (ca. 1760), the Virginia plantation of James (1751–1836) and Dolley Madison

(1768–1849), Woodlawn (1800–1805), also in Virginia, and Drayton Hall (ca. 1738), in Charleston, South Carolina.

Twenty-first-Century Trends

While early preservationists were concerned with saving properties deemed significant either through their association with a famous person or their exhibition of significant architectural styles, in the twenty-first century there is an interest in preserving other elements of the past. Efforts to save, interpret, and reuse working-class housing, factories, and other, less glamorous, structures are becoming an important part of the preservation movement.

Donna M. DeBlasio

See also Architectural History and American Architecture; Civic Architecture; Colonial Revival; Commercial Architecture; Domestic Architecture; Houses of Worship (Ecclesiastical Architecture); Materials Conservation; Museums and Museum Practice; Nostalgia; Public Monuments and Popular Commemoration; Social History

References and Further Reading

Barthel, Diane. 1996. *Historic Preservation: Collective Memory and Historical Identity.* New Brunswick, NJ: Rutgers University Press.
Fitch, James Marston. 1990. *Historic Preservation: Curatorial Management of the Built World.* Charlottesville: University Press of Virginia.
Murtagh, William J. 2006. *Keeping Time: The History and Theory of Preservation in America,* 3rd ed. New York: John Wiley.
Tyler, Norman. 1999. *Historic Preservation: An Introduction to Its History, Principles and Practice.* New York: W. W. Norton.

Holidays and Commemorations

Although *holiday* is derived from "holy day," many American holidays are not religious observations but secular *commemorations* to honor and preserve the memory of a person or event. American holidays reflect a wide diversity of cultural, ethnic and racial, and religious practices. Most holidays allow for a brief cessation of work, although many religious holidays are not observed by the wider public. American holidays are intimately tied to the consumerism that dominates other areas of American cultural life. In fact, most holidays would be unrecognizable without the trappings of the commercial material culture accompanying celebrations: from greeting cards and decorations to dress and food.

Other holidays once widely celebrated throughout the nation have disappeared from the national calendar. Bird Day (May 4), for example, was combined with Arbor Day (the last Friday in April) as a means to teach children the values of conservation. (Earth Day, instituted in 1970, revives these values by encouraging environmentalism and anticonsumption.) Still other holidays are celebrated on the state level and are growing in popularity. Juneteenth (June 19), or Emancipation Day, commemorates the end of slavery in the United States and is observed in fourteen states and many communities.

Federal Holidays

Commemorating the American Civil War (1861–1865) was the impetus for many of the national holidays now recognized in federal law. For example, George Washington (1732–1799) served as a figure to unite both North and South, leading to a national observance of his birth date. Abraham Lincoln (1809–1865) was remembered in Northern states and Jefferson Davis (1808–1889) and Robert E. Lee (1807–1882) throughout the South. During the latter half of the nineteenth century, individual state legislatures, middle-class social reformers, African Americans, immigrants, and labor activists and socialists promoted causes through the recognition of a day of commemoration.

In order of their appearance in the calendar, these days set aside by federal law to commemorate events and people are Martin Luther King Jr. Day (third Monday in January), Presidents' Day (third Monday in February), Memorial Day (last Monday in May), Independence Day (July 4), Labor Day (first Monday in September), Columbus Day (second Monday in October), Veterans Day (November 11), and Thanksgiving Day (fourth Thursday in November). As federal holidays, federal government offices and services are closed in observation of those commemorations. States are not required to recognize these commemorations, but all, in varying degrees, do.

Some of these federal holidays mark specific events in the nation's shared history, such as the patriotic observance of Independence Day, with activities from community religious services, public ceremonies, parades, and fireworks displays to picnics, baseball games, and other outdoor leisure activities. Others holidays commemorate the life and public service of the nation's leaders, such as Martin Luther King Jr. (1928–1968) Day and Presidents' Day, an observation combining in February the once-individually celebrated birthdays of Abraham Lincoln (February 12) and George Washington (February 22). Others demarcate military sacrifice, such as Veterans Day and Memorial Day, on which tributes of music, parades, ceremonies, and flowers are held at the nation's cemeteries. Labor Day, introduced by the Knights of Labor in 1882, observed contributions of the labor movement but has in the late twentieth century recognized the American worker.

National, regional, and state holidays and historical commemorations define and recognize the collective consciousness of the American people and thus, holidays are sometimes the focus of debate. For example, the meanings of two holidays, Columbus Day and Thanksgiving, are today contended. Columbus Day, initiated by descendants of Italian immigrants to honor the arrival of Christopher Columbus (1451–1506) to the New World, was legally recognized as a federal holiday in 1937 by President Franklin Delano Roosevelt (1882–1945) at the behest of the Knights of Columbus. In recent years, Native American groups have protested Columbus Day, arguing that decimation of indigenous peoples by Christopher Columbus and other European explorers should not be celebrated. The celebration of Thanksgiving is based on a New England tradition but linked also to the English colonists of Plymouth, Massachusetts. These "Pilgrims" shared a festive meal with Native Americans in 1621. The modern Thanksgiving, replete with a "New England" meal of turkey and cranberry sauce, pumpkin pie and stuffing, was promoted by Sarah Josepha Hale (1788–1879), editor of *Godey's Lady's Book*, as a means by which the nation could unite in the midst of the Civil War. President Abraham Lincoln proclaimed the observance in 1863. Full of historical inaccuracies, Thanksgiving has been criticized for its simplistic rendering of the complex relationships between Native Americans and European colonizers.

Public and Commercialized Holidays

The historical development of many commercialized holidays reflects a variety of traditions in their celebration and the importance of consumerism in American culture. St. Valentine's Day (February 14) is a recognized holiday in the Roman Catholic calendar commemorating two martyrs named Valentine. The symbols of Valentine's Day reflecting images of the Roman god of erotic love, Cupid, typically depicted as a young winged boy equipped with quiver, bow, and arrows, are often used on cards and other decorations. In the United States, Valentine's

Day (as it is commonly called) became a secular holiday marked by small handmade gifts, and by the mid-nineteenth century cards and gifts were manufactured specifically in observance of friendship and love on that day. By the early twentieth century, the holiday was celebrated in schools, workplaces, and homes. Since the 1980s, other "holidays" introduced by the card, flower, and gift industries imitate Valentine's Day: Secretary's Day (now Administrative Assistant's Day, the third or fourth Wednesday in April), the idea of an advertising executive; and Boss's Day (October 16), instituted by an insurance industry employee, also recognize changes in the workplace as well as between work and social life in the United States.

Mother's Day (second Sunday in May) was created after West Virginia native Anna Jarvis (1864–1948) sought recognition for the holiday. It was first celebrated in 1908, as was Father's Day (third Sunday in June). A presidential proclamation in 1914, linking through the display of flags the commemoration of mothers to the sons they lost in war as World War I (1914–1918) itself began to rage in Europe, cemented the holiday's place in the national calendar. Promotion by department store magnate John Wanamaker (1838–1922) ensured its celebration through the wide availability of manufactured cards, gifts, flowers, and candy.

Halloween (October 31) was a European folk tradition marking the shift from late summer and fall into winter, but in the early twentieth century it became increasingly commercialized. The holiday has grown to be a nearly national celebration of manufactured costumes, elaborate house decorations, adult and children's parties, and an increased consumption of "trick or treat" candies. Criticisms of the holiday, mostly from fundamental Christians, focus on its folk ("pagan")

roots, which persist in the symbols of witches, ghosts, and animated pumpkins.

Religious Holidays

In recent years, official (that is, in the form of school and work breaks) notice of religious holidays has shifted from a Christian-centered tradition to one encompassing other religious traditions. Christmas (December 25), marking Jesus' birth, and Easter Sunday (late March or early April), marking Jesus' resurrection, were often the only religious holidays for which accommodations were made, but today Jewish, Hindu, Muslim, and other religious traditional days are increasingly noted.

Though little observed in the first two centuries of European settlement in North America, the celebration of Christmas in the United States since the mid-nineteenth century has become a thoroughly commercialized event. Much of the nation's retail industry's profit is derived in the shopping season commencing on the day after Thanksgiving through Christmas Eve, symbolized, perhaps, by the appearance of Santa Claus at the end of the Macy's Thanksgiving Day parade. The modern Christmas, with its decorated and lighted tree (dating from the 1820s–1850s), Santa Claus, holiday lights, greeting cards, and, of course, wrapped presents, serve as material evidence of the secularization of the observance.

Ethnic Holidays

Holidays reflect the cultural diversity of the nation's population. Ethnic celebrations are regional, marking culturally and historically immigrant groups' settlement in the United States. Some of the more common include Chinese New Year (sometime between January 21 and February 19), Mardi Gras (February/March), St. Patrick's Day

(March 17), El Cinco de Mayo (May 5), and Kwanzaa (December 26–January 1).

Mardi Gras (French for "Fat Tuesday") combines religious tradition with a carnival or festival to welcome spring, held the last day before Lent begins (usually sometime in February), although the parades and parties can start after the Christmas season ends. The most notable Mardi Gras in the United States is the carnival in New Orleans, Louisiana, with the parades and parties; it may be considered a minor version of Carnival in Brazil and in other Latin American countries. Mardi Gras is a state holiday in Alabama and Florida, and a holiday in eight Louisiana parishes.

St. Patrick's Day is observed in cities, mostly in the Northeast, with a large population of Irish Americans. St. Patrick's Day parades are held in New York City, Boston, and Chicago and are often venues in which politicians serve as honorary parade marshals. El Cinco de Mayo marks Mexican independence in 1862. Local celebrations are not limited to the Southwest, where there is a high concentration of Mexican American population, but occur throughout the nation. Kwanzaa is celebrated by some African Americans. *Kwanzaa* is a Swahili word meaning "first fruit of the harvest," and the holiday occurs annually from December 26 through January 1.

Specially designated months honor racial and ethnic groups. These months are usually observed with speeches and special events, and all are heralded by a proclamation by the United States president, noting their particular significance. These are Black History (February); Women's History (March); Asian Pacific American Heritage (May); Hispanic Heritage (September); and Native American Heritage (November).

Martin J. Manning

See also Consumerism and Consumption; Folklore and Folklife; Gifts and Gift Giving; Nostalgia; Public Monuments and Popular Commemoration; Religion, Spirituality, and Belief; Rite, Ritual, and Ceremony; Tradition

References and Further Reading

Bellenir, Karen, ed. 1988. *Religious Holidays and Calendars: An Encyclopedic Handbook,* 2nd ed. Detroit, MI: Omnigraphics.
Dennis, Matthew. 2002. *Red, White and Blue Letter Days: An American Calendar*. Ithaca, NY: Cornell University Press.
Litwicki, Ellen M. 2000. *America's Public Holidays: 1865–1920*. Washington, DC: Smithsonian Institution Press.
Schmidt, Leigh Eric. 1995. *Consumer Rites: The Buying and Selling of American Holidays.* Princeton, NJ: Princeton University Press.

Homeless Residences

Homeless residences include any shelter constructed or utilized to house temporarily people without permanent, private housing. Urban homeless residences can include government-assisted housing, commercial and private lodging houses, makeshift tents and huts, and areas beneath bridges and highway overpasses. Charting the availability, quality, and material aspects of homeless residences throughout American history helps chronicle changing cultural attitudes toward, and create a complete image of homelessness in American culture.

American myth and history are replete with stories of wanderers and explorers kept perpetually mobile by the pioneer spirit (while in reality more often by poverty and unemployment) in search of new prospects and frontiers. The romanticized notion of tramps or hoboes is of young, white, male, migratory laborers following the call of independence and opportunity, crisscrossing the nation on freight trains, sleeping under open skies or in country barns, wearing oversized suits and weathered felt or tomato-can hats, carrying rolled-up blankets and kerchiefs on a stick, smoking pipes, and wearing shoes with holes in them. Industrialization and urbanization changed the stereotype and the reality of homelessness in the United States by providing men and women the promise of steady employment in factories and shops and inexpensive housing in burgeoning cities.

Commercial and charitable lodging houses provided temporary room and board of the urban poor and homeless in the late nineteenth and early twentieth centuries. Lodging houses were usually multistoried, renovated commercial spaces in the downtown districts of larger cities. Large dormitory-style rooms were filled with wooden bunks with slings of canvas across the frame or canvas cots. Hundreds of residents shared crowded, unsanitary conditions with one indoor bathroom, one exit, and no secure storage for possessions. Some flophouses, workingmen's hotels, and boardinghouses constructed crude partitions between bunks for single-room occupancy to provide privacy. The area around the lodging houses became known as the *main stem* or *skid row*. The *main stem* was usually a downtown city street on which lodging houses or boarding hotels, saloons, restaurants, charity clothing shops, employment offices, missions, and entertainment halls such as movie houses were built. Many skid row streets evolved into contemporary neighborhoods such as the Bowery in New York and Chinatown in San Francisco.

During the years of the Great Depression, displaced homeless persons and families constructed makeshift dwellings in shantytowns or Hoovervilles, named after President Herbert Hoover (1874–1964), across the American landscape. With names like Slab City, Tinkersville, and Darby's Patch, shantytowns were built on empty lots, near water-

front bridges, in parks, or in and around abandoned buildings and provided the urban homeless with shelter and community, complete with grocers, taverns, and schools. The rows of residences were shacks made from found scrap building materials such as sheets of tin, bricks, shingles, paper, and canvas tarps and were not connected to sewage or other utilities.

The Servicemen's Readjustment Act of 1944 (the "GI Bill of Rights") provided World War II veterans with education and employment opportunities, health benefits, and cheap housing in the new and growing suburbs, driving the numbers of homeless to record lows. As a result of the suburban exodus, commercial interest in urban renewal, and the regentrification of downtown centers, many skid row tenements and lodging houses were systematically demolished between 1950 and 1970. A historically white, male demographic of the homeless was now augmented with African American and Asian American populations and women and children.

The 1980s recession and changing political attitudes toward welfare lessened the role of federal relief agencies. In turn, private charities and agencies like the Young Men's Christian Association (YMCA), Young Women's Christian Association (YWCA), and the Salvation Army constructed emergency short-stay shelters. These multistoried functional buildings included separate male and female sections, small private rooms for families, and larger dormitory-style rooms for women with children. The shelters housed on-site administrative and employment offices, a clinic, a sundries shop, media rooms with television and reading materials, a schoolroom, and storage for donated clothing.

Many emergency shelters maintained strict rules and schedules, were open to residents only at night, and rarely provided secure storage of personal effects. During the day, residents of the shelters sat outside or roamed the streets, usually carrying their worldly possessions in plastic bags or in found shopping carts. The need for adequate, temporary emergency housing was highlighted in the Hurricane Katrina experience (U.S. landfall August 29, 2005), when tens of thousands of people from Louisiana, Mississippi, and other affected regions required immediate shelter aid.

For the homeless who chose not to, or were unable to, live in shelters, abandoned buildings, cars, alleyways, and highway and bridge underpasses became the space for home building and provided a ceiling or a wall to which cardboard strung on wire, found plywood, blankets, sheets, or tarps can be attached. "Dumpster diving" can provide a homeless person with the accoutrements for living, from flatware and dishes for eating to blankets and rags for cover and shack roofs to pillows and mattresses for bedding and furniture. Countless journalistic and artistic photographic images depict entire bedrooms, living rooms, and makeshift kitchens organized and arranged in open-air settings. Beyond the basic necessities for subsistence, these images also portray the neat and orderly residences of individuals. The photographs portray the distinct likes and dislikes of the residents through the inclusion of toys, magazines, books, and decorations, as well as a flair for the architectural.

In the late twentieth century, innovative charitable organizations like Atlanta's Mad Housers, the Student Housing Alliance in San Jose, California, and the Chicago Coalition for the Homeless teamed up with homeless residents and homeless associations like Homeless on the Move for Equality to draw attention and assistance from public, political, and civic organizations. After consulta-

tion with local homeless communities, civic-minded architects and city planners designed and built portable, secure huts, complete with foam mattresses, shelves, ventilation, and porches. While natural disasters have been at times the cause of homelessness, the very architecture developed for temporary housing after the San Francisco earthquake of 1906 is being used to house the city's homeless population. Ingenious architects are constructing unique communities in Los Angeles using manufactured fiberglass panels for domed dwellings.

Victoria Estrada-Berg

See also Boardinghouses; Cities and Towns; House, Home, and Domesticity; Poverty

References and Further Reading

DePastino, Todd. 2003. *Citizen Hobo: How a Century of Homelessness Shaped America.* Chicago: University of Chicago Press.
Kusmer, Kenneth L. 2002. *Down & Out, on the Road.* Oxford, UK: Oxford University Press.
Levinson, David, ed. 2004. *Encyclopedia of Homelessness.* 2 vols. Thousand Oaks, CA: Sage.
Morton, Margaret. 2000. *Fragile Dwelling.* New York: Aperture.

House, Home, and Domesticity

House, home, and *domesticity,* in American usage, are related terms referring to the physical, symbolic, and ideological aspects of shelter. A *house* is a building for human habitation, though historically the word has defined any building that contains human occupation—a bakehouse, for example. In addition, *house* defined one's family as well as rooms within a building occupied by a family. *House* and *home* are often employed interchangeably; *home* is applied generally to one's (often family) residence, whether a city apartment or town house, suburban bungalow or ranch, or rural farmhouse or trailer.

Home, though once associated more with one's region or land of birth, came to connote by the nineteenth century the physical, mental, and emotional comforts associated with one's life amidst a family at its hearth, that is, in its (seemingly) permanent shelter. As a site of nurture, *home* is also applied to institutions that tend to the needs of the poor, the elderly, the sick, and the indigent. *Domestic*, derived from the Latin for "of the house," referred to one's membership in or relation to a house, whether *house* meant a family or a structure. *Domestic* also described devotion to the home life or duties, and thus its usage delineates the ideological separation of the private, the intimate, and the feminine from the public, the political, and the masculine. *Domesticity* as an ideology has influenced historically the definition of gender roles in the United States.

Houses and Nation Building

Coined in 1931, the phrase "American Dream" is now employed to include home ownership. The possession of land from the very beginning of European settlement in North America has endowed political rights and civic obligation, tying householders to a larger political entity, be it a town, colony or (later) state, or nation. *House* and *home* have been synonymous terms, as have *home(land)* and *nation*. British colonists claimed the land not through ceremonies with flags and oaths but through the construction of dwelling houses, gardens, and fences that "improved" the land and symbolized permanent occupancy. The household, the members of which included family, servants, and slaves, was thought to be the basis of the social and political order. Though the log cabin has been popularly mythologized since the 1840 presidential campaign of William Henry Harrison (1773–1841) as the quintessential American pioneer shelter, the practice was brought by

Swedish settlers two centuries earlier in what would become Pennsylvania and Delaware. The earliest European inhabitants of North America lived in impermanent dwellings—dugouts, grass-covered huts of bent saplings, and tipis, the construction of which was borrowed from Native American practice. In the subsequent two centuries, houses, overwhelmingly one or two rooms with a hearth, would be primarily constructed of wood, plentiful in supply; the use of brick and stone depended on availability but also signaled wealth. In the southern colonies, dwellings varied greatly on the region's plantations, from elegant brick mansion houses to the rude cabins of poor white farmers and the mean slave cabins and barracks built of wood with stick-and-mud chimneys or merely a hole in the roof. Brick was the preferred building material of row houses and town houses in cities such as Philadelphia, Pennsylvania, and Charleston, South Carolina, to deter the spread of fires that always threatened to ravage densely populated areas.

After the Revolution, the federal government both encouraged and controlled permanent, primarily agricultural settlement west of the Appalachian Mountains. The Northwest Ordinance of 1787 created the Northwest Territory, whereby land was divided in six-mile-square townships in which lots were reserved for public buildings and the rest were offered for sale. Many Americans moved to what was then the West: Ohio, Michigan, Indiana, Illinois, Wisconsin, and Minnesota. The nation's increasing national domain was settled through the provisions of the Homestead Act (1862). This legislation offered 160 acres to any head of household who was at least twenty-one years of age, improved his or her claim through the construction of a house, improvement of the land, and could prove habitation for five years. When the act was repealed in 1976 (with provisions remaining for Alaska homesteading until 1986), more than two million people had filed claims for public domain lands in thirty states. About 783,000 individuals successfully "proved up" their claims. The use of the balloon frame after 1833, a construction method that required less material and labor, aided in the settlement of the treeless prairies, though "soddies," houses and dugouts made of dense prairie sod, called *prairie marble*, provided shelter for many prairie homesteaders.

Turn-of-the-twentieth-century Progressives employed the new insights of sociology, psychology, and home economics to rethink home ownership and household management. The suburbs were often the location of the small, efficient, and technologically modern family dwelling, symbolized by the bungalow. Concerned with shrinking family size, lack of home ownership, and the rise of single persons needing shelter, Progressive reformers in 1911 inaugurated the National Conference on Housing. In 1922, the Better Homes movement linked private initiative and the federal government through the sponsorship of conferences and publications and the use of demonstration houses. The movement offered forums on mortgage financing and affordable house design. At the same time, the exponential growth of the suburbs led to the establishment of the Architects' Small House Service Bureau in 1919, which offered standardized designs for modern and affordable houses. In popular culture as well as sociological theory, suburban houses offered mostly middle-class white Americans safety, convenience, and comfort; housing starts were soon to become a measure of the nation's economic well-being.

The emphasis on better and more modern housing culminated in a series of reports produced in 1931–1932 by President Herbert C. Hoover's (1874–1964) Conference on Home Building and Home Ownership. The problems cited in these publications worsened during the Great Depression of the 1930s. The nation's housebuilding industry was destroyed and did not fully recover until after World War II (1939–1943). Mortgage foreclosures in 1933 numbered 1,000 per week. In response, President Franklin Delano Roosevelt (1882–1945) signed the National Housing Act (1934), which instituted both a public housing program and, through the Federal Housing Administration (FHA), a program of affordable mortgages. The linkage of home ownership and national prosperity and security would reach full fruition after World War II, when the Servicemen's Readjustment Act of 1944 (commonly known as the "GI Bill of Rights") offered veterans low-cost, federally supported home loans (administered also by the FHA). Despite a housing construction boom aided by prefabrication, new building technologies, and innovative building materials (as evident in the Levittown, New York, development), the nation experienced a short-term housing shortage: Veterans and their wives moved in with parents; shared with other couples; and even lived in barns, garages, and chicken coops. The boom was not democratic: The FHA endorsed racial and ethnic segregation through the use of restrictive covenants governing new developments and neighborhoods. With varying degrees of success, federal housing legislation, governing single-family houses as well as multiunit apartment houses, still seeks to remedy economic disparities and racial, ethnic, and gender discrimination and raise living standards.

Home and Domesticity

Throughout the nineteenth century Americans were made aware of fashionable houses through print culture. Popular builder's manuals, pattern books, household manuals, and domestic periodicals such as *Godey's Lady's Book* (1830–1898) published house designs and offered readers complete drawings of the designs. The advice of Catharine E. Beecher (1800–1878), the fiction of her younger sister Harriet Beecher Stowe (1811–1896), and the architectural guides of Andrew Jackson Downing (1815–1852) all contributed to a Romantic understanding of home as a place of repose and family coziness, as a symbol of Christian morality and prosperity (through the Gothic Revival style), and as an important symbol of independence. Domesticity was allied with (feminine) nature, as opposed to the competitive grittiness of the (masculine) city; the suburban home, whether villa, cottage, or farmhouse, was to be situated in the midst of a landscape of beauty. In the suburban home, a woman governed by tending to the morals of family and servants and instilling the sentiments linking material culture to love of family. Women as wives, mothers, and daughters also labored, though in the ideology of domesticity such labor as cooking, cleaning, laundry, and other related activities, difficult before electrification and indoor plumbing, rendered these activities invisible in novels, lithographs, and other popular culture forms. The ideological association of women with the home proved a political barrier to women's full civil rights.

Home as Popular Culture

Since the early twentieth-century professionalization of real estate selling, real estate agents have exploited the sentiments and symbolism of home and the independence of ownership to promote house buying. Banks and other lenders also play up these ideals, and their efforts were mirrored in the years immediately following World War II. The popular film *It's a Wonderful Life* (1946), though about life and redemption, revolves also around the nature of the American family home. The lead character, George Bailey, surrenders a European honeymoon with his new wife, Mary, to aid his neighbors when the stock market crashes in 1929; throughout the 1930s Bailey's savings and loan company makes home ownership possible for immigrant families while he lives in a "fixer upper" of a nineteenth-century house with all the "Victorian" trappings. *Mr. Blandings Builds His Dream House* (1948) humorously captures one New York City family's efforts to build a traditional house in Connecticut, defying the good intent of the family friend and attorney, the architect, and the builder. In *The Best Years of Their Lives* (1946), veteran Al Stephenson returns to his old employer, a bank, but is now placed in charge of managing home loans for other veterans as he wrestles with his readjustment to his beloved but changed family. The established Stephenson family lives in a large, exclusive apartment, but one with all the trappings of a self-contained detached dwelling; another veteran, Fred Derry, visits his father and stepmother in a dismal shack near a railroad track and lives with his wife in a very small apartment; only Homer Parrish returns to a single-family dwelling, that of his parents. By the end of the film Fred Derry, leaving his cheating wife, finds a job converting old war materiel into housebuilding materials. Though the war had caused family separation and permanent loss and required often painful readjustment to civilian life, the promise in this film was the assurance of the vitality of the American Dream, realized through marriage, family, and home ownership.

Shirley Teresa Wajda

See also Agricultural Architecture; Apartments, Tenements, and Flats; Architectural History and American Architecture; Colonial

Revival; Domestic Architecture; Gender;
Gothic Revival; Homeless Residences;
Literary Studies and American Literature;
Mobile Homes and Trailer Parks; Suburbs
and Suburbia

References and Further Reading
Hornstein, Jeffrey M. 2005. *A Nation of Realtors:
A Cultural History of the Twentieth-Century
American Middle Class.* Durham, NC: Duke
University Press.
Matthews, Glenna. 1987. *Just a Housewife: The
Rise and Fall of Domesticity in America.* New
York: Oxford University Press.
Rybczynski, Witold. 1986. *Home: A Short History
of an Idea.* New York: Viking.
Wright, Gwendolyn. 1981. *Building the Dream:
A Social History of Housing in America.*
Cambridge, MA: MIT Press.

Houses of Worship (Ecclesiastical Architecture)

Houses of worship provide communal prayer
space for a variety of religious groups. The
diversity of form and use of these structures
has been a unique feature of the American
built environment from the seventeenth century to the present. Various factors, including
theology and beliefs, architectural trends,
and region, have shaped the forms that these
buildings took over the past four centuries.
The structures themselves have expressed
some of the deepest values of the historical
groups that built them. Regional cultures
and theology were the most prominent factors in determining the architectural forms
of churches and meetinghouses in colonial
America. As religious life has become more
varied in the United States, however, architectural fashions have influenced houses of
worship, making them more similar, even as
individual congregations continue to shape
broad architectural trends to fit their own
theological needs and styles of worship.

The Colonial Period: Theology and Regionalism

In colonial Virginia, the Anglican parish
church dominated the religious landscape.
Virginians built their churches in a vernacular style that combined local considerations,
traditional Gothic elements, and the newest
Georgian styles that were based on neoclassical ideas about symmetry. While theological considerations were important, Virginia's
colonists also modeled their churches on
gentlemen's houses to reflect their ideas
about hospitality and the local social order.
Thus, churches were seated according social

*Williamsburg's Bruton Parish Church, begun in 1715,
served Anglicans in the Virginia colony and serves
Episcopalians today. This 1930s photograph shows the
restored building's cruciform (Christian cross-like)
shape, intended to open the interior space to all con-
gregants. The building's exterior incorporates Gothic
and Georgian elements. (Historic American Buildings
Survey/Library of Congress)*

rank, with the most prestigious parishioners sitting nearest the pulpit and those with the least status sitting the farthest away.

Colonial New Englanders called their houses of worship *meetinghouses* to imply that they were not sacred spaces, but simply buildings in which New Englanders met to participate in both worship services and secular activities such as town meetings. Puritans built their meetinghouses with wood and eschewed the longitudinal orientation of churches, instead orienting their meetinghouses so that worshippers entered through the long sides of the building and were immediately confronted not with an altar but with a massive central pulpit. The pews were simple benches situated on all sides of the meetinghouse, except where the pulpit stood. Like the Anglican churches of Virginia, New England meetinghouses were also seated according to social standing, although in New England this was measured according to piety, official standing, age, and social and family distinctions, in addition to wealth.

In the middle colonies (New York, Pennsylvania, Maryland, Delaware, and New Jersey), where a diverse array of religious groups lived and worshipped side by side, a variety of social considerations and stylistic trends shaped church and meetinghouse forms. Quakers, like Puritans, called their houses of worship *meetinghouses* and built them, like the Old Haverford Friends Meeting House (1697) in Oakmont, Pennsylvania, on a domestic model without exterior steeples or interior pulpits. Quaker meetinghouses had two doors, and the interior consisted of wooden benches facing one another. During the eighteenth century, some Georgian decorative features appeared on Quaker meetinghouses, and brick was newly employed as a building material, but on the whole, Quaker worship spaces continued to be built on a plain domestic model.

Other groups, such as German Lutherans in Pennsylvania and Presbyterians and Dutch Calvinists in New York, employed different architectural styles. Lutheran churches in Pennsylvania, embracing a liturgical mode of worship, were built in a more traditional Georgian style similar to that of Anglican churches of the region. The Presbyterians of New York, on the other hand, built their worship spaces on a model more like that of eighteenth-century New England, with small towers often set in the middle of the buildings. Dutch Calvinists of New York included typically Dutch architectural forms such as the double-pitch roof, while also making use of regional building materials such as stone.

The Nineteenth Century: Respectability, Diversity, and National Convergence

When Methodists, Baptists, and other evangelical denominations first emerged in the American South in the eighteenth century, they challenged the established social order not only through their theology but also by occupying the crudest of structures, such as tobacco houses and rough-hewn log cabins. In the early nineteenth century, however, evangelical churches began to adopt the Greek Revival style that featured a portico of imposing and unornamented Doric columns inspired by the buildings of the ancient democracies in a newly born republic. This style had first become popular among Congregationalists and Episcopalians, the descendants of the colonial Puritans and Anglicans. Thus the emergence of Greek Revival churches across the nation indicated the emergence of national architectural trends and implied that once-marginal evangelical denominations had established themselves as respectable.

In the later nineteenth century, houses of worship often were built in the Gothic and

Romanesque revival styles. The Gothic Revival, also known as neo-Gothic, first began in Pennsylvania and New York where High Church Anglicanism, a movement focusing on hierarchy and the sacraments, became popular in the middle of the century. This style looked back to the great medieval Catholic cathedrals for its inspiration. Another popular nineteenth-century style was neo-Romanesque, in use as early as the 1840s, which combined rounded arches with elaborate stonework, and had pyramidal towers. This eclectic style became popular in a variety of denominations by the end of the century, its most notable example being architect Henry Hobson Richardson's (1838–1886) design for Boston's Trinity Episcopal Church (1877–1886).

These styles found ready acceptance in Catholic churches of the era as well, beginning with the influx of Irish immigrants in the 1840s. Having fled an oppressive British government in their homeland, Irish Catholics in New England drew upon European continental styles, rather than English patterns, in designing their churches. In the late nineteenth century, Catholic immigrants from eastern and southern Europe erected churches that represented their own ethnic identities through ornamental details such as inscriptions in their native languages and depictions of national saints in statues and stained glass windows, while also tapping into the vogue for neo-Gothic and neo-Romanesque popular in late nineteenth-century America.

Jewish immigrants of the nineteenth century also participated in the broad architectural trends of the day. Although there had been a small number of Jews in North America during the colonial period (Newport, Rhode Island's Touro Synagogue was dedicated in 1763), the major influx of central and eastern European Jews in the nineteenth cen-

tury led to the construction of new synagogues. The interiors of all synagogues were focused on the pulpit and the Ark that holds the Torah scrolls, but the layout and decorative forms varied according to popular trends and ethnic backgrounds. The earliest nineteenth-century synagogues followed the popular Greek Revival. By the 1840s, however, synagogues across the nation began to tap into the Gothic and Romanesque Revival styles made popular in New York and Pennsylvania. In the later nineteenth century synagogues like Temple Emanu-El in San Francisco (1866) began to incorporate oriental elements such as bulbous tower domes on otherwise neo-Gothic buildings. Although these styles seem to suggest Middle Eastern origins, they are a result of European Jews bringing an oriental revival movement from their native Germany.

The Twentieth Century: Continuity, Suburbanization, and Increasing Diversity

In the twentieth century national trends continued to influence a wide variety of houses of worship. The first major new trend of the twentieth century to find its way into the design of houses of worship began in the Midwest with architects like Frank Lloyd Wright (1869–1959). His Unitarian Unity Temple (1906–1909) in Oak Park, Illinois, combined the models of ancient temples, those of contemporary Japan, and the idea of the New England meetinghouse.

Another new trend of the twentieth century was the adaptation of these similar designs to the needs of suburban congregations. When evangelical Christians adapted the auditorium-style seating of their turn-of-the-century congregations to modern design they created the suburban "megachurch" of the second half of the twentieth century. Such structures appeared in large numbers across the South and Midwest. Willow Creek Community Church (1981), a nondenominational megachurch in South Barrington, Illinois, harkens back to the Puritan meetinghouse in its lack of religious iconography or sacral associations. Instead, Willow Creek focuses on creating a comfortable environment for up to 12,000 weekly worshippers who sometimes watch the service on television screens located throughout the auditorium.

Christians were not the only group to adapt twentieth-century architectural styles to new suburban circumstances. Jews also began to build suburban synagogues in the 1950s and 1960s that attempted to combine the functions of a synagogue with that of a Jewish community center and school in one convenient location. Such buildings, like Beth El (1950) in Flint, Michigan, used modern minimalist styles and materials to create complexes that housed central worship spaces connected to classrooms and social halls. These minimalist styles, with their relative lack of iconography, also began to be used by multidenominational chapels that sought to provide one worship space for various religious groups. The twentieth century also saw the first sustained building of mosques and temples by new immigrants to the United States. In the West, Japanese and Chinese immigrants built both traditional Buddhist and Shinto temples and ones that, like the Soto Mission Temple (1953) in Honolulu, Hawaii, harmonized American popular styles of the period with traditional Buddhist motifs. Immigrants from Muslim countries have begun building mosques, like Dar al-Islam (1980) in Abiquiu, New Mexico, that adapt regional and sometimes modern designs to Muslim religious practices by combining them with the traditional layouts and decorative motifs of their native lands.

Alexis Antracoli

See also Architectural History and American Architecture; Classical Revival (Neo-classicism); Georgian Style; Gothic Revival; Religion, Spirituality and Belief; Rite, Ritual, and Ceremony

References and Further Reading

Hayes, Bartlett. 1983. *Tradition Becomes Innovation: Modern Religious Architecture in America.* New York: Pilgrim Press.
Kahera, Akel Ismail. 2002. *Deconstructing the American Mosque: Space, Gender, and Aesthetics.* Austin: University of Texas Press.
Williams, Peter W. 1997. *Houses of God: Region, Religion, and Architecture in the United States.* Urbana: University of Illinois Press.
Wischnitzer, Rachel. 1955. *Synagogue Architecture in the United States: History and Interpretation.* Philadelphia, PA: Jewish Publication Society of America.

Human Aging and the Aged

Recognition of *aging*—becoming old—as a distinct developmental period in human life, and the consequent scholarly interest, is relatively recent. Early discussions were almost exclusively medical in focus and tended to emphasize decline and dysfunction. Gerontology, initially grounded in psychological and medical models, has become an increasingly interdisciplinary subject. Anthropology, sociology, social and economic history, folklore, and archaeology have informed gerontological research; material culture has become an important tool of analysis. Inquiry about the role and status of the aged has further benefited from gender studies, disability studies, and consumer history. Material culture has been particularly important to cultural and sociohistorical analyses of aging. Historians have considered clothing and other aspects of personal image, housing, furnishings, and, more recently, the plethora of appliances and supportive equipment designed for the elderly.

While not easily classified, this vast body of evidence tends to fall into three general categories: material culture that is about, by, and for older adults. A number of scholars have used artifacts to describe and interpret the roles and status of the aged. Another large body of research examines works produced by the elderly themselves. Analysts in this category are interested in issues of creativity in late life as well as the role of memory. Finally, a vast amount of research has been conducted on appliances, supportive equipment, and architectural design specifically for the aged. With the clear exception of housing and architecture, this last category includes many ephemeral sources such as catalogues and has not been systematically analyzed.

Material Culture about the Aged

Some of the most compelling studies of aging in what is now the United States have been provided by social historians and art historians, who have tended to emphasize the colonial and preindustrial experience. They have used architecture, clothing, tombstones, and portraits to determine general social attitudes toward and status of the aged. Historians John Demos (1986) and David Hackett Fischer (1978) have employed an analysis of clothing, hairstyles, and even meetinghouse seating arrangements to support their conclusion that the elderly in early America enjoyed relatively high status and authority within their families and communities. Social status, economic power, and religious dictum all merged in early America to create what Fischer describes as "veneration" of the aged.

Colonial American portraits and surviving clothing indicate that parents dressed their children in clothing similar to their own. Powdered hair and white wigs were a regular feature of a well-dressed male's wardrobe —not just old men, but men of any age, sometimes including adolescents. A well-known colonial portrait, dating from about 1710, depicts the adolescent Jonathan Benham in breeches, knee-length coat, and white hair. Such practices comment upon the relatively undifferentiated state of childhood in the eighteenth century, as well as issues of class and gender, as they do about veneration for the aged. They reinforce a positive view of the image of age in this time, albeit a view that was often tempered by realistic descriptions of decline and failing powers. In Anne Bradstreet's (ca. 1612–1672) poetic discourse on "The Four Ages of Man" (1650), an elderly man grimly observes, "My grinders now are few, my sight doth fail / My skin is wrinkled, and my cheeks are pale."

Age is not always or completely a variable of status or image and thus may not necessarily suggest enhanced status for the aged. Some groups such as the Amish, who immigrated to the United States in the eighteenth century, continue to maintain minimal differences in dress among various age groups. Generic clothing, whether in a traditional setting or a convent, is a way of muting differences between individuals.

Prescriptive literature provides insight to expectations and practices in a particular era, although we need to be cautious about assuming that most people actually followed their dictates. In 1869, Catharine E. Beecher (1800–1878) and her sister, Harriet Beecher Stowe (1811–1896), published the housekeeping guide *The American Woman's Home*. Significantly, an entire chapter was devoted to the care of the aged. The discussion emphasizes "decay" and "loss of usefulness," echoing changes in the larger society that had displaced so many elderly citizens. An underlying assumption of the chapter is that many older relatives had nowhere else to go, and it was the duty of the family to house them.

Paintings and (after 1839) photographs have provided important insights into the experiences and status of the aged. The portraits of Anne Pollard (1621–1725), a Puritan elder who sat for her likeness in 1721 at the age of 100, and Elizabeth Fenimore Cooper (1752–1817), who had her likeness depicted by George Freeman in 1816, are straightforward, with no attempt to soften or "youthen" their appearances. Works of art are also useful in documenting the changes in attitudes and circumstances that confronted the elderly with the onset of industrialization. By the mid-nineteenth century, respect began to give way at times to a more sentimental and romantic view, and occasionally to open ridicule. Currier & Ives (1834–1907) printed a widely distributed series of images in 1868 entitled *The Four Seasons of Life*. The final panel, *Old Age*, depicts a cozy domestic scene with an elderly man and woman seated in front of the fire of a comfortable home, looking adoringly at a young child, probably their granddaughter. Both adults wear spectacles and are dressed warmly with coat and shawl in contrast to the child's short-sleeved frock. These are people who have earned rest and comfort at the end of long lives. A very different message is provided in William Sidney Mount's 1847 painting, *Loss and Gain*. Although Mount's purpose was to lend support to the temperance movement, his choice of an elderly man awkwardly climbing a fence to retrieve a jug of liquor as the focus of the painting was significant. The man is a comical figure, almost a buffoon, hardly worthy of respect and admiration.

Material Culture Created by the Aged

The elderly have created art as well as been its subjects. Their works have often been used in the discussions of aging, memory, and creativity. A body of "memoir" art has been created by individuals who often began painting later in life and used their art as a means of telling their life stories. Anna May Robertson "Grandma" Moses (1860–1961) is perhaps the best known; others include "Aunt Clara" McDonald Williamson (1875–1976), Emma Serena "Queena" Stovall (1887–1980), Daisy Sifferman Cook (1902–1977), and Clementine Hunter (1886–1988). As this list suggests, many of these artists, especially in the twentieth century, are women who create nostalgic scenes of domestic life. Their works fall within a folk genre that is arguably not "geriatric" in subject matter or technique, but the paintings, as well as the voices of the painters themselves, have been employed by those who seek to understand creativity and memory in later life. A far grittier body of work was produced by "Grandma" Elizabeth Layton (1910–1993) of Topeka, Kansas; she used her painting as a therapy that ultimately lifted her out of clinical depression. Layton's self-portraits tackle a number of social issues, including modern perceptions of the aged and particularly of elderly women.

Material Culture for the Aged

The increasing social segregation of the aged, as a consequence of modernization, is evident in a variety of ways, from changing visual images to the development of special housing. The "plight" of the aged was a more frequent subject of historical and contemporary public discourse. The transition era, from the late nineteenth century to the early twentieth, was a particularly uncertain and often difficult period for older Americans. Small-town and family support gradually grew unreliable but were not immediately replaced by other services and financial support such as pensions.

Housing has been a focus of gerontologists and material culture scholars. Historians have documented the evolution of the "old-age home" that, along with other specialized service institutions, became a regular feature of American life. The earliest form of housing specifically intended for the aged was usually not much more than the county poor farm, although some attempts at housing for the "worthy" poor were early instituted. A considerable body of sociological and anthropological research focuses on congregate housing in the twentieth century. Sociological analyses of congregate living tend to be concerned with issues such as life satisfaction and social arrangements. Other studies have elaborated the differences between the circumstances of the urban and rural elderly. In varying degrees, these studies acknowledge the vast differences within the aged population by stressing the importance of physical layout, arrangements of facilities and adaptive environments that include a spectrum of environments from independent-living apartments to full nursing care units.

American twentieth-century material culture should prove a valuable resource to future scholars of aging. As their numbers and wealth have increased, older Americans have been identified and targeted as a market with particular needs and interests. Several product categories in particular illuminate the circumstances of the aged as well as attitudes about how those circumstances should be met: those items that are designed to support and enhance the quality of life, and those products such as greeting cards that reinforce ideas of what age means. Many products are intended to overcome or at least alleviate the declines of age: boosters to help an individual rise from a sitting position, magnification and illuminating devices, utensils designed for arthritic hands, accessories for walkers and canes, safety adaptations for the bath and toilet, and personal alarms and call systems. While not always intended exclusively for use by the elderly, these items reinforce the assumption that old age need not be a time of debility—an assumption further underscored by catalogue models who are often attractive and vigorous gray-haired women and men dressed in stylish clothing.

Age Groups

The postmodern world has been characterized by age segregation or association of age peers. Whether attending fourth grade or moving to an assisted living facility, Americans tend to be grouped with people of similar age. A variety of age milestones have further institutionalized the arbitrary division of age groups: the legal age to drive, vote, consume alcohol, marry, retire, collect Social Security and other pensions, and be eligible for Medicare are all determined by one's years. As a consequence, the relative recent phenomenon of heralding birthdays, and certain birthdays in particular, with festivities and an abundance of products providing all sorts of messages about the merits and deficits of one's age has become commonplace. The greeting card industry, for example, has played a major role in defining age milestones and periods of life. Cards targeted to older consumers may offer congratulations, but also declare that "You're Over the Hill."

Material Culture as Metaphor for the Aged

When she was eighty-two years old, Florida Scott-Maxwell (1883–1979) drew upon familiar images to make the following entry into her diary: "As I do not live in an age when rustling black silk skirts billow about me, and I do not carry an ebony stick to strike the floor in sharp rebuke, as this is denied me, I rap out a sentence in my note book and feel better. If a grandmother wants to put her foot down, the only safe place to do it these days is in a note book" (Scott-Maxwell 1968, 20).

The meanings attached to the things Scott-Maxwell described—skirts, ebony stick—had endured far beyond their time of use. Perhaps no other stage of life has so evoked the metaphorical use of the language of things to describe its conditions and circumstance. Old age is a time both anticipated and feared, and those dual expectations reveal the complexity and subtleties that attend the use of material culture in interpreting that time of life. Objects have function, and objects have meaning. Objects can provide insight into understanding the last stage of life.

Linna F. Place

See also Adolescence; Adulthood; Childhood; Children's Dress; Disability and Disability Studies; Human Body; Social History

References and Further Reading
Achenbaum, W. Andrew. 1978. *Images of Old Age in America: 1790 to the Present*. Ann Arbor, MI: Institute of Gerontology, University of Michigan/Wayne State University.
Achenbaum, W. Andrew. 1978. *Old Age in a New Land: The American Experience since 1790*. Baltimore, MD: Johns Hopkins University Press.
Calvert, Karin. 1992. *Children in the House: The Material Culture of Early Childhood, 1600–1900*. Boston: Northeastern University Press.
Chudacoff, Howard P. 1989. *How Old Are You? Age Consciousness in American Culture*. Princeton, NJ: Princeton University Press.
Demos, John. 1970. *A Little Commonwealth: Family Life in Plymouth Colony*. New York: Oxford University Press.
Demos, John. 1986. "Old Age in Early New England." In *Past, Present and Personal: The Family and the Life Course in American History*. New York: Oxford University Press.
Fischer, David Hackett. 1978. *Growing Old in America*, exp. ed. New York: Oxford University Press.
Premo, Terri L. 1990. *Winter Friends: Women Growing Old in the New Republic, 1785–1835*. Urbana: University of Illinois Press.
Scott-Maxwell, Florida. 1968. *The Measure of My Days*. New York: Alfred A. Knopf.
Spicker, Stuart F., Kathleen M. Woodward, and David D. Van Tassel, eds. 1978. *Aging and the Elderly: Humanistic Perspectives in Gerontology*. Atlantic Highlands, NJ: Humanities Press.

Human Body

The *body* refers to the human organism. The body is the primary material of human culture and, in terms of material culture—that is, physical manifestations of cultural and social life—the body functions in three ways. First, the body's impulses can be expressed in material form; second, the body can be confined or restrained for social purposes; and third, the body itself can be modified better to suit cultural standards.

The Body Externalized in Material Culture
Philosopher Karl Marx (1818–1883), in his various writings, including *Das Kapital* (1867) and *Grundrisse* (1857–1858), understood material objects to be expressions of the physical body. Economic relations, such as when a human body's labor is "bought" for a monetary exchange (or salary), resulted in the production of material goods that in turn would be sold in a further exchange of value. For Marx, economic life was about human bodies producing material goods that were then transacted in economic relations. The body was externalized, or expressed outwardly in material form. The great tragedy of industrial, modern life in Marx's view was that individual, bodily production was

hidden when a body's output was measured by monetary exchange value.

Many folk art historians have explored how physical objects represent bodily expressions. For example, the terminology of house architecture reflects its origin in human bodies. Windows are seen as "eyes" to a house, while doors are often figured as the "mouth" of the building, through which material and life enter and depart. Chairs, built to accommodate and display the human body, have "arms," "legs," a "back," and a "seat." Folk art directly expressed an individual's bodily experience rendered into material form. A quilt, for example, created to warm and cover the body, was in its minute stitches, its physically laborious piecing together of scraps of cloth, and the patterns of shapes and colors joined by thread, the human body's labor made into a material object.

The Body Restrained by Culture

The human body is subject to infinite varieties of social control and restraints. Most social control is seemingly innocuous. Children learn bodily etiquette that may seem "natural" but is socially constructed behavior. For example, blowing one's nose into a piece of fabric or, in contemporary times, a woven piece of soft paper, is a modern invented behavior. Prior to the Renaissance (fourteenth-century Europe), noses were emptied of mucus by blowing them on the sleeve of a garment or on one's fingers. The handkerchief and its proper use reflected new, modern standards of hygiene, cleanliness, social appearance, and bodily control. Other forms of deportment, such as different postures and forms of greeting such as the formal bow or curtsy, represent how the human body performs social actions.

Human bodies have been subject to far more direct and intrusive forms of control.

Prisons, for example, not only physically confine the human body but prison architecture symbolically represents cultural beliefs in how restraint of the body can inform moral or spiritual restraint. Michel Foucault (1926–1984), a cultural theorist, argued that social understandings of the self and its potential for moral rehabilitation were reflected in how prisons confined the bodies of those who would not conform to social standards. Individual cells, for example, increasingly characterized modern Western prisons from the mid-1800s and symbolically represented an intensification of society's ability to control the individual body and, thus, self.

Punishment of individuals, of course, often takes bodily form. Foucault discussed the extraordinary physical ruination of prisoners' bodies as a public display of state power. In the 1700s, executions were often public, endured for long periods of time, and featured the systematic dismembering and torturing of the prisoner's living body. By the 1900s, and especially in the United States in the late 1900s and early 2000s, executions took place in silence, without a large public audience, and ideally without the graphic evidence of physical torture. Foucault argued that while these new methods of bodily punishment were understood as more humane, they also represented the enlarged scope of society's control of individual bodies.

The Body Modified By Culture

American culture today is characterized by extreme forms of commodification, that is, economic and social systems characterized by commodity exchange. Since the mid-twentieth century, American culture has commodified nearly everything, including the human body. Advertising has since the 1920s wedded display of idealized human bodies with manufactured products and promises of social happiness. Advertising and other forms of media, such as cinematic films, television, and the World Wide Web, use human bodies to attract attention to various other commodities. In this system of selling, the human body is valued for its ability to sell not only products but itself to the consumer. Contemporary American culture is dominated by spectacle in which human bodies are merely objects to be looked at. In this cultural and economic environment, extreme body types (often artificially modified bodies) are valued. On one hand are bodies designated as "beautiful." In the 1920s, the ideal female body was short, childlike, and thin; the 1950s idealized female body was curvaceous with exaggerated indentations at the waist; the contemporary female ideal body type of the early 2000s is extremely thin, with disproportionately large breasts, flat hips, and an absence of abdominal flesh. These various body types are natural to only a very few women at any given time, but in each example, women not naturally endowed sometimes went to extreme measures to modify their bodies to suit these standards with the withholding of food, very high levels of physical activity, artificial padding, physical restraints of their bodies (with undergarments such as corsets, girdles, or today's control underwear), and with surgical augmentations or deletions.

On the other hand, physically anomalous bodies, or "freaks," have been displayed as objects to be consumed for entertainment. Especially in the nineteenth-century United States, the freak show, with its display of fat women, tiny adults, bearded ladies, and strong men, evoked both pity and admiration from onlookers. Today, Michael Jackson's self-created freakish appearance of extremely pale skin (in spite of Jackson's African American heritage) and distorted facial features connects contemporary American culture to its past tradition of freak dis-

play. By dint of extreme body modification, Jackson has created a body freakish in its transgression of boundaries: Is Jackson male or female, white or black, real or fake? He is in some ways the bearded lady of the nineteenth century, socially unrecognizable as male or female.

Through the use of different fabrics, cuts of material, and tailoring, clothing can dramatically modify the appearance and behavior of the body it covers to meet social needs. Consider, for example, how the contemporary men's suit, through the use of heavier fabrics, stiff linings, and structured tailoring, renders most men's bodies as similar units. Almost any man, no matter his natural body shape, can have broad shoulders (through the strategic use of padding, stiff cloth, and tightly sewn lines) and a narrow waist.

Other forms of body modification range from tanning, popular since the 1920s (wherein Caucasian people darken their skin color through exposure to sunlight or artificial light) to various hair styles (from African American styles of braiding, corn rowing, Afros, straightened hair, etc., to Caucasian hair styles of artificially curling, frizzing, straightening, or otherwise modifying the hair). Women's makeup (introduced commercially in the 1930s and socially acceptable since the 1940s) artificially modifies the skin's appearance and is sometimes used to modify the appearance of the face's physical structure (such as applying dark shades to create the illusion of high cheekbones).

Direct and permanent modification of the body includes tattooing, piercing, branding, and stitching the skin. Practiced in North America since the colonial period, since the 1980s such body modification traditions have characterized specific youth subcultures, and sometimes, as in the case of body piercing, reached mainstream popularity. So has cosmetic surgery to reshape the body and face.

Finally, the body is modified in death. By the end of the nineteenth century, embalming the body by applying preservative chemicals allowed for more elaborate presentations of the dead body and intensified funeral rituals. Coffins, and later caskets, physically represented the body enclosed within. Body parts, including baby teeth and locks of hair, were and are often saved as memorials to infant or deceased human bodies. In the case of hair, nineteenth-century Americans often made elaborate decorative objects, including jewelry, from the hair of loved ones, living or dead, as memorials to their presence.

American Slavery

No discussion of the human body as material culture can ignore the unique circumstances of American slavery. Slavery involved the legal ownership of another's body and self. In the British American colonies that would form the United States, slave ownership was gradually limited to allow only for those of African descent to be legally owned as slaves. Legal restraints of slave owners who abused the bodies of their slaves were often exerted with a light hand. The United States continued the practice of legal ownership of human beings' bodies long after other European countries ceased the practice. Bioarchaeology (the archaeological study of bodily remains) has revealed that African slaves in the United States were often physically mistreated. African slave skeletons dating from the eighteenth century uncovered in a Manhattan cemetery reveal bodies physically deformed by extreme hard work, including the constant carrying of heavy loads. In addition, these skeletons reveal that African slaves continued African body modifications, such as the selective filing of front teeth. But the imposed deformations of bones graphically reveal the bodily consequences of being owned by another.

Helen Sheumaker

See also Adolescence; Adulthood; Bodily Cleanliness and Hygiene; Body Modification; Children's Dress; Child's Body; Commodity; Cosmetics, Toiletries, Perfumes, and Colognes; Disability and Disability Studies; Dress, Accessories, and Fashion; Etiquette and Manners; Funerals; Military Dress; Mourning; Mourning and Ethnicity; Penitentiaries and Prisons; Religious Dress; Slavery

References and Further Reading

Foucault, Michel. 1977. *Discipline and Punish: The Birth of the Prison*, trans. Alan Sheridan. New York: Pantheon Books.

Lurie, Alison. 2000. *The Language of Clothes*, 2nd ed. New York: Henry Holt.

Marx, Karl. 1976 (1867). *Das Kapital (Capital: A Critique of Political Economy)*. New York: Penguin.

Marx, Karl. 2000 (1857–1858). *Grundrisse (Working: Its Meaning and Its Limits)*. Notre Dame, IN: University of Notre Dame Press.

Slavery's Buried Past. 1996. Videocassette (60 minutes). Chicago: WTTW and Kurtis Production Ltd.

Thomson, Rosemarie Garland. 1996. *Freakery: Cultural Spectacles of the Extraordinary Body*. New York: New York University Press.

I

Illicit Pleasures and Venues

Buildings; costumes and dress; printed materials such as broadsides, advertisements, lithographs, and guide books; the accoutrements of alcohol consumption and production; and artifacts from brothels and gambling dens tell us that Americans in the past participated in *illicit pleasures,* those activities proscribed, restricted, or regulated by government, ecclesiastical, or moral authority.

Early American Sins

Early Americans were tempted by a variety of activities deemed sinful. Acting in accord with religious precept, colonial authorities passed a variety of laws to forbid or curtail such activities, especially those undertaken in public places. The sin of idleness provided the rationale for colonial laws regarding what would now be termed leisure activities. High tavern license fees ensured that such establishments were owned and operated by responsible persons. Taverns throughout the colonies were restricted in dispensing alcohol to certain days, to certain patrons, and in certain amounts. Tobacco, once legalized, was very popular, and under penalty of fines, tobacco "abuse" was restricted to "private rooms" in taverns and at safe distances away from houses, barns, and hay- and corn stacks, for fear of fire as well as idleness. Horse racing was discouraged, yet the activity was popular. Philadelphia's original Sassafras Street was commonly called Race Street for the activity that occurred there; this name was formally adopted in 1853. The colonial Virginia gentry reveled in gambling on horse races and cards. Laws restricting gaming to the wealthy failed, however, to curb the practice by the white middling and lesser sorts and by slaves.

The Industrial Revolution in the early nineteenth century led to the growth of urban areas and to more and dedicated leisure time for many Americans. Houses of ill repute, gambling establishments, and other venues grew in popularity due to these changes. All classes, races, and ethnicities of citizens participated in illicit entertainment, although obviously not all individuals did so. While the church and the family dwelling remained the axis of rural and frontier life, in urban areas much leisure entertainment moved out of the domestic sphere and into public space. Along with the acceptable decorous behaviors associated with urban parks, libraries, and museums, various forms of public entertainment emerged throughout the nineteenth century that became associated with illicit pleasures.

Nineteenth-Century Prostitution

In most metropolitan areas, port cities, and frontier towns, houses of ill repute could be found in *red-light districts*, a term coined from the practice of railroad workers who would hang their lanterns outside brothels. Establishments contained a combination of elements that came to mark houses of ill repute: drinking, prostitution, and gambling. The ubiquity and variety of nineteenth-century houses of ill repute indicate that class differences were embodied in the geographic and architectural details of the city.

Generally, three classes of brothels served different classes of clients. Prostitutes' clothing and accessories reflected the clientele they served. First-class prostitutes housed in elegantly appointed brothels, called *parlor houses*, were expected to maintain a high level of fashionable dress and elegant style. Second-class street walkers dressed in a conservative fashion to integrate more easily into the social fabric. First- and second-class brothels were located on main thoroughfares near respectable businesses and hotels, while lower-class brothels, also called *bawdy houses*, were primarily found in slum districts and were often connected with saloons and gambling houses.

In addition to brothels, prostitutes could be found in public entertainment venues such as theaters, concert saloons, and concert and dance halls. Concert saloons featured entertainment, the consumption of alcohol, and "waiter girls" who often doubled as performers and as prostitutes. As evident from the architecture of concert saloons, the free or low-cost entertainment was an afterthought, a way to attract business rather than the primary purpose of the space. The third tiers or galleries of theaters were frequented by prostitutes. As theaters placed restrictions on prostitution, the back rooms or upper floors of saloons and halls increasingly served the demand for those seeking prostitutes. There was a strong connection in the public imagination between performers and houses of ill repute, and the label *actress* became a euphemism for prostitute.

Nineteenth-Century Gambling

Gambling, offered in houses of ill repute and venues in cities, on steamboats (called "floating palaces"), and in frontier towns, catered to all tastes and purse sizes. The architectural style of gambling dens ran the gamut from the well appointed to the dingy and reflected the social conditions of their locale and clientele. In the western territories and states, gambling represented the rapid acquisition and loss of money associated with the California gold rush (1848–1850) and other mining booms. The large proportion of men to women, the transient lifestyle of mine workers, and the absence of family life for many in frontier towns increased the demand for venues of illicit pleasure.

Twentieth-Century "Slumming"

In the early 1900s, a national temperance movement investigated and eliminated neighborhoods of ill repute. Beginning with Chicago in 1912, urban cities throughout the nation abolished red-light districts. Despite Prohibition (1920–1933), cabarets, speakeasies, and, in northern towns, Black-and-Tans (clubs that allowed for the mingling of blacks and whites) provided patrons with liquor and bawdy entertainment. The emergence of the liberated "new woman," the Jazz

Age, and the increased visibility of homosexual culture contributed to a proliferation of risqué entertainment, public promiscuity, and the penchant for slumming. Many cabarets and speakeasies featured gay performers and catered to both heterosexual and homosexual clientele. In large urban cities, drag (or transvestite) balls, where men and women cross-dressed, became popular public expressions of homosexual culture and contributed to the public's perception of what constituted illicit activities. In burlesque theaters, the striptease and the "bump 'n' grind" (a pelvic movement of circles and thrusts accented by live music and jeweled costumes) became dominant features.

During World War II (1939–1945) pinup girls made tawdry images patriotic and burlesque stars were featured in United Service Organization shows that entertained troops overseas. The growth of suburbia in the 1950s and the introduction of television as both entertainment and furniture shifted the primary location of entertainment away from urban centers and into the home. The variety of burlesque, with its comedians, skits, and live music that catered to both male and female patrons, waned, and strip clubs came to feature topless dancing. Adult publications and movie houses provided mostly male patrons with sexually explicit printed and visual images. The explicit display of the nude female form was no longer couched within a theatrical context, and the paraphernalia of burlesque, with its elaborate costumes, sets, and stage props, became obsolete.

Lynn Sally

See also Cities and Towns; Gender; Human Body; Leisure, Recreation, and Amusements; Popular Culture; Sex and Sexuality

References and Further Reading

Allen, Robert. 1991. *Horrible Prettiness: Burlesque and American Culture.* Chapel Hill: University of North Carolina Press.

Chauncey, George. 1994. *Gay New York: Gender, Urban Culture, and the Making of the Gay Male World, 1890–1940.* New York: Basic Books.

Hill, Marilyn Wood. 1993. *Their Sisters' Keepers: Prostitution in New York City, 1830–1870.* Berkeley: University of California Press.

Shteir, Rachel. 2004. *Striptease: The Untold History of the Girlie Show.* New York: Oxford University Press.

Industrial Design

Industrial design is the conceptualization and development of objects for mass production and distribution. The first step in industrial design is to develop a concept, either for a new product or a modification to an existing product, for which there is a market demand. Designers then develop sketches, models, and specifications so that the product can be efficiently manufactured while also being attractive and useful to the consumer. Industrial design thus forms a bridge between industrial production and the consumers' desires. While aesthetic appeal is one aspect of industrial design, utility, safety, ease and cost effectiveness of manufacture, and durability are other commonly addressed issues. Industrial designers work in many fields, from housewares to consumer electronics, medical devices, furniture, and automobiles, although most designers will focus on one area. Designers often work in teams with engineers and other specialists, contributing their knowledge of materials, manufacturing, and aesthetics to the development process.

Industrial design had its origins in the Industrial Revolution, when factory production began to supplant craft production of housewares, textiles, tools, and other consumer goods. Early nineteenth-century industrial design was often technology driven and largely decorative. New processes introduced

Industrial designer Viktor Schreckengost designed the Torpedo pedal car for the Murray Ohio Manufacturing company in Cleveland, Ohio, aiding the company to become, by 1949, the largest producer of toys. Schreckengost bridged the gap between industrialized production and consumers' desires by gathering information about children's body measurements and having children test prototypes for pedal cars. (Viktor Schreckengost Foundation)

by mid-century, such as machining and casting, were used to mimic ornate decorative effects, such as carving, that had formerly been done by hand. Late nineteenth-century design reform challenged such machine-driven mimicry. Members of the Arts and Crafts Movement in England, other nations in Europe, and the United States reacted strongly against the proliferation of ornate yet shoddily manufactured goods; they emphasized quality over quantity, the use of appropriate materials, and the integration of structural and decorative elements, setting the stage for further development of the design profession.

The German Bauhaus (1919–1933) was an avant-garde art and design school that laid the foundations of modern industrial design education. Bauhaus designs were intended to be at once mass producible, useful, and attractive. With the rise of the Nazi regime, the Bauhaus was forced to close, but many of its teachers, including Ludwig Mies van der Rohe (1886–1969), Josef (1888–1976) and Anni Albers (1883–1969), Walter Gropius (1883–1969), and László Moholy-Nagy (1895–1946) immigrated to the United States, bringing the school's Modernist philosophy across the Atlantic.

Increased market competition during the 1910s–1920s proved to manufacturers that industrial designers could add value to their goods by improving visual appeal, styling, function, and/or usability. Industrial design was formally recognized as a profession with the establishment of professional societies such as Council of Industrial Design (Great Britain, 1944). In the same year, the Society of Industrial Designers was founded in the United States, under the leadership of Walter Dorwin Teague (1883–1960). In 1965, this group merged with two other design groups to form the Industrial Designers Society of America, whose first president was Henry Dreyfuss (1904–1972).

The dramatic rise in consumer electronics and information technology in the late twentieth and early twenty-first centuries has enlisted industrial designers to design the casings and physical interfaces for electronic devices, including computers and cellular phones. New technologies have also affected the design profession, as industrial designers now use computer software to model and test their designs virtually rather than building physical models and prototypes. Computer-aided designs can then be used to program computer-controlled machines in a process known as *CAD/CAM*.

The future brings new challenges to the industrial design profession, particularly concerning sustainability and the environment. Traditionally, the design and manufacture of consumer goods has followed a "cradle to grave" model whereby raw materials are manufactured into a product that is sold, and later disposed of at the consumer's convenience. Over the long term, this cycle of design and consumption wastes materials and may cause environmental damage. Some industrial designers have become increasingly interested in developing more sustainable design strategies that will conserve resources and minimize environmental impact.

Hsiao-Yun Chu

See also Consumerism and Consumption; Decorative Arts; Design History and American Design; Graphic Design; Interior Design; Style; Technology

References and Further Reading
Byars, Mel. 2004. *The Design Encyclopedia.* New ed. New York: Museum of Modern Art.
Heskett, John. 1980. *Industrial Design.* London: Thames & Hudson.
Ulrich, Karl T., and Steven D. Eppinger. 2003. *Product Design and Development,* 3rd ed. Boston: Irwin/McGraw Hill.
Woodham, Jonathan M. 1987. *Twentieth-Century Design.* Oxford, UK: Oxford University Press.

Interior Design

The professional field of *interior design* encompasses the planning of space and the selection of finished materials, furnishings, colors, and decorative objects found within the interiors of residential, commercial, civic, and public environments.

For much of American history the interior elements of a given building were designed by the architect, the upholsterer (workrooms of whom supplied all manner of furnishings, finishes, and fabrics for residential interiors), the business owner, and/or the lady of the house if for her own residence. Beginning in the late nineteenth century, individuals such as William Morris (1824–1879) in England, and Americans Louis Comfort Tiffany (1848–1933) and Candace Wheeler (1827–1923) designed many interiors without having major involvement in the architectural process and design of the structures. Amateur tastemakers with wealth, artistic training, and social position were the subjects of magazine articles and newspaper society and women's pages and were often emulated. Some of them also offered decorating advice, as was the case of society matron and novelist Edith Wharton (1862–1937) who, with her friend, architect Ogden

Codman, Jr. (1863–1951), penned the successful treatise *The Decoration of Houses* in 1897. Former actress Elsie de Wolfe (1865–1950), the first individual identified as an interior decorator, published *The House in Good Taste* in 1913. De Wolfe counseled, among other influential collectors of American decorative arts, Henry Francis du Pont (1880–1969) in the historic interiors of his Delaware estate, Winterthur. In the twentieth century, people identified as interior decorators became increasingly prominent in the process of outfitting interior spaces, first in residential spaces and eventually becoming involved in commercial design ventures. Interior decorator Dorothy Draper (1889–1969) is identified as the first woman to specialize in commercial interiors in the 1920s.

Professional organizations for interior designers first appeared in the 1930s with the formation of the American Institute of Interior Decorators. Through various transformations, a number of professional organizations were created in the twentieth century to serve specialized segments of the interior designers. In the early twenty-first century, the primary organization that serves a broad cross-section of the profession in the United States is the American Society of Interior Designers (founded 1975).

At the beginning of the twenty-first century, the field of interior design and those who practice it have gained a popular following as exposure through television, the World Wide Web, and print media has brought increased attention to the underlying concepts and principles of design. The popular perception of residential interior design, as often promoted in the media, deals with surface treatments, materials, and furnishings, with emphasis on the aesthetics of the designed spaces. Functionality is discussed, particularly with reference to work spaces such as kitchens and entertainment

areas (as in family/media rooms). The professional organizations stress the importance of protecting the health, safety, and welfare of the public in the practice of interior design. In commercial work, the concepts of space planning—the efficient utilization of space for a given task or use—play a major role in the development of the interior design. For civic and public design, the perceived image of the interiors—formal, inviting, forbidding, comfortable, and so forth—is an essential design consideration for acceptance by the public. The selection of appropriate materials, colors, and finishes for specific uses is an important component of all types of interior design.

Terrence L. Uber

See also Aesthetic Movement; Arts and Crafts Movement; Bathrooms; Bedrooms; Chippendale Style; Classical Revival (Neoclassicism); Decorative Arts; Design History and American Design; Dining Rooms; Eastlake Style; Industrial Design; Kitchens and Pantries; Living Rooms; Parlors

References and Further Reading
Kilmer, Rosemary, and W. Otie Kilmer. 1992. *Designing Interiors*. Fort Worth, TX: Harcourt Brace Jovanovich College Publishers.
Pile, John. 2003. *Interior Design*, 3rd ed. Upper Saddle River, NJ: Prentice-Hall and Harry N. Abrams.
Pile, John. 2005. *A History of Interior Design*, 2nd ed. Hoboken, NJ: John Wiley.
Piotrowski, Christine M. 2001. *Professional Practice for Interior Designers*, 3rd ed. Hoboken, NJ: John Wiley.

International Style

International style describes the American version of European architectural Modernism in the 1920s and 1930s. The term was first used by architect Philip Johnson (1906–2005) and critic Henry-Russell Hitchcock (1903–1987)

The Farnsworth House, designed by Ludwig Mies van der Rohe and built in 1951 in Plano, Illinois, exemplifies the International style with its flat roofs, open spaces, and walls of windows. (Farnsworth House/Jon Miller, Hedrich Blessing Photographers)

in their 1932 catalogue of the Metropolitan Museum of Art's exhibition on contemporary architecture. This movement was initiated by the members of the German Bauhaus, who sought to reconcile mechanization, industrialization, and craft traditions in the face of international trade and modernization. International style encompassed a set of ideas that transcended national boundaries and attempted to remedy the economic and social dislocations caused by modernization. The Swiss-born architect Le Corbusier (1887–1975) provided theoretical leadership for this style; his journal *L'Esprit Nouveau* in the 1920s asserted the use of industrial techniques and strategies to eradicate poverty and transform society into a more efficient, comfortable environment. It was Corbusier

who stressed functionalism in his dictum that houses were "machines for living."

This revolutionary aesthetic movement ended the dominance of the ornate architecture of the prevailing European Beaux-Arts tradition. International style emphasized structure and form, rationality and asymmetry. Its goal was a "weightless" structure with dynamic open spaces and a lightening of mass, accomplished through the use of flat roofs, rectilinear forms, and walls of windows.

Taking advantage of new materials and building technologies, Modernist architects such as Walter Gropius (1883–1959) and Ludwig Mies van der Rohe (1886–1969) employed methods of mass construction with materials such as glass, concrete, and steel. Both men, who immigrated to the United

States in the 1930s, developed further the skyscraper by recasting it as a steel-frame building with open interior spaces and high-density occupancy.

This new architectural style embraced unornamented surfaces and construction. Modernist architects adopted the ideas of truth in materials and honesty in construction. According to this idea, derived from the writings of critics John Ruskin (1819–1900) and Eugène Emmanuel Viollet-le-Duc (1814–1879), the architecture is excellent only if the viewer can see how it is put together. Commercial examples of this style include what many assert is the first International style skyscraper in the United States, the Philadelphia Savings Fund Society Building (1932), designed by George Howe (1886–1955) and William Lescaze (1896–1969), and Mies van der Rohe's Seagram Building (1958) in New York City. Residential examples include Mies van der Rohe's 1951 Farnsworth House in Plano, Illinois, and Philip Johnson's 1949 Glass House in New Canaan, Connecticut.

Mohammad Gharipour

See also Architectural History and American Architecture; Civic Architecture; Commercial Architecture; Design History and American Design; Domestic Architecture; Industrial Design; Modernism (Art Moderne)

References and Further Reading
Hearn, Fil. 2003. *Ideas That Shaped Buildings.* Cambridge, MA: MIT Press.
Johnson, Philip, and Henry R. Hitchcock. 1997 (1932). *International Style.* New York: W. W. Norton.

J

Junk, Scrap, and Salvage

Junk, scrap, and *salvage* define materials that are discarded but can be put to some use. Though Americans commonly employ these terms interchangeably with *garbage, rubbish, trash,* and *waste,* each word historically possessed specific meanings. *Garbage* originally defined the offal of animals used for food; it is most often used to refer to human and animal filth and unusable food and kitchen waste. The waste matter of a building's repair or decay was called *rubbish*; that term has most often been used to define refuse and debris found in towns and cities. *Trash* once characterized the material broken or cut in the process of preparing an object for use. *Waste* refers to the useless by-product(s) of a process. *Trash* and *waste* are common synonyms for all the terms discussed here. Importantly, *garbage, rubbish,* and *trash,* as well as *refuse,* define materials that are deemed worthless and thrown away.

Junk, scrap, and *salvage,* however, designate materials or goods that have some value, in that they can be recycled and reused. *Junk* defines any waste material that can be put to use. Often, an object is called junk because the owner/user cannot or does not have any use for it, although this does not mean that the object is ultimately useless. The remains of a meal are called *scraps*. So, too, are the remnants of larger segments of a material, such as the detached pieces of a bolt of cloth, wallpaper roll, or sheet metal. Pieces of printed paper, carrying images or text, are commercially created for the leisure activity of "scrapbooking." Originally payment or compensation to those who voluntarily saved a ship or its cargo from wreck or capture, *salvage* is now defined as the property rescued from such an effort. In addition, *salvage* sometimes refers to recyclable waste.

Historical archaeologists have explored past societies through the examination of refuse pits, privy pits (in which Americans discarded household trash as well as bodily waste), and areas outside windows and doorways of domestic dwellings and other sites. (In the era before organized refuse collection or legal restriction, trash could be easily tossed out of doors without fear of fine or complaint.) Historians of dress and furniture have uncovered the constant altering, mending, and "making over" American women undertook to prolong the life of clothing or chairs and other household goods, or to keep up with fashion. Household guides, popular periodicals, diaries and letters, and other documents instruct and describe what historian Susan Strasser has called "the stewardship of objects": the care of objects to prolong use value. In the main, however, material culture scholars concentrate their studies on the new object, its initial manufacture, physical appearance, and intended firsthand use, and not its secondary or tertiary uses, the processes and meanings of its conversion to a new purpose, and, often, its remade physical characteristics.

Recycling: The Many Lives of Discarded Objects

Junk shops and junkyards are sites at which discarded objects are collected until they may once again be used. Junk, then, has some value yet to be determined. The same may be said of scrap, though scraps tend to be considered "odds and ends"—cloth, paper, metal—that need to be pieced together to create a new object, while junk items are objects that tend to require disassembly to be reused. Salvage, on the other hand, is assumed always to possess some value and use and may not necessarily need to be altered. What Americans have discarded, especially in the twentieth century, may be called *junk* or *trash* but is in reality useful, if unfashionable or unwanted, goods. The rise of what is termed *planned obsolescence* to stress "the latest thing" and to promote consumption had over the course of the twentieth century increased disposal of usable goods. Many of these items are donated to charity, sold at flea markets, yard sales, or consignment shops, or given away to friends and family members. All else, perhaps, may rightly be termed *junk*, the value of which to be determined by "dumpster divers" and other trash pickers in city and suburb alike.

In the American colonies and throughout the nineteenth century, certain materials were recycled. Rags were saved by households and sold to "rag men," peddlers who traveled circuits to gather the material and deliver it to paper mills. Not until the late nineteenth-century shift to using wood pulp paper was this practice threatened. Metal objects were also collected and melted down to create other products. In the nation's growing cities, bands of ragpickers and scavengers (mostly the poor, children, and by the end of the century, immigrants) sought cloth and metal scraps, rubber, bones (to create fertilizer), and other potentially valuable objects to sell to dealers. These groups struggled against the increasing government oversight of trash collection, removal, and disposal. The ease and convenience of trash collection led many middle-class Americans, who were also purchasing rather than making the objects they used, to throw out more, to give unwanted possessions to charity, and to equate the collection and use of waste with poverty.

During World War II (1939–1945) the collection of metals, paper, rubber, and even cooking fats became a patriotic act of sacrifice shared by many Americans on the home front. President Franklin Delano Roosevelt (1882–1945) called for several national salvage or scrap drives early in the war; local drives were conducted until the war's end in 1945. Americans learned what household materials could be converted into war materiel, and as Strasser observes, they learned that waste could be valuable. Voluntary recycling was revived in the 1960s and 1970s, when members of the counterculture and environmentalists opened and supported recycling centers for glass, paper, metals, and plastics. These small cooperative ventures and businesses could not compete with the corporations that had, since the turn of the century, managed the nation's waste. Nevertheless, recycling programs are popular, if only to educate Americans about the need to preserve the environment.

Salvagers, especially those rescuers of materials necessary to industry and to maintain discontinued automobile, truck, and tractor models, are both reviled and revered. Communities do not like salvage yards, yet for many patrons these yards provide the only opportunity to find a replacement part or to adhere to a thrifty "do it yourself" ethic. Of particular note is the popularity of historical salvage. Since the 1970s, when federal laws allowed tax credits for historic preservation of buildings, architectural salvage has become a specialty enterprise. The home-building booms of later decades aided the careful removal of stained or leaded glass windows, doors, mantels, columns, plumbing, and other features of aesthetic and historical value from structures slated for demolition. Salvage from shipwrecks is often romanticized as treasure seeking, though marine archaeologists protest commercial salvagers' activities for the loss of evidence and opportunity for scholarly research.

"Found Art" and Crafts

Artist Marcel Duchamp (1887–1968) is credited with coining the term *readymade* to refer to found objects used as art. Though not the first example of Duchamp's readymades, *Fountain*, a "sculpture" of a urinal presented on its back, signed "R. Mutt," is well known. Artist Joseph Cornell (1903–1972) filled glass-fronted boxes with salvaged objects in what is called *assemblage*. Other artists throughout the twentieth century have created collages of manufactured ephemera and paint or sculpture with discarded goods. At century's end the twin processes of globalization and multiculturalism have been encoded in "outsider art" and "folk art" and other "art" goods

by non-Anglos who may or may not be trained artists.

Middle-class Americans have not entirely abandoned their stewardship of goods; newspaper columns such as household adviser Heloise's (Heloise Bowels Cruse [1919–1977] and her daughter, Poncé Kiah Cruse) "Helpful Hints" have contained, for more than forty years, readers' advice about the myriad uses for old pantyhose and other common objects. Since the late 1980s, popular domestic periodicals such as *Martha Stewart Living* embrace both the do-it-yourself ethic and the conversion of old objects to new uses.

The relationship of words to things has provided scholars a means to explore historical change and cultural meaning. Despite the secondhand economy's growth, the interchangeability of terms such as *junk*, *scrap*, and *salvage* reveals contemporary Americans' lack of specific knowledge of the life, death, and afterlife of the objects they discard. Exploring the specific, historically situated meanings of these terms allows for a better understanding of Americans' relationships with the material world.

Shirley Teresa Wajda

See also Commodity; Consumerism and Consumption; Ephemera; Poverty; Scrapbooks; Secondhand Goods and Shopping

References and Further Reading

Lucas, Gavin. 2002. "Disposability and Dispossession in the Twentieth Century." *Journal of Material Culture* 7 (1): 5–22.

Rathje, William, and Cullen Murphy. 2001. *Rubbish! The Archaeology of Garbage*. Tucson: University of Arizona Press.

Strasser, Susan. 1999. *Waste and Want: A Social History of Trash*. New York: Metropolitan Books.

Thompson, Michael. 1979. *Rubbish Theory: The Creation and Destruction of Value*. Oxford, UK: Oxford University Press.

K

Kitchens and Pantries

The *kitchen* is the room in domestic dwellings, restaurants, hotels, and other commercial establishments where food preparation and storage take place. The *pantry*, a small room or closet used to store or hold food, tableware, cookware, linens, and other like items, is (when included in a house design) located next to the kitchen. Over time, the kitchen has most often been defined in the United States as a hub of household activity and the space in which new technology is often introduced to the American family.

In colonial America, cooking generally took place in multipurpose living spaces equipped with broad hearths where household members often gathered to eat, sleep, or warm themselves. Women and girls, whether goodwives, slaves, or servants, performed a variety of tasks in addition to cooking, such as sewing, spinning, and laundry. Only the wealthiest households had rooms dedicated to cooking and the storage of cooking equipment. Foodstuffs were often stored elsewhere, such as the pantry, cellar, chambers, or buttery, or outbuildings like smokehouses and dairies.

Hearth cooking was skilled work. Boiling was done in kettles and pots hung over wood fires from poles set low in the chimney or iron cranes attached to the side wall of the fireplace. Most other cooking was done in vessels with legs set over piles of hot coals on the floor of the hearth. Meat could be roasted in front of the fire. The wealthiest households roasted meat on spits turned by mechanical jacks.

Small amounts of baking could be done in a Dutch oven, a covered iron vessel set on the hearth with a pile of coals below and on top of the lid. The earliest brick bake ovens were built into the walls of the fireplace, making use of the main chimney flues. Later bake ovens were built beside the hearth and had their own flues. In the Southwest, bake ovens, or *hornos*, were built of adobe and were located in the *placita*, or courtyard.

Kitchens varied according to regional, cultural, and socioeconomic factors. In towns and cities, where land was scarce, kitchens were sometimes in the basement. Some families moved cooking outdoors or into a summer kitchen to help keep the house cool in warm weather. Owners of large southern plantations almost always built their kitchens as outbuildings separated from the main house to distance themselves from the heat, mess, and most importantly the enslaved Africans and African Americans who worked in the kitchens and cooked over open hearths well into the nineteenth century.

Elsewhere in the United States, the Industrial Revolution brought wood- or coal-burning cast iron cookstoves to most middle- and upper-class households. Cookstoves were more energy efficient and required less crouching and bending. Other conveniences included sinks, hot water tanks, iceboxes, and a variety of gadgets, as well as new and more plentiful food supplies. Staples and luxury items were stored in pantries or other auxiliary spaces. Pantries, increasingly designed with built-in shelves, drawers, and cabinets, were also used to store expensive tablewares.

Just as cookstoves changed the nature of kitchen work, the Industrial Revolution changed the nature of work and family life in general. Men increasingly worked in offices, factories, and shops, and children attended school. Kitchens became the domain of middle-class women and domestic servants (who were often young female immigrants). No longer drawn to the company or atmosphere of the kitchen, middle-class families retired to the parlor. Along with the new conveniences came increased expectations about the complexity of meals. Catharine E. Beecher (1800–1878), who wrote *A Treatise on Domestic Economy* (1841) and with her sister Harriet Beecher Stowe (1811–1896) wrote *The American Woman's Home* (1869), developed systems for efficient kitchen design, and encouraged women to economize housekeeping. Other reformers like Melusina Fay Peirce (1836–1923), Ellen Swallow Richards (1842–1911), and Charlotte Perkins Gilman (1860–1935) rejected the single-family kitchen,

arguing that only socialized housework (cooperative housekeeping) and "kitchenless houses" could free women from economic inequality.

At the end of the nineteenth and beginning of the twentieth centuries, Progressive reformers like Christine Frederick (1883–1970) applied scientific management principles to housework, undertaking time-motion studies and redesigning the kitchen to increase efficiency. The kitchen, now the focus of the home economics movement, became a workshop or laboratory intended to relieve cooks of drudgery. The Hoosier cabinet united built-in storage for tools and ingredients and a work surface. Gas and electric ranges replaced the cookstove. Streamlined modular designs, continuous counters, built-in cabinets rather than closets and pantries, and efficient floor plans are legacies of this movement.

Following World War II (1939–1945), American houses boasted fitted kitchens, often in a U- or L-shape, with bright color schemes and sleek electric appliances. Middle-class houses, whether the venerable Cape Cod style or the new ranch form, were designed with open floor plans allowing easy access to, and interaction between, the kitchen and the living and dining areas. In the 1970s, microwave ovens made food preparation even more convenient.

In the late twentieth and early twenty-first centuries, the kitchen is no longer a hidden space. It is often the first and most costly room to be remodeled. Cooking has become a popular activity. Nevertheless, restaurants and prepared foods have become convenient substitutes for kitchen work.

Melinda Talbot Nasardinov

See also Cellars and Basements; Commercial Food Venues; Halls; Service Industry Work and Labor; Technology

References and Further Reading

Brewer, Priscilla J. 2000. *From Fireplace to Cookstove: Technology and the Domestic Ideal in America.* Syracuse, NY: Syracuse University Press.

Cowan, Ruth Schwartz. 1983. *More Work for Mother: The Ironies of Household Technology from the Open Hearth to the Microwave.* New York: Basic Books.

Hayden, Dolores. 1981. *The Grand Domestic Revolution: A History of Feminist Designs for American Homes, Neighborhoods, and Cities.* Cambridge, MA: MIT Press.

Phipps, Frances. 1972. *Colonial Kitchens, Their Furnishings, and Their Gardens.* New York: Hawthorn.

Plante, Ellen M. 1995. *The American Kitchen, 1700 to the Present: From Hearth to Highrise.* New York: Facts on File.

L

Land and Landscape

Land is a general term referring to the physical or geographic aspect of solid earth. *Landscape* is defined as a selected view or constructed scenery created by humans using the physical land or its representation in art, photography, film, and other media. Both terms have particular importance in American history in that they are perhaps the largest material component of American culture, playing into such political and societal notions as nationalism and civic identity.

Land

The history of the United States is the history of profound changes in the relationship between its inhabitants and its shifting borders. Land was a key factor in the creation of American identity. Owning land was a possibility that did not exist for most of Europe's population. In the new nation, founded on the premise that "all men are created equal" and encouraged by the immense landmass, possessing land quickly came to represent the promise of freedom and opportunity.

The pursuit of land built the nation geographically as it created American national identity. Daniel Boone's (1734–1820) passage through the Cumberland Gap (1775) opened the frontier on the eve of the American Revolution. In the late eighteenth and early nineteenth centuries, Thomas Jefferson (1743–1826) encouraged his ideal of a society of independent yeoman farmers. Land acquisition through diplomatic means—Jefferson's Louisiana Purchase (1803) and the later Gadsden Treaty (1853)—extended both the power of the presidency and the reach of the nation. Nevertheless, Americans began to shape the land in unprecedented ways in pursuit of the benefits of industry. The Erie Canal was completed in 1825, railroad construction necessitated earthworks essential to laying track, and countless river rapids and waterfalls throughout the national domain were harnessed to support mill production —which in turn spawned a stronger desire to acquire land in the western United States. Land became the material of prosperity.

Moving west on the overland trails was the type of aggressive quest for land that Americans understood as Manifest Destiny. This phrase was coined by newspaper editor John O'Sullivan (1813–1895) in an 1845 essay advocating the annexation of Texas and the

Oregon Territory. He wrote that it was the nation's "manifest destiny to overspread the continent allotted by Providence for the free development of our yearly multiplying millions." Although usually described as a mission of ideals, Manifest Destiny encouraged Euro-Americans to immigrate into the far western United States. It also encouraged the Mexican-American War (1846–1848), the spoils of which also added to the United States' territory.

Facilitated by the Homestead Act (1862), which offered Americans the possibility of owning land on the basis of settlement and improvement, the completion of a transcontinental railroad (1869), and the land runs of the later nineteenth century, the abundance of land became a national characteristic—freedom, equality, individualism, opportunity, prosperity—as Americans attempted to distinguish themselves from Europeans.

Contested Land

American land has been historically associated with such words as *virgin* and *wild*, but perhaps the most contested notions of land in the nation's history are that it was "empty." Settlers at different times and in different locations believed the land a *tabula rasa*—a cultural blank slate onto which the Euro-American immigrants could imprint or create their own burgeoning collective identity. The land was not empty, however; diverse Native American peoples populated the continent. Especially in the West, where Euro-Americans saw the land as valuable in natural resources, disagreement over land rights was a source of immense tension and bloody conflict. Native American claims to various lands across the nation and the history of conflict, both culturally and militarily, have shaped today's patterns of land use and habitation.

The frontier has come to reflect the tensions inherent in political and cultural boundaries. Historian Frederick Jackson Turner (1861–1932) declared in 1893 that the frontier was the single most defining factor of American character. He also claimed that the frontier ceased to exist in 1890, based on federal census reports of six or more persons per square mile, indicating that the land was settled. Contemporary scholars continue to reevaluate Turner's thesis. Rather than referring to the frontier as the demarcation between civilization and wilderness, American land, as concept and as material, has come to represent the history of the shifting spaces of cultural hegemony based on use and occupation. The frontier is still a hotly contested and scrutinized concept, demonstrating how land still figures largely into the American purview.

Landscape

Landscape denotes scenery. Although the word has a lengthy and varied etymological history in the Dutch and German languages, the English use of the word is more pointed. The term originally referred to the representation of an outdoor scene. In American painting (as in European painting) of the eighteenth century, landscape was lower on the hierarchy of genres than the more coveted history painting. By the mid-nineteenth century, it became clear that history painting was not as applicable to the relative newness of American culture as it was to the European cultural past. Due to the perceived lack of a meaningful history, American artists turned to representations of the land. No ancient ruins of Euro-Americans dotted the countryside, so American artists began to envision waterfall and canyons, rock formations and giant sequoia trees as the symbols of a national heritage. By the 1860s, landscape painting took center stage in the United States.

A landscape view, actual or represented, is generally understood to embody cultural notions. That is, because of the selectivity implied by an artistically chosen or created view, landscape is defined as a view of nature seen through the lens of culture and often shaped by ideals and expectations.

Cultural Landscapes

Historically, Euro-Americans' responses to the landscape have mimicked their changing responses to the land, metamorphosing from the early Puritan distrust of the New England woods, to a pragmatic approach to property and prospect in the eighteenth century, to the nineteenth-century Romantic notions about the relationship between landscape, nationalistic identity, and spirituality.

American landscapes have meant different things at different times to distinct cultural subgroups. Some would argue that there is no such thing as an unbiased view of nature and that all views of the land are, in fact, cultural landscapes, colored by the visual conventions of various human groups, and as such, different cultures can have distinctly different responses to the landscape, producing distinctly different conceptual content. Thomas Jefferson's interpretation of the views from his mountaintop plantation, Monticello (1769–1809), undoubtedly differed from those of his slaves from their quarters on Mulberry Row. It is safe to assert that in 1847 the notorious Donner party experienced the Sierra Nevada Mountains quite differently from the modern tourist who takes in the same surroundings. As well, European immigrants, schooled in the Continental tradition of visual culture that included framing devices, point of view, and linear perspective, had a vastly different response to the land than did the indigenous peoples of North America.

Gendered Landscapes

Early visual and literary representations of the American landscape were often personified as a highly Europeanized "Indian princess." This visual sexualization of land went hand in hand with the gendered language that described America as "virgin"—untainted, passive, and ready for conquest. As well, the overarching metaphor of "mother earth" portrays land in a gender-specific way.

Scholars have argued that men and women have envisioned the land differently during different eras. For instance, women imagined the western "frontier" differently in that they were not likely to think of the view as a "prospect" of industry or natural resource. Rather, the "feminized" landscape was tempered and "civilized," and located in the home and garden.

Landscape Theory

By the late eighteenth century, artists and theorists had largely defined the European and American landscape. Edmund Burke (1729–1797) differentiated landscapes in his 1757 treatise *A Philosophical Enquiry into the Origin of Our Ideas of the Sublime and Beautiful*. His ideas were not unique in Western thought and dated to the first century with the writings of Longinus. More important for the United States was the work of William Gilpin (1813–1894) and Uvedale Price (1747–1829), English advocates of the picturesque. Gilpin's 1792 treatise, *Three Essays on Picturesque Beauty*, and Price's 1794 *Essay on the Picturesque, As Compared With the Sublime and the Beautiful*, also instructed Englishmen and Americans how to see the land. According to Gilpin, the prototypical picturesque landscape was rough in texture, irregular, and

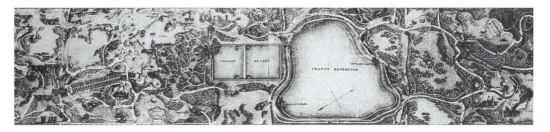

Frederick Law Olmsted's and Calvert Vaux's winning Greensward Plan for New York City's Central Park was largely informal and picturesque. This 1857 plan created a landscape with curvilinear paths tracing different use areas of the park, while vehicular traffic was kept at bay by sunken roads. (Archive Photos/Getty Images)

asymmetrical, producing an effect of charming serendipity.

Medieval farmsteads and ancient ruins did not exist in the United States, however. Instead of simply representing the past, landscapes came to represent potential. The "prospect view," for example, is one from an elevated point that allows uninhibited examination of the land. As the word *prospect* implies, the point of view shows the viewer the possibilities, where one can go physically—as on a journey, and metaphorically— as a view of future opportunity.

Beyond representation, *landscape* also engages the experience of natural scenery. Through the practice of framing, painters and photographers aesthetically represented the land, training their audiences to understand the land as selected vignettes. By the mid-nineteenth century, Americans were largely in love with their landscapes, finding in them the exceptionalism that distinguished the new country from Old World precedents. Landscapes provided a "green" antiquity and inspired the utopian mysticism of the American Transcendentalists. Landscape views were popularly thought to provoke spiritual experiences, and the search for inspiring views spawned the "picturesque tourist," who sought out the most palliative landscapes in the United States.

Americans as citizens and as tourists not only sought out picturesque landscapes but they also went to great lengths to create them. Beginning in the 1830s, picturesque parks and cemeteries became standard features of urban design. Central Park in New York City is perhaps the most famous American example of picturesque landscape design. Frederick Law Olmsted (1822–1903) and Calvert Vaux (1824–1895) deftly designed in 1857 a space of paths and broad avenues, groves of trees, and rocky outcroppings that provided opportune views across a pond or an expanse of lawn. Similar to picturesque landscapes all over the nation, the land was constructed to look un-constructed, as a tonic for the woes of modern life, offering peaceful, serene settings for the overly urbanized East.

The American penchant to find and create views eventually led to the state and national park systems. Beginning with the 1872 establishment of Yellowstone National Park as the first, these governmentally sanctioned lands provided morally edifying natural experiences while at the same time bolstered national sentiment. The scenery at these parks came to signify the most sought-after and aesthetically valuable landscape views in the United States. Along with the development of landscape architecture, the prescribed viewing locations created in the parks best exemplify the malleability of natural space inherent in the concept of landscape.

Contemporary Landscapes

The cultural meanings of landscape continue to change with the shifting notions about the value of land—as a source of natural resources, as an ecological preserve, or as a national symbol. As well, landscape studies now consider urban, domestic, and vernacular landscapes and encompass such fields as geography, anthropology, art history, the environmental sciences, and more. Americans still envision and construct the landscape, with contemporary culture and revised cultural histories informing the way we frame the modern view.

Rachel Sailor

See also Art History and American Art; City Parks; Cultural Geography; Photography; Printmaking and American Prints; Space and Place; Tourism and Travel; Visual Culture Studies

References and Further Reading
Burke, Edmund. 1759 (1757). *A Philosophical Enquiry into the Origin of Our Ideals of the Sublime and Beautiful*, 2nd ed. London: Robert and James Dodley.
Gilpin, William. 1792. *Three Essays: On Picturesque Beauty; On Picturesque Travel; and On Sketching Landscape*. London: Printed for R. Blamire.
Jackson, John Brinkerhoff. 1984. *Discovering the Vernacular Landscape*. New Haven, CT: Yale University Press.
Kolodny, Annette. 1984. *The Land Before Her: Fantasy and Experience of the American Frontiers, 1630–1860*. Chapel Hill: University of North Carolina Press.
Marx, Leo. 1964. *The Machine in the Garden: Technology and the Pastoral Ideal in America*. New York: Oxford University Press.
Nash, Roderick. 1967. *Wilderness and the American Mind*. New Haven, CT: Yale University Press.
O'Sullivan, John. 1845. "Annexation." *United States Magazine and Democratic Review* 17 (1): 5–10.
Price, Uvedale. 1794. *An Essay on the Picturesque, As Compared With The Sublime and The Beautiful; and on the Use of Studying Pictures, for the Purpose of Improving Real Landscape*. London: J. Robson.
Turner, Frederick Jackson. 1920. *The Frontier in American History*. New York: H. Holt.
Wilton, Andrew, and Tim Barringer. 2002. *American Sublime: Landscape Painting in the United States, 1820–1880*. London: Tate Publishing.

Land Transportation

Land transportation in the United States has evolved from the early days of colonial travel, when travelers walked or were conveyed by animals or animal-pulled vehicles on narrow paths; unpaved, often rutted roads; and cobblestoned streets of towns and cities. Roads generally connected to places of supply and commerce. Few bridges were built; ferries and shallow fords supplied transport routes over and through water. Overland travel was difficult and expensive for the first two centuries of European settlement on the densely forested North American continent. Rivers and lesser waterways, especially in the Chesapeake region, provided cheap means of transporting both goods and people. The natural barrier of the Appalachian Mountains deterred overland travel to and occupation of the Ohio Valley; westward migrating settlers traveled overland to Pittsburgh, Pennsylvania, and then traveled the Ohio River. The construction of the Erie Canal and other waterways spurred the movement of people and goods to the West in the 1820s.

Nevertheless, after the Revolutionary War (1775–1783), American land transportation underwent a metamorphosis that included corduroy roads, turnpikes, and improved human- and horse-drawn vehicle designs;

railroads, locomotives, and Pullman cars; urban omnibuses, streetcars, and subways; and the mass-produced automobile and other motorized vehicles.

Roads, Carriages, Carts, and Wagons

Turnpike roads, first used in England, were implemented more fully at the turn of the nineteenth century to finance roadwork in New York and Pennsylvania. The Philadelphia and Lancaster Turnpike, opened in 1794, was the first road that charged users a fee in order to maintain the thoroughfare. In the following year, seventy-two turnpike corporations were founded throughout the Northeast. Turnpike roads connected commercial centers; local roads were more traveled and in need of improvement, a state made clear in the War of 1812 when the American military found it difficult to transport troops in a timely and dependable fashion.

The Cumberland Road (1806, now known as the National Road) originated in the city of Cumberland, Maryland, and provided the first interstate highway crossing what was then the extreme edge of the United States. The road was mapped and constructed through the Appalachian Mountains and ended in Vandalia, Illinois. The duty of constructing this road fell first to the Treasury Department and in the end to the Army Corps of Engineers. The corps also mapped and constructed federal post roads throughout the lower South in the early nineteenth century.

By 1820, the entire eastern seaboard was interconnected with reliable roads due to the proliferation of turnpikes and improved road surfaces. Following the successful examples of turnpike companies, bridge companies were formed, taking advantage of improved technology to construct covered bridges of wood and stone, iron truss bridges, and suspension bridges. Private companies were also created to construct, after 1844, plank toll roads intended for short distances. Wood, a cheap construction material, was laid flat against the roadbed in three-inch-thick planks of eight feet in length, parallel with the direction of the road. Ten-plank, or corduroy, roads were built in western states in the early 1850s. Seven thousand miles of plank roads were laid by 1857. These roads, essentially existing dirt roads covered with wood, were rendered obsolete after the Panic of 1857.

Horse-drawn vehicles rolled over the nation's roads. Heavy Conestoga wagons, meant to haul freight and pulled by teams of four to six horses, and lighter and smaller but similar "prairie schooners" (so called because their beds were boat shaped), carried families and their goods westward. Omnibuses and stagecoaches that charged fares and traveled specific routes were public conveyances. Wood buckboards, carts, and wagons were primarily used to carry goods over short distances; by the end of the nineteenth century, wagons were specialized to the variety of goods transported and delivered: *wagon* was preceded by *ice*, *milk*, *post*, *butcher's*, and *florist's*, for example. Only the wealthy could afford private open or closed carriages or smaller buggies and the necessary equipment and horses. These luxury vehicles boasted cloth and leather upholstery, metal ornament, and spring seating. The names of carriage types convey luxury and in the twentieth century were adapted to automobiles: *brougham*, *cabriolet*, *landau*, and *phaeton*, for example. Sleighs and fast cutters were used in winter.

Rails in City and Country and Underground

The railroad became the ultimate sign of national reunion and progress following the Civil War (1861–1865), as the once-severed nation looked westward for economic prosperity. Introduced to the United States by British engineers George Stephenson (1781–1848) and his son Robert (1803–1859) in 1825, the rail car revolutionized travel in the expanded United States. Small railroad lines had been created in the Northeast and in the Great Lakes states. In 1830, 23 miles of rail was laid in America; by 1860, 30,626 miles of rail were in use. On May 10, 1869, at Promontory, Utah, the Union Pacific and the Central Pacific railroads were joined by a golden spike, creating the first transcontinental rail line. The rapid and extensive reach of the railroad increased the affluence and political influence of a small group of industrialists and financiers like J. P. Morgan (1837–1913), George Pullman (1831–1893), and Cornelius Vanderbilt (1794–1877). The railroad required the improvement of manufacturing techniques and the implementation of standard time zones in 1883. By 1890, the railroad was the predominant mode of commerce and travel. Train travel, though hot, smoke-filled, and uncomfortable with wood bench seats, was made more attractive by the creation of elegantly appointed, upholstered, and spring-seated Pullman Palace cars: "drawing room cars," "hotel cars," and dining cars that appealed to women and helped to establish "first class" railroad travel. Pullman also created a "sleeping car" (*car* short for *carriage*) for comfortable long-distance travel. "Pullman service" translated hotel service to the rails and employed for more than a century primarily African Americans as porters, waiters, and cooks on the nation's passenger trains.

Short-distance railways were constructed within cities, between cities, and between cities and newly built suburbs in the latter half of the nineteenth century. Major cities such as Chicago and New York had elaborate trolley systems used by both the suburban middle class and by the working class of the center city. Samuel Insull (1859–1938),

president of the Chicago Edison Company, ran his trolley car system of Chicago in order to protect the electric business. This attempt to utilize the trolley car for economic gain, like the railroad, led to increased agitation for reform. Concerns over the expansion of the city far beyond the city center were also part of this agitation. In some cities the internal combustion engine helped replace streetcars with buses. This, in addition to the adoption of private transportation provided by automobiles, made reform unnecessary, and private speculation in trolleys subsided. Nevertheless, large cities such as Boston, New York, Chicago, and San Francisco retained their public transportation systems of streetcars; New York would, in 1900, build the first subway to move the system of elevated railways and congested street rails underground.

Private Transportation: The Automobile
Henry Ford (1863–1947) and the Ford Motor Company began selling the Model T automobile in 1908. Ford's implementation of mass production by assembly lines, interchangeable parts, and generous employee benefits made the Model T ubiquitous within a few years and made his company an enviable organization. Ford's innovations led to the rise of the trucking industry during World War I (1914–1918), the improvement of roads in the 1920s, and the rise of competing vehicle companies.

The increasing need for roads for commerce led to the interstate highway system that continues to expand. The first highway travel surveys began in 1944, and the Federal Aid Highway Act of 1956 was the largest development of the highway system in American history. The Highway Act of 1962 was the first act to tie highway funding to federal aid in an effort to ensure motor safety.

Nicholas Katers

See also Air and Space Transportation; Automobile Camping (Auto-Camping); Automobiles and Automobility; Highways and National Highway System; Tourism and Travel; Water Transportation

References and Further Reading

Davison, Janet, and Michael Sweeney. 2003. *On the Move: Transportation and the American Story.* Washington, DC: National Geographic.

Goddard, Stephen B. 1994. *Getting There: The Epic Struggle between Road and Rail in the American Century.* New York: Basic Books.

Leisure, Recreation, and Amusements

Leisure (free time, or time for personal, noncompensated activities) choices have grown exponentially over the course of American history. Leisure time can be spent in *recreation* (refreshing or regenerating the mind or body through activity) or *amusement* (entertainment or a pleasurable diversion). Many historic artifacts of leisure activities, recreational pursuits, and amusement are housed in museums and private collections, but others exist in their own right as part of the built environment and are still in use today: One may still experience firsthand the amusement park of Coney Island (ca. 1895) in Brooklyn, New York, or watch a baseball game at Fenway Park (1912) in Boston. Different groups have chosen, or been allowed access to, different activities to amuse themselves, and the divisions have tended most noticeably to fall along class, gender, and racial lines.

Colonial-Era Pastimes

Seventeenth-century New England Puritans feared idleness, but productive recreation in moderation was perfectly acceptable. Husking bees and quilting bees, which would become mainstays of preindustrialized rural American society, were not problems in their eyes. The Puritans did, however, frown on other early recreational activities in which people throughout the colonies, and later the nation, partook.

Tavern games were popular throughout North America. In addition to being a place to drink alcohol, taverns provided the setting for cockfighting, card playing, dog fighting, bearbaiting, prizefighting, horse racing, and in the early 1800s, billiards. These activities were brought from England, were male dominated and violent, and generally involved gambling. While the majority of the physical structures that served as settings for these games are now gone, many manuals, ephemera, and images of these activities survive. Other material evidence includes old decks of cards, silver "spurs" that fighting cocks were fitted with to make them more deadly, and any number of horse-related artifacts. In more rural, less organized settings, the equivalents to tavern games were turkey shoots, wrestling, and gouging (trying to gouge your opponent's eyes out before he gouged out yours). Apart from old hunting firearms, these rural activities left far fewer artifacts, since wrestling and gouging required no special tools or clothing.

Nineteenth-Century Leisure

The nation's expanding and mobile population made feasible large organized gatherings of people in two uniquely American phenomena: camp meetings (beginning in 1802) and Chautauquas (organized series of speakers, named after the western New York State town that hosted both camp meetings and secular gatherings starting in 1874). While both phenomena had ostensibly practical and didactic purposes—strengthening religious fervor or expanding the intellect—they also served as a much-anticipated break in the participants' regular routines and social gatherings. Broadsides, many of which have survived, were posted in conspicuous areas for people to see well in advance of the event.

While Chautauquas and camp meetings had nominally elevated goals, circuses, traveling theater troupes and shows such as Buffalo Bill's (William F. Cody, 1846–1917) Wild West Show (begun in 1883) did not. Though photography offered still glimpses of the distant and the exotic, such shows constituted the only way most people experienced extraordinary spectacles without extensive, expensive, and time-consuming travel. Entrepreneur Phineas T. Barnum (1810–1891) would bring exotic animals, unusual humans, and impressive talent acts on tour, and eventually established a museum for them in New York City, which burned to the ground in 1865. Traveling thespians rarely brought much with them other than their meager stock of costumes, but as they became more organized over the course of the nineteenth century, traveling and eventually permanent vaudeville shows again brought singing, dancing, and comedy to Americans.

Twentieth-Century Commercial and Amateur Leisure Activities

With the turn of the twentieth century, recreation and entertainment opportunities began increasing at an astonishing rate. Commercially viable professional sports became a fixture in many urban areas, and organized amateur athletics became available to the masses. Baseball was the most popular American sport in the first half of the century, but in the decade following World War II games like football, basketball, and hockey also began attracting vast numbers of both participants and spectators. All of these sports have left copious artifacts, such as uniforms, equipment, and programs, in their respective halls of fame and in collections across the nation.

Amusement parks became popular after the Chicago World's Fair in 1893, with Coney Island the most famous but certainly not the only park inspired by the fair. Then, just as now, people could ride roller coasters; play midway games; eat delicious, unhealthy food; and listen to live music. One of the most popular aspects of amusement parks was that they were affordable to almost anyone. They also often included beaches—cheap and fun for all, though sometimes segregated.

Reserved for the wealthy classes were such leisure activities as coaching, which required a highly skilled driver to direct a team of four highly trained horses, pulling a large coach through public thoroughfares. Yachting, sailing large personal vessels, is another leisure activity that was reserved for the wealthy, although yacht racing did gain a wider spectator base than just those who could afford to participate. Yet another expensive sport, still popular in the twenty-first century, is polo, similar to soccer on horseback, but with mallets to reach the small, hard ball on the ground. Each polo player needs to be able to afford an entire string of ponies (six per player per match), which puts a strain on even deep pocketbooks. All of these sports, each leaving much material culture to be studied, had devoted fan bases.

Yet the most significant leisure activity of the twentieth century, available to all but the poorest of Americans, was provided by the entertainment media of movies, radio, and television, all of which have left and continue to create a cornucopia of material culture. Movies, from the early nickelodeons (ca. 1905) to ornate theaters to contemporary multiplexes, have provided an inexpensive way for the average person to escape his or her own life, even if it was only for a few minutes, or now a few hours. Radios still entertain people with never-ending dramas, music, news, and discussions. When television came along in the 1940s, it, like radio, offered free escape after the initial invest-ment in the machine itself. Program sched-ules, recordings, fan magazines, and many machines are found in collections open to the public. In the twenty-first century, television sets are outfitted with digital technology capabilities and can accommodate the tastes and leisure time of viewers.

Elizabeth Redkey

See also Agricultural Fairs and Expositions; Automobile Camping (Auto-Camping); Children's Material Culture; Children's Toys; City Parks; Collecting and Collections; Games; Holidays and Commemorations; Illicit Pleasures and Venues; Popular Culture; Public and Commercial Leisure, Recreation, and Amusement Venues; Recreation Rooms; Scrapbooks; Sports; Tourism and Travel; World's Fairs and Expositions

References and Further Reading

Aron, Cindy S. 1999. *Working at Play: A History of Vacations in the United States*. New York: Oxford University Press.
Dulles, Foster Rhea. 1965. *A History of Recreation: America Learns to Play*, 2nd ed. New York: Appleton-Century-Crofts.
Nasaw, David. 1993. *Going Out: The Rise and Fall of Public Amusements*. New York: Basic Books.

Light, Lighting Devices, and Lighting Systems

The day's light has been utilized and artifi-cially reproduced by man to extend sight, work, and safety into the night, into the darkness of shelter and other buildings, and along urban streets and country roads through the adaptation of fuels, the techno-logical innovation and design of lighting devices, and the establishment of energy sys-tems. Consisting of waves and particles, *light* is a form that is not fully understood by scientists. Nevertheless, light has served many functions in American society: Besides the ordinary usages, light is a necessary feature in the creation and display of art, photographs, and film; in television broad-casting; as a medical therapy for depression; and, concentrated in a laser, as a surgical tool. The light produced by liquid crystals (liquid crystal display, or LCD) enlivens alarm clock displays and computer screens. Light remains alternately an evocative meta-phor of warmth and hospitality, of knowl-edge and wisdom, of hope and a divine being, and of freedom.

Natural Light: Sun, Moon, Stars, and Fire

From the very beginning of the North Amer-ican colonization to well into the nineteenth century, men and women used primarily natural daylight and moonlight, moving their work in the course of a day and even at night to take advantage of the best light. Artificial light was sparingly used. The light of a hearth fire was enhanced through its reflection in windows, mirrors, and other surfaces. "Candlewood" (pitch pine knots) was burned for additional light. Candles were expensive and carefully used. Candle making, or dipping, was a pungent, all-day chore; a family would make a large quantity, often in the fall, when sheep or beef tallow was available after slaughter and in prepa-ration for the darker days of winter. Wicks would be dipped in the hot tallow until the tapers were large enough to set aside and cool. Tin and pewter candle molds were also used. Candles were also made of beeswax, spermaceti (whale oil), and stearine (beef tallow). Tallow candles were tasty to house-hold rodents and pets, so storage, such as candleboxes, was necessary. In urban areas where tallow was in short supply, candles were commercially made and sold.

Metal drip pans, called *chambersticks* or *hand candlesticks*, fitted to hold the smoking, burning taper and catch its drippings, were often employed to ensure the safety of carrying a lit candle. The dripping wax of brilliant chandeliers could burn a person or ruin clothing. Candles required frequent snuffing to remove the wick's charred end so as to prevent "guttering" and the diminution of light. Lanterns contained the candle and protected its light for use out of doors and in outbuildings. Despite these precautions, candles were hazardous, causing fires and death.

Night into Day: Artificial Lighting

Hand and table lamps (astral, solar, moderator, argand) provided the means with which to light one's way and work and, although available in the mid-eighteenth century, predominated in nineteenth-century urban dwellings. Rural households made use of animal fat as the fuel for lamps. Spermaceti, though expensive, provided lamp fuel. It burned unevenly, smoked if not well managed, and required that lamps be regulated and cleaned. Nevertheless, lamps became a status good; portraits and advertisements by the 1820s and daguerreotypes after 1839 show the practice of using ornamental table lamps on the parlor center table.

By the 1850s urban areas were served by gas (introduced ca. 1800); gas jets appeared in houses that were connected via pipes to the gas supply. Gas lighting, however, was inconsistent: Gas jets could leak, the gas supply was haphazard in inclement weather, and the odor of the gas was unpleasant. By 1870 kerosene was widely available and used, guaranteeing many hours of lamp maintenance, mostly by women and servants. Kerosene was especially useful in lanterns for work and traveling out of doors.

A lighting device, whether candle or lamp, rarely illuminated a whole room. Wealthy American colonists hung mirrored globes in their public rooms to aid illumination. Many more Americans used other devices, such as cheap wall-mounted tin reflectors, more expensive mirrors and cut glass, highly polished woodwork and furniture surfaces, and later in the nineteenth century, gilded furniture surfaces, to reflect and magnify the original light source. Even wallpaper and textiles sported glossy finishes to reflect light. Not until the introduction of electric lighting in the 1870s to 1880s did Americans enliven their houses with lighter furnishings that showed more dirt; electricity allowed for a cleaner, smokeless interior environment.

Public gas lighting was available in the United States in the early nineteenth century. Artist and entrepreneur Rembrandt Peale (1778–1860) lit his Baltimore, Maryland, studio and gallery by gas, setting an example for the safe use of gas lighting and inviting the establishment of private gaslighting companies. Baltimore would have public lighting in 1816. These private companies solved the problems of bringing gas lighting to the cities by conceptualizing and constructing a system with which dwellings and businesses were connected to a central, replenishable reservoir; creating uniform standards in fuel purity as well as in piping and fixture; standardizing measures of consumption; calming public fears of leaks and explosions; and teaching safety to consumers. (Thinking the lit gas fixture operated like a candle, some extinguished the flame without shutting off the gas valve, with disastrous consequences.)

Electric Lighting and Twentieth-Century Consumer Culture

Accustomed to the softer glow of gaslight, Americans disliked the brilliance of electric light when first introduced. Thomas Alva Edison's (1847–1931) incandescent filament light bulb (1879) was cheaper (as was electricity) because it could be mass produced, but the light bulb had to await the construction of power stations and networks. The light bulb did not smoke, smell, or otherwise harm humans or ruin interior furnishings. Electricity available room by room made it possible to extinguish lights at one switch, rather than the tedious turning off of each gas jet.

Light in the American domestic dwelling comforted. The design of electric lamps and lighting fixtures both disguised and restyled the novel, if plain, light bulb. From 1899 onward, Louis Comfort Tiffany's (1848–1933) Art Nouveau table and floor lamps filtered electric light through a variety of color-stained (especially blues, greens, and lavenders) or opalescent semitransparent glass molded in a variety of exotic, naturalistic shapes. Glass shades directed light downward onto a table or desk top, creating soft pools of warm light. Arts and Crafts designers used light as warm focus points throughout the house through the use of lampshades and wall sconces of leaded stained glass, and metalwork (copper and bronze) and mica. Kitchens, as efficient laboratories, were lit by bare, bright light bulbs, sometimes covered by translucent glass shades, from ceiling fixtures. Art Deco lighting in the 1920s and 1930s shifted the way light was filtered: Rather than using stained glass or other materials, Art Deco sconces and lamps of modern metals (chromium and aluminum) and translucent glass projected light against another surface to diffuse it. The use of cloth, canvas, and other materials in lampshades would expand over the course of the twentieth century, fitting the stylistic wishes of the consumer as well as responding to technological improvements in electric lighting.

Factory owners and city business owners were the first to invest in electric lights to further work hours and shopping hours. Fear of fire, especially in textile mills, was greatly diminished with the shift to electricity. Spectacular light shows were popular at the late nineteenth- and early twentieth-century world's fairs and amusement parks (such as Coney Island in New York), equating light with progress, consumerism, and leisure. With the introduction of plate glass, department stores featured large, well-lit windows that dazzled—and consumed—passersby. The idea of using bright electric illumination for advertising was implemented: Electric signs were part of Broadway's "Great White Way," first lit by arc lamps in the 1880s, and Times Square, teeming with billboards and theater marquees, dazzled. By the 1930s the use of cooler and colorful neon lights (a noble gas captured in a vacuum tube) advertised a variety of commercial services and venues; Las Vegas, Nevada, in the 1950s was constructed for living at night, through artificial light, and sleeping during nature's hours of illumination. Today, the nation's artificial lighting in some areas, as "light pollution," renders the night sky's display of stars invisible.

Shirley Teresa Wajda

See also Advertisements and Advertising; Art Deco; Art Nouveau; Arts and Crafts Movement; Base Metalwork and Metalware; Cities and Towns; Consumerism and Consumption; Department Stores; Interior Design; Technology; World's Fairs and Expositions

References and Further Reading

Archibald, Sasha. 2006. "Blinded by the Light." *Cabinet Magazine* 21. http://www.cabinetmagazine.org/issues/21/archibald.php.

Blühm, Andreas, and Louise Lippincott. 2000. *Light! The Industrial Age, 1750–1900: Art & Science, Technology & Society*. London: Thames and Hudson; Pittsburgh: Carnegie Museum of Art; and Amsterdam: Van Gogh Museum.

Duncan, Alastair. 1986. "Art Deco Lighting." *Journal of Decorative and Propaganda Arts* 1: 20–31.

Garrett, Elisabeth Donaghy. 1990. *At Home: The American Family 1750–1850*. New York: Harry N. Abrams.

Nylander, Jane C. 1993. *Our Own Snug Fireside: Images of the New England Home 1760–1860*. New York: Alfred A. Knopf.

O'Dea, William T. 1958. *The Social History of Lighting*. New York: Macmillan.

Literary Studies and American Literature

The objects that Americans possessed, used, and coveted have served as literary tropes and central themes in American literature from the early nineteenth century to the present. American literature offers a rich source of specific information to reconstruct the practices and beliefs with which possessions are imbued. Conversely, authors have employed material objects—household decor, clothing and jewelry, artwork—as motifs indicative of education, class, status, morality, and personality in realist fiction and didactic journalism.

Literature and the Market Revolution

In the early republic, industrialization and an expanding market culture converged with the emergence of new literary forms. American fiction reflected the increasing availability of manufactured goods, the growth of a mercantile and industrial middle class (and aspiring working class), and information media including magazines and instructional manuals. Descriptions of material objects betrayed the tension between rough-hewn American independence and glossy European sophistication. In James Fenimore Cooper's (1789–1851) *The Pioneers*

(1823), Judge Temple's household represents the pretensions of new settlements through its "sideboard of mahogany, inlaid with ivory, and bearing enormous handles of glittering brass, and groaning under the piles of silver plate" and "heavy, old-fashioned, brass-faced clock, encased in a high box." In *A New Home, Who'll Follow?* (1839), Caroline Kirkland (1801–1864) describes a house on the Michigan frontier boasting "a harp in a recess," its "white-washed log-walls hung with a variety of cabinet pictures." Rarefied objects were invoked to dispel the assumption that American life was invariably crude and provisional.

Simultaneously, utopians brooded that the new nation was sacrificing its soul to acquisitiveness; Ralph Waldo Emerson (1803–1864) fulminated against materialists who appreciated "sensible masses" but not abstract ideals. In a lighter vein, widely read authors of didactic fiction cautioned readers to avoid naive assessments of character based on externals. A magazine author, Eliza Leslie (1787–1848), warned against misreading apparel; in her serialized novel *Althea Vernon* (1838), "a very ill-dressed man, in gray speckled stockings, thick clumsy shoes, buckled on to his ankles, chequered pantaloons of surpassing coarseness, and the shortest possible frock coat, closely buttoned" is a nobleman, and a distinguished suitor is unimpressed by the heroine's "elegant pocket handkerchief."

At the mid-nineteenth century, Henry David Thoreau (1817–1862) eschewed "a certain number of superfluous glow-shoes, and umbrellas, and empty guest chambers for empty guests" and other paraphernalia of modern society in favor of the "essential facts of life" in his classic *Walden* (1854). Yet the materialism Thoreau scorned filled the works of his contemporaries, who interrogated household objects as emblems of competing values. The ideology of domesticity in which the home was at once women's natural sphere and a locus of spirituality and emotional sustenance focused attention beyond fine furniture to the symbolism of dishpans, towels, and other housekeeping tools. In Nathaniel Hawthorne's (1804–1864) *The House of the Seven Gables* (1851), the young heroine's housewifely talents "gild pots and kettles with an atmosphere of loveliness and joy." A more radically realist novel, Susan Warner's (1819–1885) *The Wide, Wide World* (1851), parsed the semiotics of milk strainers, flatirons, and a "coverlid made of homemade white and blue worsted mixed with cotton."

Gilded Age Literature and Consumer Culture

Following the Civil War (1861–1865), the proliferation of manufactured and imported objects afforded authors an expanding vocabulary with which to explore the tensions between social or aesthetic aspirations and integrity. Magazines, from *Godey's Lady's Book* (1830–1898) to *Harper's New Monthly Magazine* (1850–1899) guided readers to select the right belongings and interpret those of peers. While status objects grew more elaborate and complex, domestic authors asserted that even the most modest households could evince refinement through newly available, inexpensive decorations or through homemade creations combining purchased and scavenged elements. In her 1875 novel *We and Our Neighbors*, Harriet Beecher Stowe (1811–1896) portrayed the "unfashionable" yet stylish home contrived by a thrifty housewife through adroit arrangements of knickknacks and houseplants. In literature set among the upper social echelons, the iconography comprised a remarkable range of precious and exotic objects. For many authors,

imported antiques were the unmistakable sign of cultivated taste, but also connoted Old World decadence. In Augusta Evans Wilson's (1835–1909) *St. Elmo* (1866), the title character's corrupt worldliness is encapsulated in a catalogue of the relics he has acquired: "A huge plaster Trimurti stood close to the wall, on a triangular pedestal of black rock, and the Siva-face and the writhing cobra confronted all who entered. Just opposite grinned a red granite slab with a quaint basso-relivo taken from the ruins of Elora." Henry James (1843–1916) employed a similar device in *The Portrait of a Lady* (1881): The sinister aesthete, Gilbert Osmond, occupies "a seat of ease, indeed of luxury, containing a variety of those faded hangings of damask and tapestry, and those chests and cabinets of time-polished oak." In *The Gilded Age* (1873), Mark Twain (1835–1910) and Charles Dudley Warner (1829–1900) excoriated the ostentatiousness of upper-middle-class American culture. In their novels of urban life and local color William Dean Howells (1837–1920) and Sarah Orne Jewett (1849–1909) portrayed more affectionately the appurtenances of middle-class aspiration.

Twentieth-Century Realism

Social realist authors of the first half of the twentieth century offer detailed portraits of the material culture of the emerging consumer society that was, and is, the United States. In *Main Street* (1920), Sinclair Lewis (1885–1951) symbolized the intellectual barrenness of Gopher Prairie, Minnesota, through detritus including "canvas shoes designed for women with bulging ankles, steel and red glass buttons upon cards with broken edges, a cottony blanket, a graniteware frying-pan reposing on a sun-faded crêpe blouse." Willa Cather (1873–1947),

Dorothy Canfield Fisher (1879–1958), and John Steinbeck (1902–1968) described the belongings of working or impoverished Americans. In fiction and journalism after World War II (1939–1945), brand names became increasingly powerful signifiers, reflecting the intensification of advertising, target marketing, and branded identities. Best-selling novelists including Philip Roth, Tom Wolfe, Stephen King, Bret Easton Ellis, and Terry McMillan have studded their works with allusions to trademarked products, metonymically connoting precise social niches through the auras of various brands.

Many American realist authors fell from critical favor in the 1940s and 1950s, when Formalist approaches to literary studies dictated that literary value be divorced from the particular cultural and historical contexts from which texts arose, and the canon emerging from New Criticism centered on Romantic, Transcendentalist, and Modernist works. Since the 1970s, the emergence of interdisciplinary American studies and cultural studies programs has aroused new interest in popular and topical literatures that vividly represent the material objects—and the practices, aspirations, and values associated with them—of specific eras. Of special note is the emergence of "thing theory," which explores the relationship of the materiality of an object to its literary representation as a means to apprehend the epistemological relationships of humans and things—to paraphrase literary scholar Bill Brown (2004), to investigate the role of things in human lives and the role of humans in the lives of things.

Jane Weiss

See also Books; Consumerism and Consumption; Fanzines; House, Home, and Domesticity; Popular Culture; Print Culture

References and Further Reading
Brown, Bill. 2004. *A Sense of Things: The Object Matter of American Literature*. Chicago: University of Chicago Press.
Merish, Lori. 2000. *Sentimental Materialism: Gender, Commodity Culture, and Nineteenth-Century American Literature*. Durham, NC: Duke University Press.
Shi, David E. 1995. *Facing Facts: Realism in American Thought and Culture, 1850–1920*. New York: Oxford University Press.

Living Rooms

Living rooms are spaces within domestic dwellings primarily designated for social activities. As a type of culture space, living rooms have a history dating back to the fourteenth century and have, in different times and nations, been known as *parlours* (or *parlors*), *sitting rooms*, *front rooms*, *salons*, and *lounge rooms*. The contemporary living room, like its predecessors, has served as a space associated with a family's sociability and cultural refinement. Its development, however, both complements and diverges from the parlor.

In fourteenth-century Europe a living room, then called a *parlour*, was a private space within a monastery in which monks and/or visitors withdrew for conversation. Although houses of the poor and wealthy had social living quarters, the use of a space purely for social interaction and separate from food preparation, dining, and sleeping did not become common until the eighteenth century. Even then, parlours were usually only in the houses of the very wealthy. As the middle class expanded in the nineteenth century, parlours (in the United States, *parlors*) as symbols of social status, became standard features of house plans.

Andrew Jackson Downing's (1815–1852) popular treatise, *The Architecture of Country*

Houses (1850), offers clues to the evolution of the living room in the United States. In his floor plans and descriptions of cottages, the term *living room* appears. "A Working-man's Model Cottage" shows both a parlor and a living room; importantly, the latter space is linked to the kitchen as well as the entryway, while the parlor, opposite the living room on the other side of the entryway, is more private and connected to the bedroom. This living room–kitchen link echoes the traditional multiuse hall and appears to incorporate the necessity of eating; these plans do not contain dining rooms. Downing's designs for farmhouses also connect the kitchen to the living room, a contrast from the formality implied in his inclusion of dining rooms and parlors in city villas.

In the early decades of the twentieth century, the impact of public transportation and automobiles, the rise of commercial amusements, the lengthening of the period of mandatory schooling, and the entrance of women into the public sphere combined to transform the domestic dwelling. It was at this time that the term *living room* gained popularity. The parlor became obsolete as a new informality reigned. The same accoutrements that embellished parlors and signaled a middle-class family's good taste were now considered by tastemakers as "clutter." House designers purposefully chose not to use the term *parlor* in their plans and marketing for suburban dwellings because of the symbolic association of the parlor as an overly ornate, stiffly formal, and thereby outmoded room. The efficient, open floor plan of the bungalow, in which the front door often led directly into the living room, which itself was often connected to the dining room and the kitchen, would also be used in popular styles such as the Cape Cod cottage, the Colonial Revival

house, and the suburban ranch throughout the century. Suburban living rooms often boasted picture windows or window walls, signaling the house's relaxed social space therein.

During the mid-twentieth century, the living room was where the family gathered to watch television as well as receive visitors. When a family entertained a large number of guests, the living room was the major site of activity. House designs often included an elaborate bar within the living room space with easy access to the kitchen but apart from the private zone of bedrooms and bathrooms. With the addition of family rooms, dens, recreation rooms, and great rooms to American houses of the later twentieth century, family togetherness and television viewing has moved from the living room. In the late twentieth century, it became common to characterize the living room as a formal room, purely for receiving and entertaining guests.

Kirin Makker and Shirley Teresa Wajda

See also Domestic Architecture; Halls; Parlors; Recreation Rooms

References and Further Reading

Bushman, Richard L. 1992. *The Refinement of America: Persons, Houses, Cities.* New York: Alfred A. Knopf.

Clark, Edward Clifford, Jr. 1986. *The American Family Home, 1800–1960.* Chapel Hill: University of North Carolina Press.

Downing, Andrew Jackson. 1969 (1850). *The Architecture of Country Houses; including designs for cottages, and farmhouses, and villas, with remarks on interiors, furniture, and the best modes of warming and ventilating.* New York: Dover.

Grier, Katherine C. 1988. *Culture and Comfort: Parlor Making and Middle-Class Identity, 1850–1930.* Washington, DC: Smithsonian Institution Press.

M

Mail Order Catalogues

Mail order catalogues brought a variety of consumer goods and services to Americans' doorsteps, beginning in 1872 with Aaron Montgomery Ward's (1844–1913) single-sheet price list of merchandise and ordering instructions. Also called *consumer guides*, these ever-growing paperback publications contained within their pages elaborate descriptions, numerous illustrations, and competitive prices with which the consumer could shop from home and receive the goods through mail delivery, whether to their address, the post office, or the local retail store.

Mimicking in print (and later, with color) the classification and variety of goods offered by late-nineteenth-century urban department stores, mail order catalogues provided rural Americans the promise and practice of modern consumption. Chicago supply houses such as Montgomery Ward and Sears, Roebuck and Co. (which produced its first catalogue in 1886) annually issued several editions. Business boomed, bringing into the nation's cash economy rural Americans who had long utilized barter and local credit. By 1910, 10 million Americans shopped by mail.

The mail order system benefited from the introduction of bulk mail rates that facilitated cheaper costs of catalogue distribution, postal money orders with which consumers could pay for goods, and parcel post and rural free delivery (1896) that allowed mail to be delivered to every house in the nation. Installment buying, already instituted in the nation's urban department stores, was introduced to the rest of the nation through the mail order system. After widespread adoption of the telephone, orders could be more quickly placed and delivered.

Americans worried about the quality of merchandise offered through mail order catalogues. Country store owners exploited this worry in their battles against competition from mail order houses, citing also the need for economic support of local stores to ensure community prosperity. Dependent in part on brand name recognition, mail order houses countered with their guarantees of consumer satisfaction and offered cash refunds to disappointed customers.

Relatively little is known, however, about what items sold and what items gathered dust in warehouses. Sears, Roebuck & Co. returned customers' order forms with their purchases, leaving little record of inventory, sales trends, and consumer preferences. Often scholars use these works as reference guides to date or characterize artifacts rather than as key evidence of an emerging national consumer culture in the late nineteenth and early twentieth centuries. For example, some patterns of consumption and mass marketing may be charted through analysis of the shifting placement and description of a given item in catalogues over time. The catalogues chart availability and variety as well as provide images and descriptions of consumer goods. Last, these "wish books" (as Sears, Roebuck and Co.'s Christmas catalogues were called) reflect merchants' and consumers' desires in the housekeeping advice and uplifting verse included within their covers.

Of note are the mail order catalogues of houses, garages, and other domestic outbuildings that appeared first in 1908, with Sears, Roebuck and Co. in the lead, followed by Aladdin Homes (Bay City, Michigan) and other house plan and building firms across the nation. The smaller bungalow became the most popular mail order house: Customers received plans and construction manuals through the mail, while the house materials arrived by rail. The Great Depression and the onset of World War II (1939–1945) effectively ended this practice.

In the late twentieth century, the Home Shopping Network and the rise of the Internet have replaced the general mail order catalogue. Specialty and seasonal sales catalogues still reach millions of Americans, but Sears, Roebuck and Co.'s last general merchandise catalogue was issued in 1993.

Shirley Teresa Wajda

See also Advertisements and Advertising; Consumerism and Consumption; Domestic Architecture; Patents, Trademarks, and Brands; Print Culture; Trade Cards; Trade Catalogues

References and Further Reading
Schlereth, Thomas J. 1980. "Mail-Order Catalogs as Resources in Material Culture Studies." In *Artifacts and the American Past*, 48–65. Nashville, TN: American Association for State and Local History.
Schlereth, Thomas J. 1989. "Country Stores, County Fairs, and Mail-Order Catalogs: Consumerism in Rural America." In *The Consumer Culture and the American Home, 1890–1930*, ed. Glenda Dyer and Martha Reed, 27–45. Beaumont, TX: McFaddin-Ward House Museum.
Strasser, Susan. 1989. *Satisfaction Guaranteed: The Making of an American Mass Market*. New York: Pantheon Books.

Mannerism

Mannerism describes a style of decorative arts and painting that was popular in the British colonies for much of the seventeenth century. Derived from the Italian *maniera* ("style" or "grace"), Mannerism incorporated classical forms discovered and embraced in the sixteenth century while it embellished those forms with heavy and exaggerated (*grotesque*) ornament. Mannerism stressed the intellect of the artist and the craftsman as well as the richness and refinement of invention in technique.

Grotesque is derived from the first-century palace of the Roman emperor Nero (37–68), found in the 1480s in Rome. The ruins' rooms, called grottoes (hence *grotesque*), were decorated in ornate frescoes showing patterns of fantastic creatures amid exotic foliage, urns, and other elements. A new vocabulary of ornament was born, and its popularity spread from Italy through print sources to other parts of Europe such as Germany and the Netherlands. In the early seventeenth century, Protestant German and Dutch craftsmen fled from the Catholic Spanish invasion of their countries to a fervently Protestant

England and there furthered the popularity of Mannerist style as a Protestant style.

Furniture, silver, ceramics, pewter, brass, and textiles carried to, crafted in, and used in New England were decorated with grotesque ornament. Geometric patterns of emblems, heraldry, and other iconography were measured and applied with ruler and compass; the popularity of Mannerist designs in Europe, England, and the American colonies led to standardization and the marketing of patterns. Books and other printed materials were also engraved with Mannerist designs.

With a special interest in subjective expression, Mannerist artists applied deformed shapes and elongated figures in complex poses as an attempt to pass the boundaries of natural reality. With stress on the role of color in showing emotions, forms became less tangible in Mannerist paintings. According to art historian Jonathan L. Fairbanks (1982, 422), New England portraits contain evidence of the "canons of proportion, compositional devices, artful posture, and foreshortening" characteristic of the Mannerist style developed in Renaissance Italy.

Mohammad Gharipour

See also Art History and American Art; Decorative Arts; Style

References and Further Reading

Fairbanks, Jonathan L. 1982. "Portrait Painting in Seventeenth-Century Boston: Its History, Methods, and Materials." In *New England Begins: The Seventeenth Century*, vol. 3, 413–426, 443–455. Boston: Museum of Fine Arts.

Trent, Robert F. "The Concept of Mannerism." In *New England Begins: The Seventeenth Century*, vol. 3, 368–379. Boston: Museum of Fine Arts.

Wundram, Manfred. 2005. "Mannerism." In *Grove Art Online Encyclopedia*. Oxford, UK: Oxford University Press.

Maritime Material Culture

American *maritime material culture* encompasses a broad range of objects related to human interaction with the oceans, the coastal zone, and the inland waterways. These material resources provide intellectual access to the beliefs and ways of life of a variety of cultures that rely upon the water. The range of objects, while very broad, is idiosyncratic and often rooted in traditional local knowledge. Each object has its own story to tell—a story that provides a window into a distinct maritime culture, shaped by the water that surrounds it.

Perhaps the most significant factor influencing maritime material culture is the environment. Water covers nearly 70 percent of the surface of the planet in a wide variety of forms. Vast tracts of ocean have been both a barrier and a highway for human use. Prevailing winds, currents, and swells influence both the design of watercraft—ships and small craft—and navigation techniques. The maritime world, however, does not end at the American coastline; it penetrates deep into the nation's interior. The North American continent contains an immense riverine system that requires an altogether different mode of transportation and navigational skills from that of the high seas. It also touches on very important commercial aspects of American history such as the highly competitive fur trade, for which products were brought from the interior for shipment overseas. The majority of maritime communities, however, have developed along the nation's coastal areas where the rivers meet the sea.

Watercraft: Design and Culture

The most recognizable and most common examples of maritime material culture are the ships and boats that have been developed for a variety of general and specific purposes.

Onboard each of these craft is an entire category of equipment that aids in the control and propulsion of the vessel (oars, propellers, sails, or engines), in loading or hauling cargo (rigging, cargo booms, and block and tackle), and in carrying passengers (cabins, staterooms, lifeboats, and dining and recreation areas). Many craft carry highly specialized features for gathering sustenance. Many ships—yachts in particular—feature more luxurious appointments and equipment.

Dramatically different marine environments create unique situations and objects. As different as oceans are from rivers and lakes, so are the available materials. For example, bark from the birch tree provided the perfect hull material for canoes traveling on inland rivers, whereas live oak and other hardwoods provided immense strength to many oceangoing ships. Likewise, each regional culture greatly influences the material it produces, and although there are many objects of the same general type, each local community adapts certain features over others. In addition, work, survival, recreation, and competition on the water necessarily require special equipment and clothing.

The most common and well-known objects of maritime life are the watercraft that people have created and used for exploring, commerce, gathering sustenance, warfare, or recreation. Some of the most famous American watercraft are *Bear of Oakland* (Admiral Richard E. Byrd's [1888–1957] ship in which he began his 1934 Antarctic exploration); SS *United States* (one of the most famous passenger liners); Chesapeake Bay skipjacks (the only sailing vessels allowed to dredge oysters on the bay); USF *Constitution* (the world's oldest commissioned warship); and *Courageous* (two-time defender of the America's Cup). The development and evolution in shipbuilding reflects mankind's ability not only to fashion larger and more complex

vessels but also the ability to navigate them and to harness multiple power sources. Early vessels relied upon either the wind or manpower for propulsion. Later ships and boats employed various forms of mechanical power to augment or replace sails.

Local, traditional watercraft, however, are the most indicative of a maritime community. Boats reflect not only the ideas and influences of those who commissioned, built, or used them but those of the larger society as well. The objective for building a boat, the materials from which it is made, and its general style and design are all culturally based decisions. Traditions handed down from generation to generation have led to many watercraft becoming recognized as specific regional types. Perhaps the most significant American regions where multiple types of local watercraft have developed include the Chesapeake Bay and its Tilghman Island (Maryland) five-log canoe, Poquoson (Virginia) three-log canoe, skipjack, Sinepuxent skiff (Wachapreague, Virginia), bugeye, railbird skiff, and crab skiff; coastal New England and its birch-bark canoe, New Haven (Connecticut) sharpie, Grand Banks dory, Penobscot (Maine) lumberman's bateau, Friendship sloop (Maine); and the Louisiana bayous with their dugout or plywood pirogue, creole skiff, Louisiana lugger (New Orleans), Atchafalaya swamp bateau, and Laffite-style jon boat.

Art and Decorative Arts

Maritime material culture extends beyond the watercraft and all of the specialized equipment and nomenclature that have evolved. The waterways inspire unique aesthetic sensibilities and artistic and decorative works. Most notable among these are ship models, paintings, drawings, photographs, and "sailor's art." Many models, having been built prior to the actual ship, provide

Built in 1910, the two-sail, V-bottomed skipjack (or bateau) E. C. Collier *is one of the oldest vessels in Maryland's oyster dredging fleet. The vessel, depicted here in 1957, was one of the last of a commercial sailing fleet in the nation, due to Maryland's law against oyster dredging under power. It is now on display at the Chesapeake Bay Maritime Museum in St. Michaels, Maryland. (Chesapeake Bay Maritime Museum)*

valuable information. Half-hull models are scale representations of half of a ship's hull (only half is needed, as most watercraft are symmetrical). The physical measurements for many packet ships, clipper ships, and sailing yachts were taken directly from these models. A model offers a three-dimensional view of a vessel in the same manner offered by a marine painting.

For centuries artists have drawn inspiration from the sea. Marine paintings cover many styles: from documentary or narrative depictions of particular places and events to paintings where the ship is a metaphor for speed, power, or national ambition to sea-

scapes that depict ports, coastlines, or the many moods and colors of sea and sky. In many respects, marine photography grew out of the same traditions as painting and drawing. These forms of imagery, including the ship models, provide important data on the cultures they depict and from which they derive.

Sailor's art refers to any number of types of artistic work created aboard ship by seafarers. The range includes drawings, decorative ropework, painted sea chests, sailor's valentines—sea shells decoratively arranged into a remembrance for wives and sweethearts left behind—and embroidery of clothing and sea bags. Perhaps the most notable sailor's art is scrimshaw, the art of etching and inking a scene or portrait into a piece of ivory—usually a whale's tooth or a walrus' tusk. The teeth were among the few parts of a whale without commercial value. Besides decorated teeth, many sailors used the ivory and bone to fashion useful objects like pie crimpers, cribbage boards, small models, and walking cane handles. Sailor's art is an important facet of the decorative arts and provides a unique entrée into the lives of sailors aboard whaleships during the nineteenth and twentieth centuries.

Lyles Forbes

See also Art History and American Art; Decorative Arts; Tools, Implements, and Instruments; Water Transportation

References and Further Reading
Bauer, K. Jack. 1988. *A Maritime History of the United States: The Role of America's Seas and Waterways.* Columbia: University of South Carolina Press.
Bunting, William H. 2000. *A Day's Work: A Sampler of Historic Maine Photographs, 1860–1920, Part Two.* Portland, Maine: Tilbury House.
Gillmer, Thomas C. 1994. *A History of Working Watercraft of the Western World.* Camden, ME: International Marine Publishing.
Glassie, Henry. 1968. *Pattern in the Material Folk Culture of the Eastern United States.* Philadelphia: University of Pennsylvania Press.
Glassie, Henry. 1973. "The Nature of the New World Artifact: The Instance of the Dugout Canoe." In *Festschrift fur Robert Wildhaber,* ed. Walter Escher, Theo Gantner, and Hans Trumpy, 153–170. Basel, Switzerland: Verlag G. Krebs AG.
Henderson, J. Welles, and Rodney P. Carlisle. 1999. *Jack Tar: A Sailor's Life 1750–1910.* Woodbridge, Suffolk, UK: Antique Collectors' Club.
Johnson, Paula J., ed. 1988. *Working the Water: The Commercial Fisheries of Maryland's Patuxent River.* Charlottesville: University Press of Virginia.
McManus, Michael. 1997. *A Treasury of American Scrimshaw: A Collection of the Useful and Decorative.* New York: Penguin Studio.
Taylor, David A. 1992. *Documenting Maritime Folklife.* Washington, DC: Library of Congress.

Materials Conservation

An object deemed culturally or historically significant or socially valuable can be preserved or restored by varying scientific methods of conservation. Conservation practices range widely, dependent on the desired or necessary extent of the alterations and the levels of preservation chosen or available. Conservation practices take into account the object's original configuration of time, space, and matter. From minor acts of preventative conservation that strive to maintain the original material integrity to the more invasive practices of full-blown restorations, the resulting work has a potential to transform an object into a distant echo of its original state.

Time, Space, and Material

The goal of most conservation and restoration work is to return an object to its original condition. Professional conservators make informed decisions or assumptions about the object's original material configuration in time and space. The desired result of conservation is the moment when the maker, the material, and the space are joined to create one object. Nevertheless, conservators first consider a work in the most immediate sense: the physical components of the work's material, such as paint, canvas, or clay. The physical properties are addressed first and foremost, generally before the aesthetic issues. Form, color, and texture are a few examples of some more aesthetic qualities that are considered later in the conservation work.

Process

Each object subject to conservation necessitates different sets of procedures. Attempts to generalize practices into universal guidelines and to create a formula in conservation work have proved to be ineffectual.

Material elements have a finite existence. Knowledge of materials science also has limitations that may dictate how long the life of an object may be extended. When the condition of an object is assessed, an estimated life expectancy of the object is determined. Condition reports, often maintained from at least the time of accession into a museum's collection, are commonly referred to at this point. Long- and short-term conservation plans are devised and weighed, dependent on the urgency of needed or desired restoration, the value of the object, and the use of the object in exhibition, among other factors. Value is determined not only in the physical condition of an object but also in the object's social, historical, and cultural significance and pecuniary worth.

Advances in technology throughout the twentieth century have helped the development of conservation as a process and as a field. Implementing all known methods of restoration can prolong the life of an object to some extent, though conservation should not sacrifice the integrity of the object. Cases of overrestoration, overpaintings, or excessive reconstructions have led to problematic misinterpretations and misrepresentations of cultural materials. The more recent practice of clearly marking restored areas from the original is becoming common, by contrasting the color or material of the restored area to the original, for example.

Variations in Results

Differences in the operations of the particular institution, the working guidelines of the particular conservator, and the education and tastes of the conservator are a few elements that may lead to variations in the results of conservation work. When working within the subjective realm of art, personal taste and perception may be pertinent factors. Recent trends in certain conservation departments include increased documentation and the responsibility of the ethical obligation of the individual conservator to maintain the integrity of the work.

Reversibility

Today's conservators adhere to one major guideline: to ensure the capability of reversing the applications of conservation. Glues, paints, bonds, and other materials used during conservation and restoration practices should be easily removable.

Some conservators follow the "6 and 6 rule." From six feet away, the object appears to be in the original state to a passing viewer, yet from six inches the restoration work should be perceptible to a professional or an extremely observant visitor. This rule attempts to hide the restoration, however, by creating a simulated look of an authentic work in the use of similar colors, materials, or replicated textures. The perceived illusion of the state of the original is often disguised in overly restorative methods, attempting to blend seamlessly into the original.

Prevention versus Restoration

The difference between preventative and restorative conservation is in the action(s) taken directly on the material surface of an object. Conservation work is not always strictly one or the other, for some processes entail both methods of conservation.

Preventative methods strive to create and maintain a stable, sterilized environment by providing a durable physical structure in the object, maximizing its use, and retaining its integrity. The goal of preventative conservation is to inhibit further damage and deterioration without physical alteration of or addition to the material surface. This prevention extends then to the storage, exhibition, handling, and transport of the object. Environmental factors such as light, humidity, temperature, pests, and atmospheric pollution are monitored in the near-clinical environment of the museum.

Restorative methods re-create damaged or missing elements by material evidence such as photographs, condition reports, purchase agreements, and sales records. Restorative conservation attempts to re-create, in whole or part, missing elements based on historical, literary, graphic, pictorial, oral, archaeological, and scientific evidence to a chosen earlier state of a work. Reconstructive work is essentially subjective, as no methods of in-depth research or science can replicate delicate aesthetic properties. As a work is continually restored, layer upon layer of subjective visual illusion is built over the original. Restoration work ultimately depreciates the original work, losing the fundamental qualities in the newer fabricated layers.

Material Destruction

Material change should not be viewed as damage, but a part of existence. Death and destruction are not negative occurrences, but merely natural processes. The unpredictable nature of life includes loss, chance, and change. The eventual destruction of material signifies the real and tangible limitations of all matter.

As conservators work within the changing requirements and needs, and as scientific and historical knowledge changes, the methods and ethics of conservation are modified. In practice, each conservator tries to maintain and enforce his or her own working practical guidelines of conservation and ethics, often referring primarily to the codes

set by organizations such as the International Council of Museums, the Museums Association, and the European Confederation of Conservator-Restorers' Organisations for general guidelines.

Virginia Dressler

See also Fakes; Historic Preservation; Museums and Museum Practice

References and Further Reading
Ashley-Smith, Jonathan. 1999. *Risk Assessment for Object Conservation*. Oxford, UK: Butterworth-Heinemann.
Benjamin, Walter. 1992 (1936). "The Work of Art in the Age of Mechanical Reproduction." In *Art in Modern Culture: An Anthology of Critical Texts*, ed. Francis Frascina and Jonathan Harris, 297–307. London: Phaidon.
Gombrich, E. H. 1962. "Blurred Images and Unvarnished Truth." *British Journal of Aesthetics* 2 (2): 170–179.
Kubler, George. 1962. *The Shape of Time: Remarks on the History of Things*. New Haven, CT: Yale University Press.

Medical Instruments

Medical instruments enable the diagnosis of illness and injury in human and animal bodies. They also enable the delivery of medicine and related care, such as physical therapies, to a body should it be found to require treatment. In the seventeenth century, physicians depended on what patients said and what they could see on the patient's body for diagnosis. In the eighteenth century, a physician's hands were instruments, in that *percussion*—the manipulation of the body to hear sounds—was employed to detect disease and ailments.

Since the nineteenth century, health-care providers, as well as researchers in science and medicine, use medical instruments to carry out the mission of their related professions. All medical professionals use instruments of one kind or another to peer inside (x-rays), measure (thermometers to gauge body temperature; blood pressure and heart monitors), evaluate (laboratory tests dependent on centrifuges and microscopes), and administer treatments (cancer chemotherapy; plaster casts for broken bones; hypodermic needles). Individuals across different specialties use similar instruments, such as stethoscopes (also dependent on sound) and thermometers as primary diagnostic tools. Some instruments, such as the ophthalmoscope—a lighted device that optometrists, ophthalmologists, and opticians use to look inside the eye—are unique to one professional group.

Whereas surgical instruments like scalpels, forceps, and clamps; dental instruments such as curettes and tooth extractors; and other handheld tools may be considered basic devices in terms of their structure and the metal, glass, and plastic materials from which they are made, other instruments are relatively complex, multisystem tools that consist of a variety of materials and often function through specialized computer hardware and software. Examples of such devices include lasers used for surgery and magnetic resonance imaging machines used for producing high-quality images of the inside of the human body. Such machines translate the body's condition into numeric indices for evaluation.

Medical instruments are products of caregiving knowledge and practice. They are also the result of knowledge and experience gained in fields such as physics, mathematics, computer science, chemistry, and engineering. Medical instruments are therefore central to defining what it means to be a health-care professional, whether a doctor, a nurse, a veterinarian, or a physical therapist. Medical instruments therefore represent professional identity while they reflect the intellectual development and practice of medicine and the allied health sciences.

Jeffrey Reznick

See also Human Body; Technology; Tools, Implements, and Instruments

References and Further Reading

Davis, A. 1981. *Medicine and Its Technology: An Introduction to the History of Medical Instrumentation*. Westport, CT: Greenwood Press.
Lawrence, G. 1993. *Technologies of Modern Medicine: Proceedings of a Seminar Held at the Science Museum, London, March 1993*. London: Science Museum.
Webster, John G., ed. 1988. *Encyclopedia of Medical Devices and Instrumentation*. 4 vols. New York: John Wiley.

Memory and Memorabilia

The activity and organization of human thought has, for centuries, been premised on memory. English philosopher John Locke (1632–1704), for example, understood memory as an essential accessory to reason, as a "storehouse of . . . ideas" from which thoughts are made "actual again" in their "annexation" to new thoughts (Locke 1975). *Memory* is both the cognitive ability to remember and the mental representation of that which is remembered. It is shaped by language and by imagery. To *re-collect* or *re-member* is to assemble for varying purposes objects stored in the repository that is memory; to *re-call* is to summon. Borrowing from the Renaissance concepts of memory (in turn borrowed from ancient Greece and Rome), the colonists of North America understood memory as rhetorical, in the form of mnemonics learned by schoolboys and utilized in oratory.

Among the genteel in the late eighteenth and early nineteenth centuries who read, wrote, and engaged in the polite letters and conversation of the salon, memory was understood as spatial, arranging the objects of what was to be remembered in, for example, the rooms of a house, and naming or linking those rooms to topics. This "art of memory" was paralleled in the practice of keeping a commonplace book, in which pages were devoted to various subjects, under which headings the book's keeper would copy pertinent passages from books and periodicals for further reference. Personal memory was also sustained through the exchange of gifts that served metonymically: A miniature portrait or mirror, for example, was the figure of speech for the giver's face; a silhouette portrait, the giver's heart. Through such exchange and symbolism relations were sustained and memories anchored in tangible objects.

In the early nineteenth century, the marketplace increasingly provided the material means with which to construct personal and collective memory—that is, shared remembering by a group, institution, society, or nation. The print revolution in this era facilitated social memories beyond one's family or community. So, too, did the introduction of the "mirror with a memory," the daguerreotype, a form of photograph created in the silvery surface of a copperplate. Daguerreotypic images had to be viewed in a specific way so that the image could be seen; held otherwise the surface reflected the viewer. Photography revolutionized how Americans remembered by providing the means through which change over time could be visually chronicled. One's childhood, for example, could be represented with images of one's changing body. Hairwork, pieces of cloth from a loved one's dress, pressed flowers, verse and autographs saved in an album, among other handcrafted objects, were replaced over the course of the century by market goods such as gift books and portrait photographs. Personal memory was increasingly mediated by the market.

Collective Memory

Not surprisingly, the concept of *collective memory* arose with mass culture, the modern nation-state, and psychology at the beginning of the twentieth century. Rather than the Freudian view that memory resides in the unconscious and the individual mind actively works to forget or repress, collective memory is social, according to Maurice Halbwachs (1877–1945), and exists in social institutions—the family or the church, for example. Halbwachs' works, *Social Frameworks of Memory* (1925) and *On Collective Memory* (1950), promote a definition of memory as a structure in which people find meaning for their present experiences. Memory is constructed with and against other narratives of memory, including those of history, art, literature, newspapers and periodicals, television, radio, film, the Internet, personal reminiscences and gossip, diaries, and letters. It is Halbwachs' formulation of collective memory that serves as a starting point for more recent discussions of the nature of memory in postmodern society. Historians and culture critics in particular debate the nature of public memory of the nation's peoples, exploring, for example, the roles of politics, gender, race, class, and ethnicity in public commemorations and the debates over historic monuments and memorials. Some critics employ the term *popular memory* to disengage from Halbwachs' functionalist definition as well as to engage the influence of mass media and culture in creating, sustaining, and altering memory. How we remember—how we make sense of the seemingly endless representations produced by media—interests many scholars today. What events have been forgotten but reclaimed by scholars are also keys to understanding how Americans, as individuals and as a people, remember.

Memorabilia

The mass-produced material culture associated with historical events, popular entertainment, and culture is termed *memorabilia*. Items such as playbills and posters, rock concert T-shirts and baseball caps, commemorative ceramic plates and mugs, and printed matter such as newspaper clippings are valued and kept for their connections to an event or phenomenon meaningful to the collector. Memorabilia is intentionally produced to advertise an event, a television program or a film, a concert, a political campaign, or a protest march. The existence of memorabilia of a specific event that then becomes newsworthy and historic heightens the meaning and popular memory of that event. Memorabilia in a media-saturated age can be said to be collective memory; no one need participate or witness the event to be able to purchase or possess its associated memorabilia.

Shirley Teresa Wajda

See also Collecting and Collections; Ephemera; Funerals; Holidays and Commemorations; Mourning; Nostalgia; Photography; Political Ephemera; Print Culture; Public Monuments and Popular Commemoration; Scrapbooks; Souvenirs; Tourism and Travel

References and Further Reading
Bodnar, John. 1992. *Remaking America: Public Memory, Commemoration, and Patriotism in the Twentieth Century.* Princeton, NJ: Princeton University Press.

Halbwachs, Maurice. 1952 (1925). *Les Cadres Sociaux de la Memoire (The Social Frameworks of Memory).* Paris: Presses Universitaires de France.

Halbwachs, Maurice. 1992 (1950). *On Collective Memory,* ed. and trans. Lewis A. Coser. Chicago: University of Chicago Press.

Kammen, Michael. 1991. *Mystic Chords of Memory: The Transformation of Tradition in American Culture.* New York: Alfred A. Knopf.

Landsberg, Alison. 2004. *Prosthetic Memory: The Transformation of American Remembrance in the Age of Mass Culture.* New York: Columbia University Press.

Lipsitz, George. 2001 (1990). *Time Passages: Collective Memory and American Popular Culture,* rpt. ed. Minneapolis: University of Minnesota Press.

Locke, John. 1975 (1690). *An Essay Concerning Human Understanding,* ed. Peter H. Nidditch. Oxford, UK: Clarendon.

Lowenthal, David. 1985. *The Past is a Foreign Country.* Cambridge, UK: Cambridge University Press.

Sheumaker, Helen. 2007. *Love Entwined: The Curious History of Hairwork.* Philadelphia: University of Pennsylvania Press.

Stabile, Susan M. 2004. *Memory's Daughters: The Material Culture of Remembrance in Eighteenth-Century America.* Ithaca, NY: Cornell University Press.

Military Dress

Military dress encompasses highly distinctive uniforms, manufactured of a variety of textiles and mandated for members of a nation's armed forces. Since the mid-1600s in Europe, different nations' armed forces have adopted uniform clothing codes. Uniforms function to set service members apart from the civilian population, to increase the perceived solidarity of the armed services, and to reinforce a hierarchy of authority seen as necessary to the military services. Uniform clothing provides an appearance of efficiency and makes each nation's forces recognizable to civilian and enemy alike. Uniforms also reify the ideology and organizational history of the military branches as well as designate special skills, awards, and units of the armed forces' members. Military dress usually does not reflect contemporary clothing styles. Nevertheless, as in the case of the United States, military uniforms have at times reflected changing styles and fashions and the gender and various obligations of military service members. Each branch of the U.S. armed forces has developed its own uniform, including color, style, and insignia. Officers in each branch have more decorative uniforms than military service members, reflecting their higher status and greater power. Officers provide their own uniforms, while the branches of the armed forces provide enlisted men and women with a variety of purpose-defined dress.

United States Army

As the first branch of the nation's armed forces (established in 1775), the United States Army's uniforms have a long history of change in style and color. Adapted from gentleman's dress, the Continental Army uniform was originally dark blue with contrasting color in button-back lapels and cuffs. Coats sported metal buttons and shoulder belts crossed the torso, providing the means to carry weaponry. The tricornered hat of the Continental army was changed in 1832 to a cap. During the Mexican-American War (1846–1848), soldiers wore blue uniforms, but volunteer militias clothed themselves in an assortment of uniforms. The Texas volunteers were most recognizable in buckskins, pants, shirts, forage caps, and straw hats. During the Civil War (1861–1865), the army of the Confederacy also regulated its own uniforms, often a gray color (inexpensive and the color of West Point cadets' uniforms), to differentiate itself from the Union forces' blue uniforms. More than twenty-six styles of Confederate uniforms were worn, but a shortage of cloth often caused Confederate regiments to wear mixed clothing. After the Spanish-American War (1898), the United

States Army distinguished dress from field uniforms. Field uniforms were changed to account for season and climate and the nature and venue of warfare. Textile weight changed as well as color to conceal soldiers in battle. Olive drab was replaced in 1956 by a darker green called Army Green–44); the use of khaki ended in 1985. Dress uniforms remained blue.

The United States Army currently has multiple uniforms: full dress (used on ceremonial occasions), dress, service, and service fatigues. Dress uniforms have historically incorporated a series of decorations including wings on the shoulders, epaulets, knots, aiguillettes (looped cords attached to one shoulder), sashes, and fourragères (braided cords worn on the left shoulder) that marked a unit's awards. Dress uniforms of all branches used brass buttons, which signaled status and authority. In the 1970s tropical camouflage-patterned battle dress was adopted, though "battle fatigues" had been introduced in World War II (1939–1945). Fatigue jackets were worn by antiwar protesters during the era to protest the Vietnam conflict. The contemporary role of the army, however, has led to the increased use of camouflage-patterned uniforms and a decline of the multipurpose dress uniform.

United States Navy

Established as the Continental navy in 1775, the United States Navy took as models for its early dress the blue British Royal Navy uniform and other seafaring entities. Officers wore the costume of military high rank: Blue coat with red facing marked the navy officer from the army officer in the Revolution. Throughout the nineteenth century the coat was replaced with a jacket and replaced again with a double-breasted blue coat after World War I (1914–1918). White was worn in the summer months. Khaki as battle dress was adopted in World War II.

Navy sailors originally wore blue uniforms with shirts with large, square collars and wide-legged pants. Reflecting the work required of ships and sailing, sailors' uniforms fit more loosely than those of the other branches; canvas hats protected from sun and storm. The "pea coat" was adopted in 1885, as was the white stitched hat. During World War II sailors wore denim dungarees. The white uniform with bell-bottom trousers was replaced in 1975 with a coat and tie. So iconic was the bell-bottom uniform that it was readopted in 1978. The United States Coast Guard uniform shares many characteristics with its navy counterpart.

United States Marine Corps

The members of the United States Marine Corps (USMC), a separate part of the United States Navy, originally wore green coats faced with red or white, only to change by the end of the eighteenth century to a blue dress coat used throughout the nineteenth century. USMC service uniforms borrow from both the army and the navy, as befits their service on land and sea. Forest green uniforms were adopted in 1912; a cloth belt was included during World War II. Today the uniform of the Marines is olive green with a khaki shirt like that of the army, but the marine uniform lacks a beret and insignia marking their unit or special training. Their dress uniforms are blue with brass buttons and red piping.

United States Air Force

The uniform of the United States Air Force is currently blue with a light blue shirt, and aeronautical badges are mandatory. Before the air force was created as a service independent of the other armed forces in 1947, pilots adopted a variety of dress that had less to do with identity with a service branch or the United States and more with the dan-

ger and romance of aviation. For example, the leather "bomber jacket" became an icon of the "devil may care" attitude attributed to flyers in World War II; the jacket remains popular as dress for civilian men and women.

Women's Uniforms

Women's military uniforms have been through many styles and colors because their uniforms were more subject to fashion and societal norms. During World War I, women wore the "Norfolk suit," a costume borrowed from Englishmen's sporting dress. Women's uniform colors matched those of men's uniforms in the various service branches. During and after World War II, designers such as Hattie Carnegie (1889–1956) and Mainbocher (1891–1976) created fashionable uniforms for women. With the increased acceptance of women in the armed forces, dress uniforms now include maternity versions.

Kelly J. Baker

See also Dress, Accessories, and Fashion; Gender

References and Further Reading

Elting, John R., ed. 1974–1988. *Military Uniforms in America*. 4 vols. San Rafael, CA: Presidio Press.

Emerson, William. 1996. *Encyclopedia of United States Army Insignia and Uniforms*. Norman: University of Oklahoma Press.

Fussell, Paul. 2002. *Uniforms: Why We Are What We Wear*. Boston: Houghton Mifflin.

Mill Towns

Mill towns are physical relics of the United States' nineteenth- and early twentieth-century industrial past, when a single company or enterprise planned and built a community. These communities provided employment and attempted to support all of the social needs of its workers. This paternalistic relationship allowed for strict social and economic control over a workforce that was largely dependent on the company as employer, landlord, moral leader, and shopkeeper. Concentrated on a single extraction or manufacturing process, mill towns produced such materials as lumber, paper, steel, coal, and textiles. Early examples of mill towns, such as Lowell, Massachusetts, were architecturally vernacular expressions of industrial pragmatism and a hierarchical social order. The industrial mill building served as the center of daily life and economic generator of livelihood. Surrounding the mill was the social realm of small, identical workers' houses, a schoolhouse, churches, and a company store. Sited on a hill above the mill and surrounding the company town buildings was the superintendent's house, which symbolically maintained surveillance over daily activities.

After the Civil War (1861–1865), the textile industry expanded, and its factories were found in the Southeast as well as in the North. Some towns were founded to serve a textile mill factory, such as Cliffside, North Carolina, which was built in 1899 to host Henrietta Mills. Older towns became quite different cities, such as New Bedford, Massachusetts, which by the 1880s was no longer a town dependent upon the whaling industry but the host of Wamsutta Mills. By the end of the nineteenth century, mill towns were experiencing serious environmental problems, due to industrial waste and indiscriminate dumping of materials into waterways. Lawsuits and fishing closures were symptoms of these problems.

In the 1930s, a changing industrial economy, the Great Depression, and challenges by organized labor effectively ended the company town system. Mill towns either

transformed to meet new needs or they disappeared. While mill towns may have represented a highly controlled, if not oppressive, living environment for workers of the time, currently well-preserved mill buildings are increasingly re-used by preservationists and developers. The large open interior spaces with high ceilings and well-crafted architectural detailing are now seen as an attractive venue for museums, loft apartments, office space, boutique shops, and restaurants.

Jeffrey Blankenship

See also Cities and Towns; Company Towns; Factory and Industrial Work and Labor; Historic Preservation; Work and Labor

References and Further Reading

Crawford, Margaret. 1995. *Building the Workingman's Paradise: The Design of American Company Towns.* New York: Verso.
Garner, John S., ed. 1992. *The Company Town: Architecture and Society in the Early Industrial Age.* New York: Oxford University Press.
Norkunas, Martha. 2002. *Monuments and Memory: History and Representation in Lowell, Massachusetts.* Washington, DC: Smithsonian Institution Press.

Mobile Homes and Trailer Parks

Trailer park describes a dedicated piece of land upon which a collection of prefabricated manufactured trailers, or *mobile homes*, each of which are towed on their own wheels and able to connect to utilities but have no permanent foundation, are gathered. Facilities in these parks can range from basic utilities and paved roads to luxurious amenities, such as playgrounds, golf courses, and clubhouses. Tracing the evolution of the trailer park and its stigma in society underscores the importance of home ownership as an American cultural tenet.

From Recreational Shelter to Emergency Housing

While the history of the trailer park begins with recreation and camping, the challenges posed by the Great Depression in the 1930s necessitated a shift in the use of trailers from temporary vacation shelter to permanent residence. Migrant laborers in ad hoc and homemade trailers congregated outside towns along main rural roads, looking for work and creating communities of covered wagons, shanties on wheels, and small manufactured trailers. Impromptu trailer parks or camps caused consternation among residents and farmers on whose land the travelers would park and whose crops the travelers would eat. Private land owners and local municipal bodies responded by providing dedicated parking camps with access to water and communal bathrooms in order to meet the needs of the recreational traveler and migrant laborer with trailer in tow. While progressive, the placement and structure of the vehicles, along with sewage, drainage, garbage collection, and open fire cooking facilities, were not regulated. As a result, living conditions for park residents were dangerous and unsanitary, with flood and fire being two of the greatest dangers.

During World War II (1939–1945), the United States experienced a building and employment boom at factories and military bases, prompting federal agencies like the National Housing Authority (NHA) and the United States military to assemble neighborhoods of prefabricated trailers equipped with only basic necessities in order to house the influx of workers. The speed at which these mobile trailers were built allowed communities to develop quickly in both urban and remote locations near the factories and military installations. Overseen by federal agencies like the NHA, these communities were much more regulated and civic minded than the camps of the 1920s and 1930s and included schools, playgrounds, and other amenities for the workers who brought their families. When the war ended, this temporary solution would become a permanent housing solution for many returning war veterans and lower-income Americans.

The Servicemen's Readjustment Act of 1944 (known as the "GI Bill of Rights") provided World War II veterans with financial aid for housing and education. Many veterans and their new families moved into trailers or mobile homes purchased from the federal government by private owners or college campuses. These communities of trailers, usually arranged in U-shaped patterns, were erected on parceled land set aside for trailer parks to provide temporary housing for the masses of veterans and their families. They included suburban amenities like playgrounds, a recreation house, and the ubiquitous shuffleboard court. Considered by the majority of the residents as a temporary fix while the nation weathered material and housing shortages, trailer parks became the only permanent housing option for many lower-middle-class Americans at mid-century. As the reality of permanence set in, the public perception of trailer parks and mobile home camps changed from viewing these residential areas as a necessary evil to a blight of suburbia.

Mobile Homes as Permanent Housing

Two types of mobile home parks emerged in America at mid-century: the semipermanent residence-oriented park and the service-oriented park. The latter, created specifically for retirees, consisted of planned, luxurious, year-round, permanent resortlike communities established in warmer climes of the southern and western United States.

Conversely, the residence-oriented park was meant to house predominantly young families who were on their way to traditional suburban home ownership. When the temporary solution to the housing shortage became a real permanent solution for many families, the outlook for residents and for suburban outsiders changed for the worse.

Most residence-oriented parks were zoned and built on cheaper, less attractive industrial and commercial land, due to the fact that a trailer is technically a vehicle and not a residence. Many profiteering trailer park owners discriminated against racial and ethnic minorities, and thus the demographic of the postwar American trailer camps consisted of blue collar and lower-middle-class, white families. Without any federal or local regulation, land owners were free to impose an inordinate number of rules controlling anything from the allowance of pets, visitors, and even children, to landscaping and rent. Postwar American culture idealized home ownership as neat little houses in pristine, spacious, and racially white suburbs. In turn, trailer parks became reminders of decades of war and financial devastation; they were perceived as drains on public services like schools and hospitals and were viewed as the result of failure to attain the American Dream. By posing a threat and possibly debasing the sheen of true domestic suburban bliss held dear in the American subconscious, fantastic descriptions of trailer parks as lawless dens of iniquity filled with deviants with loose morals, via B movies and pulp novels, helped cement the stigma for trailer parks in American culture. Not surprisingly, few suburban neighborhoods wanted trailer parks in their vicinities.

Mobile Home Design

Through the 1960s and 1970s, residents of trailer parks attempted to emulate suburban dwellings in their 10-, 14-, and 16-foot-wide structures by adding awnings, outdoor extensions, lawn furniture, and landscaping to their lots. Typical trailer homes were either shiny metal or corrugated aluminum rectangular structures with rounded edges (remnants from the 1950s) or newer, larger rectangular homes with vinyl siding. Photographs and trailer park memoirs describe tiny lawns and concrete patios adorned with pink flamingoes, potted plants, and rusted metal lawn furniture. Though larger and with modern full-sized amenities, the newer trailer home could not escape its forced interior design. Most of the furniture was built in and stationary, giving every trailer a similar appearance and interior layout. Typically the only door entered into a small living room/dining room with adjoining kitchen. Each bedroom followed progressively back, providing entrance to the next bedroom. Most bedrooms could only fit a medium-sized bed or bunk beds. The inclusion of an indoor bathroom sealed the fate for the function of the trailer from occasional to residential use. Even construction and design advancements could not improve on the inherent lack of space and privacy, both commodities increasingly important in permanent suburban American homes.

Through the 1980s, many owners of manufactured trailer homes became trapped by the financial constraints of ownership without the benefits of appreciation and return on their investment, watching as the value of their homes depreciated and the rent for lots increased. Manufacturers building larger units to accommodate more permanent living, and residents, struggling to overcome the persistent derelict stigma of "trailer trash," intentionally adopted the terminology used to describe the parks: from *trailer* to *mobile home* to *manufactured home parks*. Yet trailer parks continue to provide the best alternative to

This 1956 photograph captures a family relaxing under the awning of their mobile home in a Miami, Florida, trailer park. Trailer parks in the postwar United States catered to vacationers but also provided permanent housing. (Bettmann/Corbis)

homelessness while manufacturers of mobile homes continue to improve and nearly mimic the structure of a traditional permanent residence.

Victoria Estrada-Berg

See also Automobile Camping (Auto-Camping); House, Home, and Domesticity; Planned Communities; Poverty; Social Class and Social Status; Tourism and Travel

References and Further Reading
Hurley, Andrew. 2001. *Diners, Bowling Alleys, and Trailer Parks: Chasing the American Dream in Postwar Consumer Culture.* New York: Basic Books.

Robinson, Newcomb. 1971. *Mobile Home Parks. Part 1: An Analysis of Characteristics.* Washington, DC: Urban Land Institute.
Wehrly, Max S. 1972. *Mobile Home Parks. Part 2: An Analysis of Communities.* Washington, DC: Urban Land Institute.
Wray, Matt, and Annalee Newitz, eds. 1997. *White Trash: Race and Class in America.* New York: Routledge.

Modernism (Art Moderne)

Modernism defines a self-conscious movement that affected art, design, literature, and the way Americans lived and thought in the years between the world wars. Art Moderne expressed the nation's economic exuberance, the rise of consumption, and the belief in progress as symbolized in the central icon of Modernism in the 1920s: the machine.

The successful and influential 1925 Paris Exposition des Arts Décoratifs et Industriel Modernes is often cited as the catalyst for this style. The exposition's organizers stipulated that no works reproducing or imitating historical styles would be accepted. Though Secretary of Commerce Herbert C. Hoover (1874–1964) declined the fair organizers' invitation, he did send a delegation to consider the exposition's emphasis for the nation's industries. The delegation saw luxurious, handcrafted products of the French Art Deco style and the geometric, socially conscious wares of the German Bauhaus (1919–1933) streamlined style.

Industrial designers in the United States quickly adopted these styles but throughout the 1930s developed a characteristic design aesthetic based on machine production. American Modernism stressed utility and abstraction over applied ornament; underused materials such as celluloid, linoleum, steel, and aluminum; new materials such as Bakelite, Formica, and Lucite; and new technologies of mass manufacture. New colors, such as cobalt blue and tangerine orange (which along with white would become the official colors of the 1939 New York World's Fair), enlivened design from housewares to textiles to wall coverings. Commercial viability marked the success of Modernist-designed goods sold from "five and dime" stores such as Woolworth's to luxury department stores such as Wanamaker's and Macy's and displayed in New York museums such as the Museum of Modern Art's 1934 Machine Art Exposition.

Industrial designers embraced the new aesthetic. Throughout the 1930s and 1940s, designers such as Raymond Loewy (1893–1986), Norman Bel Geddes (1893–1958), Russel Wright (1905–1976), and Walter Dorwin Teague (1883–1960) were actively working within the new style, embracing what was considered uniquely American forms such as the skyscraper, with its steel-framed form, soaring height, and step-back design that married form, function, and future.

Art Moderne incorporated, as designer Paul Frankl (1886–1958) noted, "(1) simplicity; (2) plain surfaces; (3) unbroken lines; (4) accentuation of structural necessity; (5) dramatization of the intrinsic beauty of materials; (6) the elimination of the meaningless and distracting motives of the Past" (Johnson 2000, 28). Drama could be found in speed; American designers "streamlined" a variety of motorized vehicles, including airplanes, locomotives, and ocean liners. This aerodynamic aesthetic was carried over to household appliances, even if they were stationary, influencing the design of radios, toasters, and fans.

American consumers hesitated in adopting the style of the machine age throughout their houses. On one hand, the American middle class embraced Art Moderne in the material culture of the apartment, the office, the nightclub, the kitchen, and the bath. Tablewares, such as the Fiesta line by The Homer Laughlin China Company, appealed through bold colors and simple lines that could be incorporated inexpensively into a household's existing collection. On the other hand, the typical American did not easily adapt the Art Moderne style into his or her living room, dining room, or bedroom, preferring instead Colonial Revival forms to remind them of comfort rather than utility and modern technology. Yet fantasy had

Early twentieth-century Modernism celebrated the machine, speed, and motion. Industrial designer Raymond Loewy poses next to the prototype of the streamlined S-1 locomotive, created for the Pennsylvania Railroad and on display in this photograph in Wilmington, Delaware, in 1937. (Library of Congress)

its role in Americans' sense of urbanity, progress, and the future. Hollywood filmmakers during the 1930s beguiled audiences with the fantastic alliance of Art Moderne with high living. For example, the set of Fred Astaire's (1899–1987) performance, "Slap That Bass" in the film *Shall We Dance* (1937), was a spotless, white, streamlined boiler room in an ocean liner. "The World of Tomorrow," celebrated at the 1939 World's Fair in New York City, was also a venue in which progress, the future, and Modernist design were celebrated.

Shirley Teresa Wajda

See also Art Deco; Decorative Arts; Design History and American Design; Industrial Design; Style; Technology

References and Further Reading

Cogdell, Christina. 2004. *Eugenic Design: Stream-lining America in the 1930s*. Philadelphia: University of Pennsylvania Press.
Johnson, J. Stewart. 2000. *American Modern, 1925–1940: Design for a New Age*. New York: Harry N. Abrams, with the American Federation of Arts.
Wilson, Kristina. 2004. *Livable Modernism: Interior Decorating and Design During the Great Depression*. New Haven, CT: Yale University Press.

Money, Currency, and Value

Money is defined as a store or symbol of value, as a medium of exchange as currency, or as a shorthand sign of the meaning of differences between goods and people. Throughout American history, the idea that money must have "intrinsic value" contested a notion of money as a pure social construction, merely a convenient symbol. Arguments for defining money as specie—gold or silver—insisted that no one could measure value without something that itself had value. Arguments for paper money countered that money was purely a social convenience—anything at all could be money if we all agreed to use it. The history of money in the United States reflects this tension between money as a real object with physical value and money as a pure symbol with an agreed value.

Colonial-Era Experiments

If the first European colonists had found gold in North America events might have turned out very differently. The original colonists claimed to have no money with which to conduct commerce. English merchants demanded payment in specie when they could get it, and the Crown insisted on gold for payments of taxes, duties, and tariffs. North American colonists, when they got gold or silver, typically did not have it for very long—it flew from their hands, they claimed, into ships headed for England to pay for necessary and luxury goods or the British Crown's taxes. Lacking real money, the colonists resorted to elaborate webs of credit. Yet they needed some convenient form of exchange.

Massachusetts settlers seized upon wampum as a form of currency. In 1637 the small clamshell beads used by the Native Americans were made legal tender for small transactions. In turn, the Native Americans began producing more wampum; so did the white settlers. Soon counterfeit wampum made its appearance, and wampum became nearly useless.

By then New England colonists had tried other forms of money, first establishing a mint in 1652 to make "pine tree shillings." The British Crown outlawed the coins in 1665. In 1690, Massachusetts began its first large experiments with paper money. Other colonies experimented as well: Virginia and Maryland issued "tobacco notes," paper bills that represented bales of tobacco. By 1755, each colony had printed paper money of various kinds, in various amounts.

In some cases these paper money issues took the form of payment to troops and suppliers, which circulated as legal tender for all public transactions (mostly taxes) for a limited term. Sometimes paper money issues took the form of interest-bearing notes. Other paper issues involved "loan offices," through which colonial governments would loan paper to men who pledged their land as security. Many kinds of paper money might circulate at the same time.

Perhaps the most radical idea was advanced by Benjamin Franklin (1706–1790) in 1729. Franklin suggested that Pennsylvania print legal tender money as it was needed, using its citizens' labor—measured by Pennsylvania's "gross colonial product"—as an index. Although some elites had misgivings about such a radical form of paper money, in general "paper currency was widely supported—by merchants as well as farmers—as a legitimate feature of the financial system" (Krooss 1983, 27). Alexander Hamilton (1757–1804) estimated that at the time of the Revolution paper made up 75 percent of the money in circulation.

Paper Money Debates in the Revolutionary Era and the Early Nation

The American Revolution shook elite confidence in paper money. Unwilling to levy taxes, the Continental Congress issued "continental dollars," which the law compelled citizens to accept. Continental dollars almost immediately began inflating, sharply undermined by British counterfeiting. By 1782 they were nearly worthless ("not worth a continental"). The experience of hyperinflation produced a new orthodoxy of fierce resistance to paper money.

Reflecting the nervousness of the founding generation's elites, the new Constitution seemingly forbade the issue of paper money, insisting that no state can "coin money; emit bills of credit [or] make anything but gold and silver coin a tender in payment of debts." It allowed Congress to "coin money" but said nothing about paper. These phrases together would seem to make paper money unconstitutional, a fact modern libertarian economists have seized on.

Americans brazenly ignored the clauses forbidding paper money over the next fifty years. Hamilton, as secretary of the treasury the primary architect of the new nation's financial system, designed a system in which a central bank, holding federal gold deposits, issued paper notes that served as the nation's money. This First Bank of the United States, chartered in 1791, was abolished in 1811 as an elitist and "English" influence. In the intervening years, private banking exploded: Five banks existed in the nation in 1791; by 1830 there were thousands.

The Age of Jackson and the Bank of the United States

Banks were closely associated with rapid rise and fall of economic fortunes, with shady enterprise, and with confidence men. The Second Bank of the United States (BUS), founded in 1816, aimed to balance fiscal conservatives who wanted gold alone, or gold-backed paper, against entrepreneurs who wanted a loose money supply and easy credit.

The BUS, a public/private hybrid, presided over an astonishing chaos of competing money forms.

Before the Civil War (1861–1865), local and state banks could—and did—issue their own paper money, backed by whatever assets they could accumulate. The money worked perfectly well if they could persuade people to accept it. Thousands of different kinds of paper money circulated along with coins of various values and the gold-backed notes of the BUS.

The BUS, according to its defenders, served as an agent of restraint, preventing overeager local banks from issuing too much paper money and providing a stable currency against which other monies could be measured. It could loan money to struggling enterprises or destroy shoddy institutions. Nicholas Biddle (1786–1844), director of the BUS, characterized the bank as a judicious check on overly enthusiastic speculators. Jacksonians denounced the BUS as an elite institution that stifled enterprise but also as, improbably, the source of corrupting paper. When he vetoed the recharter of the BUS in 1832, President Andrew Jackson (1767–1845) argued that he had freed the citizenry from oppression and that a gold standard would restore natural hierarchies.

The extraordinary "free banking" or "wildcat" era followed. Although officially a specie standard alone prevailed, between 1837 and the Civil War, as many as 8,000 different kinds of paper money circulated. The banks that issued these notes ranged from legitimate businesses to what were dubbed "wildcat" banks. Paper money issued by a well-established bank circulated at face value. A paper dollar from a "wildcat" bank bought perhaps fifty cents' worth of goods, perhaps less. Nearly every transaction involved not just questions of price but a calculation of how much the money involved might actually be worth.

In this climate, counterfeiting flourished. According to some estimates, at times more than 40 percent of the money in circulation was counterfeit. Businessmen sometimes even preferred a good counterfeit of a sound bank's bills to a genuine note from a shaky bank. In every substantial town, "note shavers" offered to exchange the traveler's out-of-town notes for local notes—at a discount. Merchants used "counterfeit detectors" to order the chaos. These monthly or biweekly periodicals contained lists of banks, descriptions of banknotes and the illustrations they bore, and a rating of the issuing bank.

The Civil War Era and "Greenbacks"

The Civil War put an end to this monetary chaos. Facing public resistance to taxes, the Union in 1862 authorized the Treasury to print and release "legal tender" paper money. The Confederacy undertook similar, less successful steps. By 1865, $450 million worth of "greenbacks" circulated throughout the North. The National Banking Act (1863) also instituted a tax on state bank issues that effectively made them unprofitable. For the first time in its history, the United States had a money supply almost entirely under the control of the federal government.

Many saw greenbacks as part of the North's wartime prosperity. More conservative (and wealthy) citizens blamed greenbacks for creating false fortunes, false values, and moral corruption. They insisted the greenbacks be "contracted," or removed from circulation, and replaced by a gold standard. Such "gold-bugs" linked paper money to political corruption in both the North and the South. Their most extreme opponents insisted that money was merely a social convenience; they formed the Greenback Labor Party in 1875.

The Gilded Age and the Silver Debate

Although businessmen increasingly used checks, paper notes, and other flexible paper instruments, the debate over gold intensified. As the use of gold or silver diminished in daily transactions, its symbolic significance increased. The greenback position lost strength in the 1870s: It offered none of the "natural" or "intrinsic" certainties gold fetishism provided, especially in wake of the Panic of 1873, which severely depressed the economy. In 1873 Congress "demonetized" the silver dollar; in 1875 the Resumption Act committed the government to redeem greenbacks for gold.

The silver movement, pushed by western mining interests, complicated the debate. Greenbackers had always favored inflation and low interest rates. "Silverites" promised that using a "bimetallic," silver *and* gold money supply would lower rates while also offering a stable basis for currency. By using the same sort of fetishized rhetoric as the gold bugs, and adding doses of conspiracy theorizing about the "Crime of '73," silverites pushed through a series of acts designed to create a metallic standard.

In the 1890s the money debate climaxed. The Populist Party, initially following the Greenback premise of legal tender paper money, entered into a merger with the freesilver Democrats, led by William Jennings Bryan (1860–1925). Gold bug Republicans marshaled their superior resources to defeat Bryan in 1896, in "the battle of the standards." Both gold and silver factions used language freighted with racial stereotyping and fantasy; again, the debate grew highly symbolic as commerce moved toward more abstract forms of money. For example, money's ambiguity forms a central theme in the work of the illusionistic painters William Michael Harnett (1848–1892), John Haberle (1856–1933), and John Frederick Peto (1854–

1907), all of whom flourished in the period. Their eye-fooling work asked the public to consider the difference between representation and reality in value. Aiming to end this ambiguity, the Gold Standard Act of 1900 formalized the nation's commitment to a gold-backed money supply.

Twentieth-Century Debates

A fond notion of social Darwinism, the self-regulating gold standard never appealed to big business, which wanted freedom from seasonal fluctuations in credit and greater stability. Pressure for a loose money supply and easy credit continued, driven by an entrepreneurial mentality. In 1913 Congress created yet another hybrid public/private institution, the Federal Reserve System. Like the BUS, the "Fed" held federal gold deposits and issued currency that became the money of the United States. It also enjoyed significant influence over interest rates. Backers emphasized the alleged judiciousness of the central bankers who made up its governing board.

Insulated from political pressures other than Wall Street's, the Fed sought the stable prices and low inflation that creditors loved. It oversaw a money supply that, although officially backed by gold, in fact looked much like the paper money Franklin had proposed in 1729. This money's stability depended partly on the Fed's curtain of secrecy and partly on the zeal of the Secret Service, which increasingly forbade representations of American money, however trivial or "artistic."

Congress passed the Gold Reserve Act (1934), which effectively ended the domestic gold standard and gave then-President Franklin Delano Roosevelt (1882–1945) the ability to control the amount of money in circulation. He also embarked on a gold-buying spree, giving the United States, by the end of World War II, the world's largest gold stock and placing it in a position of economic dominance in international exchange, where the gold standard still prevailed. The international gold standard remained in effect until 1971, when President Richard Nixon (1913–1994) enacted a law mandating that the dollar would no longer be pegged to gold—it would now "float" against other world currencies. In the 1990s, the United States government began redesigning American currency, hoping to combat massive counterfeiting after the dollar emerged as the world's de facto standard.

Michael O'Malley

See also Auctions; Commodity; Fakes

References and Further Reading
Friedman, Milton, and Anna Schwartz. 1963. *A Monetary History of the United States, 1867–1960*. Princeton, NJ: Princeton University Press.
Galbraith, John Kenneth. 1975. *Money: Whence It Came, Where It Went*. Boston: Houghton Mifflin.
Hammond, Bray. 1991 (1957). *Banks and Politics in America from the Revolution to the Civil War*. Princeton, NJ: Princeton University Press.
Krooss, Herman E., ed. 1983. *Documentary History of Banking and Currency in the United States*. 4 vols. New York: Chelsea House.
Livingston, James. 1989. *Origins of the Federal Reserve System: Money, Class, and Corporate Capitalism 1890–1913*. Ithaca, NY: Cornell University Press.
Nugent, Walter T. K. 1968. *Money and American Society, 1865–1880*. New York: Free Press.
O'Malley, Michael. 1994. "Specie and Species: The Money Question in 19th Century America." *American Historical Review* 99 (2): 369–395.
Ritter, Gretchen. 1997. *Goldbugs and Greenbacks: The Antimonopoly Tradition and the Politics of Finance in America*. New York: Cambridge University Press.
Timberlake, Richard H. 1993. *Monetary Policy in the United States: An Intellectual and Institutional History*. Chicago: University of Chicago Press.

Unger, Irwin. 1964. *The Greenback Era: A Social and Political History of American Finance, 1865–1879.* Princeton, NJ: Princeton University Press.

Wiess, Roger W. 1970. "The Issue of Paper Money in the American Colonies, 1720–1774." *Journal of Economic History* 30 (4): 770–784.

Mourning

Mourning is a term that describes two related concepts: first, feeling grief over someone's death, and second, the culturally appropriate or expected behaviors and rituals in which the bereaved participate. These behaviors can vary significantly between ethnic groups, religions, and geographic areas and have also been influenced over time by changes in societal attitudes toward death. Anglo-American mourning practices have influenced greatly the American way of death and bereavement.

Colonial American Practices

The death of anyone in the small, close-knit Puritan communities that largely made up the colonies in seventeenth-century New England was an occasion for public mourning and sorrow. In the seventeenth century, mourners simply gathered at the grave site and attended the burial. Eighteenth-century generations of English and European settlers developed more elaborate forms of mourning. Tokens were sometimes offered to mourners: gloves inscribed with the name of the deceased, scarves, mourning ribbons, or mourning rings, for example. Such rings were often gold, sometimes combined with enamel or paste gem decoration or the hair of the deceased, and were always inscribed with the name and death date of the deceased. Motifs on these rings reflect the gravestone motifs of the period such as

death's heads, hourglasses, skeletons, and coffin shapes.

Nineteenth-Century Mourning Rituals

The death in 1799 of George Washington was the first to generate widespread public mourning in the new nation. For years after Washington's death, artifacts commercially produced to commemorate Washington included lithographs, handkerchiefs, and transferware ceramic patterns showing images of mourners at Washington's grave site. Among the earliest and most decorative of the artifacts associated with the new, sentimentalized expression of mourning were mourning pictures made by young American schoolgirls. From the late eighteenth century through the mid-nineteenth century, young daughters of well-to-do families learned to embroider elaborate mourning scenes in silk thread on linen or to paint such scenes with watercolors on silk. The most popular image was one in which mourners bent over with obvious sorrow and weeping next to a monument consisting of an urn on a pedestal (a classical Greek reference to the funerary urn holding the ashes) under a large weeping willow. This motif appeared over and over in paintings, engravings, lithographs, and needlework; it was printed on cotton and porcelain and was engraved or etched on jewelry. The mourning scene of the weeping willow and urn was also a popular gravestone design in the early nineteenth century.

Cultural and religious attitudes toward death shifted over the course of the nineteenth century, from an emphasis on eternal doom to one of spiritual uplift. A new interest in Romanticism helped to soften the often harsh realities of an increasingly urbanizing, stressful society, and so sentimentalized death. This was exemplified by the popularity of the rural cemetery movement, in which pic-

This scene with a female mourner standing sorrowfully next to a looming grave marker under weeping willows was a common subject for needlework pictures in the early 1800s. Needlework memorial by Margaret Tisdale, 1804. From the collection of Robert M. Light. (Burstein Collection/Corbis)

turesque parklike landscapes appropriate for melancholy reflection replaced the previously stark and barren Puritan graveyards. Similarly, funerary monuments demonstrated a much greater range of expression of motifs, in materials such as white marble rather than the earlier dark gray slate. A new emphasis on domesticity, family life, and heaven as a place where family and friends would be reunited forever became comforting concepts. The example of Queen Victoria (1819–1901) of England was also influential. Upon the death of her husband, Prince Albert

(1819–1861), the queen embarked on a prolonged period of private mourning that lasted until her own death in 1901.

Many of the mourning practices and behaviors of the nineteenth century were centered on women, who were considered the moral arbiters of society. Widows in particular were expected to adhere to a rigid series of stages of mourning in their dress, behavior, and interactions with the outside world for up to several years. The earliest stage of mourning was referred to as *full* or *deep*, with successive stages termed *second* or *half*, and lastly, *light* mourning. Color was the primary indicator of the degree of mourning. During the full mourning period, a mourner customarily wore either all black or, occasionally, all white. Widows in deep mourning wore black veils to hide their faces. Men were also expected to wear dark clothes, but for shorter periods. Later periods of mourning allowed for a gradual return to color, first gray, then in the last stages of mourning, purple or violet.

Accessories such as gloves, hats, fans, and handkerchiefs also conformed to these colors. Specialized stores and the relatively new institution known as the department store were important purveyors of mourning goods, including the black-bordered stationery (with different-sized borders, depending on the mourning stage) used by widows for correspondence during their mourning period. Such stores also sold clothes and accessories to outfit the entire family in mourning, and for the funeral. Crepe, a type of fabric, was especially associated with the mourning costume, and with the material used to drape front doors or buildings to signify public or national mourning, such as the period following the assassination of President Abraham Lincoln (1809–1865).

Technological developments spurred the growth of another mourning-related industry, the postmortem photograph. After the introduction of daguerreotypy in 1839, photography establishments flourished in many towns and cities across the United States. One very specific service of the photographer was to visit the home of the bereaved to take a photograph of the deceased, either posed in some way to appear alive but sleeping (or if an infant, in the mother's arms) or lying in the casket, whether displayed in the home, or by the early twentieth century, in the funeral parlor. A postmortem photograph allowed a mourner to retain at least a visual representation of the deceased long after the death.

Other types of mourning artifacts were of a more ephemeral nature—that is, they were not necessarily meant to be useful beyond the period of mourning, although these objects did survive, saved by family members and friends. Such artifacts include the memorial cards that were handed out to mourners at the funeral service. These cards, usually black (or white for children and occasionally women) with gilt edging and gold print, were printed in multiples and contained the name of the deceased, birth and death dates, and usually a standard prayer. Some artifacts were widely disseminated in much greater numbers during the mourning of a national figure, for example black-edged ribbons after the assassination of President Lincoln or memorial cards for President James Garfield (1831–1881) upon his death.

Twentieth-Century and Contemporary Mass Mourning Practices

Despite differences among ethnicities and religions, the most basic functions of mourning —expressing loss or grief and remembering the deceased—remain essentially unchanged in the United States. It is still customary, though no longer rigidly prescribed, to wear dark or somber colors, particularly at the funeral. Other expressions of grief are generally at the discretion of the bereaved. One may withdraw from social activities or work for a time; another may not make any noticeable changes in his or her routine. The postmortem photograph still exists, primarily in the forms of private snapshots or of a pediatric specialty service offered to parents of stillborn or newly deceased infants. This service, like its nineteenth-century predecessor, offers the bereaved parents and other family members and friends at least one tangible vestige of the now-departed physical presence of the baby.

Mourning can take place on a national and even global scale with the use of technology. With the advent of radio, television, and more recently the Internet, news of the death of a celebrity or political or public figure spreads quickly and has a far wider impact than previously. One of the earliest deaths to generate mourning on a widespread, global scale was the assassination of President John F. Kennedy in 1963. The state funeral was broadcast around the world. Black-bordered memorial cards with a photograph of the fallen president followed traditional formats and were commercially produced. The Vietnam Veterans' Memorial in Washington, erected in 1982 and intended for sober reflection, provoked an unanticipated mourning response for its creators— the leaving of tokens, offerings, letters, and reminiscences, sometimes by friends and comrades, but just as often by strangers with no relation to the deceased soldiers whose names are etched in the black granite. (The National Park Service collects these mementoes every day and stores them for posterity.)

In recent decades, the tragic deaths of John Lennon (1940–1980) and President Kennedy's son John F. Kennedy, Jr., (1960–1999) inspired in each case gatherings of strangers united in grief and the offering of gifts, flowers, lighted candles, and written messages at meaningful locations—in Lennon's case, at Central Park's "Strawberry Fields," dedicated by New York City in his memory, and in John F. Kennedy, Jr.'s case, both at his New York apartment building and at his father's birthplace in Brookline, Massachusetts, a National Park Service museum.

Other mourning rituals emerge locally and spontaneously out of grassroots efforts. A particular example is the homemade creation of roadside memorials to mourn and honor the victims of violent deaths, particularly in car accidents. Automobiles sometimes provide the means to express grief and mourning, as when the windshield becomes an abbreviated (name and dates) mobile

obituary to a deceased friend or family member. Events such as the destruction of the World Trade Center's Twin Towers by terrorists on September 11, 2001, have also had a widespread impact on spontaneous as well as formal mourning practices.

Elise Madeleine Ciregna

See also Burial Grounds, Cemeteries, and Grave Markers; Dress, Accessories, and Fashion; Etiquette and Manners; Funerals; Funerary (Sepulchral) Monuments; Mourning and Ethnicity; Rite, Ritual, and Ceremony

References and Further Reading
Farrell, James J. 1980. *Inventing the American Way of Death, 1830–1920*. Philadelphia, PA: Temple University Press.
Kastenbaum, Robert J. 1991. *Death, Society, and Human Experience*, 4th ed. New York: Macmillan.
Pike, Martha V., and Janice Gray Armstrong. 1980. *A Time to Mourn: Expressions of Grief in Nineteenth Century America*. Stony Brook, NY: Museums at Stony Brook.
Santino, Jack, ed. 2006. *Spontaneous Shrines and the Public Memorialization of Death*. New York: Palgrave MacMillan.
Stannard, David E., ed. 1975. *Death in America*. Philadelphia: University of Pennsylvania Press.

Mourning and Ethnicity

Grief following loss is a universal human emotion. *Mourning*, however, is a culturally specific process of mediating grief through prescribed ritual, time, and/or costume. Mourning practices in the United States have varied tremendously and historically were important markers of ethnic identity. A careful examination of mourning artifacts can tell us much about social organization.

Native American Practices
The written accounts of European colonists who came in contact with Native Americans,

the findings of archaeologists, and Native American oral history traditions establish that all North American tribal people believed in an afterlife, despite differences in their funerary and mourning practices. Articles intended for use in the afterlife such as beads, iron objects, and ceramics have been found in seventeenth-century native graves in New England. As contact with Europeans increased, more European goods were found at Indian grave sites, a practice known as *syncretism*.

African American Practices

This process of syncretism also can be seen in African American mourning. Slaves brought a strong belief in the importance of mortuary practice from Africa. Elaborate funerals that were expensive and prolonged and that involved the burial of personal objects with the deceased played a prominent role in African cultures. Historians see unmistakable links between African and enslaved African practices. John Blassingame (1982, 37) cites a Georgia plantation mistress writing in the 1850s: "Negro graves were always decorated with the last article used by the departed, and broken pitchers and broken bits of colored glass were considered even more appropriate than the white shells from the beach nearby. Sometimes African Americans laid carved wooden figures or a patchwork quilt upon the grave." Slave funerals were usually held at night or before dawn both for the practical reason that slaves worked during the day and because it was believed by some that it was easier to communicate with spirits after dark. Night funerals made it possible for slaves from elsewhere in the neighborhood to come to the funeral and socialize afterward. Artifacts found at eighteenth-century slave grave sites also point to links between African and New World practices. Archaeologists have found broken bottles and jars,

often white in color, on slave graves and have argued this is an expression of the African belief that the dead are living beneath water. The most notable confluence of the slave experience and Western Christianity are spirituals, hymns through which slaves expressed their belief that they were the Bible's chosen people who would be reunited with their Savior on "the other side."

Many Cultures, Many Practices

Despite the hegemony of mourning objects and funerary practices associated with white Protestantism, distinct ethnic mourning arrived in the United States along with immigrants from Mexico, Europe, and Asia. Mexicans, concentrated largely in the Southwest, commemorate the dead through the folk culture of All Souls' Day or the Day of the Dead. Special foods are prepared such as *calabaza en tacha*, a sweetened, spicy pumpkin dish, and *pan de muerto*, a wheat bread decorated with stylized bones and tears. A popular sweet is *calaveras de azúcar*, or sugar skulls. Food is served in special black bowls and dishes. Family altars with photographs of the deceased and decorated with flowers remain in the home after All Souls' Day.

Most ethnic groups retain modified mourning practices taken from the nation of origin. Eastern European Jews, for example, traditionally rent their clothing as a gesture of mourning in the Old World. In the United States, they often pin small torn black ribbons on their clothing at a funeral or while sitting *shiva*, the prescribed seven-day mourning period. Hmong funerals are held in the afternoon, as was the tradition in Laos. Many ethnic groups struggle to reconcile traditions with American practice. For example, the Hmong are greatly distressed by autopsies, due to specific beliefs about mutilation and rebirth. Islamic tradition is that the body of the deceased must be positioned to face

Mecca, a dictum difficult to adhere to in American hospitals.

Ann Schofield

See also African America; Burial Grounds, Cemeteries, and Grave Markers; Etiquette and Manners; Funerals; Funerary (Sepulchral) Monuments; Mourning; Rite, Ritual, and Ceremony

References and Further Reading

Blassingame, John. 1982. *The Slave Community: Plantation Life in the Antebellum South.* New York: Oxford University Press.

Deetz, James. 1977. *In Small Things Forgotten: The Archaeology of Early America.* Garden City, NY: Anchor Press/Doubleday.

Hunter, Phyllis Whitman. 2001. *Purchasing Identity in the Atlantic World: Massachusetts Merchants, 1670–1780.* Ithaca, NY: Cornell University Press.

Irish, Donald P., Kathleen F. Lundquist, and Vivian Jenkins Nelsen. 1993. *Ethnic Variations in Dying, Death, and Grief: Diversity in Universality.* Washington, DC: Taylor & Francis.

Museums and Museum Practice

Museums are institutions that collect, conserve, display, and interpret objects to the public for noncommercial, educational purposes. Although some collections include art, natural history, material culture, and technology under one roof, most museums of average size focus on a specific subject area. History museums, historic houses and sites, and living history museums are among the most dedicated to collecting and interpreting material culture.

In the United States, the size of museums and their staffs vary greatly from large institutions with rosters of specialized museum professionals and scholars to small local history museums managed by one or two full-time staff and a dedicated group of volunteers. Most average-sized museum staffs include an executive director, a marketing director, an educator, a curator, a volunteer coordinator, and a museum store manager; some staff members regularly function in multiple roles. The practices of specific museums are inevitably shaped by the combination of talents and expertise present at any given time.

Museum practice as it relates to material culture focuses on the institution's collection. The curator oversees the acquisition of new objects and manages the care of those already accepted into the collection. Many museums have written collections policies to guide the scope of the collection; a historic house museum may decide to acquire or accept donations of objects only of a specific time period or with connections to certain individuals. Each object is accessioned into the collection, a process that allows its presence and status to be easily catalogued and managed. Larger institutions often have specialized registrars who oversee incoming and outgoing loans and conservators to address damage and restoration of objects. The curator (or curatorial department) also conducts historical research on the object and its context and organizes exhibitions. Resulting exhibitions, historic site restorations, and interpretive programs are complex constructions that reflect the theories and practices of the periods during which they were installed.

Visitors are attracted to museums to see "real things," authentic pieces of the past; display of collections is a critical museum practice. These institutions historically privilege the ability of material culture to "speak for itself" as a witness to or an agent in history. Through exhibitions, curators create relationships between objects that reflect a point of view, even if this message is not explicitly stated. For example, Charles Willson Peale (1741–1827), who opened the first American museum in 1786, organized his natural history collection to illustrate the Enlightenment philosophy of the "Great Chain of Being." The creators of many early exhibitions had high goals: civilizing the population, teaching it appreciation for artistic quality, and reinforcing patriotism and the values of simplicity and individualism.

The Period Room

The period room emerged as a popular way to display material culture in early twentieth-century art museums. These exhibitions attempted to re-create the domestic context of furnishings and decorative objects, either through combining objects and architectural pieces from a general period or by installing the contents of a room from a specific house inside a museum gallery. These displays emphasized the artistic qualities and craftsmanship of artifacts rather than their uses or historical significance. In 1924, the Metropolitan Museum of Art in New York City opened its American Wing, a series of sixteen rooms arranged chronologically from the seventeenth to early nineteenth centuries, which highlighted the finest American furnishings and decorative arts. Collector Henry Francis du Pont (1880–1969) chose the period room to exhibit his extensive collection of early American decorative arts at Winterthur, his country estate in Delaware. This collection became significant as a teaching tool, particularly in one of the first academic programs in material culture/museum studies.

Period rooms tended to feature material culture of the highest aesthetic standards and were not representative of the American citizenry as a whole. By the 1920s and 1930s, collectors became increasingly interested in "Americana" and objects of everyday life, which they recognized as the historical record of people who had not left documents behind. Automaker Henry Ford (1863–1947) took a strong interest in the objects and struc-

tures of "ordinary people," believing that objects offered the purest approach to teaching history. Ford's Greenfield Village (in Dearborn, Michigan), which opened to the public in 1932, celebrated the seemingly simple folk and rural life of the preindustrial era while simultaneously paying homage to technical progress.

Interpretive Exhibitions and Controversy

In 1958, the Farmers' Museum in Cooperstown, New York, opened "The Farmer's Year," a thematic exhibition that pioneered and popularized the practice of removing artifacts from rows of glass display cases and arranging them according to a narrative. Interpretive exhibitions provide historical context for material culture and a more analytical approach to the subject matter. Organization of these exhibitions is typically thematic.

Interpretive exhibitions continued to develop in the wake of the civil rights and feminist movements of the late 1960s and early 1970s. In the academic community, historians began to study history "from the bottom up" by concentrating on the stories of women, people of color, and the working class. This approach took root in museum practice when the saturated academic job market of the mid-1970s sent many individuals with new Ph.D.s looking for jobs in public history. A boom in museum growth, encouraged by the nation's bicentennial patriotism, provided them. As professional historians, some of the first to be influenced by the "New Social History," took the helm at history museums and historic sites, they expanded museum collections to include the material culture of previously underrepresented populations and held exhibition content to higher standards of academic rigor and accuracy.

In the 1980s and 1990s, the Smithsonian Institution's National Museum of American History mounted some of the most influential interpretive exhibitions based on social history. "Field to Factory: Afro-American Migration, 1915–1940" (1987) traced the experiences of African Americans who moved north by combining evocative artifacts with the stories of migrants. "A More Perfect Union: Japanese Americans and the U.S. Constitution" (1987) commemorated the Constitution's bicentennial through the history of Japanese internment camps during World War II (1939–1945). The acquisition of objects from a sweatshop raid in El Monte, California, prompted installation of "Between a Rock and a Hard Place: A History of American Sweatshops, 1820–Present" (1998). "Within These Walls" (2001) was created to tell the stories of the museum's largest artifact, a house from Ipswitch, Massachusetts, that had witnessed 200 years of history. While the Smithsonian's extensive collection of material culture was the centerpiece of these exhibitions, they were also strongly driven by specific themes and narratives.

Interpretive exhibitions have emerged as significant ways to interpret the lives of women, people of color, and the working class, whose stories and material culture had long been neglected by history museums. Creating these exhibitions motivated curators to interact with previously underrepresented groups and encouraged the involvement of new stakeholders. By providing additional context through interpretive labels, curators became better able to offer multiple points of view about one object, a technique known as "perspectivistic interpretation."

Historic House Museums

Traditionally, historic preservation has concentrated on saving the dwellings related to significant people, families, or events. At its best, this tight focus personalizes history by illustrating how social forces affected a small group of people. Nevertheless, house museum interpretation can also feature narrow, filiopietistic hero stories, or laundry lists of rare or valuable objects with no clear significance to the structure's history. Museum practices based on those used in interpretive exhibitions are slowly creating more balance in the preservation, restoration, and interpretation of historic houses.

Most house museums contain recreated period rooms, with the added authenticity of being displayed in their original domestic structure. Site administrators often choose an "interpretive period" for houses spanning long periods of time and ownership and/or occupancy by multiple families. Rooms are then restored to reflect the chosen years with the aid of archival photographs, documentary and architectural evidence, and oral histories. The collections of house museums vary greatly from site to site but often include furnishings, decorative arts, fine art pieces, and archives of letters, photographs, and other documents of domestic life. Reproduction and period furnishings and material culture substitute for originals no longer extant. House museums without extensive material culture collections have been successfully restored and interpreted as either "representative" sites or as examples of architectural preservation. Recent changes in house museum practice have been influenced by the scholarship of social historians. The residences of African Americans and immigrants have become more appealing for historic preservationists, most notably New York City's Lower East Side Tenement Museum (opened 1988), formerly home to approximately 7,000 people from twenty countries. Guided tours (the standard practice of interpreting these sites) have become more likely to include information about resident women, children, and enslaved people or domestic servants.

Historic Sites and Living History Museums

Living history museums operate much like general history museums but expand the "authenticity" of the site to include the physical activities of its interpreters. Guides at living history sites typically dress in period costume and take part in enactments of historical activities. The interpretive methods used at living history sites are either *first person*, in which the interpreter is costumed and portrays a historical character (real or fictional), or *third person*, in which he or she may wear period dress but speaks in terms of the present. Living history museums were among the first to address the history of ordinary people, such as farmers and craftsmen, before social history spread interest in their activities. Despite this achievement, the depictions of everyday life at these sites—for example, cooking programs and craft and agricultural demonstrations—have often been criticized as overly romantic.

Museum villages are made up of a variety of authentic and reproduction structures. The most common are fictional villages made up of original buildings, usually relocated from many parts of the state or region, arranged as a "typical" settlement of the interpretive period(s), most often representing the preindustrial era. Conner Prairie (established in 1934), a simulated pioneer settlement near Indianapolis, Indiana, and Old World Wisconsin (opened in 1976), a collection of ethnic settlements located outside Milwaukee, are well-known examples of this type. Plimoth Plantation (founded in 1947 in Massachusetts) is a unique site in that all structures and artifacts are reproductions and the interpreters become "living artifacts" by assuming specific personas and speaking in seventeenth-century English regional dialects. Although the village does not contain any original materials, the experience is intended to be more authentic because Plimoth Plantation allows its collection to be used and experienced by interpreters and visitors.

Since its opening in 1934, Colonial Williamsburg has been a leader in the museum profession. To date, the Virginia site's historic area consists of eighty-eight original buildings, several major reconstructed buildings, and modern museum buildings to display collections of material culture and folk art. Colonial Williamsburg staff members regularly review its restoration projects, material culture exhibitions, and interpretive programs, resulting in an institutional history that reflects the path of American museum practice. What began as a collection of buildings and material culture dedicated to the preservation of American patriotism has grown into a complex institution that attempts to represent the lives of enslaved people, women, and the poor in addition to the city's famous revolutionaries.

Jennifer Pustz

See also Collecting and Collections; Fakes; Historic Preservation; Materials Conservation; Public Monuments and Popular Commemoration

References and Further Reading

Alexander, Edward P. 1996. *Museums in Motion: An Introduction to the History and Functions of Museums.* Walnut Creek, CA: AltaMira Press.

Anderson, Gail. 2004. *Reinventing the Museum: Historical and Contemporary Perspectives on the Paradigm Shift.* Walnut Creek, CA: AltaMira Press.

Anderson, Jay. 1991. *A Living History Reader. Volume One: Museums.* Nashville, TN: American Association of State and Local History.

Conn, Steven. 1998. *Museums and American Intellectual Life, 1876–1926.* Chicago: University of Chicago Press.

Donnelly, Jessica Foy. 2002. *Interpreting Historic House Museums*. Walnut Creek, CA: AltaMira.

Handler, Richard, and Eric Gable. 1997. *The New History in an Old Museum: Creating the Past at Colonial Williamsburg*. Durham, NC: Duke University Press.

Leon, Warren, and Roy Rosenzweig. 1989. *History Museums in the United States: A Critical Assessment*. Urbana: University of Illinois Press.

Music and Musical Instruments

Music has served to consolidate gatherings of congregations, friends, and family for occasions both festive and somber, in private dwellings and in public venues. From parlor concerts to the antics of minstrelsy and vaudevillian sideshows to operas and symphonic music, a wide array of musical entertainments were available for consumption in the nineteenth century. Although the music of orchestras and quartets continued to be performed in upscale venues around the country, it was popular dance music of various manifestations that was crucial to American culture in the twentieth century as it brought together diverse audiences in speakeasies, dance halls, and auditoriums or was played at home on phonographs and radios, which by the 1920s had supplanted domestic musicmaking.

Folk Music, Ethnic Music, and Musical Instruments

Folk music, or *traditional music*, describes music that was not commodified, but rather shared, learned, and performed within a community and, like oral tradition, conveyed through direct participation and by word of mouth. The first folk music in North America originated with indigenous peoples, whose musical practices generally placed greater emphasis on song with instrumental music and rhythms as accompaniment. Because instruments were made from natural sources —hollowed-out tree trunks, animal hides, and bones—few ancient examples remain today. As Native Americans' lands were seized in the nineteenth century, their artifacts, including musical instruments, were collected by museums and individuals in large quantities. Their meanings and uses were not always fully understood by Euro-Americans, because these instruments frequently served in sacred functions often closed to outsiders (healing ceremonies, initiations, celebrations of birth, rituals for death, and other social events). Flutes, for example, were said to be courtship instruments in some native tribes including the Lakota Sioux. The choice of natural materials for musical instrument design was symbolic as well as utilitarian, as was the case of the carapace and the enclosed pellets used for a Seneca turtle rattle, which had spiritual importance for the False Face Societies of the Northeast and was played by striking the instrument against a log.

Music was integral to the lives of African Americans in the nineteenth century, evidenced through work songs, celebrations, and recreation, which often recalled folk traditions of the many African peoples. Work song rhythms alleviated monotony; call-and-response forms, derived from counterparts in African tradition, invigorated the mind despite the tedium and hard labor of domestic chores and fieldwork. Congo Square in New Orleans, Louisiana, held some of the largest gatherings for African American celebrations in the antebellum United States. Accounts of these events described the use of banjos, drums, fiddles, bones, and bells, which had African antecedents. Plucked lutes, called *bangelo* ("bangeos" in the eighteenth century), and bowed, fiddlelike lutes were common instruments in western Sudan, as were various drum styles. Bone instruments were standard in Dahomey, Morocco, and South Africa, fashioned from animal bones that were split, hollowed, and dried; when held two in each hand and clapped together they sounded similar to castanets.

European immigrants brought music traditions specific to their ethnic identities and celebrations. Songwriters like Thomas Moore (1779–1852) and John Hill Hewitt (1801–1890) created parlor songs for piano that borrowed from European models. Moore's *Irish Melodies* (1808) used traditional Irish folk songs that were sentimental and nostalgic airs about his beloved homeland like "My Gentle Harp," whose original melody dates to the 1600s and was also rekindled in the early 1900s by Barry Taylor for the now-classic "Danny Boy." One of Stephen Foster's (1826–1864) many poignant parlor songs, "My Old Kentucky Home, Good Night" (1853), tells a story of the loss of a loved one, the missing person being a slave father who has been sold and forced to leave his family. Its deeply sentimental message was meant to demonstrate to white audiences the depth of feeling black families held for their loved ones.

Popular Music

Popular music is widely accessible and diverse in its manifestations and can include parlor tunes, band repertory, songs of minstrelsy, show tunes, and dance music. In the 1840s and 1850s, concerts combined theater with popular song. Prompted by the inspirational lectures of the Lyceum movement, songs of moral uplift and social relevance included themes of westward migration ("A Life in the West"), the nefarious treatment of Native Americans ("The Indian Hunter"), and love for family ("The Old Armchair").

Concert singer Jenny Lind (1820–1887), the "Swedish Nightingale," debuted in New York in 1850 and performed sentimental and national favorites like "Home Sweet Home" under the direction of showman P. T. Barnum (1810–1891). Likewise, African American Elizabeth Taylor Greenfield (1819 or 1824–1876) sang Bellini's "Oh! Native Scenes," Donizetti's "Salut a La France," as well as "Home Sweet Home" throughout the United States and Europe. She opened doors for other artists like opera diva Sissieretta Jones (1869–1933), whose venues included the White House, Madison Square Garden in New York, and the 1893 World's Columbian Exposition in Chicago.

The 1890s also ushered in *ragtime*, music written for piano with a syncopated rhythm that stressed the unaccented beats. Ragtime's lively tunes supported the new mania for dancing, and titles mirrored the events of the day: for example, "The Aeroplane Rag," and "Ragadora," which celebrated dancer Isadora Duncan's (1878–1927) popularity. Scott Joplin's (1868–1919) classics "Maple Leaf Rag" and "The Entertainer" secured his title "King of Ragtime." After World War I ended in 1918, ragtime gave way to *jazz*. Unlike ragtime, which was written music and dependent upon the piano, jazz's improvisational character was not easily reproduced for sheet music and could include a wide range of instruments.

In the 1920s, record companies that had previously resisted recording black performers began to do so. Mamie Smith (1883–1946) started the blues craze when she recorded "Crazy Blues" in 1920. Rock and roll music forerunners like Joe Turner (1911–1985) found their roots in blues bands and Count Basie's (1904–1984) boogie-woogie. By the 1970s, rock and roll was a catch-all for popular music culture in United States as played on "Top 40" radio and could be as different as Elton John, Carlos Santana, or Carole King.

Music and Musical Instruments in the Home

Musical soirees were common domestic entertainment in the nineteenth century as they showcased family talent and amateur musicians and singers, and for the wealthy could include professional quartets or even orchestras. Upright pianos, introduced in 1830 by Chickering and Sons of Boston, eventually replaced the square piano. Early in the century, the instrument's high price made it a prized possession in the parlor. Piano manufacturing firms grew in number from 110 in 1860 to 294 by 1909, producing sturdier instruments for home use, driving down the price, and making the piano a ubiquitous instrument in middle- and upper-class homes.

Less expensive than the upright piano, the parlor organ, or reed organ, also appealed to Americans. The organ bellows, controlled by pedals, provided a wider tonal range and modified its volume, depending on the pace of the pedaling. Guitars, too, were popular parlor instruments, less costly than pianos and organs, and more versatile in their portability. Early in the century, the Spanish guitar came into vogue and replaced the lutelike, tear-shaped English guitar. The Spanish guitar maintained its distinctive incurved waist and sound hole, but its string design was simplified to accommodate the myriad amateur musicians who adopted it. Guitars lost their domestic importance in the twentieth century. Once electric amplifiers were introduced in 1930s, the guitar became the preeminent instrument for stage musicians in the second half of the century.

Twentieth-century technology challenged conventional, manual modes of music enjoyment at home. Along with mechanized player pianos and organs, the 1887 patent for the phonograph, which played flat disks as opposed to Thomas Edison's (1847–1931) earlier music cylinders, began the trend away from performing music and toward listening to prerecorded music. Companies like the Edison Home Phonograph and the Gramophone Company (eventually becoming RCA, whose logo was Nipper the Dog listening to his master's voice on a gramophone), advertised their machines as providing family-centered entertainment. By the 1920s, home music included the radio (in 1927, radios were introduced in automobiles); by the mid-1930s, 67 percent of American houses had radios, increasing to 81 percent by 1939. Like the upright piano of the previous century, the radio became the central feature around which families gathered. Radios and phonograph records continued to be Americans' primary source for home music entertainment throughout the twentieth century. The high-fidelity record player ("hi-fi") allowed radio hits to be played at home, until eight-tracks, cassette tapes, CDs, DVDs, and the home computer's Internet access supplanted these technologies.

War Songs and Musical Instruments

Music has been an important part of military experience in America, inspiring tunes that date from the Revolution ("Yankee Doodle") and the War of 1812 (Francis Scott Key's "The Star-Spangled Banner"). Many Civil War regiments had bands that were generally ensembles of brass and percussions, occasionally including stringed instruments but rarely woodwinds. Fifes, drums, and bugles were standard instruments for field musicians, who could be boys as young as twelve but who transmitted various musical commands and signals important to the daily routine of the camp and on the battlefield. The Vietnam conflict (1959–1975) divided the country and incited numerous antiwar and progovernment songs. Pete Seeger's "Where Have All the Flowers Gone" is possibly the best-known Vietnam protest song; written in 1955 as an anti-military song, when recorded in 1961 became emblematic of anti-war resistance.

Art Music, Concert Halls, and Performance Centers

While most large eastern cities had at least one performance hall or large church to accommodate musical events before the Civil War, the postwar zeal to remake the nation placed emphasis on the urban experience and "culture building," which included the creation of concert halls and performance centers. Music critics like John Sullivan Dwight (1818–1893) promoted music of a European-classical tradition, called *art music*, or *cultivated music*, as a means to educate and refine the general populace. Likewise wealthy investors like Andrew Carnegie (1835–1919) financed projects such as New York City's Carnegie Hall, designed in 1891, to improve society through the cultural arts. By extension, the symphonies of Beethoven, the sonatas of Schubert, Mendelssohn's oratorios, and Handel's *Messiah* were believed to have civilizing effects and could correct the crudities of the populace and raise the cultural standards of the nation. The rectangular, "shoe-box" design of Boston Symphony Hall (1900), by the architectural firm McKim, Mead, and White (est. 1879), incorporated the improved acoustical designs of Harvard physics professor Wallace Sabine (1868–1919). The building is considered one of the finest music halls in the world. The acoustically disastrous Philharmonic Hall in New York City was originally built in 1962 and patterned after Boston's Symphony Hall. Architects Philip Johnson and John Burgee revamped the earlier structure to the specifications of acoustician Cyril Harris to reopen the new Avery Fisher Hall in 1976. Harris' designs were used in other shoe-box halls, including John F. Kennedy Center in Washington DC and Orchestra Hall in Minneapolis, Minnesota. In the end, the acoustical results of Avery Fisher Hall did not match the warm, reverberant sound produced in Boston. Rather the sharp, comprehensible sounds of Avery Fisher Hall are common to other concert halls in North America, ideally suited for contemporary popular music.

Tamara Wilde

See also African America; Civic Architecture; Folklore and Folklife; Music Ephemera; Popular Culture; Technology; Tools, Implements, and Instruments

References and Further Reading
Forsyth, Michael. 1985. *Buildings for Music: the Architect, the Musician, and the Listener from the Seventeenth Century to the Present Day.* Cambridge, MA: MIT Press.
Levine, Lawrence W. 1988. *Highbrow/Lowbrow: The Emergence of Cultural Hierarchy in America.* Cambridge, MA: Harvard University Press.
Libin, Lawrence. 1994. *Our Tuneful Heritage: American Musical Instruments from the Metropolitan Museum of Art.* Provo, UT: Museum of Art, Brigham Young University.
Roell, Craig H. 1989. *The Piano in America, 1890–1940.* Chapel Hill: University of North Carolina Press.

Music Ephemera

Music ephemera is defined as those printed documents, such as sheet music, flyers, programs, advertising posters, and tickets, associated with the promotion of music. These items provide crucial documentation of

American musical culture, particularly the historical culture that existed prior to the advent of recorded sound during the 1890s. During the seventeenth, eighteenth, and nineteenth centuries, music could only be heard live; music ephemera furnish us with a printed record of these acoustical experiences. This body of evidence reveals much about American popular culture, shifting tastes, political concerns, and leisure as well as the technological advances in printing and distribution.

Piano sheet music has been the most widely studied and catalogued type of music ephemera. Pianos were a necessary accoutrement for cultivated middle-class American households during the latter half of the nineteenth century. Women in particular were expected to become proficient on the piano as evidence of their gentility. During the 1870s more than sixty-five sheet-music publishing firms in the United States produced perhaps 200,000 individual published compositions for piano. This sheet music can be analyzed in a number of ways. It provides evidence of middle-class tastes, in terms of both musical styles and subject matter. For example, popular song forms were waltzes and Scottish and Irish ballads; frequent song subjects were romantic love, sentimental portrayals of mother and home, and patriotic odes to contemporary or historical political leaders. Many sheet-music pieces were minstrel or "coon" songs, written by white composers, with covers and lyrics that featured derogatory caricatures of African Americans. This music exemplified the racism of the white middle class while suggesting that it held a fascination with African American culture.

Piano sheet music has been used by historians to explore nineteenth-century, middle-class gender relationships. Songs were often performed as sing-alongs in the parlor, with

This sheet music cover for the quickstep song, "McClellan is the Man," by Henry Cromwell, dates from 1864. General George B. McClellan, who served under Abraham Lincoln in the Civil War, lost the presidential election of 1864 as the Democratic candidate, despite this song's assurance that he "is the Man." Popular music often reflected larger social, political, and economic life in the United States. (Library of Congress)

the entire family involved; sometimes young couples participated together in sing-alongs as part of their courtship. Widely popular songs can thus be seen as an acceptable form of discourse between the sexes.

With the advent of lithography in the 1840s, posters, sheet music, and programs were elaborately illustrated. The analyses of the images, music, and lyrics reveal at times conflicting ideals and realities in American culture and specifically within nonnative, nonwhite groups. For example, musicologist

Irene Heskes (1984) has studied the Yiddish sheet-music industry that thrived in New York City between 1880 and 1920. Yiddish sheet music revealed simultaneously the desire of Jewish immigrants to acculturate and their concerns about what they had found in the United States. The covers were often patriotic and optimistic, featuring symbols such as the Statue of Liberty. But the song lyrics themselves often told stories of disappointment, about men failing to find work, street crimes, and industrial accidents.

Music ephemera documents the ways in which music has been marketed to consumers. For example, the Pekin Theater in Chicago, opened in 1904 as the first black-owned, black-patronized musical theater in the United States, appealed to the middle-class aspirations of its audiences by issuing lavish program books, filled with advertisements for banks and high-grade cigarmakers. Much more recently, "indie rock" labels eschew the slick promotional materials common to major record labels, using amateurish-looking flyers and posters as signs of their authenticity—an authenticity that will presumably be passed on to their customers.

Tom Collins

See also Ephemera; Graphic Design; Music and Musical Instruments; Popular Culture; Print Culture

References and Further Reading
Heskes, Irene. 1984. "Music as Social History: American Yiddish Theater Music, 1882–1920." *American Music* 2 (4): 73–87.
Krummel, Donald William, and Stanley Sadie. 1990. *Music Printing and Publishing*. New York: W. W. Norton.
Tatham, David. 1973. *The Lure of the Striped Pig: The Illustration of Popular Music in America, 1820–1870*. Barre, MA: Imprint Society.
Wolfe, Richard J. 1980. *Early American Music Engraving and Printing: a History of Music Publishing in America from 1787 to 1825 with Commentary on Earlier and Later Practices*. Urbana: University of Illinois Press.

N

Native America

Before European explorers and exploiters set foot on the North American continent, 500 nations of indigenous peoples, with greatly varying languages, religious beliefs, social organizations, and cultures, lived in what would become the United States. Modern knowledge of these peoples, who have been dubbed *Native Americans*, has been acquired through personal and official letters, manuscripts, drawings, and published works written by Europeans, including Jesuit missionaries; Spanish conquistadores; and English, French, and Dutch colonists from the sixteenth century through American independence. The movement westward of Euro-Americans and continuing waves of immigrants from primarily Europe elicited similar evidence, including oral history, art, and photography of Native American housing, dress, daily life, and ceremonies. The United States government and state governments, in efforts to control the peoples commonly called *Indians* (a misnomer attributed to explorer Christopher Columbus's (1451–1506) error of believing he had found a passage to India), enacted legislation, conducted surveys, and used military force, all of which have left an enormous written record but resulted in a relatively small percentage of Native Americans living where their ancestors flourished.

The history of Europeans and Euro-Americans and indigenous peoples is one of brutality and racism. Yet it is also a chronicle of cultural contact and exchange and survival, evident primarily in material culture. Native peoples actively sought to preserve their identities through their traditions and material culture, surviving at times through accommodation and at times through physical removal to new locations, especially in the nineteenth century. Archaeological investigations undertaken at many sites throughout the United States and study of collections of Native American–made and –used artifacts offer much insight into the material practices of indigenous peoples. Collectors, especially in the early twentieth century, elevated specific native crafts (which were erroneously dubbed *primitive*) into art, so much so as to misrepresent the complexity of native peoples' cultures and in their collecting promote the long-standing romantic idea of the "vanishing Indian." This was

This photogravure image, "Baskets in the Painted Cave," appears in photographer Edward S. Curtis's multivolume The North American Indian *(1924). The Yokuts of central California's Tule River Reservation created these baskets. By the time Curtis posed these baskets within the sacred space of a painted cave, Euro-Americans had developed an interest in Native American goods as collectible and decorative art. (Library of Congress)*

also true of projects undertaken by artist George Catlin (1796–1872) and photographer Edward S. Curtis (1868–1952), both of whom traveled westward to portray Native Americans, fearing their disappearance.

The historical study of Native America is based on two models: language and culture area. Linguists have used language families to classify peoples, but in the study of material culture, the concept of culture area is more useful. A *culture area* is a region defined by ecology and geography in which groups interact through intermarriage and trade,

war and diplomacy. Through such activities cultural characteristics are shared and may be traced. Though extensive and complete coverage is impossible in this essay, especially of the indigenous peoples of what are now Alaska and Hawaii, what follows is a discussion of key examples of material life.

Precontact Material Life: The Moundbuilders

The sophistication of the people known as the Moundbuilders is confirmed in the remains of the great mounds they created before European contact. Archaeological excavation has yielded evidence of moundbuilding throughout the Eastern Woodlands, but these forms are found primarily in the Ohio and Mississippi river valleys. Appearing singly or grouped together, designed in squares, circles, rectangles, and octagons, these mounds served their builders as sacred ritual and burial sites. Serpent Mound, in southeastern Ohio, is over 1,330 feet long, rising an average of 4 to 5 feet high, and ranging between 20 and 25 feet wide.

Inside these earthen constructions is evidence of an extensive trade network. For example, copper from the northern Great Lakes region, mica from what is now North Carolina or Mexico, and obsidian from what is now Wyoming have been found by archaeologists in these mounds. Other sacred objects, such as human and animal effigies (carved in stone, cut out of copper and mica, or crafted in clay), pots, pipes, and engraved stone tablets, reveal a complex religion.

Hundreds of mounds near Collinsville, Illinois, mark a city of some 200 acres once protected by wooden palisades. Known as Cahokia, this city likely housed anywhere from 10,000 to 50,000 inhabitants, who built by hand these great earthen masses on which public buildings and houses were erected. Also evident are plazas. The built environment of Cahokia belies the long-held stereotype that Native Americans were nomadic.

Native American Material Life

Christopher Columbus's voyage to the New World marks the commencement of European colonization of what would become the United States. The establishment of new trade networks with colonists of France, Spain, and England altered power structures between native nations, reorganized gender roles within villages, and often augmented rather than changed material life and practices. For example, the Algonkians, who had traded with inland native nations, began trapping what English colonists desired in the early seventeenth century: beaver pelts. Increasingly, trade centers moved to the eastern seaboard, and the Algonkians spent more time on trapping beaver than hunting and preserving larger game such as deer. In turn, the Algonkians donned cotton shirts, knitted stockings, and beaver hats, diminishing to a degree their dependence on animal skins as dress. They adopted portable copper kettles and iron pots, brought by traders and considered to be better than the immovable, carved-out stumps used to heat soups and stews by dropping into the stumps heated stones. Tools carved from stone and bone were not replaced by steel knives, though the Algonkians traded for these implements. Stone implements were still used to scrape hides, prepare food, and build housing.

Still other native-made goods did not incorporate European materials. The materials and construction of houses remained more or less the same. In much of the Eastern Woodlands, houses were constructed of wood frames and covered with bark, plant fibers, and animal skins. The Iroquois, centered in what is now New York State, employed elm bark to cover *longhouses*, large buildings that re-created, through spatial organization,

village society. Along the southern eastern seaboard, the Catawbas framed dome-shaped houses with bent tree saplings, which were in turn covered with bark. *Tipis* (or tepees) of the Plains Indians were created using buffalo hides. In the Pacific Northwest, the Tlingit reinforced the social order by creating large, peak-roofed houses of planks with carved posts at each corner. These carved and decorated posts, called *totem poles*, were also created to frame doorways or stand in public areas to commemorate important events.

In the Southwest, the Navajo, once a nomadic people, built *hogans*, one-room houses constructed of earth with a door always facing east. The Apache constructed oval-shaped *wickiups* of brush covered with animal hides. Spanish colonists encountered on top of high mesas a building form they called *pueblo*, thus giving to the builders the name of Pueblos. Constructed of stone or adobe, these multihousehold buildings were the largest of their kind in North America until urban apartment buildings were erected in the late nineteenth century. Adobe pueblos were framed with heavy timber beams (transported from a distance) to support a strong, multilayer roof upon which many activities were performed. The ceremonial chamber known as the *kiva* was also constructed among the Pueblo and the Apache (who built these spaces partially beneath ground level). Kivas were hidden from the Spanish colonists, who, through Franciscan missionaries, attempted to spread Christianity. In part, the missionaries succeeded: Wooden crosses and religious prints appeared in Pueblo households.

Tree bark, wood, and other plant fibers also provided Native Americans the material to make many necessary tools, utensils, and even transport. Birchbark canoes were crafted by many native peoples of the Eastern

Woodlands. Tree saplings were bent and shaped into a frame, over which a covering of bark, stitched together, was stretched. The bark would be sealed with pitch. This method of sealing bark so as to make it waterproof was also applied to cooking and storage vessels, to housing materials, and to clothing.

Animal skins provided Native Americans with clothing, though European trade goods—cotton shirts, heavy wool blankets, leggings, capes, and ornamental glass beads—became part of Native American dress in the seventeenth and eighteenth centuries in the East. Then traders used red and blue "trade coats" to cement alliances with key native leaders. Such clothing became a sign of status, just as purple and white shell beads, called *wampum*, became currency in the increasingly competitive trade market. In the nineteenth century, Native Americans living on the Great Plains depended on the buffalo. After the Spanish introduced the domesticated horse, the buffalo could be hunted with great success. Buffalo hides offered the fabric of tepees and clothing, including capes, robes, and moccasins. The great animal's bones were used to carve shovels, knives, and war implements. Personal ornaments and rope were fashioned from buffalo hair.

Twentieth-Century Crafts

By the beginning of the twentieth century, Euro-Americans had populated the American West that had been made knowable by government surveys, photography, and the railroads. The Homestead Act (1862), wars and other military activity, and the Dawes Severalty Act (1887) had greatly diminished Native Americans' political and economic power. The tourist trade, the quest for the "authentic" by experiencing other ethnic groups' cultures, and in decorative arts (seen in the Arts and Crafts Movement's interest

in Native American handicrafts), and the emphasis on the primitive in fine art converged to re-create the relationship between Native Americans, particularly in the Southwest, in California, and in the Pacific Northwest, and Euro-Americans.

In the case of the Navajo, the demands of the tourist market altered in many cases the baskets, blankets, and metalwares that had been produced for centuries. The Navajo had grown cotton and woven blankets before the arrival of the Spanish. Wool from the churro sheep the Spanish brought with them was adapted to the Navajo women's looms, with which blankets and other textile forms were produced. Utilitarian baskets and pottery were also altered for trade, becoming smaller and more decorative to appeal to the market. By the mid-twentieth century, native craftsmen were producing stock items for sale. Silver jewelry, for example, was once pawned by Navajos for goods; the unredeemed jewelry was then sold to Euro-Americans. Its increased popularity led to mass production for the tourist trade and the use of such stock "Indian" symbols as thunderbirds and crossed arrows suggested by traders. By the 1930s and 1940s Indian boarding and reservation schools incorporated instruction in crafts such as weaving, pottery making, and jewelry making. What these forms of material culture represented was an agreement between Native Americans and Euro-Americans of what "Native American" is. In some ways, as scholars Rayna Green (1988) and Philip Deloria (1998) have argued, both groups are "playing Indian."

Shirley Teresa Wajda

See also Agricultural Fairs and Expositions; Animals; Anthropology and Archaeology; Body Modification; Child's Body; Collecting and Collections; Dress, Accessories, and Fashion; Ethnicity; Gifts and Gift Giving; Holidays and Commemorations; Land and

Landscape; Money, Currency, and Value; Mourning and Ethnicity, Music and Musical Instruments; Race; Slavery; Souvenirs; Textiles; Tourism and Travel; Water Transportation

References and Further Reading
Baxter, Paula. 1994. "Cross-Culture Controversies in the Design History of Southwestern American Indian Jewellery." *Journal of Design History* 7 (4): 233–245.

Deloria, Philip. 1998. *Playing Indian*. New Haven, CT: Yale University Press.

Green, Rayna. 1988. "The Tribe Called Wannabe: Playing Indian in America and Europe." *Folklore* 99 (1): 30–55.

Hoxie, Frederick E., ed. 1996. *Encyclopedia of North American Indians: Native American History, Culture, and Life from Paleo-Indians to the Present*. New York: Houghton Mifflin.

Isenberg, Andrew C. 2000. *The Destruction of the Bison: An Environmental History, 1750–1920*. Cambridge, UK: Cambridge University Press.

Krech, Shepard, III, and Barbara A. Hail. 1999. *Collecting Native America, 1870–1960*. Washington, DC: Smithsonian Institution Press.

Milner, George. 2004. *The Moundbuilders: Ancient Peoples of Eastern North America*. New York: Thames and Hudson.

Nash, Alice N., and Christoph Strobel. 2006. *Daily Life of Native Americans from Post-Columbian through Nineteenth-Century America*. Westport, CT: Greenwood Press.

Orchard, William C. 1975 (1929). *Beads and Beadwork of the American Indians*, 2nd ed. New York: Museum of the American Indian.

Penney, David. 2004. *North American Indian Art*. New York: Thames and Hudson.

Peterson, James B., ed. 1996. *A Most Indispensable Art: Native Fiber Industries from Eastern North America*. Knoxville: University of Tennessee Press.

Philips, Ruth B. 1998. *Trading Identities: The Souvenir in Native North American Art from the Northeast, 1700–1900*. Seattle: University of Washington Press.

Sandweiss, Martha A. 2002. *Print the Legend: Photography and the American West*. New Haven, CT: Yale University Press.

Sturtevant, William C., ed. 1978. *Handbook of North American Indians*. 20 vols. Washington, DC: Smithsonian Institution Press.

Nostalgia

The simple fact that humans age and change provides the basis of the phenomenon known as *nostalgia*. The sense that the past was somehow better, whether that past was one's childhood or a time even beyond one's lifetime, describes the phenomenon. *Nostalgia* describes a condition in which a person, community, society, or nation creates selectively a past, often because that invented past offers a pleasant or soothing alternative to the present or the future. As sociologist Fred Davis (1977, 420) observes, nostalgia "always occurs in the context of present fears, discontents, anxieties, or uncertainties even though those may not be in the forefront of the person's awareness." In short, nostalgia provides a means by which individuals and societies may create and maintain identity. For nations, this identity may be a result and a practice of accumulation, generation after generation, of key symbols and shared commemorations. Forms of material culture, such as relics, antiques, historic houses, or even replicas, offer tangible, personal links to that invented past for those who feel a sense of alienation with the present. Indeed, in modern American consumer culture, nostalgia sells.

History of Nostalgia

The concept of nostalgia is most often traced to the Swiss doctor Johannes Hofer, who in 1688 employed the German word *heimweh* to characterize the homesickness experienced by Swiss mercenaries far from their native land. *Nostalgia*, a combination of two Greek terms for return home (*nostos*) and sorrow or pain (*algos*), described physical and mental conditions that by the end of the eighteenth century were medicalized. Symptoms mirrored those of melancholy: listlessness, sadness, indifference, withdrawal from social interaction, rejection of nourishment. Many physicians thought there was no cure for nostalgia.

Nostalgia throughout the nineteenth century shifted from a physiological disease based on geographical dislocation to a social condition caused by modernization. In the United States, the economic dislocations caused by the Industrial Revolution transplanted rural folk to rapidly growing cities to which immigrants also came, created new forms of labor and new concepts of work discipline and time, and shifted financial methods to a cash economy that alienated traditional ideas of trust. In turn, many Americans sought refuge or comfort in a constructed past that was somehow better. Often this refuge was in nature, as in the writings of Ralph Waldo Emerson (1803–1882) and Henry David Thoreau (1817–1862), whose yearlong experiment at simple living at Walden Pond near Concord, Massachusetts, has remained a touchstone for many who seek a "return" to a perceived "better" time. The American landscape, as opposed to Europe's ruins, was considered superior in terms of its potential, especially on the western frontier. Yet in the long-settled East the landscape, with its constant alterations placing the old against the new, offered its inhabitants no respite against change. The picturesque parks and rural cemeteries constructed by Emerson's and Thoreau's contemporaries offered such a temporary relief.

Nostalgia as Social and Cultural Movement

Nostalgia may be simultaneously celebratory of an imagined past and critical of modern life and result in political, aesthetic, and social movements. After its defeat in the Civil War (1861–1865), the South's espousal of the "Lost Cause" as part of a regional heritage remains today a political force. The Arts and Crafts Movement of the late nineteenth and early twentieth centuries argued for a return to the world of the artisan in the face of industrialization and the concomitant degradation of labor. At the same time participants in the Colonial Revival, remembering as part of their childhoods their grandparents' houses, inaccurately framed the nation's colonial past as somewhere before 1840— that is, before industrialization and the rise of immigration from southern and eastern Europe threatened the supposed social and cultural homogeneity of Protestant whites. Colonial Revivalists pursued the establishment of museum collections of Americana and the "rescue" of historic sites such as presidents' birthplaces and Civil War battlefields, the creation of the Pledge of Allegiance and historical pageants, and the establishment of national holidays. At the end of the nineteenth century, the publication of historical fiction was matched by a great many reminiscences, memories, and recollections, especially by grandparents about "times gone by" or "folkways" or "quaint customs"—that is, removed from the present and retrievable through memory and outmoded artifacts of daily life. Indeed, the Colonial Revival and the Arts and Crafts Movement gave rise to the study of the stuff stored in "grandmother's attic": "pots and pans" history, the study of everyday life through material culture. During the Great Depression of the 1930s, the search for a national "usable past" was endorsed by New Deal programs to document and celebrate the material culture and customs of the American people.

Nostalgia and Consumption

Nostalgia, with its sense of a more authentic past, promoted new markets for historic goods. Antiques and relics, by definition hard to find or rare and often costly, were affordable for the historic elite and newly established museums. Increased middle-class prosperity and leisure widened this market throughout the twentieth century and shortened the age of what is considered an antique. The manufacture of fake antiques also increased. The application of scuff marks and dirt to objects, the creation of furniture worm holes made with nails or air guns, the fake patina of metalware through chemical oxidation, and other treatments are still employed to deceive the buyer.

As David Lowenthal (1985) has observed, historic replicas translate styles of the past to modern usage and convenience. The symbolism of the domestic hearth, for example, need not require wood chopping, ash cleaning, and ember banking. One need only turn on the gas or electricity that creates, beyond fake logs, the glow of past home fires. Plastic and linoleum are manufactured to imitate wood grain or historic patterns and forms. Other items recall the past in traditional materials. Reproduction spinning wheels, large and small, may be found in living rooms and dens next to imitation Chippendale tea tables hold never-lit hand-dipped candles perched on modern pewter candlesticks, as well as the remote control which has directed the homeowner to a televised baseball game in a "retro" ballpark such as Baltimore's Camden Yards (1992). These reproductions may have been purchased at a Georgian-style brick shopping center, or a newly built "quaint" shop on an ersatz Main Street similar to that represented in the sentimental paintings of Thomas Kinkade or at Disneyland.

Today aspects of even the recent past have become nostalgic, abetted by television shows embracing the baby boom generation (those born between 1946 and1964), from *Happy Days* (set in the 1950s) to *The Wonder Years* (the 1960s) to *That 70s Show*. Americans not even born in the 1970s and 1980s collect rock and roll memorabilia, for example, and sport various fashions from those decades. Toys and fad items such as velvet paintings, mood rings, and pet rocks are often popular. Mid-twentieth-century Modernist design is now imitated in housewares offered by Target stores and Crate and Barrel. Historical reproductions and replicas, especially in the forms of domestic furnishings, continue to appeal to the middle class eager to display its affinity with the past. Martha Stewart's celebrations of various American pasts have resulted in paint and flooring lines, K-Mart furniture lines, and even houses that seek to recall an idealized past. In what many considered a new form of the village improvement society, the planned community of Seaside, Florida, recalls late nineteenth-century American townscapes. Automobiles are banned, house styles are varied and constructed within walking distance of the community and commercial town center, and porches function as a means of informal, face-to-face sociability.

Nostalgia fuels the market for memorabilia that remind their owners of relations, events, and feelings in their own individual pasts. Scrapbooks of high school ephemera are reverently stored in drawers, and family albums of photographs recall family vacations, celebrations, and everyday life, each an edited version of experience. Keepsakes, mementos, and souvenirs have also become marketable commodities. Mall stores such as Things Remembered offer personalization through engraving of items related to weddings, birthdays, graduations, births, and anniversaries, through which "memories are made." Perhaps the best-known purveyor of nostalgic sentiment is Hallmark Cards, Inc. In its Gold Crown stores Hallmark offers greeting cards, annual Christmas "keepsake ornaments," and holiday and celebration gifts, all with wraps, bows, frames, albums, and cases with which to present and preserve the memory and sentiment contained within. Often derided as kitsch or cheap sentiment, such nostalgia-driven enterprises are big business in the United States.

Shirley Teresa Wajda

See also Antiques; Arts and Crafts Movement; Burial Grounds, Cemeteries, and Grave Markers; Colonial Revival; Consumerism and Consumption; Ephemera; Fakes; Funerals; Funerary (Sepulchral) Monuments; Heirlooms; Holidays and Commemorations; Memory and Memorabilia; Political Ephemera; Rite, Ritual, and Ceremony; Scrapbooks; Souvenirs; Tourism and Travel; Tradition

References and Further Reading

Davis, Fred. 1977. "Nostalgia, Identity and the Current Nostalgia Wave." *Journal of Popular Culture* 11 (2): 414–424.

Davis, Fred. 1979. *Yearning for Yesterday: A Sociology of Nostalgia*. New York: Free Press.

Kammen, Michael. 1991. *Mystic Chords of Memory: The Transformation of Tradition in American Culture*. New York: Alfred A. Knopf.

Lears, T. J. Jackson. 1981. *No Place of Grace: Antimodernism and the Transformation of American Culture, 1880–1920*. New York: Pantheon.

Litwicki, Ellen M. 2000. *America's Public Holidays: 1865–1920*. Washington, DC: Smithsonian Institution Press.

Lowenthal, David. 1985. *The Past Is a Foreign Country*. Cambridge, UK: Cambridge University Press.

Lynch, Kevin. 1972. *What Time Is this Place?* Cambridge, MA: MIT Press.

Stewart, Susan. 1984. *On Longing: Narratives of the Miniature, the Gigantic, the Souvenir, the Collection*. Baltimore, MD: Johns Hopkins University Press.

O

Office Work and Labor

With the rise of the corporation in the 1890s, *office work*—nonmanual clerical or administrative work—began to dominate the American economic life and American work life. Throughout the course of the nineteenth century the nature of work in the United States changed to include not only the "handwork" of manufacturing but also "headwork": those skills necessary to the conduct and management of business and commerce and increasingly associated with the growing middle class. Though men predominated as office workers for much of the nineteenth century, the establishment of business colleges in the 1880s, the increased enrollment of women in these colleges, and the urgent need for labor by rapidly growing corporations led to a two-tiered system in office labor: men as managers, and women as stenographers, typists (originally called *typewriters*, merging human and machine, and with the advent of the computer *word processors* or *data processors*), secretaries, receptionists, accounting clerks, and bookkeepers. These "working girls"—mostly native born—constituted a new urban demographic group, and insti-

tutions were created to serve their needs: The Young Women's Christian Association, for example, oversaw residences as well as recreational and educational services for working women. The women, paid less than the men working in the same occupations, were often successful in unionizing; early in the twentieth century stenographers' and typewriters' unions were established in Chicago and New York City.

Office Space and Status

The factory as the site and symbol of the United States' dependence on manufacturing was replaced with a new building and symbol. The skyscraper is the building form most closely associated with corporate work life. The first skyscraper, built in 1883 in Chicago for the Home Insurance Company, took advantage of new building techniques and materials. Soon cities across the nation had commercial centers in their downtown areas where looming skyscrapers clustered together.

The interior spaces of corporations' offices reflected both a public role of engaged citizen and a privatized role of domestic coziness. Lobbies were extravagantly appointed, with

The interior of the Johnson Wax Building in Racine, Wisconsin, was designed and constructed in 1936–1939 by architect Frank Lloyd Wright. The "lily pad" support columns provided an open and free-flowing space for secretaries. (Library of Congress)

marble columns, enormous chandeliers, and elaborately divided public work spaces for workers. Executive suites were also luxurious, but these aimed to reflect domestic spaces, with wood-lined walls, fireplaces, and hunting-themed art on the walls.

Yet corporate buildings were, above all, work spaces. In the early twentieth century the principles of "scientific management" were applied to the office as well as the factory, seeking to save costs and increase efficiency. Work spaces were thus plain and unornamented. To control work processes, large vast interior spaces were divided and subdivided to reflect the hierarchy of management levels. Today, cubicles are constructed from these interior spaces by using portable "walls," which can be configured in seemingly infinite ways.

Desks reflect the increasing depersonalization of office work. The rolltop desk with its flexible wood cover that "rolls down" over the work on the desk and can be locked was popular in the 1870s. This is a highly individualized desk that emphasizes how one worker uses one allotment of work space. By the 1880s desks were housed in "cages," slotted walls that demarcated space but allowed for communication between workers and oversight by management. Today, work spaces are nominally individualized by cubicle walls, while computer networking, phone tapping, and other forms of electronic monitoring accomplish the constant oversight management has historically sought to exert over workers.

Physical space was also used to demarcate status. For example, executives of corporations were, in the late nineteenth century as today, provided with private toilet and sink facilities, while other workers used communal toilets and bathroom facilities. In this way, workers are reminded that they lack basic privacy privileges allotted to those higher up in the management hierarchy. Gender segregation was common as well. Not only did corporations rely upon a "pink ghetto" of low-paid secretaries to staff their clerical jobs but many corporations also created separate work spaces for men and women. For example, in 1911 Metropolitan Life Insurance Company had a large "women's dining hall" that provided space for 2,000 women.

Business Uniforms

The rise of a business culture of "white collar" managerial and clerical jobs led to the establishment of the modern business ("sack") suit for men: This uniform of white shirt, coordinated suit jacket and trousers, and tie, though altered by fashion's mandates, has remained constant for more than a century. Women in business culture also adopted this uniform as they entered the pink-collar jobs of secretaries, receptionists, and clerks in the late nineteenth century. A secretary's shirtwaist, tie, and dark plain skirt together created a feminine version of the businessman's uniform. The increasing numbers of women in executive and managerial positions over the course of the twentieth century did not necessarily alter this formula. Hemlines, collars, and colors did change, but "dressing for success" advice for women in the feminist era of the 1970s and 1980s counseled traditional lines, muted colors, and a deemphasis of the female form in the adoption of the American business uniform.

Helen Sheumaker

See also Commercial Architecture; Dress, Accessories, and Fashion; Gender; Space and Place; Technology; Work and Labor

References and Further Reading

Albrecht, Donald, and Chrysanthe Broikos, eds. 2000. *On the Job: Design and the American Office*. New York: Princeton Architectural Press, and Washington, DC: National Building Museum.
Kwolek-Folland, Angel. 1994. *Engendering Business: Men and Women in the Corporate Office, 1870–1930*. Baltimore, MD: Johns Hopkins University Press.
Lupton, Ellen. 1993. *Mechanical Brides: Women and Machines from Home to Office*. New York: Cooper-Hewitt Design Museum and Princeton Architectural Press.

P

Parlors

Derived from the French *parler* ("to talk"), the *parlor* (or *parlour*), alternately known as the *best chamber, best room, front room, with-drawing room,* or *drawing room,* designated in American domestic dwellings from seventeenth-century settlement through the early twentieth century as a space dedicated to sociability and status display. Commercial parlors, appearing in the nineteenth century with the Market Revolution, were public spaces in which middle- and upper-class Americans could "see and be seen" as well as purchase services and goods meant to confirm and enhance their physical appearance and social status. In the private realm, many American houses had a formal (front) parlor that served as the family's public interface. The parlor functioned as a metaphor for polite society.

Colonial Era

In the typical seventeenth-century Anglo-American double-cell house plan, the parlor was the "inner room" accessible from the main room, or hall. Thus set apart from the daily activities of work, the parlor was accorded special status: Here was the household's best furniture, the best bedstead and bedding. In actuality a sleeping parlor, this chamber designates historically the introduction of privacy as a form of social improvement. Rural New Englanders would hold to this practice into the mid-nineteenth century.

Other colonists built new, large, symmetrical Georgian-style houses that employed the parlor as a room set aside for entertainment, accessible through an increasingly ceremonial stair passage, and as a counterpart to a dining chamber on the other side of the passage. Replacing the parlor bedstead were tables, chairs, and display furniture such as cupboards. A parlor marked the house owner as "genteel." Technological innovations, especially in heating and lighting, differentiated these lighter, airier formal spaces from production spaces within the eighteenth-century dwelling: Smaller fireplaces, larger windows, and better lighting devices allowed inhabitants to perform politeness by releasing them from fireside and window. Chairs, tilt-top tables, and other furniture forms of fine woods such as cherry and mahogany were arranged around the room against walls and were brought out when occasion dictated exercises in gentility such as tea drinking, card playing, conversations, musicales, and balls.

The Market Revolution and the Rise of the Comfortable Parlor

Nineteenth-century Americans sought more than genteel performance in their parlors in which they spent their leisure time as well as entertained others. Informality, physical ease, and the emphasis on the family came to define the parlor and its culture of comfort. The introduction of rocking chairs and easy chairs into this room heralded this new emphasis on relaxation, as did the banishment of work paraphernalia. The houses of the emerging middle class boasted front and back parlors—the former dedicated to refinement, the latter a "sitting room" or "family room" in which each member could improve one's self through conversation, reading, and other didactic pursuits, gathered at night around the light of the center table lamp.

By the 1850s the material attributes of the comfortable parlor—matched suites of upholstered furniture, textiles and carpets, wallpapers, lamps and mirrors, books and bookcases, pictures, and knickknacks—were the products of the Market Revolution. Machine-made, mass-produced goods cosseted parlor inhabitants against the competitive, masculine market that daily threatened the family stability symbolized by the feminine, domestic parlor. The Gilded Age Aesthetic Movement incorporated into the "artistic" parlor the exoticism brought to Americans' attentions through the world's fairs in Philadelphia (1876) and Chicago (1893). Japanese screens, ceramics, and prints; "Turkish corners" of large pillows and drapery decorated with scimitars; Turkish tufted and tasseled furniture; ottomans; and coffee table reflected Americans' increased political

and cultural interaction with the rest of the world. Bookcases, whatnots (etageres), wall-pockets, easels, and tabletops held the material attributes of refinement: matched sets of books, collectibles, busts of artists and authors, pictures, travel souvenirs, and natural history specimens.

The domestic parlor was an important site for sociability and the creation and maintenance of middle-class identity. Women, and to a lesser extent men, participated in a secular ritual called "calling." Several hours of a woman's day would be spent receiving visitors or visiting other women. Newspapers and social registers published regular times at which a woman would be "at home" and ready to receive visitors in the formal parlor. Dressed for the purpose and armed with calling cards and polite conversation, women circulated in towns and cities and in so doing sought or cemented social status—that is, became part of "Society." Woe to the caller who was told by a servant that the mistress of the house was "not at home"—that is, rejecting the caller's appeal to enter into this parlor ritual.

Commercial Parlors

The promise of refinement could also sell services and goods largely dedicated to promoting the disciplined body and the person of good taste. By the 1830s, urban hotels advertised "ladies' parlors" that acknowledged women as consumers and catered to families. By the 1850s steamboats and railroad cars alike were outfitted in parlor luxuries, including spring seating, expensive upholstery, and fashionable appointments. *Parlor* was employed to introduce novel services, foodstuffs, or ideas to Americans. Portrait daguerreotypists such as the famous Mathew B. Brady (1822–1896) offered visitors and patrons well-appointed reception rooms described meticulously in professional periodicals and local newspapers. (So great was the parlor's symbolic importance that photographers used parlor backdrops and furniture for portraiture.) Dry goods stores and other mercantile enterprises, including department stores such as John Wanamaker's (1838–1922) Philadelphia palace, employed fashionable furnishings to attract genteel customers to their businesses. When refrigeration and scale allowed, ice cream was sold in parlors, appealing, again, to a certain clientele based on cultivated taste and refinement and a presumed leisure budget. When the science of embalming became familiar after its wider usage during the American Civil War (1861–1865), the preparation and display of the deceased moved from the domestic dwelling to the commercial funeral parlor or funeral home.

The Demise of the Domestic Parlor

By the 1910s, if not earlier, household decoration manual writers were proclaiming the death of the parlor, now considered "cluttered" and "dusty." Men's increased attendance in the workplace, children's lengthening school day (not to mention more years of schooling), and women's increased entrance into the workplace and the public sphere refigured not only the American family but its dwelling as well. The parlor gave way to the living room. Commercial leisure, from sports to restaurants to movie theaters, accessible via public transportation and the automobile, offered other venues for sociability. The practices of the parlor remain codified in rituals associated with formality: High school graduation announcements are personalized with calling cards, for example, announcing one's entrance into society.

Shirley Teresa Wajda

See also Aesthetic Movement; Bedrooms; Etiquette and Manners; Halls; Living Rooms; Rite, Ritual, and Ceremony

References and Further Reading

Ames, Kenneth L. 1992. "First Impressions." In *Death in the Dining Room and Other Tales of Victorian Culture*, 7–43. Philadelphia, PA: Temple University Press.

Bushman, Richard L. 1992. *The Refinement of America: Persons, Houses, Cities*. New York: Alfred A. Knopf.

Cummings, Abbott Lowell. 1964. *Rural Household Inventories: Establishing the Names, Uses and Furnishings of Rooms in the Colonial New England Home, 1675–1775*. Boston: Society for the Preservation of New England Antiquities.

Garrett, Elisabeth Donaghy. 1990. *At Home: The American Family 1750–1850*. New York: Harry N. Abrams.

Grier, Katherine C. 1988. *Culture & Comfort: People, Parlors and Upholstery, 1850–1930*. Rochester, NY: Margaret Woodbury Strong Museum; Amherst: University of Massachusetts Press.

Kwolek-Folland, Angel. 1984. "The Elegant Dugout: Domesticity and Moveable Culture in the United States, 1870–1900." *American Studies* 25 (2): 21–37.

Leach, William R. 1993. *Land of Desire: Merchants, Power, and the Rise of a New American Culture*. New York: Vintage.

Wajda, Shirley Teresa. 1997. "The Commercial Photographic Parlor, 1839–1889." In *Shaping Communities: Perspectives in Vernacular Architecture*, ed. Carter L. Hudgins and Elizabeth Collins Cromley, 216–230. Knoxville: University of Tennessee Press.

Patents, Trademarks, and Brands

Property rights for inventors, innovators, and manufacturers in their discoveries have been recognized in law from the very beginnings of what would become the United States. Through the registration of patents and trademarks individuals and companies are granted legal rights to the profits of an invention as well as to its design. The United States Patent and Trademark Office grants more than 180,000 patents a year, providing an accessible record of the ever-changing material culture of the United States.

Curators consult patent records to date, describe, and interpret specific artifacts. Scholars interested in invention, technology, industrialization, and consumption find in patent and trademark records evidence of objects that changed American society, of ideas made material, and occasionally, objects that never got off the drawing board. In addition, the visual, material, and textual strategies of branding a marketable good or set of goods, from the "look" of a *brand* (often interchangeable with *trademark*) to its associated advertising campaigns to elicit product recognition and consumption, provide useful evidence of the ways in which manufacturers and advertisers gauged American consumers' needs, desires, and tastes.

Patents

A *patent* is a state-granted limited monopoly. Many of the first North American colonies were founded as land patents granted by European monarchs, guaranteeing that the joint-stock companies that sought to establish settlements for trade and riches would enjoy the protection of the monarchy against competition. In England, the monarch also issued patents for his own benefit and that of his court. Certain industries were protected through patents. Patents, unlike taxes, were ways for the monarch to raise money without incurring popular anger. The power of the monarch to issue patents was not unfettered. In 1624 the English Parliament passed a Statute of Monopolies, which limited the power of the king to grant monopolies only to "manners of new manufacture" and only for a period of fourteen years. The Massachusetts Bay Colony was granted invention patents in the 1640s.

During the Confederation period (1777–1787) the individual states had the power to grant patents. The first national patent system, "to promote the Progress of Useful Arts," was provided for in the United States Constitution and established through an act by the United States Congress in 1790. A patent was granted for a period of fourteen years to grantees who had submitted a description of the invention and, if applicable, a model. This act was repealed in 1793. In its stead was a more precise definition of what may be patented: "any new and useful art, machine, manufacture or composition of matter or any new and useful improvement on any art, machine, manufacture or composition of matter." Though altered in detail and application over time, this definition has remained in force. Applications now must include a description of the invention and an argument for its distinction from other patented inventions. Court cases and changes in law have assured that only novel inventions were granted patents and that patent infringement be rationalized rather than left to the decisions of courts. The United States Patent Office was created under the Department of State in 1836 and transferred to the new Department of Commerce and Labor in 1925.

The nation's patent system has encouraged innovation and manufacturing. Patent descriptions were made readily available throughout the nation through the Patent Act of 1836. Libraries in every state regularly received copies of new patents, thus providing public knowledge of the nation's "Progress of Useful Arts." The ever-increasing numbers of patents demanded a patent classification system, which was adopted in the United States in the late nineteenth century. Reflecting the effects of globalization, the International Patent Classification has been in use since 1968. Novel technological inventions are sorted into eight key categories: A: Human Necessities; B: Performing Operations, Transporting; C: Chemistry, Metallurgy; D: Textiles, Paper; E: Fixed Constructions; F: Mechanical Engineering, Lighting, Heating, Weapons; G: Physics; and H: Electricity.

Trademarks

Manufacturers of similar goods or providers of similar services identify and distinguish their goods and services from others through the use of *trademarks.* Trademarks guard against confusion by or deception of a consumer while reinforcing in the consumer's mind the quality or qualities of a given good as well as the goodwill between manufacturer and consumer. A trademark historically took the form of a word, a phrase, a symbol, or a design, or a combination thereof. Trademarks are usually found on a good or on its packaging. With the rise of radio, film, television, and the Internet, trademarks now may be three dimensional, a sound or series of sounds, a scent, or a color. The Internet has led to an exponential increase in trademark registration, including domain names. Unlike patents, trademarks can be renewed as long as a manufacturer or business exists.

The first trademark protected by law in the United States was for the manufacture of sailcloth. Though Thomas Jefferson (1743–1826) would argue for trademark legislation in the late eighteenth century to protect American manufacturers abroad and with trade to Native Americans, the first federal trademark law, based on patent and copyright law, was not passed until 1870, only to be repealed. In 1881, another trademark protection law was passed, this time legitimated by the United States Constitution's commerce clause. In 1883, an international trademark agreement was achieved, providing protection to manufacturers in the nations that were party to the agreement. Not until the 1905 Trademark Act, however, did domestic manufacturers file for trademark protec-

tion; this act, unlike its predecessors, included goods in interstate commerce, and not only foreign commerce. The Lanham Act of 1946, in force today, allows for federal enforcement of trademark law to end unfair competition, protects owners from consumer confusion created through the use of similar trademarks, and extends trademark protection to service marks.

A manufacturer's trademark may change over time, and thus a specific good or set of goods may be dated and the method(s) of manufacture known through research in trademark registration records. The trademarks themselves provide evidence of a given era's aesthetics, ideals, politics, and technology. Some imagery has been updated several times; in the case of General Mills' fictitious Betty Crocker, to reflect changing perceptions of the "typical" American homemaker. Trademarks employing derogatory imagery of Native Americans, African Americans, Irish, Italian, Chinese, and Jews have been generally discarded. Still other trademarks have remained constant: The cursive script of "Coca Cola" registered in 1887 is still in use. A trademark serves as a "memory hook" (Laird 1998, 15) and as such is the core element in brand marketing.

Brands

Originally a form of marking livestock with a hot iron, *branding* developed in the nineteenth century as a method of differentiating one manufacturer's goods from those of a competitor. Brands appeared in the nineteenth century, when mass production expanded markets and increased competition; integrated transportation allowed for goods to be shipped beyond the locales of their manufacture; and mass communications (including innovations in photography, lithography, and typesetting) allowed for the ready dissemination of information about goods through posters, trade cards, trade catalogues, newspapers, magazines, and packaging.

Registered trademarks endow owners with legal rights; brands, on the other hand, more often refer to a set of distinctive features of a product or service and strategies of advertising and marketing to inform consumers and induce them to buy said product or service. Brand recognition was ensured through distinctive styling and packaging; brand loyalty, it was believed, would be cultivated through familiarity, dependability, and attractiveness. Early successful brands included Ivory Soap, with its slogan "99 44/100 Pure®—It Floats" attesting to its purity. By the 1920s, advertisers were invested in creating campaigns for mass market goods and services, using music, jingles, slogans, celebrity endorsements, and mascots to persuade consumers to buy. Within a decade, advertising agencies employed the insights of social sciences such as psychology, anthropology, and sociology to create strategies of selling goods through appeals to consumer desires and lifestyles. In the twenty-first-century United States, brand experience, brand loyalty, cross-branding, product placement in movies, and branding itself is inextricable from daily life.

Shirley Teresa Wajda

See also Advertisements and Advertising; Commercials; Commodity; Consumerism and Consumption; Fakes; Mail Order Catalogues; Popular Culture; Technology; Trade Cards; Trade Catalogues

References and Further Reading

Coombe, Rosemary J. 1996. "Embodied Trademarks: Mimesis and Alterity on American Commercial Frontiers." *Cultural Anthropology* 11 (2): 202–224.
Dobyns, Kenneth W. 1994. *The Patent Office Pony: A History of the Early Patent Office*. Fredericksburg, VA: Sergeant Kirkland's Museum.
Laird, Pamela Walker. 1998. *Advertising Progress: American Business and the Rise of Consumer Marketing*. Baltimore, MD: Johns Hopkins University Press.
Phillips, Barbara J. 1996. "Defining Trade Characters and Their Role in American Popular Culture." *Journal of Popular Culture* 29 (4): 143–158.

Penitentiaries and Prisons

Penitentiaries and prisons are specifc examples of institutions in which the ownership and use of material culture are strictly controlled. Whether one building or many, whether urban or rural, the built environment of these institutions controls their temporary and permanent inhabitants. *Penitentiaries* are the dominant form today and are institutions whose aim, to some degree, is the reformation or correction of individuals convicted for breaking the law. A *prison* is a building used to forcibly confine individuals awaiting trial or serving a term of punishment. Today, prisons are used to hold individuals before a trial, and nearly all convicted felons are then sent to a penitentiary. A cell in a typical American maximum-security penitentiary contains only a few permanent objects: steel bunks, a stainless steel toilet and washbasin, a grille of steel bars across a small window, another grille of steel bars across the front of the cell. Prisoners are allowed scant possessions. They are issued bedding, hygiene items, and clothing. They are able to buy snacks and some personal care products at the prison commissary. Penitentiary authorities limit their books, magazines, photographs, and jewelry. Inmates are sometimes permitted to purchase an in-cell television or a pair of name-brand sneakers. Many commonplace objects are forbidden, for example, transparent ballpoint pens, which can be utilized as syringes, and masking tape, which can be wound around a plastic eating utensil, strengthening it so that it becomes a weapon. The objects allowed in prison all have significance. They have been proscribed by the prison authorities; they have specific functions and meanings that contribute to the prison's purposes—to incarcerate, punish, and rehabilitate inmates.

Throughout their history, these institutions —and the material culture found in them— have represented American ideas about criminality, punishment, and rehabilitation. At the same time, prisoners have occasionally found ways to use objects for their own self-expression in defiance of the structures of prison life.

Prison Design and
Prisoner Rehabilitation

The first notable American prison was the Walnut Street prison in Philadelphia, constructed in 1775. This institution looked like a large house and functioned like an unruly household. Inmates of both sexes and all degrees of criminality kept quarters together, walking about freely in their street clothes and drinking and gambling as they chose. The commonplace objects used in the prison were often of high quality; an archaeological excavation conducted at the site in 1973 found hundreds of shards of fine English creamware and oriental porcelain, which were typically owned by genteel families. Debtors, sometimes wealthy men who had fallen into financial straits, were evidently permitted to bring their accustomed lifestyles with them to prison.

The lenient character of the Walnut Street prison reflected the colonial view of criminality. Many colonists subscribed to the Calvinist belief in the innate depravity of humans and regarded crime as a sin against God. Just as sin could not be cured, criminals could not be rehabilitated. The colonists be-

lieved in punishment ranging from fines to acts of public shaming (whippings, brandings, letter wearing) to the gallows. But incarceration in a prison held no hope of redemption, and therefore the lives of prisoners within the prison walls were surprisingly unrestricted.

The American concept of criminality changed dramatically during the late eighteenth and early nineteenth centuries, informed by Enlightenment ideas about the capability of humans to shape their own destinies. Prison advocates began to envision the prison as a place where criminals could be imbued with morality and discipline. Crucial to the success of this project was the physicality of the prison, the way it was designed, and the objects found inside. Physician Benjamin Rush (1746–1813), a leading Philadelphia reformer, wrote that prisons should embody principles "of bodily pain, labour, watchfulness, solitude, and silence" (quoted in Meranze 1996, 134). Every architectural detail, from the appearance of the walls to the shape of a cell window, could be used to influence proper behavior.

The new ideas about rehabilitation were fully implemented during the 1820s, when two significant penitentiaries were completed: Philadelphia's Eastern Penitentiary at Cherry Hill and New York's Auburn Penitentiary. Eastern Penitentiary's "Pennsylvania system" called for the absolute isolation of every inmate; the rehabilitative idea was for prisoners to be confronted only with the Bible, their own conscience, and the "cheerless blank" of the walls around them. The building was a massive structure resembling a medieval military fortress. Inside was a central observation tower with seven radial cellblock arms; the positioning of the tower and guard walkways allowed for the easy surveillance of prisoners. Each cell had a

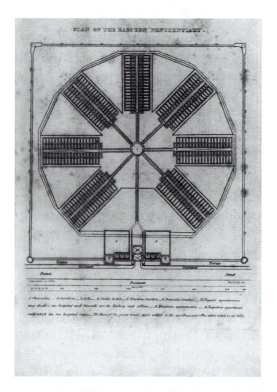

This circa 1850 plan of Philadelphia's Eastern State Penitentiary, engraved by C. C. Childs, reveals how the building's design isolated each inmate while allowing, through a central observation tower, constant surveillance. Designed by architect John Haviland and opened in 1829, the penitentiary served as the template for many structures of incarceration built in the United States and in other nations. (Library of Congress)

round window in the ceiling, known as the "eye of God," and its own attached walled-in exercise yard. Inmates remained in their cell and exercise yard for the duration of their sentence, taking their meals through a food drawer, sleeping, working, and bathing there, not once laying eyes on their fellow inmates. Silence was maintained at all times: Guards wore heavy wool socks over their shoes, and carts used on prison grounds had their wheels muffled with leather. The institution's ventilation, heating, and plumbing systems were painstakingly constructed to prevent inmates from communicating with each other, for example, by tapping on pipes. Prisoners were permitted no letters or visits from family members. The only book allowed, placed in each cell, was the Bible.

Like prisoners in Pennsylvania, those at the Auburn Penitentiary were required to be silent. To teach social discipline, inmates were placed in tempting proximity to one another while being forbidden to communicate in any way. The penitentiary was designed so that each prisoner lived in a separate cell, but there were common dining areas, work rooms, and marching yards. Material objects were essential to the penitentiary's disciplinary program. The prisoners' daily life was guided by the sound of horns and bells, which alerted them when to awaken, eat, work, and sleep; they were required to pick up their night buckets (receptacles in which bodily waste was placed), empty them, and clean them in unison; they sat at long tables in the mess room, all facing in the same direction, their backs erect, never making eye contact; they wore the same coarse striped uniform. American penitentiaries that followed the "Auburn system" devised a number of ingenious punishment devices for inmates who broke the rules. These included the iron gag, "stretcher" pulley systems, the "sweat box" (an unventilated cell next to a fireplace), and the "shower" (a chair in which an inmate was locked and then drenched with a powerful stream of ice water).

Penology in the Twentieth Century

Progressive Era reformers charged that the Pennsylvania and Auburn systems that had been widely implemented in the United States were inhumane and counterproductive. In particular, reformers believed that inmates who spent years in enforced silence and solitary confinement were utterly unprepared to reenter society. The new model held that prison life should approximate normal community life as much as possible. Altering prison design and material culture was the key to reform. Inmate possessions were now yoked to the rehabilitative process; as in the larger society, what one owned was a gauge of success. For example, a pioneering effort at the Elmira Reformatory in New York during the 1880s permitted "first grade" inmates to live in cells furnished with a cupboard, chair, and other amenities, while "third grade" inmates were consigned to cells with only a bed and night bucket. During the 1930s in some penitentiaries, well-behaved inmates were rewarded with movie nights and earphones connected to a central radio system. The design of prisons changed, although not fundamentally. Inmates still lived in enormous cellblocks, frequently monitored from control towers and catwalks by guards, but classrooms, vocational workshops, baseball diamonds, and basketball courts were added to the prison complex. The "yard" became a focal point of prison life, where inmates could easily socialize while participating in recreational activities.

Most of these innovations, while making the environment less oppressive, did little to successfully rehabilitate prisoners. Some changes were purely cosmetic. Reformers insisted that inmates be permitted to wear clothing that would make them feel more "normal"; the prisoner's striped uniform was abolished, only to be replaced by regulation-gray pants and sweaters stenciled with the prisoner's identification number. Educational programs were chronically underfunded. Vocational workshops taught how to make road signs and automobile license plates, but there were no jobs awaiting prisoners who acquired these skills, because only state prisons produced road signs and license plates.

More recent prison design has attempted to tailor incarceration to the problems and needs of particular inmate groups. Minimum-, medium-, and maximum-security facilities have been developed, each with a material culture that reflects the resident population: men or women, low-risk offenders or hardened criminals, the physically impaired, the mentally ill. For example, prisons that house nonviolent mothers often feature nurseries and playrooms for visiting children. Special units have been designed for geriatric and disabled inmates, with guard rails, grab bars and enlarged cells for those in wheelchairs. Many minimum- and medium-security prisons resemble college campuses. Rather than stand out in the landscape, bristling and forbidding, these prisons are intended to blend in with surrounding vernacular structures. Buildings are constructed from brick, stucco, and glass; the perimeter is marked by fences instead of walls. Inmates live in small cell clusters around a multiuse communal area, attractively furnished and decorated, where both inmates and staff can congregate. In contrast, "super-max" penitentiaries have been built for the worst offenders, spurred by the political enthusiasm for "get tough" policies against criminals. These penitentiaries echo the austere policies of the Pennsylvania and Auburn systems. Prisoners are locked down in solitary-confinement cells for up to twenty-four hours per day. There are no communal areas, and inmates exercise alone while wearing leg restraints and waist chains.

Objects of Defiance

American penal institutions have successfully incarcerated and punished criminals but have often failed miserably to rehabilitate them. One measure of this failure is the extent to which inmates have turned prison material culture against their jailers. Although weapons and narcotics are prohibited, in prisons today gang-related violence and drug use are endemic, a situation that has developed through the ingenuity of prisoners. Weapons have been created out of bits of sharpened plastic or rolled-up newspapers soaked in toothpaste. A homemade ball and chain is made by weighing down a plastic cup with wetted toilet paper and tying up the cup in a sweat sock. Drugs are smuggled into and around prisons in a variety of items, such as snack pies, cassette-tape cases, and tennis balls.

Commonplace objects have become the media for artistic self-expression. Wetted toilet paper and soft bread are molded into three-dimensional objects and then painted. White cotton handkerchiefs serve as a prized drawing surface, to the extent that a style of handkerchief art known as *Pano Arte* has become popular among Hispanic prisoners. In institutions that ban paints and colored pencils, inmates have made colored art by scraping glossy magazine covers and using the colored dust or soaking colored candies to release their dye, then painting an image with the resulting color, and lacquering the image with floor wax. Tattooing is a widespread means of expression; inmates concoct tattoo guns by assembling objects such as paper clips, ballpoint pens, Walkman motors, and batteries. Authorities on prison art note that the tattoo helps the inmate to retain a sense of selfhood amid dehumanizing conditions; one's own body is inscribed with a highly personal iconography. Tattooing is particularly popular because it is uniformly forbidden in American prisons.

Tom Collins

See also Body Modification; Civic Architecture; Human Body

References and Further Reading
Blomberg, Thomas G., and Karol Lucken. 2000. *American Penology: A History of Control.* Hawthorne, NY: Aldine de Gruyter.

Kornfeld, Phyllis. 1997. *Cellblock Visions: Prison Art in America.* Princeton, NJ: Princeton University Press.
Meranze, Michael. 1996. *Laboratories of Virtue: Punishment, Revolution, and Authority in Philadelphia, 1760–1835.* Chapel Hill: University of North Carolina Press.
Morris, Norval, and David J. Rothman, eds. 1995. *The Oxford History of the Prison: The Practice of Punishment in Western Society.* New York: Oxford University Press.

Photography

Photography is a method by which an image is recorded by direct light or by light directed through a camera onto a light-sensitive, chemically treated surface or, more recently, converted to a digital "memory stick" that stores images. The history of photography has typically rested on the invention of the many new and different processes and materials employed in making photography a commercially successful enterprise. The impact of photography is immeasurable and ongoing: From the earliest direct images on silver-coated copperplate to digital images saved on "memory sticks" for alteration or reproduction via computer software and printers, the photographic image since 1839 has altered humans' understanding of the earth and its inhabitants.

Though often termed a *mirror of nature*, the photographic image is the product of culture discernible in the image's framing, subject, and social relations. As a form of material culture, photographs are admired works of art; objects of display and collection; sentimental possessions; pedagogical tools; and legal, journalistic, and historical evidence. Photographs are used to create images on clothing (T-shirts), tablewares (coffee mugs), souvenirs (postcards and plates), and toys (jigsaw puzzles). Many a refrigerator in the American kitchen has become a gallery of family and humorous photographs. Desktops and walls display loved ones' portraits. Fashion shots sell clothes; mug shots and the Federal Bureau of Investigation's "Ten Most Wanted" list warn of danger. The invention of electric light allowed for photography at night; the invention of flight allowed for aerial photography. Photography is integrally intertwined with modernity in the United States, so much so that it is difficult to imagine a world without such images with which to remember, prove, defend, deny, and love.

Commercial Photography

The quest for a commercially viable means of creating portraits was undertaken by several men. In England, William Henry Fox Talbot (1800–1877) and Sir John Herschel (1792–1871) experimented separately with salted paper sensitized with silver nitrate. (Herschel coined the word *photography*.) Yet it was the work of Frenchman Louis Jacques Mandé Daguerre (1787–1851) that achieved widespread acknowledgment as the "invention" of photography. Announced in January 1839, *daguerreotypy*, through which a positive image was created directly on a chemically treated, silver-coated copperplate placed in a camera, was introduced in the United States in September of that year. By 1840, Americans had read about daguerreotypy and many individuals took up daguerreotypy as a profession.

Early daguerreotypy was plagued by an imperfect understanding of the process as well as unreliable chemicals and flawed camera lenses and plates. The necessity of having to place the plate, wet with chemicals, into the camera before removing the camera lens cover frustrated even the most patient and experienced of practitioners. Nevertheless, throughout the 1840s Americans flocked to the growing number of daguerreotype rooms in which they could sit for their likenesses or view exhibitions of daguerreotypic portraits, still lifes, and landscapes. Americans could also engage the services of itinerant daguerreotypists who lugged their equipment from town to village.

By the 1850s, daguerreotypy was being imitated in the ambrotype (in which the image was fixed on japanned glass) and the tintype or ferrotype (in which the image was fixed on sheet metal). Given the fragility of the image, which could be easily scratched, these forms were encased in leather-covered, gutta-percha-covered, or thermoplastic ("Union") cases or protected by glass, brass mats, and preservers. At mid-decade, however, these processes were replaced by photography on paper, created through the use of glass plates rather than metal ones. Photographers' reception rooms became parlors, decorated with fashionable carpets, wall and window coverings, and furniture and often featuring music in the form of pianos or songbirds (hence, for fussy children sitting for their portraits, the direction to "watch the birdie"). The appeal to genteel culture was also reflected in the uses of tables, posing chairs and stands, painted backdrops, and other properties employed in creating portraits. Albert Sands Southworth (1811–1894) and Josiah Hawes (1808–1901) of Boston, Mathew B. Brady (1822–1896) of New York City, James Presley Ball (1825–1904) of Cincinnati, and Marcus Aurelius Root (1808–1888) of Philadelphia employed these strategies for their growing middle-class clientele.

Innovations and improvements from the 1850s throughout the rest of the century confirmed photography's permanent role in American life. The adoption of the negative allowed for retouching, and this, along with the growing sophistication in the knowledge of light and pose, allowed photographers to claim the artist's mantle. The power of portraiture to re-create or confirm social relations was reflected in the small *carte de visite*, a calling-card-sized photograph that could be traded and collected in albums created for that purpose. By the 1870s, larger cabinet cards were meant to be displayed in parlors, in ornate parlor table albums, on walls and tabletops, in wall pockets and bookcase shelves, and on easels. In studios and darkrooms (in which plates were developed and "fixed"—that is, the chemical action on the surface was stopped—through the application of chemicals and heat), photographers adopted improvements such as "dry plate" glass negatives that could be prepared and stocked in quantity. Albumen prints, the most popular form of photograph, were paper coated with a mixture of egg white and silver salts. Other novel forms, such as the gem or imperial size, for images on jewelry and ceramics, or large "crayon" portraits, combining photography and paint, engaged Americans in a variety of ways to contemplate other humans and the world as created through the frame of the image.

Stereography

One of the most popular forms of commercial photography from the 1850s through the 1920s was the *stereograph*, a cardboard mount upon which two photographs of the same subject, each taken from a slightly different point of view (approximately two-and-a-half inches) with a two-lens camera, are pasted. When viewed through the binocular lenses of a stereoscope, three-dimensional depth of field is realized. Single stereograph cards of famous personages, tourist destinations, newsworthy events, and humorous scenes acted out in front of the camera were collected by Americans after the introduction of the stereograph and stereoscope at London's Crystal Palace Exhibition in 1851. By the 1870s, stereographs were made by amateur and commercial photographers and were purchased from photographers, from door-to-door salesmen, and through mail order firms such as Sears, Roebuck and Co. Stereo-

graph viewing was considered a didactic family pastime, but it was also introduced into schools as a means of exploring geography, history, and nature.

Amateur Photography

Amateurs had tried their hand at photography since the 1840s, but the pastime was expensive and time consuming, and practitioners were primarily wealthy. Professional cameras were large and usually positioned on a tripod stand. The introduction of dry-plate glass negatives led to the popularization of "detective cameras" in the 1870s and 1880s. Disguised as satchels or lunch baskets, these cameras contained five or six negatives to capture, unnoticed, what the amateur wished. The *snapshot* (a term borrowed from hunting, meaning the hunter's rifle shot at prey without aiming) engendered delight as well as public consternation; lawsuits concerning the right of privacy ensued, especially after George Eastman's (1854–1932) invention of a flexible, paper-based roll film in 1888. Eastman's box or "hand" camera, in which roll film for 100 images was packaged, was extremely popular. The camera was returned to the factory for developing, the film was reloaded, and snapshots and camera were returned to the amateur. Eastman's Kodak system, the advertising slogan of which was "You press the button, we do the rest," became synonymous with amateur photography. In 1900, the easy-to-use Brownie camera was offered to the public, with great commercial success.

Throughout the twentieth century, camera and film manufacturers created a variety of methods to facilitate amateur photography. Home movie cameras, first introduced by Eastman Kodak in 1932, were also dependent on the invention of roll film. In the main, however, it was the hand camera that Americans embraced, from the Polaroid "instant" camera with self-developing film, patented in 1947 by Edwin H. Land (1909–1991) and known originally as the Land camera, to the Kodak Instamatic (1963), which used a film cartridge for easier loading. Film itself underwent changes: Paper-based film was replaced by cellulose nitrate. In 1935, color photography was made widely available through Kodachrome film for both still and movie cameras. Flash bulbs created better lighting in which to capture images; the Instamatic would in the later 1960s facilitate the Flashcube, a rotating cube containing four flashbulbs. Automatic focus, battery-operated film advance and winding, flash, and other technological advances made photography attractive to consumers. The successful mass production of the video cassette recorder (VCR) in the late 1970s led to the "camcorder," a combination of a camera and VCR, introduced to the amateur market in 1980 by the Sony Corporation. Like the original Kodak, disposable ("single use") cameras, preloaded with film, were devised in the mid-1980s. These are sold in camera shops as well as grocery, drug, and variety stores and souvenir stands, the last venue testifying to the camera's place in the tourist's arsenal. The picture postcard, which experienced its own craze of collection at the beginning of the twentieth century, was increasingly supplanted with the points of view of tourist photographers.

The rise of amateur photography mirrored the rise of leisure time and consumption in the United States. By the mid-twentieth century, family outings and vacations and private celebrations could be captured in casual snapshots by a small, affordable, and easy-to-use camera.

Art Photography

In the late nineteenth century, "Kodakery" became a craze, and amateur photography

clubs were founded in great numbers throughout the United States. Professional photography journals carried articles and reports of the many exhibitions and meetings of these clubs, as well as criticism of amateur photographers who, professionals thought, would diminish the photographic art. Indeed, the debates about photography as a fine art were many, and it is in this era that the establishment of art photography occurred. What defined photography as an art in the nineteenth century was the practitioner's knowledge of light, chemicals, and art history applied in the framing of a landscape or the pose of a human subject. By the early twentieth century, a photograph was a fine art object if the practitioner manipulated not only the negative but the print, through retouching, airbrushing, and application of other materials. Members of the Pictorial Photographers of America such as Edward Steichen (1879–1973) and Gertrude Käsebier (1852–1934), for example, imitated established art forms through the use of printing processes and custom manipulation by hand of the photograph's surface to render it a unique work of art. In 1904 Steichen and Alfred Stieglitz (1864–1946) established the Little Galleries of the Photo-Secession at 291 Fifth Avenue in New York City. At "291," as the gallery was called, art photography was promoted. Stieglitz had founded *Camera Work* in 1903, which carried discussions of the nature of art and photography. It was with the advent of Modernism, with its establishment of critics, collections, and museums dedicated to Modernist works, that the photograph, the product of a machine, could be elevated to an art form.

Documentary Photography

The camera's ability to capture quickly the image in front of its lens (although framed by the photographer) has been lauded by many

This photograph of a young woman in colonial dress in a colonial interior is the work of Wallace Nutting, a minister turned amateur photographer turned entrepreneur of the Colonial Revival. His hand-colored "art photographs," created in his Connecticut studio, were popular gifts in the early twentieth century. (Wadsworth Atheneum Museum of Art, Hartford, Connecticut. Gift of David W. Dangremond)

as a means through which phenomena can be documented. Early photography, in the form of daguerreotypy, was indeed a slow process, but the camera immediately made its appearance on the battlefield in the American Civil War (1861–1865) as well as along the frontier that was the American West, whether as the means to record natural resources, as in the government-funded scientific explorations, or merely to recount the journey.

Yet the documentary style of photography is most often understood as that style employed by social reformers since the late nineteenth century in the United States. New York City newspaperman Jacob Riis (1849–1914), for example, employed the camera to record the deplorable conditions of the city's immigrant poor in *How the Other Half Lives* (1890). Riis' work became widely known because of the introduction of the halftone process, through which photographic images could be printed (rather than pasted) in books, newspapers, and magazines. During the Great Depression of the 1930s, the Farm Security Administration employed photographers to record Americans' daily lives in various regions of the nation affected by economic hardships. Documenting problems to encourage action and solution was the purpose of these efforts. Walker Evans (1903–1975), Margaret Bourke-White (1904–1971), Gordon Parks (1912–2006), and Dorothea Lange (1895–1965) are the best-known documentary photographers. War photographers such as Robert Capa (1913–1954) worked for *Life* magazine, continuing the practice of photography as a means of exposing problems.

Vernacular Photography

Scholarly and artistic interest in the ordinary photographs taken by amateurs has resulted in a relatively new term, *vernacular photography*, that describes the adoption of new inter- and extradisciplinary ways with which to study the ubiquitous photograph. A leading proponent of this approach, Geoffrey Batchen (2002), argues against the traditional art historical emphases on originality, aesthetics, and masterpieces, as well as histories of photography based on technological innovation. Observing that the photograph engages many aspects of human existence, Batchen proposes that scholars and critics extend their examinations beyond the United States and Europe. The increased practice in collecting ordinary photographs in a variety of venues—flea markets and yard sales, auctions and eBay, dumpsters—has lent another name to these objects: *found photography*.

Digital Photography

Digital cameras share the same original technology of early television's video tape recorders, created in the 1950s to capture live images by converting them to electric impulses and recording them on magnetic tape. With the 1969 invention of the charge-coupled device (CCD) that senses the intensity of light and color, images could be recorded on silicon microchips. Astronomers and the National Aeronautics and Space Administration were the first to use this technology, as well as computer technology, in the pursuit of science, creating digitized images of the surface of the moon and exploring other space phenomena.

Not until the 1990s was a commercially viable digital camera created for the American market. With these devices, a personal computer, not film, is now necessary to print photographic images from a camera. Digital cameras use electronic components and light sensors to capture an image and display that image immediately to the photographer, who may then choose to store or discard it. Portable cell phones may also contain this technology, allowing for recording both personal and newsworthy images. With the rise of the Internet, photographic images can be sent electronically throughout the world. While photographs were popularly understood as mirrors of nature, they never were. Through readily available software, photographs can now be altered with the click of a computer mouse. Such manipulation only continues the discussion of what, actually, a photograph captures.

Shirley Teresa Wajda

See also Art History and American Art; Computers and Information Technology; Ephemera; Modernism (Art Moderne); Parlors; Technology; Tourism and Travel; Vernacular; Visual Culture Studies

References and Further Reading

Batchen, Geoffrey. 2002. *Each Wild Idea: Writing, Photography, History*. Cambridge, MA: MIT Press.

Earle, Edward W., Jr. 1979. *Points of View: The Stereograph in America—A Cultural History*. Rochester, NY: Visual Studies Workshop.

Edwards, Elizabeth, and Janice Hart, eds. 2004. *Photographs Objects Histories: On the Materiality of Images*. London: Routledge.

Henisch, Heinz K., and Bridget A. Henisch. 1994. *The Photographic Experience, 1839–1914: Images and Attitudes*. State College: Pennsylvania State University Press.

Lipkin, Jonathan. 2005. *Photography Reborn: Image Making in the Digital Age*. New York: Harry N. Abrams.

Newhall, Beaumont. 1982. *The History of Photography from 1839 to the Present Day*, rev. ed. New York: Bulfinch Press.

Sandweiss, Martha A., ed. 1991. *Photography in Nineteenth-Century America*. Fort Worth, TX: Amon Carter Museum.

Stott, William. 1973. *Documentary Expression and Thirties America*. New York: Oxford University Press.

Plainness (Quaker)

The Religious Society of Friends (or Quakers, a pejorative term now deemed acceptable by most Friends), is a Protestant sect founded in 1652 by George Fox (1624–1691) in England. In the face of ongoing persecution of Quakers, in 1681, Quaker William Penn, an Englishman, encouraged Friends to settle on a large section of land in the English American colonies (today's Pennsylvania).

Quakers were well known in the seventeenth to the mid-nineteenth centuries for their adherence to principles of plainness. *Plainness* was a spiritual doctrine of a simple, unadorned relationship with others and with God. Materially, plainness was expressed in clothing, housing, quilts, and other material artifacts unadorned with pattern or decoration. A Quaker dress for a woman from the 1840s, for example, might consist of a solid dark color, straight sleeves, a modest-sized skirt with plain flat pleats, and a wide rectangular white collar. Patterns, lace, and the elaborate details and trimmings so popular in women's fashion of the nineteenth century are absent. In housing, the plain style was expressed again in simple rectilinear lines, a conscious effort to use vernacular building techniques and styles, and a lack of detailed adornment.

By the later nineteenth century, many Quakers found that practicing plainness was itself a form of self-pride. In addition, the pressure to conform to a social environment of increased ornamentation had its effects. Finally, while the plain style had been lauded as a spiritual path for Quakers, many Quakers, especially wealthy ones, had never fully adhered to the style. Yet even today, simplicity and plainness remain important testimonies to, or practices of, Quakers.

Helen Sheumaker

See also Dress, Accessories, and Fashion; Religion, Spirituality, and Belief; Religious Dress

References and Further Reading

Chiarappa, Michael J. 1992. "'The First and Best Sort': Quakerism, Brick Artisanry, and the Vernacular Aesthetics of Eighteenth-Century West New Jersey Pattern Brickwork Architecture." Ph.D. diss., University of Pennsylvania.

Garfinkel, Susan L. 1986. "Discipline, Discourse, and Deviation: The Material Life of Philadelphia Quakers, 1762–1781." M.A. thesis, University of Delaware.

Keller, Patricia J. 1996. *"Of the Best Sort But Plain": Quaker Quilts from the Delaware Valley, 1760–1890*. Chadds Ford, PA: Brandywine River Museum.

Lapsansky, Emma Jones, and Anne A. Verplanck, eds. 2003. *Quaker Aesthetics: Reflections on a Quaker Ethic in American Design and Consumption*. Philadelphia: University of Pennsylvania Press.

Planned Communities

Planned communities are cities, towns, villages, or neighborhoods in which all aspects of the physical organization of the community have been predetermined, often to support larger social and aesthetic principles. Planners, landscape architects, architects, and engineers determine the layout of streets and lots, the distribution of parkland and open space, the proximity to transportation infrastructure, and the mix of residential, commercial, and industrial land uses. Beginning in the United States with colonial communities such as Savannah, Georgia, and Williamsburg, Virginia, and continuing with the utopian communities of the nineteenth century, the Garden City Movement of the late nineteenth and early twentieth centuries, through early twentieth-century Greenbelt and New Towns to today's experiments with New Urbanism, planned communities reflect the larger social agendas of the era.

The modern history of American planned communities can be characterized as an effort to combine the best aspects of urban amenities and rural life. Often viewing the city as an unhealthy environment of pollution, overcrowding, and noise and the rural landscape as too isolated, planners in the United States have attempted to create an idealized "middle landscape" that balances development with green open space while maintaining a strong sense of community. The American preference for these middle landscapes has resulted in some of the unforeseen negative impacts of standardized suburban development and urban sprawl. There is, for example, a widespread nostalgia among the middle class in the United States for the iconography of "small-town America." The Florida communities of Seaside and Celebration are examples of this phenomenon. The current planning movement known as New Urbanism, based on pedestrian-oriented, mixed-use planning principles, often utilizes nostalgic architectural forms and details such as front porches and late nineteenth-century cottage-style aesthetics in an effort to re-create a lost residential landscape.

Jeffrey Blankenship

See also Cities and Towns; Company Towns; Mill Towns; Suburbs and Suburbia; Utopian Communities

References and Further Reading

Bressi, Todd, ed. 2002. *The Seaside Debates: A Critique of the New Urbanism: The Seaside Institute, Seaside, Florida.* New York: Rizzoli.

Forsyth, Ann. 2005. *Reforming Suburbia: The Planned Communities of Irvine, Columbia, and The Woodlands.* Berkeley: University of California Press.

Parsons, Kermit C., and David Schuyler, eds. 2002. *From Garden Cities to Green City: The Legacy of Ebenezer Howard.* Baltimore, MD: Johns Hopkins University Press.

Political Ephemera

Central to United States history is participation in, and the material culture relating to, politics. It was politics—bad politics as viewed by the English colonists—that founded the nation. Political viewpoints were expressed in the Revolutionary era through symbols, images, and materials of political dissent: liberty poles and liberty trees, political cartoons, allegorical imagery, the adoption of specialized dress. The establishment of free speech and assembly principles allowed for the expression of competing political ideologies. Political campaigns became popular experiences of the early nation's public life. Since the very first American presidential election candidates have been pushing their names, parties, and platforms to the public. A wide variety of political campaign materials have been employed to win the vote. Trinkets, buttons, snuffboxes, and even cigarettes have been used by candidates to sway the undecided public and reward the decided public to check the right names on the ballot on Election Day. Collecting political ephemera, especially those materials related to election campaigns, has become one of the fastest growing hobbies in the nation.

The First National Campaigns

The inauguration of the nation's first president, George Washington (1732–1799), was commemorated by copper, brass, and pewter buttons bearing his likeness. Andrew Jackson (1767–1845) is generally credited with organizing the first campaign giveaways. Jackson, in his first failed (though controversial) bid for the presidency in 1824, distributed small medals for collars and lapels. Jackson's trinkets typically had holes in order to be tied on to the lapels and to be used as watch fobs. Jackson's other campaign medals were double sided, with an image of Jackson on one side and on the other side, a slogan such as "The Nation's Good." Jackson took advantage of this new form of advertising by also providing silk ribbons, cartoons, posters, ballots, and prints.

The 1840 campaign between Whig nominee William Henry Harrison (1773–1841) and Democrat Martin Van Buren (1782–1862) was the first (as the Smithsonian Institution's National Museum of American History claims) to associate consistent imagery with a candidate, namely, Harrison's Log Cabin Campaign. A Democratic editor said that Harrison would be just as happy with a jug of hard cider to sip in front of his log cabin as serving as president. The Whigs seized this idea, playing up Harrison's appeal to the masses with a "log cabin and hard cider" campaign by serving hard cider at campaign rallies, producing campaign imagery of jugs and log cabins, and making Harrison synonymous with the image of a log cabin. Harrison's running mate, John Tyler (1792–1862), was also brought into the campaign with what is considered to be the first slogan for a presidential candidate: "Tippecanoe and Tyler, Too."

Harrison also used tokens to discredit his opponent. Harrison's "Hard Times Token," distributed to the public, referred to the federal government's intervention in banking and the nationwide depression occurring during Martin Van Buren's (1782–1862) term (and was the first time that the Democratic Party was represented by the image of a donkey). Harrison and Tyler defeated Van Buren in 1840 by 145,000 popular votes and captured 80 percent of the electoral votes.

Campaign coins—photographs taken on a thin sheets of tin or iron (thus called ferrotypes or tintypes)—were very popular in the mid-to-late nineteenth century. Many of the coins featured the candidate's image(s) along with a slogan and sometimes another emblematic image. Abraham Lincoln (1809–1865) used a ferrotype with an image the Republicans were desperate to convey: The "Rail-Splitter of the West" image was used to appeal to western voters and show that he was a man of the people.

Commercialization and Improvements of Political Campaign Materials

By the 1870s the commercial appeal and marketing possibilities of political campaign materials was evident. In 1876, the Blackwell Durham Bull Tobacco Company made a trading card for both candidates, Republican Rutherford B. Hayes (1822–1893) and New York Democrat Samuel J. Tilden (1814–1886). These trading cards, as metamorphic cards, were designed so that as the card was moved, the image was altered.

The 1880s ushered in the era of cloth-covered buttons and the shank-backed enameled buttons. Paper images wrapped around a disc and coated with celluloid became popular. Celluloid-fronted buttons for presidential campaigns in 1888, 1892, and 1896 achieved further popularity as the full-celluloid button was put into use, the first time the modern button style was used.

Buttons were not the only popular campaign giveaways of the latter nineteenth century. Lapel pieces with moving parts—known as *mechanicals*—appealed in the 1880s and 1890s. These mechanicals featured presidential chairs, coffins, flags, and eagles. The election of 1896 also brought about mechanicals of bugs—both gold and silver—to reflect the gold versus silver controversy between candidates William McKinley (1843–1901) and William Jennings Bryan (1860–1925). McKinley's 1896 campaign also produced a flag with his face pronouncing his virtues of "patriotism, protection, and prosperity."

Theodore Roosevelt's (1858–1919) campaigns of 1904 and 1912 offered a lapel pin with a cowboy hat initialed "T.R." Buttons stamped in lithographic tin became available in 1916, and that election, featuring Woodrow Wilson (1856–1924) and Charles Evans Hughes (1862–1948), saw another win by Woodrow Wilson, after he voted down the slogan "He kept us out of war"—perhaps thinking, and correctly, that would not be possible. The 1916 election is considered to be the first election that the name and slogan pieces became popular nationwide.

The Rise and Popularity of Political Campaign Materials

Throughout the twentieth century, campaign materials grew more lavish. Attempts to appeal to voters grew, and candidates' attempts to sway voters began to appeal to voters' vices. After the repeal of Prohibition, Franklin Delano Roosevelt (1882–1945) gave out whiskey shot glasses exclaiming that "Happy Days Are Here Again." Roosevelt was such a powerful opponent for Republicans that campaign materials grew during his four terms in office. Wendell Wilkie (1892–1945) distributed over 1,000 different buttons in the 1940 election to oppose Roosevelt. Adlai Stevenson (1900–1965) offered packs of "Stevenson for President" cigarettes in his bids for the presidency in the 1950s. In

1972 Richard Nixon (1913–1994) handed out bubblegum cigars to voters. The Dwight D. Eisenhower (1890–1969) campaign was also noteworthy for the amount and variety of campaign handouts, of not only buttons and leaflets but also potholders and pencils. Eisenhower was another candidate to hand out cigarettes as a way for voters to remember his name on Election Day.

John F. Kennedy (1917–1963) was the first candidate to use television as a campaign strategy with his program "Coffee with Senator and Mrs. Kennedy." For this show, Kennedy's campaign distributed paper cups ideally for use while watching the show. Nixon was also creative in his campaign "freebies," offering a bumper sticker asking voters to select his wife "Pat for First Lady." In 1964, Barry Goldwater (1909–1998) became the first presidential candidate to use the periodic table as a form of name recognition with his AuH_2O slogan for the 1964 presidential election: Au is the elemental symbol for gold and H_2O the formula for water.

Political Reform Materials

The breadth of political material culture is not limited to presidential elections. The Elizabeth Cady Stanton Trust, established in 1999, has collected women's rights and suffrage materials in an effort to preserve and study that cause. Among the pieces collected is a windowpane sign from the early 1900s that reads, "A woman living here has registered to vote thereby assuming responsibility of citizenship." The National Women's History Museum collects material culture related to women's suffrage. These buttons and ribbons are traditionally gold in color and are adorned with simple statements such as "Votes for Women." Other objects adopt the colors of the American suffrage movement: gold, white, and purple. One gold button produced during the campaign for the referendum to allow universal suffrage in Ohio exclaimed "Let Ohio Women Vote" around an angelic figure with radiant sunlight emanating from behind her.

The nineteenth-century abolitionist societies and the civil rights movement of the 1950s and 1960s adopted the same media produced in other political forums. As far back as 1838, American abolitionists produced bronze tokens asking "Am I not a woman & a sister?" The American Colonization Society, founded in 1816, promoted moving free African Americans to Africa (ultimately Liberia) as opposed to the possibility of emancipation. To forward its cause, the society issued one-cent coins in 1833 with "Liberia" over an image of a man working with a ship approaching a shore.

Gay rights political materials have been produced since at least the 1960s. Demonstrations outside the White House, Pentagon, and the Department of State in that decade produced posters proclaiming "First Class Citizenship for Homosexuals" and "Homosexual Americans Demand Their Civil Rights." One of the most prominent collections of gay, lesbian, bisexual, and transgender materials is the Morris Kight Collection, housed at the Lesbian and Gay Historical Society in San Diego, California.

Collecting Political Memorabilia

The last thirty years have brought much in the way of candidates and slogans, but little in the way of new forms of political material culture. Still, giveaways and images are very popular among candidates. Collectible presidential memorabilia—objects kept or collected because of their historical associations or because they evoke memories of events, people, or places with which they are associated—is no longer produced by the candidates themselves. The United States Postal Service offered an Inauguration Day 2005 keepsake set with photographs of George W. Bush and Dick Cheney, a twenty-six-page booklet, and twenty 37-cent stamps. The American Political Items Collectors (APIC) was founded in 1945 to "encourage the collection, preservation, and study of political Americana;" Political memorabilia collecting grew widely in the 1960s. Today APIC has more than 3,000 members with thirty chapters nationwide.

James Yasko

See also Advertisements and Advertising; Collecting and Collections; Ephemera; Popular Culture; Print Culture; Souvenirs

References and Further Reading
American Political Items Collectors. 2005. Home page. http://www.apic.us.
Duke University. 2000. "America Votes: Presidential Campaign Memorabilia from the Duke University Special Collections Library." http://scriptorium.lib.duke.edu/americavotes/.
Fischer, Roger A. 1988. *Tippecanoe and Trinkets Too: The Material Culture of American Presidential Campaigns, 1828–1984*. Urbana: University of Illinois Press.
Melder, Keith E. 1992. *Hail to the Candidate: Presidential Campaigns from Banners to Broadcast*. Washington, DC: Smithsonian Institution Press.
National Women's History Museum. 2005. Home page. www.nmwh.org.
The Osgood File. August 2, 2004. "Political memorabilia reflects American culture of the time." http://www.acfnewsource.org/art/poli_memorabilia.html.
Stockman, Rachel. 2003. "Stanton's Memorabilia Stuffs a Family Closet." Women's E-News, August 26. http://www.womensenews.org/article.cfm/dyn/aid/1500/context/archives.
Vargas, Jose Antonio. 2005. "Signs of Progress." *Washington Post*, July 23, C1.
Warda, Mark. 2004. *200 Years of Political Campaign Collectibles*. Clearwater, FL: Galt Press.

Popular Culture

The definition of *popular culture* is hotly debated by scholars and cultural critics, but it is most often held to be one or more of the following: (1) items and activities that are widely available and appealing to the mainstream public (this includes mass-produced products that are designed specifically for the mainstream public); (2) all that is not considered "high culture"; or (3) a culture created spontaneously by the people for the people (a folk culture).

The first definition is usually associated with the American middle class, as its members are able to afford the various products and pursuits of popular culture. Much of what is produced for mass consumption is aimed directly at this economic group, which constitutes a large percentage of the nation's population. It is a quantitative definition that requires the examination of sales of products, tickets to performances, ratings of film and television, and research concerning the different types of audiences or consumers in order to define precisely what is considered "popular" at any given time.

The second definition emphasizes an important distinction between those works of art and activities that are enjoyed by different classes of people. This definition often regards popular culture as below standard or "low class" and requires us to judge an item or activity on the basis of supposed standards of high culture such as complexity, sensibility, and moral worth.

The third definition of popular culture is used to describe the handmade crafts, rituals, and amusements created for and by the working class for their own enjoyment. This definition assumes that anything created for the working class is not authentically popular. It implies that commercial popular culture is essentially forced upon them and used for purposes such as social control. The only "true" form of popular culture, according to those that espouse the third definition, is one they make for themselves. Often, critical analysts of rock and popular music use this definition to call attention to spontaneously emergent working-class musical forms like jazz or blues.

Popular culture is usually associated with things or products such as crafts, toys, and servingware, but also refers to activities such as games, rituals, festivals, and styles of dance. Most often, *popular culture* is used to describe media culture, which consists of movies, comics, novels, music, advertisements, newspapers, magazines, Web sites and television.

Historical Popular Culture in the United States

Initially, *popular culture* was defined in what today we would today call anthropological terms. When gentleman-scholars first started to examine popular culture in the late eighteenth century, they romanticized what they called *folk* or *peasant cultures* as simpler, more organic, and closer to nature. The folk songs, crafts, and rituals of American agrarian culture were seen as primitive and uncorrupted.

In the era before the advent of mass media, most forms of amusement were localized. For instance, songs were sung at home or in taverns. Evidence of early songs comes in the form of "broadside ballads" and newspaper articles. While traditional ballads were handed down orally, broadside ballads were songs put in print, on one side of a sheet of paper, with accompanying illustrations and sometimes music. With the spread of the press, songs began to be widely published. Musicians and singers often modified lyrics and music, however, changing them to reflect personal and community preferences. By the end of the nineteenth century, sheet music was produced and disseminated on a large scale, responding to the emergence of a large urban audience with pianos in their homes. The inventions of the phonograph and radio in the early twentieth century furthered the success of at-home piano entertainment.

The first form of American popular entertainment was the minstrel show. The minstrel show was the most popular form of entertainment from 1843 to 1870 patronized by the white middle and working classes. Minstrelsy was a blackface performance wherein (most often) white actors painted their faces black and depicted African Americans in grossly exaggerated and inaccurate ways. Minstrel shows portrayed slaves as either complete fools or wholly content with life on the plantation. After the Civil War (1861–1865), minstrelsy became part of other emerging traveling variety shows and continued until well into the 1950s. Evidence of these performances exists in sheet music with piano and vocal arrangements, handbills, and journalistic accounts of the performances in local newspapers.

During the nineteenth century, the United States moved from an agrarian economic base to an industrial economic base, and as a result, the middle class grew considerably and emerged more prosperous and literate. Novels, tabloids, and melodramas were created for the middle classes and were usually disparaged by critics. Technology had allowed for cheaper printing costs, driving the cost of books and newspapers down, so portions of novels were printed in both book form and serial form in newspapers. Writers of serials such as Henry James (1843–1916) were lambasted by many literary critics for printing sections of their work in newspapers, thus lowering the art form by associating

it with the middle class. Intellectuals of the day, such as Matthew Arnold (1822–1888), began to fear this unwieldy mass of people and held the perspective that these art forms and activities were at best undesirable and at worst leading to anarchy and social disintegration.

Popular Culture and American Cultural Anxieties

Like tavern singing, dancing was a participatory form of popular culture. Dancing has a long history, but as a popular amusement we can see evidence of a "dance craze" beginning in the early twentieth century. Some taverns had rooms adjacent where dancing took place, but dance halls soon emerged that could accommodate many more people.

Dance halls were another way for the urban public to experience music, but they were not like structured society dances or debutante balls, which were usually well chaperoned. Public halls were typically rented by small groups or clubs, and eventually halls were created specifically for dances, where young people met without chaperones and could experiment with romance, tobacco, and alcohol. Flyers and photographs are the principal material evidence of the dance hall craze. The dance halls were a working-class form of amusement, as the middle class generally preferred cabarets where dinner and performance were part of the experience. Just as other popular amusements, dance halls came under moral scrutiny, however, as some cities passed ordinances that limited the sale of alcohol and prohibited certain kinds of dance moves. Dancing had become associated with the moral degeneracy of youth, an association that would grow even stronger as young people began to engage in popular amusements more often on their own.

As mass forms of communication such as radio, film, and television emerged, audiences nationwide were able to view and hear broadcasts simultaneously. Material evidence of these media forms exists in many different formats. The radio itself reflects technological and stylistic changes. Some radio programs have been preserved in the form of recordings and/or scripts, as well as photographs of the performers while broadcasting.

Films and their creation, distribution, and consumption offer an abundance of material evidence, such as photographs of actors, premieres, and crowds of people in attendance at movie theaters. Posters and press photographs of stars were used to advertise films, and many of them have been reproduced. And, of course, the films themselves remain. Though some have been lost due to neglect or oversight, effort has been made to restore deteriorating films and convert them to digital format.

Television sets also illustrate the stylistic and technological changes brought about since its invention in the late 1920s. The original television set was a piece of technology that required extensive marketing in the 1940s. Televisions were promoted as handsome pieces of furniture intended as centerpieces of the communal areas of the home, quite unlike the portable handheld televisions available by the end of the twentieth century. Some television programs were also lost or never recorded—many shows were live and little priority was placed on preservation—but a great deal of television history is preserved in scripts and on film, video, DVD, and now the Internet. Television advertisements also remain, some of them for programs and networks, others for the set itself. Since television is a relatively recent and widely adopted invention, its importance as a historical subject has allowed for the accumulation of much information concerning its early innovators.

As each new form of mass media emerged, debates rehearsed the moral and aesthetic standards of mass-produced culture. By the time television became an everyday household item, for example, journalists, psychologists, and public figures had begun their debate about its effects on consumers. While some claimed that television could bring together families and create a forum for education, others felt it would lead to a sedentary culture incapable of conversation.

Journalists, public figures, and religious organizations continue to question the impact of new media forms, claiming that lax morals, low intellect, and dependency would result from their growing popularity. One result of this claim was the establishment of the Hays Code, instituted in 1934 by the major film studios, which was a specific standard of morals and "good taste" for films. Though fairly lenient on the depiction of violence, the code prohibited certain depictions of sexuality, crimes, and criminals. The Hays Code reflected a belief that popular amusements (and the public they were directed toward) held dangerous potential.

Understanding Popular Culture and Its Audiences

Many critics have sought to understand the relationship between popular amusements and the people who experience them. Early scholarship examined the content of popular culture to understand the desires of the consuming public. Later scholars concentrated on "effects" studies that mapped out a causal relationship between popular culture and negative behaviors. They conducted studies that focused on issues of crime and child rearing, such as the damaging behavioral effects of violent films, or the decreased level of physical activity in children who play video games. More recent explorations into popular culture use different kinds of material evidence to explore not just effects but also the many uses and gratifications of the consuming public.

Studies of representation work to uncover stereotypes and explore assumptions about race, class, gender, and sexuality in popular culture. Marlon Riggs' (1957–1994) documentaries, *Color Adjustment* (1991) and *Ethnic Notions* (1987), explore the representations of African Americans in popular culture, ranging from performance to postcards to film and television, while Jean Kilbourne explores representations of women in advertisements in her documentary *Killing Us Softly* (1979). Both scholars explore the dangerous social realities that result when one type of image is presented over and over again in popular texts. Feminist scholarship in the 1960s and 1970s worked to uncover ways in which popular culture misrepresented and repressed women. Kate Millett, Andrea Dworkin (1946–2005), and Molly Haskell conducted studies on pornography, claiming that the industry produced images that resulted in and perpetuated the victimization of women in the real world. Vito Russo's (1946–1990) groundbreaking book, *The Celluloid Closet* (1995), which eventually became a documentary film, explored the history and representation of gays and lesbians in Hollywood films.

Audience (or reception) studies work to understand the different ways that audiences interpret and interact with popular culture. Scholars in this field discuss all forms of audience practices and interpretations. They examine the dialogue of Internet message board threads; interviews with women about the experience of attending a rock concert; discussions at book club meetings; the fashion style of young Madonna fans in the 1980s; and the fan fiction, films,

and elaborate art and home architecture of film and television fans. All of this works to document the experience as well as the artifacts of popular culture.

As new art forms and amusements become popular, such as the Internet, video games, rap music, and rave dances, debates concerning moral decency and the decline of American civility re-emerge. But alongside the constant criticism are attempts to understand further and perhaps even defend the complex relationships between popular art forms and consumers.

Sandra M. Falero

See also Advertisements and Advertising; Animals; Body Modification; Collecting and Collections; Commercials; Consumerism and Consumption; Cultural Studies; Ephemera; Fanzines; Folklore and Folklife; Games; Illicit Pleasures and Venues; Leisure, Recreation, and Amusements; Literary Studies and American Literature; Music and Musical Instruments; Music Ephemera; Patents, Trademarks, and Brands; Political Ephemera; Print Culture; Printmaking and American Prints; Public Monuments and Popular Commemoration; Race; Religion, Spirituality, and Belief; Scrapbooks; Social History; Sports; Trade Cards; Vernacular; Visual Culture Studies

References and Further Reading
Cullen, Jim. 1996. *The Art of Democracy: A Concise History of Popular Culture in the United States*. New York: Monthly Review Press.
Fiske, John. 1989. *Understanding Popular Culture*. New York: Routledge.
Tichi, Cecilia. 1992. *Electronic Hearth: Creating an American Television Culture*. Oxford, UK: Oxford University Press.

Postmodernism

Though its coinage may be dated in English to 1914, *Postmodernism* since the late 1970s describes an eclectic movement in which architects, artists, and designers (among others) sought consciously to break from what they saw as hidebound Modernist principles of formal purity and functionalism. Many architectural historians date the Postmodern movement to the 1972 publication of *Learning from Las Vegas*, in which architects Robert Venturi and Denise Scott Brown characterize the commercial architecture of the Las Vegas Strip as a powerful form of building-as-communication akin to advertisement. Six years later, architect Philip Johnson (1906–2005) took up this observation in his model for New York City's American Telephone & Telegraph Building, according to design historian Jeffrey L. Meikle. Johnson capped the Modernist granite-clad structure with a broken pediment and installed a human-scaled classical arcade on the ground floor. Johnson's playfully historicist decoration—the tower is often referred to as the "Chippendale building"—countered the International style's intellectual and aesthetic formalism as it recalled Las Vegas' "'Motel Monticello' as 'a silhouette of an enormous Chippendale highboy . . . visible on the highway'" (Meikle 2005, 195).

Understanding building facades as a medium similar to advertising, Postmodern architects employ visual metaphor and symbol in their designs. (Form no longer followed function as Modernists had posited.) In so doing they challenge the divide between high and popular culture, between academic and vernacular, through strategies such as the eclectic use of historical styles and decorative elements and an interest in surface that results in experimentation with color, texture, and nontraditional building materials. American architects such as Venturi, Scott Brown, Michael Graves, Robert A. M. Stern, and Frank O. Gehry have created buildings that counter Modernism's adherence to simplicity and form.

Architect Philip Johnson's design for the AT&T Building (1984; now the Sony Building) in New York City subverted the International style with its broken "Chippendale highboy"–styled pediment. (David Shankbone)

Since the 1980s, Postmodern design has been applied to expensive decorative arts as well as mass-produced housewares embraced by American consumers. Designers imagined objects anew, with attention to the emotional rather than the intellectual, the superficial (surface) rather than the substance, and at times the whimsical and the parodic rather than the serious. Graves' housewares line, available at Target stores, reinterpreted his own design for the elite Italian firm Alessi, bringing affordable design, according to some cultural observers, to the many. Graphic designers, too, spurred by innovations in computer technology that challenged the relationship between function and form (even with the shape and style of the computer itself as well as what constituted a "page"), upset the grid, inverted form, and experimented with collage, pattern, image, and color. The emphasis on consumer goods and visual media by some Postmodern designers reflects the varied "rehumanization" of design after the formal austerity of Modernism. Others, however, see in Postmodernist art a critique of Modernist ideas of progress and the loss of individual agency, the result of the constant barrage of images, sound bites, and canned information of late twentieth-century mass media.

Shirley Teresa Wajda

See also Architectural History and American Architecture; Cultural Studies; Decorative Arts; Design History and American Design; Graphic Design; Industrial Design; International Style; Modernism (Art Moderne); Style; Vernacular

References and Further Reading

Aldersey-Williams, H., ed. 1988. *New American Design: Products and Graphics for a Post-Industrial Age.* New York: Rizzoli.

Jencks, Charles. 1987. *Post-Modernism: The New Classicism in Art and Architecture.* New York: Rizzoli.

Meikle, Jeffrey L. 2005. *Design in the USA.* Oxford, UK: Oxford University Press.

Venturi, Robert, Denise Scott Brown, and Steven Izenour. 1972. *Learning from Las Vegas: The Forgotten Symbolism of American Form.* Cambridge, MA: MIT Press.

Poverty

Poverty presents unique challenges for material culture scholars. Poverty almost always precludes conservation; artifacts are used up until there is simply nothing of the objects left. Clothing is worn to threads; furniture is used until finally dismantled and burnt; material culture is rendered into "trash" and discarded. What material items that do survive are not the kinds of objects preserved in historical collections or assigned value in the market of collectors' items.

Poverty is the acute and/or chronic inability to meet one's own, and one's dependants', material needs. This includes acute or chronic homelessness; lack of food; and inability to attain adequate education, health care, or clothing. Poverty is experienced in degrees that range from absolute poverty, which is a chronic deprivation of all basic necessities including food, water, sanitation, education, clothing, shelter, to relative poverty, which is deprivation relative to the social and economic contexts in which a person lives.

Measures of Poverty

In the United States, poverty is measured in two ways. One method, an "absolute poverty line," is employed by the federal government. Created in 1964 by a government economist, Mollie Orshansky (1915–2006), and later amended, this measure is based on the minimal amount of income (that is, cash inflow) a family unit requires to eat the least expensive yet nutritionally sound diet available. That figure is tripled (since in 1964 most families spent about one-third of their income on food) to determine the poverty line. The resulting figure is quite low and, critics argue, does not reflect real-life family-unit expenses in the twenty-first century. In 2005, a household of a single person, aged over 65, is federally defined as poor if his or her income is at or lower than $9,367; a family unit of four individuals, three of whom are related children, is poor when its income is at or lower than $19,874.

Another measure of poverty is relative poverty. *Relative poverty* is to have significantly less financial resources than others in the society. The absolute poverty measure is reliant upon food prices, which have fluctuated over time but have in general decreased as a portion of family income expenditure. Other costs, such as transportation, education, and health care, have dramatically increased, however. Serious calls for a re-evaluation of poverty measures have been voiced. About 37 million Americans, or 12.7 percent of all Americans, live below the federal poverty line (2004–2005).

Historical Poverty and Material Culture in the United States

Extreme conditions of poverty have created unusual relationships with material culture. For example, there was the deliberate imposition of material deprivation of slavery experienced by Africans and African Americans from the 1600s to 1865. Slaves existed in a daily world of material culture that at times reflected their own cultural traditions (as in extant examples of beads, religious symbols decorating pottery, and the like) but usually reflected Euro-American material life (experienced in the architecture of farms and plantations, clothing given to slaves, and such). For poor whites as well as indentured servants during this period, material life could be scanty as well. While probate records of wealthy families speak of an increasingly rich material life filled with imported furniture, American and European books, printed music, domestic items, and clothing, the poor lived in a material world that could be considered medieval. Belongings were often limited to single changes of clothing, bedding, and housewares.

Poverty in the twentieth century was likewise experienced by an absence or lack of access to material possessions and comfort; poverty was evidenced not only in inadequate sanitation, health care, and nutrition but also in the non-existence of furniture, housewares, and the accoutrements of daily life. While material life burgeoned for most

Americans in the twentieth century, the poor remained isolated by their lack of access to material goods. This is made clear in two Depression-era accounts that record the material life of Americans: the Farm Security Administration (FSA) photographic projects, and James Agee (1909–1955) and Walker Evans' (1903–1975) *Let Us Now Praise Famous Men: Three Tenant Families* (1941). The FSA photographs often depict the material hardships experienced by the poorest in the country, while Agee and Evans' text records the experience of living with inadequate material supplies. They graphically narrate what it was like to wear torn and much-mended clothing whose fabric was worn thin with use, what it was like to walk in a house with floors warped by moisture and heat, and what it was like to sleep on hard mattresses smelly with years of overuse.

In the contemporary United States, the material culture of poverty is most evident in the millions of homeless citizens who either construct elaborate domestic spaces from refuse and trash or transport their belongings in wagons or shopping carts. At the same time, most poverty is experienced away from the public eye.

Poverty has given rise to exceptional creations of material culture. Folk art and crafts have persisted in part because of traditions encouraged by poverty. Indeed, the popularity of such crafts is tied to the perception that the poor, especially the historically poor cultural groups, are somehow distinct and different from others in American culture. The popular 1970s series *The Foxfire Books*, for example, focused on poor white and black southerners who were practicing traditional crafts, including many relating to material culture. Appalachian crafts, such as those which appear in the *Foxfire* series, have been particularly popular as evidence of a Euro-American past of stalwart struggle and honest values. As one historian, Jane S. Becker (1998, 7), pointed out, "it was the idea of *tradition* that sold mountain handicrafts and defined southern Appalachian folk as cultural 'others.'" At the same time, folk crafts and art have been recognized for their aesthetic beauty, use of natural and manufactured materials, and distinction from more formal art traditions.

Relieving Poverty

One common method of addressing poverty has been material relief. Donated, often used, clothing and household items are given to the poor or sold to the poor at low prices. This kind of poverty relief has been practiced by Euro-Americans since the earliest colonial period to the present. Two impulses govern material relief. The first assumes that it is a moral duty on the part of those fortunate to have resources to provide for others. In the eighteenth and nineteenth centuries, for example, women's sewing societies (or sewing circles) repaired or created clothing for the poor as a spiritual duty. The second impulse argues that the poor are themselves improved through the act of possessing and improving donated goods. This approach was used beginning in the late 1800s, especially by community groups that were part of the Associated Charities movement (begun in 1877). These groups argued poverty had to be addressed holistically; simply giving material relief created dependence. This argument informed the social work movement and then quasi-religious charities such as the Goodwill Industries (begun in the early 1900s by Reverend Edgar Helms [1863–1942]). Groups like Goodwill hired poor or handicapped individuals to repair donated goods, which were then either sold in a local Goodwill store or purchased by the employees themselves.

The Modern Landscape of Poverty

The American landscape reflects the persistence of poverty. In urban areas this is visible, either with historically poor areas in urban centers (such as Manhattan's tenement buildings) or with landscapes that call attention to the presence of the poor (for example, the high-rise "projects" built to house the poor in the 1970s). In rural areas, poverty similarly marks the landscape, although often with less visibility. Historically, poor families lived far from local roads, often isolated from even the smallest towns. Today, poverty in rural areas is evidenced with late-model trailer homes, transient worker housing, and farmhouses in disrepair.

Helen Sheumaker

See also Agricultural Work and Labor; Folklore and Folklife; Homeless Residences; Junk, Scrap, and Salvage; Mobile Homes and Trailer Parks; Secondhand Goods and Shopping; Slavery

References and Further Reading

Agee, James, and Walker Evans. 1941. *Let Us Now Praise Famous Men*. Boston: Houghton Mifflin.

Becker, Jane S. 1998. *Selling Tradition: Appalachia and the Construction of an American Folk, 1930–1940*. Chapel Hill: University of North Carolina Press.

Finnegan, Cara A. 2003. *Picturing Poverty: Print Culture and FSA Photographs*. Washington, DC: Smithsonian Books.

Iceland, John. 2006. *Poverty in America: A Handbook*, 2nd ed. Berkeley: University of California Press.

Smith, Billy G., ed. 2004. *Down and Out in Early America*. University Park: Pennsylvania State University Press.

Strasser, Susan. 1999. *Waste and Want: A Social History of Trash*. New York: Metropolitan Books.

United States Census Bureau, Housing and Household Economic Statistic Division. 2006. "Poverty." http://www.census.gov/hhes/www/poverty/poverty.html.

Wigginton, Eliot, ed. 1972–2004. *The Foxfire Book*, vols. 1–12. New York: Anchor Books/ Random House.

Print Culture

Print culture entails a web of dynamic relationships linking culture, communications, and technology formed by the production, distribution, and consumption of printed matter. It includes phenomena such as authorship, graphic design, printing and binding, publishing, distribution, copyright, literacy, reading practices, and even librarianship and personal book collecting. Print culture draws attention to the profound impact that the development of printing has had on intellectual processes and social relations since the fifteenth century. Sometimes referred to as the *history of the book*, the study of print culture is a vigorous interdisciplinary field currently engaging students from a variety of disciplines and perspectives.

Why Study Print?

Scholars have long examined the impact of oral communications and the transition to a scriptural or manuscript culture revolving around European monastical life. The academic concept of print culture has been evolving since the 1970s as scholars have become increasingly intrigued by the influence of different forms of communication. For example, scholars now argue that the transformative importance of Johannes Gutenberg's (ca. 1398–1468) innovation of printing from movable type in the 1540s comes from print's more extensive and intensive impact on social relations, cultural forms, intellectual perspectives, and political power. It is no coincidence that this interest in the cultural effects of print has been piqued in an era of

transition from the dominance of words on printed pages to the emergence of ubiquitous forms of digital communication, especially hypertext.

History of American Print Culture

Scholars in the United States have been particularly interested in how print culture played a unique and powerful role in the creation and evolution of the United States as a democratic republic. While a printing press did not appear in the British colonies until 1638, the impact of the printed page was evident early in colonial life. Seventeenth- and early eighteenth-century print served to help create self-identity among colonial groups, particularly religious groups. From the 1750s on, the press, especially newspaper and pamphlet publishing, was a key player in creating and disseminating political knowledge about the issues that culminated in the American Revolution. After the Revolution, the role of print in conducting political life assumed center stage, and issues such as freedom of the press and protection of copyright were written into the foundational documents of the United States.

The development of iron hand presses and then machine presses in the late 1820s, coinciding with the introduction of the so-called penny press newspapers, increased the speed of print production and the range of distribution. The later expansion of the public school system and the postal system increased Americans' exposure to print culture. During the course of the nineteenth century, print evolved into a method of communication with varying appeals to diversity, authority, and influence. Evangelicals were major publishers early in the century, but by mid-century the federal government had become one of the largest and most influential purveyors of printed matter. In the twentieth century, the expanded growth of mass-market magazines, the proliferation of special-interest magazines, and the popularity of book clubs vastly expanded the market for printed matter and influenced, as well as reflected, changing patterns of consumption.

There are several categories of printed material—religious tracts, governmental publications, newspapers, magazines, books—and numerous genres within each to be considered. Each category requires its own analysis of authorship and authority, methods of production, design and physical characteristics, methods of marketing and distribution, and consumer reception. In addition, students of the consumption of print are well advised to be alert to issues of gender, class, age, race and ethnicity, political affiliation, and individual and group self-identification. Common themes addressed in studies of print culture include orality, writing, and print; literacy and illiteracy; youth culture and print; print and "the public"; authorship and intellectual property; and the revolutions in reading practices.

William S. Pretzer

See also Advertisements and Advertising; Books; Ephemera; Fanzines; Graphic Design; Literary Studies and American Literature; Mail Order Catalogues; Printmaking and American Prints; Scrapbooks; Technology; Trade Cards; Trade Catalogues

References and Further Reading
Amory, Hugh, and David D. Hall, eds. 2000. *The Colonial Book in America*, vol. 1 of *A History of the Book in America*, 5 vols, ed. David D. Hall. Cambridge: Cambridge University Press.
Casper, Scott E., Joanne D. Chaison, and Jeffrey D. Groves, eds. 2002. *Perspectives on American Book History: Artifacts and Commentary*. Amherst: University of Massachusetts Press, in association with the American Antiquarian Society and the Center for the Book, Library of Congress.
Danky, James P., and Wayne Wiegand, eds. 1998. *Print Culture in a Diverse America*. Urbana: University of Illinois Press.
Davidson, Cathy N., ed. 1989. *Reading in America: Literature and Social History*. Baltimore, MD: Johns Hopkins University Press.

Printmaking and American Prints

Prints are composed images on a surface (wood, linoleum, metal plates, etc.) onto which inks are applied and then pressed by machine or hand onto paper. Prints historically have served Americans as decorative objects for middle-class houses, as political propaganda, and as fine art objects. A particular characteristic of prints is the ability to make multiples, giving prints a more democratic appeal and affordability. That prints could exist as multiple originals proves to be a benefit and a hindrance for an art medium so long treated as an artistic stepchild to painting and even sculpture.

Printmaking Processes

Four main printmaking processes are practiced. The first is *relief*: the artist uses metal gouging tools to carve away sections of (usually) a block of wood, leaving an image, in reverse, to be inked with a roller. The wood block is pressed against paper, or paper is laid on the block and rubbed with a hard tool.

Intaglio employs sharp metal tools to incise directly into a metal plate or onto a plate predipped in acid-resistant solution. Lines of various depths and widths are created by cuts made directly into the metal plate with the sharp tool or by acid, which eats away the metal (exposed from scraping away the acid-resist). In this case, the ink pools and channels into the incisions in the metal so that the paper is pressed against and into the grooves in the metal plate. This process results in engravings, etchings, mezzotints, and aquatints.

Lithography involves drawing directly onto a polished stone or slick surface with an oil-based crayon or pigment, in reverse. The stone or surface is inked and pressed against paper, transferring the image onto paper.

Silkscreening or *silkprinting* requires applying stencils onto a very fine screen, usually made of silk. Using a squeegee, the printmaker forces ink across the screen so that any part of the screen not covered by the stencil transfers ink to the paper, placed under the screen. This technique produces silkscreens or screenprints.

Etching and silkscreening have historically been the most popular techniques employed by American artists. Etchings were popular among middle- and upper-class patrons in the eighteenth and nineteenth centuries, while silkscreening cemented the reputations of many American artists of the 1960s.

Colonial Printmaking Practices and Images

Early colonial America supported few printmakers, print shops, and paper mills, which left the bulk of the production and sales of prints to Europe. The tendency for Americans to look to Europe for aesthetic style and fashion persisted through the mid-twentieth century. The most popular printmaking subjects in early and mid-eighteenth-century America were etchings of maps, usually sold in bookstores. The maps depicted European cities and, later, the cities and coasts of North America. Ownership of framed etchings and engravings, recorded copiously in the personal inventories and diaries of early Americans, reflected the owner's curiosity, class, and education. After 1775, American cities boasted printmaking shops filled with European-trained printmakers who influenced American taste for portraits, land-scapes, and reproductions of satirical European and historical American paintings and prints, available as grayscale and color engravings.

The Rise of Commerce and Art: Nineteenth-Century Printmaking Innovations

Lithography, imported from Germany in the early nineteenth century, provided a cheaper, faster, and more versatile printing technique that allowed printers more flexibility and opportunity for larger editions. The lithographic process also enabled the reproduction of the look of intaglio printmaking and dominated commercial printing in the nineteenth-century United States. The New York City firm of Currier & Ives (1857–1907) flooded the American market with popular hand-colored lithograph images ("Colored Engravings for the People") of historic events, daily life, and sentimental ideals for the firm's primarily middle-class customers. German immigrant Louis Prang (1824–1909) revolutionized commercial printing, popularizing chromolithography (printing in colors) and giving Americans after the Civil War (1861–1865) business cards, greeting cards, trade cards, and scraps. The invention of photography and the proliferation of the photomechanical reproduction process in the mid-nineteenth century halted the need for traditional printmaking (i.e., etching and engraving techniques) in newspapers, advertisement, and illustration and for portraiture. The dominance of lithography in commercial printing liberated intaglio techniques such as etching to act as vehicles for printmakers to pursue artistic production.

As early as the 1820s, enterprising American print dealers opened galleries and hosted exhibitions specifically for the sale of art prints, increasingly produced by American artists. An important proponent of printmaking and especially of etching as an aesthetic pursuit was the American expatriate artist James McNeill Whistler (1834–1903). Whistler innovated methods of applying and removing etching acid to create subtle, delicate textures and gradation. Whistler himself pressed his works, allowing for freedom of manipulation at every stage of the process. The result was a unique image in small editions with a clear mark of the artist's hand. This helped elevate and differentiate fine art printmaking from commercial printing. While landscape and the nature prints of John James Audubon (1785–1851) and Currier & Ives continued to be popular among middle-class clientele, subject matter in American printmaking in the late nineteenth century began to embrace realist genre scenes of the dynamic urban life in the nation's modern cities.

Twentieth-Century Printmaking as Fine Art

A boon to the artistic potential of printmaking came in the form of the 1930s Works Progress Administration's Federal Art Project (FAP) under the auspices of the New Deal. Based mostly out of the New York City workshop, the artists working in the FAP's Graphic Arts Division created thousands of works. Aside from providing needy artists with employment, the FAP helped expose many artists to relief printing, lithography, and silkscreening, thus establishing their popularity as fine art techniques in the United States. The FAP artists produced thousands of federally sanctioned works of art depicting contemporary American life, serving as a social and cultural mirror and important historical record. The resulting works of art moved the American artistic identity from under its European shadow. Printmakers combined uniquely American iconography and abstraction (a European

influence) to enhance the reputation of printmaking as a fine art medium in the United States.

Groups of printmakers like the Painter-Gravers of America (1917) and the Associated American Artists (AAA) formed in 1934 to enhance the status of printmaking as a viable fine art medium and to reestablish print patronage. The AAA, for example, collected a series of editions and sold them cheaply at department stores, while the Society of American Graphic Artists (originally the Brooklyn Society of Etchers, 1915) and the Chicago Society of Etchers (1910) mounted exhibitions. Professional printmaking workshops grew larger in number throughout the country. Their success encouraged Stanley William Hayter (1901–1988) to move his Atelier 17 to New York City in 1944. In turn, the success of Hayter's printmaking workshop served as the impetus for entrepreneurial artists like June Wayne to open the famous Tamarind Lithography Workshop in California in 1960 and Tatyana Grosman (1904–1982) to pursue the greatest contemporary American artists at mid-century, like Robert Rauschenberg, Jasper Johns, Helen Frankenthaler, Lee Bontecou, Jim Dine, and Grace Hartigan. These artists produced what would become revolutionary artworks at the Universal Limited Arts Edition studio in New York in 1959.

Frankenthaler and Rauschenberg accommodated traditional printmaking techniques to their contemporary pursuits. Frankenthaler produced large, abstract color-field woodcuts combining the texture of wood blocks with the hard-edge painting style of the 1950s and 1960s. Rauschenberg used photomechanical processes to print onto canvas and in doing so succeeded in conflating any difference between painting and printmaking. Perhaps the most well-known

American printmaker of the twentieth century, Andy Warhol (1928–1987) exploited the appearance of artistic detachment in the process of silkscreening to celebrate and critique simultaneously the iconic commercialization of people and products in American society. Warhol and Rauschenberg exposed the technique and process of printmaking, seen in the skewed layers of Warhol's infamous prints of Hollywood siren Marilyn Monroe and in Rauschenberg's overlapping political and cultural scenes of many of his works from the late 1950s, as part of their artistic aesthetic. No longer seen as merely reproductive or illustrative, printmaking techniques had found a place of their own within the hierarchy of fine art media.

Victoria Estrada-Berg

See also Art History and American Art; Ephemera; Graphic Design; Music Ephemera; Popular Culture; Print Culture; Scrapbooks; Trade Cards; Visual Culture Studies

References and Further Reading
Fowble, McSherry E. 1987. *Two Centuries of Prints in America, 1680–1880.* Charlottesville: University Press of Virginia.
Griffiths, Antony. 1996 (1980). *Prints and Printmaking: An Introduction to the History and Techniques.* Berkeley: University of California Press.
Hansen, Trudy V., David Mickenberg, Joann Moser, and Barry Walker. 1995. *Printmaking in America: Collaborative Prints and Presses 1960–1990.* New York: Harry N. Abrams.
Johnson, Deborah J. 1987. *Whistler to Weidenaar: American Prints 1870–1950.* Providence: Museum of Art, Rhode Island School of Design.
Marzio, Peter C. 1979. *The Democratic Art: Pictures of a 19th-Century America: Chromolithography, 1840–1900.* Boston: David R. Godine.
Walker, Barry. 1983. *The American Artist as Printmaker.* Brooklyn, NY: Brooklyn Museum.

Probate Records, Probate Inventories, and Wills

Probate records have been kept by courts designed to judge the validity of wills and oversee the distribution of a deceased person's estate through wills, petitions, and other legal procedures since the arrival of the British in North America in the seventeenth century. Probate courts prove or disprove the authenticity of a last will and testament of a deceased person. If the deceased left a will, the probate is called *testate*. If the deceased did not leave a will, the probate is *intestate* and in such cases probate records may contain evidence, according to prevailing inheritance laws, of the distribution of the deceased's assets including real estate and personal possessions. The probate court oversees the distribution of these assets, once the value of the deceased's estate is established and debts are paid.

A probate record may include a will and codicils, a petition for an estate executor, a probate of the will, a list of heirs, court documents for estate division if heirs cannot agree, receipts from heirs, the court's concluding statement, and an inventory of the deceased's estate at time of death. Probate records are usually kept in county courthouses and county and state archives.

Probate Inventories

The *probate inventory* or household inventory has proved very useful to material culture scholars and curators wishing to analyze domestic furnishings and personal possessions. Given the laws and customs of inheritance from the seventeenth to the mid-nineteenth century, men were property owners, but women's names do occasionally appear in probate records. Widows' dower rights, for example, were part of the probate record and depended on the value of their deceased husbands' estates.

Scholars have utilized the records of probate courts to analyze how Americans lived, especially in the seventeenth, eighteenth, and early nineteenth centuries. Genealogists may trace family lineage through such records. Social and economic historians find in probate records evidence of family relationships and wealth through wills and other legal documents concerning real and personal estates. The methodical "room by room" nature of inventorying the material culture within a house and its outbuildings have aided curators in understanding the naming and historical evolution of rooms and buildings.

Nevertheless, probate inventories are not comprehensive or exact descriptions of a decedent's possessions. Personal items with sentimental value or no market value at all and items bequeathed by the deceased to others are not listed. Some household goods, such as clothing, utensils, or dishes, are combined and given a monetary value, thwarting specific identification. Historians have puzzled over historical nomenclature, illegible handwriting, and inconsistent spelling in these documents.

Wills

The *will and last testament* is a legal document through which a person (testator) directs to others his or her wealth, possessions, and wishes after death. *Testament* applies to the disposition of personal property, but the distinction between *testament* and *will* has been erased over time. Wills generally provide a means of regulating property (and thus people) after the testator's death. As such, wills prove useful to historians seeking to understand familial relationships through particular inheritances or through patterns of inheritance over time. Material culture scholars have analyzed wills in re-creating

domestic interiors in historic houses and to comprehend a family's material life.

Shirley Teresa Wajda

See also Dower Right; Gender; Heirlooms

References and Further Reading
Cummings, Abbott Lowell, ed. 1964. *Rural House Inventories: Establishing the Names, Uses and Furnishings of Rooms in the Colonial New England Home, 1675–1775*. Boston: Society for the Preservation of New England Antiquities.
Demos, John. 1970. *A Little Commonwealth: Family Life in Plymouth Colony*. New York: Oxford University Press.
Izard, Holly. 1997. "Random or Systematic? An Evaluation of the Probate Process." *Winterthur Portfolio* 32 (2–3): 147–167.
Main, Gloria T. 1975. "Probate Records as a Source for Early American History." *William and Mary Quarterly* 31 (1): 88–99.
Stapp, Carol Buchalter. 1993. *Afro-Americans in Antebellum Boston: An Analysis of Probate Records*. New York: Garland Publishing.

Public and Commercial Leisure, Recreation, and Amusement Venues

Public and commercial venues for leisure, recreation, and amusement include permanent, often single-purpose spaces such as amusement parks and county fairgrounds, sports arenas, racetracks, ballparks, dance halls, game arcades, casinos, movie theaters, symphony halls, public gymnasiums, and temporary, multiuse spaces, such as the parade route through the center of town or an impromptu camping ground. The architectural characteristics of purpose-built structures and environments, as well as the movable material culture of the activities undertaken within them, offers much evidence of how Americans played. The specific locations and purposes of these venues, their uses, and their temporary inhabitants also offer evidence of how Americans, as participants, spectators, and employees, have organized historically their time and their society.

The dedication of specific places and times to a leisure activity is predicated on a given society's definition of leisure, recreation, and amusement. The historical material culture of tavern amusements, bowling greens, and horse racing, as well as much documentation of celebratory and commemorative parades, reveals that Americans enjoyed leisure pursuits and set aside time and space for them.

Venues as Sites of Social Definition and Social Conflict

In the United States, public and commercial spaces for leisure, recreation, and amusement were, and remain, sites of debates about societal structure and appropriate behavior. The rise of industrialization in the first half of the nineteenth century distinguished working-class and immigrant leisure activities and spaces as towns and cities reordered their environments to segregate groups and control their leisure activities. From the end of the Civil War (1861–1865) to the mid-1960s, segregation in the South led to separate theaters and other types of recreation venues and institutions for African Americans. In the South, the segregation of institutions was legally established, but in the North, informal segregation also limited African Americans' access to public spaces such as parks. In California and other Pacific Coast states, similar exclusionary practices affected Chinese and Japanese immigrants to the United States in the nineteenth century. Thus, the presence of theater, film, and sports venues record America's history of racial segregation and integration.

Class identity and segregation could also be reified in public and commercial leisure venues. Who should enjoy city parks was debated in newspapers as well as encoded in architectural barriers, signs limiting access to grassy areas or to activities, the competition between pedestrian and coach traffic on paths and roads, and the discussions concerning the types of activities to be enjoyed in a given area.

Over the course of the nineteenth century, concert halls, formerly buildings in which many classes mingled, became preserves of the refined, if not only the wealthy. Decorous behavior was expected in these halls of high culture. Immigrants established their own music halls, singing societies, and other leisure venues, testifying to the relationship of ethnicity and class in late nineteenth- and early twentieth-century American social hierarchy. Gender also played a role; whereas white middle- and upper-class women and men tended to engage in homosocial activities, working-class women and men indulged in the heterosocial worlds of commercial amusements increasingly available in or near the nation's cities and towns. Dance halls and amusement parks such as New York City's Coney Island provided new means of displaying one's body in public as well as enjoying one's well-earned leisure.

Leisure Venues as Urban Revitalization

Currently, sports arenas serve as central institutions for the revitalization of the nation's inner cities. Further, in these new venues, such as Baltimore, Maryland's Oriole Park at Camden Yards (1992), architectural design reflects a Postmodern combination of old and new aesthetics. Since most of these new baseball parks and football stadiums receive substantial public subsidies, these institutions are at the center of debates about which people should directly receive public assistance and whether such revitalization plans truly benefit all city residents.

Tourism

The rise and popularity of the national and state parks in the twentieth century have encouraged Americans to "take to the road" to get "back to nature" through hiking, camping, or touring. Recreational cityscapes such as Las Vegas, Nevada; theme parks such as Sea World; and the various Disney parks are also the focus of cultural landscape studies exploring the creation of tourist landscapes and corporate public spaces.

Krista M. Park

See also Cities and Towns; City Parks; Illicit Pleasures and Venues; Leisure, Recreation, and Amusements; Sports; Tourism and Travel

References and Further Reading

Kasson, John F. 1978. *Amusing the Million: Coney Island at the Turn of the Century.* New York: Hill and Wang.

Richmond, P. 1993. *Ballpark: Camden Yards and the Building of an American Dream.* New York: Simon & Schuster.

Rosenzweig, Roy. 1985. *Eight Hours for What We Will: Workers and Leisure in an Industrial City, 1870–1920.* Cambridge, UK: Cambridge University Press.

Public Markets

A *public market* is often defined as an urban site designated and regulated by a municipality for the sale and purchase of foodstuffs and goods. Open-air marketplaces were established in the British American colonies soon after initial settlement. Boston created its town market in 1634; a little over a century later, the city built Faneuil Hall (1742; rebuilt 1763), an enclosed market. Public markets were centrally located, easily accessible, and regulated. Market houses varied greatly in size. The brick Faneuil Hall rented stalls to vendors on its ground floor; the second floor was used for public meetings.

Other towns built small open-walled market sheds. By the mid-nineteenth century the nation's major cities boasted more than one market and many more towns supported a central market. For much of American history when dependable refrigeration was nonexistent, going to market was a daily activity. Public markets were necessary, central locations for the sale and distribution of food.

Early market activity was conducted directly between producers and consumers. Farmers brought fresh produce to town; butchers offered a variety of meats, but live poultry and livestock often competed with sellers for the attention of consumers. By the nineteenth century, middlemen owned permanent stalls and bought farm foodstuffs and goods now more easily accessible by improved roads, canals, and railroads. Farmers still rented stalls, and their wives and daughters sold foodstuffs, such as butter and applesauce, and household necessities, such as brooms, goose feathers, soap, potted plants, baskets, and, in New England, palm leaf hats.

Hours of operation, locations, types of sellers, and goods were subject to the authorities; vendors were required to purchase licenses to sell their goods, and in some cities market stalls were auctioned. Public health officials charged with inspection of public markets found problems of sanitation. Buyers did have some recourse to complaints of short weighting or problematic foodstuffs and goods. "Hucksters" were a constant problem; these unlicensed street vendors attempted to circumvent market hours or sell to the public without renting market stalls, often working just beyond the market grounds. Over the course of the nineteenth century, city ordinances preventing private shop development were abandoned, thus providing competition for market vendors as well as reducing the central political and commercial importance of the public market.

Market houses were civic structures dedicated to the public good as well as commerce. Architectural styles chosen for these buildings emphasize this purpose: Boston's Quincy Market (1824–1826), for example, was built of granite and red brick and designed as a Greek Revival temple by its architect, Alexander Parriss (1780–1852). City directories and foreign visitors' accounts throughout the nineteenth century lauded the size and cleanliness of America's public markets, converting these places into tourist sites as well as measures of the nation's health, wealth, and progress.

Shirley Teresa Wajda

See also Cities and Towns; Civic Architecture; Commercial Architecture; Consumerism and Consumption; Food and Foodways; Grocery Stores

References and Further Reading

Strasser, Susan. 1982. *Never Done: A History of American Housework*. New York: Pantheon Books.

Tangires, Helen. 2003. *Public Markets and Civic Culture in Nineteenth-Century America*. Baltimore, MD: Johns Hopkins University Press.

Public Monuments and Popular Commemoration

Among the most visible examples of material culture in the United States, *public monuments* constitute those structures (often the core of a memorial environment housing museums, exhibits, and other interpretive centers) designed to honor or pay tribute to a person, group, or event regarded as central to a nation's, state's, or people's foundational myths, patriotic ideals, or collective history. If public monuments are broadly construed as "sacred places," then it is possible to view the Grand Canyon; Yosemite;

Elvis Presley's (1935–1977) Graceland; and the giant replicas of the mythic Paul Bunyan and Babe, the Blue Ox, in Minnesota as examples. Traditionally, however, *monument* refers to an edifice, designed and constructed by individuals, as a concrete expression (often literally) of a people's shared memory, derived from strategies to bind the act of remembrance to specific places in order to preserve that memory. Monuments are best understood in relation to all those associated practices (such as design contests, funding and campaign drives, construction and dedication events, rituals of remembrance carried out at the site, subsequent alterations and controversies) intended to offer contemporary spectators as well as later generations a guide for understanding the cultural, social, and national meanings of the structure.

The last three decades have witnessed heightened interest in the political dimension of American monuments and memorials. This is the result of a number of significant transformations in the post–Vietnam conflict (1959–1975) era, such as the greater scrutiny of state-funded art by government officials, cultural critics, and a public increasingly defined as comprising taxpayers and consumers rather than citizens and workers. Public debates over the appropriate representation of historical events or figures within "official" national culture became common, perhaps most famously the controversy over Maya Lin's spare design for the Vietnam Veterans Memorial ("the Wall," 1982). A decade later, challenges to the Smithsonian Institution's exhibition of the *Enola Gay* and objections to the National Park Service's renaming of the "Custer Battlefield National Monument" (erected in 1881) as the "Little Bighorn Battlefield National Monument" garnered much media attention. Veterans and nonveterans alike responded ambivalently to the stark white facades of

The Vietnam Veterans Memorial, designed by Maya Lin and dedicated in 1982 in Washington, D.C., has evoked strong emotions among visitors. Though monuments and memorials as "sacred spaces" may unite individuals in collective rites of memory, history, and mythmaking, these structures at times are controversial and have incited the construction of "counter monuments" to represent the past. (Department of Defense)

the National World War II Memorial (2004) on the National Mall, which to some observers was ironically reminiscent of Nazi Germany's neoclassical Third Reich architecture. Memorialization may be a crucial material practice in the United States during its late twentieth-century ascendancy as the "last global superpower."

Yet the memorial landscape of the United States has long been a dense terrain. Since the founding of the nation, statues, obelisks, friezes, cenotaphs, and the ubiquitous roadside historical markers have served as constant reminders of what must not be forgotten. The loss of lives in armed conflict in order to protect the nation is particularly favored; wars, battlefields, soldiers, generals,

and even nonmartial sites of political violence (e.g., President Abraham Lincoln's [b. 1809] assassination at Ford's Theatre in 1865) are often the subject of memorialization. Commemorative sites in the United States frequently pay homage to protracted episodes of struggle and violence between and within nations, a paradox well illustrated by poet William Stafford's (1914–1993) paean to tranquil United States relations with its northern neighbor, *At the Un-National Monument along the Canadian Border* (1977): "This is the field where the battle did not happen, / where the unknown soldier did not die. . . . No people killed—or were killed—on this ground / hallowed by neglect and an air so tame / that people celebrate it by forgetting its name."

Monuments and Memory

The issue of forgetting, that is, the processes of defining who and what is deemed not worthy of remembering, is key to understanding memorialization as not just selective but also characterized by tension and strife. Although public monuments and commemorative rituals are tangible expressions of a unified "collective memory," in fact *their* respective histories are frequently as conflicted as the event being commemorated. Any culture comprises multiple constituencies that have different and sometimes competing views of historical incidents, although not all have the requisite power and access to advance this perspective in the public sphere. As historian Edward Linenthal (2001, 560) notes, "the ideology of memorial space and commemorative ritual does not simply emerge naturally but is produced, most often by elites who are culturally and politically empowered to claim ownership of the means of representation." Thus, most memorials promote state-sponsored "myths of origin" or constitutive narratives promoting a particular vision of the nation's past or its founders. This is not to say, however, that commemoration as a cultural practice represses alternative expressions of tribute and is wholly uncontested by competing if marginalized groups. Many public monuments retain varying traces of this negotiation between official culture and what historian John Bodnar (1992, 14) has called *vernacular culture*: "[such] expressions convey what social reality feels like rather than what it should be like. Its very existence threatens the sacred and timeless nature of official expressions."

Monuments and Space

This engagement between the "sacred and timeless" attributes of the traditional memorial and the more immediate and temporal expressions of grief, loss, and remembrance is seen in varying degrees and for different purposes in nearly all forms of popular commemoration. Historian Pierre Nora has suggested that "memory attaches itself to sites," which become consecrated space; such *lieux de memoire* or "sites of memory" (Nora 1989, 22) are regarded as uncorrupted proclamations of a nation's political and social ideals. Yet many monuments function less as hermetically sealed shrines than as dynamic terrain, public settings for the personal expression of "what social reality feels like." One recent example is the "people's memorial," a chain-link fence originally erected around the ruins of the Alfred P. Murrah Building in Oklahoma City to keep visitors from entering the "sacred" memorial site. As the monument was being constructed, those who had lost loved ones in the 1995 bombing left personal items on or near the fence, creating an "intimate devotional space" (Linenthal 2001, 565). Eventually, at the request of the survivors, some of the items were placed within the memorial's permanent exhibition center.

In other contexts, expression of the vernacular in a commemorative site runs counter to what nationalist and patriotic elites regard as the appropriate requirements of a national memorial. In 1982, many observers felt that the proposed Vietnam Veterans Memorial (described by one as "a black gash of shame") did not accurately reflect the experiences of returning veterans, nor represented the ideals of the nation-state in celebrating the heroism of the soldiers who fell. In response, the Vietnam Veterans Memorial Foundation modified the original design to include an American flag, the inscription "God Bless America," and a statuary group featuring combatants in fatigues (Bodnar 1992, 4–9).

In many instances, the "sacred" qualities of a memorial gloss over the more troublesome aspects of a foundational event or figure so that the site sanctifies national unity or glorifies the sacrifice of those lost at the expense of historical accuracy. Probably the best example of this is the Lincoln Memorial on the National Mall; the text surrounding the solemn statue of the Great Emancipator does not mention the abolition of slavery nor pursuit of racial justice as the ideological raison d'être of the Civil War (1861–1865). Rather, Lincoln is the embodiment of the unity between North and South, and the monument a testament to national consensus. At the dedication ceremonies in 1922, a period when segregation was socially and judicially sanctioned, African American attendees were seated separately from whites. By 1939, however, the memorial began to function as a "site of protest, a place to call the nation back to its ideals" (Linenthal 2001, 560), when in response to the Daughters of the American Revolution's rejection of her request to perform at Constitution Hall, Marian Anderson (1897–1993) gave an Easter Sunday concert on its steps. Reverend Martin Luther King, Jr., (1929–1963) delivered his "I Have a Dream" speech on the memorial steps in 1963, and subsequently a variety of movements dedicated to social and economic justice, such as the Poor People's Campaign in 1968 and multiple antiwar protest marches, have chosen this memorial landscape as a symbolic backdrop.

Monuments and Time

All monuments have a complicated relationship to time, subject to revision by subsequent generations in order to reflect changing perspectives on historical events. This process seldom occurs without controversy, not only because such alterations seem to violate the "timeless" quality required of monuments but also because they reveal changing power relations among privileged and emergent groups who typically have very different stakes in how the past is remembered. Memorial sites in the American South in particular have been subject to such revisionism, as black and white residents debate the appropriateness of battlefields, statues, and monuments commemorating the events and leaders of the Confederacy (1861–1865). Ultimately, all commemorative practices (including changes to or even erasures of memorial sites) strive to "reproduce the past for present-day aims" (Zelizer 1995, 217). At both the time of a monument's construction and at subsequent stages, historical accuracy is deemed less important than "the establishment of social identity, authority, solidarity, [and] political affiliation" (Zelizer 1995, 219).

Perhaps the best recent example of this is the World Trade Center commemorative project. Controversy erupted over the International Freedom Center (IFC), proposed as part of architect Daniel Libeskind's "memorial quadrant," whose exhibitions were meant as a "celebration of the human aspiration to liberty" (Solomon 2005, 27). Some constituencies were angered by the center's critical, albeit historically informed, inquiry into America's successes as well as failures to live up to its ideals of freedom and used media outlets (the *Wall Street Journal*, television talk shows, Internet sites, and blogs) to suggest that the center's exhibits were an apologia for the terrorists' actions on September 11, 2001. The IFC responded by revising its programming to be "appropriately celebratory of our nation and its leading role in the global fight for freedom" (Solomon 2005, 27). The World Trade Center memorial controversy shows how "culturally and politically empowered elites" can promote a particular vision of the nation's past expressed in the memorial landscape—in this instance as a means to sanction the actions of a current political or economic order.

Monuments and Media

The use of mass media to circulate a particular perspective on the historical past and render it significant and worthy of consumers' attention is crucial to memorialization. This is not a recent phenomenon; the role of newspapers and mass-market publishing in the promotion of nationalism dates at least back to the mid-nineteenth century. Concomitantly, commemorative practices and forms of memorialization were becoming the province of emerging technologies in the modern industrial age: first still photography, then motion pictures and subsequent innovations challenged the traditional view of the monument as a physical structure with a privileged, univocal link to a bygone era. Historian Alison Landsberg (2003, 146) has noted, "the cinema and the technologised mass culture that it helped inaugurate transformed memory by making possible an unprecedented circulation of images and narratives about the past." Motion pictures and their attendant technologies did not displace monuments and memorials; rather, across the twentieth century public remembrance of definitive events and individuals necessitated media representation as both a sign of its national aspect and its legitimacy as civic tribute.

Yet beyond the publicizing of various commemorative practices associated with the creation of memorials, media's ability to concretize the past in compelling ways for broad audiences has meant that Nora's "sites of memory" are increasingly found in the domain of screen culture, wherein official culture not only mediates but often competes with vernacular visions. At the close of the twentieth and into the twenty-first century, viewers pay tribute to foundational events and figures by accessing them in "virtual space." To a great extent, the amelioration of episodes in the nation's past evoking loss and trauma is now the task of the television miniseries (e.g., *Roots* [1977]) and the subgenre of historical filmmaking associated with Oliver Stone (*Born on the Fourth of July* [1989], *JFK* [1991], *Nixon* [1995]) and Steven Spielberg (*Saving Private Ryan* [1998]). In the summer of 2006, Stone released *World Trade Center*, about the events of September 11, 2001; Spielberg will direct a feature based on historian Doris Kearns Goodwin's biography of Abraham Lincoln and produced an adaptation of *Flags of Our Fathers* (2006), the stories of the soldiers depicted in the Iwo Jima Memorial directed by Clint Eastwood. As motion pictures and television give way to the Internet and digital technologies, a citizenry at once local and global may welcome the broadened sphere for critical examination of and exchange about the social and political uses of historical commemoration.

Heidi Kenaga

See also Civic Architecture; Community; Historic Preservation; Holidays and Commemorations; Land and Landscape; Memory and Memorabilia; Nostalgia; Popular Culture; Souvenirs; Space and Place; Tourism and Travel

References and Further Reading

Bodnar, John. 1992. *Remaking America: Public Memory, Commemoration, and Patriotism in the Twentieth Century*. Princeton, NJ: Princeton University Press.

Hass, Kristin Ann. 1998. *Carried to the Wall: American Memory and the Vietnam Veterans Memorial*. Berkeley: University of California Press.

Kammen, Michael. 1991. *Mystic Chords of Memory: The Transformation of Tradition in American Culture*. New York: Alfred A. Knopf.

Landsberg, Alison. 2003. "Prosthetic Memory: The Ethics and Politics of Memory in an Age of Mass Culture." In *Memory and Popular Film*, ed. Paul Grainge, 144–161. Manchester, UK: University of Manchester Press.

Linenthal, Edward. 1991. *Sacred Ground: Americans and Their Battlefields*, 2nd ed. Urbana: University of Illinois Press.

Linenthal, Edward. 2001. "Monuments and Memorials." In *Encyclopedia of American Cultural and Intellectual History*, ed. Mary Kupiec Cayton and Peter W. Williams, vol. 3, 559–566. New York: Charles Scribner's Sons.

Nora, Pierre. 1989. "Between History and Memory: Les lieux de memoire." *Representations* 26 (1): 13–25.

Solomon, Alisa. 2005. "Memorial Chauvinism." *The Nation*, September 26, 26–28.

Zelizer, Barbie. 1995. "Reading the Past against the Grain: The Shape of Memory Studies." *Critical Studies in Mass Communication* 12 (2): 214–238.

Q

Queen Anne Style

The *Queen Anne,* or Early Georgian, style (1725–1760) reflected a new American colonial sensibility for late Baroque design. Good design was defined by refined proportions, selective ornamentation, and an adherence to classical architectural ideas, broadly based on the vogue of furniture and interiors found in England during the reign of Queen Anne (1702–1714) and her successors, kings George I and II (1714–1760). It continued to be a popular style after the American Revolution, especially evident in fashionable Newport, Rhode Island, furniture. Made of fine walnut and mahogany, Queen Anne furniture balanced curved and linear elements, solid and void spaces, and plain or decorative surfaces that served to enhance visual appreciation. The serpentine, or S-curve, of the furniture forms and decoration reflected the new ideas and attitudes about beauty that were espoused in England by William Hogarth (1697–1764) in his *Analysis of Beauty* (1753). The incorporation of a more linear classical architectural vocabulary, along with the introduction of the shell motif, was inspired by Andrea Palladio (1508–1580), the

Italian architect whose illustrated works were beginning to be republished in London.

In America, regional preferences also played a determining role in the aesthetic appearance of furniture. Extending from New England to New York, Philadelphia and farther south, distinctions are clearly expressed in decorative designs in the shape of backsplats and seats of chairs, the size and scale of cabriole legs and claw-and-ball feet, the appearance or elimination of stretcher frames, as well as the overall amount of carved ornament. The elaborate treatment of writing bureaus and high chests brought them out of bedchambers and into the house's more public spaces for admiration. Fine upholstery, hardwood veneered finishes and expensive woods, as well as reflective looking glass mirrors, created refined and opulent interior spaces that demonstrated Americans' ideals of a comfortable and distinguished life.

Evie T. Joselow

See also Decorative Arts; Furniture; Style

References and Further Reading
Fairbanks, Jonathan L., and Elizabeth Bidwell Bates. 1981. *American Furniture, 1620 to the Present.* New York: R. Marek.

In this plate from English artist William Hogarth's Analysis of Beauty *(London, 1753), the serpentine or S-curve characteristic of the furniture form known as the Queen Anne style is portrayed in the images bordering the classical statues Hogarth features as epitomes of classical beauty. (Burstein Collection/Corbis)*

Hayward, Helena. 1977 (1965). *World Furniture*. Secaucus, NJ: Chartwell.

Kirk, John T. 2000. *American Furniture: Understanding Styles, Construction, and Quality*. New York: Harry N. Abrams.

Vandal, Norman. 1990. *Queen Anne Furniture: History, Design, and Construction*. Newtown, CT: Taunton Press.

R

Race

Race is a genetically meaningless but socially significant method of categorizing humans and is generally based on phenotypical differences in skin color, hair texture, and eye shape. From the seventeenth century through the beginning of the twentieth century, many scientists tried to develop systems for measuring racial differences. While these attempts have been abandoned, the cultural belief in racial categories continues, shaping the settlement patterns, material culture, and media depiction of different racial groups in the United States and throughout the world.

Legal Definition of Race

Currently, the United States federal Office of Management and Budget has the responsibility for creating the nation's legal definition of race. The United States' official racial categories as of the 2000 federal census were American Indian or Alaska Native, Asian, Black or African American, Native Hawaiian or Other Pacific Islander, and White. Ethnicity is counted separately; questions on ethnicity capture whether a respondent is Hispanic. New to the 2000 census was the option to claim a multiracial identity, an option previously discontinued in 1920, when segregation mandated the creation of a clear distinction between whites and blacks.

Evolution of Race in the United States

Race, as first used in the late Middle Ages, referred to breeding animals; when applied to humans it originally carried the same connotation as *people* or *nation*. The modern idea of race as biological, inherited qualities of persons took shape after the sixteenth century, during the colonial expansion of Europe. The United States' classification of race has several unusual qualities: a historical refusal to acknowledge race mixing, a tendency to conflate race with ethnicity, and the development of the "one-drop rule"—which labels anyone with any African ancestry as black—to classify African Americans and no other group. This system had roots in the early settlement patterns of English colonists and their creation of a permanent serving class composed of Africans, and became refined as membership in a racial group defined access to freedom and other civil, social, political, and property rights.

The English colonists generally arrived in family groups and encountered small, nomadic, indigenous populations. The English settlers were not likely to intermarry with people outside their ethnic group, and they gradually developed a bias against any such mixing. English colonists found it ill advised to enslave Native Americans, whose geographic knowledge, strength in numbers, and susceptibility to European diseases made them dangerous or unprofitable servants. English and Irish indentured servants fell out of favor after Bacon's Rebellion in Virginia in 1676 revealed the dangers inherent in mistreating servants who would eventually be free and armed. Africans, readily available due to a renewal of slavery practices by Europeans, and skilled in subtropical agriculture, became the slaves of choice. As the colonists developed an economic system based on perpetual servitude of this group, however, they also developed a political ideology mandating equality. The new idea of racial difference smoothed over this contradiction. Colonial laws testify to this gradual process. Slavery was legalized in some colonies by 1640, but early legal distinctions between free and slave status were based on ethnicity defined as nationality or religion. *White* as a descriptor of free peoples does not appear in Virginia's laws until 1691.

Scientific Attempts to Classify Race

Beginning in the late sixteenth century, as the scientific method spread across Europe via the Enlightenment, many scientists attempted to define race based on various systems of measurement. Scientific racism in the United States was used to support slavery of blacks, the removal of Native Americans to reservations, and the exclusion of most Asian groups from the country.

Some early classificatory systems were based on physical traits such as variations in skin color, hair, form, and general appearance. Other systems, like those of Bernard Varen (1622–1650) and John Ray (1627–1705) in the mid-seventeenth century and Swedish botanist Carl Linnaeus (1707–1788) a century later, classified humans by both physical traits and cultural traits such as diet and habits. Georges-Louis Leclerc (1707–1788), the Comte de Buffon, is generally credited with introducing *race* into the terminology of natural sciences in 1749; he thought racial differences were superficial, based on climate, geography, and culture. Anthropologists such as Paul Broca (1824–1880), a founder of the Anthropological Society of Paris, invented instruments to further *anthropometry*—the science of measuring human bodies.

In the United States, these scientific systems created religious controversy. Some scientists, convinced of a huge chasm between the races, decided that different races were actually different species formed in separate creations (polygenesis). Others saw this as heretical, believing that there was one creation, as specified in the Bible, and racial differences were therefore the result of gradual degeneration (monogenesis). The polygenesis versus monogenesis debate continued until general acceptance of the theory of evolution rendered it moot.

Major polygeneticists included Dr. Samuel Morton (1799–1851), a physician and anatomist, Morton's student Dr. Josiah Nott (1804–1873), and Harvard scientist Louis Agassiz (1807–1873). Morton, working in the 1830s and 1840s, founded the science of *craniometry* and amassed the largest collection of human skulls in the world. Morton claimed that each race had a distinct skull size, shape, and cranial capacity, and that these physical differences endowed each race with permanently different moral and intellectual capacities. Other measurements used to distinguish between races included prognathism (a measure of the jutting of jaw related to incline of forehead), the cephalic index (a measurement of a skull's roundness versus length), and phrenology (a measure of capabilities assigned through assessment of the bumps on a person's skull). Not all scientists believed in theories of racial inferiority and superiority. Around the turn of the twentieth century, anthropologists such as Franz Boas (1858–1942) discovered that anthropometric measurements changed between parent and child, indicating the influence of environmental factors such as nutrition and climate on such measurements. Others questioned the legitimacy of craniometry and the accuracy of earlier measurements.

Even though some anthropologists and biologists began to distance themselves from the idea of race, scientific racism still influenced the broader society. For example, Prudential Insurance Company statistician Frederick Hoffman (1865–1946) predicted the eventual extinction of the black race based on analysis of death rates. Scientific ideas about race powered the American eugenics movement, whose ideologies provided fodder for antimiscegenation laws, the forced sterilization of undesirables, and eventually the Nazis' Final Solution during World War II (1939–1945). Although most scientists now believe that the idea of race is biologically meaningless, attempts to locate biological regularities connected to race have not vanished, as some studies of racial differences in cytology, hematology, and genetics continue.

Representations of Race

Material culture helps create and circulate ideologies of race. In the United States, it has been fairly common for whites to use images of racialized "others" in print culture, from travel brochures to commercial advertisements to instruction manuals to trade cards. Images of Africans and African Americans, Native Americans, and Chinese were particularly likely to be used in advertising from the eighteenth century through the 1960s. Linkage of nonwhite peoples with consumer products was especially common when the advertised product was associated with either colonial trade (such as tobacco, sugar, coffee, and tea) or the labor of nonwhite ethnic groups (for example, cotton or railroads). Other advertisements lack even this tenuous connection between the advertised product and racial representation: Representation of Africans, Asians, and American Indians frequently showed these groups as savage, sinister, or vacuous, outside the world of modern commodities, and occupying comic or servile positions.

Racial hierarchies also were revealed in more subtle ways through the use of consumer goods. As the color line assumed greater importance in early colonial life, consumers began to associate whiteness with quality and refinement in the products they bought, from dishes to clothing to paint. Middle- and upper-class whites developed a preference for white porcelain, whitewashed houses, and white clothing. Racial boundaries were defined and reified through access to more refined material objects; lower races and classes were defined as those who used darker, rougher material goods.

Racial and Ethnic Creations

American material culture historically has shown the influence of the nation's various racial and cultural groups. In the colonial South, slave artisans and craftsmen continued African traditions to create textiles, musical instruments, carvings, houses, and food, mixing their styles and techniques with those of European craftspeople. Many slaves preferred to use African farming implements rather than adapting to English tools, and whites and blacks adopted Native American agricultural techniques, and later, their textiles, pottery, basketry, and other art forms. The houses of slaves, free blacks, and lower-class whites tended to mix elements of both English and African architecture.

Because of historical influences such as the legally mandated illiteracy of slaves and the deculturation programs aimed at American Indians, whites have been more able to express themselves through various material artistic forms, which has meant that white depictions of other races dominated United States culture for much of its history. Blacks, American Indians, Hispanics, and Asian Americans have frequently appeared in the mass media in distorted forms, represented as buffoons in minstrel shows, savages or sidekicks in Westerns, or dragon ladies in detective films. Jim Crow segregation was supported by films such as D. W. Griffith's (1875–1948) influential film *Birth of a Nation* (1915). The film, taken as history by many viewers, showed a post–Civil War South in which savage freed slaves committed atrocities against whites until the Ku Klux Klan arrived to restore order and decency.

Cultural products are open to multiple interpretations, however, so it is never a given that everyone will read implied racial messages in the same fashion. For example, research shows that people generally identify with the heroes of films, no matter what their respective races. Cultural forms produced by nonwhites have frequently been interpreted using the preexisting semiotic codes of white culture; thus the Afro has been interpreted as "natural," while Native American textiles and pottery are evaluated through the Eurocentric idea of authenticity. The identification of whiteness with commodity culture, while a measure of the relative power of whites, has also created

negative images of whiteness, as it is associated at times with the blander and over-processed products of consumer society.

While whites still dominate major media companies, blacks, Asian Americans, and Native Americans have produced their own narratives using smaller companies, a trend that began between the two world wars, when black audiences flocked to "race movies" that reversed Hollywood's negative images. These films were paralleled by an explosion of literature, music, art, and theater, notably centered in the Harlem Renaissance that flourished during the interwar period.

Dispersion of Goods and Land Use

In the United States, race influences what people own and where they live. Income and wealth are distributed more unequally in America than in other industrialized nations (despite a common belief that the opposite is true), and inequality follows racial lines. The median incomes of white Americans and some Asian Americans (Japanese and Chinese Americans) are far above the median incomes of African Americans, Native Americans, and Hispanic Americans. Even when income is similar, a wealth gap exists between whites and blacks.

Concentration of land ownership in the hands of whites and patterns of segregation have deep roots in the United States. The English settlers who colonized North America did not recognize American Indians' group stewardship of land as a legitimate use, and therefore justified their confiscation of the lands of Native Americans and the subsequent removal of tribes to reservations. This removal was accomplished through more than 370 treaties between the federal government and different American Indian tribes, and also by the imposition of European standards of land ownership and group membership: Indians were identified by a blood quantum, and land was parceled out to individuals rather than to tribes. Today, many American Indians remain concentrated on western reservations.

In the antebellum era, the majority of blacks lived in the South; in 1870, 80 percent of blacks were rural and southern. A combination of push and pull factors, including industrialization, crises in agriculture, and the harsh Jim Crow segregation of the South, caused a massive migration of African Americans to the North and to cities. By 1970, 80 percent of blacks were urban, and half lived outside the South. A variety of forces have led to extreme segregation between whites and blacks; these include violence, racial zoning (ruled unconstitutional in 1917), boycotts, restrictive covenants, and redlining practiced by government agencies such as the Home Owners' Loan Corporation.

Katherine Walker

See also African America; Consumerism and Consumption; Ethnicity; Native America; Popular Culture; Slavery; Suburbs and Suburbia

References and Further Reading

Deetz, James. 1977. *In Small Things Forgotten: The Archeology of Early American Life.* Garden City, NY: Anchor Press/Doubleday.

Fields, Barbara, 1990. "Slavery, Race, and Ideology in the United States of America." *New Left Review* 181: 95–118.

Fontana, Bernard L. 1978. "Artifacts of the Indians of the Southwest." *Material Culture and the Study of American Life,* ed. Ian M. G. Quimby, 75–108. New York: W. W. Norton.

Frankenberg, Ruth. 1993. *White Women, Race Matters: The Social Construction of Whiteness.* Minneapolis: University of Minnesota Press.

Heneghan, Bridget T. 2003. *Whitewashing America: Material Culture and Race in the Antebellum Imagination.* Jackson: University Press of Mississippi.

Massey, Douglas, and Nancy Denton. 1993. *American Apartheid: Segregation and the Making of the Underclass.* Cambridge, MA: Harvard University Press.

O'Barr, William. 1994. *Culture and the Ad: Exploring Otherness in the World of Advertising.* Boulder, CO: Westview Press.

Oliver, Melvin L., and Thomas M. Shapiro. 1997. *Black Wealth, White Wealth: A New Perspective on Racial Inequality.* New York: Routledge.

Omi, Michael, and Howard Winant. 1994. *Racial Formation in the United States: From the 1960s to the 1990s.* New York: Routledge.

Shively, JoEllen. 1992. "Cowboys and Indians: Perceptions of Western Films among American Indians and Anglos." *American Sociological Review* 57 (6): 725–734.

Sobel, Mechal. 1987. *The World They Made Together: Black and White Values in Eighteenth-Century Virginia.* Princeton, NJ: Princeton University Press.

Smedley, Audrey, 1999. *Race in North America: Origin and Evolution of a Worldview,* 2nd ed. Boulder, CO: Westview Press.

Recreation Rooms

More familiarly called *rec room, rumpus room, game room,* and *playroom,* a *recreation room* is an enclosed space designated and used for a variety of leisure activities. These activities include but are not limited to play, hobbies, games, dancing, parties, and other informal entertainments. *Canteen* and *club room* are more often used specifically to describe a recreation room for public use. When located within a domestic dwelling, the recreation room is often found in the basement.

Many middle-class houses in the nineteenth-century United States contained a room used by the family for recreation. Such rooms were designated by the type of recreation each housed: smoking room, billiards room, sitting room, drawing room, or parlor. Nevertheless, the multiuse room known as the recreation room did not appear until the early twentieth century. After World War I, the smaller bungalow increasingly became the housing style of choice. The suburban bungalow and its simply arranged interior rooms reflected a trend toward informality and openness in social interactions among the family and guests. Bungalow living rooms could not always accommodate the varied and growing needs of families with more free time and more ways to occupy it. The recreation room harbored an unrestrained environment in which all age groups could participate in multiple recreational activities.

As single-family home ownership, family leisure time, and discretionary funds increased, the recreation room became a popular "do it yourself" project. It reached the height of its popularity in the post–World War II era when the Servicemen's Readjustment Act of 1944 (the "GI Bill of Rights") allowed unprecedented numbers of families to purchase their own suburban homes and automation in the workplace helped to create the forty-hour work week. The postwar baby boom and the concomitant emphasis on the teenager rendered the rec room a necessity for intergenerational harmony: Teenagers could enjoy privacy or entertain friends with the latest music without disrupting other family members' activities.

Many American middle-class dwellings today contain basement rec rooms; these spaces remain devoted mainly to the children and adolescents. The family (or "great") room located adjacent to the living room has replaced the recreation room in many instances as the place for leisure-time activities with and among family members. One wonders whether the rec room is passing into nostalgia and history, with its central role in the popular television series *That '70s Show* (1998–2006) and in the 1992 film *Wayne's World*.

Pamela Dorazio Dean

See also Cellars and Basements; House, Home, and Domesticity; Leisure, Recreation, and Amusements

References and Further Reading

Clark, Clifford Edward, Jr. 1986. *The American Family Home, 1800–1960*. Chapel Hill: University of North Carolina Press.
Dulles, Foster Rhea. 1965. *A History of Recreation: America Learns to Play*, 2nd ed. New York: Appleton-Century-Crofts.

Religion, Spirituality, and Belief

The interplay of religion, spirituality, and belief within American material life can be difficult to discern. First and foremost the terms, while interrelated, are not interchangeable. Religious people may cultivate a spiritual life that articulates, and is reinforced by, their beliefs about humanity, the world, the supernatural, and the cosmos. Does this mean, however, that all beliefs are necessarily spiritual, or that all spiritualities are necessarily affiliated with a religious worldview? Further, religious institutions grow and decline throughout history, and beliefs evolve over time. So does material life. As historian Colleen McDannell (1995, 3) notes in her *Material Christianity*, "The artifacts, landscapes, architecture, and arts that make up material culture are not discrete units. Each . . . interacts with the others to produce an array of physical expressions." Like religion, material culture is far from being easily explained. Both are "constantly changing as people invent, produce, market, gift, or dismantle" them (McDannell 1995, 3).

Religion

Religion itself defies definition, making it all the more difficult to map the relationship of religion and material culture. Sociologist

Emile Durkheim (1858–1917) formulated a definition of *religion* with which social scientists both agree and disagree. In *The Elementary Forms of Religious Life* (1912, 47), Durkheim delineates the sacred and the profane when he defines religion as "a unified system of beliefs and practices relative to sacred things, that is to say, things set apart and forbidden—beliefs and practices which unite into one single moral community called a Church, all those who adhere to them."

McDannell takes issue with Durkheim's model of religion. "The assumption that true Christian sentiments can be, must be, set apart from the profane," she writes, "cannot be upheld when we look at how people use material culture in their religious lives" (McDannell 1995, 6). The American nation is a cultural matrix within which sacred religious life is "frequently fus[ed]" with and "scrambled" into the vast sea of allegedly secular culture. For example, Catholics employ printed Mass cards, crucifixes and relics, and both prints and photographic images portraying lives and shrines of saints, in constructing home shrines (McDannell 1995, 28–33). Jews mark their religious affiliation and identity through such objects as the *mezuzah*, a small container with a parchment upon which prescribed prayers are written; it is posted on a door lintel (*mezuzah* is Hebrew for "doorpost"). Protestants, whose denominations have traditionally eschewed representations of Jesus or dismissed portrayals of other religious figures as "idolatry," have employed "the social exchange of religious goods"—for example, nineteenth-century Methodists displaying a teapot commemorating the life of the denomination's founder, John Wesley (1703–1791)—in order to declare denominational affiliation as well as confession of Christian belief (McDannell 1995, 43–44). The phenomenon is by no means limited to traditional Western religions.

The number of books endorsing various schools of Buddhism (albeit often for Western audiences), for example, has exploded since the 1950s (Prothero 2001).

Durkheim's narrow definition of religion assumes that "the American landscape and consumer culture are devoid of religious forms" (McDannell 1995, 7). McDannell provides two crucial observations about American religious life. It has, of course, a rich "material dimension," and it exists within a marketplace of ideas and objects that compete for the hearts and minds of Americans *and* for a place within American life. Sociologists Roger Finke and Rodney Stark (2005) champion a view of America as a "marketplace" in which various religions, protected by the First Amendment to the United States Constitution, compete for market share (Stark and Finke, 2005). Religious studies scholar Ninian Smart (1996, 10–12) formulated a model of the religious "phenomenon" by identifying various dimensions of the religious life, the last of which is the "material or artistic dimension" within which "[a] religion or worldview will express itself [in] material creations, from chapels to cathedrals to temples to mosques, from icons and divine statuary to books and pulpits."

Smart did not foresee the ascendancy of the Internet as a means through which Americans could construct "virtual" community bonds. Buddhist studies scholar Charles S. Prebish (1999, 203) charts the growth since the early 1990s of the online Buddhist *sangha* from online discussion forums to Web sites that provide a community "never imagined by the Buddha [yet] unit[ing] practitioners and scholars into one potentially vast community." Providing a more general arena for various traditions, *Beliefnet* is an online resource combining historical introductions to various religious traditions with both commentaries from representatives of various perspectives on current events and discussion forums through which the curious may connect with people from various worldview communities, as well as from their own (www.beliefnet.org).

Spirituality

Spirituality may be distinguished from *religion* in that it does not necessitate the community ties or rituals that are root features of the latter. As Durkheim (1912, 44) concluded, "religion [is] an eminently collective thing." Wade Clark Roof, a sociologist of religion, notes that, with the maturation of the baby boomers in the last two decades of the twentieth century, the United States became a "spiritual marketplace" within which a "quest culture" operated. "Disenchantment" with the traditional religions, or the lack of any religious tradition within which they were raised, encouraged many Americans to explore "*both* inside *and* outside of" traditional organizations or places of worship a way of life that would provide inward "meaning and strength" (Roof 2001, 57). Stark and Finke (2000, 43, 51) argue that this spiritual quest is the evaluation by "rational consumers" of religious goods and the selection of a religious affiliation and identity dependent upon whether the spiritual "benefits" outweigh the social "costs" of making such a purchase. High demand among consumers for a high-risk investment yielding a generous return fuels the spiritual marketplace. Roof disputes this, however. Whether, he notes, they "reawaken" and come "home" to traditions in which they were raised, embrace wholly new traditions, assemble personal "religious" identities by "eclectically" picking and choosing from various traditions or beliefs, or remain free agents of the spirit, these questers have emphasized a personal experience of feeling connected with something transcending or greater than themselves. This may be done within a religious community—however, a feeling of individual completeness is prioritized and privileged (Roof 2001, 17–33).

Regardless of whether the motives are more external or more internal, the American religious fabric is currently undergoing a profound transformation. According to a 2005 *Newsweek* poll, 79 percent of Americans identify themselves as "spiritual," while 64 percent identify themselves as "religious" and perhaps no more than 20 percent attend religious service every week (*Newsweek* 2005, 50). Further, while Christianity retains far more American adherents than any other tradition, the Protestantism that has shaped American social and cultural life since the nation's founding—due to immigration, conversion, and changes of individual religious affiliation, all of which reflect increased competition—may no longer hold its traditional majority (Smith and Kim 2004, 1–3).

The result of this exponential explosion of choice in the American spiritual marketplace is reflected in American material and consumer culture. Religious studies scholar Thomas Tweed (2002, 71) notes that popular interest in Buddhism has allowed for the emergence of "night-stand Buddhists," people who get their knowledge of and affiliation with Buddhism from books written for popular consumption and read in the bedroom after work and at night (Tweed 2002, 71). Historian Stephen Prothero (2001) notes that much popular "Boomer Buddhism" centers around one's self-identification and one's individual experience of "enlightenment" rather than the rigorous study of the *dharma* of non-self toward attaining liberation from rebirth. The popular Kabbalah movement stresses the individual's awareness of the "presence of God" within his or her life without the rigorous study of Torah and Talmud traditionally considered foundational and obligatory before one could begin to study the *Zohar* (www.kabbalah.org). Recognizing that "conversation about God . . . is being increasingly found outside the Church as well as within it," theologian Robert K. Johnson encourages those Christians who have habitually shunned the "corrupt" "secular" cinema to "better connect with" a "Hollywood" that could—when one becomes a conscientious critic, of course—facilitate rather than negate meaningful dialogue about human nature and "divine encounter" (Johnson 2000, 14–15, 57–58). The common thread joining all of these approaches by spiritual seekers from diverse traditions is one's personal relationship with reality in order to craft an individual meaning that provides him or her with inward fulfillment.

Belief

As Durkheim noted, *belief* unites and keeps together religious communities. Beliefs also impel seekers to initiate a spiritual quest after a personal truth. And, as Stark and Finke (2000) write, beliefs form the stuff of the advertisement and public relations campaign, the marketing strategy that a religious tradition uses to lure clients.

As each of these theories of religion illumines, however, belief in and by itself is no equivalent of religion. The first is a matter of opinion or doctrine that may or may not be held by all members of a religious community; the latter denotes a social system in which several beliefs may operate (Durkheim 1995, 34; Stark and Finke 2000, 137). Therefore, one's expression of beliefs is not necessarily a reflection of a religious tradition as a whole. More than 90 percent of Americans claim belief in "God." But given the vast range of and disparity among beliefs circulating in the United States about what "God" *is*, this statistic does not speak deeply about what the religions say about God. Sev-

enty-nine percent, according to the *Newsweek* poll, "believe that someone of another faith can attain salvation or go to heaven." This is a slightly more specific statement that, as broken down among Evangelical Protestants and non-Christians, for example, expresses a narrower range of ideas. Yet it still does not speak to specific tenets of faith held by respective traditions; rather it reflects a general trend (*Newsweek* 2005, 49). In the end, the beliefs behind these statistics are the equivalents of more general statements made on bumper stickers proclaiming that "Jesus Loves You" or the label of a bottle of "Dr. Bronner's Magic Soap" prophesying that we are "ALL ONE!" on "God's spaceship Earth" (www.drbronner.com). They express beliefs that are themselves expressions of an individual's spirituality. This is perhaps why they may find popularity that transcends religious distinctions in the marketplace of goods and in meaningful material culture.

Matt Stefon

See also Burial Grounds, Cemeteries, and Grave Markers; Community; Consumerism and Consumption; Funerals; Funerary (Sepulchral) Monuments; Holidays and Commemorations; Houses of Worship (Ecclesiastical Architecture); Mourning; Mourning and Ethnicity; Popular Culture, Religious Dress; Rite, Ritual, and Ceremony

References and Further Reading

Chidester, David, and Edward T. Linenthal, eds. 1995. *American Sacred Space*. Bloomington: Indiana University Press.

Durkheim, Emile. 1995 (1912). *The Elementary Forms of Religious Life*, trans. Karen E. Fields. New York: Free Press.

Finke, Roger, and Rodney Stark. 2005. *The Churching of America, 1776–2005: Winners and Losers in our Religious Economy*, 2nd ed. New Brunswick, NJ: Rutgers University Press.

Johnson, Robert K. 2000. *Reel Spirituality: Theology and Film in Dialogue*. Grand Rapids, MI: Baker.

Material History of Religion Project. 2001.
Home page. http://www.materialreligion
.org/.

McDannell, Colleen. 1995. *Material Christianity:
Religion and Popular Culture in America*. New
Haven, CT: Yale University Press.

Newsweek. 2005. "In Search of the Spiritual."
Newsweek, August 29, 50.

Prebish, Charles S. 1999. *Luminous Passage: The
Practice and Study of Buddhism in America*.
Berkeley: University of California Press.

Prothero, Stephen. 2001. "Boomer Buddhism."
Salon, February 26. http://archive.salon
.com/books/feature/2001/02/26/
buddhism/print.html.

Roof, Wade Clark. 2001. *Spiritual Marketplace:
Baby Boomers and the Remaking of American
Religion*. Princeton, NJ: Princeton University
Press.

Smart, Ninian. 1996. *Dimensions of the Sacred:
An Anatomy of the World's Beliefs*. Berkeley:
University of California Press.

Smith, Tom W., and Seokho Kim. 2004. "The
Vanishing Protestant Majority." Conducted
for the National Opinion Research Center,
University of Chicago. *GSS Social Change
Report No. 49* (July).

Stark, Rodney, and Roger Finke. 2000. *Acts of
Faith: Explaining the Human Side of Religion*.
Berkeley: University of California Press.

Tweed, Thomas. 2002. "Who Is a Buddhist?
Night-stand Buddhists and Other Crea-
tures." In *Westward Dharma: Buddhism
Beyond Asia*, ed. Charles Prebish and Martin
Baumann, 17–33. Berkeley: University of
California Press.

Religious Dress

Dress has historically functioned for mainstream, utopian, and sectarian religious
groups as a way to identify inclusion and
roles in a religious community as well as to
reify the boundaries of a community. The
numerous Protestant denominations that
settled in early North America employed
dress as symbols of dissent and identity.
Puritans rejected the finery and vestments
for ministers as a form of protest against the
Catholic leanings of the Church of England.
New England Puritan clergy wore black robes
to signal their moral and religious authority.
Clothing in colonial America reflected both
religious affiliation and social hierarchy; thus
dissent could be registered through dress.
The Religious Society of Friends (or Quakers), pietists, and evangelicals used "plain"
dress to counter fine clothing as well as to
proclaim their egalitarianism. Quakers were
the most consistent in their use of plain dress
as separation from "worldly" society. Itinerant Quaker ministers discarded clerical garb
to protest the distinction between clergy and
laity.

Liturgical and Ceremonial Dress

Though Protestant denominations range
widely in the adoption of clerical garments,
Christian ministers and priests tend to dress
in dark clothing and wear clerical ("Roman")
collars; in the performance of religious rites
they wear white gowns (albs) and a variety
of surplices, scarves or stoles, tunics, and
other symbolic, color-meaningful garb related
to specific ceremonies throughout the Christian calendar. The Roman Catholic Church
has historically identified its clergy by dress.
The church's hierarchical structure is reified
in the various costumes used to designate
priests, monsignors, bishops, cardinals, and
the pope when performing the various rites
and celebrations within the church. Jewish
rabbis do not wear distinctive clothing; during such major observances as Rosh Hashanah
and Yom Kippur, rabbis don a white robe
called a *kittel*.

Religious Commitment
and Affiliation

Some Christian monks and nuns register
their devotion to God through their adoption
of robes and, for nuns, habits. After the Sec-

ond Ecumenical Council of the Vatican (Vatican II, 1962–1965), habits were no longer required from Catholic religious women, although some communities have since readopted the habit. Most Catholic schools require uniforms, and students' popular culture is replete with memoirs, plays, and jokes about the implied discipline of the uniform and the transgressions of raising hemlines, unraveling sweaters, loosening ties, and wearing shirttails out.

The adoption of specific dress and accessories signals commitment and membership to a particular faith. Over the centuries some Jews have assimilated to American culture by giving up traditional forms of dress. Nevertheless, Jewish men may choose to wear a skullcap, called a *yarmulke*, as well as *tzitzit*, fringes attached to an undershirt, part of the medieval tradition of the *tallit*, a fringed shawl. Hasidic Jews have not surrendered distinctive forms of clothing. In Hasadism, women cover their hair. Hasidic men wear beards and side-locks, fur hats, long silk coats, slipper-style shoes, and white knee socks.

Male and female members of the Church of Jesus Christ of Latter Day Saints (Mormons) daily wore sacred garments similar to long underwear, and many adhere to this practice today. In the late nineteenth century, the Salvation Army, identifying its members as God's Christian soldiers, mandated military uniforms for its members. Though diverse, their uniforms reflected the organization's theology in colors: blue (purity), red (Christ's blood), and yellow (the Holy Spirit).

Religion, Modesty, and Gender

Modesty of thought and dress for men and for women is a constant precept in the world's major religions. Women's dress, however, has been a particular topic of attention. Women's clothing was and is a way to display piety through modesty, humility, and devotion. Fashion was thought to lead women astray. In the seventeenth century, Puritans believed that immodest dress was a feminine sin, and this belief about female dress reappeared in many utopian movements in the nineteenth century, most notably the Oneida community. Founder John Humphrey Noyes (1811–1886) implemented the "short dress," which consisted of a short skirt and pantalettes, or bloomers, underneath the skirt. For Noyes, women's dress reform reflected their spirituality and moved women away from the sin of pride in dress. In the nineteenth century, members of the African Methodist Episcopal Church, in particular women, used dress as a tool to help present conversion as well as to claim their authority as leaders. Women preachers relied on plain dress and on respectable dress, which was fashionable but chaste. For these African American women, dress represented the nature of their soul.

For Muslims in the United States, women's dress has also been a special concern. The Koran dictates modesty in dress for both men and women, but the concern surrounds the issue of whether women have to wear the *hijab*, the head scarf, to be good Muslims. Moreover, women wearing the *hijab* have been discriminated against in the workplace because of this visible marker of their devotion to Islam.

"Dressing up" to attend religious services has had a long tradition in the United States. This does not require special clothes, but it does mark the importance of the service to the wearer. Moreover, Christian retailing has led to a variety of T-shirts, hats, armbands, and jewelry that proclaim one's faith.

Kelly J. Baker

See also Dress, Accessories, and Fashion; Gender; Plainness (Quaker); Religion, Spirituality, and Belief; Rite, Ritual, and Ceremony

References and Further Reading

Arthur, Linda B., ed. 1999. *Religion, Dress and the Body*. Oxford, UK: Berg.

Fischer, Gayle V. 2001. *Pantaloons and Power: A Nineteenth-Century Dress Reform in the United States*. Kent, OH: Kent State University Press.

Kuhns, Elizabeth. 2003. *The Habit: A History of the Clothing of Catholic Nuns*. New York: Doubleday.

McDannell, Colleen. 1995. *Material Christianity: Religion and Popular Culture in America*. New Haven, CT: Yale University Press.

Schmidt, Leigh Eric. 1989. "'A Church-Going People Are a Dress-Loving People': Clothes, Communication, and Religious Culture in Early America." *Church History* 58: 36–51.

Smith, Jane I. 1999. *Islam in America*. New York: Columbia University Press.

Winston, Diane. 2000. *Red-Hot and Righteous: The Urban Religion of the Salvation Army*. Cambridge, MA: Harvard University Press.

Renaissance Revival

A style based on the architecture of sixteenth-century Italy and France (which, in turn, was based on the styles of ancient Rome and Greece), the Renaissance Revival in the United States influenced architecture and the decorative arts from the mid-nineteenth century through the first decade of the twentieth century. With grand proportions, elaborate ornamentation, and expensive materials, Renaissance Revival buildings symbolized the permanence of the institutions and businesses within; structures in this style included civic buildings such as McKim, Mead, and White's (est. 1879) Boston Public Library (1887–1895) and the St. Louis, Missouri, City Hall (1892–1904). This style

Boston Public Library was designed by the architectural firm McKim, Mead, and White. Completed in 1895, this monumental Renaissance Revival structure stands as a testament to Charles Follen McKim's description of a "palace for the people." (Library of Congress)

well suited urban commercial blocks of cast-iron facades behind which department stores and specialty stores celebrated rising wealth and consumption. Architects also designed late nineteenth-century grand mansions for America's Gilded Age wealthy in this style. The Breakers (1893–1895), designed by Richard Morris Hunt (1828–1895) for Cornelius Vanderbilt II (1843–1899), in Newport, Rhode Island, stands as the premier example of this taste.

Furniture and other decorative arts in this style were monumental and elaborate. Often massive and rectilinear in form, Renaissance Revival furniture featured columns, cartouches and medallions, and veneer panels and applied molding, as well as carvings featuring flowers and fruits, caryatids and classical busts, and animal heads. This style was particularly effective in the dining room, conveying middle- and upper-class Americans' sense of distance between civilization and savagery through the iconography of the hunt and the harvest carved into sideboards that seemed more sacred altar than utilitarian server and storage cabinet. Matched parlor suites of furniture were affordable through the mass production made available via centers of furniture making on the East Coast and, by the 1870s, in Grand Rapids, Michigan. The display of Grand Rapids furniture in this style at the Centennial Exposition in Philadelphia in 1876 guaranteed the Midwest's primacy in production of this style. Critics within the Aesthetic Movement would label this popular style "Grand Rapidism," arguing that it lacked creativity and beauty in its reliance on historicism and overuse.

Shirley Teresa Wajda

See also Civic Architecture; Commercial Architecture; Decorative Arts; Furniture; Style

References and Further Reading
Ames, Kenneth L. 1974. "The Battle of the Sideboards (1851–1876)." *Winterthur Portfolio* 9 (1): 1–27.
Carron, Christian, with Kenneth Ames, Jeffrey Kleiman, and Joel Lafever. 1998. *Grand Rapids Furniture: The Story of America's Furniture City*. Grand Rapids, MI: Public Museum of Grand Rapids.
Gelernter, Mark. 1999. *A History of American Architecture: Buildings in Their Cultural and Technological Context*. Hanover, NH: University Press of New England.
Seale, William. 1995 (1881). *The Tasteful Interlude: American Interiors through the Camera's Eyes, 1860–1917*. Walnut Creek, CA: AltaMira Press.

Rite, Ritual, and Ceremony

The study of historical and contemporary American life through a consideration of experiences defined as rite, ritual, and ceremony offers insight to the beliefs Americans have held and hold about themselves, the groups with which they engage, and their membership in communities and the nation. A *rite*, a formal procedure or act, often, but not always, is religious and provides a means of achieving transcendence. *Ritual*, derived from and often synonymous with *rite*, qualifies objects or practices connected with a rite. Rites and rituals are repetitive, learned via instruction and practice as a means to ensure continuity.

Scholarship on rite and ritual historically focused on religious belief and practice. Since the 1970s scholars have explored *secular ritual*, those activities that may or may not have transcendence as a goal or incorporate symbols. In this sense *ritual* also qualifies habitual or repetitive acts that may not possess symbolic meaning but characterize social expectations and cultural norms. A *ceremony* is a sacred or secular rite, but it also refers to those social interactions in which deference to rank or common courtesy is symbolized through polite gestures and acts. (To *stand on ceremony* is to acknowledge the necessity to observe such formalities.) A *rite* is a special ceremony; *ceremony* is not necessarily always special but certainly courteous and formal. In the United States courtesy has been codified in etiquette guides. These activities employ material culture as meaningful symbolic objects that connect individuals to one another as well as to intangible ideas or beliefs. Rite, ritual, and ceremony not only structure human behavior but they also attempt to structure the way people think about social life (Moore and Myerhoff 1977, 4). Rituals may alleviate anxieties and foster social coherence and harmony, but they also may reify emotions or ideologies deemed fractious and threatening. The Ku Klux Klan's ritual of cross burning constitutes an extreme example.

Religious Rites

A religious rite is a body of customary observances that defines a particular religion, its community of believers, and that community's relationship to the sacred. Material objects are often used in the many ceremonies, from the ever-present sacred texts to prayer beads used daily to specific vestments and spaces (mosques, temples, synagogues, meetinghouses, and churches) to celebrate specific observances. The world's major religions share the observation of life transformations: birth, coming of age, marriage, and death.

The material culture of religion has become a field in itself, exploring the art and objects Americans used in their various religious practices. Not all religious material culture is used in ritual; nevertheless, the question of the separation of the sacred and the profane that is symbolically erased through religious rites may be explored through the study of this body of material culture. Spontaneous roadside shrines are often considered sacred spaces by family members and friends. As such, they may become sites of mourning commemorations.

Civic Rites

Federal holidays such as Independence Day, Memorial Day, Veterans Day, and Labor Day are observed throughout the United States. Though observances may differ from place to place, the ceremonies adopted inscribe membership in the nation, whether through the playing of "Taps" to honor war dead, to parades of bands playing patriotic music, to the commemoration of the nation's founding. Other civic rites are government officials' swearing-in ceremonies, presidential inaugurations, the cutting of ribbons to open new public facilities, and the awarding of the "keys to the city" to honor individuals. Given baseball's primacy as "the nation's pastime," even the ceremonial first pitch by a sitting president or his representative to mark the beginning of the Major League Baseball's season may be seen as a civic rite.

Parades—celebratory, often ceremonial processions that a group or groups assume for a time a public thoroughfare to display symbols and themselves—have a long history. Such "street theater" was evident in colonial Boston's anti-Catholic "Pope's Day" parades and in New York City's Gay Pride parade today. As festive, public activities, parades—in their participants, order of presentation, and symbolism—represent the groups and the structures of power in a community. At the same time, however, the "off stage" political debates and social problems of a given community offer clues to the parade—its theatrical, orderly procession of dignitaries, bands, and floats—as anything but unchanging.

Family Rituals

Family rituals may be private or be conducted in the presence of others or in relationship to a public rite or to holidays. These observances may celebrate the family: birthdays and wedding anniversaries, family reunions on the Fourth of July, and Christmas gifting are all rituals that have changed over time and are as varied as the families who participated in these celebrations. Historian Elizabeth H. Pleck has found three historical phases of family rituals in the United States: the seventeenth- and eighteenth-century carnivalesque public celebrations; the rise of the "sentimental" ritual, beginning in the early nineteenth century; and the "postsentimental" ritual, discernible after World War I but especially evident in the 1970s. As Pleck (2000, 2) writes, "these transformations in how the family is celebrated and how the family celebrates holidays and special events were the result of changes in many fronts—in the family, in women's roles, in ethnic group consciousness, and in nationalism, consumer culture, and popular entertainment." The very definition of *family* is explored in these types of rituals.

Rites of Passage

Rites of passage symbolically facilitate a transition in social status. Such rites are usually public in character; ordered through a formal ceremony; and dependent on symbolic actions, symbolic objects such as specialized dress, and dedicated spaces for the purpose. Religious rites of passage include Christian baptism and confirmation, Jewish bar and bat mitzvahs, and marriage. French folklorist Arnold van Gennep (1873–1957) was one of the first, in 1908, to analyze rites of passages as performances. Anthropologist Victor Turner (1920–1983) elaborated van Gennep's insights. A rite of passage possesses a three-part sequence based on the idea of *liminality* —a term borrowed from the Latin *limen*, meaning threshold. First, the individual undergoing a rite of passage is separated from his or her former status (separation) and is, secondly, "outside" social structure (transition). Last, the individual is integrated into a new group or, having a new status, reintegrated into his or her previous group, but with a new identity (aggregation). Turner's idea of *communitas* describes the social bonds created through liminality, that state of being "betwixt and between." Rites of passage thus serve as agents of socialization.

A well-known example of a rite of passage in contemporary American society is high school graduation. Though meant to commemorate the fulfillment of a state-required education, graduation marks the end of the liminal status of adolescence. During a public ceremony appropriately named *commencement*, students on the brink of graduation wear identical regalia—robes and flat-topped, tasseled headwear called "mortar boards"—that set them apart from school administrators, teachers, family members, and other spectators. Commencement speakers commend the students' individual and shared accomplishments and offer advice for their new roles as graduates. The receipt of diplomas, the public declarations of administrators certifying the fulfillment of requirements, and the moving by hand of the mortar board tassel from right to left signals the transition of high school student to high school graduate, a status that is equated with adulthood and coinciding with the acquisition of civic duties such as voting.

Some rites of passage are specific to gender and ethnic origins. The *debut*, also known as "coming out" or "bowing to society," is for adolescent girls a coming-of-age or puberty rite that signals girls' marriageability. Historically the practice of royalty seeking to align themselves with other powerful families, the debut was adopted by elite American families. Now the debut is a widespread practice—the high school prom (short for *promenade*, a public stroll), the "sweet sixteen" party, and the Latina *quinceañera*. Minority groups in the United States have adopted these practices; Polish American and African American clubs, for example, hold debut ceremonies every year. The prescribed (often white) dress, shoes, gloves, and flowers; the precise performance of the ceremony (including a deep curtsy when announced); knowledge of various cotillion dances and graceful bearing were key to a successful presentation. By the late twentieth century these ceremonies became exaggerated, expensive, and fully engaged with the consumption of costly goods and services.

Ritual in Contemporary America

Recent scholarly work in ritual has considered the phenomenon of ritual as an agent of culture, in that the seemingly formal and traditional aspects of ritual change over time. The symbolic meaning of a ritual may change as well, as rituals are adopted by new groups or altered to changing social, political, and economic circumstances. The challenges to the political and religious meanings of marriage since the 1960s have altered traditional religious rites as well as introduced new secular ones. Some women, for example, do not include *obey* in traditional wedding vows or have their fathers "give them away" to be married, seeing these acts as a vestige of historical legal and economic powerlessness. *Jumping the broom* is sometimes incorporated

in African American wedding ceremonies; like any tradition, its origins are debated but its meaning for those who adopt it as a reminder of the African American historic experience as an enslaved people is the important factor.

Some Americans eschew religious ritual and create through various folk traditions *secular life ceremonies* with which to celebrate rites of passage from birth, marriage, and death to getting a new job, moving to a new home, or returning to health after grave illness. Critics note that the syncretism of picking and choosing from a variety of traditional rituals threatens to dilute the symbolism and meanings encoded in such rites. Scholars note that some "invented traditions," such as Valentine's Day, are created or co-opted by commercialism and that greeting card makers, florists, and other businesses have introduced consumption on belief and in social relationships. Nevertheless, the ready or debated adaptation of standing rites and ceremonies to new circumstances has always occurred; the Puritan rejection of certain aspects of the Church of England's theology and concomitant attitude that ritual practices as merely rote and thereby meaningless was based on the Puritans' understanding of the early Christian Church and helped to establish the American colonies and later nation. As many scholars have more recently observed, ritual is a process: contingent, historical, and changing. Perhaps a better question is why certain rites and ritual practices have disappeared. Certainly a question always to be posed is whether a ritual "works," for in such a question is the frame through which social tensions and cultural meanings may be analyzed.

Shirley Teresa Wajda

See also Community; Etiquette and Manners;
Holidays and Commemorations; Human
Body; Public Monuments and Popular

Commemoration; Religion, Spirituality, and Belief; Religious Dress; Tradition

References and Further Reading

Geertz, Clifford. 1973. "Religion as a Cultural System." In *The Interpretation of Cultures: Selected Essays*, 87–125. New York: Basic Books.

Marling, Karal Ann. 2004. *Debutante: Rites and Regalia of American Debdom*. Lawrence: University Press of Kansas.

Material History of American Religion Project. 1995–2001. Home page. www.materialreligion.org.

Moore, Sally F., and Barbara G. Myerhoff. 1977. "Secular Ritual: Forms and Meanings." In *Secular Ritual*, 3–24. Assen, Netherlands: Van Gorcum.

Pleck, Elizabeth H. 2000. *Celebrating the Family: Ethnicity, Consumer Culture, and Family Rituals*. Cambridge, MA: Harvard University Press.

Schmidt, Leigh Eric. 1995. *Consumer Rites: The Buying and Selling of American Holidays*. Princeton, NJ: Princeton University Press.

Turner, Victor W. 1995 (1969). *The Ritual Process: Structure and Anti-Structure*, rpt. ed. Chicago: Aldine Transactions.

Van Gennep, Arnold. 1961. *The Rites of Passage*, trans. Minika B. Vizedom and Gabrielle L. Caffee. Chicago: University of Chicago Press.

Rococo Revival

American decorative arts in the mid-nineteenth-century Rococo Revival style drew design elements from eighteenth-century French furnishings popular during the reign

The Rococo Revival style was a fashionable choice for parlor furniture in the mid-nineteenth century. These parlor armchairs, made of laminated rosewood by German-born cabinetmaker John Henry Belter in New York City, feature elaborately carved and curved elements. (Peter Harholdt/Corbis)

(1715–1774) of Louis XV (1710–1774), also known as the Rococo period. Typical motifs include serpentine S-scrolls and C-scrolls as well as naturalistic designs taken from flowers, fruit, and foliage. Cabriole legs terminating in scrolled feet are common.

Rosewood was the predominant wood used in Rococo Revival furniture created in the mid-nineteenth century, often synonymous with the work of John Henry Belter (1804–1863), an immigrant cabinetmaker from Germany who perfected the process of wood lamination that made possible elaborate carved and curved elements. Thin veneers of wood were glued together with the grains of the layers laid in alternating directions to form a thick panel. This panel was subjected to a steambending process and fitted into a curved mold. When the furniture form had taken on the undulating shape of the mold, carved decorations were added onto the frame.

Rococo Revival furniture was often used in the parlor and purchased in sets that could include a center table, armchairs, sofas, fire screens, and mirrors. It was known as the "Modern French" style during the mid-nineteenth century and was popularized through international exhibitions and illustrated periodicals. Alexander Roux (1813–1886) was another well-known New York City cabinetmaker working in the style.

Other items produced in the Rococo Revival style include silver, cast iron and other metalwork, wallpapers, textiles, and porcelain.

H. Christian Carr

See also Decorative Arts; Furniture; Style

References and Further Reading

Ames, Kenneth L. 1992. *Death in the Dining Room and Other Tales of Victorian Culture.* Philadelphia, PA: Temple University Press.

Schwartz, Marvin D. 1981. *The Furniture of John Henry Belter and the Rococo Revival: An Inquiry into Nineteenth-Century Furniture Design through a Study of the Gloria and Richard Manney Collection.* New York: E. P. Dutton.

Voorsanger, Catherine Hoover, and John K. Howat, eds. 2000. *Art and the Empire City.* New York: Metropolitan Museum of Art.

S

Scrapbooks

Scrapbooks are books with originally blank pages, which are then filled with various "scraps" of paper from commercially produced advertisements, photographs, and illustrations, newspaper and magazine clippings; autographs and hand-drawn images; and decorations. Since the early nineteenth century, scrapbook compiling has provided opportunities for remembrance, practical instruction, and self-created entertainment. Scrapbooks compiled by a single person might express individual creativity, while scrapbooks that contain materials gathered by a group express shared experiences, interests, or sensibilities.

Historical scrapbooks reflect the changes in printing technology in the United States and attest to rising literacy rates after 1800. Some early scrapbooks (1800–1850) contained recycled illustrations dating back to the American Revolution. *Fugitive scraps*, unattributed scraps that have fallen from scrapbooks or those that do not have any known provenance, date back to the 1790s. Creating and keeping scrapbooks became popular in the later nineteenth century, with the introduction of colorful and affordable commercially printed scraps. These chromolithographed relief papers, also called *chromos* and known as *true scraps*, were printed and sold in sheets. Printers and entrepreneurs quickly saw how chromolithography, though at first a costly and time-consuming process, could be adapted for other purposes. Louis Prang (1824–1909) introduced chromolithographed business cards at the 1873 Vienna Exposition. That year Prang's Christmas greeting cards were introduced in England and quickly crossed the Atlantic to become popular in the United States. The New York firm of McLoughlin Brothers (circa 1855–1910), followed the example of Louis Prang, becoming successful for its affordable paper dolls, postcards, books, and scraps. McLoughlin Brothers similarly produced imagery that were sold in sheets, booklets, and boxes and portrayed religious life, school life, home life, nature, geography, patriotism, sexism, racism, and every facet of American life—all the while advertising a new consumer product.

While some scraps were sold in die-cut embossed sheets to be cut or torn, others were individually precut and sold or given away, to be affixed to cards or other paper-work projects. Greeting cards, bookmarks, calling cards, magazine illustrations, and advertisements all became fodder for scrapbook making. Advertising trade cards dominated advertising during the 1880s and 1890s, and scrapbook compilers became the most avid collectors of these printed images bearing brand names. Postcards and greeting cards were often arranged in scrapbooks and collected for their images as well as for their personal messages.

Nineteenth- and twentieth-century educators promoted scrapbooks as a means for teaching art skills. By arranging images, colors, and text in tidy little blank books, students could learn design, perspective, and composition and have something to do to prevent boredom. Creating scrapbooks was viewed as an ideal parlor activity: quiet, neat, and organizational in character. Today, scrapbook compiling (scrapbooking) has re-emerged as a popular pastime, especially for women. The scrapbooking industry is composed of commercially produced tools, blank books, scraps, and even professional scrapbookers who will create personalized memory books for customers.

Meredith Eliassen

See also Books; Collecting and Collections; Ephemera; Leisure, Recreation, and Amusements; Memory and Memorabilia; Popular Culture; Print Culture; Printmaking and American Prints; Trade Cards

References and Further Reading
Allen, Alistair, and Joan Hoverstadt. 1983. *The History of Printed Scraps.* London: New Cavendish Books.
Garvey, Ellen Gruber. 1996. *The Adman in the Parlor: Magazines and the Gendering of Consumer Culture, 1880 to 1910s.* New York: Oxford University Press.
McClinton, Katharine Morrison. 1973. *The Chromolithographs of Louis Prang.* New York: Clarkson N. Potter, Inc.
Tucker, Susan, Katherine Ott, and Patricia B. Buckler, eds. 2006. *The Scrapbook in American Life.* Philadelphia, PA: Temple University Press.

Secondhand Goods and Shopping

Secondhand goods—not-new goods that were previously used by others—are acquired in four ways. First, one can receive hand-me-downs—used goods informally given to a person. Second, one can attain goods in informal, temporary venues besides auctions, such as garage sales, church sales, and flea markets. Third, used goods are acquired from charity stores, such as the Salvation Army or church thrift shops. Fourth, used goods are purchased from for-profit retailers, such as thrift stores and Internet sellers such as eBay.

Throughout much of American history, charities more often gave used goods to the needy without expecting cash payment. Ideas about the poor and charity changed in the early twentieth century. Benevolent groups argued that it was denigrating to the poor to be given something but uplifting for the impoverished to purchase an item with cash. Thus, national charity groups opened charity stores. These stores were open to the general public and sold donated or salvaged goods for cash. In 1902 Boston's Morgan Chapel opened such a store to raise money for its charity work; this was the beginning of Goodwill Industries, which by the 1910s had opened stores across the nation. Around 1900, impermanent stores, such as rummage sales that sold used goods to accrue funds for charitable work, began to be regularly seen.

For-profit retailers were established in North America as soon as European settlers set up trade. Colonial-era and nineteenth-century Americans also relied upon traveling peddlers who bartered new goods for used goods. In urban areas, most used goods were sold to pawn shops, which then would resell the items. New York City's first pawnshop (or hockshop) opened in 1822. Other stores sold used goods without the pawning mechanism. These stores often specialized in clothing and appeared in urban areas in the 1870s. After the Civil War (1861–1865), fear arose that soldiers' clothing was being sold illegally at these used clothing stores. During the Great Depression of the 1930s, for-profit used goods stores proliferated, as many Americans found little cash available to purchase new products.

In the 1980s and 1990s, both for-profit and nonprofit secondhand stores professionalized, with cleaner stores, marketing efforts such as coupons, and national chains. EBay, an Internet auction and retail site founded in 1995, has become a major outlet of secondhand goods transactions.

For many Americans, used goods are a way to continue to participate in the market of goods even with constrained incomes. Many poor families rely almost entirely upon secondhand shopping to buy necessary clothing and goods. For others, used goods are a way to subvert the power of a materialistic society. In the late 1980s, secondhand clothing was a way for teenagers, particularly punk teens, to express their rejection of mass-marketed clothing. In the 1990s, "hipster" culture embraced secondhand shopping and an aesthetic of kitsch and retro fashions. In addition, various environmental and/or ethical movements, from freegans (those opposed to capitalistic participation who attain goods for "free" by dumpster diving or other means) to voluntary simplicity participants (who limit their expenditures on new items), have used the secondhand markets to clothe themselves, furnish their abodes, and provide basic material life without purchasing newly produced commodities.

Helen Sheumaker

See also Auctions; Consumerism and Consumption; Flea Markets; Junk, Scrap, and Salvage; Popular Culture; Poverty; Yard Sales

References and Further Reading
Caskey, J. P., and B. Zikmond. 1994. *Fringe Banking: Check-Cashing Outlets, Pawnshops, and the Poor*. New York: Russell Sage Foundation.
Hoff, Al. 1997. *Thrift Score*. New York: Harper-Collins.
McRobbie, Angela, ed. 1988. *Zoot Suits and Secondhand Dresses: An Anthology of Fashion and Music*. Boston: Unwin Hyman.
Strasser, Susan. 1999. *Waste and Want: A Social History of Trash*. New York: Metropolitan Books.

Servants' Spaces

Domestic dwellings may contain intended or temporary rooms designated as living spaces for enslaved or free domestic workers. In the preindustrial United States, many families hired local girls to help with labor-intensive household work and production activities. These "hired girls" lived with their employers and shared their living spaces. By the mid-nineteenth century, domestic servants were more likely to be German or Irish immigrants or African Americans; the employment of domestic servants also indicated social status for their employers. The changes in household labor and laborers resulted in the division of space into public, private (family), and production (servant) zones.

Although the styles and contents of servants' quarters varied according to the means of the employing family and region, the approach to constructing and furnishing these spaces was consistent. Servants' quarters were located in the back of the main house, in the basement or the attic, or on the uppermost bedroom floor. These rooms could be completely closed off from public and family spaces and had a separate outside entrance and interior staircase. On southern plantations throughout the seventeenth, eighteenth, and first half of the nineteenth centuries, or on country estates with field labor, servants' quarters were often separate structures constructed out of sight of the main dwelling and in the vicinity of other work, maintenance, or farm buildings.

Families with many servants generally could offer the most pleasant sleeping quarters as well as separate servants' dining rooms for meals and leisure. Quarters in multiple-servant households reflected an additional hierarchy that developed among the domestic staff. On large plantations, the overseer's quarters tended to be larger and more prominent than the dwellings of most field slaves. Enslaved people working as house servants were provided with finer sleeping spaces and amenities than those working in the fields. Similar distinctions existed in the quarters of free domestic servants. Butlers and head housekeepers, typically at the top of the servant hierarchy, were often housed in the largest and best-appointed rooms, frequently in relatively close proximity to their masters and mistresses. Maids and servants of lower status shared the poorer rooms in the servants' wing.

Overall, servants' quarters featured simple design and little ornamentation. Those located in the employer's dwelling were often built with materials inferior to those used in public and family spaces. Sloped ceilings, small windows, inexpensive wallpaper, and simple pine floors were common. By the 1920s, few middle-class families continued to hire servants, and servants' quarters were traded for smaller dwellings with new domestic technology, including indoor plumbing and electric and gas appliances and heating.

The contents of servants' quarters are not well documented, since families were less likely to record or photograph these areas than the main rooms and servants themselves left few records. Early probate inventories provide some clues to furnishings, as do household manuals and women's magazines of the late nineteenth and early twentieth centuries. Many families furnished these rooms with old or unwanted pieces or simple, economical, and easily cleaned furnishings. Servants were usually temporary residents, moving regularly to better positions, thus their personal additions to these rooms, such as religious icons and inexpensive prints, were likely minimal.

Jennifer Pustz

See also Attics; Bedrooms; Cellars and Basements; Kitchens and Pantries; Service Industry Work and Labor; Slavery

References and Further Reading

Dudden, Faye. 1983. *Serving Women: Household Service in Nineteenth-Century America.* Middletown, CT: Wesleyan University Press.

O'Leary, Elizabeth L. 2003. *From Morning to Night: Domestic Service in Maymont House and the Gilded Age South.* Charlottesville: University Press of Virginia.

Pettingill, Lillian. 1905. *Toilers of the Home: The Record of a College Woman's Experience as a Domestic Servant.* New York: Doubleday, Page & Company.

Pustz, Jennifer. 2004. "The Servant Problem: Historic House Museums and Social History," Ph.D. diss., University of Iowa.

Vlach, John Michael. 1993. *Back of the Big House: The Architecture of Plantation Slavery.* Chapel Hill: University of North Carolina Press.

Service Industry Work and Labor

Work in which the individual's labor does not produce goods but rather focuses on care of another person's needs or possessions is designated as *service*. Domestic (household)

service is among the most studied of the service occupations. Although historically rooted in the private family dwelling, the service industry has, over time, become more closely associated with commercial enterprises, including restaurants, hotels, retail outlets, beauty salons and barber shops, health spas and fitness clubs, service stations and automobile maintenance shops, commercial laundries, and housecleaning agencies.

Social position is a significant factor in service industry labor due to the relationship between the "server" and the one who is "served." Workers in these occupations have tended to be of low social status and predominantly African Americans and recent immigrants. Although the service industry is not gender specific, women have been particularly active in this sector as laundresses, maids, and waitresses. A further hierarchy often exists within the service industry itself. For example, in the early twentieth century, women working in department stores had higher status than domestic servants, even though both performed similar duties by serving other individuals. Service employees often wear uniforms, which makes them easy to locate by people seeking assistance and indicates their status. A uniformed servant who opens the door of a domestic dwelling is known not to be the owner; a uniformed chauffeur behind the steering wheel of a luxury car is recognized as a paid driver and not the car's owner. Nevertheless, these workers are regularly treated as if their labor should be unseen.

Service industry labor is primarily physical since it usually involves cleaning and care of material objects and individual persons. Industrialization and electrification have greatly changed such labor. Jobs once performed completely by hand, such as laundry, have been made less onerous through the use of machines. Higher standards for cleanliness and greater knowledge of hygiene, however, have meant that such work came to be done more frequently.

Jennifer Pustz

See also Commercial Food Venues; Department Stores; Dress, Accessories, and Fashion; Gender; Servants' Spaces; Service Stations; Technology; Work and Labor

References and Further Reading
Benson, Susan Porter. 1986. *Counter Cultures: Saleswomen, Managers, and Customers in American Department Stores, 1890–1940.* Urbana: University of Illinois Press.
Cobble, Dorothy Sue. 1991. *Dishing It Out: Waitresses and Their Unions in the Twentieth Century.* Urbana: University of Illinois Press.
Cowan, Ruth Schwartz. 1983. *More Work for Mother: The Ironies of Household Technology from the Open Hearth to the Microwave.* New York: Basic Books.
Ehrenreich, Barbara. 2001. *Nickel and Dimed: On (Not) Getting By in America.* New York: Henry Holt and Co.
Kessler-Harris, Alice. 1982. *Out to Work: A History of Wage-Earning Women in the United States.* Oxford, UK: Oxford University Press.
Sutherland, Daniel. 1981. *Americans and Their Servants: Domestic Service in the United States from 1800 to 1920.* Baton Rouge: Louisiana State University Press.

Service Stations

The first American service stations—business establishments that house the refueling, maintenance, and repair of automobiles—were little more than a single gasoline pump placed in front of a home or business. At the turn of the twentieth century, bulk supply depots provided the only source of distributing gasoline to motorists. Drivers filtered gasoline through a chamois-covered funnel into the fuel tank. By 1910, curbside gas stations with freestanding pumps dotted the landscape. Their close proximity to the street made pumps a target for careless drivers, whose numbers grew daily. Demand increased for larger stations that offered full-service maintenance facilities, and oil companies joined service station owners to construct buildings that accommodated the needs of both automobile and driver. Employees tended all aspects of automobile service, from oil changes and lubrication to window washing and fill-ups.

Station construction itself evolved into an art form, with oil companies and independent owners competing to build modern, innovative, and often unique structures—wigwams, flying saucers, and tea kettles were favorites—in an effort to capture both patrons' business and their imagination. The results of their labors stood as architectural landmarks along American highways, prompting more than a few second glances from curious passersby. The impetus to modernize came from community zoning officials, who worked to replace hazardous curbside pumps, and urban reformers, who targeted the unsightly conditions that many small, "mom and pop" stations brought to neighborhoods. Oil companies responded by constructing drive-in service stations, experimenting with prefabricated buildings. The most popular of the prefabricated forms replicated houses found in suburban neighborhoods, the most popular being the English cottage–style station popularized by the Pure Oil Company. It featured two chimneys, bay windows, shutters, flower boxes, and a gabled roof. The popularity of the English cottage exploded from its inception in 1925, and by 1930, more than 6,000 cottage-style stations graced neighborhoods across the country.

As oil companies further became committed to providing motorists with service, they hired professionals to attend to the sale and distribution of gasoline. By the mid-1920s,

they also began offering secondary-market merchandise and service such as oil, tires, and batteries. To capitalize on the growing repair market brought on by Depression-era frugality, oil companies constructed buildings that included garage bays, service counters, restrooms, and display windows. Companies found new inspiration in the streamlined, enameled, and glass exteriors industrial designer Walter Dorwin Teague (1883–1960) created for Texaco, replacing "cottages" of clapboard, stucco, and faux-stone facades. By 1940, more than 50 percent of service station buildings reflected Teague's Modernist vision.

The introduction in the 1950s of self-service stations eroded the popularity of full-service pumps and ushered in the rise of the corporate superstation. Stations took on a uniform appearance, consisting primarily of a large, canopied pull-in with multiple pumps and a small, boxlike sales counter. While many independent retailers fought the changes by continuing to offer full service, the cost appeal of self-service soon became the industry standard, making full-service stations nearly obsolete.

Susan V. Spellman

See also Automobile Camping (Auto-Camping); Automobiles and Automobility; Highways and National Highway System; Land Transportation; Tourism and Travel

References and Further Reading

Jakle, John A. 1994. *The Gas Station in America.* Baltimore, MD: Johns Hopkins University Press.

Liebs, Chester. 1985. *Main Street to Miracle Mile: American Roadside Architecture.* Boston: Little, Brown.

Margolies, John. 1993. *Pump and Circumstance: The Glory Days of the Gas Station.* Boston: Bulfinch Press.

Witzel, Michael Karl. 1992. *The American Gas Station.* Osceola, WI: MBI Publishing Company.

Sex and Sexuality

Material culture relating to sex and sexuality has been shaped both by advancements in technology and manufacture and shifting cultural values; it runs the spectrum from celebrating and/or enhancing sexual expression to attempting to prevent sexual activities or responses from occurring.

Birth Control

In colonial America, midwives and women offered herbal concoctions and shared recipes for suppositories as abortifacients. Patent claims on abortion devices such as uterine douches or syringes, which were often marketed as cleansing devices to avoid the laws banning abortion, increased in the 1830s. Beginning in the 1850s, blocking devices such as contraceptive sponges, cervical caps, and rubber diaphragms were manufactured, offering an option to homemade devices devised from plant materials and natural sea sponges. Intrauterine devices became recognized through patents in the 1860s.

The development of vulcanized rubber in 1844 was followed several years later by the availability of the first commercially developed condoms. Condoms were popularized not only as contraceptives but also because of their disease-preventing value. Despite this, condoms soon were manufactured and sold only through the underground market due to the 1873 Comstock Act, which prohibited the distribution of contraceptives. After the efforts of noted birth control advocate and nurse Margaret Sanger (1879–1966) resulted in the diminishment of the Comstock Act in the 1920s and 1930s, more developments came about in the design and manufacture of condoms, including the direct marketing to pharmacies of Trojan brand condoms for "disease prevention" by Youngs Rubber Company. The next significant era for condom manufacture and distribution came in the 1980s with the realization of the AIDS crisis in the United States. In response to the crisis, female condoms were manufactured, as well as flavored condoms, oral condoms, and a variety of latex skin barriers, from finger guards to full-body suits.

One of the most significant developments in birth control occurred through the concerted efforts of advocate Margaret Sanger and millionaire Katherine Dexter McCormick (1875–1967), who funded development for a contraceptive pill. First developed in 1951, the pill was not approved by the federal Food and Drug Administration for contraceptive use until 1960. It was regarded as revolutionary because of its success rate and because it allows women to have significantly greater control over their reproduction. In 1965, the United States Supreme Court case *Griswold v. Connecticut* affirmed the use of birth control as a legal right protected by the Court's assumption of a constitutional right to privacy. In 1973, the court used this case as a significant part of the basis for overturning antiabortion laws in the case of *Roe v. Wade*.

Antimasturbation and Chastity Devices

Pseudoscience combined with biblical interpretation fueled an opposition to masturbation in the 1800s. Parents were encouraged by clergy and physicians alike to interrupt the masturbation of children and adolescents, and were discouraged from engaging in this behavior themselves. As private rooms for children became more commonplace, inventors stepped up the development of antimasturbation devices, notably produced for males. Many patents were awarded for clothing or belts that could lock, preventing access to the genital region, while other inventors focused on mechanical devices or electric shock collars to prevent such behaviors from occurring. Concerns also existed about "seminal weakness" and other physical aberrations caused by the nocturnal emissions of males, thus inspiring the creation of products designed to prevent erections. While many of these relied on pain to end the erection (through sharp projectiles in penile rings), others relied on technology to cool the penis, set off alarms, or trigger electric shock.

The concern for females was not connected as much to self-pleasuring, but was focused on the maintenance of chastity, although most devices designed to prevent sexual intercourse also prevented masturbation. The most widely known product designed to prevent sexual intercourse for females is the chastity belt, typically made of metal (often covered in fabric or leather) and designed to be locked. While originally created to maintain the virginity of daughters and the sexual purity of wives, chastity devices were also amended to prevent rape. Many of these are of belt design, while others are "stealth" devices worn inside the vagina and designed to injure the penis.

Sex "Toys"

Devices or "toys" used for sexual pleasure exist for pleasuring both males and females. Such devices include clothing designed for visual or sexual stimulation (as well as protection from disease), furniture and harnesses designed to aid positioning, inflatable or solid life-sized sex dolls shaped into both genders as well as various nonhuman mammals, smaller devices designed to increase the pleasure of intercourse (such as ticklers designed to stimulate the clitoris and cock rings used to extend erections). Patents, however, indicate that the majority of development and manufacturing are focused on two product categories: dildos and vibrators.

Manufacture of dildos preceded the industrial age, and hand-crafted configurations formed from leather, bone, wood, and other plant materials exist today. United States patents for dildos increased in the 1960s and 1970s as the sexual revolution led to a booming "marital aid" product market, improved by advancements in synthetic materials and electronics. Not every state has welcomed these innovations. Texas still has what is commonly referred to as a "dildo law," enacted in 1973, which prohibits the possession of more than five dildos and inhibits sales. Not to be outdone, Alabama enacted a law in 1998 prohibiting the sale of sex toys. Interestingly, both laws focus on devices primarily marketed to women for sexual pleasure.

Sexual devices became linked to feminism as female masturbation became more widely discussed. In 1969 a group called the Boston Women's Health Collective authored *Our Bodies, Ourselves*, which included open discussion of female masturbation. In 1974, Betty Dodson published *Liberating Masturbation*, and by 1977, the influence of the feminist movement led to the development of the first sex store catering to women, Good Vibrations, which was opened to provide women with an alternative venue to adult bookstores in order to purchase sex toys and literature and locate information about sexuality and sexual health.

The sex toy category with the greatest variations of innovation is the personal vibrator. Earliest examples of vibrating tools are found in the 1860s. Medical practitioners in the 1800s theorized that electrical stimulation could cure a variety of ills. Notable in the development of the electromechanical vibrator was an assumption that physician-guided stimulation of the vulva could prevent hysteria in women by releasing vaginal tension. Improvements in mechanical design led to smaller units that could be purchased for private use. Vibrators sold throughout most of the twentieth century were packaged and marketed as health products. Changes in societal norms and laws opened the doors for vibrating products designed and marketed specifically for sexual pleasure to be sold from the 1970s on. Further improvements in design, batteries, synthetic materials, and computer chips have led to a market niche with thousands of variations of the former medical device.

Pornography/Erotica

The preponderance of printing presses in the United States in the 1800s, combined with the development of inexpensive paper, expanded the availability of sexual literature. Sexual-oriented fiction included copies of erotic literature from Europe, original writings of a sexual nature, and "true" accounts, including morality tales and sex-crime stories. While nude images were among the first photographic images produced in the 1840s, these images remained the domain of wealthy collectors until improvements in photographic techniques allowed for the mass production of images.

Not all texts regarded as pornographic have been fictional. Educational tracts about reproductive health authored by Margaret Sanger were confiscated by the federal government, as were a variety of tracts written by lesser-known or anonymous writers. Perhaps no books had a greater impact on sexual mores in the twentieth century than *Sexual Behavior in the American Male* (1948), and *Sexual Behavior in the American Female* (1953), both written by Indiana University researcher Alfred Kinsey (1894–1956). By documenting that average sexuality for men and women included masturbation, homosexuality, and premarital and extramarital sex, Kinsey opened up a dialogue that would significantly change American sexuality, but his work was decried as pornographic in many municipalities and states.

The first true movie cameras and projection devices were developed in the 1880s, and in 1896, *The Kiss*, a twenty-second short of stage actors kissing, became the Edison Studio's most popular film. The first demands for film censorship on the basis of sexual content quickly followed. Outside the gaze of incensed citizens were Kinetoscope parlors and vaudeville houses featuring short films of exotic dancers or nude prostitutes. The numbers of exploitation films featuring nudity and sexual content, often in the guise of hygiene or educational works, increased in the 1910s. More explicit "stag" films were often distributed through men's social clubs and military bases and clubs.

Mainstream films were allowed to include nudity and sexual content until the enforcement of the Hays Code in 1934. As Hollywood adhered to the restrictions of the code, small entrepreneurs responded to audience interest in the restricted content and expanded production of stag or porn reels. Organized crime became involved in the distribution of these films, and adult bookstores with film booths became commonplace in American cities. In 1968, the Motion Picture Association of America developed a voluntary ratings system following the abolition of the Hays Code the prior year. Coinciding with the sexual revolution, legitimate theaters began showing films to audiences of men and women with explicit content from Sweden and Denmark.

The 1970s, a decade of crossover success of hard-core pornography into the mainstream, are known among pornographic film critics as the "golden age" of pornography because of high production values, well-developed scripts, and competent acting. The most successful of these films was *Deep Throat*, released in 1973 to theaters across the United States. In addition to being the most widely viewed hard-core movie thus far, *Deep Throat* was such a significant cultural icon that Mark Felt, then associate director of the Federal Bureau of Investigation, used "Deep Throat" as his anonymous moniker when he leaked information about the Nixon-era Watergate break-in to *Washington Post* reporters.

The "golden age" of pornography came to an end not by the increasing attempts to return to censorship but by the technological development of video. Video cameras allowed consumers to make private sex tapes, while video players increased the convenience of showing hard-core productions in the home and increased the demand for quickly produced hard-core content. Video lowered the costs of producing sexually oriented moving images, and soon the San Fernando Valley in California became the home to a sizable population of video entrepreneurs, and thus became popularly known as "Porn Valley." As distribution transitioned from adult theaters to mail-order operations, the influence of organized crime on the rapidly expanding industry was dramatically reduced. By the 1990s, the typical "money men" investing in the adult video industry were mainstream corporations rather than mafiosi.

Increased efforts to limit or ban the distribution of sexually explicit materials marked the 1980s. President Ronald Reagan's (1911–2004) Meese Commission picked up where the previous administration's commission on pornography and obscenity left off, and an interesting commingling of conservatives and feminists occurred when radical feminist antipornography advocates joined with pro-censorship forces, resulting in antipornography ordinances developed by Andrea Dworkin (1946–2005) and Catherine MacKinnon being adopted. These were immediately vetoed in Minneapolis in 1984,

debated in a number of cities, and implemented in Canada. This same decade, "pro-sex feminists" argued against the philosophy of "antipornography" feminists, with many developing their own pornographic magazines, books, and videos for both heterosexual and lesbian audiences.

Since the late 1990s, the next revolution of the distribution of sexually explicit content has been connected to the Internet. Estimated to be a $2.5 billion industry, Internet pornography has democratized the industry by allowing gays and lesbians, feminists, and various fetish aficionados to have access to the same distribution as do established industry forces.

Molly Merryman

See also Bedrooms; Consumerism and Consumption; Gay Consumerism; Gender; Human Body; Illicit Pleasures and Venues; Photography; Popular Culture; Print Culture; Technology

References and Further Reading
Berry, Mary Frances. 2000. *The Pig Farmer's Daughter and Other Tales of American Justice: Episodes of Racism and Sexism in the Courts from 1865 to the Present.* New York: Vintage.
Friedman, Laurence M. 1993. *Crime and Punishment in American History.* New York: Basic Books.
Levins, Hoag. 1996. *American Sex Machines: The Hidden History of Sex at the U.S. Patent Office.* Holbrook, MA: Adams Media Corporation.
Maines, Rachel P. 1999. *The Technology of Orgasm: "Hysteria," the Vibrator, and Women's Sexual Satisfaction.* Baltimore, MD: Johns Hopkins University Press.
Muller, Eddie, and Daniel Faris. 1996. *Grindhouse: The Forbidden World of "Adults Only" Cinema.* New York: St. Martin's Press.
Ulrich, Laurel Thatcher. 1990. *A Midwife's Tale: The Life of Martha Ballard, Based on Her Diary, 1785–1812.* New York: Vintage.
Weddington, Sarah. 1992. *A Question of Choice.* New York: Grosset/Putnam.

Shopping Centers and Shopping Malls

A *shopping center* is a collection of retail and business establishments in a concentrated area under the ownership and management of a single individual or organization. A *shopping mall* is an enclosed, privately owned and managed commercial structure housing stores, restaurants, and services lined along well-lit and landscaped walkways with benches and constructed in American suburbs.

At the turn of the twentieth century, most burgeoning American suburban residential neighborhoods did not have shopping nearby. The main shopping districts remained inside the city center. Only the well-planned upscale developments, like J. C. Nichols' (1880–1950) Country Club Plaza in Kansas City from 1922, incorporated shopping centers into their initial designs, including essential stores and services at the center of the residential development. Independent neighborhood shopping centers began with small shops—grocery, pharmacy, candy—in neighborhood buildings. Architects preferred to give the entire center a cohesive facade that blended in with the surrounding residences. These neighborhood centers were small, open-air complexes that served the immediate neighborhood and were arranged in a strip near public transportation stops, on a main road, or on a town square. Though they were equipped with parking, the design of the centers still catered to pedestrian traffic.

As dependence on the automobile increased and suburban neighborhoods grew by the mid-twentieth century, shopping centers grew in number and size and incorporated parking areas. Beginning with large department stores that built smaller versions of their downtown stores, retail followed residents down the highway and away from downtown shopping districts. As larger versions of the neighborhood centers, intermediate malls included either one department store or a large grocery store and several specialty shops.

Smaller strips of shops existed along main roads from the 1920s through the 1940s. A building boom for commercial real estate occurred in the 1950s. Enormous federal income tax breaks for commercial real estate developers in 1954 made development of retail centers and shopping malls a very lucrative business. Together with an abundance of cheap land and weak zoning laws, suburban shopping malls proliferated—including the first enclosed shopping mall.

The enclosed shopping mall was the creation of Viennese designer Victor Gruen (1903–1980). Gruen envisioned the shopping mall as a place for retail and for respite. His first creation, Southdale (1956), was set in suburban Minneapolis, Minnesota. The mall incorporated gardens and trees among a two-story, climate-controlled, 679,000-square-foot shopping wonderland. Taking a cue from Gruen, developers all over the nation constructed regional malls, multistory constructions with ample parking in garages or in large lots. They consisted of several anchor or key stores (usually large department stores) and up to a hundred smaller boutiques and specialty or variety shops along open walkways somewhat resembling sidewalks, plus a centralized food court and entertainment venues, such as video arcades and movie theaters. Regional malls were intended to serve larger populations than the intermediate or neighborhood centers and were constructed near highway intersections providing easy access by automobile, leaving little access to pedestrian traffic. While the malls of suburban America recalled downtown shopping districts in their design and layout, they provided shelter from the elements, were kept clean by maintenance staff, and were perceived as safer than most city retail districts.

While a main motivation of suburban expansion was to escape the commercialism and congestion of the city center, regional shopping centers were intended to provide not only a commercial but also a civic function. Shopping malls served suburbanites not just with shopping convenience but also as an equivalent to the town center where traditional, seasonal activities, like photographs with the Easter Bunny and Santa Claus or beauty and fashion pageants, traditionally took place. They also provided a place for America's suburban youth to meet and spend hours in shopping, eating, and amusement without concerns about the weather or time of day, especially since shopping malls were, from the beginning, open until at least nine o'clock at night.

While shopping malls provided both economic and social benefits, culturally they tended to follow segregationist tendencies seen in American suburbia as a whole. Private owners could discriminate against ethnic and racially diverse populations and markets by leasing only to white merchants and white businesses. By carefully selecting tenants, mall managers could guarantee clientele of specific demographics, essentially white, middle-class women. Choice of stores, products, and availability of public transportation from the city helped keep shopping malls as racially segregated as the suburbs they served. Also, mall owners with private security forces were better able to enforce rules and laws concerning soliciting, loitering, and lawlessness than in public, downtown city shopping districts.

After the mid-century boom came the decline of the enclosed shopping mall in the 1970s. Following an overall regentrification

of urban spaces, developers in the 1980s attempted to rejuvenate urban shopping centers using suburban models. The numbers of new malls declined in the 1980s, in part as a result of competition from "big box" stores in strip malls that specialized in a single type of product, like office supplies, toys, or pet-related products. Much renovation to the architecture, facades, and amenities of existing malls occurred during the 1990s, in the face of the introduction of high-end stores, which had previously stayed in downtown shopping centers in part to ensure their elite, high-class clientele. Today, malls face additional competition from factory outlet malls, situated even farther out from the city, and shoppers' Internet shopping capabilities.

The shopping mall remains a uniquely American phenomenon whose invention and proliferation are cemented in the national landscape. They have become an integral part of the social, economic, and commercial life in the United States, as can be described by their ubiquitous representations in now-classic American teenage movies like *Fast Times at Ridgemont High* (1982), *Valley Girl* (1983), *Dawn of the Dead* (1978), and *Mallrats* (1995).

Victoria Estrada-Berg

See also Automobiles and Automobility; Cities and Towns; Civic Architecture; Commercial Architecture; Consumerism and Consumption; Race; Suburbs and Suburbia

References and Further Reading
Cohen, Lizabeth. 1996. "From Town Center to Shopping Center: The Reconfiguration of Community Marketplaces in Postwar America." *American Historical Review* 101 (4): 1050–1081.
Gruen, Victor. 1960. *Shopping Towns USA: The Planning of Shopping Centers*. New York: Reinhold.
Hanchett, Thomas W. 1996. "U.S. Tax Policy and the Shopping-Center Boom of the 1950s and 1960s." *American Historical Review* 101 (4): 1082–1110.

Hayden, Dolores. 2003. *Building Suburbia: Green Fields and Urban Growth, 1920–2000*. New York: Pantheon Books.

Jackson, Kenneth T. 1996. "All the World's a Mall: Reflections on the Social and Economic Consequences of the American Shopping Center." *American Historical Review* 101 (4): 1111–1121.

Longstreth, Richard. 1997. *City Center to Regional Mall: Architecture, the Automobile, and Retailing in Los Angeles, 1920–1950*. Cambridge, MA: MIT Press.

Steinhauer, Jennifer. 1997. "Spending It: On Long Island, the Mall as History Book." *New York Times*, December 21, Sec. 3.

Silverwork and Silverware

Silver is a malleable and ductile white noble metal found primarily in ore. Silver is now generally extracted as a by-product of lead, gold, copper, and zinc. Pure silver is too soft to be used in the creation of objects. Silver alloys, such as sterling silver, which is 92.5 percent silver and 7.5 percent copper, are most often used in the creation of tablewares, ornamental pieces, and works of fine art. As a precious metal, silver possesses a long history as money and, like gold, was coined. Its value was legally regulated in the British colonies of North America, and so silver objects, commonly called *plate*, carry *hallmarks*, legal stamps designating that the object has been officially assayed to ascertain the amount of silver in the object. Until 1850, the centers for silver production and consumption were Boston (the Revolutionary Paul Revere [1735–1818] was a silversmith), New York City, and Philadelphia. Wrought silver could be easily melted and reconstituted as newly fashionable objects or as currency but it more often served, and continues to serve, as the valuable material with which desirable and beautiful objects (including jewelry), signifying wealth and social status,

Tea-drinking was a genteel ritual in the eighteenth-century British American colonies. John Singleton Copley's 1768 portrait of Paul Revere depicts the Boston silversmith in the process of completing the silver teapot he holds. The tools near Revere's right elbow were used to engrave silver pieces with the refined owner's monogram, emblem, or coat of arms. (Freelance Photography Guild/Corbis)

are made. The "family silver," in common American usage, is passed from one generation to the next, its age perhaps revealed in patina and wear but testifying to the family's claim of historical longevity and social legitimacy.

Manufacturing Silver Objects

Historically a silversmith had at his disposal several labor-intensive and time-consuming techniques through which to create objects of silver, or *silverwork*. A sheet or disc of silver may be shaped by *raising:* after blocking the sheet into a concave form, the sheet is hammered with a mallet over a wooden block and creased—that is, crimped around an anvil. A smaller hammer, called a *crimping hammer* or *neck hammer*, is then used to shape the sheet against a convex wooden form. Alternately, *sinking*—creating a hollow form through stretching the metal by hammering on the inner concave surface—may be used, producing holloware. These processes required that the silver be annealed (heated) several times before the object was finished. The object may then be planished, or smoothed. Silver may also be cast. Ornamentation, called *repoussé work* or *embossing*, is then added. The surface may be decorated from the back by using punches, hammers, and snarling irons (long irons with curved ends inserted in vessels with narrow openings and hit with hammers so that the vibrations travel through the iron to shape the vessel). Chasing is performed on the front, using finer punches for detail. Silver's malleability allows for the controlled stretching caused by embossing. Silver objects may also be ornamented through engraving, etching, piercing, and gilding.

Silver manufacturing was time consuming and costly in the American colonies; only the wealthy could afford to purchase plate. With the advent of steam-powered machinery and piecework in the nineteenth century, two methods were created to mechanize the production of silver objects: *spinning* (circa 1800), in which a silver sheet was made into a hollow form by a spinning lathe against which a wooden form was placed to create the desired final shape, and *electroplating*, in which a coating ("plate") of silver through the use of electricity and chemical reactions is achieved.

Silver in Religious Observance
Silver was used to manufacture Christian communion vessels (chalice, salver, flagon, and basin) in colonial America. In Anglican churches, as in Roman Catholicism, these vessels were consecrated and handled by priests. Members of New England's Puritan meetings, which had rejected Anglican communion practice, passed among the covenanted ordinary wine cups, tankards, and, borrowing from Dutch practice, beakers. The wealthy made gifts of communion vessels and other wrought silver objects to their congregations; often these ornate pieces were inscribed. This practice continued in specific Protestant denominations (in particular, the Episcopal Church) into the twentieth century.

Other early ecclesiastical silverwork included Protestant altar pieces, candlesticks, baptismal basins, alms basins, and, in Catholic missions and churches founded by the French and the Spanish, crucifixes, censers, monstrances, and reliquaries. Silver was used to create the crown of the Torah, its scroll bells (*rimonim*), breastplate, and pointer in Jewish observance. The Kiddush cup and circumcision tools historically were also manufactured of silver. Design and decoration were balanced between ceremonial function and contemporary fashion.

Silver in the Decorative Arts
Wealthy European settlers in the New World (especially the English) brought with them items of silver, from dining pieces and candlesticks to rings and shoe buckles. Throughout the colonial period silver pieces were commissioned; imported from London; or manufactured in Boston, New York City, and Philadelphia. Silver in the forms of tankards and cups, spoons, and dishes was used on special occasions and to commemorate special events. With the eighteenth-century rise of genteel society and its use of exotic goods, silversmiths dedicated their energies to tea and coffee services, sugar bowls, salt cellars, and snuffboxes. The estab-

lishment of colonial government (and later state and national governments) required implements of state, including state seals, ink stands, and medals.

The establishment of the nation, however, led to depletion of the supply of silver, in the form of coin, with which the new nation's silversmiths worked. French francs and Spanish dollars (from Mexico) substituted for American currency and helped silversmiths manufacture flatware and dishes to meet demand. The quality of silverwork available to Americans was thus dependent on the legally mandated alloy of silver with other metals in coins allowed by the United States government. The words *coin standard* or *standard* stamped on a spoon verified the silversmith's adherence to the law. Not until 1907, however, did the government delineate coin from sterling based on the percentage of pure silver to another alloy metal.

The introduction of electroplating led to the mass production of silverplated goods, especially tablewares, and the coinage, in 1860, of the term *silverware*. Gorham Manufacturing Company (founded 1831), Reed & Barton (established 1824), Oneida (incorporated 1881), and other companies created for the status-conscious American middle and upper classes a wide variety of silverplated goods for use in the home, available in specialty and department stores as well as through mail order catalogues by the end of the nineteenth century. A middle-class dining table could become a figurative wonderland: From napkin rings and serving pieces to flatware, silverplated diningware was adorned with whimsical forms of flora and fauna, mythical and allegorical imagery, and historical and contemporary designs. Weddings, wedding anniversaries, and other life milestones could be marked by the purchase and the presentation of engraved sil-

ver goods such as serving trays, loving cups, jewelry and watches, and monogrammed flatware and serving pieces.

The term *presentation silver* applies to any silverwork given to commemorate persons, occasions, and achievements. Especially after the Civil War (1861–1865), though, when silver was discovered in great quantities in the frontier West, wealthy captains of industry commissioned firms such as Tiffany & Company (founded 1837) and Gorham to commemorate the creation of railroads and bridges or events such as world's fairs in the one-of-a-kind forms of monumental loving cups, vases, plates, trays, plaques, and punch bowls. The Great Depression of the 1930s redefined this practice as ostentatious, rendering it nearly an obsolete corporate ritual. The advent of the second world war in 1939 diminished greatly the supply of silver, and American factories, long the largest producers of silverwares in the world, shifted their production due to shortages. Yet, throughout the twentieth century the American silver industry and individual craftsmen have explored the material through the century's major stylistic movements, both traditional and avant garde. Indeed, as silver historian Charles L. Venable has pointed out, the association of the traditional and the commemorative with this precious, ancient metal has often deterred its adaptation, except in small, aesthetically progressive circles of consumers and makers, to Modernism and futuristic styles.

Shirley Teresa Wajda

See also Decorative Arts; Money, Currency, and Value

References and Further Reading

Fennimore, Donald L. 1978. "Religion in America: Metal Objects in Service of the Ritual." *American Art Journal* 10 (2): 20–42.

Hood, Graham. 1989 (1971). *American Silver: A History of Style, 1650–1900.* New York: E. P. Dutton.

Stern, Jewel. 2005. *Modernism in American Silver: 20th-Century Design,* ed. Kevin W. Tucker and Charles L. Venable. Dallas, TX: Dallas Museum of Art; New Haven, CT: Yale University Press.

Trench, Lucy, ed. 2000. *Materials and Techniques in the Decorative Arts: An Illustrated Dictionary.* Chicago: University of Chicago Press.

Venable, Charles L. 1994. *Silver in America, 1840–1940: A Century of Splendor.* Dallas, TX: Dallas Museum of Art.

Warren, David B., Katherine S. Howe, and Michael K. Brown. 1987. *Marks of Achievement: Four Centuries of American Presentation Silver.* Houston, TX: Museum of Fine Arts and Harry N. Abrams.

Waters, Deborah Dependahl. 1977. "From Pure Coin: The Manufacture of American Silver Flatware, 1800–1860." *Winterthur Portfolio* 12: 19–33.

Slavery

Slavery, the legal ownership of one human being by another human being, was practiced in the North American colonies and later United States from the earliest colonial years to 1865. This ancient practice was resurrected on modern, capitalistic lines in the 1500s by Europeans, who imported at least 10 to 15 million individuals to the New World. The North American colonies began to define slavery as a racialized practice (that is, only humans of African descent could be legally enslaved) in the early 1600s. By the end of the 1600s, slaves were defined as being of African descent, determined matrilineally, and as beings without legal rights. Slaves were chattel, the personal property of their owners.

The material culture of American slavery reflects three distinct cultural phenomena.

Material things were used to subjugate African enslaved peoples; the material culture record attests to the persistence of African traditions; and acculturation and complex social interactions affected the material culture of African Americans held in slavery. In addition, the effort to end slavery led to the creation of numerous artifacts that sought to inform the public as to the evils of enslaving human beings.

Control and Domination

African and African American slaves lived in a world in which white slave owners struggled to maintain control over other human beings. Slave owners created landscapes of domination that were intended to remind, visually and physically, slaves of their lower positions. For example, large southern plantations typically had the "big house," not necessarily the grandiose, white-pillared mansion depicted in nostalgic images of the South but certainly the best structure on the grounds. Arrayed behind this house were small, carefully arranged slave quarters, work houses, and other outbuildings that encompassed the labor of the plantation.

Clothing identified slaves as such; most slaves were deliberately clothed in inferior fabrics and untailored clothing, which offered sharp contrast with the finer fabrics and close cuts reserved for white owners and free whites. One former slave, Harriet Jacobs (1813–1897), recalled the "linsey-woolsey [a rough, loosely woven wool fabric] dress given every winter" as "one of the badges of slavery" (1987, 20). Food was equally simple and spartan, especially in comparison with the foodstuffs provided for owners—and prepared by slaves. Plantation records outline a simple diet of weekly allotments of maize (corn), very rarely portions of meat, and no other regular food. Slaves usually augmented this diet with their own garden-grown produce and animals attained through hunting.

Other material culture included tools of confinement, punishment, and death, such as bell harnesses that encircled a slave's body with iron rings and suspended bells above his or her head in an effort to curtail movement. Iron chains, rings, clamps, and other devices were used to restrain slaves as well. The bodies of enslaved individuals were demarcated with brands, piercings, and other imposed bodily modifications to ensure identification of ownership. Bodily abuse resulted in physical deformations such as whip scars, missing teeth, digits removed in punishment, and facial scars. Ironically, such marks were viewed by potential white owners as a warning of a disruptive or uncontrollable slave, rather than as graphic evidence of a white owner's violent tendencies. Urban slave markets across the United States were located in trading areas and typically consisted of small barred pens with a central open space for the viewing of slaves.

Retention of African Traditions

In the seventeenth and eighteenth centuries, African slaves brought to the Americas created material culture that reflected their cultural traditions. Africa, a continent of vastly differing cultural groups, had an ancient past and diverse, sophisticated contemporary traditions that enslaved Africans attempted to retain in their new lives. Foodways, especially those of the American South, often reflected African food traditions, with similar foodstuffs, cooking techniques, and presentation. Holidays practiced by enslaved Africans also retained some traditions. Music was especially persistent, and Africans created instruments similar to those from their home cultures, such as the *bangoe*. Dances such as the *juba*, depicted in a well-known painting of slaves dancing in South Carolina,

reflect West African (especially Yoruba) traditions. Further emphasizing the African traditions of the scene, the women in the painting wear traditional African headwraps, while men dance with a cane (another Yoruban tradition) while a man plays the *molo*, a form of banjo, and a West African drum.

African traditions of spirituality were also retained. Archaeological studies have found intriguing if inconclusive evidence of the retention of African, especially West African, religious traditions. Buttons carved with pentagrams (five-sided figures with spiritual connotations), pottery bowls with geometric designs inscribed on the surface, amber bead necklaces, and other artifacts suggest that African enslaved people deliberately replicated specific ritual items from their home traditions. In Texas, one study found an array of items from a fly whisk, "oracle bones," and other objects that suggest the continuation of African and Afro-Caribbean traditions.

Architecture has also demonstrated how African slaves retained their traditional cultures. The most well-known example of this is the shotgun house. Shotgun houses are narrow, one-room-wide houses in which the rooms are arranged linearly with no interior hallway and the front door is on the gable end facing the street. Shotgun houses are found throughout the South and up through the Ohio and Mississippi river valleys and have been used by African Americans since the 1700s. There has been debate for several decades about the origin of this housing style. It is similar to housing used in Haiti, which suggests a Creole or New Orleans origin, while other scholars point to Yoruban (West African) traditions. While specific cultural traditional origins are disputed by scholars, it is agreed that the distinctive American architectural form is African and African American, that is, the product of the interplay of different African traditions in the Americas.

While the landscape of slavery was created and maintained by slave owners, African slaves were able to manipulate their use of space to reflect their own needs and cultural traditions. Slave owners typically laid out slave quarters in the familiar, Euro-American grid pattern of rows of houses. When enslaved people were allowed to organize their own living quarters, they tended to string houses in a meandering line that was positioned near the edges of wooded areas. Plantation landscapes had a public face of grand architecture, formal gardens, and sweeping paths, but the working side of plantations, which were productive farms and small industrial factories, was demarcated with slaves' work paths, hidden escape routes, and wooded areas that afforded slaves some privacy.

Acculturation

Acculturation is the interplay of different cultural traditions in which new cultural pathways are made. For example, the various African cultural groups forcibly brought together through enslavement formed new, distinctive, African American cultures in the United States. But this process did not affect Africans alone; Native American and white cultures were also changed by their interactions with the enslaved Africans. Artifacts track these cultural changes. For example, basketry in the South reflects how Native American and African basket making interacted to create distinctive new patterns and styles of basket weaving. This intermixing of style is particularly evident in seagrass basketry of the coastal Southeast.

Colonoware is a rough-textured, lightly fired, unglazed pottery made during the colonial period of the United States. Colono-

ware was Native American pottery used by both Native Americans and African Americans in the seventeenth, eighteenth, and early nineteenth centuries and is found along the East Coast of North America. Archaeologists disagree about its specific cultural origin, in that it is unclear whether enslaved Africans manufactured colonoware for their own use, or attained it by bartering with Native Americans. Yet colonoware does provide fascinating evidence of the interplay of cultural traditions and is an example of how material culture artifacts are shared across cultural lines.

Abolition and Antislavery Efforts

Abolition, the legal eradication of slavery, was a movement that began in the United States upon its founding as a colonial outpost. Many enslaved and free blacks participated in this long movement, and many abolitionist leaders were individuals who had at one point in their lives been slaves. The antislavery movement relied upon personal testimony, graphic portrayals of the violent nature of slavery, and material artifacts such as handkerchiefs, children's toys and readers, broadsheets, musical numbers, and other entertaining memorabilia to convey their message. Ex-slave, abolitionist, and women's rights advocate Sojourner Truth (Isabella Baumfree, 1797–1883), for example, sold photographic images of herself to raise money. Women in the abolitionist movement created and sold goods with antislavery themes at fairs dedicated to the cause. Historians have long relied upon these artifacts to document and learn more about the strategies of the antislavery movement.

The antislavery movement also included rebels who created the famed Underground Railroad, an informal but highly organized transport system that moved slaves from the

South to freedom in the North. Begun in the 1810s, by 1831 the name *Underground Railroad* was given to this effort, in which free blacks, enslaved blacks, Native Americans, and whites fought against slavery. Understandably, few artifacts remain of the effort, but numerous houses have been officially recognized as "stations" in the Underground Railroad system. Many of these houses have modifications to accommodate escaped slaves, such as the small door in the upper bedroom of the Levi Coffin (1798–1877) House in Indiana that could be easily hidden when a bedstead was pushed up against it.

Helen Sheumaker

See also African America; African American Foodways; Agricultural Work and Labor; Human Body; Race; Service Industry Work and Labor; Work and Labor

References and Further Reading

Deetz, James. 1977. *In Small Things Forgotten: The Archaeology of Early American Life*. Garden City, NY: Anchor Books/Doubleday.

Ferguson, Leland. 1992. *Uncommon Ground: Archaeology and Early African America, 1650–1800*. Washington, DC: Smithsonian Institution Press.

Horton, James Oliver, and Lois E. Horton. 2005. *Slavery and the Making of America*. New York: Oxford University Press.

Jacobs, Harriet. 1987. *Incidents in the Life of a Slave Girl: Written by Herself*. Edited by L. Maria Child, ed. Jean Fagin Yellin. Cambridge, MA: Harvard University Press.

Singleton, Theresa A., ed. 1985. *The Archaeology of Slavery and Plantation Life*. New York: Academic Press/Harcourt Brace Jovanovich.

Vlach, John Michael. 1993. *Back of the Big House: The Architecture of Plantation Slavery*. Chapel Hill: University of North Carolina Press.

White, Shane, and Graham White. 1995. "Slave Clothing and African-American Culture in the Eighteenth and Nineteenth Centuries." *Past and Present* (148): 149–186.

Social Class and Social Status

Social class may be defined simply as a division in society. Historically, those who were members of a social class such as the nobility, aristocracy, or the "middling sorts" were considered apart from, or above, the masses. Thus, *class* in historical colloquial usage has long been used to apply to persons of higher rank. To *have no class* is to be of little or no worth, even vulgar; to *have class* or *be classy* is to be noted for one's admirable demeanor or actions. Often, *social status* is used interchangeably with *social class*, though *class*, following Max Weber's (1864–1920) formulation, is an economically based system or structure related to the market, while *status* is an ascribed or earned quality based on non-economic criteria. *Status* refers to one's standing, *social status* one's position in society, implying the fluid and at times impermanent nature of human relations. Status may include such attributes as religious belief, age, kinship, and other factors. Individuals belonging to a social class may not share the same status; "old money" families, for example, have historically disdained "new money," though both groups may share the same class position. Fear of losing one's social position has been called *status anxiety*; *status seekers* are those who search for improvement of their position in society, often by demonstrating through education, taste, and material possessions their rightful membership in a class.

American society, past and present, has been considered classless—that is, one's condition of birth or wealth is not a factor in one's political or personal identity. Benjamin Franklin (1706–1790), after all, rose from a poor runaway apprentice to a wealthy and internationally known man of letters in the eighteenth century. Colonial American society was ordered not by birth but by wealth and by religious affiliation; one was one of the "better sorts" or "middling sorts" or "lower sorts." Timothy Shay Arthur's (1809–1885) morality tales of character triumphing over wealth and Horatio Alger's (1832–1899) "rags to riches" stories counseled nineteenth-century readers that education, hard work, manners, a clean body, attire, and surroundings were the means to wealth and success. Success manuals, even today, offer similar advice, and Gilded Age captains of industry such as Andrew Carnegie (1835–1916) and John D. Rockefeller (1839–1937), were real-life examples of the worth of such instruction. On the other hand, American society has historically been divided not only by political, economic, and social inequality due to racial and ethnic biases but also due to the great disparity of wealth. American capitalism has long been subject to Marxist theory, in which classes are created in relation to the modes of production: a ruling class of capitalists and a working class whose labor is sold to subsist. With its history of middle-class prosperity and values (at odds with Marxist theory), Americans have believed that democracy trumps aristocracy and that whatever class lines exist are ever changing and permeable.

Historical Class Formation in America

Americans historically have employed material culture as markers of social class. Mercantilism created fortunes for many families in colonial seaports such as Boston; Providence, Rhode Island; New York City; Philadelphia; and Charleston, South Carolina, and on large southern plantations. Part of those fortunes were invested in genteel imitation of English aristocratic practice: family portraits, mimicking noble lineage; specialized tablewares, including silver or ceramic tea sets; fashionable clothing; books; and spa-

cious houses dedicated to conviviality and comfort. Deference to wealthy elites—the "better sorts"—was displayed by members of the "middling" and "lower sorts" by the removal of hats and the bowing of heads in public. In turn, religious and cultural mores dictated that the middle and lower ranks enjoy the protection and charity of those elites. Still, many colonists, themselves originally from the middling sorts in England, rejected or challenged this reciprocity. Advertisements for runaway slaves, servants, and wives testify not only to the inequalities of American society encoded in law but also indicate the clothing and personal effects of these individuals who could not afford to be immortalized through portraiture.

Luxury was equated with aristocracy in the new nation and was thus inimical to republicanism. As industrialization and the rise of a cash economy allowed more Americans access to cheaper status goods such as clocks, chairs, carpets, textiles, portraits, and mirrors, Americans worried about how those goods, once considered luxuries, were becoming necessities of life. The rise of the factory system and unskilled labor further delineated "headwork" (nonmanual labor) from "handwork" (manual labor) in the first decades of the nineteenth century. The craft system of masters, journeymen, and apprentices was also threatened and would eventually disappear; the "working classes" earned wages rather than learned a trade or craft in the hope of opening businesses. The construction of urban factories and of factory towns in the countryside segregated more distinctly workers from the rest of society.

By mid-century, middle-class businessmen sought in their increasingly suburban houses to imitate the country estates or the fashionable townhouses of the wealthy. Workers remained within the walking city, living in aging freestanding dwellings, row houses, and tenements. In the latter half of the nineteenth century, the phenomenal wealth of the Gilded Age's "captains of industry" stood in stark contrast to the poverty of the working poor, both native born and immigrant, in the nation's cities. *Society* itself became a somewhat rigid category, as elites established such measures of membership as the Social Register, genealogy-based organizations such as the Society of Mayflower Descendants (est. 1897) and the Daughters of the American Revolution (est. 1890), and private country clubs. Newspapers across the United States established "Society" pages, in which the activities of elites and the middle class (often in emulation) were chronicled. The elite became trendsetters, with their taste in clothing, house design and furnishings, and leisure pursuits copied by the middle class. But many families also subscribed to the tenet of *noblesse oblige* and founded museums, libraries, hospitals, schools, and philanthropies to fight social problems such as poverty, education, and disease. The "nouveau riche" were suspect and often characterized as vulgar in their interests in indulging and displaying their wealth rather than putting it to good works. Middle-class Americans distanced themselves from the "blue collar" working class through the purchase and display of status goods in their homes. The struggle for middle-class distinction in this era is evidenced in the proliferation of etiquette guides, domestic periodicals exalting middle-class values, and novels by writers such as William Dean Howells (1837–1920) and Edith Wharton (1862–1937), the latter of whom also penned house decoration guides.

Industrial workers gained increases in wages due to labor union strength and federal regulation (including minimum wage laws) in the first decades of the twentieth century. The urgent necessity of labor after the United States entered World War II in 1941, combined with rationing and shortages, led to increased wages and savings—and postwar prosperity. Blue-collar workers were able to purchase suburban homes and leisure goods (especially automobiles and televisions), take vacations, allow their children to complete school and in many instances attend college, and enjoy overall a more comfortable life. At the same time, office workers, teachers, and other "white collar" and "pink collar" workers were ill paid and received little in the way of benefits. These men and women struggled to appear respectably middle class at work and in public but shared dwellings, ate poorly, and took advantage of any opportunity to cut costs by buying goods on sale. Since the 1970s, the demise of the nation's major industries (such as steel and automobile manufacturing in the Midwest "Rust Belt") and the rise of new technologies and the service industry have complicated the categories of headwork and handwork, so that social status markers and class boundaries are again inchoate. A new nouveau riche has arisen in the late twentieth-century New Economy, its members involved in the technology revolution and Wall Street, while the established elite have retreated ever more into private life.

Material Culture as Class Status Markers

Historians, sociologists, and economists have studied class systems by charting quantifiable measures such as education, income, and club membership. They have also begun to consider patterns of consumption and the social power of status goods in defining self and group. The leisure classes, as economist Thorstein Veblen (1867–1929) observed in his 1899 treatise *The Theory of the Leisure Class*, participated in a competitive acquisition he called *invidious comparison* and a display of possessions he called *conspicuous consumption*. These formulations have greatly influenced studies of the social and cultural meanings of forms of material culture in the United States. High fashion and luxury goods, for example, are often copied or imitated with cheaper materials and through mass production to be sold at lower prices to those (according to Veblen) who wish to emulate the wealthy or show their knowledge of trends. On the other hand, scholars argue that the intent or desires of these consumers cannot always be known, so the issue of emulation as a motive in selecting specific goods is more variable than constant. Anthropologist Grant McCracken (1990) also points out that the wealthy will respond by choosing new means through which to demarcate class—less Georg Simmel's (1858–1918) "trickle down" theory and more a constant "flight and pursuit" strategy to distinguish class boundaries.

French sociologist Pierre Bourdieu's (1930–2002) concept of *habitus* places class in a historical and cultural framework by positing a system in which class and status are based within a society's structure and become encoded in the patterns of behavior of that society's members. For French society, Bourdieu (1984) found that there was an unequal distribution of *cultural capital*—what the middle class has achieved through education are skills in handling symbols, from bodily deportment to defining and displaying taste to articulating and explaining beliefs in ways that appear instinctive or natural rather than learned—related to social positions of power.

Other scholars, especially those interested in advertising, marketing, and business, have explored lifestyle as a way of understanding the relationship between people, consumption, and material culture. *Lifestyle*, originally a term of childhood development

coined in 1929 by psychologist Alfred Adler (1870–1937) to counter Sigmund Freud's (1856–1939) deterministic theories, was understood by Adler as the personality created in early childhood and based not only on heredity, environment, and other factors but also on the meanings the person determines in a given situation. With its fundamental belief in conscious choice, Adler's concept of lifestyle could be easily borrowed over the course of the twentieth century to refer to consumer activity. Since the 1970s, *lifestyle marketing* is a field in which manufacturers, retailers, and advertisers poll and measure consumers' attitudes, interests, activities, and spending habits to match more closely their products and services to various consumers. In turn, class position may be measured in what brands consumers use in a given time and place.

Shirley Teresa Wajda

See also Consumerism and Consumption; Dress, Accessories, and Fashion; Ethnicity; Etiquette and Manners; Gender; Poverty; Race; Style

References and Further Reading
Blumin, Stuart M. 1988. *The Emergence of the Middle Class: Social Experience in the American City, 1760–1900.* New York: Cambridge University Press.
Bourdieu, Pierre. 1984. *Distinction: A Critique of the Judgement of Taste,* trans. Richard Nice. Cambridge, MA: Harvard University Press.
Conroy, Marianne. 1998. "Discount Dreams: Factory Outlet Malls, Consumption, and the Performance of Middle-Class Identity." *Social Text* 54 (1): 63–83.
McCracken, Grant. 1990. *Culture and Consumption: New Approaches to the Symbolic Character of Consumer Goods and Activities.* Bloomington: Indiana University Press.
Mills, C. Wright. 1951. *White Collar: The American Middle Classes.* New York: Oxford University Press.
Nickles, Shelley. 2002. "More Is Better: Mass Consumption, Gender, and Class Identity in

Postwar America." *American Quarterly* 54 (4): 581–622.

Simmel, Georg. 1904. "Fashion." *International Quarterly* 10: 130–150.

Weber, Max. 1958 (1924). "Class, Status and Party." In *From Max Weber: Essays in Sociology*, ed. Hans Gerth and C. Wright Mills, 180–195. New York: Oxford University Press.

Social History

Social history (sometimes called *local history*) is the study and interpretation of the historic everyday life of ordinary people, often at the level of the community—village, town, or county. American social history has since the 1960s been defined against prevailing historical study that created and sustained what is most often defined as "traditional" or "standard" topics and approaches. Political events, movements, and leaders; diplomacy; and economic change, as well as the overwhelming emphasis on the written and printed word and periodization dependent largely on wars and political events, have shaped the history of the nation. Social history challenged this definition by asserting that ordinary Americans make and possess their own history and indeed help to shape the nation's history. That challenge was bolstered by the inclusion of material culture as historical evidence with which to comprehend the history of those without access to literacy and/or power—to write history, in the words of the New Social Historians, "from the bottom up." Americans overlooked in traditional narratives of national history—women, African Americans, slaves and indentured servants, industrial laborers, rural farmers, immigrants, the poor— became the subjects of the social historian's study. The nation as the primary subject and purpose of historical analysis was challenged by social historians' emphasis on communities in specific times and places, albeit in service to writing a different, "total" history. The perspectives of the people rather than leaders were engaged and legitimated. These perspectives are not dismissed as false, fantastic, or inconsequential, but rather examined within the people's own experiences. Material culture was and is fundamental to this inquiry.

"Pots and Pans" History

Though the phrase *social history* is most often associated with historians' work of the 1960s and 1970s, the study of the everyday life of anonymous Americans has always occurred. Local and regional historical societies were established in great numbers in the United States after the Civil War (1861–1865). Influenced by the Colonial Revival Movement, Americans began to collect artifacts as well as collect themselves into societies, libraries, and museums devoted to the study and protection of these historical relics; the Society for the Preservation of New England Antiquities (now Historic New England), founded in 1910, is only one of many such organizations.

In this same era, historians began to join university faculties and, influenced by German historian Leopold von Ranke (1795–1886), stressed a "scientific method" that depended entirely on documents rather than artifacts. Those collectors and amateurs who labored to write American history with material culture were redefined as antiquarian rather than scientific and modern; in short, they were marginalized pejoratively as "pots and pans" historians by scholars who were themselves seeking professional legitimacy through the doctorate, university affiliation, and participation in professional organizations such as the American Historical Association (founded in 1884).

Nevertheless, the study of the everyday life of everyday people was popular and successful, if the establishment of museums such as Henry Ford's (1863–1947) Greenfield Village (founded in 1929), John D. Rockefeller, Jr.'s (1874–1960) Colonial Williamsburg (founded in 1926), and the opening of the American Wing of New York City's Metropolitan Museum of Art in 1924 are any measure. Even more popular were studies published by collectors and nonaffiliated historians early in the twentieth century. Alice Morse Earle's (1851–1911) eighteen volumes on colonial life in New England represent well this body of work. Everyday life and work are chronicled through the collection and analysis of artifacts, diaries and letters, town and tax records, immigration lists, and business records. Due to the false separation of local history from political and national history, mirrored in the separation between museums' collecting practices and professional historians' emphasis on the verbal and the political, social history is often but erroneously associated with the study of domestic life.

The New Social History

Energized by the civil rights movement of the 1960s and by the nation's bicentennial in 1976, historians in the United States challenged "standard" historical practice. The personal was, for many champions of this New Social History, political, in that it also could be practiced by historians beyond the university. Federal, state, local, and philanthropic monies for historic preservation, museum exhibitions, and other public history projects and inquiries helped to democratize the practice of history and to include material culture in that practice.

The New Social Historians turned to scholarship beyond the nation's shores as examples of a new type of "total history": that of structures rather than events. French historian Fernand Braudel's (1902–1985) magisterial study of the Mediterranean world (1949) and his three-volume *Civilization and Capitalism, 15th–18th Centuries* (1979) argued against event-driven history and for the consideration of geographic factors and economic relations as agents of change, as well as the works of Braudel's colleagues who published in the journal *Annales: Economies, sociétés, civilizations* (changed recently to *Annales: histoires, sciences sociales*), also argued for a history of *mentalité*. Borrowing from Karl Marx (1818–1883) his ideas about class and social change, the works of Edward P. Thompson (1924–1993) and other British labor historians promised also to change the shape of history and of historical practice.

The emphasis on structure is at its core a consideration of the system of economic relations within and geographical location of a historical community or society. New Social Historians adapted the theories and methods of the social sciences—economics, sociology, and anthropology—to the study of marginalized groups and of communities who would no longer be portrayed as victims or as passive but as agents of change. Demography and other quantitative and statistical methods were widely adopted as a means with which to analyze large amounts of historical data, discern patterns of all human behavior, and re-create historical economic and social systems. Census records, tax records, probate inventories, and court records were subjected to quantitative analysis to chart over time rates of birth, marriage, and death; foodways and diet; the shape of family life; and the standards of living through wealth distribution, clothing, and material possessions. The town or county became the focus of this method to explore class, labor, race relations, and other categories of analysis; studies of the Massachusetts towns of Concord, Dedham, Lynn, and Plymouth were early examples. Such historical community studies, however, were faulted in two areas: Separate studies on separate towns in the same era (and in the same state or region) were considered microcosms of larger, national trends and issues but resulted in different conclusions about historical change, while some studies were constructed so insularly as to ignore momentous and surely instrumental factors such as war.

A second aspect of the New Social History was the analysis of consciousness—what the *Annales* historian Lucien Febvre (1878–1956) called *mentalité*—a group's mode of thought. Adapting sociology theories of collective consciousness and worldview and anthropological practices of ethnography, New Social Historians analyzed official records to chart patterns of human behavior through narrative structure, repetition, and language. A simple court case about theft could reveal much more than an illegal act: Witness testimony may reveal evidence of family relations, class structure, city life, leisure, and perceptions, for example. Stressing non-elite perspectives also legitimated the study of popular culture in its various forms or in interaction with "learned" (high or elite) culture.

Impact of the New Social History
Though the New Social Historians in the United States overwhelmingly produced works in eighteenth- and nineteenth-century history, the methods of oral history and ethnography were employed in preserving the recollections and experiences of living Americans. African American history, women's history, ethnic history, and lesbian and gay history were established in the wake

of the New Social History. At its heart a political movement to democratize historical practice, the New Social History also aided the establishment of graduate programs in historic preservation and in *public* or *applied history*, the practice of history in museums, historical societies, and state and federal agencies. American material culture studies courses were created, and a few programs dedicated to the field were also established as a result of this movement.

Nevertheless, the divide between university scholars and museum scholars remains. For the many works written by university-affiliated social historians, only a relative few employed artifacts or analysis of material life as evidence. John Demos' *A Little Commonwealth: Family Life in Plymouth Colony* (1970), an early contribution, employed probate inventories to capture the Plymouth colonists' domestic life in relation to their Puritan beliefs. Exhibitions in museums and historical societies provide more accessible venues in which to present American social history with and through artifacts.

Recent Trends
American historical practice in the 1980s and 1990s was swept by what has been termed the "cultural turn" or the "linguistic turn." The very language of the documents the New Social Historians studied was itself a tool of the powerful rather than a benign system of signs conveying meaning. To understand power in a society one had to investigate that society's system of discourse that language both shapes and represents. This shift away from experience to text was accompanied by the implication that the agency of an individual or group was, at best, debatable, bound up as it was in discourse.

Social history has adapted to these changes: the stress on the qualitative rather than quantitative and the cultural over the economic, and the rise of *microhistory*—the intensive study of phenomena on a greatly reduced scale. Many historians point to Carlo Ginzburg's *The Cheese and the Worms* (1980), a study, in the vein of the history of *mentalités*, of a sixteenth-century Italian miller's understanding of religion and the world reconstructed through the records of the Inquisition, as the seminal work in this field; others invoke influential anthropologist Clifford Geertz's (1926–2006) emphasis on the ethnographic practice of "thick description" that eschews theory and praises the particular. Still others see in microhistory a return to narrative as it accounts for complexity in people's lives. These adaptations, however, beg the question of whether these forms are now better defined as *cultural history*.

Shirley Teresa Wajda

See also Anthropology and Archaeology; Cultural History; Cultural Studies; Ethnicity; Folklore and Folklife; Gender; Historic Preservation; Popular Culture; Poverty; Race; Social Class and Social Status

References and Further Reading
Demos, John. 1970. *A Little Commonwealth: Family Life in Plymouth Colony*. New York: Oxford University Press.
Gardner, James B., ed. 1983. *Ordinary People and Everyday Life: Perspectives on the New Social History*. Nashville, TN: American Association for State and Local History.
Henretta, James. 1979. "Social History as Lived and Written." *American Historical Review* 84 (5): 1293–1323.
Kessler-Harris, Alice. 1997 (1990). "Social History." In *The New American History: Critical Perspectives On the Past*, rev. and exp., ed. Eric Foner, 231–256. Philadelphia, PA: Temple University Press.
Scott, Joan W. 1991. "The Evidence of Experience." *Critical Inquiry* 17 (4): 773–797.
Stearns, Peter N. 2003. "Social History Present and Future." *Journal of Social History* 37 (10): 9–19.

Souvenirs

A *souvenir* is a small object of remembrance. Souvenirs materially represent relationships, as in the case of an image of a mother treasured by her child; represent experiences, as when tourists purchase small artifacts from areas they are visiting or when a moviegoer saves a ticket from a show; and represent accomplishments, as when an athlete is given an ornamental trophy to commemorate a performance in a competition.

Owning and collecting souvenirs is an ancient activity, with artifacts found in ancient Roman and ancient American sites. Why do humans collect souvenirs? Some scholars point to the same impetus behind ritualistic ownership. To own a representation of something or someone is to exert power over that original source. In this way, souvenirs are an attempt to control not only the past but the future. Because of this, souvenirs are not neutral objects.

For example, white tourists traditionally have collected souvenirs representing their travels among people they have defined as "other"—that is, different and lesser than themselves. In these cases, the desired souvenirs represent a complicated longing for the supposed "simpler life" of the indigenous people and yet an assertion of supremacy on the part of the white collector. Thus, a nineteenth-century souvenir of a hand-woven rug from the Diné people was prized for its representation of the distance between supposedly civilized white society and the supposedly less-advanced native culture, while the rug was appreciated for its value as an object of beauty and fine craftsmanship.

At the same time, such ethnic souvenirs were rendered into western commodities of exchange. Collectors sought, purchased, and then traded objects of another culture whose original purposes were often distant from the object of a collector's passion. An example of this would be the "souvenir" of a white Euro-American tourist on an 1894 Alaska cruise who purchased a basket from a local Tlingit woman. The basket, originally created to hold foodstuffs, is taken out of its specific context and used for other purposes. Our hypothetical tourist returns to her home in San Francisco, and sells the basket for far more money to a local wealthy collector of Native American artifacts. Once a souvenir, the basket has been transformed into a commodity twice over (at the point of original purchase and the secondary exchange), and the culture that produced the basket likewise has been rendered a commodity for sale and trade.

Some souvenirs were deliberately manufactured to be purchased as souvenirs. Artifacts emblazoned with the name of a locale, such as a plaque with an image of the Niagara Falls, were common from the early nineteenth century on. Curios were often created, sometimes by indigenous peoples, for the tourist trade. For example, one dealer in Santa Fe, New Mexico, in the 1880s had a large stock of pottery figures called "rain gods" that had been created specifically to be sold to tourists. Another form of souvenir was the souvenir or gift book, which was not tied to a specific locale. These were small, commercially produced books with sentimental images of children, nature, and women, and poems and short moral essays. The frontispiece invariably had a commercially printed page that said, "A Gift From _____."

Souvenirs, purchased and treasured for their ability to recall specific moments of the past and to embody unfamiliar contexts, are in fact about the owner of the souvenirs. Ultimately, souvenirs tell a story about the self as told through others.

Helen Sheumaker

See also Collecting and Collections; Commodity; Consumerism and Consumption; Gifts and Gift Giving; Memory and Memorabilia; Native America; Nostalgia; Tourism and Travel

References and Further Reading
Hitchcock, Michael, and Ken Teague, eds. 2000. *Souvenirs: The Material Culture of Tourism.* Aldershot, UK: Ashgate.
Phillips, Ruth B. 1998. *Trading Identities: The Souvenir in Native North American Art from the Northeast, 1700–1900.* Seattle: University of Washington Press.
Phillips, Ruth B., and Christopher B. Steiner. 1999. *Unpacking Culture: Art and Commodity in Colonial and Postcolonial Worlds.* Berkeley: University of California Press.
Stewart, Susan. 1984. *On Longing: Narratives of the Miniature, the Gigantic, the Souvenir, the Collection.* Baltimore, MD: Johns Hopkins University Press.

Space and Place

Contemporary academic studies within the humanities and the social sciences have borne witness to a geographical turn, an increased awareness of the geography of social processes writ large and the politics of daily life. These studies, no longer bound to the discipline of geography itself, can be characterized by their analytical use of the terms *space* and *place* and the degrees to which disputes about the meanings of these terms form academic debates. *Space*, briefly defined, can be cited as a geographical category concerned with large-scale social, economic, and environmental processes—"the space of modernity," for example. In contrast, *place* can be defined as a geographical category concerned with distinctly narrower and more humanistic understandings of the geography of everyday life—as in "a sense of place." The use of this space/place dialectic is the geographical equivalent to philosopher Karl

Marx's (1818–1883) understanding of history as *epochal* and *historical*: *epochal* in that history may be read as a *longue durée* process of social and evolutionary change, and *historical* in the sense that there are punctuated time- and place-bound moments in history that may be cited as specific case examples (Roseberry 1997). In this reading, space may be considered as a form of long-term process, whereas place may be seen as a form of daily praxis—in the study of geography either conceptualization may be appropriate for different kinds of problems.

The academic debate surrounding the definitions of *space* and *place* arose in the 1960s, with what can be described as a generalized shift toward a quantitative approach to the study of geography (Crang 1998). Mirroring a shift toward structuralism throughout the social sciences, quantitative approaches to geography sought to impose spatial models and to uncover underlying broad spatial patterns. This shift recast geography as a positivist spatial science, and in particular was built from a Cartesian view of space that separated mind and body. Space in this light was a category taken to be *a priori* to human creation and thought and existed solely as a physical terrain or backdrop for human activity (Casey 1996). Space as a scientized category negated human activity and implied the idea of a sense of originality, in short that there could be a pure unthought-of space.

Countering the idea of a space outside human creation, Marxist and phenomenological philosophers in the 1970s began to reemphasize the importance of place. Mirroring a backlash against the dominance of structuralism within the social sciences, the use of the abstracted analytical category of space was criticized for its dehumanizing effects and for failing to take account of everyday life. Early influential works triggering this shift in thought can be seen in

Henri Lefebvre's *The Production of Space* (1974), Yi-Fu Tuan's *Space and Place: The Perspective of Experience* (1977), Edward Relph's *Place and Placelessness* (1976), and Michel de Certeau's *The Practice of Everyday Life* (1984). In these accounts, the modernist predilection for space was challenged in favor of views of place that were politically contingent, perceived through embodied experience, pregnant with cultural history and metaphor, and thus deeply personal. Of particular influence were the works of Lefebvre—notably his reworking of Marxian dialectics to include an understanding of space that posits the notion that space is socially produced and conditional to varying modes of production —in short, a form of spatial thinking that attempts to regain a unity between the physical, the mental, and the social (Lefebvre 1974; Soja 1989). Likewise, the work of de Certeau challenged notions of *a priori* space by positing that everyday space was something that was practiced on the ground through what he termed *pedestrian speech acts*—the daily tactics and strategies that individuals used to negotiate urban environments.

Following in the wake of these theoretical works, geography has often been cited to have taken a cultural turn; while the humanities and the social sciences—in particular anthropology, archaeology, American Studies, and sociology—have been cited as having taken a geographical turn. In each case it was taken to be axiomatic of the importance of the spatiality of everyday life, as well as the cultural and social conditions from which that spatiality was understood. In this sense place came to be the dominant geographical category of analysis since the 1980s. Corresponding to an increased concern with the proliferation of globalization, the lasting effects of modernity, and an uncertain shift toward notions of postmodernity, spatial scholars began to address the construction, maintenance, contestation, and erosion of places in what was termed a changing world. In many instances spatial scholars began to utilize the phrase, *a sense of place*, as a means of contextualizing the geographical location of social and cultural groups and to emphasize the importance of place in the creation of social and cultural identity. Debates focusing on the politics of place included the study of gendered place, postmodern places, new forms of urbanism, and the impact of globalization on what were seen to be traditional places. Prominent scholars responsible for shaping place debates since the late 1980s include David Harvey (1990), Edward Soja (1989), Mike Davis (1990), Doreen Massey (1994), and Linda McDowell (1999).

Further problematizing the notion of place, the French anthropologist Marc Augé has coined *non-place* (1995). Read as a result of the proliferation of individuated places and increasingly transient everyday lives devoid of interpersonal contact in what he terms *super-modernity*, non-place is seen as resulting in a loss of a sense of place. Read in a number of diverse places—from highways to ATM machines to fast-food restaurants—the idea of non-place challenges established notions of place as geographically rooted and socially constructed. Non-place in Augé's reckoning reemphasizes the importance of long-term social and economic processes and the potential effects of degradation of unique senses of place that might result from them.

Matthew David Cochran

See also Cultural Geography; Cultural Studies; Land and Landscape

References and Further Reading

Adams, Paul C., Steven Hoelscher, and Karen E. Till, eds. 2001. *Textures of Place: Exploring Humanist Geographies*. Austin: University of Texas Press.

Augé, Marc. 1995. *Non-Places: Introduction to an Anthropology of Supermodernity*, trans. John Howe. London: Verso.

Casey, Edward S. 1996. "How to Get from Space to Place in a Fairly Short Stretch of Time: Phenomenological Prolegomena." In *Senses of Place*, ed. Steven Feld and Keith H. Basso, 13–52. Santa Fe, NM: School of American Research Press.

Crang, Mike. 1998. *Cultural Geography*. London: Routledge.

Crang, Mike, and Nigel Thrift, eds. 2000. *Thinking Space*. London: Routledge.

Cresswell, Tim. 2004. *Place: A Short Introduction*. Oxford, UK: Blackwell.

Davis, Mike. 1990. *City of Quartz: Excavating the Future in Los Angeles*. London: Verso.

de Certeau, Michel. 1984. *The Practice of Everyday Life*, trans. Steven Rendall. Berkeley: University of California Press.

Harvey, David. 1990. *The Condition of Postmodernity: An Enquiry into the Origins of Cultural Change*. Cambridge, MA: Blackwell.

Hayden, Dolores. 1995. *The Power of Place: Urban Landscapes as Public History*. Cambridge, MA: MIT Press.

Hubbard, Phil, Rob Kitchin, and Gill Valentine, eds. 2004. *Key Thinkers on Space and Place*. London: Sage.

Lefebvre, Henri. 1991 (1974). *The Production of Space*, trans. Donald Nicholson-Smith. Oxford, UK: Blackwell.

Low, Setha M., and Denise Lawrence-Zúñiga, eds. 2003. *The Anthropology of Space and Place: Locating Culture*. Oxford, UK: Blackwell.

Massey, Doreen. 1994. *Space, Place and Gender*. Minneapolis: University of Minnesota Press.

McDowell, Linda. 1999. *Gender, Identity and Place: Understanding Feminist Geographies*. Minneapolis: University of Minnesota Press.

Relph, Edward. 1976. *Place and Placelessness*. London: Pion.

Roseberry, William. 1997. "Marx and Anthropology." *Annual Review of Anthropology* 26: 25–46.

Soja, Edward W. 1989. *Postmodern Geographies: The Reassertion of Space in Critical Social Theory*. London: Verso.

Tuan, Yi-Fu. 1977. *Space and Place: The Perspective of Experience*. Minneapolis: University of Minnesota Press.

Sports

Sports are competitive and noncompetitive games and exercises. The material culture of sports, whether sports equipment, dress, or playing fields, reflects larger social changes, technological and manufacturing developments, an increasing professionalization of sports, and the dominance of consumerism in American history and life.

Native American Sports

Native Americans played sports, often with elaborate rules and protocol. Many different tribal nations played these games for both entertainment and as parts of rituals. Lacrosse, a stick and ball game, was played by the Six Nations of the Iroquois and was called *baggataway*. In the 1860s, the game was introduced to a larger American public and in the 1880s was adopted by several prominent eastern universities and colleges, such as Harvard.

Native Hawaiians lay upon, sat upon, and stood upon boards that "surfed" on the waves in the Pacific Ocean beginning around 1000 CE. Forced Christianization of the Hawaiians in the 1820s lessened surfing's popularity, but in the early 1900s the pastime was revived by Hawaiians, and later introduced by them to several Anglo men on the California coast. Duke Kahanamoku (1890–1968) was an extraordinary athlete who won three Olympic gold medals and two Olympic silver medals in swimming categories. Kahanamoku specialized in stand-up surfing, and his prominence as an athlete and later movie star led to the popularization of this style of Hawaiian surfing.

Seventeenth- and Eighteenth-Century Euro-American Sports

Sports in Europe, and later the North American colonies, were rarely standardized. For example, Dutch colonists in New Amsterdam (later New York) played nine pins. The object of this game was to knock down as many of the nine pins as possible with a ball. The size, shape, and weight of the pins and balls were not standardized, and rules of play were created as the game was in process. Other sports in the North American colonies reflected games played in Europe, especially England.

Sport hunting, an activity of aristocrats and the wealthy, was also imported from Europe. Hunting dogs were bred for this activity; the Treeing Walker Coonhound, for example, was bred selectively to chase its quarry into trees. Hunting gear, by the late eighteenth century, was personalized with carved designs and elaborate monograms on gun stocks. Horses, too, were bred for sporting purposes, not only for hunting but also for racing. Formal racetracks were built as early as 1665 on Long Island, New York.

Nineteenth- and Twentieth-Century Professionalization

After the Civil War (1861–1865), new sports, venues, and ways to participate were created. By the late nineteenth century, sports were not only a major American leisure activity but also the impetus for new consumer goods. A general trend toward greater professionalization of participants, further organization and regulation of professional and amateur players, and a proliferation of highly specialized equipment occurred over the course of the twentieth century.

The historical development of baseball, usually considered the quintessential American sport, epitomizes these trends. Baseball was most popular in the United States during the nineteenth and twentieth centuries, but its roots are in eighteenth-century England and the American colonies. The game of "base-ball" was depicted in children's books in England in the 1740s, and bat-and-ball games were played by Americans in the late 1700s. *Rounders* was a game popularized by an English children's book in the 1830s and is first mentioned in an American text in the 1840s. And then in 1845 American baseball took shape when a New Yorker, Alexander J. Cartwright (1820–1892), organized a baseball team, the New-York Knickerbocker Base Ball Club, and wrote down rules governing play. By the 1850s, baseball clubs were found not only in the New York City area but across the country. After the Civil War, baseball became a reunification tool for the country. It was popular in both the North and South, and the game was increasingly commercialized and professionalized, with baseball parks, ticket sales, and professional players.

By the 1880s, a national league had taken shape (although it took decades of struggles for the different leagues to achieve national status), minor leagues were formed, and players became fully professionalized and often celebrities in their own right. African American players were a part of these early years, playing on national as well as minor league teams, with white colleagues or on all-black teams. By the early 1900s, however, segregation had taken hold. Until player Jackie Robinson (1919–1972) and Branch Rickey (1881–1965), the president of the Brooklyn Dodgers, reintegrated baseball immediately after World War II, talented black players and others struggled to make careers in the Negro Leagues. Women began playing baseball by the 1860s and very occasionally were placed on professional teams in the late 1890s and early 1900s. After the United States entered World War II in 1941, men left the ball field for the battlefield and a women's league was formed; however, it was short lived. Baseball today remains popular, although other professional sports such as basketball have challenged its position as the most popular sport in the United States.

The equipment used to play baseball has been dramatically modified over the years. Baseball was played bare handed until the 1860s. As baseball's rules changed, so did its equipment. Position-specific equipment, such as catcher's mitts, chest protectors, and various sizes and shapes of fielding gloves, as well as bats, batting helmets, and batting gloves testify to the shifting specifications of play. Even uniforms have been the focus of technological development. Baseball equipment has always been popular among amateur players and was readily available to consumers beginning in the 1850s.

In the twenty-first century, sports are practiced by amateurs and professionals alike, and new sports are being created, such as *parkour*, an urban gymnastics obstacle race. The commercialization of sports has included consumer products, such as designer running shoes, twenty-four-hour access to television broadcasting of sports events, and increasing levels of corporate sponsorship of even obscure sports and the athletes who participate.

Sports Equipment

Sports equipment has become increasingly specialized and more readily available to amateur participants as well as professional athletes. In the North American colonies, sports equipment, such as fishing hooks, was imported from England, while gun manufacture began early in the colonies. For many Americans, fishing and game hunting was a necessary daily task, but for wealthier Americans, participation in these sports was considered leisure activity modeled upon practices by the elite in England. By the 1850s billiard tables were manufactured and sold in the United States, and after the Civil War, as sports became more popular, stores specializing in selling sporting goods appeared in major cities.

Sports equipment was a technological product, and advances in materials and manufacture changed not only what kinds of equipment were available but how a particular sport was played. For example, in 1898 the A. G. Spalding Company, started by a former baseball player, Albert G. Spalding (1850–1915), manufactured a new kind of golf ball—the gutta-percha ball. *Gutta-percha* is an organic material that, when heated, becomes plastic (that is, flexible) and water resistant. Luckily, The Spalding Company did not stop with the gutta-percha ball. By 1903 Spalding created golf balls out of rubber, another organic, elastic material, and devised a way to cover the balls with balata, a natural rubber that becomes hard and leatherlike. By 1905 the company was selling the now-familiar white golf ball. These and other technological innovations changed how golf was played, since the new balls traveled farther when hit, became easier to control, and were more durable.

In the 1970s and 1980s, changes in sports equipment were not only in technological developments but in marketing. Brand names, designer names, and the selling of an image were perhaps the most influential changes introduced. Companies such as Nike and Adidas relied upon status as well as the quality of their products in maintaining market shares. In addition to the intensified commercialization of sports equipment was an increasing tendency to professionalize even children's sports. For example, for several decades soap box derbies required that the children participating design and construct their own cars. The contests, begun in the 1930s, were held on a local basis, with a single national championship race. In 1976 the governing association, the All-American Soap Box Derby, introduced car kits with patterns

and hardware for participants to purchase and use (if they chose to). Children no longer had to create their own vehicles, but rather could assemble similar, professionally designed machines with which to compete. Most sports played by children, such as baseball, softball, kickball, and even jumping rope, are now organized by adults, subject to regulation, and the focus of formal competitions.

Unfortunately, another technological aid to sports competition has been the use of chemical enhancers such as anabolic steroids. In 1869 six-day bicyclists were taking "speedballs" (a mixture of cocaine and heroin) to enhance their performance. Amphetamine use was widespread in the 1950s and 1960s and resulted in several investigations of professional sports leagues. Today all professional and college leagues have a system of penalties to punish the use of chemical enhancers. Nevertheless, most observers agree that drug use in sports, even on the amateur level, is present and sometimes tolerated.

Sports Participation

Sports participation reflected American realities such as discrimination against African Americans, ethnic minorities, and women. On the other hand, sports has proved to be amazingly effective at creating shared identities, such as when a city's population backs its professional team or a high school homecoming centers around a football game. The material culture of sports reflects the ways in which sports has encompassed a diverse array of citizens, and at times has excluded individuals and groups.

Most Americans are introduced to sports and athletic play through their local neighborhood or school playground. The playground movement was born out of the park movement of the 1850s, which argued that outdoor parks improved physical and moral health and lessened crime rates. In the 1880s

Massachusetts began building nursery parks intended for use by small children. In 1893 Jane Addams (1860–1935) built a large playground at Hull House in Chicago, and by 1899 Boston had built twenty-one playgrounds. These playgrounds included swing sets, slides, and other permanent equipment for young children. Women's groups and charitable organizations began funding playgrounds in larger cities. By the late 1800s, organized sports and games were offered at these playgrounds, now intended for use by older children as well. During the Great Depression, the federal government funded the construction of elaborate playgrounds that included softball and baseball fields, tennis courts, and swimming pools.

The development of sports for the physically challenged reflects another aspect of how sports develop to accommodate individuals. In 1948, the first organized competitive wheelchair race took place in England, and the first international contest was held in 1976. Paralympics today is an international competition organized into six disability groups. Highly specialized equipment has been developed to aid athletes in their training and competitions, and many of these innovations, such as racing wheelchairs, have affected standard equipment as well.

For individuals with intellectual disabilities, the Special Olympics provides competitive opportunities for play. The organization was founded in 1968 by Eunice Kennedy Shriver, and today 2.25 million athletes from across the globe participate year-round. Special Olympics athletes train throughout the year and compete on local, national, and international levels.

Many Americans of all ages and abilities participate in amateur sports and purchase equipment unique to their chosen sport. In addition, even more Americans view sports in person, through televised broadcasts, and in webcasts. Americans may purchase an extraordinary range of sports-related memorabilia, from souvenirs to trading cards to figurines to clothing emblazoned with a favorite team's logo or a player's image. Home decor, team-related decals for vehicles, and a wide array of other sports-fan-related products are offered.

Elizabeth Redkey and Helen Sheumaker

See also Disability and Disability Studies; Education and Schooling; Games; Leisure, Recreation, and Amusements; Memory and Memorabilia; Public and Commercial Leisure, Recreation, and Amusement Venues

References and Further Reading

Adelman, Melvin L. 1986. *A Sporting Time: New York City and the Rise of Modern Athletics, 1820–1870.* Urbana: University of Illinois Press.

Guttmann, Allen. 2004. *Sports: The First Five Millennia.* Amherst: University of Massachusetts Press.

Riess, Steven A. 1989. *City Games: The Evolution of American Urban Society and the Rise of Sports.* Chicago: University of Illinois Press.

Style

Style is a means by which to describe an object by placing it into a categorical framework that articulates relationships among objects that are similar in their combination of physical characteristics, methods of production, and meaning. In order to assess whether an object illustrates a particular style, it may therefore be necessary to have more than visual information about the object. For example, an analysis of visual factors for a simple, unornamented, utilitarian wooden chair may suggest no particular stylistic reference in its design due to a lack of distinctive physical characteristics. We might also conclude, however, that such a chair illustrates the American Arts and Crafts style if it meets the requisite criteria. In this case such criteria include the exhibition of a plain, rectilinear form, probably in oak, and possibly with exaggerated joints as its ornament. The chair in question would also need to demonstrate a method of manufacture, either by hand or machine, that does not explicitly express mechanized production. Finally, the chair would demonstrate the Arts and Crafts style if it can be determined that it represents the simple, unornamented design created to counter explicitly the detailed and highly referential or ornamental furniture styles that were being produced at the same time, usually through mechanized processes.

The terms used to designate the various categories of style are sometimes descriptive, as in *Arts and Crafts*, which poses its philosophical opposition to mass industrial production. Often style terminology makes reference to a particular place or time, as in *American Colonial*. Still other style labels are derived from the name of the particular individual or a group considered the originator of the style, such as the terms *Chippendale* or *Eastlake*. Many terms locate a particular style in relationship to those that have preceded it—either immediately or in the distant past—such as *Postmodern, Greek Revival,* or *Neoclassical*.

Disciplines such as art history and architectural history and fields such as material culture studies that rely on visual evidence have long made use of style-based frameworks to organize their subject matter. These frameworks are usually linear in their structure, suggesting that the evolution of the characteristics of a style is chronological. Early twentieth-century charts explaining the styles of objects such as furniture sometimes replicated genealogical relationships among their various components as though

a subsequent style should be understood as the offspring of its predecessor and as a member of a larger family of styles.

Style and Connoisseurship

For all its emphasis on description and definition, style is a relative concept. Objects that meet the accepted criteria of a known style without any exceptions are uncommon. It is an object's ability to align closely with the characteristics defined within an accepted framework that determines the level to which it exemplifies a particular style. As a means of defining and categorizing artifacts, the relationships between objects from a similar place or from a common time period are articulated in a manner that emphasizes their similarities, but this does not negate the possibility that differences exist. The level to which an object follows the criteria of a particular style can, therefore, be used as a characteristic to judge the explicit and inherent value of an object. This process of judgment, known as *connoisseurship*, is practiced by collectors and appraisers.

Decorative arts scholar, curator, and connoisseur Charles F. Montgomery (1910–1978) formalized a process of evaluation based on fourteen criteria, including style, to be used to determine the success or significance of an object (Montgomery 1961, 149–150). Connoisseurs use the premise that the more closely an object aligns with a style's particular set of characteristics, the more "pure" or valuable that object is as an artifact of study. This premise also provided a foundation for twentieth-century historic preservation practice in the United States, since preservationists usually considered buildings that more completely illustrate the characteristics of their assigned styles to be more historically significant contributions to the built environment.

Historical and Contemporary Definitions of Style

Views of the concept of style have shifted over time. In the nineteenth century, art historians tended to emphasize the essential characteristics of an object. Critics such as John Ruskin (1819–1900) and Owen Jones (1809–1874) in England and the art historian Alois Riegl (1858–1905) in Austria attempted to fit historic objects and artistic works into generalized abstract categories of style that focused on the dichotomy between the natural and the geometric or synthetic. The character of the ornament illustrated in the forms and on the surfaces of objects received preferential consideration in this analytical approach.

The modern movement in art and design generated a different view of style. Modern designers viewed the association of the concept of style with their works as detrimental to their goal of creating designs that avoided references to the past. As a result, an association of style with the imitative and the superficial emerged in the early twentieth century. A rift occurred in the interpretation of modern objects and those that were created in the popular decorative or referential "period" styles that emulated objects of previous eras.

The rise of material culture studies created an argument for the significance of style as a defining characteristic of an object. Art historian Jules David Prown asserted that connecting an object to a style goes beyond the definition of physical properties to include the role it plays in a particular culture. In 1980, Prown's essay "Style as Evidence" articulated an argument for the significance of style to the understanding of material culture due to its ability to communicate cultural values (Prown 1980, 207). By noting correlations between stylistic shifts and changes in socioeconomic conditions of various periods of history, Prown asserted that it is possible to use style to map and interpret people's attitudes and beliefs along with their circumstances.

Over the course of the twentieth century, the concept of style also served as a rhetorical tool used by designers, manufacturers, and advertisers to generate interest in new products. Objects that exhibit the accepted characteristics of trends or fashions can be said to *have style*. Serving as both a noun and a verb, *style* has played a key role in encouraging consumption by seeming to necessitate the frequent replacement of goods by implying that objects that do not express current stylistic trends are obsolete.

Mary Anne Beecher

See also Architectural History and American Architecture; Art History and American Art; Decorative Arts; Historic Preservation

References and Further Reading

Calloway, Stephen, and Elizabeth Cromley, eds. 1991. *The Elements of Style: A Practical Encyclopedia of Interior Architectural Details, from 1485 to the Present*. New York: Simon & Schuster.

Montgomery, Charles F. 1982 (1961). "The Connoisseurship of Artifacts." In *Material Culture Studies in America*, ed. Thomas J. Schlereth, 143–152. Nashville, TN: American Association for State and Local History.

Poppeliers, John C., and S. Allen Chambers, Jr. 2003. *What Style Is It? A Guide to American Architecture*. Hoboken, NJ: John Wiley.

Prown, Jules David. 1980. "Style as Evidence." *Winterthur Portfolio* 15 (3): 197–210.

Schafter, Debra. 2003. *The Order of Ornament, the Structure of Style: Theoretical Foundations of Modern Art and Architecture*. Cambridge, UK: Cambridge University Press.

Suburbs and Suburbia

A *suburb* is a purposeful development of a residential district of single-family dwellings outside the legal boundaries of an urban center. *Suburbia* describes the suburban phenomenon, with accompanying utility and community services like sewage, schools, libraries, and telephone, plus consumer services like retail and industry and the lifestyles of those living in such communities. The existence of suburbia is predicated on escape, both geographic and psychological: escape from the slums, traffic, pollution, crime, and physical constriction of the urban setting.

History of the American Suburb

The first suburban developments in the United States began in the mid-eighteenth century as undesirable slums on the outskirts of the metropolitan city core. In the eighteenth century, with the exception of the wealthiest Americans' summer country house, living outside the comforts and conveniences of the city—made essential by the lack of transportation—was considered cultural exile and relegated to outcasts and the lower classes. This attitude shifted in the mid-nineteenth century. As cities outgrew their limits and capacities, the city center became increasingly congested and unhealthy. Advances in transportation technology and availability, such as the omnibus, railroad, and trolley, created the real possibility of commuting to the city from a residence beyond its industrial and commercial center, as well as the lower-class housing that surrounded it. *Railroad suburbs*, or residential districts built around railroad or trolley rail systems coming out from the city, developed. Close proximity to public transportation meant that blue-collar and professional heads of households could commute to work from stations within walking distance of their suburban dwellings. The place of work and the place of refuge were thus separated.

Advances in transportation were practical and logistical characteristics of suburbanization, but commercial and moral motives proved to be of great influence in the United States. Early entrepreneurial real estate agents and land developers assisted this important cultural change. Suburbia's privacy, space, and luxury of land were selling points to families of moderate means. By implanting the idea of the suburb as a haven from the city's ills, suburbs were sold not just as parcels of land but also as a mind-set. A specifically American sanctity for the home as a moral refuge, a desire for privacy, and an increasing skepticism about the virtues of public life also encouraged suburban residential developments. Especially for the middle class, suburbs offered physical and psychological relief from the pressures of city life.

While living on the city's edge away from the congestion was a great advantage, the location of suburban dwellings of the late nineteenth century was still limited to within walking distance of public transportation. Travel for groceries and other goods remained a difficult venture. The automobile encouraged suburban living because it allowed movement within and beyond the suburbs themselves. Suburban residences were no longer restricted in location by proximity to public transportation. Greater popularity and availability of automobiles throughout the twentieth century encouraged the evolution from the railroad suburb to more insolated, detached suburban neighborhoods extending farther and farther from the city core and from transportation hubs.

The federal government encouraged suburban development with financial assistance aimed at building up the suburban ideal through the early twentieth century. Herbert Hoover's (1874–1964) President's National Conference on Home Building and Home

Ownership in 1931 influenced the attitude toward home ownership as not just a financial symbol but as a patriotic and anti-Communist symbol. The Federal Housing Administration, started in 1934, encouraged lenders to lower payment and interest rates and extend loan repayment agreements. The agency also established construction industry standards for safety and structural stability of dwellings. Especially generous to returning World War II veterans through the Servicemen's Readjustment Act of 1944 (or the "GI Bill of Rights"), this kind of governmental financial aid directed potential homeowners specifically to the suburbs. The duties of the Home Owners Loan Corporation, another federal agency, were to appraise land value and lender credit. As such the agency established zones of residential properties based on desirability and helped establish strictly segregated neighborhoods by approving loans only to certain racial populations in certain neighborhoods. Other kinds of federal assistance included the Federal Highway Act of 1916, and later the Federal-Aid Highway Act of 1956, which encouraged the use of automobiles by providing large, well-paved thoroughfares connecting the suburbs to the city.

Material and Popular Characteristics of the Suburb

Building on nineteenth-century innovations in construction techniques, like the balloon frame method (which consisted of numerous 2 × 4–inch posts supporting ceiling beams; it quickened the pace for construction and lowered the cost of residential manufacturing materials and labor), housebuilding, especially after World War II, became an industry of its own. Sears, Roebuck and Co. sold kits for entire houses, whereby families could follow the instructions and build the house themselves or hire labor to erect it.

Utilizing the same kind of mass production and prefabrication, the Levitt and Sons, Inc., family business began a revolution in design and availability. The Levitts created a suburban development, Levittown, New York, from 1946 to 1951. By the 1950s, suburbs were characterized by Levittown's residential architecture with houses that were mostly single-story or split-level structures with roomy lots for front and back yards and built on concrete slabs. Most homes had two or three bedrooms, one bath, a kitchen in front and living room in rear, plus a large prominent garage with a concrete driveway that led out onto the street. The new residential construction, with low roofs, plenty of windows, large yards, and carports or garages, became extremely popular with architects and homeowners alike.

As regional design styles gave way to architectural homogeneity, the ethnic and economic demographics in the suburbs approached uniformity. Zoning and land-use restrictions were used as foils for discrimination against blacks, Hispanics, and lower-income housing like apartments and trailer parks. While suburban homeowners did attempt individuality through home and yard decoration and landscaping, living in a neighborhood with people of similar age, race, income bracket, and moral habits threatened to estrange suburbanites to ethnic diversity. Even within suburbia, variations follow larger cultural and socioeconomic hierarchies. While traditionally suburbia has been described as staunchly middle class, neighborhoods, villages, and incorporated subdivisions exist for the upper- and upper-middle classes. As well, lower- and lower-middle-class neighborhoods fall within the broad definition of a suburb. Still, demographics in each kind of suburb remain respectively homogeneous.

This aerial photograph of Levittown, New York, was taken in 1948, shortly after the planned community was completed on Long Island farmland near Manhattan. Real estate developer William J. Levitt created mass-produced, low-cost, tract housing to address the housing crunch after World War II. (AP/Wide World Photos)

Television and popular culture help reiterate cultural stereotypes of American suburban living. Magazines like *Good Housekeeping* (begun in 1885) and *House Beautiful* (begun in 1896) advertised and encouraged specific roles for women as housewives. Housekeeping and laundry chores using the latest appliances, with the occasional Tupperware party, filled the days and nights of many American suburban women. Conversely, lawn care and barbeques filled the weekends of many American suburban males. Though consumerism was not a uniquely suburban phenomenon, certain products and goods were directed specifically to the homeowner in suburbia who had a large lawn that necessitated a riding mower or kitchen space for an electric dishwasher. Television programs like *Leave it to Beaver* (1957–1963), *The Brady Bunch* (1969–1974), and *The Wonder Years* (1988–1993) attempted to depict an ideal home life for children and adults alike, content to play in their yards with little need to leave the safe confines of their village or subdivision.

Yards play a crucial role in the dichotomy between privacy and social conformity in American suburbia. A well-kept lawn symbolizes a healthy, normal, productive, and industrious family. The pride of landscaping and yard mowing remains a staple in the persistent competition between the "Joneses" in every subdivision. The back yard, which in traditional Levitt construction was accessible through the family or living room in the rear of the home, provides a private oasis for the family. Though traditionally the white picket fence is a staple in representation of early suburban living, the popularity, size, and material of fencing yards ebbs and flows depending on the economic level of the neighborhood and the amount of consumer goods (e.g., swing sets, trampolines, pools, lawn furniture) families amassed in their ample back yards. While upper-middle-class neighborhoods may have tall wooden privacy fences, poorer neighborhoods may have chain link, and rural subdivisions may prefer no fencing to break up their plentiful lots.

Commercial Aspects of American Suburbs

The same cheap and abundant land that enticed domestic building encouraged commercial services to develop in the suburbs. Undeveloped land also encouraged an exodus of factories and industry headquarters to the suburbs, where company workers enjoyed ample parking, parklike settings, and the convenience of proximity to their suburban homes. By 1970, many corporate headquarters and manufacturing plants moved closer to the suburbs, creating a decentralization of industry and a greater reliance on the automobile. To accommodate the growing industrial and domestic population, the landscape of the suburbs changed and began to incorporate necessary services like shopping, eating, hotels, and entertainment. The "mom-and-pop" shops located near the transportation hubs gave way to drive-in theaters and drive-up or drive-thru fast food chain restaurants and retail and grocery centers surrounded by large parking lots. This development was fueled in part by an increasingly ingrained car culture. The closest approxi-

mation to pedestrian-friendly commerce allowed in the suburbs is the large-sized, indoor shopping mall. Removed from cultural attractions of the city, suburban children and teenagers devoted a majority of their time either to watching television or hanging out in the malls.

Starting with housing, then industry, then retail, a continuous exodus from the city center meant a consistent sprawling and decentralization of the nonurban environment. The ubiquity of subdivisions and shopping centers with the same group of fast food restaurants makes it difficult to distinguish one suburb from another and blurs the distinctions between states, cities, and neighborhoods. The extension of retail and industry to the suburbs, while providing its residents with some conveniences, has also negated the domestic refuge that initially motivated the move from the city into peripheral and outlying areas.

The American suburb has become a mini-city of single-family residences on curving streets and cul-de-sacs, with its own utilities, school districts, shopping malls, strip centers, and series of staple fast food restaurants nestled within a web of superhighways and freeways. Many social scientists and cultural historians question the idea of the suburb as a separate entity from the city and instead declare that suburbs, with their residences, commerce, and transportation systems, are mini-cities connected to each other and to large cities by highways. Still others point out the decline of suburban living after the 1980s in some areas of the nation in favor of urban renewal and regentrification.

Victoria Estrada-Berg

See also Automobiles and Automobility; Domestic Architecture; Highways and National Highway System; House, Home, and Domesticity; Planned Communities; Shopping Centers and Shopping Malls

References and Further Reading

Hayden, Dolores. 2003. *Building Suburbia: Green Fields and Urban Growth, 1820–2000*. New York: Pantheon Books.

Jackson, Kenneth T. 1985. *Crabgrass Frontier: The Suburbanization of the United States*. Oxford, UK: Oxford University Press.

Sies, Mary Corbin. 2001. "North American Suburbs, 1880–1950: Cultural and Social Reconsiderations." *Journal of Urban History* 27 (3): 313–346.

Supermarkets

Prior to the 1930s, grocery stores generally were small in size and limited in the quantity and variety of goods for sale. Changes in mass food production and distribution, technology, and transportation in the 1910s and 1920s transformed the scale and scope of grocery stores, leading to the development of the supermarket. These stores were large-scale ventures conducted on a cash-and-carry basis, with customers picking and choosing goods from open shelving. Unlike small independent and early chain grocery stores, supermarkets traded in large volume, offering a greater diversity of goods and choices to consumers. Store owners profited from bulk buying, passing discounted prices on to their customers. Additionally, improved organizational methods separated supermarkets by department, leading to more efficiently operated stores.

Supermarkets first appeared in the 1930s on the West Coast with Ralphs Grocery Company establishing markets that covered 5,000 to 6,000 square feet of building space, or nearly ten times the size of conventional grocery stores. Given their large size, these stores tended to locate in suburban neighborhoods, where ample parking space could accommodate shoppers' automobiles. Supermarkets allowed customers the convenience of one-stop shopping, with separate meat, produce, bakery, and grocery departments housed under one roof. Shoppers could purchase more than a day's worth of groceries, thanks to in-home electric refrigerators, available beginning in the 1920s. This enabled customers to take advantage of volume discounts. The sheer size of supermarkets and consumer purchases required the use of shopping carts, invented in 1935 to hold ample grocery orders. By the 1950s, supermarkets dominated trade because of the convenience, location, and economical benefits they offered customers.

"Big box" chain stores such as Wal-Mart, K-Mart, and Target stores have introduced "superstores," which boast the inclusion of full supermarkets. Fully 20 percent of groceries in the United States are now purchased in these superstores.

Susan V. Spellman

See also Cities and Towns; Commercial Architecture; Consumerism and Consumption; Food and Foodways; Grocery Stores; Suburbs and Suburbia

References and Further Reading

Mayo, James M. 1993. *The American Grocery Store: The Business Evolution of an Architectural Space*. Westport, CT: Greenwood Press.

Tedlow, Richard S. 1990. *New and Improved: The Story of Mass Marketing in America*. Boston: Harvard Business School Press.

Zimmerman, M. M. 1955. *The Super Market: A Revolution in Distribution*. New York: McGraw-Hill.

T

Technology

Technology, broadly defined, includes tools and machines of all sorts; the use of those artifacts; and the skills and knowledge to design, make, and use them. Material culture —tools, machines, and other useful artifacts— is thus central to an understanding of technology and its place in culture. What does it mean that technology depends on objects? How does the material base of technology affect the nature of technological knowledge, technological systems, and technological actions? How have historians used artifacts to understand technology and technological change over time?

Much of material culture might be called technology. Define *technology* as it often is defined—as useful things—and it might include not just the obvious tools and machines but also much of the material covered in this encyclopedia. For example, one might consider clothing as the technology of dress, or furniture as the technology of domestic life. Thus it is useful to define *technology* in a narrower way. *Technological artifacts* are those the purposes of which are, for the most part, utilitarian. Folklorist Henry Glassie (1977, 47)

suggests that artifacts are like poetry, "explosive with ambiguity and uneasy in the confines of time." Technological artifacts, narrowly defined, would be more like prose. This is not to say that there is not poetry— symbolism, art, politics, and even ambiguity —in technology, but rather that utility of some sort is essential.

Some students of material culture have put technology not at the center of their studies but at its edges, suggesting that technology obeys the rules of science or economics, and not of culture. Yet technological artifacts, like other material culture, are cultural artifacts, and that while they may be, because of their practical uses, more strongly shaped by natural law and economics than some artifacts, much of what makes them interesting is shaped by culture.

The Historiography of Technology in the United States

In part because the study of the history of technology has long had a strong base in museums, material culture has been an important element in its historiography. Late nineteenth-century ethnologists at the Smithsonian Institution, for example, displayed the history of technology as a progression of improvements reflecting racial categories, with European and American culture supposedly developing the most sophisticated technology. While anthropology still depends on archaeology to a large extent, the early interest in technology diminished in the early twentieth century when anthropology became an academic field with emphasis on human relations rather than artifacts, especially technological artifacts. Anthropology-based exhibitions were replaced, at the Smithsonian and other museums, with historical displays that focused on technological invention and innovation; individual invention, not the invention of "the race." Artifacts continued to play a strong role in these displays.

In the second half of the twentieth century, historians of technology generally have put more emphasis on culture and context, whether economic, business, or labor—the settings of artifacts—and on skills and expertise—the knowledge that is encapsulated in artifacts or required to design or use them. Especially as issues of design came to be viewed as more interesting than issues of use, and science-based technologies more interesting than simpler technologies, artifacts seemed less important. Enthusiasts have continued to approach the material culture of technology with a version of connoisseurship that focuses on identification and operation of antique machines. The field of industrial archaeology, with its emphasis on surviving industrial artifacts and structures, has partially filled the gap between connoisseurship and contextualism.

In recent years, historians have begun to pay more attention to the way that technological artifacts are used, not just to the way they are designed. That, and recent theoretical trends in the "social construction of technology," have also helped revive an interest in the material culture of technology and have helped to bring the history of technology back to issues of more general interest to historians.

Using Artifacts to Understand History

Material culture has been most prominent in recent technological history in the work of scholars who use the close study of artifacts to answer historical questions about work, skills, and design. Historians interested in industrial work have undertaken some of the most interesting analyses of the material culture of technology, examining tools and machines closely for wear marks and other indications of use to reconstruct the lives and skills of the men and women who operated them. They have examined the design of machines to gain a better understanding of managerial oversight and labor relations; they have examined machines themselves to understand the choices made by their designers, and to understand technological skills and knowledge, a key theme in the history of technology.

Some of the central questions in the history of American technology have been addressed with the use of material culture. Close examination of muskets made by Eli Whitney (1765–1825) has debunked the widely held belief that they were produced using interchangeable parts, as Whitney had claimed. William Kelly's (1811–1888) claim, accepted for more than 150 years, that he had invented the steel converter before Henry Bessemer (1813–1898), was proved false by close examination of his surviving apparatus.

In a few cases, historical artifacts or copies of them have been operated to determine something of the knowledge and skills of their creators and users. Replicating historical artifacts and using them is a long-standing tradition in archaeology, where it has fostered a better understanding of everything from flint-knapping (the making of stone tools) to mastodon hunting. Historians have operated historic lathes, looms, and other machines to determine levels of skill and attentiveness they demanded of the men and women who operated them, making more complex notions of "deskilling" based on other kinds of sources.

Understanding Technological Artifacts: Theoretical Issues

Many of the significant theoretical issues in technology studies incorporate consideration of material culture. Politics, style, and the social construction of technology have placed artifacts at the center of contemporary theoretical debates. Recent work examining technology and gender, especially the *consumption junction* of design, marketing, and use, has suggested some of the ways that technology has shaped people's lives. Political theorist Langdon Winner's 1980 seminal article "Do Artifacts Have Politics?" raised a central question for the material culture of technology. To what extent, he asked, are political choices embedded in the design of technological artifacts? His example of the way that bridges on the Long Island Expressway were designed to keep buses from Long Island parks have led to many studies of the political design of landscapes and architecture, especially vernacular and factory architecture. More generally, his question has been applied to studies of the ways politics shape artifacts and the way those artifacts in turn intentionally or unintentionally shape society.

The physical design of technological objects is another issue that has attracted considerable attention, following on art historian Jules David Prown's (1980) discussions of style in domestic material culture. Physical laws, students of technological style argue, do not determine the shape of technological artifacts. Rather, they argue, these artifacts reflect styles in the same way that decorative arts do. Historian of science Eric Schatzberg's (1999) analysis of the shift from wood to metal airplanes makes material choice a key element of technological style.

In recent years, the "social construction of technology" approach, first outlined by sociologist Trevor Pinch and social scientist Wiebe Bijker (1987), has been central to the historiography of technology. Followers of this approach have focused on the "interpretive flexibility" of technological artifacts. Artifact design is "contingent," not determined, they argue, and thus interest groups of all sorts shape technological artifacts. Technological artifacts, according to this school of thought, mean different things to different groups; they have no intrinsic meaning, though, over time, as society comes to consensus on a technology, interpretive flexibility decreases, and the artifact—its meaning and use—becomes more stable.

Historian of technology Ruth Schwartz Cowan (1987) has developed this approach further, using the notion of the consumption junction. The *consumption junction* is the point in a technological network where a technological artifact, its producer, and its consumer interact. Both designer and consumer are enmeshed in a web of social relations that shape their interactions. Cowan puts the consumer and his or her choices at the center and urges that the meaning and value of technological artifacts be understood as issues of use, not merely design or production.

Cowan's work, and that of those who follow her, have helped to bring the study of technological artifacts into the mainstream of the study of twentieth-century American history. The examination of artifacts standing at the nexus of gender, race, and class suggests an intersection between historians of technology and others interested in American social and cultural history. In part because of its long-standing interest in artifacts, the history of technology can bring new perspectives to understanding the past.

Steven Lubar

See also Agricultural Work and Labor; Air and Space Transportation; Anthropology and Archaeology; Automobiles and Automobility; Bathrooms; Computers and Information Technology; Consumerism and Consumption; Disability and Disability Studies; Factory and Industrial Work and Labor; Food and Foodways; Graphic Design; Human Body; Industrial Design; Kitchens and Pantries; Land Transportation; Medical Instruments; Office Work and Labor; Print Culture; Service Industry Work and Labor; Time, Timekeeping, and Timepieces; Tools, Implements, and Instruments; Water Transportation; Work and Labor

References and Further Reading
Basalla, George. 1988. *The Evolution of Technology.* Cambridge, UK: Cambridge University Press.
Bijker, Wiebe E., Thomas P. Hughes, and Trevor F. Pinch. 1987. *The Social Construction of Technological Systems: New Directions in the Sociology and History of Technology.* Cambridge, MA: MIT Press.
Glassie, Henry. 1977. "Meaningful Things and Appropriate Myths: The Artifact's Place in American Studies." *Prospects* 3: 1–49.
Lubar, Steven, and W. David Kingery, eds. 1993. *History from Things: Essays on Material Culture.* Washington, DC: Smithsonian Institution Press.
Prown, Jules David. 1980. "Style as Evidence." *Winterthur Portfolio* 15 (3): 197–210.
Pye, David. 1968. *The Nature and Art of Workmanship.* Cambridge, UK: Cambridge University Press.
Schatzberg, Eric. 1999. *Wings of Wood, Wings of Metal: Cultural and Technical Choice in American Airplane Materials, 1914–1945.* Princeton, NJ: Princeton University Press.
Winner, Langdon. 1980. "Do Artifacts Have Politics?" *Daedalus* 109 (1): 121–136.

Textiles

Textiles (structures made of interlaced fiber) have played an important role in American history and culture beginning in the precontact, fur trade, and colonial eras. The most distinctive developments and traditions in textile production emerged with industrialization. New technologies and inexpensive cloth production simultaneously spurred on utopian visions and prolonged slavery, democratized handwork, and led to the explosion of expressive forms such as quilts. In the late nineteenth and early twentieth centuries, an anti-industrial craft revival built on an imagined simpler colonial and native past was popular. In the twenty-first century, American textiles are merging the handmade and the commercial. Increasingly, however, the textile world is internationalized.

Precontact, Fur Trade, and Colonial Eras
Strong textile traditions existed on the North American continent well before European contact. The basket makers working around 1000 AD made sophisticated containers and garments in what is now the southwestern United States. European explorers' reports included admiring descriptions of natives' decorated clothing. During the fur trade era, beaver pelts (used in stylish European hats) were traded for warm woolen blankets and other cloth. Natives transformed such materials into syncretic forms—trade beads and imported fabric were used in American Indian beadwork, for example, but the beadwork evinces Native aesthetics.

In the colonial period, most American textiles came from Europe. "Homespun" goods were briefly fashionable as a sign of resistance during the Revolutionary War (1775–1783), but it was never the case that every family produced its own fabrics, though home spinning and weaving of wool and linen were undertaken. An abundance of cloth usually indicated a wealthy household, as did the presence of decorative textiles; only well-off women had time to produce crewel embroidery (e.g., on bed hangings) or other forms of ornamentation. Well into the first decades of the nineteenth century, European-styled yet sparely wrought needlework samplers and pictures were framed and displayed as markers of a genteel education, since refined embroidery was taught at female academies that only prosperous families could afford.

Industrialization

The 1793 invention of the cotton gin was simultaneous with the opening of the first factory to process cotton yarn. Soon after, gins were powered by steam engines. Southern planters found it cost effective to replace tobacco with cotton, resulting in its precipitous rise from 140,000 pounds in 1791 to 35 million in 1800. This decision reinvigorated the faltering slavery system; the "need" for more slaves increased as this labor-intensive industry grew (the United States was growing three-quarters of the world's cotton by the middle of the century). This in turn fed much of the North-South tension that led to the Civil War (1861–1865) and affected subsequent international allegiances. To help supply its own textile industry, England, despite its own antislavery laws, threw much of its support to the cotton-producing Confederacy.

A utopian vision lay behind the early textile industry. The first large-scale mills were built in Lowell, Massachusetts, in the 1830s. Determined to avoid the English model of "dark satanic mills," these entrepreneurs recruited young (ages 15–25), single women from New England farming communities. Envisioned as a revolving temporary workforce rather than a permanent underclass, the women were housed in supervised board-inghouses, and many participated in self-improvement activities in nonworking hours. This experiment lasted only a few decades but was a telling part of the American tradition of self (re)invention. Notably, many utopian and religious separatist communities, including the Shakers, Mormons, and Harmonists, were also successful textile manufacturers. Just as idealistic was the "mulberry tree craze" of the 1830s. Excited by the success of the cotton mills, thousands of people invested in the trees that silkworms feed on, hoping to share in the prosperity of a nation that could produce its own luxury fiber. This widespread speculation was a failure, for sericulture proved to be too labor intensive and climate sensitive. Successful American silk factories, relying on imported raw materials, did arise later in the century.

Decorative textile practices also flourished with industrialization. Embroidery was significantly democratized in the 1830s with inventions that enabled the reproduction of colored patterns and the widespread dissemination of printed instructions; one no longer needed personal instruction to produce fashionable needlework. By mid-century, many forms of "fancywork" were not only popular but common enough to serve as hallmarks of middle-class status. Most fancywork was used to make small, ostensibly functional items that decorated the home. Techniques ranged from beadwork to (human) hairwork to crochet. The last, introduced to North America by Irish immigrants, was relatively simple to do and was worked with the ubiquitous cotton thread. It was thus a "democratic" type of embellishment, sometimes referred to as "American lace."

The quilt, considered by many the distinctively American textile form, was similarly dependent on industrial technologies.

The combination of the everyday and the special is evident in women's expressive textile work. The use of plain and printed cottons and silk and wool embroidery thread in this mid-nineteenth-century "album quilt" created in Baltimore, Maryland, functioned as a personal memory device as well as a form of women's art. (Peter Harholdt/Corbis)

A small number of true "scrap" quilts had always existed, and some fine quilts were produced by wealthy women (or their slaves) before 1830, but quilt production exploded with the abundance of inexpensive printed cotton cloth. Quilt making spread to every level of society by mid-century, and unique styles and traditions developed. A syncretic form, American quilts were influenced by (among other things) African appliqué traditions introduced by slaves. Quilts became an important part of the nation's social life, serving as instruments of community cohesion (e.g., when church or organization members made a "presentation" quilt or raised money through quilt raffles) or, in the form of "album" quilts, as personal memory devices.

The woven coverlet tradition that is often thought of as colonial was also most significant in the mid-nineteenth century. While some coverlets were made by housewives on hand looms, the distinctive pictorial coverlets that featured printed names and images were produced by professional (mostly male) weavers from the Mid-Atlantic states who worked on technologically sophisticated Jacquard looms.

Late Nineteenth-Century Aesthetic Reform

Prevalent textile practices changed as the nation became truly a culture of consumption rather than production. In some instances the products reflected the commercialism of the broader society. The most popular type of quilt was no longer a practical cotton bed cover but a decorative silk "throw," typically worked in "crazy" patterning. The then-thriving domestic silk industry produced a relatively cheap product, and many quilts were made from precut scraps provided by manufacturers of tie and dress fabrics. These same companies also published patterns and instructions for luxurious-looking but affordable silk embroidery. Popular textiles also began to reflect nostalgia for the seemingly nobler preindustrial era. Following the model of the English Arts and Crafts Movement, American aesthetic reformers began to look to older textile forms as examples of good design. "Decorative arts societies" produced new versions of these quality products, usually by employing needy individuals. By the turn of the twentieth century, many of these societies turned specifically to the American past for their aesthetic models. The founders of the Deerfield, Massachusetts, Blue and White Society (1896) adapted patterns and techniques from colonial crewelwork and employed local women to stitch their line of commercially viable "art" textiles. Other supposedly early American textile forms were also produced in this way. (Some, such as hooked rugs and patchwork quilts, actually dated from a post-colonial, industrialized period, but Colonial Revivalists did not make such distinctions.) Well into the 1930s, the production of "old-fashioned" textiles was encouraged as suitable work for "underdeveloped" people. Reformers helped start "home industries" in rural areas like Maine and Appalachia with the idea that they would raise the general level of taste and the area's standard of living. Appalachian mountain coverlets, touted as colonial products, were among those that found a ready market.

The same nostalgia also fed a marked interest in handmade native textiles. Once the West had been "won" and Indians confined to reservations, Americans romanticized the "primitive" native past. Coupled with the belief that Indians were a "vanishing race," this resulted by the turn of the century in a collecting boom of Indian baskets and beadwork. Ironically, many of the most collectible forms were actually new products that had evolved in response to changing native lifeways and new markets. Navajo rugs are a case in point. Prior to government intervention and extensive Anglo settlement in the Southwest, the Navajo had woven blankets and wearable textiles. Navajo rug production only began with the intervention of nonnative traders, who introduced Oriental textiles as models of saleable products. These new forms were only one example of the fluorescence of Indian art in this period, despite—or in part as a response to—the stress Native cultures were experiencing. In turn, Native design and craft came to be seen as iconically American. The Boy Scouts and Campfire Girls (both founded in 1910) taught Indian-style beadwork and basketry, making them seem part of an American childhood, and commercial manufacturers like the Pendleton Company positioned their "Indian design" blankets as nationally resonant symbols.

Colonial Revival interest in folk textiles continued until World War II (1939–1945), but decorative textile traditions increasingly followed commercial models. "Traditional" cotton quilts were revived in the 1920s and 1930s, but most of the new generation of quilters relied on preprinted patterns; it was even possible to piece a predesigned quilt top and send it away to be stitched. Newly popular samplers now came in kits, demanded little sewing skill, and contained sentimental homilies and romantic iconography. A new type of professional woman textile entrepreneur arose to market these items. Individuals like Anne Orr (1875–1946), needlework editor of *Good Housekeeping* for twenty years, and quilt expert Carrie Hall (1866–1955) were media figures (they even appeared on radio programs) and ran successful pattern and design companies. Their influence on contemporary American home decor was sizable. In other cases textile manufacturers continued to encourage forms of handwork that utilized their new and easy-to-work materials. The Dennison Company, for example, touted its newly developed crepe paper as a "valuable fabric" for craft projects and simple household furnishings. Felt was promoted in a similar manner.

Modern and Postmodern Textiles

In the mid-twentieth century, American textile manufacturing became associated with informal, "easygoing" fabrics. The United States was the unquestioned leader in the ready-to-wear industry by the 1930s and was especially identified with leisure wear and casualness. The "American" or "California look" in fashion (which was heavily influenced by Hollywood) went hand in hand with bright, cheerful fabrics and playful iconography (e.g., as seen in Hawaiian shirts) or the kind of sturdy denim worn by cowboys and lumberjacks. In addition, American industry was the leader in the postwar development of easy-care synthetics and "miracle fibers."

The United States was also at the forefront of the craft revival of the 1960s, in which the particular expressive qualities of fiber were rediscovered and thoughtfully explored. This revival was influenced by the civil rights movement, since native and minority groups began to reclaim and reinvigorate their unique textile traditions, and by the feminist movement, which looked with fresh eyes on the often underappreciated woman-made items. Over the next few decades industrial designers and individual artists collaborated; figures like Jack Lenor Larsen (1927–) articulated the idea of the "art fabric" (*fiber art* and *art quilt* are roughly parallel terms) and manufactured textiles used ubiquitously in commercial products like airplane upholstery. Larsen and other late twentieth-century designers drew eclectically from worldwide textile and craft traditions. Twenty-first-century textiles are marked by an even stronger synthesis of hand and commercial technologies and now often represent global production partnerships. Increasingly, "American textiles" are in truth "international textiles," as world travel, artistic cross-fertilization, and globalized manufacturing practices make national boundaries less meaningful in this form of material culture.

Beverly Gordon

See also Children's Dress; Decorative Arts; Design History and American Design; Dress, Accessories, and Fashion; Folklore and Folklife; Handicraft and Artisanship; Native America; Technology

References and Further Reading

Berlo, Janet Catherine, and Patricia Cox Crews, with Carolyn Ducey, Jonathan Holstein, and Michael James. 2003. *Wild by Design: Two Hundred Years of Innovation and Artistry in American Quilts*. Lincoln, NE: International Quilt Study Center at the University of Nebraska–Lincoln; Seattle: University of Washington Press.

Constantine, Mildred, and Jack Lenor Larsen. 1973. *Beyond Craft: The Art Fabric*. New York: Van Nostrand Reinhold.

Dockstader, Frederick J. 1978. *Weaving Arts of the North American Indian*. New York: Crowell.

Ferrero, Pat, Elaine Hedges, and Julie Silber. 1987. *Hearts and Hands: The Influence of Women & Quilts on American Society*. San Francisco: Quilt Digest Press.

Gordon, Beverly. 1980. *Shaker Textile Arts*. Hanover, NH: University Press of New England.

Gordon, Beverly. 1998. "Spinning Wheels, Samplers, and the Modern Priscilla: The Images and Paradoxes of Colonial Revival Needlework." *Winterthur Portfolio* 33 (2/3): 163–194.

Kent, Kate Peck. 1983. *Prehistoric Textiles of the Southwest*. Santa Fe, NM: School of American Research.

Kiracofe, Roderick, Mary Huff, and Elizabeth Johnson. 1993. *The American Quilt: A History of Cloth and Comfort, 1750–1950*. New York: Clarkson Potter.

Macdonald, Anne L. 1988. *No Idle Hands: The Social History of American Knitting*. New York: Ballantine Books.

Montgomery, Florence M. 1984. *Textiles in America, 1650–1870: A Dictionary Based on Original Documents: Prints and Paintings, Commercial Records, American Merchants' Papers, Shopkeepers' Advertisements, and Pattern Books with Original Swatches of Cloth*. New York: W. W. Norton.

Ring, Betty. 1993. *Girlhood Embroidery: American Samplers & Pictorial Needlework, 1650–1850*. 2 vols. New York: Alfred A. Knopf.

Sheumaker, Helen. 2007. *Love Entwined: The Curious History of Hairwork*. Philadelphia: University of Pennsylvania Press.

Vincent, Margaret. 1987. *The Ladies' Work Table: Domestic Needlework in Nineteenth-Century America*. Allentown, PA: Allentown Art Museum.

Weissman, Judith Reiter, and Wendy Lavitt. 1987. *Labors of Love: America's Textiles and Needlework, 1650–1930*. New York: Alfred A. Knopf.

Wheat, Joe Ben. 2003. *Blanket Weaving in the Southwest*, ed. Ann Lane Hedlund. Tucson: University of Arizona Press.

Time, Timekeeping, and Timepieces

The apprehension of time has attracted the attention of philosophers, physicists, musicologists, and literary critics. Perhaps the most significant body of scholarly literature on the subject has emerged from distinguished anthropologists and sociologists such as Pierre Bourdieu (1930–2002), Emile Durkheim (1858–1917), Clifford Geertz (1926–2006), Anthony Giddens, Marcel Mauss (1872–1950), and Eviatar Zerubavel. They have denaturalized time and have reminded us that it is not an immutable category. Societies and individuals construct temporal systems that order and make sense of experience. These temporal systems provide points onto which individuals can fix meaning, organize experience, and synchronize and coordinate behavior. As such they are subject to historical processes. The fashioning of temporal communities—and the processes of negotiation, resistance, and accommodation to these temporalities—provide a lens through which scholars can illuminate and reinterpret social, cultural, and political events, patterns, and systems. While we have a sophisticated literature on the time of the non-Western "other," there are but a handful of historical studies of the temporal systems and rhythms of the West and of the United States.

The almanac, calendar, clock, and watch are the technological manifestations of the dominant temporal systems that Americans have followed since the colonial period. During the colonial period most Americans were attuned to nature's time, as manifested in both the seasons and the sun's movement across the sky. Many communities read the sun's time from a sundial, which was known as "local time." Each community's time differed from its neighbor's, except in those rare instances when two communities shared the same latitude. Thus New York City was a few degrees east and 10 minutes and 27 seconds ahead of Baltimore. The few people, such as surveyors, who needed to know the exact time, had to refer to the stars (for sidereal time) to correct for the slight tilt in the earth's rotation around the sun, which resulted in days that were longer or shorter than twenty-four hours. Almanacs, the most common timepiece during the colonial period, published *ephemerides*, which provided the equations of time necessary for correcting solar time so that the "true time" could be ascertained. The almanac prevailed until the advent of machine production, rapid communications and transportation, and consumer capitalism created the conditions that at once stimulated demand for mechanical timepieces and made the mass production of clocks and watches possible. Almanacs codified seasons, tides, new moons, solar eclipses, holy days, college commencements, court dates, and other such marks of time that the natural world, the church, and the state mandated.

During the first decade of the nineteenth century, mass-produced and therefore inexpensive wooden clocks were used alongside, rather than replaced, almanacs. Over several decades improvements in the manufacture of clocks, along with dramatic changes in the American economy, ushered in the regularity of artificial, mechanical time. Americans' behavior began to change; they were less time obedient and more time disciplined. The former required bells, drums, whistles, and whips, each employed to communicate that it was time to work, or attend church services. Time discipline, on the other hand, gave individuals more autonomy: They knew at what hour they should be in their places. So, with the help of published schedules, public clocks, and above all watches, they marshaled their time accordingly in order to make the train or begin work. In the 1870s, at about the same time that the wall and pocket calendar appeared and trumped the almanac for good, the machine production and mass marketing of watches heralded the triumph of hours, minutes, and seconds over seasons and sabbaths in the widely variegated time consciousness of Americans.

Clocks and Industrialization

Few colonists owned clocks, in large part because few artisans had the skills necessary for such intricate production and because the price of imported clocks was prohibitive. But this changed during the first few decades of the nineteenth century, when several Americans revolutionized the production of clocks. The Willard brothers—Aaron (1757–1844/48), Simon (1753–1848), Ephraim (1755–?), and Benjamin Jr. (1743–1803)— having learned the craft from their father Benjamin in North Grafton, Massachusetts, perfected the shelf clock and the "banjo" clock by 1802 and lowered the costs of production by using wood rather than metals to manufacture the movements. The wooden movements ran for thirty hours without winding, rather than eight days, as did more expensive clocks. Other artisans, especially in Connecticut, began manufacturing wooden clocks as well; they followed the innovations of Eli Terry (1772–1852), Seth Thomas (1785–1859), and Silas Hoadley (1786–1870), who pioneered the use of water-powered machinery to make interchangeable parts for clocks. The machine production of wooden movements transformed the clockmaking industry: No longer artisanal, it was in the vanguard

of the industrial revolution. Further innovations in production, such as Chauncey Jerome (1793–1868) and his brother Noble's (1800–1860) perfection of the method for making weatherproof brass movements in the 1840s, the substitution of coiled springs for falling weights for power in the 1840s, and the annual changes in clock designs beginning in the 1870s, extended the reach of the clock.

Due to the plummeting price, more than half the households in the state of Connecticut and New York State's Hudson Valley came to own a clock, usually purchased from an itinerant peddler. Southerners acquired their clocks somewhat later than did their northern counterparts, but by the 1840s more than half of southern nonslave households, both rural and urban, also owned clocks. Clocks were status symbols, denoting gentility, self-control, and individualism, which were all values at a premium in the early republic. While mostly acquired for decorative and symbolic purposes, clocks soon transformed the ways that rural and urban Americans did their work, synchronized their activities, and experienced the passage of time.

Overseers and masters controlled and motivated their enslaved workforce through a combined use of the clock and the whip; farmers began to measure productivity as the relationship between their expenditure of time and money in relation to their profits; and bankers, mill owners, post office officials, and a host of others began to keep set hours, post schedules, and impose fines for tardiness. These and myriad other changes catalyzed by the widespread dissemination of clocks heralded the arrival of time discipline and are among the finest examples of how the sheer presence of material goods can change consciousness, as well as practices and experiences. The authority for time, then, as historian Michael O'Malley (1996) has argued, shifted from God to man, from nature to machine.

Clock Towers

Contemporaneous with domestic and office clocks was the appearance of public timepieces, typically clock towers, but not infrequently technologies such as bells and time balls meant to communicate the arrival of a certain time, such as noon or nine in the evening. Church societies, local authorities, and voluntary groups raised subscriptions for the purchase, erection, and maintenance of these expensive symbols of a community's commitment to punctuality and order. Bells were less expensive and were part of the older habit of time obedience, and so many communities relied on them to provide the

This circa 1860 clock tower, constructed as part of the Boott Cotton Mills (built 1835) in Lowell, Massachusetts, was a reminder to employees of the need for timeliness, as well as a marker of time itself. (Historic American Engineering Record/Library of Congress)

public with its sense of time. A visual, rather than an aural, time signal with which more than two dozen American cities experimented was the *time ball*—a large painted sphere hoisted to the top of a pole perched on the tallest and most visible building and released via a telegraphic signal daily, except Sundays, at noon. Public clocks, on towers, streets, and the facades of buildings, in railroad stations and office buildings, dominated however, and through their presence further demanded of citizens that they interiorize clock time. As of the writing of this essay no systematic survey of the number and kinds of public clocks has been undertaken, and so the geography of public timepieces in the United States, which has been so well mapped out for Europe, remains terra incognita.

Watches

Individuals, who possess highly variable senses of time, found it necessary to conform to newly defined, homogenous, and set time. *Watches* are tools that enable the coordination of self with public schedules, expectations, and timetables. Typically people rely on watches, rather than on internal clocks, to achieve time discipline. Scholars have not yet determined how many Americans owned watches. Before the middle of the nineteenth century the vast majority of watches were imported from England, Switzerland, or France. No more than 1,000 watches were made in the United States before the 1850s, when watchmakers and mechanics at the American Watch Company in Waltham, Massachusetts, perfected the process and machinery for the mass production of watches. The rampant demand for Waltham watches among Union soldiers during the Civil War (1861–1865) boosted the firms' profits and reputation, and a score of rivals sprang up, seeking to capture a share of the market for watches. Only a few companies survived the heated competition of the 1870s and 1880s, including Elgin, Hamilton, and Ingersoll. To dispose of the surplus, companies innovated in advertising; exported hundreds of thousands of watches to Europe, Latin America, and Asia; and cut their prices so dramatically that their profit margins were minuscule. Raising the tide of watches that flooded the United States was the active secondhand trade. Men tucked their watches into a pocket, attached to a chain and fob; women wore theirs on chains around their necks, pinned as brooches to their bodices, or tucked into specially tailored pockets near the waistband of their dresses. Watch "wristlets" or bracelets were in vogue for women in the 1890s, and American soldiers began to wear their watches on their wrists after the United States entered World War I in 1917. By the 1950s the pocket watch was obsolete. To this day, however, watches tantalizingly combine utilitarian and ornamental impulses and are among the most personal of possessions, willed as keepsakes for children, and cherished far beyond their monetary worth.

Industrial Needs and Government Standards

Through much of the nineteenth century, local time, usually known through the use of a sundial and ephemeris but in some places provided by astronomical observatories, prevailed, thus confusing many a train passenger and shipping agent. It was only near the end of 1883 that standard time and time zones were introduced by a consortium of railroad companies and adopted throughout most of the United States. Daylight saving time, a system meant to extend the amount of daylight during winter months, was first imposed on Americans by an act of Congress during World War I, and it was

not until well into the 1960s that it became the norm for most of the nation.

Alexis McCrossen

See also Agricultural Work and Labor; Cities and Towns; Factory and Industrial Work and Labor; Mill Towns; Technology

References and Further Reading
Landes, David S. 2001 (1983). *Revolution in Time: Clocks and the Making of the Modern World*. Cambridge, MA: Harvard University Press.
McCrossen, Alexis. 2000. *Holy Day, Holiday: The American Sunday*. Ithaca, NY: Cornell University Press.
O'Malley, Michael. 1996. *Keeping Watch: A History of American Time*. Washington, DC: Smithsonian Institution Press.
Stephens, Carlene E., and the Smithsonian Institution. 2005. *On Time: How America Has Learned to Live by the Clock*. New York: Bulfinch Press.
Thompson, E. P. 1967. "Time, Work-Discipline and Industrial Capitalism," *Past and Present* 38: 56–97.

Tools, Implements, and Instruments

Tools, implements, and *instruments* are the objects or systems made by and with which humans shape their environments. This category of material culture implies portability, specialization, and refinement of function and purpose and encompasses a broad range of items, from written language to hammers, from chemicals to needles, and from saxophones to levers. The words *tool, instrument,* and *implement* suggest devices of relative simplicity, as opposed to the words *machine* or *technology* that connote relative complexity and perhaps the ability to accomplish multiple tasks at once. Yet even the simplest tools are also machines and technologies, because they augment or redirect the force applied by a human user. While most implements are material, both tools and instruments do not have to be. Language or other technical systems are tools, and laws are often understood to be instruments. Together, tools, implements, and instruments extend the power of humans to explore, improve, rearrange, inhabit, and destroy the physical world. They are basic building blocks of material culture: the things by which all other things are made or unmade, the methods by which processes of greater complexity are accomplished. They are objects that effect critical transformations in raw materials, such as the transition from a "natural" found material to a finished, man-made thing.

Tools

Scholars have argued that the use of tools was the dividing line between humans and other species, since the evolution of opposable thumbs combined with the use of tools made humans highly flexible and adaptable. Tools, by this logic, are extensions of the human body. Today, some researchers challenge this context for understanding tools, but the history of tools remains strongly influenced by the findings of archaeologists and anthropologists. Early definitions of what constituted a tool stressed a similar mode of producing the tool (e.g., all early ax heads from a particular time and place are chipped in nearly the same manner), but even that dividing line is blurred by the argument that some naturally occurring materials can be used effectively as tools with little or no additional shaping.

Some of the first tools used in the Americas were spear points made of stone that are at least 13,000 years old. These points have become a central object in researchers' attempts to date the population of North and South America by humans, figure out the connections between peoples of the Western and Eastern hemispheres, and trace the

spread of different techniques for making and using tools from one population group to another and through generations. Early tools were made of rock, and probably also made of wood, bone, and shell, although tools made of these last three materials have rarely survived in the historical record. As with peoples of the ancient Middle East and Mediterranean, the indigenous peoples in the Americas made some tools out of common and precious metals. With the invention and adoption of metal tools came a revolution in the manufacture of tools, as tools could be cast by pouring molten metals into a mold.

The development of steam engines powered by coal in eighteenth-century England set in motion a host of innovations in multipart tools (or mechanical devices) in the nineteenth century. Tools could be run not only by human power but also by horsepower, waterpower, steam power, and, by the late nineteenth century, electricity. As more tools depended upon these other sources of energy, and as new materials such as plastics and improved metal alloys were developed, highly specialized tools proliferated. At the same time, after the American Civil War (1861–1865), mass production used cheaper materials to produce standardized tools.

In the twentieth century, scholars have studied tools to learn about people who left little trace in the written historical record. Pre–Civil War tools were made, distributed, used, repaired, and occasionally discarded by a limited number of people in local or regional networks, and the unique markings or shapes they bear can provide a window into the daily workings of entire communities that are otherwise obscure.

Implements

An *implement* is a tool that is an essential part of completing a given job. Implements outfit or equip a person or place and include kitchen utensils, furnishings for offices, weapons of war, farming equipment, and accessories for the disabled, as well as other similar categories of material artifacts. They can be obviously task oriented, like a fork, or they can finish something less obviously task oriented, as when a priest's vestments complete the visual cues to his authority and prepare him for the performance of sacred rites. Due to their association with a general category of knowledge or activity, implements function as symbols of that knowledge or activity. As with tools, implements sometimes have distinct gender, class, racial, ethnic, religious, geographic, or other associations connected to their possession or use, and thus help establish boundaries and norms of behavior in society.

Instruments

Instruments are tools associated with a single profession, occupation, field, or discipline. Instruments often require highly specialized knowledge and refined skill sets to deploy them in a culturally and/or socially appropriate or expected manner. Aeronautical, agricultural, dental, drawing, electronic, medical, musical, meteorological, navigational, scientific, surgical, surveying, and ultrasonic instruments are defined by the associated expertise, whether that expertise is knowledge or a skill set. Each of these categories of instruments (and more) can be further sub-

Carpentry, as with other tradescrafts, required an array of specialized tools and knowledge. Here, young men learn the carpentry trade at the Berry School in Georgia, circa 1915. (Library of Congress)

divided into specific subcategories, which are subdivided into specific objects. For example, four categories of musical instruments exist: wind, electronic, percussion, or stringed; stringed instruments include violins, violas, pianos, and harps, which all are made with taut cords that are strummed, plucked, or hit.

Instruments, as this system of classification suggests, help humans accomplish and organize detailed work, access information, or create novel expressions of human values. More than tools or implements, instruments contribute to the construction of social and cultural boundaries and mark status. In doing so, they both create and reflect attributes like accuracy and compartmentalization that humans associate with modernity.

Tools, implements, and instruments provide information about changing technologies, but sometimes there are cultural reasons for how tools develop over time. They can all be appropriated for unusual or unexpected uses in the service of social and/or cultural commentary or resistance, a process that both affirms societal norms and seeks to redefine them. And they all function abstractly, embodying knowledge, and at the same time concretely, as the human body adapts them and adapts *to* them.

Katherine Stebbins McCaffrey

See also Agricultural Work and Labor; Computers and Information Technology; Factory and Industrial Work and Labor; Handicraft and Artisanship; Medical Instruments; Music and Musical Instruments; Native America; Office Work and Labor; Service Industry Work and Labor; Technology; Work and Labor

References and Further Reading

Baird, Davis. 2004. *Thing Knowledge: A Philosophy of Scientific Instruments.* Berkeley: University of California Press.

Childe, Vere Gordon. 1944. *The Story of Tools.* London: Cobbett Publishing Co.

Rolt, L. T. C. 1986. *Tools for the Job: A History of Machine Tools to 1950.* London: H.M.S.O.

Tourism and Travel

Tourism and *travel* are related processes defined by separation from home, the workplace, and from what is personally familiar to individuals as they journey across spatial distance. The reasons for travel are many: business and family obligations, the quest for improved health, leisure and recreational pursuits, and—especially when travel is dedicated to touring—the desire to discover and experience other cultures, scenic landscapes, and historic landmarks. The material culture of tourism and travel may be categorized in three ways: (1) the means of transporting and supporting people and their belongings; (2) the objects providing basic facts and sensory descriptions about unknown locations, attractions, and peoples, transforming alien landscape and cultures into consumable products and inducing desires to experience them through the process of touring; and (3) the objects that store and evoke the memory of travel and tourist encounters for an undetermined span of time.

Travelers' Transportation

Besides walking and riding on horseback, specialized horse-drawn vehicles met the needs of travelers well into the nineteenth century. Two-wheeled chaises transported affluent travelers in early America, but by the end of the eighteenth century stagecoaches provided a common means of carrying passengers and luggage. Early coaches had exposed sides with roll-up leather blinds to protect passengers from inclement weather. Metal and wood springs offered little cushioning from the jolts from rough roads. By the mid-1800s, the innovative Concord coach, with its leather suspension system, upholstered seats, and sliding glass windows, brought fame to New Hampshire carriage makers Lewis Downing (1792–1873) and J. Stephens Abbot (1804–1871) as it increased passengers' comfort. Even in better coaches, travel progressed at a slow pace, usually covering little more than nine miles per hour.

Steam power improved water and land travel during the nineteenth century. Steamships and rail cars began as simple, uncomfortable means of travel. By the 1850s, well-appointed rooms greeted even middle-class passengers, with upholstered seats, oil lamps, carpets, and wallpapers. Some railroads provided luxury amenities into the twentieth century. The New York Central Railroad, which traveled the Hudson River Valley, kept pace with modern design by hiring industrial designer Henry Dreyfuss (1904–1972) to create the Twentieth Century Limited. This luxury rail line, which debuted in 1938, featured Art Deco styling. Passenger car interiors offered areas for conversation and reading and a bar for socializing. At the same time, airlines began to attract increasing numbers of travelers. While airline interiors were modest compared to rail cars, the time-saving transportation they provided made airlines desirable, but they were not widely affordable.

Also competing with railroads, automobiles offered travelers the freedom to go where and when they wished. Following World War I (1914–1918), automobile ownership in the United States increased. Auto tourists could travel on miles of expanded and maintained roads and stop to enjoy sites and nature as they pleased. Enhancing auto touring was specially designed camping equipment, such as tents that connected to automobiles to provide convenient sleeping and eating quarters for those who liked

"roughing it." Trailers and mobile homes equipped with cooking appliances, tables and chairs, beds, and eventually bathroom facilities brought homelike amenities on the road. The Airstream trailer, first marketed in 1936 by Wally Byam (1896–1962), set a high standard. His streamlined aluminum trailers, still manufactured today, feature luxurious interiors.

Commercial air travel connecting Americans to each other and to Europe began in earnest after Charles Lindbergh's (1902–1974) transatlantic flight in 1927. Though passenger travel by dirigible (also called *airship* or *zeppelin*) was available in the 1920s, it was not until 1939, when Pan American Airlines' luxurious Yankee Clipper crossed the ocean to Ireland, that transatlantic travel became commercially viable. Nevertheless, the era of international passenger air service would have to wait until after World War II (1939–1945). Then, American airlines shortened travel time within North America as well as to the other continents (save Antarctica). Commercial airlines promoted tourism through posters, guidebooks, and television commercials. Airports, in the 1920s merely hangars and basic shelters, evolved to accommodate both the necessity of airplanes and jets and increased passenger traffic. To offset the stress of traveling, airport designers have increasingly exploited space, light, and the lure of consumer goods and even exhibits of local crafts and museum collections to occupy waiting travelers' time.

Amenities

Taverns, inns, hotels, and restaurants have furnished basic amenities to travelers. Inns and taverns offering shared board and sleeping spaces appeared in the American colonies during the first half of the seventeenth century. Some colonial governments required the establishment of inns. In 1644, Connecticut enacted a law ordering towns "to keepe an Ordinary, for pruisio [praise] and lodgeing" of passengers and strangers. In the early nineteenth century hotels began replacing inns and taverns in commercial centers. Hotels differed from their predecessors by offering private rooms, elegantly decorated lobbies, and halls for gatherings and entertainment. By the early twentieth century, railroad companies partnered with government and private business to construct hotels to encourage the tourist trade. The Northern Pacific Railroad joined with the Yellowstone Park Association to build the Old Faithful Inn in 1904. It appealed to tourists with its usage of local materials: rough log construction, Navajo rugs, and rustic furniture. In addition to commodious hotels, smaller "motels" (motor lodges), tourist cottages, and cabins appeared along the nation's roadways. Some imitated Indian *tipis* (tepees), miniature colonial homes, and other fanciful forms, which connoted to travelers the discovery of exotic lands, people, and a distant past.

Signs to guide travelers have been essential. Several years after Connecticut ordered towns to establish inns, it passed legislation in 1672 requiring the inns to erect signs. Until the second quarter of the nineteenth century, innkeepers generally used imagery like lions or a rising sun as identification. Some iconography referred directly to the accommodations. Horses indicated the presence of stables; punch bowls and wineglasses signified libations. Following the Revolution, patriotic eagles and state seals became common and contributed to the formation of a national identity. As the American population shifted in the nineteenth century from a visual culture to a textual culture, inn signs changed. Frequently just the name of the inn or hotel appeared, painted in gold across a black background. Travel and tourist signs proliferated in the twentieth century, the

highway billboard being one of the most noticeable. Yet the plethora of signs has frequently detracted from tourist sites. Vermont, for example, passed legislation in 1968 banning roadway signs to ensure a more visually pleasing landscape.

Luggage and storage containers evolved with modes of travel. Leather satchels that could be slung over horses held personal belongings prior to the widespread use of coaches. The stagecoach provided space for small trunks and boxes and advanced the development of such articles. The colorful bandbox became one of the most visible in the early nineteenth century. Made of pasteboard bent into ovals and covered with wallpaper, bandboxes held clothing, bonnets, and accessories and were used by both men and women. Railroads and steamships allowed the use of large wooden trunks, as both offered more storage space for travelers' possessions. Modern airports forced yet other changes in luggage design, most noticeably the adaptation of small wheels and collapsible handles for pulling suitcases through long corridors.

Conveying Information

One of the few travel books published prior to the nineteenth century was *The Vade Mecum for America, or a Companion for Traders and Travellers* (1732). Published travel accounts became more common after the Revolution. Timothy Dwight (1752–1817) wrote *Travels in New-England and New-York* (four volumes; 1821–1822), while novelist James Fenimore Cooper (1789–1851) produced *Notions of the Americans Picked Up by a Traveling Bachelor* (1828). These accounts described American society and culture as much as they did the landscape and tourist sites. Late nineteenth-century guidebooks offered travel advice along with travel narratives. William Henry Harrison Murray's (1840–1904) *Adventures in the Wilderness; or, Camp-Life in the Adirondacks* (1869) provided such a mixture and has been credited with starting a mass migration of summer vacationers to the Adirondack Mountains. During this same period, several publications advocated the healthfulness of specific climates and guided travelers who sought relief from certain ailments, especially respiratory conditions. In the face of World War I, the interest in domestic tourism, especially automobile touring, led the Page Company, Boston publishers, to embark on its twenty-one-volume See America First series (1912–1931). Volumes featured photographic halftones and colorful stamped covers depicting idealized scenery.

Railroads printed their own travel literature to promote their services and the scenery and tourist sites along their routes. By the late nineteenth century, promotional booklets frequently included colorful pictures of scenery, hotels, and American Indians. The tourism and travel industries often commissioned artists to capture sites and scenery for colorful posters that evoked a sense of discovery and adventure. German-born graphic designer Ludwig Hohlwein (1874–1949) was commissioned by the Yellowstone Park Transportation Company in the early twentieth century to create such a poster. His image, featuring a stagecoach loaded with passengers, captured a romantic spirit of the "Old West." Travel posters often included representations of the hotels and transportation services that issued them.

The American reading public could turn to popular magazines to find travel advice and descriptive articles, often enhanced with engravings or photographs. Nineteenth-century gift books, published with ornate covers and prints, informed Americans about tourist destinations. In 1840, Nathaniel P. Willis (1806–1867) produced *American Scenery*, which included 121 steel-engraved prints by

William H. Bartlett (1809–1854), showing picturesque landscape and tourist sites located in the eastern United States, including the Natural Bridge in Virginia, Baltimore's Battle Monument, and Sing-Sing Prison along the Hudson River. Willis's accompanying descriptions instructed readers why the locations were worthy of seeing. William Cullen Bryant's (1794–1878) edited *Picturesque America* (1872–1874) continued the trend. Some periodicals, such as *Outing Magazine* and *Forest and Stream* (now *Field and Stream*) of the nineteenth century, and *Condé Nast Traveller* of the late twentieth and twenty-first centuries have specialized in travel information.

The fine and decorative arts have informed viewers about distant locations and exotic cultures. English Staffordshire potters filled the nineteenth-century American market with ceramicwares decorated with American landscapes and architecture. Throughout much of the nineteenth century, annual art exhibits hosted by the Pennsylvania Academy of the Fine Arts and the National Academy of Design included American landscape paintings by such notables as Thomas Cole (1801–1848), Frederick Edwin Church (1826–1900), and others. These artists' canvases, depicting locations such as Maine's Mount Desert Island and New York State's Catskill Mountains, helped foster tourism. Fairs and expositions installed art galleries of paintings and photographs of scenic landscapes and American Indians. The 1893 World's Columbian Exposition in Chicago displayed Thomas Moran's (1837–1926) 1872 painting, *The Grand Canyon of the Yellowstone*. The exposition also displayed part of a large California sequoia tree cut near the boundary of the newly created Sequoia National Park. Natural history specimens and ethnographic collections fascinated viewers and elicited the desire to travel to see their original habitats.

Evoking Memory

Tourists have typically sought ways to preserve their memories of their adventures. Souvenirs validate tourists' extraordinary experiences and provide proof of their visits to sites and encounters with alien cultures.

Souvenirs encompass the handcrafted, self-gathered, and mass-produced commercial goods. With natural history specimens, such as rocks and pressed flowers, tourists literally preserve aspects of the sites visited. Natural flora and fauna have also been used to craft utilitarian and decorative arts objects, like model birchbark canoes and picture frames made by American Indians in Maine, Minnesota, and other destinations. Fragrant balsam needles, sewn into pillows for the tourist trade, offer in the needles' sweet fragrance an aide-memoire of sojourns in northern forests and camping excursions and connote a pure, invigorating environment.

Indian nations throughout the Northeast have made products to sell to tourists at destinations like Niagara Falls and Saratoga Springs. By the late nineteenth century, southwestern Indians began a similar production for the tourist market. The Fred Harvey Company and the Santa Fe Railroad encouraged native craftwork for tourist consumption and promoted the process itself as an attraction. Pueblo pottery and Navajo rugs have remained popular souvenirs at southwestern trading posts.

The photographic image, whether a personal snapshot or a mass-printed postcard, has become the ubiquitous tourist souvenir. Small, handheld cameras, first developed by George Eastman (1854–1932) in 1888, made picture taking accessible to most Americans. By the early twentieth century, tourists could easily capture on film the events, sights, and cultures witnessed during their travels. By organizing photographs in albums and scrapbooks, tourists have been able to reconstruct the itinerary of their trips as a visual narrative.

Professionally produced photographic postcards and stereographs have likewise served tourists. Such media generally capture idealized, generic views not specific to individuals or their personal travel experiences; they function as surrogate images. The postcard remains one of the most popular souvenirs. When carried home by tourists, postcards evoke memories of personal experiences, but when mailed to friends and relatives, they communicate knowledge about destinations and peoples not personally encountered.

W. Douglas McCombs

See also Air and Space Transportation; Automobile Camping (Auto-Camping); Automobiles and Automobility; Commercial Food Venues; Handicraft and Artisanship; Highways and National Highway System; Land and Landscape; Land Transportation; Memory and Memorabilia; Native America; Nostalgia; Photography; Print Culture; Scrapbooks; Souvenirs; Water Transportation

References and Further Reading

Aron, Cindy S. 1999. *Working at Play: A History of Vacations in the United States.* New York: Oxford University Press.

Belasco, Warren J. 1979. *Americans on the Road: From Autocamp to Motel, 1910–1945.* Cambridge, MA: MIT Press.

Brown, Dona. 1995. *Inventing New England: Regional Tourism in the Nineteenth Century.* Washington, DC: Smithsonian Institution Press.

Conron, John. 2000. *American Picturesque.* University Park: Pennsylvania State University Press.

Grief, Martin. 1979. *The Airport Book: From Landing Field to Modern Terminal.* New York: Mayflower Books.

Hassrick, Peter H. 2002. *Drawn to Yellowstone: Artists in America's First National Park.* Los Angeles: Autry Museum of Western Heritage.

Herman, Daniel Justin. 2001. *Hunting and the American Imagination*. Washington, DC: Smithsonian Institution Press.

Hochschild, Harold K. 1962. *Life and Leisure in the Adirondack Backwoods*. Blue Mountain Lake, NY: Adirondack Museum.

Löfgren, Orvar. 1999. *On Holiday: A History of Vacationing*. Berkeley: University of California Press.

MacCannell, Dean. 1989. *The Tourist: A New Theory of the Leisure Class*. Rev. ed. New York: Schocken Books.

McKinsey, Elizabeth. 1985. *Niagara Falls: Icon of the American Sublime*. New York: Cambridge University Press.

Nash, Roderick. 1982. *Wilderness and the American Mind*. New Haven, CT: Yale University Press.

Phillips, Ruth B. 1998. *Trading Identities: The Souvenir in Native American Art from the Northeast, 1700–1900*. Seattle: University of Washington Press; Montreal: McGill-Queen's University Press.

Runte, Alfred. 1979. *National Parks: The American Experience*. Lincoln: University of Nebraska Press.

Rydell, Robert W. 1984. *All the World's a Fair: Visions of Empire at American International Expositions, 1876–1916*. Chicago: University of Chicago Press.

Schoelwer, Susan P. 2000. *Lions & Eagles & Bulls: Early American Tavern & Inn Signs*. Hartford: Connecticut Historical Society.

Sears, John F. 1989. *Sacred Places: American Tourist Attractions in the Nineteenth Century*. New York: Oxford University Press.

Shaffer, Marguerite S. 2001. *See America First: Tourism and National Identity, 1880–1940*. Washington, DC: Smithsonian Institution Press.

Stewart, Susan. 1984. *On Longing: Narratives of the Miniature, the Gigantic, the Souvenir, the Collection*. Baltimore, MD: Johns Hopkins University Press.

Trade Cards

Trade cards are small-scale printed notices of businesses and the goods and services available. Typically 2 × 4- or 3 × 5-inch cards, trade cards were imprinted on one or both sides with the name and address of a retailer or manufacturer and a picture. The colorful cards were widely collected and saved in sometimes elaborate albums, in part because color itself was valuable and a source of pleasure. Trade cards were a dominant form of advertising in the United States from the late 1870s until they were displaced by national magazine advertising in the 1890s.

As nationally distributed goods played a larger role in the market from the 1880s on, manufacturers sought to attract consumers to buy their products beyond advertising in local newspapers. Advertising trade cards, initially engraved or single-color cards used primarily by retailers, took on a larger role with the development of color (or chromo) lithography. As trade cards created recognition of brand name products, they helped to override habits of shopping in which articles were requested generically or, before the self-service grocery, in which the shopper relied on the grocer to choose or recommend what to buy.

Some cards were nationally distributed by the drummers or salesmen who sold the merchandise to the storekeepers, who then bestowed cards on customers; others came as premiums with products. Some cards were made specifically for a product, while others were *stock cards*—cards with an attractive or humorous picture that could be imprinted by a local letterpress printer with the advertiser's name.

High-art oil paintings and watercolors reproduced by the same process were soon the target of elite scorn, but the cards occupied a different niche. Calling cards and biblical psalm and proverb cards were made by the same process, looked very similar, and were collected in the same albums as advertising trade cards. Cigarette cards more often had images of bare-legged women. Trade

The Chicago soapmaker James S. Kirk & Company employed both humor and the eye-catching color printing afforded by chromolithography in this circa 1880 trade card. Trade cards were distributed by retailers and inserted with products, and familiarized consumers with national brand names. (Library of Congress)

cards are a rich source of late nineteenth-century images, offering insight into what was thought of as eye-catching and enticing. Some used racist imagery, caricaturing African Americans and Chinese immigrants.

Trade cards have again attracted present-day collectors. They offer evidence of a variety of manufactured goods available to Americans and as such reveal the nation's material life and its inhabitants' aspirations.

Ellen Gruber Garvey

See also Advertisements and Advertising; Collecting and Collections; Consumerism and Consumption; Ephemera; Patents, Trademarks, and Brands; Popular Culture; Print Culture

References and Further Reading

Garvey, Ellen Gruber. 1996. *The Adman in the Parlor: Magazines and the Gendering of Consumer Culture, 1880s to 1910s*. New York: Oxford University Press.
Jay, Robert. 1987. *The Trade Card in Nineteenth-Century America*. Columbia: University of Missouri Press.
Laird, Pamela. 2001. *Advertising Progress: American Business and the Rise of Consumer Marketing*. Baltimore, MD: Johns Hopkins University Press.

Trade Catalogues

Ranging from single-sheet price lists to full-color booklets, a *trade catalogue* is a publication that promotes a manufacturer's, wholesaler's, or retailer's wares to a consumer, whether that consumer is another business, an organization, or an individual.

Trade catalogues, through text and/or drawn, printed, or photographic image, describe the wealth of wares available to Americans, particularly in the nineteenth and twentieth centuries. More than a mere account of merchandise, a trade catalogue is also a form of advertisement. Certain industries, such as nursery and seed companies, employed chromolithography in their catalogues to enliven with color the images of fresh plants, verdant vegetables, and delectable fruits. The words of satisfied customers were often quoted, testifying to the quality of the products revealed therein. Also found in trade catalogues are instructions on how to use products and price lists (which were often detached by readers, a reflection of shifting pricing over time).

The great variety and numbers of trade catalogues, considered printed ephemera by curators and librarians, reflect the growth of American industry and manufacturing, particularly after 1870. The catalogues themselves are the products of improvements in printing technology that reduced costs and facilitated mass distribution. Trade catalogues reveal the growth also of consumer culture in the United States. As primary evidence, this genre serves to enhance understanding of the history of modernization, everyday life, business and economics, and advertising.

Shirley Teresa Wajda

See also Advertisements and Advertising; Consumerism and Consumption; Mail Order Catalogues; Patents, Trademarks, and Brands; Print Culture; Trade Cards

References and Further Reading
Ames, Kenneth L. 1986. "Trade Catalogues and the Study of History." In *Accumulation and Display: Mass Marketing Household Goods in America, 1880–1920*, ed. Deborah Anne Federhen et al., 7–14. Winterthur, DE: Winterthur Museum.
Crom, Theodore R. 1989. *Trade Catalogues, 1542–1842.* Melrose, FL: T. Crom.
Romaine, Lawrence B. 1960. *A Guide to American Trade Catalogs 1744–1900.* New York: R. R. Bowker.

Tradition

Tradition is the "received wisdom" that ensures cultural continuity by linking a society's beliefs, conventions, and institutions to the past; "that which . . . is handed down; a statement, belief, or practice transmitted (esp. orally) from generation to generation" (*Oxford English Dictionary*). This linkage is a necessary component in tradition's influence on a society's ideas of normal practices and beliefs. Tradition creates and maintains collective identity, establishes social relations, and promotes social cohesion, often through formal rituals. Since the 1980s, the concept of *invented tradition* serves historians by positing historical contexts in which specific practices that serve the modern nation-state are created. More recently, cultural studies scholars, focused on the mass consumption, mass media, and popular culture, have employed the concept of invented tradition to criticize industrial, capitalist societies through the study of specific cultural, often consumer practices of subalterns and their relations to power.

The concept of tradition informs the study of American material culture. Objects are often defined as mute declarations of culture, and this definition invokes folklorists' assumptions about orality. Observable in the processes of making and using objects is evidence of traditional practices and beliefs. Too, objects serve as necessary ritual adjuncts and are endowed with meanings to be preserved through tradition. In other words, objects "speak."

Tradition is historical, but, as the anthropologist Claude Lévi-Strauss observed in his study of myth, not necessarily in and of itself history. For folklorists and anthropologists, tradition is a dynamic process synonymous with oral culture. Historians, on the other hand, have understood tradition as the product of modernity. Eric Hobsbawm defines "invented tradition" as "a set of practices, normally governed by overtly or tacitly accepted rules and of a ritual or symbolic nature, which seek to inculcate certain values and norms of behavior by repetition, which automatically implies continuity with the past" (Hobsbawm and Ranger 1983, 1). Invented traditions, in Hobsbawm's view, occur when a society experiences rapid transformation, and these new practices are often related to the establishment and support of the modern nation-state. National holidays and the repetitive use of patriotic symbols, for example, are legitimated by reference to the past, formalization by law, or repeated use.

Hobsbawm distinguishes between *genuine* and *invented* tradition. Those traditions Hobsbawm deems genuine are those rites of passage he considers practices of premodern society—marriages and funerals, for example. Not only does Hobsbawm ignore the historical evolution of such rites of passage but his definition of genuine tradition feminizes those practices as private and somehow unaffected by the nation-state. Yet marriages and funerals possessed symbolic power by tradition's legitimacy in a premodern past as it instantiated political and economic power within the nation-state.

Folklorist Richard M. Dorson (1916–1981) delineated the genuine and invented in his discussion of "fakelore": those materials, often consumer goods, sold as "traditional." Cultural studies scholars have seized upon these materials to explore how corporations, governments, and consumers maintain, change, or challenge specific political or cultural ideologies through the marketplace. The recent scholarly interest in collective memory and social memory has influenced, and in some fields, supplanted the employment of *tradition* to refer to those cultural practices of identity and identification through reference to the past. Indeed, as folklorist Simon J. Bronner (1998, 10) has observed, the many meanings of *tradition* have rendered the term "conceptually soft."

Shirley Teresa Wajda

See also Folklore and Folklife; Holidays and Commemorations; Memory and Memorabilia; Mourning; Mourning and Ethnicity; Nostalgia; Rite, Ritual, and Ceremony

References and Further Reading
Bronner, Simon. 1998. *Following Tradition: Folklore in the Discourse of American Culture.* Logan: Utah State University Press.
Dorson, Richard M. 1976. *Folklore and Fakelore: Essays toward a Discipline of Folk Studies.* Cambridge, MA: Harvard University Press.
Glassie, Henry. 1995. "Tradition." *Journal of American Folklore* 108: 395–412.
Hobsbawm, Eric, and Terence Ranger, eds. 1983. *The Invention of Tradition.* Cambridge, UK: Cambridge University Press.
Lévi-Strauss, Claude. 1965. "The Structural Study of Myth." In *Myth: A Symposium,* ed. Thomas A. Sebeok. Bloomington: Indiana University Press.
Western Folklore. 2000. "The Meanings of Tradition." *Western Folklore* 59 (special issue): 2.

U

Utopian Communities

Historically, *utopian communities* in the United States were founded by dissident groups seeking an idealized place apart from the dominant culture. These communities were based on a collective or socialist form of collective settlement and on a common belief that the community was the physical manifestation of a religious or secular social ideology. The organization of the landscape, the design of buildings, and the crafting of tools and domestic furnishings served to reinforce a sense of order, a belief in collective endeavor, and a motivation to illustrate morality through technical innovation. In this context, a formal garden becomes a replica of Eden, a building facade represents ideological stability, and a cleverly designed agricultural tool is seen to reflect human potential or divine inspiration. The golden age of communal experiments in the United States was the nineteenth century, especially between 1820 and 1850, when proponents of various reform movements found an outlet for their experimental notions through communitarian rather than individual or confrontational approaches to social change.

The first utopian experiments were based in religious dissent from widely held Christian doctrine. One of the most successful, the United Society of Believers in Christ's Second Coming (founded in 1774 and known as the Shakers), believed their communities to represent literally a small corner of the Garden of Eden. Traditional Shaker building and craftsmanship strove to create a heavenly space within an earthly sphere, and their characteristic aesthetic of functional simplicity reflected a perfectionist desire for order that can be found in the detail of a straight-back chair as well as the layout of villages and the design of buildings.

In 1820, the British social theorist Robert Owen (1771–1858) proposed a plan for the ideal secular community based on a belief that the potential for human happiness is molded by external factors and living conditions that could be shaped to encourage proper character formation. His plan called for an internally focused, walled community organized with communal housing, dining, and meeting rooms surrounding a large public square. Owen's ideas became the model for many secular communities, especially those based on the writings of Charles

Fourier (1772–1837) of France, who believed that a science of human relationships would lead to a harmonious balancing of human passions. For both Owen and Fourier, the creation of these sociopetal, or inwardly focusing, public spaces, encouraged beneficial human relationships. Fourier called his proposed ideal community the Phalanx. At the center of community life was the phalanstery, a social palace with dining rooms, meeting rooms, a library, and a winter courtyard. The surrounding wings would be for workshops, education rooms, and residences.

The Oneida Community (1848–1881), established in Oneida, New York, was also established with the ideal of communal property not only of material things but of another human being within marriage. Oneida challenged gender conventions by asserting equality for men and women. The large "mansion house" accommodated the slowly growing sect; the building, now a museum, has more than 200 rooms. Members engaged in farming and industry, activities ranging from dairying to light manufacture. Indeed, the community, faced with moral charges against founder John Humphrey Noyes (1811–1886) as well as internal strife, reorganized as a joint-stock company in 1881. Known as Oneida Community Ltd., the new enterprise enjoyed success in trapmaking, fruit preservation, and silverware manufacture. In 1940 Oneida Ltd. joined the New York Stock Exchange and persists today as a world-renowned maker of silver and stainless steel tableware. As with the Shakers, who increasingly engaged the mar-

ket for fashionable domestic goods during the Gilded Age, the emphasis on the spiritual over the material was difficult to maintain in a capitalist nation.

The "back to the land" movements of the 1960s and 1970s had their bases both in Henry David Thoreau's (1817–1862) writings (*Walden, Or Life in the Woods* [1854]) and in Scott (1883–1983) and Helen (1904–1995) Nearing's works, especially *Living the Good Life: How to Live Sanely and Simply in a Troubled World* (1954). A reaction against war's destruction of the earth's natural resources, industrialization, and urbanization, Nearings' book preached conservation and self-sufficiency, aligning those practices with the peace movements during the Vietnam conflict (1959–1975). Younger Americans in the era created or joined communes, practiced cooperative living, adopted vegetarianism, and sought to live on less or to create their own foodstuffs, shelter, and clothing.

Jeffrey Blankenship

See also Cities and Towns; Planned Communities; Religion, Spirituality, and Belief

References and Further Reading
Fogarty, Robert S. 1990. *All Things New: American Communes and Utopian Movements, 1860–1914.* Chicago: University of Chicago Press.
Hayden, Dolores. 1976. *Seven American Utopias: The Architecture of Communitarian Socialism, 1790–1975.* Cambridge, MA: MIT Press.
Holloway, Mark. 1966. *Heavens on Earth: Utopian Communities in America, 1680–1880,* 2nd ed. New York: Dover.

V

Vernacular

Despite its use by scholars, the term *vernacular material culture* has yet to emerge into common usage. If it did, the term could well be applied to either a subset of material cultural forms or to an area of study drawing on such interdisciplinary fields as folklore and folklife, decorative arts, and American Studies. Instead, many aspects of what we might usefully understand as the vernacular within material culture or its study remain underexplored or scattered within the larger field and still in need of synthesis.

Background

Why is the vernacular significant to material culture study? If *vernacular* is "the everyday expression of cultural groups, from language to architecture," then vernacular material culture might be seen as the everyday objects that serve as expressions of a group (Louisiana Division of the Arts 2005). Such everyday objects are sufficiently widespread that it is irresponsible to ignore them, especially if they embody an overtly expressive function. As implied by the concept of a culture group, *vernacular* also means local—either local to the people in a certain physical place and time or local in the sense that it is specific in creation, meaning, or use to members of a distinct set of people. Since so much of material culture research is focused on recovering context, a strategy that emphasizes both physical and cultural locations offers great promise as a way to enhance future studies.

The concept of vernacularity is also useful because it helps us to break out of the high-versus-low dichotomies and folk/popular/elite triads by which previous generations have tried to define "levels" of art and culture. *Low art* is openly pejorative, while the implication of increased sophistication from folk through popular to elite is a misleading oversimplification of cultural processes—one that also privileges the origins of artifact forms while downplaying their actual uses. While it is crucial to identify cultural boundaries in context, the biases embedded in terms like *high* and *low* can quickly get in the way of thoughtful, and respectful, user-based analysis. The concept of the vernacular bridges such distinctions and allows us to think about everyday objects—or indeed the customary uses of all manner of artifacts—

in ways that emphasize the specific cultural locations where meanings are created and shared.

Are only some objects inherently vernacular? Might not all objects be vernacular to the extent that they are used or understood in vernacular ways? Here scholars may openly disagree but may also fail to recognize this fundamental distinction. Such differentiation, however, is crucial to material culture studies. It is neither acceptable to categorize and study objects simply as forms nor to analyze objects by context alone. There has been, for example, a concerted movement away from looking at static items of folklore, be they ballads, tales, proverbs, or artifacts, to looking at folklore as a communicative process based in shared genres of expression. This newer approach invites attention to artifact meanings as they emerge in real time, thus bringing form and context together while also necessarily foregrounding the local, shared components of material culture in use.

Sources and Studies to Date

Historically *vernacular* has been applied to that which is local, domestic, or indigenous to a particular place, especially language. Nineteenth-century scholars observed broad patterns of linguistic distribution mapped to history and place. Early folklorists, such as Germans Wilhelm (1785–1859) and Jacob (1786–1863) Grimm (the Brothers Grimm), likewise noticed that variations in folktales, folk songs, or proverbs correlate with physical geography. The careful documentation of local variations in language and oral genres became a widely used technique for exploring the evolution of expression across space and time. Studies of material forms soon followed in this same mode.

The closest thing to a formalized study of vernacular material culture has emerged through the field of vernacular architecture study, and in this sense it is closely aligned not only to folklore and folklife but also to art and architectural history. The Vernacular Architecture Group was founded in Great Britain in 1952, and its American counterpart, the Vernacular Architecture Forum, celebrated its twenty-fifth anniversary in 2005. The impetus for their formation was the need to consider every building worthy of study regardless of the artistic reputation of its architect (if it even had one, as most pre-nineteenth-century and many later ordinary buildings do not). In the United States, everything from agricultural outbuildings to workers' housing to suburban garages was considered worthy of attention, while monographs such as architectural historian Abbott Lowell Cummings' *Framed Houses of Massachusetts Bay* (1979) and especially folklorist Henry Glassie's *Folk Housing in Middle Virginia* (1975) served to establish a particular interest in historical domestic architecture and a stress on research through fieldwork. The first collection of essays on vernacular architecture appeared in 1986 as *Common Places: Readings in American Vernacular Architecture*, edited by architectural historian Dell Upton and folklorist John Michael Vlach; it remains the classic textbook.

The field of vernacular architecture has grown beyond its early focus on primarily rural, preindustrial buildings to encompass both a larger range of building types—urban, industrial, institutional, and so forth—as well as an expanded set of related material forms. Techniques have also moved beyond solely creating typologies and analyzing forms. Folklorist Thomas Carter (1991, 419) highlights the strong traditional component in vernacular design "whether it be folk or popular in origin," arguing that with the advent of industrialism, such influences are rarely isolated. Rather, he explains, the characteristics of formerly folk design processes continue through the intertwining of tradition and innovation. Glassie (1975, 21) writes that "the study of vernacular architecture is an approach to the whole of the built world. It favors completeness, recognizes diversity, and seeks ways to use buildings as evidence in order to tell better versions of the human story." A second set of influences for students of the vernacular comes from the various fields that study popular culture, especially American Studies, British cultural studies, and sociology, as well as history and literary studies. Add to this interdisciplinary mix the less academic but often detailed work of pop culture collectors and enthusiasts, and, as well, the practices developed by public historians working in museums or historic preservation. Especially through the field of American Studies and its still influential early efforts to explore a uniquely American ethos in art and culture, scholars have looked for what is distinctively American about the artifacts used and produced across the United States. Design historian Jeffrey L. Meikle (2005) outlines the history of what some have called an American vernacular style, recognized through the years for its streamlining of ornament and focus on functional innovation. French traveler Alexis de Tocqueville (1805–1859) "meditated on the 'virtuous materialism' of Americans" (Meikle 2005, 26) while scholar John A. Kouwenhoven (1909–1990) "identified 'a democratic-technological vernacular' style whose functional simplicity . . . exemplified the best, most typically American examples of 'the design of useful things'" (Meikle 2005, 28). Yet such observers, according to Meikle, overstressed this idealized aesthetic while failing to recognize an equally significant interest in material luxury and ornament. More recently, scholars have looked at identity formation through material life more

broadly, with influential contributions from British scholars including *Subculture* (1979) by Dick Hebdige and the recent works of anthropologist Daniel Miller.

Finally, studies of consumerism, commodities, and the circulation of goods have played an important role in raising the profile of vernacular aspects of material culture—again with an emphasis on process and performance. Historical works such as McKendrick, Brewer, and Plumb's *The Birth of a Consumer Society* (1982) and anthropologist Arjun Appadurai's edited collection *The Social Life of Things* (1986) have been especially influential, as have recent trends in the study of historical archaeology. These approaches tend to focus on exchange as much as situated use and to recognize that the same objects can have very different meanings as they move from location to location or continue to exist at a given site through time. Finally, just as United States vernacular architecture studies are becoming multinational in scope, material culture is increasingly seen through the lenses of multiple viewpoints, with special attention to meaning creation that involves mediated or adaptive transplantations of original forms and uses.

Looking Ahead

As we pay more attention to objects in motion, our need to correlate effectively meanings to specific locations increases. At the same time, the processes of mediation that seem to go with modern life can significantly complicate our understanding of how communities develop and function. Material culture is everywhere, yet the basic work of bringing nonverbal, material expressions into their proper place as fully recognized primary sources for cultural and historical studies continues. A developed approach to the study of vernacular material culture offers to address directly these concerns, given its necessary emphasis on locations in time and space and the move to break down scholars' own categories in favor of fieldwork on the ground. With the rise of interdisciplinary perspectives across the humanities and social sciences and a growing interest in theorizing material culture more fully, the study of vernacular material culture likewise presents an opportunity to bring the overall field into broader recognition.

Susan Garfinkel

See also Anthropology and Archaeology; Architectural History and American Architecture; Art History and American Art; Consumerism and Consumption; Cultural Geography; Cultural Studies; Decorative Arts; Domestic Architecture; Folklore and Folklife; Historic Preservation; Museums and Museum Practice; Popular Culture

References and Further Reading
Appadurai, Arjun, ed. 1986. *The Social Life of Things: Commodities in Cultural Perspective.* New York: Cambridge University Press.
Asquith, Lindsay, and Marcel Vellinga, eds. 2005. *Vernacular Architecture in the 21st Century.* New York: Routledge.
Carter, Thomas. 1991. "Traditional Design in an Industrial Age: Vernacular Domestic Architecture in Utah." *Journal of American Folklore* 104 (3): 419–442.
Cummings, Abbott Lowell. 1979. *The Framed Houses of Massachusetts Bay, 1625–1725.* Cambridge, MA: Belknap Press.
Glassie, Henry. 1975. *Folk Housing in Middle Virginia: A Structural Analysis of Historic Artifacts.* Knoxville: University of Tennessee Press.
Glassie, Henry. 2000. *Vernacular Architecture.* Bloomington: Indiana University Press.
Gregson, Nicky, and Louise Crewe. 2003. *Second-Hand Cultures.* London: Berg.
Hebdige, Dick. 1979. *Subculture: The Meaning of Style.* London: Methuen.
Lantis, Margaret. 1960. "Vernacular Culture." *American Anthropologist* 62 (2): 202–216.
Louisiana Division of the Arts. 2005. "Louisiana Voices." http://www.louisianavoices.org/edu_glossary.html.
McKendrick, Neil, John Brewer, and J. H. Plumb. 1982. *The Birth of a Consumer Society: The Commercialization of Eighteenth-Century England.* Bloomington: Indiana University Press.
Meikle, Jeffrey L. 2005. *Design in the USA.* New York: Oxford University Press.
Miller, Daniel. 2001. *The Dialectics of Shopping.* Chicago: University of Chicago Press.
Upton, Dell, and John Michael Vlach, eds. 1986. *Common Places: Readings in American Vernacular Architecture.* Athens: University of Georgia Press.

Visual Culture Studies

Scholars shaping the interdisciplinary field of *visual culture studies* assess images, image-making technologies, technologies of seeing, and visual experiences to explain historical and contemporary culture. The study of *visual culture* is based on the notion that the typical cultural artifacts used to understand the past and the present, such as written and printed documents, are important, but new insights emerge by analyzing the predominant, and historically underexamined, visual realm. Visual culture provides another site in which cultural meanings are created and debated. As scholar Eilean Hooper-Greenhill (2000, 14) observes, "Visual culture works toward a social theory of visuality, focusing on questions of what is made visible, who sees what, how seeing, known and power are interrelated. It examines the act of seeing as a product of the tensions between external images or objects, and internal thought processes."

Visual culture studies is not only interested in what is seen. It also explores how ever-changing technology creates new permutations and alterations within the milieu of looking. How an individual interacts with technology in what art historian Nicholas Mirzoeff (1999, 3) calls "visual events" may be gleaned from a range of sources, including film, television, art, design, fashion, architecture, animation, cartoons, public celebrations, museum displays, advertising, and the Internet. Distinctions between *high* and *low* or the *popular* are merged in the acknowledgment that humans experience the visual as a system of cross-mediation of many visual forms and technologies. In addition, proponents of visual culture studies extend its evidence to consider things that are visualized but are not themselves visual—that is, to comprehend what human eyes may not be able to see except through such technologies as the microscope, the telescope, the x-ray, or the computer.

Theory and Debates

Sifting through visual culture to get at what should be included under its giant umbrella of interpretative possibilities is a difficult task. Art historian Keith Moxey (1996, 57) advises that the new "discipline might concern itself with all images for which distinguished cultural value has been or is being proposed. Such a model would respect the tradition on which the discipline is founded, namely that certain objects have been and are given special cultural significance, but [we should] refuse to accept the corollary that aesthetic experience is derived from a universal response." Like so many scholars who deal with the visual, Moxey straddles the fine line between a desire to study those images that have been deemed special by culture (works of fine art, for example) and claiming that the concept of universal beauty can no longer be understood as axiomatic. The irony is that the two ideas are not mutually exclusive camps. Placing an image in the category of *distinguished*, to use Moxey's terminology, usually requires some level of acceptance when it comes to universal truths. After all, "special cultural significance" does not emerge in a vacuum and necessitates a belief in the qualitative assessment of what constitutes significance.

If we are to accept Moxey's premise about the need to expand the study of the visual realm, then we should also consider other ways in which scholars explain visual culture. Cultural studies scholar Donna Haraway has written about how vision signifies with the help of new technologies. In her important manifesto *Simians, Cyborgs, and Women*, Haraway argues the need for science to be aware of its cultural assumptions, which she couches in her strong belief that there is no a priori conception of pure science. Given this observation, she declares, "The instruments of visualization in multinationalist, postmodernist culture have compounded . . . meanings of dis-embodiment. The visualizing technologies are without apparent limit; the eye of any ordinary primate like us can be endlessly enhanced by sonography systems, magnetic resonance imaging, artificial intelligence-linked graphic manipulation systems . . . colour enhancement techniques, satellite surveillance systems . . ." (Haraway 1991, 188–189). In the technological arena of "enhanced" vision, chronologically stretching from the early days of corrective lenses to the recent advent of the visually guided smart bomb, the study of visual culture can help us decipher history.

Moxey's ideas about expanding the possibilities of what constitutes the visual archive and Haraway's contention about the need to look at the technological aspects of vision are two different, yet interrelated, positions. Moxey wants us to look at the past more broadly, while Haraway sees vision as integrally related to the scientific devices that magnify our experience of the visual. This distinction about what constitutes the study of visual culture has a similar corollary within American cultural studies, specifically as connoted by the subtle variances that historians make between visual and material culture.

Visual Culture and American Material Culture Studies

Material culture has traditionally been that field of inquiry that assesses tangible objects. Chairs, tables, toys, houses, scientific instruments, and other assorted things, from books to computers, are usually thought of as *material culture*. *Visual culture*, however, has been thought of as the study of objects' surfaces that signify through the medium of the visual. Paintings, sculpture, photographs, postcards, stereographs, and other visually mediated artifacts are understood as part of visual culture.

Visual culture studies and material culture studies are interconnected, and can and should inform each other in ways that will bring new insights to the past and the present. Indeed, the best work done under the rubric of material culture studies and visual cultural studies engages in a conversation that fluctuates between the concerns of the visual and the material. Projects, such as art historian Alexander Nemerov's (2001) book on the painter Raphaelle Peale, assess their subject matter by scrutinizing both the system of visuality inherent to the object as well as its materiality. Nemerov interprets Peale's paintings by examining the historical context of Peale's images as well as the physical construction of some of the frames on which Peale stretched his canvases. Outside the realm of fine art scholarship, critic Mike Davis's (1990) work on the city of Los Angeles, for example, carefully observes both the visual and material aspects of Los Angeles' contemporary landscape to explain the city as a site of racial and socioeconomic segregation enforced through the apparatus of architectural control. For instance, Davis understands that rounded bus stop benches in Los Angeles are an "innovation" whose sole purpose is to keep overnight guests out of "public" spaces in the city by enforcing a no-sleeping policy through their uncomfortable surfaces. Davis also looks at buildings and gated communities where the visual presence of physically imposing obstacles sends a clear message about who is allowed where in Los Angeles through a type of physical demarcation strongly suggested through architectural intimidation. Davis also turns to new technology, such as the police helicopter and its deployment of a visual vantage point for heightened surveillance, as another example of Los Angeles' militaristic state. Like Nemerov, Davis examines the visual and the material to give the reader a better understanding of his subject.

This admixture of visual and material culture approaches can lead to new knowledge. To think critically about objects and spaces—from the perspective of both materiality and visuality—is to engage everyday life in new ways and apprehend one's own role in a given time and place. This possibility becomes clear after thinking about the role of the gaze as mediated through the advent of what may be one of the most important technological innovations of the modern era, the motion picture.

One film repeatedly used by scholars to teach the role of the gaze is filmmaker Alfred Hitchcock's (1899–1980) *Rear Window* (1954). Hitchcock staged the film on a set that looked like a typical interior city block in New York City where it is easy to survey neighbors by looking out the window and into others' lives. Photographer L. B. Jeffries (actor James Stewart) has just broken his leg. Confined to a wheelchair and a problematic relationship with a society doyenne named Lisa Fremont (actress Grace Kelly), Jeffries desperately searches for an escape from his forced domesticity. To make the time pass, he looks out at the apartments that surround the courtyard beyond his large windows. At first, his looking is a game, one that his nurse Stella (actress Thelma Ritter) mocks and decries as unnatural. Soon Jeffries sees what he believes are a series of events that reveal how a man directly across the way has killed his wife. An innocent man has been brought into the midst of a crime, yet here that naive involvement comes to the fore as a result of the main character's gaze. The eye is what gets Jeffries into trouble.

The camera in *Rear Window*, film scholars argue, enhances the protagonist's voyeurism. The camera makes the audience aware that Jeffries becomes sexually aroused by the act of looking. Queries about the gendered nature of Jeffries' vision (for instance, his falling in love with the beautiful Lisa Fremont at the moment she becomes an object to be looked at from across the block's interior) have dominated discussion about this Hitchcock classic (Mulvey 1975).

The materiality of the film's set, which Hitchcock cleverly designed to allow for maximum directorial control, further elucidates how this is a movie about looking. The proximity of the set's buildings and the manner in which the camera moves the audience throughout this urban environment increase the sense of claustrophobia and narrative tension in the film. In other words, how the set is the ideal stage for a peeping Tom, and how the camera works to give us the perspective of that peeping Tom, are easier to grasp after thinking about the material and visual concerns raised by the film.

The idea of visual culture, especially when studied with an understanding of material culture, leads to new ways of expanding the historical record and defining the nature of history. It is becoming increasingly critical to look at cultural artifacts without accepting these artifacts as naive manifestations of cultural "truths." At a time when television and the mass media infiltrate everyday experience, it is appropriate to think about approaches to cultural criticism that will incite individuals to look carefully, think critically, and engage politically with the visual.

David Brody

See also Art History and American Art; Cultural Studies; Land and Landscape; Photography; Printmaking and American Prints; Technology

References and Further Reading
Cartwright, Lisa, and Marita Sturken. 2001. *Practices of Looking: An Introduction to Visual Culture.* New York: Oxford University Press.
Crary, Jonathan. 1990. *Techniques of the Observer: On Vision and Modernity in the Nineteenth Century.* Cambridge, MA: MIT Press.
Davis, Mike. 1990. *City of Quartz: Excavating the Future in the City of Los Angeles.* London: Verso.
Hooper-Greenhill, Eilean. 2000. *Museums and the Interpretation of Visual Culture.* London: Routledge.
Haraway, Donna J. 1991. *Simians, Cyborgs, and Women: The Reinvention of Nature.* London: Routledge.
Mirzoeff, Nicholas, ed. 1988. *The Visual Culture Reader.* London: Routledge.
Mirzoeff, Nicholas. 1999. *Introduction to Visual Culture.* London: Routledge.
Moxey, Keith. 1996. "Animating Aesthetics." *October* 77: 56–59.
Mulvey, Laura. 1975. "Visual Pleasure and Narrative Cinema." *Screen* 16 (3): 6–18.
Nemerov, Alexander. 2001. *The Body of Raphaelle Peale: Still Life and Selfhood, 1812–1824.* Berkeley: University of California Press.

W

Wallpaper

Wallpaper decorates interior room partitions of domestic, commercial, and civic buildings in the early American colonies and later United States. Affixed with paste or glue to walls and sometimes ceilings and other surfaces, wallpaper, painted or printed with a pattern or a scene, has reflected a given society's aesthetic tastes, political and social concerns, and adaptation of technological innovation. Wallpaper has been and is used in combination with other wall treatments, including paint, textiles, stenciling, wainscoting (wood paneling), and plaster ornamentation. Wallpaper is one of the most ephemeral of domestic furnishings. The common practice of papering over, rather than stripping, extant wallpaper means that it is rarely collected except by museums and commercial manufacturers of reproduction wallpapers. The collection and study of wallpaper are hampered by wallpaper's use as well as the lack of manufacturers' records.

Wallpaper Manufacture and Use

Wallpaper was introduced in sixteenth-century Europe as a cheaper substitute for woven tapestries, leather, and canvas coverings. Early wallpapers were sheets of paper block printed in black ink with pictures, in imitation of paintings. These decorative papers were not intended for removal or reuse, and they often served as a backdrop rather than a feature or focus of a room. Glue, paste, smoke from heating and lighting devices, and other everyday wear affected wallpaper's "life," as did changing tastes. The European colonists in North America employed the decorative strategies of their homelands: Tapestries matched seating furniture upholstery, woven textiles, and leather-adorned walls. After 1700 wallpaper was increasingly imported in easily portable rolls to the American colonies from England, France, and China. In the 1760s wallpaper was produced by "paper stainers" who purchased "hanging paper" made of unbleached textile rags (rendering the paper blue, gray, or tan) and covered them with colors, either by hand or through wood block printing. Sizes varied, from individual sheets to rolls of 12 yards. *Flocking*—wool or silk affixed by paste to create a textured pattern—imitated cut velvet and brocades. Early American-made wallpaper patterns borrowed from the then-fashionable naturalistic designs found in textiles and from architectural ornamental designs. These designs were made widely available through the publication of illustrated books and paintings.

To compete with imported papers American paper stainers underpriced their wares. Sold by booksellers, stationers, and upholsterers, American wallpapers into the early nineteenth century were "plain" (one color); "architectural" (imitating architectural forms such as the popular Neoclassical "pillar and arch" motif); borders (imitating architectural moldings or repeating patterns); and "common" (repeating patterns of flowers, stripes, checks, and textile weaves, among others). Blue and green were popular colors. Landscapes (imitating painted murals) and imitation drapery and textiles became popular choices in the early nineteenth century. Wallpapers adorned entryways, stairways, halls, and rooms in domestic dwellings, large and small. Wallpaper provided the wealthy with a means of staying in fashion; for landlords and renters, wallpaper easily made new a set of rooms; for everyone, wallpaper faded over time and had to be replaced.

Wallpaper patterns were standardized in the 1840s, a reflection of the interest in understanding and codifying aesthetics in Europe and England exemplified in Englishman Owen Jones's (1809–1874) 1856 treatise, *The Grammar of Ornament*. American Andrew Jackson Downing (1815–1852) included illustrations of papers in *The Architecture of Country Houses* (1850). In 1839, the introduction of cylinder printing through the adaptation of a press used to print calico mechanized wallpaper production. At mid-century, bold, dark Gothic Revival designs, large floral patterns, and contrasting bold stripes were embraced by middle-class Americans who heeded the advice of a growing number of tastemakers. After 1880, wallpaper prices de-

creased dramatically as wood-pulp paper replaced textile-based papers. Other improvements in ink, paper, and, later, the use of lithography and silkscreen printing, served to widen the market for wallpaper. By the end of the century, wallpaper had adapted to the Aesthetic Movement's imperatives: "Art wallpapers" adorned with abstracted natural forms or conveying *japonisme* became popular. In addition, the Arts and Crafts ideals of plain "earth" colors or bold striping, as well as a revival of a soft, "colonial" palette were evident in wallpaper choices.

Throughout the twentieth century wallpaper patterns have reflected a variety of tastes. Particularly in the 1950s "theme papers" covered the gamut of popular interests, from martinis to gardening to hobbies to kitchen equipment. Testifying to the growing power of the youth market, wallpaper manufacturers created theme papers displaying teenagers' interests in cars, the prom, rock and roll, and sports. These were also called *conversationals*, intended to cover only one wall of a room. Biomorphic forms, adaptations of abstract paintings, as well as traditional patterned wallpaper, borders, and like treatment, offered Americans a seemingly endless variety of moods and interests to be indulged on their walls.

Shirley Teresa Wajda

See also Aesthetic Movement; Decorative Arts; Design History and American Design; Interior Design; Printmaking and American Prints; Textiles

References and Further Reading

Cooper-Hewitt Museum. 1995. *Kitsch to Corbusier: Wallpapers from the 1950s.* New York: Cooper-Hewitt National Design Museum, Smithsonian Institution.

Hoskins, Lesley, ed. 1994. *The Papered Wall: The History, Patterns and Techniques of Wallpaper.* New York: Harry N. Abrams.

Lynn, Catherine. 1980. *Wallpaper in America: From the Seventeenth Century to World War I.*

New York: W. W. Norton, for Cooper-Hewitt Museum.

Nylander, Richard C., Elizabeth Redmond, and Penny J. Saner, eds. 1986. *Wallpaper in New England*. Boston: Society for the Preservation of New England Antiquities.

Schoeser, Mary. 1986. *Fabrics and Wallpapers: Twentieth-Century Design*. New York: E. P. Dutton.

Water Transportation

Transporting humans and goods by water has historically encompassed the use of a variety of watercraft and, at times, the construction of artificial waterways to accommodate movement and trade. Travel over water—oceans, seas, lakes, ponds, rivers, and canals—provided through much of American history the most economical and fast means through which to carry goods and people to and from what would become the United States as well as within its borders.

Vessels Powered by Wind, Water, and Humans

European settlement in what would become the United States required oceangoing vessels such as caravels and larger galleons. Until the nineteenth century ocean ships, primarily constructed of oak, were powered by sail affixed to pine masts. The deforestation of England and Europe and the rise of international trade by the end of the sixteenth century had spurred exploration for new sources of wood for increased shipbuilding in addition to wood's many other uses in this era.

Native American peoples employed small, light, shallow-draft canoes or kayaks created of local materials: Cedar logs and animal skins were used in the Northwest, while birchbark was employed among the Eastern Woodlands peoples. Dugout canoes were created of logs that were felled and then burned and scraped with stones. Native peoples utilized an extensive network of canoe trails based on the continent's river system to carry on trade. Canoes and other small watercraft were the dominant form of inland river, stream, and lake transportation before the nineteenth century.

Artificial Waterways: Canals and Canal Boats

Three short commercial canals, totaling 100 miles, were built in the two centuries before the great Erie Canal was completed in 1825. The Erie Canal, stretching 364 miles across upstate New York and containing eighty-eight masonry locks, broke through the barrier of the Appalachian Mountains and facilitated increased settlement and commerce in the Great Lakes region. As segments were completed, evidence of its future success was witnessed in overcrowded traffic. The canal's success spurred canal building throughout the Northeast, where up-country towns were connected across the fall line to tidewater areas; to the Midwest, linking eastern commercial centers to the Great Lakes region; and in the Great Lakes region linking to the Ohio and Mississippi rivers. More expensive than turnpikes and other roads to build and maintain, and challenged by railroad construction in the 1850s, canals became inefficient and expensive.

The romance of the canal era is pictured in images of flat-bottomed canal boats and barges that traveled the nation's canals during their heyday before 1860. Towpaths alongside canals were trod by horses, mules, and humans pulling or walking beside (and given, at times, traffic jams, ahead of) open and covered wood boats.

Steamboats

Following the American Revolution and the rise of industry in the United States, the steam engine became a fascination of inventors throughout the new nation. More functional ships, such as river flat boats and oceangoing keel ships such as the swift clipper, were used until steamboats were perfected.

Robert Fulton's (1765–1815) steamboat, the *Clermont*, was not the first steam-powered boat in the United States. It was, however, the first steamboat to work successfully and it traveled the Hudson River in 1807. Fulton and Robert Livingston (1746–1813) were responsible for the first successful steamboat route on the Mississippi. The steamboat *New Orleans* traveled from Pittsburgh, Pennsylvania, to Louisiana and completed its route in January 1812. Fulton's successful steamboat trips, along with the necessity to expand westward, led to the astronomic rise in steamboat usage on the nation's rivers, even in the western territories.

A National Water Transportation System

The rise in steamboats was paralleled by the rise of the United States Army Corps of Engineers and engineering projects throughout the nation. The corps, created in 1802 by the United States Congress, was given the job of surveying transportation routes and overseeing road, bridge, and canal development throughout the United States. The corps created a system of safety along the nation's coastline, constructing lighthouses and piers and mapping navigation harbor channels for safe passage of ships. In the 1820s, the corps was given responsibility to survey the nation's waterways for military and commercial uses and to improve navigation. It began to clear the Ohio and Mississippi rivers of sandbars and other obstacles, construct dams, and undertake dredging.

The need for hydroelectric power in the early twentieth century led to the corps' design and construction of dams and reconfig-

uration of navigation on the nation's western rivers. Flood control projects were undertaken in the 1920s and 1930s, through the construction of levees to protect cities, especially along the Mississippi River, and the construction of reservoirs, which have become in many areas popular lakes on which Americans boat. Along with the creation of the St. Lawrence Seaway in 1959, the corps is responsible for the shape of the nation's water transportation system. These canals, seaways, and other projects were, and are, vital to American commerce and transportation.

Nicholas Katers

See also Air and Space Transportation; Land Transportation; Maritime Material Culture; Technology; Tourism and Travel

References and Further Reading
Bauer, Karl J. 1988. *A Maritime History of the United States: The Role of America's Seas and Waterways.* Columbia: University of South Carolina Press.
Taylor, George Rogers. 1951. *The Transportation Revolution: Industry, 1815–1860.* New York: Rinehart.

William and Mary Style

The William and Mary style greatly influenced colonial American furniture design. Between 1690 and 1725 the forms and methods of European Baroque craftsmen popularized during the short reign (1689–1702) of William of Orange and Mary Stuart in England filtered into American workshops. The new profession of *cabinetmaker* required a mastery of furniture-making techniques including elaborate turning, dovetail joinery, veneered finishes, and inlay work. Simple and symmetrical furniture forms were transformed by this new interest in ornamentation. Ornate carvings, fancy wood turnings in trumpet, bowl, and cup shapes, and burled

This chest on frame, made in 1726 by Philadelphian John Head, possesses the emphasized verticality, elaborate turning, and walnut veneer finish of the William and Mary style. (Philadelphia Museum of Art/Corbis)

and other faux veneers (including the imitative lacquer technique of japanning) embellished furniture that was now more formal and larger in scale and proportion than previous styles.

The redesign of American furniture to imitate that of European courts defined the new social position and status of America's rising merchant class. Its members chose to furnish their residences with the fashionable forms including daybeds (or couches), dressing tables, and high and low chests on frames. For reasons of economy as well as comfort, chair forms were adapted from Anglo-Flemish styles and included copies of high-back great chairs (imitating medieval thrones) and banister chairs with upholstered or caned seats, as well as the easy chair,

with down-filled cushions and winged sides designed specifically for the elderly and infirm. Bureau cabinets with drawers and interior compartments, sometimes with attached bookcases, were signs of business success, as were other more luxurious novelties such as spice cabinets and tea tables. Interiors became more formal and were designed for specific functions. Furniture was arranged symmetrically around the space, emphasizing a rational design. Chambers were made more lavish with the addition of textile furnishings, showing the virtuosity of the upholsterer, another new craft. In such spaces furniture achieved a grander stature as well as attained an important presence and purpose for its occupants.

Evie T. Joselow

See also Decorative Arts; Furniture; Style

References and Further Reading
Fairbanks, Jonathan L., and Elizabeth Bidwell Bates. 1981. *American Furniture, 1620 to the Present*. New York: R. Marek.
Hayward, Helena. 1977 (1965). *World Furniture*. Secaucus, NJ: Chartwell.
Kirk, John T. 2000. *American Furniture: Understanding Styles, Construction, and Quality*. New York: Harry N. Abrams.

Work and Labor

Although used interchangeably to refer to the physical or mental exertion in the production or accomplishment of a task, *work* and *labor* have subtly charted the historic shift in the types of activities and the social definitions of the individuals who and the animals that perform them in the United States. *Labor*, for example, is most often defined as work for wages and as work that is exhausting or difficult. *Labor* is also employed to define unionized workers and historic movements, beginning in the latter half of the nineteenth century, for worker rights in the United States.

Almost any place—from the factory to the farm, from the office building to the department store, from the church to the home, from the school to the coal mine—may be a site where work and labor are performed. Artifacts relating to work and labor also range from tools to clothing, from books to sacred objects, from office equipment to safety gear, and from cash registers to fork lifts. Examining workplaces as well as objects can help interpret the nature of work and labor throughout American history. The material culture of work and labor can tell much about the character of work, the historical development of an industrial society, and the contemporary evolution of the dominant service economy as American communities rapidly deindustrialize.

Work and labor have greatly altered the built environment. The layout of the rural farm often speaks to the kind of agriculture practiced (dairy, wheat, ranching, etc.). Farm structures can also suggest the relative wealth of the owners, how daily life is organized, the evolution of farming, even if tenant farmers or sharecroppers are also working the land. Much of what we know about the daily work of rural slavery is evident in the historic built environment.

Besides the actual labor relating to farming itself, the rural built environment can help interpret domestic work as well, which raises discussions about gender roles. The rural landscape also includes small towns associated with farming communities. These towns' plans and structures offer much evidence about the work needed to sustain rural life. Churches, schools, commercial buildings, transportation-related facilities, and recreational venues were all places that provided livings for the people who supported agricultural life.

Industrialization

Prior to the massive industrialization of the nineteenth century, industrial structures like blast furnaces and their associated facilities, distilleries, sawmills, and other small-scale production facilities dotted the landscape. The relatively small capacity of the facilities hint at the size of the workforce and the various skills required to carry out production. With the Industrial Revolution, the built environment changed radically, albeit over a long period of time. Mass production needed an increasingly larger workforce and correspondingly immense facilities. The steel industry, emblematic of most large-scale industries, required huge tracts of land located near water sources in order to feed the other industries reliant on this basic product. The size and scale of mass industry altered not only the landscape but the way people worked. Connected with the rise of mass industry is growing unionization. We can learn much about organized labor through not only the union halls and other gathering places but also the sites of labor conflict.

Large-scale industrialization in the late nineteenth and early twentieth centuries occurred in growing urban areas, which spawned new workplaces such as offices and department stores as well as larger public facilities like hospitals and schools. New building types like skyscrapers emerged, changing the landscape as much as did the huge industrial facilities. New entertainment venues like amusement parks and movie theaters also need employees to make them operate, thus providing other sources to study and interpret labor history. The same is true of sporting venues such as ballparks, stadiums, and arenas. Saloons and bars, gambling establishments, and houses of prostitution, although they are the sites of illegal and/or illicit entertainment, are workplaces as well.

Workers lay out steel on a hot bed at a plate mill in a circa 1909 to 1915 photograph. Large-scale machinery of the early twentieth-century industrial workplace dwarfed workers, symbolizing the historic shifts in technology, the nature of work, and the daily lives of workers on the job. (Library of Congress)

Workers' and Laborers' Housing

Housing can be used to examine the lifestyles of various classes of workers. Indeed, company towns and company housing are the outward expressions of industrial welfare capitalism and tell much about the relationship between the employers and the employees, raising questions about workers' control and control of workers. Working-class housing can also reveal information about domestic life in working-class communities, women's work in the home, and the care of boarders.

Tools and Technology

Interpreting workplaces gives only part of the picture of work and labor. Tools, equip-

ment, machines, and protective gear are valuable primary source materials. Clothing, for example, has changed not only with fashion but also with the work environment. The use of uniforms for service workers as diverse as health care employees and those employed in the food industry as well as blue-collar workers is one avenue of exploration to look at changes in work and labor over time.

Technology, of course, greatly changed the nature of work, as well as how people get to work, which in turn changed the places that workers live. In many industries, for example, new technologies meant that labor itself was deskilled, leading to a need for more unskilled workers in larger numbers, which significantly altered labor-management relations. Technology also led to greater opportunities to exert more control over workers. The timeclock (1889) is one mechanism that contributed to the regimentation of workers' time. The moving assembly line (1913) further increased the monotony of industrial work, which opens a whole host of issues in understanding the nature of labor over time.

Technology can also help interpret gender roles in the workplace; the typewriter alone contributed greatly to the increased number of women in the workforce, thus affecting societal relationships as well as contributing to the rise of organizations like the Young Women's Christian Association (YWCA). Rural Americans also saw their lives changed by technology. New tools for farming not only increased output but also decreased the number of people needed to work the land and increased farm debt as farmers required more credit to buy the new machinery.

The material culture of work and labor thus encompasses a host of objects, structures, spaces, and images—all of which help to humanize one of the most basic facets of life. How Americans earn their living (whether paid or unpaid) is a topic of great interest. The nature of workers and work often goes unmentioned in written historical sources. Material culture allows historians to offer the fullest possible picture of the evolution of work and labor in the United States.

Donna M. DeBlasio

See also Agricultural Work and Labor; Factory and Industrial Work and Labor; Handicraft and Artisanship; Office Work and Labor; Service Industry Work and Labor; Slavery; Technology; Tools, Implements, and Instruments

References and Further Reading
Bradley, Betsy Hunter. 1999. *The Works: The Industrial Architecture of the United States.* New York: Oxford University Press.

Dubofsky, Melvyn, and Foster Rhea Dulles. 2004. *Labor in America: A History.* Wheeling, IL: Harlan Davidson.
Jones, Jacqueline. 1998. *American Work: Four Centuries of Black and White Labor.* New York: W. W. Norton.

World's Fairs and Expositions

Works of the fine and applied arts, scientific and technological inventions, and historic relics have long served to chart and legitimate a nation's history and progress as well as provide material proof for that nation to exist as a geopolitical entity. Novel, beautiful, and historic items have been chosen and displayed in world's fairs and expositions since the Great Exhibition of the Works of Industry of All Nations was held at the Crystal Palace in London in 1851. Especially in the nineteenth and early twentieth centuries, these international spectacles celebrating industrialization influenced greatly Americans' interest in the arts, artifacts, and manufactures of other nations, as they also became venues for the United States to showcase its own claims as a political actor on the world stage. These events also abetted mass consumption of the goods, foods, and designs displayed by manufacturers and commercial entertainment providers.

Though considered peaceful events of unity and cooperation, world's fairs and expositions were fraught with competition between organizers, contributors, and constituents, both within individual nations' borders and between nations, especially those nations in the industrialized West. As "worlds in miniature" constituted of representative objects and peoples, international fairs and expositions offered various groups the opportunity to be represented or, if not, the opportunity for protest. As several historians have observed, the physical sites of the fairs categorized the many peoples and nations of the world according to prevailing Western notions of gender, race, and ethnicity. As complex material expressions of modernity, world's fairs and expositions offer historical "snapshots" of the ways in which nations represented through material and visual culture, architecture, and the built environment their status to their subjects, their citizens, and other nations' governments and peoples.

Rarely profitable, world's fairs and expositions celebrated the material culture of participating nations. Nations understood the events as competitions, and medals were awarded; the displays, the demonstrations, and the ever-increasing size and complexity of successive fairs attest to this understanding. The built environment of each fair—the locations, types, and designs of buildings; the gardens, walkways, and vistas of the fairgrounds; and the technological wonder of the transportation systems— asserted relationships among nations and peoples as well as categorized the material universe. In the latter half of the nineteenth century, the view of industrialization and imperialism as progress celebrated scientific invention and technology and was applied to categorize people on a scale from the "primitive" to the "civilized." On the eve of World War II (1939–1945) fairs began to offer utopian visions of the future and to explore peaceful coexistence and cross-cultural exchange. By the end of the twentieth century, these events presented nations as "brands" through which to assert specific images and ideas. Host cities benefited greatly from the investment in preparing for and in some cases building new infrastructures to accommodate these large fairs. New ideas about urban planning, transportation, light, and color were introduced at world's fairs and expositions.

The United States in the World/The World in the United States

World's fairs, especially in the nineteenth century, commemorated historical events as they surveyed the Western world's industrial progress. The United States display at the 1851 Crystal Palace fair in London introduced to the world the Colt revolver and the McCormick reaper, for example. The United States Centennial International Exhibition in Philadelphia in 1876 celebrated the nation's first one hundred years as it displayed the United States' industrial prowess. Following the popular historical exhibitions of the Civil War's United States Sanitary Commission fairs, the world's fairs of 1876 and 1893 boasted (respectively) a "New England kitchen" and a log cabin, among other exhibitions of American historic relics and commemorative artwork that would spur the Colonial Revival movement. Yet American fairgoers marveled at the great Corliss steam engine that powered the 1876 Centennial fair's Machinery Hall, a building that also contained innovations such as the elevator, electric lights, the calculator, the typewriter, and the telephone. The 1893 Columbian Exposition in Chicago, with its centerpiece of the Beaux-Arts "White City," emphasized a model city designed not only by engineers and architects but also by artists and sculptors. In the many pavilions dedicated to the world's nations, Americans became entranced with the exotic styles of Middle Eastern and Asian exhibitions, adapting Turkish and Japanese aesthetics to their architecture and interior design in the following decades. Exoticism was also embraced in Chicago via the Midway Plaisance, where dancers at the "Street in Cairo," Buffalo Bill's (William F. Cody, 1846–1917) Wild West show, and the Ferris wheel treated Americans to new, sensual experiences.

Major World's Fairs and Expositions in the United States Since 1853

Title	Location	Dates
Exhibition of the Industry of All Nations	New York City, NY	1853
International Exhibition of Arts, Manufactures, and Products of the Soil and Mine (Centennial Exposition)	Philadelphia, PA	1876
International Cotton Exposition	Atlanta, GA	1881
The American Exhibition of the Products, Arts, and Manufactures of Foreign Nations	Boston, MA	1883–1884
Southern Exposition	Louisville, KY	1883–1887
World's Industrial and Cotton Centennial Exposition	New Orleans, LA	1884
Franklin Institute International Electrical Exhibition	Philadelphia, PA	1884
World's Columbian Exposition	Chicago, IL	1893
California Midwinter International Exposition	San Francisco, CA	1894
Cotton States and International Exposition	Atlanta, GA	1895
Tennessee Centennial and International Exposition	Nashville, TN	1897
Trans-Mississippi and International Exposition and Indian Congress	Omaha, NE	1898
Inter-State and West Indian Exposition	Charleston, SC	1901–1902
Pan-American Exposition	Buffalo, NY	1901
Louisiana Purchase International Exposition	St. Louis, MO	1904
Lewis and Clark Centennial and American Pacific Exposition and Oriental Fair	Portland, OR	1905
Jamestown Tercentennial Exposition	Hampton Roads, VA	1907
World's Pure Food Exposition	Chicago, IL	1907
Alaska-Yukon-Pacific Exposition	Seattle, WA	1909
Negro Historical and Industrial Exposition	Richmond, VA	1915
Panama-Pacific International Exposition	San Francisco, CA	1915
Panama California Exposition	San Diego, CA	1915–1916
Sesquicentennial International Exposition	Philadelphia, PA	1926
Century of Progress International Exposition	Chicago, IL	1933–1934
California Pacific International Exposition	San Francisco, CA	1935–1936
Great Lakes Exposition	Cleveland, OH	1936–1937
Texas Centennial Central Exposition (Sesquicentennial)	Dallas, TX	1936
New York World's Fair	New York City, NY	1939–1940
Golden Gate International Exposition	San Francisco, CA	1939–1940
Century 21 Exposition	Seattle, WA	1962
New York World's Fair	New York City, NY	1964–1965
HemisFair '68	San Antonio, TX	1968
Expo '74	Spokane, WA	1974
International Energy Exposition	Knoxville, TN	1982
Louisiana World Exposition	New Orleans, LA	1984

The future was also a topic of fairs, especially in the twentieth century. New York's "Building the World of Tomorrow" in 1939–1940 celebrated progress in the form of technology and consumer products that promised not only ease and leisure but prosperity; this was despite the fact that the fair also commemorated the 150th anniversary of George Washington's (1732–1799) presidential inaugural. Practitioners of a new profession, industrial design, constructed a streamlined Modernist vision of the future. Noted and successful industrial designers and fair board members Norman Bel Geddes (1893–1958), Raymond Loewy (1893–1986), Henry Dreyfuss (1904–1972), and Walter Dorwin Teague (1893–1960) sought to create a vision of the future that adapted consumer society to the machine. Bel Geddes' design of Futurama, part of General Motors' contribution to the fair, projected a United States in 1960 that linked corporations with the nation's wealth and its citizens' daily lives. The Century 21 Exhibition of 1962 also presented the future through the exploration of space and the changing face of architecture, including the Space Needle, which now symbolizes the host city, Seattle, Washington. Nevertheless, fairs after World War II, both in the United States and abroad, were more commercial and spectacular than utopian, more about national branding than historical identity.

The proliferation of international exhibitions led to the creation of the Bureau International des Exhibitions (BIE) in 1928 to promote human knowledge and global goodwill as well as to regulate the number and quality of these events. Located in Paris, the organization currently represents ninety-eight nations that recognize the BIE's governance to regulate international expositions. With the exception of the 1964–1965 New York World's Fair, since 1928 the international

Building the World of Tomorrow was the theme of the 1939 New York World's Fair. This poster depicts the Fair's utopian symbols, the Trylon and Perisphere buildings designed by Wallace K. Harrison and J. André Fouilhoux. These buildings appeared on other forms of World's Fair advertising, including paperweights, salt and pepper shakers, bookends and lamps. (Library of Congress)

expositions held in the United States were approved by the BIE.

Shirley Teresa Wajda

See also Agricultural Fairs and Expositions; Colonial Revival; Consumerism and Consumption; Decorative Arts; Design History and American Design; Industrial Design; Popular Culture; Technology; Tourism and Travel

References and Further Reading

Ames, Kenneth L. 1974. "The Battle of the Sideboards." *Winterthur Portfolio* 9: 1–28.

Brown, Julie K. 2001. *Making Culture Visible: Photography and Display at Industrial Fairs, International Expositions and Institutional Exhibitions in the U.S., 1847–1900.* Amsterdam: Harwood Academic.

Burris, John P. 2001. *Exhibiting Religion: Colonialism and Spectacle at International Expositions, 1851–1893.* Charlottesville: University Press of Virginia.

Findling, John E., and Kimberly Pelle, eds. 1990. *Historical Dictionary of World's Fairs and Expositions, 1851–1988.* Westport, CT: Greenwood Press.

Haddow, Robert H. 1997. *Pavilions of Plenty: Exhibiting American Culture Abroad in the 1950s.* Washington, DC: Smithsonian Institution Press.

Mattie, Erik. 1998. *World's Fairs.* New York: Princeton Architectural Press.

Rydell, Robert W. 1984. *All the World's a Fair: Visions of Empire at American International Expositions, 1876–1916.* Chicago: University of Chicago Press.

Rydell, Robert W., and Nancy E. Gwinn, eds. 1994. *Fair Representations: World's Fairs and the Modern World. European Contributions to American Studies,* vol. 27. Amsterdam: VU University Press.

Y

Yard Sales

Also called *curb, driveway, estate, garage, jumble, moving, porch, rummage,* or *tag sales, yard sales* are informal, temporary venues in which homeowners or neighborhoods offer for public sale used household goods. Often held on weekends or holidays in the spring, summer, and fall when housecleaning and good weather coincide, yard sales are popularly viewed as a means for owners to rid themselves of "clutter" and for consumers to find "bargains." An *estate sale* differs slightly in this purpose: A deceased person's possessions are sold by direction of the estate executor. Yard sales may also be held primarily to profit sellers, and consumers may elect to participate as a form of recreation or as a lifestyle practice. Organizations such as churches, charities, and service groups as well as entire communities have also adapted this activity (commonly called a *rummage sale*) to raise funds for often philanthropic purposes through the donation of used (and sometimes new) goods.

A central feature of yard sales is bargaining for price rather than paying a fixed monetary amount. (One exception is the metropolitan New York/New England practice of *tag sales,* in which sale items are priced.) Although some items may be marked as having a nonnegotiable "firm price," many more items are sold through the give and take of "haggling." Thus these venues counter economists' assertion that the United States has a rational economic system, one in which the market allows or directs the consumer to seek the best price for a given good. Rather, yard sales, very much like auctions, car sales, and real estate sales, depend on factors such as information, emotion, timing, need, and want, as well as competition. By being categorized as a practice marginal to the social norm of paying fixed prices, yard sale activity historically carried with it a taint or lack of respectability. Bargaining itself is fraught with social miscues, with sellers being insulted with offers of prices below their expectations of their personal possessions, and both sellers and buyers seeking the "fair price" being considered greedy, aggressive, and rude. The imperative of friendliness and the inequality of material advantage collide, as do gender roles and class position.

Nevertheless, in the last three decades of the twentieth century, yard sales were elevated by the popularization of collecting and the rise of flea markets throughout the United States. Rather than a degraded consumer practice exercised out of financial necessity and associated with the poor, yard sales offer primarily middle- and working-class Americans the sense of adventure in "questing" for "lost treasure." Yard sales now celebrate affluence and increased consumerism. Since the 1980s, popular domestic advice experts such as Martha Stewart embrace tag sales as a means to find decorative and utilitarian goods. Television shows such as *Antiques Roadshow* endorse the practice by featuring individuals who paid very little at a yard sale for a highly appraised object. The popular style of the 1990s, "shabby chic," so dubbed by its originator, Rachel Ashwell, invited adherents to blend the new with remade "finds" purchased at yard sales, flea markets, architectural salvage warehouses, and auctions. A welter of published "how to" guides and Web sites devoted to yard and garage sales offer advice and anecdotes about *thrifting*—finding bargains, kitsch, collectibles, and antiques. The practice itself has created a vocabulary ("early birds," for example, are those consumers who appear before a yard sale's stated time seeking the best selection) and specific etiquette for such events. The songwriter Kristi Morris recorded the song "Garage Sale" in 2001. *Zen in the Art of Yardsailing* (in development in 2007 by Thunderground Films), explores, in the words of the independent filmmakers, "the cutthroat world of prosumer yardsale shopping." The "world's longest yard sale" takes place every August on Route 127 between Covington, Kentucky, and Gadsden, Alabama. Introduced by Fentress County, Tennessee, executive Mike Walker in 1987, this 450-mile event (also called the Highway 127 Corridor Sale) sought to pull tourists and their dollars away from the interstate highway system and onto the region's scenic byways. The event has been featured on House and Garden Television and is annually noted in the national news.

Shirley Teresa Wajda

See also Antiques; Consumerism and Consumption; Flea Markets; Junk, Scrap, and Salvage; Secondhand Goods and Shopping

References and Further Reading
Herrmann, Gretchen M. 1995. "His and Hers: Gender and Garage Sales." *Journal of Popular Culture* 29: 127–145.
Herrmann, Gretchen M. 1997. "Gift or Commodity: What Changes Hands in the U.S. Garage Sale?" *American Ethnologist* 24 (4): 910–930.
Herrmann, Gretchen M. 2003. "Negotiating Culture: Conflict and Consensus in U.S. Garage-Sale Bargaining." *Ethnology* 42 (3): 237–252.
Herrmann, Gretchen M., and Stephen M. Soiffer. 1984. "For Fun and Profit: An Analysis of the American Garage Sale." *Urban Life* 12 (4): 397–421.
Soiffer, Stephen M., and Gretchen M. Herrmann. 1987. "Visions of Power: Ideology and Practice in the American Garage Sale." *Sociological Review* 35: 48–83.
Strasser, Susan. 1999. *Waste and Want: A Social History of Trash*. New York: Metropolitan Books.
Wajda, Shirley Teresa. "Repo Culture." *Material History Review/Revue d'histoire de la culture materiélle* 54 (2): 110–118.

Bibliography

The wide-ranging scholarship in American material culture studies is difficult to categorize in a neat and forthright manner. The study of physical things and material practices is undertaken by a variety of scholars with wide-ranging training and interests across many traditional academic disciplines. Material culture specialists work in museums, historical societies, libraries, and universities; in historical preservation and conservation; and in marketing, advertising, and other business-related professions. Some work independently as collectors, connoisseurs, and appraisers. All bring different perspectives and approaches to the study of material culture in the United States.

This bibliography is intended as an introductory survey, rather than a comprehensive statement, of the immense field of American material culture studies. We begin with "Origins, History, and Statements of the Field." Much of this work is found in essay form. Neither monolithic nor static, American material culture studies has often been characterized through collections of essays representative of various approaches prevalent at the collections' publication dates. Each collection serves as a sort of historiographical snapshot of this multifaceted field. Works under "Theory and Methodology" reveal the field's range and adaptations, borrowing and benefiting greatly from theoretical positions and methodology across the disciplinary spectrum.

In our attempt to comprehend the field of American material culture studies apart from, but with all due respect to, its historic antecedents, we have chosen to exclude studies of specific makers and artists and of specific regions characteristic of traditional connoisseurship, conventional art history, and historical archaeology, except those studies that otherwise served or serve as innovative or exemplary models of scholarship. We have excluded popular collector's, antiquer's, and restoration guides. Although these guides often prove useful in providing images, typologies and taxonomies, and their publication often precedes scholarly study, such publications, often written with the market in mind, are not consistently reliable as scholarship.

"Bibliographies, Research Guides, Encyclopedias, Dictionaries, Glossaries, Directories, and Reference and Field Guides" offers lists of works within specific subfields as well as useful research tools. The latest scholarship may be found in the periodicals dedicated to American material culture studies and its many subfields. These are listed under "Journals." Rather than reproduce here the entire contents of these periodicals or list individual articles under various headings, we provide readers with journals' World Wide Web sites.

With its emphasis on all the physical senses, material culture is best experienced, or at least better seen rather than read about, and to that end we have included the category "Pictorial Sources, Exhibition Catalogues, and Checklists." General overviews of material culture that chart over time specific forms, techniques, and materials—that is, take objects as subjects—are listed under "Historical Surveys and Studies of Materials, Forms, and Objects."

Echoes of traditional disciplinary inquiry, however, sound in the section titles organizing the remaining bibliographical entries. Of course, many works listed here may be listed under several categories, reflecting the field's interdisciplinarity. Under "Historical Approaches" are works that engage forms of material culture as evidence in chronological explanations of other human phenomena. "Social, Cultural, and Ethnographic Approaches" characterizes those works that explore a form or forms of material culture synchronically (that is, these studies are not primarily concerned with change over time). Works listed as "Linguistic and Literary Approaches" engage objects through their textual representations, while studies that explore style, design, appearance, the built environment, and aesthetics appear under "Visual, Spatial, and Aesthetic Approaches." Books, essays, and articles found under "Technology, Economics, Business, and Consumption" comprehend materialist systems and their consequences.

Theories of collecting and the collection, as well as studies of specific collections as reflections of their individual and institutional creators/curators, have increased in the last two decades, as have the number of works on museum history and museology. Professional practice in conservation and preservation has expanded greatly knowledge of materials, manufacture, and use. These subfields are covered in the sections "Collecting, Collections, Museums, Museum Studies, and Public History" and "Historic Preservation and Materials Conservation."

Readers should, of course, consult first the "Further Reading" sections of individual entries for specific topics of interest.

Origins, History, and Statements of the Field

Alpers, Svetlana. 1977. "Is Art History?" *Daedelus* 1: 1–13.

Ames, Kenneth L. 1977. *Beyond Necessity: Art in the Folk Tradition*. Winterthur, DE: Winterthur Museum.

Appadurai, Arjun, ed. 1986. *The Social Life of Things: Commodities in Cultural Perspective*. Cambridge, UK: Cambridge University Press.

Armstrong, Robert Plant. 1971. *The Affecting Presence: An Essay in Humanistic Anthropology*. Urbana: University of Illinois Press.

Berger, Arthur Asa. 1992. *Reading Matter: Multidisciplinary Perspectives on Material Culture*. New Brunswick, NJ: Transaction Publishers.

Brewer, John, and Roy Porter, eds. 1993. *Consumption and the World of Goods*. New York: Routledge.

Bronner, Simon J. 1985. *American Material Culture and Folklife: A Prologue and Dialogue*. Ann Arbor, MI: UMI Research Press.

Corn, Wanda. 1988. "Coming of Age: Historical Scholarship in American Art." *Art Bulletin* 70 (2): 188–207.

Davis, John. 2003. "The End of the American Century: Current Scholarship on the Art of the United States." *Art Bulletin* 85 (1): 544–580.

DeCunzo, Lu Ann, and Bernard L. Herman, eds. 1996. *Historical Archaeology and the Study of American Culture*. Winterthur, DE: Winterthur Museum.

De Cunzo, Lu Ann, and John H. Jameson, Jr., eds. 2005. *Unlocking the Past: Celebrating Historical Archaeology in North America*. Gainesville: University Press of Florida.

Dewey, John. 1979 (1934). *Art as Experience*. New York: Paragon Books.

Dorson, Richard. 1976. *Folklore and Fakelore: Essays toward a Discipline of Folk Studies*. Cambridge, MA: Harvard University Press.

Elias, Norbert. 1978 (1939). *The Civilizing Process: The History of Manners*, trans. Edmund Jephcott, rpt. ed. New York: Urizen Books.

Fleming, E. McClung. 1958. "Early American Decorative Arts as Social Documents." *Mississippi Valley Historical Review* 45 (2): 276–284.

Glassie, Henry. 1977. "Meaningful Things and Appropriate Myths: The Artifact's Place in American Studies." *Prospects* 3: 1–49.

Jackson, Peter. 1999. "Commodity Cultures: The Traffic in Things." *Transactions of the Institute of British Geographers* (new series) 24 (1): 95–108.

Kouwenhoven, John. 1967 (1948). *The Arts in Modern American Civilization*, rpt. ed. New York: W. W. Norton.

Margolin, Victor. 1988. "A Decade of Design History in the United States 1977–87." *Journal of Design History* 1 (1): 51–72.

Martin, Ann Smart. 1996. "Material Things and Cultural Meanings: Notes on the Study of Early American Material Culture." *William and Mary Quarterly*, 3rd ser. 53 (1): 5–12.

Martin, Ann Smart, and J. Ritchie Garrison, eds. 1997. *American Material Culture: The Shape of the Field*. Winterthur, DE: Winterthur Museum.

Martinez, Katherine, and Kenneth L. Ames, eds. 1997. *The Material Culture of Gender, the Gender of Material Culture*. Winterthur, DE: Winterthur Museum.

Miller, Daniel. 1995. "Consumption and Commodities." *Annual Review of Anthropology* 24: 141–161.

Miller, Daniel, ed. 1998. *Material Culture: Why Some Things Matter*. Chicago: University of Chicago Press.

Oswalt, Wendell H. 1982. "Material Culture in Anthropology." In *Culture and Ecology: Eclectic Perspectives*, ed. John Kennedy and Robert B. Edgerton, 56–64. Washington, DC: American Anthropological Association.

Pearce, Susan M., ed. 1997. *Experiencing Material Culture in the Western World*. London: Leicester University Press.

Pocius, Gerald R., ed. 1991. *Living in a Material World: Canadian and American Approaches to Material Culture*. St. John's, Newfoundland: Institute of Social and Economic Research.

Prown, Jules David. 1982. "Mind in Matter: An Introduction to Material Culture Theory and Method." *Winterthur Portfolio* 17 (1): 1–19.

Prown, Jules David. 1994. "In Pursuit of Culture: The Formal Language of Objects." *American Art* 9 (2): 2–3.

Prown, Jules David. 2001. *Art as Evidence: Writings on Art and Material Culture*. New Haven, CT: Yale University Press.

Prown, Jules David, and Kenneth Haltman. 2000. *American Artifacts: Essays in Material Culture*. East Lansing: Michigan State University Press.

Quimby, Ian M. G., ed. 1978. *Material Culture and the Study of American Life*. New York: W. W. Norton.

Rathje, William L. 1981. "A Manifesto for Modern Material Culture Studies." In *Modern Material Culture: The Archaeology of Us*, 51–66. New York: Academic Press.

Schiffer, Michael B. 1999. *The Material Life of Human Beings: Artifacts, Behavior, and Communication*. London: Routledge.

Schlereth, Thomas J. 1980. *Artifacts and the American Past*. Nashville, TN: American Association for State and Local History.

Schlereth, Thomas J. 1982. *Material Culture Studies in America: An Anthology*. Nashville, TN: American Association for State and Local History.

Schlereth, Thomas J., ed. 1985. *Material Culture: A Research Guide*. Lawrence: University Press of Kansas.

Schlereth, Thomas J. 1985. "Material Culture Research and Historical Explanation." *Public Historian* 7 (4): 21–36.

Schereth, Thomas J. 1989. *Cultural History and Material Culture: Essays on Everyday Life, Landscapes, and Museums*. Ann Arbor: University of Michigan Press.

St. George, Robert Blair. 1988. "Introduction." In *Material Life in America, 1600–1850*, 3–13. Boston: Northeastern University Press.

Tilley, Christopher. 2006. *Handbook of Material Culture*. London: Sage.

Tuan, Yi-Fu. 1980. "The Significance of the Artifact." *Geographical Review* 70 (4): 462–472.

Theory and Methodology

Anderson, Benedict. 1991. *Imagined Communities: Reflections on the Origins and Spread of Nationalism*, rev. ed. New York: Verso.

Arvatov, Boris, and Christina Kiaer. 1997. "Everyday Life and the Culture of the Thing (Toward the Formulation of the Question)." *October* 81: 119–128.

Bachelard, Gaston. 1994 (1969). *The Poetics of Space*, trans. Maria Jolas, rpt. ed. Boston: Beacon Press.

Barthes, Roland. 1977. *Image, Music, Text*, ed. Stephen Heath. New York: Hill and Wang.

Barthes, Roland. 1985. *The Fashion System*. Trans. Matthew Bard and Richard Howard. London: Jonathan Cape.

Barthes, Roland. 1986. *Mythologies*. London: Paladin.

Baudrillard, Jean O. 1995. *Simulacra and Simulation*, trans. Sheila Faria Glaser. Ann Arbor: University of Michigan Press.

Baudrillard, Jean. 1996 (1968). *The System of Objects*, trans. James Benedict. London: Verso.

Benes, Peter, ed. 1987. *Early American Probate Inventories: The Dublin Seminar for New England Folklife Annual Proceedings, July 11 and 12, 1987*. Boston: Boston University.

Benjamin, Walter. 1969 (1936). "The Work of Art in the Age of Mechanical Reproduction." In *Illuminations*, ed. Hannah Arendt, trans. Harry Zohn, 217–251. New York: Schocken Books.

Berger, John, et al. 1972. *Ways of Seeing*. London: British Broadcasting Corporation and Penguin Books.

Berger, Peter L., and Thomas Luckmann. 1967. *The Social Construction of Reality: A Treatise in the Sociology of Knowledge*. New York: Anchor Books.

Bourdieu, Pierre. 1984. *Distinction: A Social Critique of the Judgment of Taste*, trans. Richard Nice. Cambridge, MA: Harvard University Press.

Bronner, Simon J. 1986. "Material Culture and Region: Lessons from Folk Studies." *Kentucky Folklore Record* 32 (1–2): 1–16.

Buisseret, David. 1990. *From Sea Charts to Satellite Images: Interpreting North American History through Maps*. Chicago: University of Chicago Press.

Burke, Edmund. 1759 (1757). *A Philosophical Enquiry into the Origin of Our Ideals of the Sublime and Beautiful*, 2nd ed. London: Robert and James Dodley.

Burke, Peter. 2001. *Eyewitnessing: The Use of Images as Historical Evidence*. Ithaca, NY: Cornell University Press.

Carter, Thomas, and Elizabeth Collins Cromley. 2005. *Invitation to Vernacular Architecture: A Guide to the Study of Ordinary Buildings and Landscapes*. Knoxville: University of Tennessee Press.

Cartwright, Lisa, and Marita Sturken. 2001. *Practices of Looking: An Introduction to Visual Culture*. New York: Oxford University Press.

Daniels, Bruce. 1976. "Probate Court Inventories and Colonial American History: Historiography, Problems and Results." *Social History* [Canada] 9 (18): 387–405.

Danzer, Gerald A. 1997. *Public Places: Exploring Their History*. Walnut Creek, CA: AltaMira Press, publishing in cooperation with the American Association for State and Local History.

De Certeau, Michel. 2002. *The Practice of Everyday Life*, trans. Steven Rendall. Berkeley: University of California Press.

Debord, Guy. 1995. *The Society of the Spectacle*, trans. Donald Nicholson-Smith. New York: Zone Books.

Donald, Moira, and Linda Hurcombe, eds. 2000. *Gender and Material Culture in Archaeological Perspective*. Houndsmill, UK: MacMillan Press Ltd.

Donald, Moira, and Linda Hurcombe, eds. 2000. *Gender and Material Culture in Historical Perspective*. Houndsmill, UK: MacMillan Press Ltd.

Douglas, Mary. 1972. "Deciphering a Meal." *Daedalus* 101: 61–81.

Fleming, E. McClung. 1973. "Artifact Study: A Proposed Model." *Winterthur Portfolio* 9: 153–173.

Foucault, Michel. 1972. *Archaeology of Knowledge: The Discourse on Language*, trans. A. M. Sheridan Smith. New York: Pantheon Books.

Foucault, Michel. 1994 (1972). *The Order of Things: An Archaeology of the Human Sciences*. New York: Vintage.

Fountain, Daniel L. 1995. "Historians and Historical Archaeology: Slave Sites." *Journal of Interdisciplinary History* 26 (1): 67–77.

Frank, Isabelle. 2000. *The Theory of Decorative Art: An Anthology of European and American Writings, 1750–1940*. New Haven, CT: Yale University Press.

Geertz, Clifford. 1973. *The Interpretation of Cultures: Selected Essays*. New York: Basic Books.

Gieryn, Thomas F. 2002. "What Buildings Do." *Theory and Society* 31 (1): 35–74.

Goffman, Erving. 1959. *The Presentation of Self in Everyday Life*. New York: Anchor Books/Doubleday.

Gombrich, E. H. 1985. *Meditations on a Hobby Horse and Other Essays on the Theory of Art*, 4th ed. Chicago: University of Chicago Press.

Gosden, Chris, and Yvonne Marshall. 1999. "The Cultural Biography of Objects." *World Archaeology* 31 (2): 169–178.

Groover, Mark D. 2003. "Identifying Consumption Differences between Social Groups." *North American Archaeologist* 24 (3): 245–257.

Habermas, Jurgens. 1991. *The Structural Transformation of the Public Sphere: An Inquiry into a Category of Bourgeois Society*. Cambridge, MA: MIT Press.

Hall, Edward T. 1959. *The Silent Language*. Garden City, NY: Doubleday.

Hall, Edward T. 1966. *The Hidden Dimension*. Garden City, NY: Doubleday.

Hebdige, Dick. 1979. *Subculture: The Meaning of Style*. New York: Routledge.

Howe, Barbara J., et al. 1987. *Houses and Homes: Exploring Their History*. Nashville, TN: American Association for State and Local History.

Izard, Holly V. 1997. "Random or Systematic? An Evaluation of the Probate Process." *Winterthur Portfolio* 32 (2–3): 147–167.

Johnson, Byron A. 1978. "Probate Inventory: A Guide to Nineteenth-Century Material Culture." *Curator* 21 (3): 181–190.

Jones, Michael Owen. 1997. "How Can We Apply Event Analysis to 'Material Behavior,' and Why Should We?" *Western Folklore* 56 (3/4): 199–214.

Kingery, W. David, ed. 1996. *Learning from Things: Method and Theory of Material Culture Studies*. Washington, DC: Smithsonian Institution Press.

Kirk, John T. 2000. *American Furniture: Understanding Styles, Construction, and Quality*. New York: Harry N. Abrams.

Kubler, George. 1962. The *Shape of Time: Remarks on the History of Things*. New Haven, CT: Yale University Press.

Lefebvre, Henri. 1991. *The Production of Space*, trans. Donald Nicholson-Smith. London: Blackwell.

Leone, Mark P., and Neil Asher Silberman. 1995. *Invisible America: Unearthing Our Hidden History*. New York: Henry Holt.

Lévi-Strauss, Claude. 1965. "The Structural Study of Myth." In *Myth: A Symposium*, ed. Thomas A. Sebeok. Bloomington: Indiana University Press.

Lubar, Steven, and W. David Kingery, eds. *History from Things: Essays on American Culture*. Washington, DC: Smithsonian Institution Press.

MacCannell, Dean. 1989. *The Tourist: A New Theory of the Leisure Class*, rev. ed. New York: Schocken Books.

Marx, Karl. 1976 (1867). *Das Kapital (Capital: A Critique of Political Economy)*. New York: Penguin Books.

Marx, Karl. 2000 (1857–1858). *Grundrisse (Working: Its Meaning and Its Limits)*. Notre Dame, IN: University of Notre Dame Press.

Mauss, Marcel. 2000. *The Gift: The Form and Reason for Exchange in Archaic Societies*, trans. W. D. Halls. New York: W. W. Norton.

McCusker, John J. 1992. *How Much Is that in Real Money? A Historical Price Index for Use as a Deflator of Money Values in the Economy of the United States*. Worcester, MA: American Antiquarian Society.

Miller, Naomi Frances, and Kathryn L. Gleason, eds. 1994. *The Archaeology of Garden and Field*. Philadelphia: University of Pennsylvania Press.

Mirzoeff, Nicholas, ed. 1988. *The Visual Culture Reader*. London: Routledge.

Moe, John F. "'They Sang To My Eye': A Humanistic Approach to the Study of Material Artifacts." *International Journal of Social Education* 1 (1): 37–54.

Montgomery, Charles F. 1962. "Some Remarks on the Practice and Science of Connoisseurship." *The Walpole Society Notebook 1961*, 56–69.

Mugerauer, Robert. 1995. *Interpreting Environments: Tradition, Deconstruction, Hermeneutics*. Austin: University of Texas Press.

Mulvey, Laura. 1975. "Visual Pleasure and Narrative Cinema." *Screen* 16 (3): 6–18.

Orser, Charles E., Jr. 1998. "The Challenge of Race to American Historical Archaeology." *American Anthropologist* (new series) 100 (3): 661–668.

Prown, Jules David. 1980. "Style as Evidence." *Winterthur Portfolio* 15 (3): 197–210.

Pye, David. 1964. *The Nature of Design*. New York: Reinhold Publishing.

Pye, David. 1995 (1968). *The Nature and Art of Workmanship*, rev. ed. Bethel, CT: Cambium Press.

Reynolds, Barrie, and Margaret A. Stott, eds. 1987. *Material Anthropology: Contemporary Approaches to Material Culture*. Lanham, MD: University Press of America.

Richards, Elizabeth, Sherri Martin-Scott, and Kerry Maguire. 1990. "Quilts as Material History: Identifying Research Models." *Uncoverings* 11: 149–163.

Riggins, Stephen Harold, ed. 1994. *The Socialness of Things: Essays on the Socio-Semiotics of Objects*. Berlin: Mouton de Gruyter.

Schein, Richard H. 1997. "A Conceptual Framework for Interpreting an American Scene." *Annals of the Association of American Geographers* 87 (4): 660–680.

Scott, Elizabeth M. 1997. "'A Little Gravy in the Dish and Onions in a Tea Cup': What Cookbooks Reveal about Material Culture." *International Journal of Historical Archaeology* 1 (2): 131–155.

Scott, Joan Wallach. 1986. "Gender: A Useful Category of Analysis." *American Historical Review* 91 (5): 1053–1075.

Simmel, Georg. 1904. "Fashion." *International Quarterly* 10 (1): 130–155.

Simmel, Georg. 1990. *The Philosophy of Money*. London: Routledge.

Smith, Merritt Roe, and Leo Marx, eds. 1994. *Does Technology Drive History?* Cambridge, MA: MIT Press.

Soja, Edward W. 1989. *Postmodern Geographies: The Reassertion of Space in Critical Social Theory*. London: Verso.

Stearns, Peter N., ed. 2006. *A Day in the Life: Studying Daily Life through History*. Westport, CT: Greenwood Press.

Storey, John. 2001. *Cultural Theory and Popular Culture: An Introduction*. Athens: University of Georgia Press.

Thompson, Michael. 1979. *Rubbish Theory: The Creation and Destruction of Value*. New York: Oxford University Press.

Tilley, Christopher, ed. 1990. *Reading Material Culture: Structuralism, Hermeneutics, and Post-Structuralism*. Cambridge, MA: Blackwell.

Tuan, Yi-Fu. 1982. *Segmented Worlds and Self: Group Life and Individual Consciousness*. Minneapolis: University of Minnesota Press.

Upton, Dell. 1992. "The City as Material Culture." In *The Art and Mystery of Historical Archaeology: Essays in Honor of James Deetz*, ed. Anne Elizabeth Yentsch and Mary C. Beaudry, 51–74. Boca Raton, FL: CRC Press.

Upton, Dell. 1996. "Ethnicity, Authenticity, and Invented Tradition." *Historical Archaeology* 30 (2): 1–7.

Veblen, Thorstein. 1899. *The Theory of the Leisure Class: An Economic Study in the Evolution of Institutions*. New York: Macmillan.

Zimmerman, Philip D. 1981. "Workmanship as Evidence: A Model for Object Study." *Winterthur Portfolio* 16 (4): 283–307.

Bibliographies, Research Guides, Encyclopedias, Dictionaries, Glossaries, Directories, and Reference and Field Guides

Ames, Kenneth L., and Gerald W. R. Ward, eds. 1989. *Decorative Arts and Household Furnishings in America, 1650–1920: An Annotated Bibliography*. Winterthur, DE: Winterthur Museum.

Anderson, Clarita S. 1984. "Coverlet Bibliography." *Ars Textrina* 2: 203–215.

Anderson, Clarita S. 2002. *American Coverlets and Their Weavers: Coverlets from the Collection of Foster and Muriel McCarl: Including a Dictionary of More than 700 Coverlet Weavers*. Williamsburg, VA: Colonial Williamsburg Foundation.

Baker, John Milnes. 1994. *American House Styles: A Concise Guide*. New York: W. W. Norton.

Barber, Edwin AtLee. 1904. *Marks of American Potters*. Philadelphia, PA: Patterson and White Co.

Belden, Louise Conway. 1980. *Marks of American Silversmiths in the Ineson-Bissell Collection*. Charlottesville: University Press of Virginia for the Henry Francis du Pont Winterthur Museum.

Berger, Michael L. 2001. *The Automobile in American History and Culture: A Reference Guide*. Westport, CT: Greenwood Press.

Bjerko, Ethel Hall, with John Arthur Bjerkoe. 1957. *The Cabinetmakers of America*. Garden City, NY: Doubleday.

Bronner, Simon J. 1984. *American Folk Art: A Guide to Sources*. Garland Reference Library of the Humanities, vol. 464. New York: Garland Publishing.

Burnham, Dorothy K. 1980. *Warp and Weft: A Textile Terminology*. Toronto: Royal Ontario Museum.

Byars, Mel. 2004. *The Design Encyclopedia*, new ed. New York: Museum of Modern Art.

Cable, Carole. 1989. *Architectural Pattern Books: An Annotated Survey of Recent Scholarship, 1975–1988*. Monticello, IL: Vance Bibliographies.

Calasibetta, Charlotte Mankey. 1986. *Essential Terms of Fashion: A Collection of Definitions*. New York: Fairchild Publications.

Calloway, Stephen, and Elizabeth Cromley, eds. 1991. *The Elements of Style: A Practical Encyclopedia of Interior Architectural Details, from 1485 to the Present*. New York: Simon & Schuster.

Cameron, Elisabeth. 1986. *Encyclopedia of Pottery and Porcelain, 1800–1960*. New York: Facts on File.

Carley, Rachel. 1994. *The Visual Dictionary of American Domestic Architecture*. New York: Henry Holt and Co.

Clabburn, Pamela. 1976. *The Needleworker's Dictionary*. New York: William Morrow.

Clayton, Michael. 1971. *The Collector's Dictionary of the Silver and Gold of Great Britain and North America*. New York: World Publishing.

Crom, Theodore R. 1989. *Trade Catalogues, 1542–1842*. Melrose, FL: T. R. Crom.

Cummings, Abbott Lowell, ed. 1964. *Rural Household Inventories: Establishing the Names, Uses, and Furnishings of Rooms in the Colonial New England Home, 1675–1775*. Boston: Society for the Preservation of New England Antiquities.

Cuthbert, John A., Barry Ward, and Maggie Keeler. 1985. *Vernacular Architecture in America: A Selective Bibliography*. Boston: G. K. Hall.

Darbee, Herbert C. 1965. *A Glossary of Old Lamps and Lighting Devices*. Technical Leaflet No. 30. Nashville, TN: American Association for State and Local History.

Davis, Audrey B. 1986. *The Finest Instruments Ever Made: A Bibliography of Medical, Dental, Optical, and Pharmaceutical Company Trade Literature, 1700–1939.* Arlington, MA: Medical History Publishing Associates.

Derwich, Jenny B. 1984. *Dictionary Guide to United States Pottery and Porcelain (Nineteenth and Twentieth Century).* Franklin, MI: Jenstan.

Dillistin, William H. 1949. *Bank Note Reporters and Counterfeit Detectors, 1826–1866; with a Discourse on Wildcat Banks and Wildcat Bank Notes.* New York: American Numismatic Society.

Distin, William H., and Robert Bishop. 1976. *The American Clock: A Comprehensive Pictorial Survey, 1723–1900, with a Listing of 6,153 Clockmakers.* New York: E. P. Dutton.

Doumato, Lamia. 1987. *Vernacular Houses in the U.S.A.* Monticello, IL: Vance Bibliographies.

Dow, George Francis. 1967 (1927). *The Arts and Crafts in New England, 1704–1775: Gleanings from Boston Newspapers Relating to Painting, Engraving, Silversmiths, Pewterers, Clockmakers, Furniture, Pottery, Old Houses, Costume, Trades and Occupations.* New York: Da Capo Press.

Emerson, William. 1996. *Encyclopedia of United States Army Insignia and Uniforms.* Norman: University of Oklahoma Press.

Evans, Charles. 1903–1959. *American Bibliography. A Chronological Dictionary of All Books, Pamphlets and Periodical Publications Printed in the United States of America from the Genesis of Printing in 1639 Down to and Including the Year 1820.* 12 vols. Chicago: Blakely Press.

Evans, Paul. 1974. *Art Pottery of the United States: An Encyclopedia of Producers and Their Marks.* New York: Charles Scribner's Sons.

Fleming, John, and Hugh Honour. 1989. *The Penguin Dictionary of Decorative Arts.* London: Penguin Books.

Franklin, Linda Campbell. 1978. *Antiques and Collectibles: A Bibliography of Works in English, 16th Century to 1976.* Metuchen, NJ: Scarecrow Press.

Gitner, Fred, ed. 1995. *Medical Trade Catalogs at The New York Academy of Medicine Library: A Bibliography.* New York: New York Academy of Medicine.

Gordon, Beverly. 1978. *Domestic American Textiles: A Bibliographic Source-Book.* Pittsburgh, PA: Center for the History of American Needlework.

Gottfried, Herbert, and Jan Jennings. 1988. *American Vernacular Design, 1870–1940.* Ames: Iowa State University Press.

Graham, Joe S. 1989. *Hispanic-American Material Culture: An Annotated Directory of Collections, Sites, Archives, and Festivals in the United States.* Westport, CT: Greenwood Press.

Groce, George C., and David H. Wallace. 1957. *The New York Historical Society's Dictionary of Artists in America, 1564–1860.* New Haven, CT: Yale University Press; London: Oxford University Press.

Harris, Dianne. 1999/2000. "The Postmodernization of Landscape: A Critical Historiography." *Journal of the Society of Architectural Historians* 58(3): 434–443.

Hayden, Dolores. 2004. *A Field Guide to Sprawl.* New York: W. W. Norton.

Hobbie, Margaret. 1992. *Italian American Material Culture: A Dictionary of Collections, Sites, and Festivals in the United States and Canada.* Westport, CT: Greenwood Press.

Jakle, John A., Robert W. Bastian, and Douglas K. Meyer. 1989. *Common Houses in America's Small Towns: The Atlantic Seaboard to Mississippi Valley.* Athens: University of Georgia Press.

Jakle, John A., Douglas K. Meyer, and Robert W. Bastian. 1981. *American Common Houses: A Selected Bibliography of Vernacular Architecture.* Monticello, IL: Vance Bibliographies.

Jerde, Judith. 1992. *Encyclopedia of Textiles.* New York: Facts on File.

Karmason, Marilyn G., and Joan B. Stacke. 1989. *Majolica: A Complete History and Illustrated Survey.* New York: Harry N. Abrams.

Karpel, Bernard, ed. 1979. *Arts in America: A Bibliography.* 4 vols. Washington, DC: Smithsonian Institution Press.

Krooss, Herman E., ed. 1983. *Documentary History of Banking and Currency in the United States.* 4 vols. New York: Chelsea House.

Leggett, M.D., comp. 1976 (1874). *Subject-Matter Index of Patents for Inventions Issued by the United States Patent Office from 1790–1873, Inclusive.* 3 vols, rpt. ed. New York: Arno.

Lewis, Philippa, and Gillian Darley. 1986. *Dictionary of Ornament*. New York: Pantheon Books.

Maddex, Diane, ed. 1985. *Built in the U.S.A.: American Buildings From Airports to Zoos*. Washington, DC: National Trust for Historic Preservation.

Marshall, Howard Wight. 1981. *American Folk Architecture: A Selected Bibliography*. Washington, DC: American Folklife Center, Library of Congress.

Marti, Donald. B. 1986. *Historical Directory of American Agricultural Fairs*. Westport, CT: Greenwood Press.

McAlester, Virginia, and Lee McAlester. 1989. *A Field Guide to American Houses*. New York: Alfred A. Knopf.

McKinstry, E. Richard. 1984. *Trade Catalogues at Winterthur: A Guide to the Literature of Merchandising, 1750–1980*. New York: Garland Publishing.

Mergen, Bernard. 1980. *Play and Playthings: A Reference Guide*. Westport, CT: Greenwood Press.

Montgomery, Florence M. 1984. *Textiles in America, 1650–1870: A Dictionary*. New York: W. W. Norton.

Nash, Ray. 1959. *American Writing Masters and Copybooks; History and Bibliography Through Colonial Times*. Boston: Colonial Society of Massachusetts.

Nelson, Robert, and Richard Shiff. 2003. *Critical Terms for Art History*, 2nd ed. Chicago: University of Chicago Press.

Newman, Harold. 1977. *An Illustrated Dictionary of Glass*. London: Thames and Hudson.

Newton, Sarah E. 1994. *Learning to Behave: A Guide to American Conduct Books before 1900*. Westport, CT: Greenwood Press.

Noble, Allen G., and Richard K. Cleek. 1995. *The Old Barn Book: A Field Guide to North American Barns and Other Farm Structures*. New Brunswick, NJ: Rutgers University Press.

Noël Hume, Ivor. 1969. *A Guide to Artifacts of Colonial America*. New York: Alfred A. Knopf.

Oliver, Valerie. 1996. *Fashion and Costume in American Popular Culture: A Reference Guide*. Westport, CT: Greenwood Press.

Oshins, Lisa Turner, comp. 1987. *Quilt Collections: A Directory for the United States and Canada*. Washington, DC: Acropolis Books.

Peterson, Harold Leslie. 1956. *Arms and Armor in Colonial America, 1526–1783*. Harrisburg, PA: Stackpole.

Poppeliers, John, and S. Allen Chambers, Jr. 2003. *What Style Is It? A Guide to American Architecture*, rev. ed. Hoboken, NJ: John Wiley and Sons.

Rainwater, Dorothy T. 1975. *Encyclopedia of American Silver Manufacturers*. New York: Crown Publishers.

Reiff, Daniel D. 2000. *Houses from Books: Treatise, Pattern Books, and Catalogs in American Architecture, 1738–1850: A History and Guide*. University Park: Pennsylvania State University Press.

Revi, Albert Christian. 1964. *American Pressed Glass and Figure Bottles*. New York: Thomas Nelson and Sons.

Revi, Albert Christian. 1967. *Nineteenth Century Glass: Its Genesis and Development*, rev. ed. New York: Galahad Books.

Revi, Albert Christian. 1968. *American Art Nouveau Glass*. Camden, NJ: Thomas Nelson and Sons.

Richter, Paula Bradstreet. 2001. *Painted with Thread: The Art of American Embroidery*. Salem, MA: Peabody Essex Museum.

Rickards, Maurice, and Michael Twyman, eds. 2000. *The Encyclopedia of Ephemera: A Guide to the Fragmentary Documents of Everyday Life for the Collector, Curator and Historian*. New York: Routledge.

Rifkind, Carole. 1980. *A Field Guide to American Architecture*. New York: New American Library.

Romaine, Lawrence B. 1960. *A Guide to American Trade Catalogues, 1744–1900*. New York: R. R. Bowker.

Rudmin, Floyd W., Russell W. Belk, and Lita Furbey. 1987. *Social Science Bibliography on Property, Ownership, and Possession: 1580 Citations from Psychology, Anthropology, Sociology, and Related Disciplines*. Monticello, IL: Vance Bibliographies.

Rullo, Guiseppina. 1987. "People and Home Interiors: A Bibliography of Recent Psychological Research." *Environment and Behavior* 19 (2): 250–259.

Schimmelman, Janice G. 1999. *Architectural Books in Early America: Architectural Treatises and Building Handbooks Available in American Libraries and Bookstores through 1800*. New Castle, DE: Oak Knoll.

Shortridge, Barbara G., and James R. Shortridge. 1995. "Cultural Geography of American Foodways: An Annotated Bibliography." *Journal of Cultural Geography* 15 (2): 79–108.

Shumsky, Neil Larry, ed. 1998. *Encyclopedia of Urban America: The Cities and Suburbs*. Santa Barbara, CA: ABC-CLIO.

Smart, Charles E. 1962, 1967. *The Makers of Surveying Instruments in America since 1700*. 2 vols. Troy, NY: Regal Art Press.

Snodgrass, Mary Ellen. 2004. *Encyclopedia of Kitchen History*. New York: Fitzroy Dearborn.

Steele, Valerie, ed. 2005. *Encyclopedia of Clothing and Fashion*. Farmington Hills, MI: Charles Scribner's Sons.

Strong, Susan R. 1983. *History of American Ceramics: An Annotated Bibliography*. Metuchen, NJ: Scarecrow Press.

Trench, Lucy, ed. 2000. *Materials and Techniques in the Decorative Arts: An Illustrated Dictionary*. Chicago: University of Chicago Press.

Walker, Lester. 1981. *American Shelter: An Illustrated Encyclopedia of the American House*. Cambridge, MA: MIT Press.

Webb, Pauline, and Mark Suggitt. 2000. *Gadgets and Necessities: An Encyclopedia of Household Innnovations*. Santa Barbara, CA: ABC-CLIO.

Webster, John G., ed. 1988. *Encyclopedia of Medical Devices and Instrumentation*. 4 vols. New York: Wiley.

Weidner, Ruth Irwin, comp. 1982. *American Ceramics before 1930: A Bibliography*. Westport, CT: Greenwood Press.

Wertkin, Gerard C., ed. 2004. *Encyclopedia of American Folk Art*. New York: Routledge.

Williams, Raymond. 1983. *Keywords: A Vocabulary of Culture and Society*, rev. ed. New York: Oxford University Press.

Worrell, Estelle Ansley. 1980. *Children's Costume in America 1607–1910*. New York: Charles Scribner's Sons.

Journals

American Antiquity
http://www.saa.org/publications/AmAntiq/amantiq.html
American Art
http://www.journals.uchicago.edu/AmArt/
American Ceramic Circle Journal
http://www.amercercir.org/publications.htm
American Furniture
http://www.chipstone.org/publications/AFALL.html
American Indian Art Magazine
http://www.aiamagazine.com
Ceramics in America
http://www.chipstone.org/framesetpublications.html
Clothing and Textiles Research Journal
http://www.itaaonline.org
Collections: A Journal for Museum and Archives Professionals
http://www.altamirapress.com/RLA/Journals/Collections/
Curator: The Museum Journal
http://www.altamirapress.com/RLA/Journals/Curator/
Design Issues
http://www.mitpressjournals.org/loi/desi
Dress: The Journal of the Costume Society of America
http://www.costumesocietyamerica.com/Bookstore/bookstorepages/publicationarea.htm

Food, Culture and Society
http://www.bergpublishers.com/us/food/food_about.htm
Gastronomica
http://www.ucpress.edu/journals/gfc/
Historical Archaeology
http://www.sha.org/Publications/sha_ha.htm
Home Cultures
http://www.bergpublishers.com/us/material/material_about.htm
IA: Journal for the Society for Industrial Archeology
http://www.sia-web.org/iajournal/siaia.html
Journal of the American Institute for Conservation
Journal of Consumer Culture
http://www.sagepub.com/journal.aspx?pid=265
Journal of Consumer Research
http://www.journals.uchicago.edu/JCR/home.html
Journal of Cultural Geography
http://www.geog.okstate.edu/users/culture/culture.htm
Journal of Decorative and Propaganda Arts
http://www.wolfsonian.fiu.edu/education/publications/dapa.main.html
Journal of Design History
http://jdh.oxfordjournals.org/
Journal of Early Southern Decorative Arts
http://www.oldsalem.org/about/esda.htm
Journal of the History of Collections
http://www.oxfordjournals.org/hiscol/about.html
Journal of Material Culture
http://www.sagepub.com/journal.aspx?pid=112
Journal of Museum Education
http://www.lcoastpress.com/wst_page10.html
Journal of Planning History
http://www.sagepub.com/journal.aspx?pid=341
Journal of the American Planning Association
http://www.planning.org/japa/index.htm
Journal of the Society of Architectural Historians
http://www.sah.org
Journal of Visual Culture
http://www.sagepub.com/journal.aspx?pid=264
Landscape Journal: Design, Planning and Management of the Land
http://www/wisc/edu/wisconsinpress/journals/journals/lj.html
The Magazine Antiques
http://www.magazineantiques.com/
Material History Review
http://www.sciencetech.technomuses.ca/english/about/hreview.cfm
Material Religion: The Journal of Objects, Art and Belief
http://www.bergpublishers.com/us/material/material_about.htm
Museums and Social Issues: A Journal of Contemporary Controversies
http://www.lcoastpress.com/wst_page10.html
Northeast Historical Archaeology
http://www.smcm.edu/Academics/soan/cneha/publ.htm
Perspectives in Vernacular Architecture
http://www.vernaculararchitectureforum.org/publications.html

Preservation: The Magazine of the National Trust for Historic Preservation
   http://www.nationaltrust.org/Magazine/index.htm
The Public Historian
   http://www.ucpress.edu/journals/tph/
Senses and Society
   http://www.bergpublishers.com/uk/senses/senses_about.htm
Space and Culture: International Journal of Social Spaces
   http://www.sagepub.com/journal.aspx?pid=287
Studies in the Decorative Arts
   http://www.bgc.bard.edu/academic/journal.shtml
Studies in the History of Gardens and Designed Landscapes
   http://www.tandf.co.uk/journals/titles/14601176.asp
Textile: The Journal of Cloth & Culture
   http://www.bergpublishers.com/us/textiles/textile_advise.htm
Winterthur Portfolio: A Journal of American Material Culture
   http://www.journals.uchicago.edu/WP/home.html

Pictorial Resources, Exhibition Catalogues, and Checklists

Barquist, David L. 1985. *American and English Pewter at the Yale University Art Gallery: A Supplemental Checklist*. New Haven, CT: Yale University Art Gallery.

Bates, Elizabeth Bidwell, and Jonathan L. Fairbanks. 1981. *American Furniture, 1620 to the Present*. New York: R. Marek Publishers.

Battison, Edwin A., and Patricia E. Kane. 1973. *The American Clock, 1725–1865: The Mabel Brady Garvan and Other Collections at Yale University*. Greenwich, CT: New York Graphic Society.

Baumgarten, Linda. 2002. *What Clothes Reveal: The Language of Clothing in Colonial and Federal America: The Colonial Williamsburg Collection*. Williamsburg, VA: Colonial Williamsburg Foundation.

Berlo, Janet Catherine, and Patricia Cox Crews, with Carolyn Ducey, Jonathan Holstein, and Michael James. 2003. *Wild by Design: Two Hundred Years of Innovation and Artistry in American Quilts*. Lincoln: International Quilt Study Center at the University of Nebraska–Lincoln; Seattle: University of Washington Press.

Bishop, Robert. 1972. *Centuries and Styles of the American Chair, 1640–1970*. New York: E. P. Dutton.

Blühm, Andreas, and Louise Lippincott. 2000. *Light! The Industrial Age, 1750–1900: Art & Science, Technology & Society*. London: Thames and Hudson; Pittsburgh: Carnegie Museum of Art; Amsterdam: Van Gogh Museum.

Blum, Stella, ed. 1974. *Victorian Fashions and Costumes from Harper's Bazaar: 1867–1898*. New York: Dover Publications.

Blum, Stella, ed. 1985. *Fashions and Costumes from* Godey's Lady's Book. New York: Dover Publications.

Botwinick, Michael, et al. 1979. *The American Renaissance, 1876–1917*. New York: Brooklyn Museum.

Bruhn, Thomas P. 1979. *American Decorative Tiles, 1870–1930*. Storrs, CT: William Benton Museum of Art, University of Connecticut.

Buhler, Kathryn C., and Graham Hood. 1970. *American Silver: Garvan and Other Collections in the Yale University Art Gallery*. 2 vols. New Haven, CT: Yale University Press for the Yale University Art Gallery.

Burke, Doreen Bolger, Jonathan Freedman, and Alice Cooney Frelinghuysen. 1986. *In Pursuit of Beauty: Americans and the Aesthetic Movement*. New York: Metropolitan Museum of Art.

Byron, Joseph. 1976. *New York Interiors at the Turn of the Century*. New York: Dover Publications in cooperation with the Museum of the City of New York.

Clark, Robert Judson, ed. 1972. *The Arts and Crafts Movement in America, 1876–1916*. Princeton, NJ: Princeton University Press.

Cooper, Wendy A. 1980. *In Praise of America: American Decorative Arts, 1650–1930; Fifty Years of Discovery Since the 1929 Girl Scouts Loan Exhibition*. New York: Alfred A. Knopf.

Cooper, Wendy A. 1993. *Classical Taste in America, 1800–1840*. New York: Abbeville Press.

Cooper-Hewitt Museum. 1995. *Kitsch to Corbusier: Wallpapers from the 1950s.* New York: Cooper-Hewitt National Design Museum, Smithsonian Institution.

Denker, Ellen Paul. 1989. *Lenox China: Celebrating a Century of Quality, 1889–1989.* Trenton: Lenox China and New Jersey State Museum.

Denker, Ellen, Charles L. Venable, Stephen G. Harrison, and Katherine C. Grier. 2000. *China and Glass in America, 1880–1980: From Table Top to TV Tray.* New York: Harry N. Abrams.

Fairbanks, Jonathan L., and Robert F. Trent. 1982. *New England Begins: The Seventeenth Century.* 3 vols. Boston: Museum of Fine Arts.

Feld, Stuart P. 1999. *Boston in the Age of Neo-Classicism, 1810–1840.* New York: Hirsch & Adler Galleries.

Forman, Benno M. 1988. *American Seating Furniture, 1630–1730: An Interpretive Catalogue.* New York: W. W. Norton.

Fowble, McSherry E. 1987. *Two Centuries of Prints in America, 1680–1880.* Charlottesville: University Press of Virginia.

Frelinghuysen, Alice Cooney. 1989. *American Porcelain, 1770–1920.* New York: Metropolitan Museum of Art.

Frelinghuysen, Alice Cooney, et al. 1986. *In Pursuit of Beauty: Americans and the Aesthetic Movement.* New York: Metropolitan Museum of Art.

Garvan, Beatrice B. 1987. *Federal Philadelphia, 1785–1825: The Athens of the Western World.* Philadelphia, PA: Philadelphia Museum of Art.

Hanks, David A. 1981. *Innovative Furniture in America from 1800 to the Present.* New York: Horizon Press.

Haskell, Barbara. 1999. *The American Century: Art & Culture, 1900–1950.* New York: Whitney Museum of American Art in association with W. W. Norton.

Heckscher, Morrison H. 1985. *American Furniture in the Metropolitan Museum of Art, Late Colonial Period: The Queen Anne and Chippendale Styles.* New York: Metropolitan and Random House.

Heckscher, Morrison H., and Leslie Greene Bowman. 1992. *American Rococo, 1750–1775: Elegancy in Ornament.* New York: Harry N. Abrams.

Heisey, John W., comp. 1978. *A Checklist of American Coverlet Weavers,* ed. Gail C. Andrews and Donald R. Walters. Williamsburg, VA: Colonial Williamsburg Foundation.

Heisinger, Kathryn B., and George H. Marcus, eds. 1983. *Design since 1945.* Philadelphia, PA: Philadelphia Museum of Art.

Historic American Buildings Survey/Historic American Engineering Record. 1995. *American Preserved: A Checklist of Historic Buildings, Structures, and Sites: Recorded by The Historic American Buildings Survey/Historic American Engineering Record.* Washington, DC: Library of Congress.

Hosley, William. 1990. *The Japan Idea: Art and Life in Victorian America.* Hartford, CT: Wadsworth Atheneum.

Howe, Katherine S., and David B. Warren. 1976. *The Gothic Revival Style in America, 1830–1870.* Houston, TX: Museum of Fine Arts.

Kaplan, Wendy. 1987. *"The Art That Is Life": The Arts and Crafts Movement in America, 1875–1920.* Boston: Little, Brown for the Museum of Fine Arts.

Kaplan, Wendy, ed. 1995. *Designing Modernity: The Arts of Reform and Persuasion, 1885–1945.* New York: The Wolfsonian and Thames and Hudson.

Kaplan, Wendy, et al. 2004. *The Arts and Crafts Movement in Europe and America: Design for the Modern World.* New York: Thames and Hudson in association with the Los Angeles County Museum of Art.

Kardon, Janet, ed. 1994. *Revivals! Diverse Traditions, 1920–1945: The History of Twentieth-Century American Craft.* New York: Harry N. Abrams.

Kardon, Janet, et al., eds. 1993. *The Ideal Home 1900–1920: The History of Twentieth-Century Craft in America.* New York: Harry N. Abrams for American Craft Museum.

Kirk, John T. 1982. *American Furniture and the British Tradition to 1830.* New York: Alfred A. Knopf.

Lash, Stephen, et al. 2005. *America and the Sea: Treasures from the Collections of Mystic Seaport.* New Haven, CT: Yale University Press.

Libin, Laurence. 1994. *Our Tuneful Heritage: American Musical Instruments from the Metropolitan Museum of Art*. Provo, UT: Museum of Art, Brigham Young University.

MacDougall, Elisabeth Blair. 1990. *The Architectural Historian in America*. Washington, DC: National Gallery of Art.

Martin, Ann Smart. 1999. *Makers and Users: American Decorative Arts, 1630–1820, from the Chipstone Collection*. Madison, WI: Elvehjem Museum of Art.

Mayhew, Edgar de N., and Minor Myers, Jr. 1980. *A Documentary History of American Interiors from the Colonial Era to 1915*. New York: Charles Scribner's Sons.

Meyer, Marilee B., ed. 1997. *Inspiring Reform: Boston's Arts & Crafts Movement*. Wellesley, MA: Wellesley College Museum.

Newark Museum Association. 1963. *Classical America, 1815–1845*, text by Berry B. Tracy and William H. Gerdts. Newark, NJ: Newark Museum.

Nichols, Sarah. 2000. *Aluminum by Design: Jewelry to Jets*. Pittsburgh, PA: Carnegie Museum of Art and Harry N. Abrams.

Nickel, Douglas. 1998. *Snapshots: The Photography of Everyday Life, 1888 to the Present*. San Francisco: San Francisco Museum of Modern Art.

Palmer, Arlene. 1993. *Glass in Early America: Selections from the Henry Frances du Pont Winterthur Museum*. Winterthur, DE: Winterthur Museum.

Papert, Emma. 1972. *The Illustrated Guide to American Glass*. New York: Hawthorn Books.

Peterson, Harold L. 1971. *American Interiors from Colonial Times to the Late Victorians: A Pictorial Source Book of American Domestic Interiors with an Appendix on Inns and Taverns*. New York: Charles Scribner's Sons.

Phillips, Lisa. 1999. *The American Century: Art & Culture, 1950–2000*. New York: Whitney Museum of American Art in association with W. W. Norton.

Reps, John W. 1998. *Bird's Eye Views: Historic Lithographs of North American Cities*. Princeton, NJ: Princeton University Press.

Ring, Betty. 1987. *American Needlework Treasures: Samplers and Silk Embroideries from the Collection of Betty Ring*. New York: E. P. Dutton in association with the Museum of American Folk Art.

Robinson, Julian. 1998. *The Quest for Human Beauty: An Illustrated History*. New York: W. W. Norton.

Schoelwer, Susan P. 2000. *Lions & Eagles & Bulls: Early American Tavern & Inn Signs*. Hartford: Connecticut Historical Society.

Schreier, Barbara A. 1994. *Becoming American Women: Clothing and the Jewish Immigrant Experience, 1880–1920*. Chicago: Chicago Historical Society.

Seale, William. 1981. *The Tasteful Interlude: American Interiors through the Camera's Eyes, 1860–1917*, 2nd ed., rev. and enl. Nashville, TN: American Association for State and Local History.

Severa, Joan L. 1995. *Dressed for the Photographer: Ordinary Americans & Fashion, 1840–1900*. Kent, OH: Kent State University Press.

Spillman, Jane Shadel. 1981. *American and European Pressed Glass in the Corning Museum of Glass*. Corning, NY: The Corning Museum of Glass.

Spillman, Jane Shadel, and Suzanne K. Frantz. 1990. *Masterpieces of American Glass*. New York: Crown Publishers.

Stern, Jewel. 2005. *Modernism in American Silver: 20th-Century Design*, ed. Kevin W. Tucker and Charles L. Venable. Dallas: Dallas Museum of Art; New Haven, CT: Yale University Press.

Thornton, Peter. 1984. *Authentic Decor: The Domestic Interior, 1620–1920*. New York: Viking Penguin.

Tracy, Berry B., Marilynn Johnson, Marvid D. Schwartz, and Suzanne Boorsch. 1970. *19th-Century America: Furniture and Other Decorative Arts: An Exhibition in Celebration of the Hundredth Anniversary of the Metropolitan Museum of Art, April 16 through September 7, 1970*. New York: Metropolitan Museum of Art.

Venable, Charles L. 1994. *Silver in America, 1840–1940: A Century of Splendor*. Dallas: Dallas Museum of Art; New York: Harry N. Abrams.

Vincent, Margaret. 1987. *The Ladies' Work Table: Domestic Needlework in Nineteenth-Century America*. Allentown, PA: Allentown Art Museum.

Voorsanger, Catherine Hoover, and John K. Howat, eds. 2000. *Art and the Empire City*. New York: Metropolitan Museum of Art.

Ward, Barbara McLean, and Gerald W. R. Ward, eds. 1979. *Silver in American Life: Selections from the Mabel Brady Garvan and Other Collections at Yale University*. Boston: David R. Godine in association with the Yale University Art Gallery and the American Federation of Arts.

Ward, Gerald W. R. 1988. *American Case Furniture in the Mabel Brady Garvan and Other Collections at Yale University*. New Haven, CT: Yale University Art Gallery.

Ward, Gerald W. R., and William N. Hosley, Jr., eds. 1985. *The Great River: Art and Society of the Connecticut Valley, 1635–1820*. Hartford, CT: Wadsworth Athenaeum.

Warren, David B., Katherine S. Howe, and Michael K. Brown. 1987. *Marks of Achievement: Four Centuries of American Presentation Silver*. New York: Harry N. Abrams, for the Museum of Fine Arts, Houston, TX.

Watkins, Malcolm. 1952. *Artificial Lighting in America, 1830–1860*. Washington, DC: Smithsonian Institution.

Wilson, Kenneth M. 1995. *American Glass, 1760–1930: The Toledo Museum of Art*. New York: Hudson Hills Press.

Wright, John L., ed. 1992. *Possible Dreams: Enthusiasm for Technology in America*. Dearborn, MI: Henry Ford Museum and Greenfield Village.

Yale University Art Gallery. 1965. *American Pewter: Garvan and Other Collections at Yale*. New Haven, CT: Yale University Art Gallery.

Historical Surveys and Studies of Materials, Forms, and Objects

Adams, Jonathan. 2001. "Ships and Boats as Archaeological Source Material." *World Archaeology* 32 (3): 292–310.

Allen, Alistair, and Joan Hoverstadt. 1983. *The History of Printed Scraps*. London: New Cavendish Books.

Amory, Hugh, and David D. Hall, eds. 2000. *The Colonial Book in America*, vol. 1 of *A History of the Book in America*, ed. David D. Hall. 5 vols. Cambridge, UK: Cambridge University Press.

Angeloglou, Maggie. 1970. *A History of Make-Up*. London: Macmillan Co.

Arthur, Linda B., ed. 1999. *Religion, Dress and the Body*. Oxford, UK: Berg.

Aslet, Clive. 1990. *The American Country House*. New Haven, CT: Yale University Press.

Bailey, Chris H. 1875. *Two Hundred Years of American Clocks and Watches*. Englewood Cliffs, NJ: Prentice-Hall.

Barber, Edwin AtLee. 1909. *The Pottery and Porcelain of the United States: An Historical Review of American Ceramic Art from the Earliest Times to the Present Day; to Which is Appended a Chapter on the Pottery of Mexico*, 3rd ed., rev. and enl. New York: G. P. Putnam's Sons.

Beldon, Louise Conway. 1983. *The Festive Tradition: Table Decorations and Desserts in America, 1650–1900*. New York: W. W. Norton.

Berlo, Janet Catherine, and Ruth B. Phillips. 1998. *Native North American Art*. New York: Oxford University Press.

Bjelajac, David. 2005. *American Art: A Cultural History*, 2nd ed. Upper Saddle River, NJ: Prentice-Hall.

Bolton, Ethel Stanwood, and Eva Johnston Coe. 1921. *American Samplers*. Boston: Massachusetts Society of the Colonial Dames of America.

Bradford, Nancy. 1968. *Costume in Detail: Women's Dress 1730–1930*. Boston: Plays, Inc.

Breward, Christopher. 1995. *The Culture of Fashion: A New History of Fashionable Dress*. Manchester, UK: Manchester University Press.

Brown, Ann Eckert. 2003. *American Wall Stenciling, 1790–1840*. Hanover, NH: University Press of New England.

Butler, Joseph T. 1967. *Candleholders in America, 1650–1900: A Comprehensive Collection of American and European Candle Fixtures used in America*. New York: Crown Publishers.

Claney, Jane Perkins. 2004. *Rockingham Ware in American Culture, 1830–1930: Reading Historical Artifacts*. Hanover, NH: University Press of New England.

Cohen, Nancy E. 2002. *America's Marketplace: The History of Shopping Centers*. Lyme, CT: Greenwich Publishing Group.

Colby, Averil. 1971. *Quilting*. New York: Charles Scribner's Sons.

Constantine, Mildred, and Jack Lenor Larsen. 1973. *Beyond Craft: The Art Fabric*. New York: Van Nostrand Reinhold.

Cooke, Edward S., Jr., ed. 1987. *Upholstery in America and Europe from the Seventeenth Century to World War I*. New York: W. W. Norton.

Cooper, Grace Rogers. 1976. *The Sewing Machine: Its Invention and Development*. Washington, DC: Smithsonian Institution Press for the National Museum of History and Technology.

Cranz, Galen. 1982. *The Politics of Park Design: A History of Urban Parks in America*. Cambridge, MA: MIT Press.

Cummings, Abbott Lowell. 1961. *Bed Hangings; a Treatise on Fabrics and Styles in the Curtaining of Beds, 1650–1850*. Boston: Society for the Preservation of New England Antiquities.

Cummings, Abbott Lowell. 1979. *The Framed Houses of Massachusetts Bay, 1625–1725*. Cambridge, MA: Belknap Press.

Denker, Ellen, and Bert Denker. 1979. *The Rocking Chair Book*. New York: Mayflower Books.

Dockstader, Frederick J. 1978. *Weaving Arts of the North American Indian*. New York: Crowell.

Earle, Alice Morse. 1968 (1903). *Two Centuries of Costume in America*. 2 vols. New York: B. Blom.

Edmonds, Mary Jaene. 1991. *Samplers and Samplermakers: An American Schoolgirl Art, 1700–1850*. New York: Rizzoli.

Ehrlich, Cyril. 1990. *The Piano: A History*. Oxford, UK: Clarendon Press.

Ensminger, Robert F. 2003 (1992). *The Pennsylvania Barn: Its Origin, Evolution, and Distribution in North America*, rev. ed. Baltimore, MD: Johns Hopkins University Press.

Evans, Nancy Goyne. 2006. *Windsor-Chair Making in America: From Craft Shop to Consumer*. Hanover, NH: University Press of New England.

Ewing, Elizabeth. 1977. *History of Children's Costume*. New York: Charles Scribner's Sons.

Fales, Dean A., Jr. 1972. *American Painted Furniture, 1660–1880*. New York: E. P. Dutton.

Fales, Martha Gandy. 1973. *Early American Silver*, rev. and enl. ed. New York: E. P. Dutton.

Farrell-Beck, Jane, and Colleen Gau. 2002. *Uplift: The Bra in America*. Philadelphia: University of Pennsylvania Press.

Ferrero, Pat, Elaine Hedges, and Julie Silber. 1987. *Hearts and Hands: The Influence of Women & Quilts on American Society*. San Francisco: Quilt Digest Press.

Fischer, Claude S. 1992. *America Calling: A Social History of the Telephone to 1940*. Berkeley: University of California Press.

Fischer, Roger A. 1988. *Tippecanoe and Trinkets Too: The Material Culture of American Presidential Campaigns, 1824–1984*. Urbana: University of Illinois Press.

Fiske, Patricia L. 1976. *Imported and Domestic Textiles in Eighteenth-Century America*. Washington, DC: Textile Museum.

Fitzgerald, Oscar P. 1982. *Three Centuries of American Furniture*. Englewood Cliffs, NJ: Prentice-Hall.

Formanek-Brunell, Miriam. 1993. *Made to Play House: Dolls and the Commercialization of American Girlhood, 1830–1870*. New Haven, CT: Yale University Press.

Foster, Vanda. 1982. *Bags and Purses*. Costume Accessories Series, ed. Aileen Ribiero. London: B.T. Batsford.

Frasko, Mary. 1994. *Daring Do: A History of Extraordinary Hair*. New York: Flammarion.

Frelinghuysen, Alice C. 1989. *American Porcelain, 1770–1920*. New York: Metropolitan Museum of Art.

Gelertner, Mark. 1999. *A History of American Architecture: Buildings in Their Cultural and Technological Context*. Hanover, NH: University Press of New England.

Gerdts, William H. 1990. *Art Across America: Two Centuries of Regional Painting, 1710–1920*. New York: Abbeville Press.

Gere, Charlotte. 1975. *American and European Jewelry, 1830–1914*. New York: Crown.

Gillmer, Thomas C. 1994. *A History of Working Watercraft of the Western World*. Camden ME: International Marine Publishing.

Goodsell, Charles T. 2001. *The American Statehouse: Interpreting Democracy's Temples*. Lawrence: University Press of Kansas.

Gordon, Beverly. 1980. *Shaker Textile Arts*. Hanover, NH: University Press of New England.

Gowans, Alan. 1976 (1964). *Images of American Living: Four Centuries of Architecture and Furniture as Cultural Expression*. New York: Harper and Row.

Greer, Georgeanna H. 1981. *American Stonewares: The Art and Craft of Utilitarian Potters*. Exton, PA: Schiffer Publishing.

Gutjahr, Paul. 1999. *An American Bible: A History of the Good Book in the United States, 1777–1880*. Stanford, CA: Stanford University Press.

Hanks, David A. 1981. *Innovative Furniture in America from 1800 to the Present*. New York: Horizon Press.

Hedges, Ernest S. 1964. *Tin in Social and Economic History*. New York: St. Martin's Press.

Heininger, Mary Lynn Stevens. 1986. *At Home With a Book: Reading in America, 1840–1940*. Rochester, NY: The Strong Museum.

Henisch, Heinz K., and Bridget A. Henisch. 1994. *The Photographic Experience, 1839–1914: Images and Attitudes*. State College: Pennsylvania State University Press.

Herlihy, David V. 2004. *Bicycle: The History*. New Haven, CT: Yale University Press.

Hewitt, Karen and Louise Roomet. 1979. *Educational Toys in America: 1800 to the Present*. Burlington VT.: Robert Hull Fleming Museum, University of Vermont.

Hofer, Margaret K. 2003. *The Games We Played: The Golden Age of Board and Table Games*. New York: Princeton Architectural Press.

Hood, Graham. 1971. *American Silver: A History of Style, 1650–1900*. New York: Praeger Publishers.

Hooker, Richard J. 1981. *Food and Drink in America: A History*. Indianapolis: Bobbs-Merrill.

Horan, Julie L. 1996. *Porcelain God: A Social History of the Toilet*. Toronto: Carol Publishing Group.

Hoskins, Lesley, ed. 1994. *The Papered Wall: The History, Patterns and Techniques of Wallpaper*. New York: Harry N. Abrams.

Hunter, Christine. 1999. *Ranches, Rowhouses & Railroad Flats: American Homes: How They Shaped Our Landscape and Neighborhoods*. New York: W. W. Norton.

Issenman, Betty Kobayashi. 1997. *Sinews of Survival: The Living Legacy of Inuit Clothing*. Vancouver: University of British Columbia Press.

Ivins, William H., Jr. 1953. *Prints and Visual Communication*. Cambridge, MA: Harvard University Press.

Jacobs, Flora Gill. 1965. *A History of Dolls' Houses*. New York: Charles Scribner's Sons.

Jacobs, Flora Gill. 1974. *Dolls' Houses in America: Preservation in Miniature*. New York: Charles Scribner's Sons.

Jakle, John A., and Keith A. Sculle. 1999. *Fast Food: Roadside Restaurants in the Automobile Age*. Baltimore, MD: Johns Hopkins University Press.

Jay, Robert. 1987. *The Trade Card in Nineteenth Century America*. Columbia: University of Missouri Press.

Jenkins, Virginia Scott. 1994. *The Lawn: A History of an American Obsession*. Washington, DC: Smithsonian Institution Press.

Jumonville, Florence M. 1993. "The Wastebasket and the Grave: Funeralia in the South." *Southern Quarterly* 31 (2): 98–118.

Kane, Adam I. 2004. *The Western River Steamboat*. College Station: Texas A & M Press.

Kane, Patricia E. 1976. *Three Hundred Years of American Seating Furniture: Chairs and Beds from the Mabel Brady Garvan and other Collections at Yale University*. Boston: New York Graphic Society.

Kaszynski, William. 2000. *The American Highway: The History and Culture of Roads in the United States*. Jefferson, NC: McFarland and Company.

Kauffman, Henry J. 1966. *Early American Ironware: Cast and Wrought*. New York: Weathervane Books.

Kauffman, Henry J. 1972. *The American Fireplace: Chimneys, Mantelpieces, Fireplaces, and Accessories*. Nashville, TN: Thomas Nelson.

Kauffman, Henry J. 1979 (1968). *American Copper and Brass*, rpt. New York: Bonanza Books.

Kent, Kate Peck. 1983. *Prehistoric Textiles of the Southwest*. Sante Fe, NM: School of American Research.

Kinney, Thomas A. 2004. *The Carriage Trade: Making Horse-Drawn Vehicles in America*. Baltimore, MD: Johns Hopkins University Press.

Kiracofe, Roderick, Mary Huff, and Elizabeth Johnson. 1993. *The American Quilt: A History of Cloth and Comfort, 1750–1950*. New York: Clarkson Potter.

Kuhns, Elizabeth. 2003. *The Habit: A History of the Clothing of Catholic Nuns*. New York: Doubleday.

Landes, David S. 1983. *Revolution in Time: Clocks and the Making of the Modern World*. Cambridge, MA: Harvard University Press.

Landreau, Anthony N. 1976. *America Underfoot: a History of Floor Coverings from Colonial Times to the Present*. Washington, DC: Smithsonian Institution Press.

Lasansky, Jeannette, et al. 1988. *Pieced by Mother: Symposium Papers*. Lewisburg, PA: Oral Traditions Project.

Laughlin, Ledlie I. 1940. *Pewter in America*. 2 vols. Cambridge, MA: Riverside Press.

Little, Nina Fletcher. 1952. "Lighting in Colonial Records." *Old-Time New England* 42: 96–101.

Little, Nina Fletcher. 1967. *Floor Coverings in New England before 1850*. Sturbridge, MA: Old Sturbridge Village.

Loesser, Arthur. 1954. *Men, Women and Pianos: A Social History*. New York: Simon & Schuster.

Loveland, Anne C., and Otis B. Wheeler. 2003. *From Meetinghouse to Megachurch: A Material and Cultural History*. Columbia: University of Missouri Press.

Lynn, Catherine. 1980. *Wallpaper in America: From the Seventeenth Century to World War I*. New York: W. W. Norton.

Maddock, Archibald M., II. 1962. *The Polished Earth: A History of the Pottery Fixture Industry in the United States*. Trenton, NJ: n.p.

McClellan, Elisabeth. 1937. *History of American Costume 1607–1870*. New York: Tudor Publishing Company.

McGurn, James. 1987. *On Your Bicycle: An Illustrated History of Cycling*. New York: Facts on File.

McKearin, George S., and Helen McKearin. 1941. *American Glass*. New York: Crown.

McKearin, George S., and Helen McKearin. 1950. *Two Hundred Years of American Blown Glass*. Garden City, NY: Doubleday.

McKearin, Helen, and Kenneth M. Wilson. 1978. *American Bottles and Flasks and Their Ancestry*. New York: Crown.

McManus, Michael. 1997. *A Treasure of American Scrimshaw: A Collection of the Useful and Decorative*. New York: Penguin Studio.

Meikle, Jeffrey L. 1995. *American Plastic: A Cultural History*. New Brunswick, NJ: Rutgers University Press.

Meikle, Jeffrey L. 2005. *Design in the USA*. Oxford: Oxford University Press.

Mintz, Sidney W. 1995. *Sweetness and Power: The Place of Sugar in Modern History*. New York: Penguin.

Monkhouse, Christopher P. 1982. "The Spinning Wheel as Artifact, Symbol, and Source of Design." *Nineteenth Century* 8 (3–4): 154–172.

Montgomery, Charles F. 1978. *A History of American Pewter*, rev. and enl. ed. New York: E. P. Dutton.

Montgomery, Florence M. 1970. *Printed Textiles: English and American Cottons and Linens, 1700–1850*. New York: Viking Press.

Morison, Stanley. 1951. *American Copybooks: An Outline of Their History from Colonial to Modern Times*. Philadelphia, PA: W. F. Fell Co., Printers.

Moylan, Michele, and Lane Stiles. 1996. *Reading Books: Essays on the Material Text and Literature in America*. Amherst: University of Massachusetts Press.

Mulholland, James A. 1981. *A History of Metals in Colonial America*. Tuscaloosa: University of Alabama Press.

Murray, Harold James Ruthven. 1952. *A History of Board-Games Other Than Chess*. Oxford, UK: Clarendon Press.

Nylander, Richard C., Elizabeth Redmond, and Penny J. Saner, eds. 1986. *Wallpaper in New England*. Boston: Society for the Preservation of New England Antiquities.

O'Brien, Richard. 1993. *The Story of American Toys from the Puritans to the Present*. London: New Cavendish Books.

Orchard, William C. 1975 (1929). *Beads and Beadwork of the American Indians*, 2nd ed. New York: Museum of the American Indian.

Orlofsky, Patsy, and Myron Orlofsky. 1974. *Quilts in America*. New York: McGraw-Hill.

Orvell, Miles. 2003. *American Photography*. New York: Oxford University Press.

Parlett, David. 1999. *Oxford History of Board Games*. Oxford, UK: Oxford University Press.

Peers, Juliette. 2004. *The Fashion Doll: From Bébé Jumeau to Barbie*. Oxford, UK: Berg.

Pillsbury, Richard. 1990. *From Boarding House to Bistro: The American Restaurant Then and Now*. Boston: Unwin Hyman.

Plante, Ellen M. 1995. *The American Kitchen, 1700 to the Present: From Hearth to Highrise*. New York: Facts on File.

Pohl, Frances K. 2002. *Framing America: A Social History of American Art*. New York: Thames and Hudson.

Punch, W. Howard, ed. 1992. *Keeping Eden: A History of Gardening in America*. Boston: Little, Brown.

Quimby, Ian M. G., ed. 1972. *Ceramics in America*. Charlottesville: University Press of Virginia for the Henry Francis du Pont Winterthur Museum.

Rice, Kym S. 1983. *Early American Taverns: For the Entertainment of Friends and Strangers*. Chicago: Regnery Gateway.

Ring, Betty. 1993. *Girlhood Embroidery: American Samplers and Pictorial Needlework, 1650–1850*. 2 vols. New York: Alfred A. Knopf.

Robins, Trina. 1999. *From Girls to Grrrlz: A History of Women's Comics from Teens to Zines*. New York: Chronicle Books.

Roell, Craig H. 1989. *The Piano in America, 1890–1940*. Chapel Hill: University of North Carolina Press.

Rogers, Gay Ann. 1983. *An Illustrated History of Needlework Tools*. London: John Murray.

Rosenzweig, Roy, and Elizabeth Blackmar. 1992. *The Park and the People: A History of Central Park*. Ithaca, NY: Cornell University Press.

Roth, Leland M. 1979. *A Concise History of American Architecture*. New York: Harper & Row.

Roth, Rodris. 1967. "Floor Coverings in Eighteenth-Century America." In *United States National Museum Bulletin 250. Contributions from the Museum of History and Technology*, Paper 59, pp. 1–64. Washington, DC: Smithsonian Institution Press.

Rybczynski, Witold. 1986. *Home: The Short History of an Idea*. New York: Viking Press.

Sandweiss, Martha A., ed. 1991. *Photography in Nineteenth-Century America*. Fort Worth, TX: Amon Carter Museum; New York: Harry N. Abrams.

Schoeser, Mary. 1986. *Fabrics and Wallpapers: Twentieth-Century Design*. New York: E. P. Dutton.

Schoeser, Mary, and Celia Rufey. 1989. *English and American Textiles: From 1790 to the Present*. London: Thames and Hudson.

Sheumaker, Helen. 2007. *Love Entwined: The Curious History of Hairwork*. Philadelphia: University of Pennsylvania Press.

Simpson, Pamela H. 1999. *Cheap, Quick, and Easy: Imitative Architectural Materials, 1870–1930*. Knoxville: University of Tennessee Press.

Sonn, Alfred H. 1978 (1928). *Early American Wrought Iron*. 3 vols. New York: Hacker Art Books.

Steele, Valerie. 2003. *The Corset: A Cultural History*. New Haven, CT: Yale University Press.

Swan, Susan. 1995. *Plain and Fancy: American Women and Their Needlework, 1650–1850*. Rev. ed. Austin, TX: Curious Works Press, 1995.

Tangires, Helen. 2003. *Public Markets and Civic Culture in Nineteenth-Century America*. Baltimore, MD: Johns Hopkins University Press.

Taylor, Colin F. 2001. *Native American Weapons*. Norman: University of Oklahoma Press.

Towner, Donald. 1978. *Creamware*. London: Faber and Faber.

Tucker, Susan, Katherine Ott, and Patricia P. Buckler, eds. 2006. *The Scrapbook in American Life*. Philadelphia, PA: Temple University Press.

Turner, Noel D. 1972. *American Silver Flatware, 1837–1910*. South Brunswick, NJ: A. S. Barnes.

Upton, Dell. 1998. *Architecture in the United States*. Oxford, UK: Oxford University Press.

Von Rosenstiel, Helene. 1978. *American Rugs and Carpets from the Seventeenth Century to Modern Times*. New York: William Morrow.

Wallis, Alan D. 1991. *Wheel Estate: The Rise and Decline of Mobile Homes*. New York: Oxford University Press.

Weissman, Judith Reiter, and Wendy Lavitt. 1987. *Labors of Love: America's Textiles and Needlework, 1650–1930*. New York: Alfred A. Knopf.

Wischnitzer, Rachel. 1955. *Synagogue Architecture in the United States: History and Interpretation*. Philadelphia, PA: The Jewish Publication Society of America.

Wyckoff, Alexander, ed. 1965. *The History of American Dress*. 3 vols. New York: B. Blom.

Historical Approaches

Adelman, Melvin L. 1986. *A Sporting Time: New York City and the Rise of Modern Athletics*. Chicago: University of Illinois Press.

Agnew, Jean-Christophe. 1993. *Worlds Apart: The Market and the Theater in Anglo-American Experience*. London: Verso.

Allen, James B. 1966. *The Company Town in the American West*. Norman: University of Oklahoma Press.

Ames, Kenneth L., ed. 1983. *Victorian Furniture: Essays from a Victorian Society Autumn Symposium*. Philadelphia, PA: Victorian Society in America.

Aresty, Esther B. 1970. *The Best Behavior: The Course of Good Manners—from Antiquity to the Present—as Seen through Courtesy and Etiquette Books*. New York: Simon & Schuster.

Aron, Cindy S. 1999. *Working at Play: A History of Vacations in the United States*. New York: Oxford University Press.

Banner, Lois. 1983. *American Beauty*. Chicago: University of Chicago Press.

Becker, Jane. 1998. *Selling Tradition: Appalachia and the Construction of an American Folk, 1930–1940*. Chapel Hill: University of North Carolina Press.

Belasco, Warren. 1979. *Americans on the Road: From Autocamp to Motel, 1910–1945*. Cambridge, MA: MIT Press.

Belasco, Warren. 1989. *Appetite for Change: How the Counterculture Took On the Food Industry, 1966–1988*. New York: Pantheon Books.

Benes, Peter, ed. 1984. *Foodways in the Northeast, Dublin Seminar for New England Folklife Annual Proceedings 1982*. Boston: Boston University.

Bentley, Amy. 1998. *Eating for Victory: Food Rationing and the Politics of Domesticity*. Urbana: University of Illinois Press.

Blanchard, Mary Warner. 1998. *Oscar Wilde's America: Counterculture in the Gilded Age*. New Haven, CT: Yale University Press.

Blumin, Stuart M. 1989. *The Emergence of the Middle Class: Social Experience in the American City, 1760–1900*. Cambridge, UK and New York: Cambridge University Press.

Bodnar, John. 1992. *Remaking America: Public Memory, Commemoration, and Patriotism in the Twentieth Century*. Princeton, NJ: Princeton University Press.

Bolton, Richard, ed. 1989. *The Contest of Meaning: Critical Histories of Photography*. Cambridge, MA: MIT Press.

Boris, Eileen. 1986. *Art and Labor: Ruskin, Morris, and the Craftsman Ideal in America*. Philadelphia, PA: Temple University Press.

Bowers, Brian. 1998. *Lengthening the Day: A History of Lighting Technology*. Oxford, UK: Oxford University Press.

Boydston, Jeanne. 1990. *Home and Work: Housework, Wages, and the Ideology of Labor in the Early Republic*. New York: Oxford University Press.

Breen, T. H. 1988. "'Baubles of Britain': The American Consumer Revolutions of the Eighteenth Century." *Past & Present* 119: 73–104.

Brown, Dona. 1995. *Inventing New England: Regional Tourism in the Nineteenth Century*. Washington, DC: Smithsonian Institution Press.

Brumberg, Joan Jacobs. 1997. *The Body Project: An Intimate History of American Girls*. New York: Random House.

Buggeln, Gretchen Townsend. 2003. *Temples of Grace: The Material Transformation of Connecticut's Churches, 1790–1840*. Hanover, NH: University Press of New England.

Burman, Barbara, and Carole Turbin, eds. 2003. *Material Strategies: Dress and Gender in Historical Perspective*. Oxford, UK: Blackwell.

Bushman, Richard L. 1992. *The Refinement of America: Persons, Houses, Cities*. New York: Alfred A. Knopf.

Bushman, Richard L., and Claudia M. Bushman. 1988. "The Early History of Cleanliness in America." *Journal of American History* 74 (4): 1213–1238.

Calvert, Karin. 1992. *Children in the House: The Material Culture of Early Childhood, 1600–1900*. Boston: Northeastern University Press.

Carson, Barbara G. 1990. *Ambitious Appetites: Dining, Behavior, and Patterns of Consumption in Federal Washington*. Washington, DC: American Institute of Architects Press.

Carson, Cary, Ronald Hoffman, and Peter J. Albert, eds. 1994. *Of Consuming Interests: The Style of Life in the Eighteenth Century*. Charlottesville: University Press of Virginia.

Chapman, Roger. 1999. "From Vietnam to the New World Order: The GI Joe Action Figure as Cold War Artifact." *State University of West Virginia Studies in the Social Sciences* 36: 47–55.

Clark, Clifford E., Jr. 1976. "Domestic Architecture as an Index to Social History: The Romantic Revival and the Cult of Domesticity in America, 1840–1870." *Journal of Interdisciplinary History* 7: 35–56.

Clark, Clifford Edward, Jr. 1986. *The American Family Home, 1800–1960*. Chapel Hill: University of North Carolina Press.

Clarke, Alison J. 2001. *Tupperware: The Promise of Plastic in 1950s America*. Washington, DC: Smithsonian Institution Press.

Cohen, Lizabeth A. 1980. "Embellishing a Life of Labor: An Interpretation of the Material Culture of American Working-Class Homes, 1885–1915." *Journal of American Culture* 3 (4): 752–775.

Collins, Cary C. 2003. "Art Crafted in the Red Man's Image: Hazel Pete, the Indian New Deal, and the Indian Arts and Crafts Program at Santa Fe Indian School, 1932–1935." *New Mexico Historical Review* 78 (4): 439–470.

Crowley, John E. 2001. *The Invention of Comfort: Sensibilities and Design in Early Modern Britain and Early America*. Baltimore, MD: Johns Hopkins University Press.

Cunningham, Patricia A. 2003. *Reforming Women's Fashion, 1850–1920: Politics, Health, and Art*. Kent, OH: Kent State University Press.

Darrah, William. 1964. *Stereo Views: A History of Stereographs in Ameria and Their Collection*. Gettysburg, PA: Times and News Publishing Company.

Darrah, William. 1977. *The World of Stereographs*. Gettysburg, PA: William Darrah Publisher.

Davis, Philip John. 2002. "The Material Culture of U.S. Elections: Artisanship, Entrepreneurship, Ephemera and Two Centuries of Trans-Atlantic Exchange." *Journal of Political Marketing* 1 (2–3): 9–24.

Davis, Susan G. 1986. *Parades and Power: Street Theatre in Nineteenth-Century Philadelphia*. Philadelphia, PA: Temple University Press.

Dawson, Melanie. 2005. *Laboring to Play: Home Entertainment and the Spectacle of Middle-Class Cultural Life, 1850–1920*. Tuscaloosa: University of Alabama Press.

Deetz, James. 1977. *In Small Things Forgotten: The Archaeology of Early America*. Garden City, NY: Anchor Press/Doubleday.

Deloria, Philip. 1999. *Playing Indian*. New Haven, CT: Yale University Press.

Deloria, Philip. 2004. *Indians in Unexpected Places*. Lawrence: University Press of Kansas.

Demos, John. 1970. *A Little Commonwealth: Family Life in Plymouth Colony*. New York: Oxford University Press.

Denenberg, Thomas Andrew. 2003. *Wallace Nutting and the Invention of Old America*. New Haven, CT: Yale University Press and the Wadsworth Atheneum of Art.

Dennis, Matthew. 2002. *Red, White and Blue Letter Days: An American Calendar*. Ithaca, NY: Cornell University Press.

DePastino, Todd. 2003. *Citizen Hobo: How a Century of Homelessness Shaped America*. Chicago: University of Chicago Press.

Douglas, Ann. 1977. *The Feminization of American Culture*. New York: Avon.

Dulles, Foster Rhea. 1965. *A History of Recreation: America Learns to Play*, 2nd ed. New York: Appleton-Century-Crofts.

Earle, Edward E., ed. 1979. *Points of View: The Stereograph in America, A Cultural History*. Rochester, NY: Visual Studies Workshop Press.

Ferguson, Leland. 1992. *Uncommon Ground: Archaeology and Early African America, 1650–1800*. Washington, DC: Smithsonian Institution Press.

Fischer, Gayle V. 2001. *Pantaloons and Power: A Nineteenth-Century Dress Reform in the United States*. Kent, OH: Kent State University Press.

Foster, Helen Bradley. 1997. *New Raiments of Self: African American Clothing in the Antebellum South*. Oxford, UK: Berg.

Foy, Jessica, and Thomas J. Schlereth, eds. 1992. *American Home Life, 1880–1930: A Social History of Spaces and Services*. Knoxville: University of Tennessee Press.

Fried, Robert M. 1998. *The Russians Are Coming! The Russians Are Coming! Pageantry and Patriotism in Cold-War America*. New York: Oxford University Press.

Friedman, Alice T. 1998. *Women and the Making of the Modern House: A Social and Architectural History*. New York: Harry N. Abrams.

Gamber, Wendy. 2002. "Tarnished Labor: The Home, the Market, and the Boardinghouse in Antebellum America." *Journal of the Early Republic* 22 (2): 177–204.

Garrett, Elisabeth Donaghy. 1990. *At Home: The American Family, 1750–1870*. New York: Harry N. Abrams.

Gelber, Steven M. 1999. *Hobbies: Leisure and the Culture of Work in America*. New York: Columbia University Press.

Gillis, John R. 1997. *A World of Their Own Making: A History of Myth and Ritual in Family Life*. New York: Oxford University Press.

Glassberg, David. 1990. *American Historical Pageantry: The Uses of Tradition in the Early Twentieth Century*. Chapel Hill: University of North Carolina Press.

Goddard, Stephen B. 1994. *Getting There: The Epic Struggle between Road and Rail in the American Century*. New York: Basic Books.

Goings, Kenneth W. 1994. *Mammy and Uncle Mose: Black Collectibles and American Stereotyping*. Bloomington: Indiana University Press.

Goldstein, Carolyn M. 1998. *Do It Yourself: Home Improvement in 20th-Century America*. Washington, DC: National Building Museum; New York: Princeton Architectural Press.

Gordon, Beverly. 1998. *Bazaars and Fair Ladies: The History of the American Fundraising Fair*. Knoxville: University of Tennessee Press.

Green, Harvey. 1983. *The Light of the Home: An Intimate View of the Lives of Women in Victorian America*. New York: Pantheon Books.

Green, Harvey. 1986. *Fit for America: Health, Fitness, Sport, and American Society*. New York: Pantheon Books.

Grier, Katherine C. 1997. *Culture and Comfort: Parlor Making and Middle-Class Identity, 1850–1930*. Washington, DC: Smithsonian Institution Press.

Grier, Katherine C. 2006. *Pets in America: A History*. Chapel Hill: University of North Carolina Press.

Grover, Kathryn, ed. 1987. *Dining in America, 1850–1900*. Amherst: University of Massachusetts Press; Rochester, NY: Margaret Woodbury Strong Museum.

Haber, Barbara. 2002. *From Hardtack to Homefries: An Uncommon History of American Cooks and Meals*. New York: The Free Press.

Halttunen, Karen. 1982. *Confidence Men and Painted Women: A Study of Middle-Class Culture in America, 1830–1870*. New Haven, CT: Yale University Press.

Handlin, David P. 1979. *The American Home: Architecture and Society, 1815–1915*. Boston: Little, Brown.

Handlin, David P. 1985. *American Architecture*. New York: Thomas and Hudson.

Harris, Neil. 1990 (1966). *Cultural Excursions: Marketing Appetites and Cultural Tastes in Modern America*. Chicago: University of Chicago Press.

Harris, Neil. 1992 (1966). *The Artist in American Society: The Formative Years 1790–1860*. Chicago: University of Chicago Press.

Heininger, Mary Lynn Stevens, et al. 1984. *A Century of Childhood, 1820–1920*. Rochester, NY: Margaret Woodbury Strong Museum.

Hemphill, C. Dallett. 1999. *Bowing to Necessities: A History of Manners in America, 1620–1860*. New York: Oxford University Press.

Herman, Daniel Justin. 2001. *Hunting and the American Imagination*. Washington, DC: Smithsonian Institution Press.

Hindle, Brooke. 1984. "A Retrospective View of Science, Technology, and Material Culture in Early American History." *William and Mary Quarterly*, 3rd ser. 41 (3): 422–435.

Hoganson, Kristin. 2003. "Food and Entertainment from Every Corner of the Globe: Bourgeois U.S. Households as Points of Encounter, 1870–1920." *Amerikastudien* 48 (1): 115–135.

Holt, Marilyn Irvin. 1995. *Linoleum, Better Babies & the Modern Farm Woman, 1890–1930*. Albuquerque: University of New Mexico Press.

Hornstein, Jeffrey M. 2005. *A Nation of Realtors: A Cultural History of the Twentieth-Century American Middle Class*. Durham, NC: Duke University Press.

Horowitz, Helen Lefkowitz. 1984. *Alma Mater: Design and Experience in the Women's Colleges from their Nineteenth Century Beginnings to the 1930s*. New York: Alfred A. Knopf.

Hoy, Suellen. 1995. *Chasing Dirt: The American Pursuit of Cleanliness*. New York: Oxford University Press.

Hurley, Andrew. 2001. *Diners, Bowling Alleys, and Trailer Parks: Chasing the American Dream in Postwar Consumer Culture*. New York: Basic Books.

Hutchins, Catherine E., ed. 1994. *Everyday Life in the Early Republic*. Winterthur, DE: Winterthur Museum.

Hutchison, Janet. 1997. "Building for Babbitt: The State and the Suburban Home Ideal." *Journal of Policy History* 9 (2): 184–210.

Ibson, John. 2002. *Picturing Men: A Century of Male Relationships in Everyday American Photography*. Washington, DC: Smithsonian Institution Press.

Isaac, Rhys. 1982. *The Transformation of Virginia, 1740–1790*. Chapel Hill: University of North Carolina Press.

Jackson, Kenneth T. 1985. *Crabgrass Frontier: The Suburbanization of the United States*. New York: Oxford University Press.

Jeffrey, Julie Roy. 2003. "'Stranger, Buy . . . Lest Our Mission Fail': The Complex Culture of Women's Abolitionist Fairs." *American Nineteenth Century History* 4 (1): 1–24.

Jensen, Joan M. 1980. "Cloth, Butter and Boarders: Women's Household Production for the Market." *Review of Radical Political Economics* 12 (2): 14–24.

Jordan, Terry G. 1989. "New Sweden's Role on the American Frontier: A Study in Cultural Preadaptation." *Geogragiska Annaler. Series B, Human Geography* 71 (2): 71–83.

Kammen, Michael. 1993. *Mystic Chords of Memory: The Transformation of Tradition in American Culture*. New York: Vintage Books.

Kasprycki, Sylvia S. 1996. "'Matters of Faith': Notes on Missionaries and Material Culture." *European Review of Native American Studies* [Germany] 10 (2): 45–50.

Kasson, John F. 1978. *Amusing the Million: Coney Island at the Turn of the Century*. New York: Hill & Wang.

Kasson, John F. 1990. *Rudeness and Civility: Manners in Nineteenth-Century Urban America*. New York: Hill & Wang.

Kenney, William Howland. 1999. *Recorded Music in American Life: The Phonograph and Popular Memory, 1890–1945*. New York: Oxford University Press.

Kidwell, Claudia Brush, and Margaret C. Christman. 1974. *Suiting Everyone: The Democratization of Clothing in America.* Washington, DC: Smithsonian Institution Press for National Museum of History and Technology.

Kidwell, Claudia Brush, and Valerie Steele. 1989. *Men and Women: Dressing the Part.* Washington, DC: Smithsonian Institution Press.

Kwolek-Folland, Angel. 1984. "The Elegant Dugout: Domesticity and Moveable Culture in the United States, 1870–1900." *American Studies* 25 (2): 21–37.

Kwolek-Folland, Angel. 1994. *Engendering Business: Men and Women in the Corporate Office, 1870–1930.* Baltimore, MD: Johns Hopkins University Press.

Labaree, Benjamin W., et al. 1998. *America and the Sea: A Maritime History.* Mystic Seaport, CT: Mystic Seaport Museum Publications.

Laderman, Gary. 2003. *Rest in Peace: A Cultural History of Death and the Funeral Home in Twentieth-Century America.* New York: Oxford University Press.

Larkin, Jack. 1988. *The Reshaping of Everyday Life 1790–1840.* New York: Harper and Row.

Leach, William R. 1994. *Land of Desire: Merchants, Power, and the Rise of a New American Culture.* New York: Vintage Books.

Lears, T. J. Jackson. 1981. *No Place of Grace: Anti-Modernism and the Transformation of American Culture, 1880–1920.* New York: Pantheon Books.

Lears, T. J. Jackson. 1994. *Fables of Abundance: A Cultural History of Advertising in America.* New York: Basic Books.

Levenstein, Harvey A. 1988. *Revolution at the Table: The Transformation of the American Diet.* New York: Oxford University Press.

Levine, Lawrence W. 1988. *Highbrow/Lowbrow: The Emergence of Cultural Hierarchy in America.* Cambridge, MA: Harvard University Press.

Litwicki, Ellen M. 2000. *America's Public Holidays: 1865–1920.* Washington, DC: Smithsonian Institution Press.

Löfgren, Orvar. 1999. *On Holiday: A History of Vacationing.* Berkeley: University of California Press.

Longmore, Paul, and Lauri Umansky, eds. 2001. *The New Disability History: American Perspectives.* New York: New York University Press.

Lowenthal, David. 1985. *The Past Is a Foreign Country.* Cambridge, UK: Cambridge University Press.

Luchetti, Cathy. 1993. *Home on the Range: A Culinary History of the American West.* New York: Villard Books.

Macdonald, Anne L. 1988. *No Idle Hands: The Social History of American Knitting.* New York: Ballantine Books.

Marling, Karal Ann. 1988. *George Washington Slept Here: Colonial Revivals and American Culture, 1876–1986.* Cambridge, MA: Harvard University Press.

Marten, James. 1998. *The Children's Civil War.* Chapel Hill: University of North Carolina Press.

Matthews, Glenna. 1987. *"Just a Housewife": The Rise and Fall of Domesticity in America.* New York: Oxford University Press.

McDannell, Colleen. 1986. *The Christian Home in Victorian America, 1840–1900.* Bloomington: Indiana University Press.

McDannell, Colleen. 1995. *Material Christianity: Religion and Popular Culture in America.* New Haven, CT: Yale University Press.

McDonald, Roderich A. 1993. *The Economy and Material Culture of Slaves: Goods and Chattels on the Sugar Plantations of Jamaica and Louisiana.* Baton Rouge: Louisiana State University Press.

McFeely, Mary Drake. 2000. *Can She Bake a Cherry Pie? American Women and the Kitchen in the Twentieth Century.* Amherst: University of Massachusetts Press.

McMurry, Sally. 1988. *Families and Farmhouses in Nineteenth Century America: Vernacular Style and Social Change.* New York: Oxford University Press.

Meranze, Michael. 1996. *Laboratories of Virtue: Punishment, Revolution, and Authority in Philadelphia, 1760–1835.* Chapel Hill: University of North Carolina Press.

Meyer, Bathasar Henry, ed. 1948. *History of Transportation in the United States before 1860*. New York: P. Smith.

Meyer, Richard E. 1992. *Cemeteries and Gravemarkers: Voices of American Culture*. Logan: Utah State University Press.

Miller, Marla R. 2006. *The Needle's Eye: Women and Work in the Age of Revolution*. Amherst: University of Massachusetts Press.

Milner, George. 2004. *The Moundbuilders: Ancient Peoples of Eastern North America*. New York: Thames and Hudson.

Morris, Norval, and David J. Rothman, eds. 1995. *The Oxford History of the Prison: The Practice of Punishment in Western Society*. New York: Oxford University Press.

Motz, Marilyn Ferris, and Pat Browne, eds. 1988. *Making the American Home: Middle-Class Women and Domestic Material Culture, 1850–1940*. Bowling Green, OH: Bowling Green State University Popular Press.

Mulrooney, Margaret M. 2002. *Black Powder, White Lace: The Du Pont Irish and Cultural Identity in Nineteenth-Century America*. Hanover, NH: University Press of New England.

Nasaw, David. 1993. *Going Out: the Rise and Fall of Public Amusement*. New York: Basic Books.

Nash, Alice N., and Christoph Strobel. 2006. *Daily Life of Native Americans from Post-Columbian through Nineteenth-Century America*. Westport, CT: Greenwood Press.

Neuhaus, Jessamyn. 2003. *Manly Meals and Mom's Home Cooking: Cookbooks and Gender in Modern America*. Baltimore, MD: Johns Hopkins University Press.

Nylander, Jane C. 1993. *Our Own Snug Fireside: Images of the New England Home, 1760–1860*. New Haven, CT: Yale University Press.

O'Dea, William T. 1958. *The Social History of Lighting*. New York: Macmillan.

O'Leary, Elizabeth L. 2003. *From Morning to Night: Domestic Service in Maymont House and the Gilded Age South*. Charlottesville: University Press of Virginia.

Orvell, Miles. 1989. *The Real Thing: Imitation and Authenticity in American Culture, 1880–1940*. Chapel Hill: University of North Carolina Press.

Pearson, Marlys, and Paul R. Mullins. 1999. "Domesticating Barbie: An Archaeology of Barbie Material Culture and Domestic Ideology." *International Journal of Historical Archaeology* 3 (4): 225–259.

Peiss, Kathy. 1986. *Cheap Amusements: Working Women and Leisure in Turn-of-the-Century New York*. Philadelphia, PA: Temple University Press.

Peiss, Kathy. 1998. *Hope in a Jar: The Making of America's Beauty Culture*. New York: Metropolitan Books.

Perkins, Elizabeth A. 1991. "The Consumer Frontier: Household Consumption in Early Kentucky." *Journal of American History* 78 (2): 486–510.

Pitzer, Donald E., ed. 1997. *America's Communal Utopias*. Chapel Hill: University of North Carolina Press.

Prude, Jonathan, and Steven Hahn, eds. 1985. *The Countryside in the Age of Capitalist Transformation: Essays in Social History*. Chapel Hill: University of North Carolina Press.

Rediker, Marcus. 1989. *Between the Devil and the Deep Blue Sea: Merchant Seamen, Pirates, and the Anglo-American Maritime World, 1700–1750*, new ed. Cambridge, UK: Cambridge University Press.

Reed, Christopher Robert. 2000. *"All the World Is Here!": The Black Presence in the White City*. Bloomington: Indiana University Press.

Reese, William J. 1995. *The Origins of the American High School*. New Haven, CT: Yale University Press.

Reiss, Steven A. 1989. *City Games: The Evolution of American Urban Society and the Rise of Sports*. Chicago: University of Illinois Press.

Reps, John W. 1965. *The Making of Urban America: A History of City Planning in the United States*. Princeton, NJ: Princeton University Press.

Restad, Penne. 1995. *Christmas in America: A History*. New York: Oxford University Press.

Rogers, J. Daniel. 1990. *Objects of Change: The Archaeology and History of Arikara Contact with Europeans*. Washington, DC: Smithsonian Institution Press.

Rose, Kenneth D. 2001. *One Nation Underground: A History of the Fallout Shelter in American Culture*. New York: New York University Press.

Roth, Rodris. 1964. "The Colonial Revival and Centennial Furniture." *Art Quarterly* 27 (1): 57–81.

Rothman, David J. 1980. *Conscience and Convenience: The Asylum and Its Alternatives in Progressive America*. Boston: Little, Brown.

Rothman, David J. 2002. *The Discovery of the Asylum: Social Order and Disorder in the New Republic*. New York: Aldine de Gruyter.

Rydell, Robert W. 1984. *All the World's a Fair: Visions of Empire at American International Expositions, 1876–1916*. Chicago: University of Chicago Press.

Samford, Patricia. 1996. "The Archaeology of African-American Slavery and Material Culture." *William and Mary Quarterly*, 3rd ser. 53 (1): 87–114.

Scharff, Virginia. 1992. *Taking the Wheel: Women and the Coming of the Motor Age*. Albuquerque: University of New Mexico Press.

Schlereth, Thomas. 1991. *Victorian America: Transformations in Everyday Life, 1876–1915*. New York: HarperCollins.

Schlesinger, Arthur Meier. 1946. *Learning How to Behave: A Historical Study of American Etiquette Books*. New York: Macmillan.

Schmidt, Leigh Eric. 1989. "'A Church-Going People are a Dress-Loving People': Clothes, Communication, and Religious Culture in Early America." *Church History* 58: 36–51.

Schrum, Kelly. 2004. *Some Wore Bobby Sox: The Emergence of Teenage Girls' Culture, 1920–1945*. New York: Palgrave Macmillan.

Scobey, David. 1994. "What Shall We Do With Our Walls? The Philadelphia Centennial and the Meaning of Household Design." *European Contributions to American Studies* [Netherlands] 27: 87–120.

Sears, John F. 1989. *Sacred Places: American Tourist Attractions in the Nineteenth Century*. New York: Oxford University Press.

Shaffer, Marguerite S. 2001. *See America First: Tourism and National Identity, 1880–1940*. Washington, DC: Smithsonian Institution Press.

Shank, Barry. 2004. *A Token of My Affection: Greeting Cards and American Business Culture*. New York: Columbia University Press.

Shapiro, Laura. 1986. *Perfection Salad: Women and Cooking at the Turn of the* Century. New York: Farrar, Straus & Giroux.

Shapiro, Laura. 2004. *Something From the Oven: Reinventing Dinner in 1950s America*. New York: Viking Press.

Shi, David. 1985. *The Simple Life: Plain Living and High Thinking in American Culture*. New York: Oxford University Press.

Silverman, Kenneth. 1976. *A Cultural History of the American Revolution: Painting, Music, Literature, and the Theatre in the Colonies and the United States from the Treaty of Paris to the Inauguration of George Washington, 1763–1789*. New York: Thomas Y. Crowell Company.

Singleton, Theresa, ed. 1999. *"I, Too, Am America": Archaeological Studies of African-American Life*. Charlottesville: University Press of Virginia.

Smith, Barbara Clark. 1985. *After the Revolution: The Smithsonian History of Everyday Life in the Eighteenth Century*. New York: Pantheon Books.

Smith, Billy G. 1990. *The "Lower Sort": Philadelphia's Laboring People, 1750–1800*. Ithaca, NY: Cornell University Press.

Smith, Gregory W. 1995. "Alcoa's Aluminum Furniture: New Applications for a Modern Material, 1924–1934." *Pittsburgh History* 78 (20): 52–64.

Sobel, Mechal. 1987. *The World They Made Together: Black and White Values in Eighteenth-Century Virginia*. Princeton, NJ: Princeton University Press.

Spigel, Lynn. 1992. *Make Room for TV: Television and the Family Ideal in Postwar America*. Chicago: University of Chicago Press.

Stabile, Susan M. 2004. *Memory's Daughters: The Material Culture of Remembrance in Eighteenth-Century America*. Ithaca, NY: Cornell University Press.

Stapp, Carol Buchalter. 1993. *Afro-Americans in Antebellum Boston: An Analysis of Probate Records.* New York: Garland Publishing.

Taft, Robert. 1938. *Photography and the American Scene: A Social History.* New York: McMillan.

Thornton, Tamara Plakins. 1989. *Cultivating Gentlemen: The Meaning of Country Life among the Boston Elite, 1785–1860.* New Haven, CT: Yale University Press.

Thornton, Tamara Plakins. 1996. *Handwriting in America: A Cultural History.* New Haven, CT: Yale University Press.

Ulrich, Laurel Thatcher. 1997. "Hannah Barnard's Cupboard: Female Property and Identity in Eighteenth-Century New England." In *Through a Glass Darkly: Reflections on Personal Identity in Early America,* ed. Ronald Hoffman, Mechal Sobel, and Fredrika J. Teute, 238–273. Chapel Hill: University of North Carolina Press.

Ulrich, Laurel Thatcher. 2001. *The Age of Homespun: Objects and Stories in the Creation of an American Myth.* New York: Alfred A. Knopf.

Waits, William B. 1993. *The Modern Christmas in America: A Cultural History of Gift-Giving.* New York: New York University Press.

Walsh, Margaret. 1979. "The Democratization of Fashion: The Emergence of the Women's Dress Pattern Industry." *Journal of American History* 66: 299–313.

Ward, Gerald W. R., ed. 1988. *Perspectives on American Furniture.* New York and London: W. W. Norton for the Winterthur Museum.

Wilkie, Laurie A. 2004. *Creating Freedom: Material Culture and African American Identity at Oakley Plantation, Louisiana, 1840–1950.* Baton Rouge: Louisiana State University Press.

Williams, Susan. 1985. *Savory Suppers and Fashionable Feasts: Dining in Victorian America.* New York: Cambridge University Press.

Wilson, Elizabeth. 2003. *Adorned in Dreams: Fashion and Modernity.* New Brunswick, NJ: Rutgers University Press.

Wilson, Sherrill D. 1994. *New York City's African Slaveowners: A Social and Material Culture History.* New York: Garland Publishing.

Wolf, Stephanie Grauman. 1993. *As Various as Their Land: The Everyday Lives of Eighteenth-Century Americans.* New York: HarperCollins.

Wouters, Cas. 1995. "Etiquette Books and Emotion Management in the 20th Century: Part One—The Integration of Social Classes." *Journal of Social History* 29 (1): 107–124.

Wouters, Cas. 1995. "Etiquette Books and Emotion Management in the 20th Century: Part Two—The Integration of the Sexes." *Journal of Social History* 29 (2): 325–339.

Wright, Gwendolyn. 1980. *Moralism and the Model Home: Domestic Architecture and Cultural Conflict in Chicago, 1873–1913.* Chicago: University of Chicago Press.

Wright, Gwendolyn. 1981. *Building the Dream: A Social History of Housing in America.* New York: Pantheon Books.

Yosifon, David, and Peter N. Stearns. 1998. "The Rise and Fall of American Posture." *American Historical Review* 103 (4): 1056–1095.

Young, James Harvey. 1961. *The Toadstool Millionaires: A Social History of Patent Medicines in America Before Federal Regulation.* Princeton, NJ: Princeton University Press.

Social, Cultural, and Ethnographic Approaches

Ames, Kenneth L. 1992. *Death in the Dining Room and Other Tales of Victorian Culture.* Philadelphia, PA: Temple University Press.

Canter, David, and Terence Lee, eds. 1974. *Psychology and the Built Environment.* New York: John Wiley.

Conner, Patrick. 1982. *People at Home: Looking at Art.* New York: Atheneum.

Conroy, Marianne. 1998. "Discount Dreams: Factory Outlet Malls, Consumption, and the Performance of Middle-Class Identity." *Social Text* 54: 63–83.

Cooper, Wendy. 1971. *Hair: Sex, Society, Symbolism.* New York: Stein and Day.

Crane, Diana. 2000. *Fashion and Its Social Agendas: Class, Gender, and Identity in Clothing*. Chicago: University of Chicago Pess.

Csikszentmihalyi, Mihaly, and Eugene Rochberg-Halton. 1981. The *Meaning of Things: Domestic Symbols and the Self*. Cambridge, UK: Cambridge University Press.

Dant, Tim. 1999. *Material Culture in the Social World: Values, Activities, Lifestyles*. Philadelphia, PA: Open University Press.

Davis, J. A. 1990. *Living Rooms as Symbols of Status*. New York: Garland Publishing.

Davis, Mike. 1990. *City of Quartz: Excavating the Future in the City of Los Angeles*. London: Verso.

Douglas, Mary. 2002 (1996). *Purity and Danger: An Analysis of the Concepts of Pollution and Taboo*. New York: Routledge.

Douglas, Mary, and Baron Isherwood. 1979. *The World of Goods: Toward an Anthropology of Consumption*. New York: Basic Books.

Duncombe, Stephen. 1997. *Notes from Underground: Zines and the Politics of Alternative Culture*. London: Verso.

Featherstone, Mike, Mike Hepworth, and Bryan Turner, eds. 1995. *The Body: Social Process and Cultural Theory*. London: Sage.

Freyer, John D. 2002. *All My Life for Sale*. New York: Bloomsbury.

Gans, Herbert J. 1974. *Popular Culture and High Culture: An Analysis and Evaluation of Taste*. New York: Basic Books.

Goffman, Erving. 1967. *Interaction Ritual: Essays in Face-to-Face Behavior*. Chicago: Aldine.

Green, Ernest J. 1993. "The Social Functions of Utopian Architecture." *Utopian Studies* 4 (1): 1–13.

Hall, Dennis. 1999. "Rites of Appraisal and Questions of Value: Public Television's *Antiques Roadshow*." *Studies in Popular Culture* 21 (31): 13–22.

Halle, David. 1993. *Inside Culture: Art and Class in the American Home*. Chicago: University of Chicago Press.

Harris, Neil. 1999. *Building Lives: Constructing Rites and Passages*. New Haven, CT: Yale University Press.

Herrmann, Gretchen M. 1995. "His and Hers: Gender and Garage Sales." *Journal of Popular Culture* 29: 127–145.

Herrmann, Gretchen M. 1997. "Gift or Commodity: What Changes Hands in the U.S. Garage Sale?" *American Ethnologist* 24 (4): 910–930.

Herrmann, Gretchen M. 2003. "Negotiating Culture: Conflict and Consensus in U.S. Garage-Sale Bargaining." *Ethnology* 42 (3): 237–252.

Herrmann, Gretchen M., and Stephen M. Soiffer. 1984. "For Fun and Profit: An Analysis of the American Garage Sale." *Urban Life* 12 (4): 397–421.

Hochschild, Arlie. 1983. *The Managed Heart: Commercialization of Human Feeling*. Berkeley: University of California Press.

Hyde, Lewis. 1983. *The Gift: Imagination and the Erotic Life of Property*. New York: Vintage.

Johnson, Norris Brock. 1980. "The Material Culture of Public School Classrooms: The Symbolic Integration of Local Schools and National Culture." *Anthropology & Education Quarterly* 11 (3): 173–190.

Kidder, Tracy. 1985. *House*. Boston: Houghton Mifflin.

Klein, Naomi. 2002. *No Logo, No Space, No Choice, No Jobs*. New York: Picador.

Kline, Stephen. 1993. *Out of the Garden: Toys, TV, and Children's Culture in the Age of Marketing*. New York: Verso.

Krech, Shepard, III, and Barbara A. Hail. 1999. *Collecting Native America, 1870–1960*. Washington, DC: Smithsonian Institution Press.

Kron, Joan. 1983. *Home Psych: The Social Psychology of Home and Decoration*. New York: Clarkson Potter.

Küchler, Susanne, and Daniel Miller. 2005. *Clothing as Material Culture*. Oxford, UK: Berg.

Laumann, E. O., and J. S. House. 1970. "Living Room Styles and Social Attributes: The Patterning of Material Artifacts in a Modern Urban Community." *Sociology and Social Research* 54 (3): 321–342.

Laurer, Robert, and Jeanette Laurer. 1981. *The Meaning of Fashion in American Society*. Englewood Cliffs, NJ: Prentice-Hall.

Lipsitz, George. 2001 (1990). *Time Passages: Collective Memory and American Popular Culture*, rpt. ed. Minneapolis: University of Minnesota Press.

Marling, Karal Ann. 2004. *Debutante: Rites and Regalia of American Debdom*. Lawrence: University Press of Kansas.

McCracken, Grant. 1989. *Culture and Consumption: New Approaches to the Symbolic Character of Consumer Goods and Activities*. Bloomington: Indiana University Press.

McCracken, Grant. 1995. *Big Hair: A Journey into the Transformation of Self*. New York: Overlook Press.

Moore, Sally F., and Barbara G. Myerhoff. 1977. "Secular Ritual: Forms and Meanings." In *Secular Ritual*, 3–24. Assen, Netherland: Van Gorcum.

Murray, David. 2000. *Indian Giving: Economies of Power in Early Indian-White Exchanges*. Amherst: University of Massachusetts Press.

Otnes, Cele, and Richard F. Beltramini, eds. 1996. *Gift Giving: A Research Anthology*. Bowling Green, OH: Bowling Green State University Press.

Philips, Ruth B. 1998. *Trading Identities: The Souvenir in Native North American Art from the Northeast, 1700–1900*. Seattle: University of Washington Press.

Postrel, Virginia. 2003. *The Substance of Style: How the Rise of Aesthetic Value is Remaking Commerce, Culture, and Consciousness*. New York: HarperCollins.

Rook, Noliwe M. 1996. *Hair Raising: Beauty, Culture, and African American Women*. New Brunswick, NJ: Rutgers University Press.

Sack, Daniel. 2000. *Whitebread Protestants: Food and Religion in American Culture*. New York: St. Martin's Press.

Schrift, Alan D., ed. 1997. *The Logic of the Gift: Toward an Ethic of Generosity*. New York: Routledge.

Smith, Charles W. 1989. *Auctions: The Social Construction of Value*. New York: Free Press.

Soiffer, Stephen M. 1987. "Visions of Power: Ideology and Practice in the American Garage Sale." *Sociological Review* 35: 48–83.

Thomson, Rosemarie Garland, ed.1996. *Freakery: Cultural Spectacles of the Extraordinary Body*. New York: New York University Press.

Titchkosky, Tanya. 2003. *Disability, Self, and Society*. Toronto: University of Toronto Press.

Turner, Victor. 1995 (1969). *The Ritual Process: Structure and Anti-Structure*, rpt. ed. Chicago: Aldine Transactions.

Van Gennep, Arnold. 1961. *The Rites of Passage*, trans. Minika B. Vizedom and Gabrielle L. Caffee. Chicago: University of Chicago Press.

Vaughn, Genevive. 1997. *For-Giving: A Feminist Criticism of Exchange*. Austin, TX: Plain View Press.

Waksman, Steven. 2001. *Instruments of Desire: The Electric Guitar and the Shaping of Musical Experience*. Cambridge, MA: Harvard University Press.

Weiner, Annette B. 1992. *Inalienable Possessions: The Paradox of Keeping-while-Giving*. Berkeley: University of California Press.

Westmacott, Richard. 1992. *African American Gardens and Yards in the Rural South*. Knoxville: University of Tennessee Press.

Willis, Susan. 1991. *A Primer for Daily Life*. London: Routledge.

Zachman, Jon B. 1994. "The Legacy and Meanings of World's Fair Souvenirs." *European Contributions to American Studies* 27: 199–217.

Zukin, Sharon. 2004. *Point of Purchase: How Shopping Changed American Culture*. New York: Routledge.

Linguistic and Literary Approaches

Avery, Gillian. 1994. *Behold the Child: American Children and Their Books 1621–1922*. Baltimore, MD: Johns Hopkins University Press.

Balshaw, Maria, and Liam Kennedy, eds. 2000. *Urban Space and Representation*. Sterling, VA: Pluto Press.

Barnes, Trevor J., and James S. Duncan, eds. *Writing Worlds: Discourse, Text, and Metaphor in the Representation of Landscape*. London: Routledge.

Bishop, Ronald. 1999. "What Price History? Functions of Narrative in Television Collectibles Shows." *Journal of Popular Culture* 33 (3): 1–27.

Bowen, Janet Wolf. 1992. "Architectural Envy: 'A Figure is Nothing without a Setting' in Henry James's *The Bostonians*." *New England Quarterly* 65 (1): 3–23.

Bowlby, Rachel. 1985. *Just Looking: Consumer Culture in Dreiser, Gissing, and Zola*. New York: Methuen.

Bowlby, Rachel. 1993. *Shopping with Freud*. London: Routledge.

Brown, Bill. 2004. *A Sense of Things: The Object Matter of American Literature*. Chicago: University of Chicago Press.

Brown, Bill, ed. 2004. *Things*. Berkeley: University of California Press.

Brückner, Martin. 2006. *The Geographic Revolution in Early America: Maps, Literacy, and National Identity*. Chapel Hill: University of North Carolina Press.

Casey, Janet Galligani. 2004. "'This Is Your Magazine': Domesticity, Agrarianism, and the Farmer's Wife." *American Periodicals* 14 (2): 179–211.

Clark, Beverly Lyon, and Margaret R. Higgonet. 1999. *Girls, Boys, Books, Toys: Gender in Children's Literature and Culture*. Baltimore, MD: Johns Hopkins University Press.

Cohn, Jan. 1979. *The Palace or the Poorhouse: The American House as a Cultural Symbol*. East Lansing: Michigan State University Press.

Davidson, Cathy N., ed. 1989. *Reading in America: Literature and Social History*. Baltimore, MD: Johns Hopkins University Press.

Diller, Christopher. 2000. "'Fiction in Color': Domesticity, Aestheticism, and the Visual Arts in the Criticism and Fiction of William Dean Howells." *Nineteenth-Century Literature* 55 (3): 369–398.

Dorst, John Darwin. 1989. *The Written Suburb: An American Site, an Ethnographic Dilemma*. Philadelphia: University of Pennsylvania Press.

Dorst, John Darwin. 1999. *Looking West*. Philadelphia: University of Pennsylvania Press.

Durso, Patricia Keefe. 2002. "Bringing Whiteness 'Home': Exploring the Social Geography of Race in Mary Gordon's 'The Other Side.'" *Modern Language Studies* 32 (1): 85–102.

Evans, Brad. 2005. *Before Cultures: The Ethnographic Imagination of American Literature, 1865–1920*. Chicago: University of Chicago Press.

Falk, Cynthia G. 2001. "'The Intolerable Ugliness of New York': Architecture and Society in Edith Wharton's *The Age of Innocence*." *American Studies* 42 (2): 19–43.

Gilmore, Michael T. 1985. *American Romanticism and the Marketplace*. Chicago: University of Chicago Press.

Gilmore, Paul. 2004. "Republican Machines and Brackenridge's Caves: Aesthetic and Models of Machinery in the Early Republic." *Early American Literature* 39 (2): 299–322.

Heneghan, Bridget T. 2003. *Whitewashing America: Material Culture and Race in the Antebellum Imagination*. Jackson: University Press of Mississippi.

Keane, Webb. 2003. "Semiotics and the Social Analysis of Material Things." *Language and Communication* 23 (3/4): 409–425.

Klimasmith, Betsy. 2005. *At Home in the City: Urban Domesticity in American Literature and Culture, 1850–1930*. Hanover, NH: University Press of New England.

Kolodny, Annette. 1975. *The Lay of the Land: Metaphor as Experience and History in American Life and Letters*. Chapel Hill: University of North Carolina Press.

Kolodny, Annette. 1984. *The Land Before Her: Fantasy and Experience of the American Frontiers, 1630–1860*. Chapel Hill: University of North Carolina Press.

Lane, Belden C. 2001 (1988). *Landscapes of the Sacred: Geography and Narrative in American Spirituality*, exp. ed. Baltimore, MD: Johns Hopkins University Press.

Marshall, Howard Wight, and John Michael Vlach. 1973. "Toward a Folklife Approach to American Dialectics." *American Speech* 48 (3/4): 163–191.

Marx, Leo. 1964. *The Machine in the Garden: Technology and the Pastoral Ideal in America*. New York: Oxford University Press.

Mayers, Ozzie J. 1988. "The Power of the Pin: Sewing as an Act of Rootedness in American Literature." *College English* 50: 664–680.

Merish, Lori. 2000. *Sentimental Materialism: Gender, Commodity Culture, and Nineteenth-Century American Literature*. Durham, NC: Duke University Press.

Moylan, Michele, and Lane Stiles, eds. 1996. *Reading Books: Essays on the Material Text and Literature in America*. Amherst: University of Massachusetts Press.

Nash, Roderick. 1967. *Wilderness and the American Mind*. New Haven, CT: Yale University Press.

Pipkin, John S. 2003. "Glances From the Shore: Thoreau and the Material Landscape of Cape Cod." *Journal of Cultural Geography* 20 (2): 1–19.

Radway, Janice. 1984. *Reading the Romance: Women, Patriarchy, and Popular Literature*. Chapel Hill: University of North Carolina Press.

Rigal, Laura. 1998. *The American Manufactory: Art, Labor, and the World of Things in the Early Republic*. Princeton, NJ: Princeton University Press.

Romero, Lora. 1997. *Home Fronts: Domesticity and Its Critics in the Antebellum United States*. Durham, NC: Duke University Press.

Romines, Ann. 1992. *The Home Plot: Women, Writing, and Domestic Ritual*. Amherst: University of Massachusetts Press.

Ryden, Kent C. 1993. *Mapping the Invisible Landscape: Folkore, Writing, and the Sense of Place*. Iowa City: University of Iowa Press.

Shi, David E. 1995. *Facing Facts: Realism in American Thought and Culture, 1850–1920*. New York: Oxford University Press.

Smith, Henry Nash. 1978 (1950). *Virgin Land: The American West as Symbol and Myth*. Cambridge, MA: Harvard University Press.

St. George, Robert Blair. 1998. *Conversing in Signs: Poetics of Implication in Colonial New England Culture*. Chapel Hill: University of North Carolina Press.

Stewart, Susan. 1984. *On Longing: Narratives of the Miniature, the Gigantic, the Souvenir, the Collection*. Baltimore, MD: Johns Hopkins University Press.

Stonely, Peter, Albert Gelpi, and Ross Posnock. 2003. *Consumerism and American Girls' Literature, 1860–1940*. New York: Cambridge University Press.

Sweeting, Adam. 1996. *Reading Houses and Building Books: Andrew Jackson Downing and the Architecture of Popular Antebellum Literature, 1835–1855*. Hanover, NH: University Press of New England.

Tichi, Cecelia. 1997. *Shifting Gears: Technology, Literature, and Culture in Modernist America*. Chapel Hill: University of North Carolina Press.

Wilson, Sarah. 2004. "Melville and the Architecture of Antebellum Masculinity." *American Literature* 76 (1): 59–87.

Zwicky, Ann D., and Arnold M. Zwicky. 1980. "America's National Dish: The Style of Restaurant Menus." *American Speech* 55 (2): 83–92.

Visual, Spatial, and Aesthetic Approaches

Albrecht, Donald, ed. 1995. *World War II and the American Dream: How Wartime Building Changed a Nation*. Washington, DC: National Building Museum; Cambridge, MA: MIT Press.

Albrecht, Donald. 2000 (1986). *Designing Dreams: Modern Architecture in the Movies*, rpt. Santa Monica, CA: Hennessey and Ingalls.

Ashwin, Clive, comp. 1984. *History of Graphic Design and Communication: A Sourcebook*. London: Pembridge Press.

Aslin, Elizabeth. 1969. *The Aesthetic Movement: Prelude to Art Nouveau*. New York: Excalibur Books.

Axelrod, Alan, ed. 1985. *The Colonial Revival in America*. New York: W. W. Norton.

Ayres, William S., ed. 1993. *Picturing History: American Painting, 1770–1930*. New York: Rizzoli in association with Fraunces Tavern Museum.

Bacon, John M. 1991. *Cellars, Garrets, and Related Spaces in Philadelphia Houses, 1750–1850*. Philadelphia, PA: Independence National Historical Park.

Badaracco, Claire. 1995. *Trading Words: Poetry, Typography, and Illustrated Books in the Modern Literary Economy.* Baltimore, MD: Johns Hopkins University Press.

Banham, Reyner. 1960. *Theory and Design in the First Machine Age.* London: Architectural Press; New York: Praeger.

Banham, Reyner. 1996. *A Critic Writes: Essays by Reyner Banham.* Berkeley: University of California Press.

Batchelor, Ray. 1994. *Henry Ford: Mass-Production, Modernism and Design.* Manchester, UK: Manchester University Press.

Batchen, Geoffrey. 2004. *Forget Me Not: Photography and Remembrance.* New York: Princeton Architecture Press.

Benton, Charlotte, Tim Benton, and Ghislaine Wood, eds. 2003. *Art Deco, 1910–1939.* Boston: Bulfinch Press.

Benton, Megan. 2000. *Beauty and the Book: Fine Editions and Cultural Distinction in America.* New Haven, CT: Yale University Press.

Bergman, David, ed. 1993. *Camp Grounds: Style and Homosexuality.* Amherst: University of Massachusetts Press.

Betsky, Aaron. 1995. *Building Sex: Men, Women, Architecture, and the Construction of Sexuality.* New York: William Morrow.

Betsky, Aaron. 1997. *Queer Space: Architecture and Same-Sex Desire.* New York: William Morrow.

Bierut, Michael, William Drenttel, and Steven Heller, eds. 1994–2002. *Looking Closer: Critical Writings on Graphic Design.* 4 vols. New York: Allworth Press and American Institute of Graphic Arts.

Blackmar, Elizabeth. 1989. *Manhattan for Rent, 1785–1850.* Ithaca, NY: Cornell University Press.

Blackwell, Lewis. 2004. *20th-Century Type,* new and rev. ed. New Haven, CT: Yale University Press.

Boime, Albert. 1987. *Art in an Age of Revolution, 1750–1800.* Chicago: University of Chicago Press.

Boyd, Sterling. 1985. *The Adam Style in America, 1770–1820.* New York: Garland Publishers.

Bradley, Betsy Hunter. 1999. *The Works: The Industrial Architecture of the United States.* New York: Oxford University Press.

Bradley, Martha. 2001. "Building Community: The Fundamentalist Mormon Concept of Space." *Communal Studies* 21: 1–19.

Breisch, Kenneth A., and Alison K. Hoagland, eds. 2005. *Building Environments: Perspectives in Vernacular Architecture, X.* Knoxville: University of Tennessee Press.

Brimhall, Janell. 2000. "'Diversity of Gifts': The Eclectic Architecture of Early LDS Churches." *Utah Historical Quarterly* 68 (Spring): 157–171.

Brown, Elspeth H. 2000. "Rationalizing Consumption: Lejaren à Hiller and the Origins of American Advertising Photography, 1913–1924." *Enterprise & Society: The International Journal of Business History* 1 (4): 715–738.

Brown, Julie K. 2001. *Making Culture Visible: Photography and Display at Industrial Fairs, International Exhibition, and Institutional Exhibitions in the U.S., 1847–1900.* New York: Routledge.

Brown, Milton W. 1970 (1955). *American Painting: From the Armory Show to the Depression.* Princeton, NJ: Princeton University Press.

Buder, Stanley. 1990. *Visionaries and Planners: The Garden City Movement and the Modern Community.* New York: Oxford University Press.

Burnham, Van. 2001. *Supercade: A Visual History of the Videogame Age 1971–1984.* Cambridge, MA: MIT Press.

Carney, George O., ed. 1995. *Fast Food, Stock Cars, and Rock-n-Roll: Place and Space in Popular Culture.* Lanham, MD: Rowman and Littlefield.

Carter, Thomas, ed. 1997. *Images of an American Land: Vernacular Architecture in the Western United States.* Albuquerque: University of New Mexico Press.

Carter, Thomas, and Bernard L. Herman, eds. 1991. *Perspectives in Vernacular Architecture, IV.* Knoxville: University of Tennessee Press.

Center for Universal Design. 1998. *The Universal Design File, Designing for People of All Ages and Abilities.* Raleigh: North Carolina State University, The Center for Universal Design.

Chidester, David, and Edward T. Linenthal, eds. 1995. *American Sacred Space*. Bloomington: Indiana University Press.

Clarke, Kenneth. 1974 (1928). *The Gothic Revival: An Essay in the History of Taste*. New York: Harper and Row.

Clay, Grady. 1980 (1973). *Close-Up: How to Read the American City*. Chicago: University of Chicago Press.

Clay, Grady. 1994. *Real Places: An Unconventional Guide to America's Generic Landscape*. Chicago: University of Chicago Press.

Clayton, Virginia Tuttle, Elizabeth Stillinger, Erika Doss, and Deborah Chotner. 2002. *Drawing on America's Past: Folk Art, Modernism, and the Index of American Design*. Chapel Hill: University of North Carolina Press.

Cloonan, Michel Valerie. 1995. "Bookbinding, Aesthetics, and Conservation." *Libraries & Culture* 30 (2): 137–152.

Cogsdell, Christina. 2005. *Eugenic Design: Streamlining America in the 1930s*. Philadelphia: University of Pennsylvania Press.

Conzen, Michael P., ed. 1990. *The Making of the American Landscape*. Boston: Unwin Hyman.

Cooke, Lynne, and Peter Wollen. 1995. *Visual Display: Culture Beyond Appearances*. Seattle: Bay Press.

Corn, Wanda M. 1999. *The Great American Thing: Modern Art and National Identity, 1915–1935*. Berkeley: University of California Press.

Cranz, Galen. 1998. *The Chair: Rethinking Cultural, Body, and Design*. New York: W. W. Norton.

Crary, Jonathan. 1990. *Techniques of the Observer: On Vision and Modernity in the Nineteenth Century*. Cambridge, MA: MIT Press.

Craven, Wayne. 1986. *Colonial American Portraiture: The Economic, Religious, Social, Cultural, Philosophical, Scientific, and Aesthetic Foundations*. Cambridge, UK: Cambridge University Press.

Crawford, Margaret. 1995. *Building the Workingman's Paradise: The Design of American Company Towns*. New York: Verso.

Cromley, Elizabeth. 1990. *Alone Together: A History of New York's Early Apartments*. Ithaca, NY: Cornell University Press.

Cromley, Elizabeth Collins. 1990. "Sleeping Around: A History of American Beds and Bedrooms." *Journal of Design History* 3 (1): 1–17.

Cromley, Elizabeth Collins, and Carter L. Hudgins, eds. 1995. *Gender, Class, and Shelter: Perspectives in Vernacular Architecture, V*. Knoxville: University of Tennessee Press.

Crouch, Dora P., Daniel J. Garr, and Axel I. Mundigo. 1982. *Spanish City Planning in North America*. Cambridge, MA: MIT Press.

Crowley, John E. 2001. *The Invention of Comfort: Sensibilities and Design in Early Modern Britain and Early America*. Baltimore, MD: Johns Hopkins University Press.

Cummings, Abbott Lowell. 1979. *The Framed Houses of Massachusetts Bay, 1625–1725*. Cambridge, MA: Belknap Press.

Davis, Alex. 1967. *Package and Print: The Development of Container and Label Design*. New York: C. N. Potter.

Davis, Sam. 2004. *Designing for the Homeless: Architecture That Works*. Berkeley and Los Angeles: University of California Press.

Domosh, Mona. 1987. "Imagining New York's First Skyscrapers, 1875–1910." *Journal of Historical Geography* 13 (3): 233–248.

Domosh, Mona. 1996. *Invented Cities: The Creation of Landscape in Nineteenth-Century New York and Boston*. New Haven, CT: Yale University Press.

Dormer, Peter. 1993. *Design Since 1945*. London: Thames and Hudson.

Doss, Erika. 1995. *Spirit Poles and Flying Pigs: Public Art and Cultural Democracy in American Communities*. Washington, DC: Smithsonian Institution Press.

Doss, Erika, ed. 2001. *Looking at* Life *Magazine*. Washington, DC: Smithsonian Institution Press.

Dunbar, Michael. 1986. *Federal Furniture*. Newtown, CT: Taunton Press.

Duncan, Alastair. 1986. *American Art Deco*. New York: Thames and Hudson.

Early, James. 2004. *Presidio, Mission, and Pueblo: Spanish Architecture and Urbanism in the United States.* Dallas, TX: Southern Methodist University Press.

Edgette, J. Joseph. 1999. "'Now I Lay Me down to Sleep . . .': Symbols and Their Meaning on Children's Gravemarkers." *Children's Folklore Review* 22 (1): 7–24.

Faulkner, Charles H. 2004. "Moved Buildings: A Hidden Factor in the Archaeology of the Built Environment." *Historical Archaeology* 38 (2): 55–67.

Ferris, William, ed., 1983. *Afro-American Folk Arts and Crafts.* Boston: G. K. Hall.

Findlay, John M. 1992. *Magic Lands: Western Cityscapes and American Culture After 1940.* Berkeley: University of California Press.

Finnegan, Cara A. 2003. *Picturing Poverty: Print Culture and FSA Photographs.* Washington, DC: Smithsonian Institution Press.

Flad, Harvey K. 1997. "Country Clutter: Visual Pollution and the Rural Roadscape." *Annals of the American Academy of Political and Social Sciences* 553: 117–129.

Fogelson, Robert M. 1989. *America's Armories: Architecture, Society, and Public Order.* Cambridge, MA: Harvard University Press.

Fogelson, Robert M. 2001. *Downtown: Its Rise and Fall.* New Haven, CT: Yale University Press.

Forty, Adrian. 1986. *Objects of Desire: Design and Society from Wedgwood to IBM.* New York: Pantheon Books.

Foy, Jessica H., and Karal Ann Marling, eds. 1994. *The Arts and the American Home, 1890–1930.* Knoxville: University of Tennessee Press.

Frank, Robin Jaffee. 2000. *Love and Loss: American Portrait and Mourning Miniatures.* New Haven, CT: Yale University Press.

Garner, John S., ed. 1992. *The Company Town: Architecture and Society in the Early Industrial Age.* New York: Oxford University Press.

Garrett, Wendell D. 1992. *Classic America: The Federal Style and Beyond.* New York: Rizzoli.

Gerdts, William H. 1973. *American Neo-Classic Sculpture: The Marble Resurrection.* New York: Viking Press.

Glassie, Henry. 1975. *Folk Housing in Middle Virginia: A Structural Analysis of Historic Artifacts.* Knoxville: University of Tennessee Press.

Glassie, Henry. 1976 (1969). *Pattern in the Material Folk Culture of the Eastern United States.* Philadelphia: University of Pennsylvania Press.

Glassie, Henry. 2000. *Vernacular Architecture.* Bloomington: Indiana University Press.

Goss, Jon. 1993. "The 'Magic of the Mall': An Analysis of Form, Function, and Meaning in the Contemporary Retail Built Environment." *Annual of the Association of American Geographers* 83 (1): 18–47.

Gowans, Alan. 1986. *The Comfortable House: North American Suburban Architecture, 1890–1930.* Cambridge, MA: MIT Press.

Greif, Martin. 1975. *Depression Modern: The Thirties Style in America.* New York: University Books.

Groth, Paul Erling. 1994. *Living Downtown: The History of Residential Hotels in the United States.* Berkeley: University of California Press.

Groth, Paul Erling, and Todd W. Bressi, eds. 1997. *Understanding Ordinary Landscapes.* New Haven, CT: Yale University Press.

Gudis, Catherine. 2004. *Buyways: Billboards, Automobiles, and the American Landscape.* New York: Routledge.

Gundaker, Grey. 1993. "Tradition and Innovation in African-American Yards." *African Arts* 26 (2): 58–71.

Gutfreund, Owen D. 2004. *Twentieth-Century Sprawl: Highways and the Reshaping of the American Landscape.* New York: Oxford University Press.

Hales, Peter Bacon. 1984. *Silver Cities: The Photography of American Urbanization, 1839–1915.* Philadelphia, PA: Temple University Press.

Hayden, Dolores. 1976. *Seven American Utopias: The Architecture of Communitarian Socialism, 1790–1875.* Cambridge, MA: MIT Press.

Hayden, Dolores. 1981. *The Grand Domestic Revolution: A History of Feminist Designs for American Homes, Neighborhoods, and Cities*. Cambridge, MA: MIT Press.

Hayden, Dolores. 1984. *Redesigning the American Dream: The Future of Housing, Work and Family Life*. New York: W. W. Norton.

Hayden, Dolores. 2003. *Building Suburbia: Green Fields and Urban Growth, 1820–2000*. New York: Pantheon Books.

Hearn, Fil. 2003. *Ideas that Shaped Buildings*. Cambridge, MA: MIT Press.

Henkin, David. 1998. *City Reading: Written Words and Public Spaces in Antebellum New York*. New York: Columbia University Press.

Hepp, John Henry, IV. 2003. *The Middle-Class City: Transforming Space and Time in Philadelphia, 1876–1926*. Philadelphia: University of Pennsylvania Press.

Herman, Bernard L. 1992. *The Stolen House*. Charlottesville: University Press of Virginia.

Herman, Bernard L. 2005. *Townhouse: Architecture and Material Life in the Early American City, 1780–1830*. Chapel Hill: University of North Carolina Press for the Omohundro Institution of Early American History and Culture.

Herzog, Lawrence A. 1999. *From Aztec to High Tech: Architecture and Landscape Across the Mexico-United States Border*. Baltimore, MD: Johns Hopkins University Press.

Heskett, John. 1980. *Industrial Design*. London: Thames and Hudson.

Hess, Alan, Robert Venturi, Denise Scott Brown, and Steven Izenour. 1993. *Viva Las Vegas: After Hours Architecture*. San Francisco: Chronicle Books.

Hoagland, Alison K., and Kenneth A. Breisch, eds. 2003. *Constructing Image, Identity, and Place: Perspectives in Vernacular Architecture, IX*. Knoxville: University of Tennessee Press.

Hollis, Richard. 2000. *Graphic Design: A Concise History*, rev. and exp. ed. New York: Thames and Hudson.

Holloway, David, and John Beck, eds. 2005. *American Visual Cultures*. New York: Continuum.

Horowitz, Helen Lefkowitz. 1984. *Alma Mater: Design and Experience in the Women's Colleges from Their Nineteenth Century Beginnings to the 1930s*. New York: Alfred A. Knopf.

Howe, Katherine S., and David B. Warren. 1976. *The Gothic Revival Style in America, 1830–1870*. Houston, TX: Museum of Fine Arts.

Hubka, Thomas C. 1984. *Big House, Little House, Back House, Barn: The Connected Farm Buildings of New England*. Hanover, NH: University Press of New England.

Hudgins, Carter L., and Elizabeth Collins Cromley, eds. 1997. *Shaping Communities: Perspectives in Vernacular Architecture*. Knoxville: University of Tennessee Press.

Isenberg, Alison. 2005. *Downtown America: A History of the Place and the People Who Made It*. Chicago: University of Chicago.

Jackson, John Brinckerhoff. 1980. *The Necessity for Ruins, and Other Topics*. Amherst: University of Massachusetts Press.

Jackson, John Brinckerhoff. 1984. *Discovering the Vernacular Landscape*. New Haven, CT: Yale University Press.

Jackson, John Brinckerhoff. 1994. *A Sense of Place, A Sense of Time*. New Haven, CT: Yale University Press.

Jackson, John Brinckerhoff. 1997. *Landscape in Sight: Looking at America*, ed. Helen Lefkowitz Horowitz. New Haven, CT: Yale University Press.

Jakle, John A. 1994. *The Gas Station in America*. Baltimore, MD: Johns Hopkins University Press.

Jeffery, R. Brooks. 2003. "From Azulejos to Zaguanes: The Islamic Legacy of the Built Environment of Hispano-America." *Journal of the Southwest* 45 (1–2): 289–327.

Jencks, Charles. 1987. *Post-Modernism: The New Classicism in Art and Architecture*. New York: Rizzoli.

Jennings, Jan. 2005. *Cheap and Tasteful Dwellings: Design Competition and the Convenient Interior, 1879–1909*. Knoxville: University of Tennessee Press.

Jennings, Jan, and Herbert Gottfried. 1988. *American Vernacular Interior Architecture, 1870–1940*. New York: Van Nostrand-Reinhold.

Johns, Elizabeth. 1991. *American Genre Painting: The Politics of Everyday Life*. New Haven, CT: Yale University Press.

Johns, Michael. 2003. *Moment of Grace: The American City in the 1950s*. Berkeley: University of California Press.

Jones, Karen R., and John Wills. 2005. *The Invention of the Park: Recreational Landscapes from the Garden of Eden to Disney's Magic Kingdom*. Cambridge, UK: Polity Press.

Jones, Michael Owen. 1975. *The Hand Made Object and Its Maker*. Berkeley: University of California Press.

Jones, Michael Owen. 1987. *Exploring Folk Art: Twenty Years of Thought on Craft, Work, and Aesthetics*. Logan: University of Utah Press.

Jussim, Estelle. 1983. *Visual Communication and the Graphic Arts: Photographic Technologies in the Nineteenth Century*. New York: R. R. Bowker.

Kahera, Akel Ismail. 2002. *Deconstructing the American Mosque: Space, Gender, and Aesthetics*. Austin: University of Texas Press.

Kamau, Lucy Jayne. 1992. "The Anthropology of Space in Harmonist and Owenite New Harmony." *Communal Studies* 12: 68–89.

Kelly, Barbara M. 1993. *Expanding the American Dream: Building and Rebuilding Levittown*. Albany: State University of New York Press.

King, Anthony D. 1980. *Buildings and Society: Essays on the Social Development of the Built Environment*. London: Routledge.

Kinsey, Joni L., Rebecca Roberts, and Robert F. Sayre. 1996. "Prairie Prospects: The Aesthetics of Plainness." *Prospects* 21: 261–297.

Kirk, John. 1980. *The Book of Shaker Furniture*. Amherst: University of Massachusetts Press.

Kisacky, Jeanne. 2005. "Restructuring Isolation: Hospital Architecture, Medicine, and Disease Prevention." *Bulletin of the History of Medicine* 79 (Spring): 1–49.

Kniffen, Fred. 1965. "Folk Housing: Key to Diffusion." *Annals of the Association of American Geographers* 55: 549–577.

Kornfeld, Phyllis. 1997. *Cellblock Visions: Prison Art in America*. Princeton, NJ: Princeton University Press.

Kostof, Spiro. 1987. *America by Design*. New York: Oxford University Press.

Lanier, Gabrielle M., and Bernard L. Herman. 1997. *Everyday Architecture of the Mid-Atlantic: Looking at Buildings and Landscapes*. Baltimore, MD: Johns Hopkins University Press.

Lapsansky, Emma J., and Anne A. Verplanck. 2003. *Quaker Aesthetics: Reflections on a Quaker Ethic in American Design and Consumption*. Philadelphia: University of Pennsylvania Press.

Lara, Jaime. 2004. *City, Temple, Stage: Eschatalogical Architecture and Liturgical Theatrics in New Spain*. Notre Dame, IN: University of Notre Dame Press.

Lavin, Maud. 2001. *Clean New World: Culture, Politics, and Graphic Design*. Cambridge, MA: MIT Press.

Lawrence, Denise L., and Setha M. Low. 1900. "The Built Environment and Spatial Form." *Annual Review of Anthropology* 19: 453–505.

Lewis, Pierce F., et al. 1973. *Visual Blight in America*. Washington, DC: Association of American Geographers.

Liebs, Chester. 1985. *Main Street to Miracle Mile: American Roadside Architecture*. Boston: Little, Brown.

Lipkin, Jonathan. 2005. *Photography Reborn: Image Making in the Digital Age*. New York: Harry N. Abrams.

Loeffler, Jane C. 1998. *The Architecture of Diplomacy: Building America's Embassies*. New York: Princeton Architectural Press.

Longstreth, Richard. 1997. *City Center to Regional Mall: Architecture, the Automobile, and Retailing in Los Angeles, 1920–1950*. Cambridge, MA: MIT Press.

Longstreth, Richard. 1999. *The Drive-In, the Supermarket and the Transformation of Commercial Space in Los Angeles, 1914–1941*. Cambridge, MA: MIT Press.

Loth, Calder, and Julius Toursdale Sadler, Jr. 1975. *The Only Proper Style: Gothic Architecture in America*. New York: New York Graphic Society.

Lovell, Margaretta M. 2005. *Art in the Season of Revolution: Painters, Artisans, and Patrons in Early America*. Philadelphia: University of Pennsylvania Press.

Low, Setha M., and Denise Lawrence Zúñiga, eds. 2003. *The Anthropology of Space and Place: Locating Culture*. London: Blackwell.

Lowes, Mark Douglas. 2002. *Indy Dreams and Urban Nightmares: Speed Mechants, Spectacle, and the Struggle over Public Space in the World-Class City*. Toronto: University of Toronto Press.

Lubin, David M. 1994. *Picturing a Nation: Art and Social Change in Nineteenth-Century America*. New Haven, CT: Yale University Press.

Ludwig, Allan I. 1966. *Graven Images: New England Stonecarving and its Symbols, 1650–1815*, 3rd ed. Hanover, NH: University Press of New England.

Lupton, Ellen. 1993. *Mechanical Brides: Women and Machines from Home to Office*. New York: Cooper-Hewitt National Museum of Design; New York: Princeton Architectural Press.

Marcus, Leonard S. 1978. *The American Store Window*. New York: Watson-Guptill Publications for the Whitney Library of Design.

Marling, Karal Ann. 1994. *As Seen on TV: The Visual Culture of Everyday Life in the 1950s*. Cambridge, MA: Harvard University Press.

Marling, Karal Ann. 1997. *Designing Disney's Theme Parks: The Architecture of Reassurance*. Paris: Flammarion.

Marling, Karal Ann. 2000 (1982). *Wall-to-Wall America: Post Office Murals in the Great Depression*. Minneapolis: University of Minnesota Press.

Marzio, Peter. 1979. *The Democratic Art: Pictures for a Nineteenth-Century America: Chromolithography, 1840–1900*. Boston: David R. Godine.

Massie, Anne. 2001. *Hollywood Beyond the Screen: Design and Material Culture*. New York: New York University Press.

Maynard, W. Barksdale. 2002. *Architecture in the United States, 1800–1850*. New Haven, CT: Yale University Press.

McDannell, Colleen. 2004. *Picturing Faith: Photography and the Great Depression*. New Haven, CT: Yale University Press.

McDowell, Linda. 1999. *Gender, Identity, and Place: Understanding Feminist Geographies*. Minneapolis: University of Minnesota Press.

McMurry, Sally, and Annmarie Adams, eds. 2000. *People, Power, Places: Perspectives in Vernacular Architecture, VIII*. Knoxville: University of Tennessee Press.

Meggs, Philip, and Alston W. Purvis. 2000. *Meggs' History of Graphic Design*, 4th ed. Hoboken, NJ: John Wiley and Sons.

Meikle, Jeffrey L. 1979. *Twentieth-Century Limited: Industrial Design in America, 1925–1939*. Philadelphia, PA: Temple University Press.

Meinig, D. W. 1986. *The Shaping of America: A Geographical Perspective in 500 Years of History*. New Haven, CT: Yale University Press.

Meinig, Donald W., and John Brinckerhoff Jackson, eds. 1997. *The Interpretation of Ordinary Landscapes: Geographical Essays*. New York: Oxford University Press.

Miller, Angela L. 1993. *Empire of the Eye: Landscape Representation and American Cultural Politics, 1825–1875*. Ithaca, NY: Cornell University Press.

Nabokov, Peter, and Robert Easton. 1989. *Native American Architecture*. New York: Oxford University Press.

Neil, J. Meredith. 1975. *Toward a National Taste: America's Quest for Aesthetic Independence*. Honolulu: University Press of Hawaii.

Newhall, Beaumont. 1976. *The Daguerreotype in America*, 3rd rev. ed. New York: Dover.

Newhall, Beaumont. 1982. *The History of Photography from 1839 to the Present Day*, 5th ed. New York: Museum of Modern Art.

Noble, Allen G. 1984. *Wood, Brick, and Stone: The North American Settlement Landscape*. Amherst: University of Massachusetts Press.

Noble, Allen G., ed. 1992. *To Build a New Land: Ethnic Landscapes in North America*. Baltimore, MD: Johns Hopkins University Press.

Nostrand, Richard L., and Lawrence E. Estaville. 2001. *Homelands: A Geography of Culture and Place in America*. Baltimore, MD: Johns Hopkins University Press.

Novak, Barbara. 1980. *Nature and Culture: American Landscape and Painting, 1825–1875*. New York: Oxford University Press.

Orne, Jerrold. 1976. "Academic Library Buildings: A Century in Review." *College and Research Libraries* 37 (4): 316–321.

Park, Marlene, and Gerald E. Markowitz. 1984. *Democratic Vistas: Post Offices and Public Art in the New Deal*. Philadelphia, PA: Temple University Press.

Penney, David. 2004. *North American Indian Art*. New York: Thames and Hudson.

Peterson, Jon A. 2003. *The Birth of City Planning in the United States, 1840–1917*. Baltimore, MD: Johns Hopkins University Press.

Pevsner, Nikolaus. 1949 (1936). *Pioneers of the Modern Movement from William Morris to Walter Gropius*. New York: Museum of Modern Art.

Pile, John. 2003. *Interior Design*. 3rd ed. Upper Saddle River, NJ: Prentice-Hall, Inc., and Harry N. Abrams.

Pile, John. 2005. *A History of Interior Design*. 2nd ed. Hoboken, NJ: John Wiley & Sons, Inc.

Poynor, Rick. 2003. *No More Rules: Graphic Design and Postmodernism*. New Haven, CT: Yale University Press.

Promey, Sally M. 1993. *Spiritual Spectacles: Vision and Image in Mid Nineteenth-Century Shakerism*. Bloomington: Indiana University Press.

Prosterman, Leslie. 1995. *Ordinary Life, Festival Days: Aesthetics in the Midwestern County Fair*. Washington, DC: Smithsonian Institution Press.

Pulos, Arthur J. 1983. *American Design Ethic: A History of Industrial Design to 1940*. Cambridge, MA: MIT Press.

Raizman, David. 2004. *History of Modern Design*. Upper Saddle River, NJ: Prentice-Hall.

Rapaport, Amos. 1969. *House Form and Culture*. Englewood Cliffs, NJ: Prentice-Hall.

Redekop, Calvin. 1986. "Mennonites, Aesthetics, and Buildings." *Mennonite Life* 41 (3): 27–29.

Reiff, Daniel D. 1986. *Small Georgian Houses in England and Virginia: Origins and Development through the 1750s*. Newark, DE: University of Delaware Press; London: Associated University Press.

Remington, R. Roger, with Lisa Bodenstedt. 2003. *American Modernism: Graphic Design, 1920–1960*. New Haven, CT: Yale University Press.

Reps, John. 1969. *Town Planning in Frontier America*. Princeton, NJ: Princeton University Press.

Richardson, M., ed. 1974. *The Human Mirror: Material and Spatial Images of Man*. Baton Rouge: Louisiana State University Press.

Rosenstein, Leon, 1987. "The Aesthetic of the Antique." *Journal of Aesthetics and Art Criticism* 45 (4): 393–402.

Rothschild, Joan, ed. 1999. *Design and Feminism: Re-Visioning Spaces, Places, and Everyday Things*. New Brunswick, NJ: Rutgers University Press.

Rotman, Deborah L., and Ellen-Rose Savulis. 2003. *Shared Spaces and Divided Places: Material Dimensions of Gender Relations and the American Historical Landscape*. Knoxville: University of Tennessee Press.

Ruby, Jay. 1995. *Secure the Shadow: Death in Photography in America*. Cambridge, MA: MIT Press.

Rudisill, Richard. 1971. *Mirror Image: The Influence of the Daguerreotype in American Society*. Albuquerque: University of New Mexico Press.

Rybczynski, Witold. 1995. *City Life: Urban Expectations of North American Cities*. New York: Scribner's.

Samuels, Gayle Broandow. 1999. *Enduring Roots: Encounters with Trees, History, and the American Landscape*. New Brunswick, NJ: Rutgers University Press.

Sandweiss, Martha A., ed. 1991. *Photography in Nineteenth-Century America*. Fort Worth, TX: Amon Carter Museum.

Sandweiss, Martha A. 2002. *Print the Legend: Photography and the American West*. New Haven, CT: Yale University Press.

Sasser, Elizabeth Skidmore, and Sara Elizabeth Sasser. 1976. "The Aesthetics of Adobe." *Southwestern Art* 5 (2): 11–16, 62.

Saunders, Richard H., and Ellen G. Miles. 1987. *American Colonial Portraits: 1700–1776*. Washington, DC: Smithsonian Institution Press for the National Portrait Gallery.

Savage, Kirk. 1997. *Standing Soldiers, Kneeling Slaves: Race, War, and Monument in Nineteenth Century America*. Princeton, NJ: Princeton University Press.

Scanlan, John. 2005. *On Garbage*. London: Reaktion Books.

Schlereth, Thomas J. 1997. *Reading the Road: U.S. 40 and the American Landscape*, rev. ed. Knoxville: University of Tennessee Press.

Scully, Vincent. 1971. *The Shingle Style and The Stick Style: Architectural Theory and Design from Richardson to the Origins of Wright*. New Haven, CT: Yale University Press.

Senie, Harriet F., and Sally Webster, eds. 1993. *Critical Issues in Public Art: Content, Context, and Controversy*. New York: HarperCollins.

Simons, D. Brenton, and Peter Benes. 2002. *The Art of Family: Genealogical Artifacts in New England*. Boston: New England Historic Genealogical Society and Northeastern University Press.

Smith, Terry. 1993. *Making the Modern: Industry, Art, and Design in America*. Chicago: University of Chicago Press.

Sorkin, M., ed. 1994. *Variations on a Theme Park: The New American City and the End of Public Space*. New York: Hill & Wang.

Spain, Daphne. 1992. *Gendered Spaces*. Chapel Hill: University of North Carolina Press.

Sparke, Penny. 1986. *An Introduction to Design and Culture in the Twentieth Century*. New York: Harper & Row.

Sparke, Penny. 1995. *As Long as It's Pink: The Sexual Politics of Taste*. London: HarperCollins.

Spens, Iona, ed. 1994. *Architecture of Incarceration*. London: Academy Group.

Stanton, Phoebe B. 1968. *The Gothic Revival and American Church Architecture: An Episode in Taste, 1840–1856*. Baltimore, MD: Johns Hopkins University Press.

Stein, Roger B. 1967. *John Ruskin and Aesthetic Thought in America, 1840–1900*. Cambridge, MA: Harvard University Press.

Sternberger, Paul Spencer. 2001. *Between Amateur and Aesthete: The Legitimization of Photography as Art in America, 1880–1900*. Albuquerque: University of New Mexico Press.

Stilgoe, John R. 1981. "Fair Fields and Blasted Rock: American Land Classification Systems and Landscape Aesthetics." *American Studies* 22 (1): 21–33.

Stilgoe, John R. 1982. *The Metropolitan Corridor: The Railroad and the American Scene*. New Haven, CT: Yale University Press.

Stilgoe, John R. 1983. *Common Landscape in America, 1580–1845*. New Haven, CT: Yale University Press.

Stilgoe, John R. 1990. *Borderland: Origins of the American Suburb, 1820–1939*. New Haven, CT: Yale University Press.

Stilgoe, John R. 1999. *Outside Lies Magic: Regaining History and Awareness in Everyday Places*. New York: Walker and Company.

Stilgoe, John R. 2005. *Landscape and Images*. Charlottesville: University Press of Virginia.

Tangney, Shaunanne. 2004. "But What Is There to See? An Exploration of a Great Plains Aesthetic." *Great Plains Quarterly* 24 (1): 31–41.

Tatham, David, 1973. *The Lure of the Striped Pig: The Illustration of Popular Music in America, 1820–1870*. Barre, MA: Imprint Society.

Thompson, Ellen Mazur. 1997. *The Origins of Graphic Design in America, 1870–1920*. New Haven, CT: Yale University Press.

Thompson, Emily. 2002. *The Soundscape of Modernity: Architectural Acoustics and the Culture of Listening in America, 1900–1933*. Cambridge, MA: MIT Press.

Thompson, Susan Otis. 1996. *American Book Design and William Morris*, 2nd ed. New Castle, DE: Oak Knoll Books.

Trachtenberg, Alan. 1989. *Reading American Photographs: Images as History, Mathew Brady to Walker Evans*. New York: Hill & Wang.

Tuan, Yi-Fu. 1977. *Space and Place: The Perspective of Experience*. Minneapolis: University of Minnesota Press.

Turner, Patricia A. 1994. *Ceramic Uncles and Celluloid Mammies: Black Images and Their Influence on Culture*. New York: Anchor.

Turner, Paul Venable. 1984. *Campus: An American Planning Tradition*. Cambridge, MA: MIT Press.

Upton, Dell. 1984. "White and Black Landscapes in Eighteenth-Century Virginia." *Places: A Quarterly Journal of Environmental Design* 2 (2): 59–72.

Upton, Dell. 1986. *Holy Things and Profane: Anglican Parish Churches in Colonial Virginia*. Cambridge, MA: MIT Press.

Upton, Dell, ed. 1987. *America's Architectural Roots: Ethnic Groups that Built America*. Washington: Preservation Press.

Upton, Dell, and John Michael Vlach, eds. 1986. *Common Places: Readings in American Vernacular Architecture*. Athens: University of Georgia Press.

Valentine, Gill, ed. 2000. *From Nowhere to Everywhere: Lesbian Geographies*. Binghamton, NY: Haworth Press.

Van Hook, Bailey. 2003. *The Virgin & the Dynamo: Public Murals in American Architecture, 1893–1917*. Athens: Ohio University Press.

Van Slyck, Abigail A. 1995. *Free to All: Carnegie Libraries & American Culture, 1890–1920*. Chicago: University of Chicago Press.

Venturi, Robert, Denise Scott Brown, and Steven Izenour. 1998. *Learning From Las Vegas: The Forgotten Symbolism of Architectural Form*, rev. ed. Cambridge, MA: MIT Press.

Vermeule, Cornelius. 1971. *Numismatic Art in America: Aesthetics of the United States Coinage*. Cambridge, MA: Belknap Press.

Vlach, John Michael. 1978. *The Afro-American Tradition in Decorative Arts*. Cleveland, OH: Cleveland Museum of Art.

Vlach, John Michael. 1993. *Back of the Big House: The Architecture of Plantation Slavery*. Chapel Hill: University of North Carolina Press.

Vlach, John Michael. 2002. *The Planter's Prospect: Privilege and Slavery in Plantation Paintings*. Chapel Hill: University of North Carolina Press.

Walker, Lynne. 2002. "Home Making: An Architectural Perspective." *Signs: Journal of Women in Culture and Society* 27 (3): 823–835.

Wallace-Sanders, Kimberly Gisele, ed. 2002. *Skin Deep, Spirit Strong: The Black Female Body in American Culture*. Ann Arbor: University of Michigan Press.

Weiss, Ellen. 1987. *City in the Woods: The Life and Design of an American Camp Meeting on Martha's Vineyard*. New York: Oxford University Press.

Weiss, Marc. 1987. *The Rise of the Community Builders: The Real Estate Industry and Urban Land Planning*. New York: Columbia University Press.

Weissbach, Lee Shai. 2003. "The Architecture of the *Bimah* in American Synagogues: Framing the Ritual." *American Jewish History* 91 (1): 29–51.

Wharton, Annabel Jane. 2001. *Building the Cold War: Hilton International Hotels and Modern Architecture*. Chicago: University of Chicago Press.

White, Shane, and Graham White. 1998. *Stylin': African American Expressive Culture from its Beginnings to the Zoot Suit*. Ithaca, NY: Cornell University Press.

Williams, Peter W. 2000. *Houses of God: Religion and Architecture in the United States*. Urbana and Chicago: University of Illinois Press.

Willis, Deborah. 1994. *Picturing Us: African American Identity in Photography*. New York: New Press.

Wilson, Chris, and Paul Groth, eds. 2003. *Everyday America: Cultural Landscape Studies after J. B. Jackson*. Berkeley: University of California Press.

Wilson, Kristina. 2004. *Livable Modernism: Interior Decorating and Design During the Great Depression.* New Haven, CT: Yale University Press in association with Yale University Art Gallery.

Wilson, Richard Guy, Shaun Eyring, and Kenny Marotta, eds. 2006. *Re-Creating the American Past.* Charlottesville: University Press of Virginia.

Wilton, Andrew, and Tim Barringer. 2002. *American Sublime: Landscape Painting in the United States, 1820–1880.* London: Tate Publishing.

Wood, Ghislaine. 2003. *Essential Art Deco.* London: V & A Publications.

Wood, Marcus. 2000. *Blind Memory: Visual Representations of Slavery in England and America, 1780–1865.* New York: Routledge.

Woodham, Jonathan M. 1997. *Twentieth-Century Design.* Oxford, UK: Oxford University Press.

Yamin, Rebecca, and Karen Bescherer Metheny, eds. 1996. *Landscape Archaeology: Reading and Interpreting the American Historical Landscape.* Knoxville: University of Tennessee Press.

Young, Terence, and Robert Riley, eds. 2002. *Theme Park Landscapes: Antecedents and Variations.* Washington, DC: Dumbarton Oaks.

Zelinsky, Wilbur. 1973. *The Cultural Geography of the United States.* Englewood Cliffs, NJ: Prentice-Hall.

Zukin, Sharon. 1991. *Landscapes of Power: From Detroit to Disney World.* Berkeley: University of California Press.

Technology, Economics, Business, and Consumption

Abelson, Elaine S. 1989. *When Ladies Go A-Thieving: Middle Class Shoplifters in the Victorian Department Store.* New York: Oxford University Press.

Ackerman, Marsha. 2002. *Cool Comfort: America's Romance with Air Conditioning.* Washington, DC: Smithsonian Institution Press.

Anderson, Oscar Edward. 1972 (1953*). Refrigeration in America: A History of a New Technology and Its Impact.* Port Washington, NY: Kennikat Press.

Andrews, William D., and Deborah C. Andrews. 1974. "Technology and the Housewife in Nineteenth-Century America." *Women's Studies* 2 (3): 309–328.

Atherton, Lewis E. 1939. *The Frontier Merchant in Mid-America.* Columbia: University of Missouri Press.

Barrow, Mark V. 2000. "The Specimen Dealer: Entrepreneurial Natural History in the Gilded Age." *Journal of the History of Biology* 33 (3): 493–534.

Barry, Kit. 1994. *The Snake Oil Syndrome: Patent Medicine Advertising.* Hanover, MA: Christopher Publishing.

Belasco, Warren, ed. 2001. *Food Nations: Selling Taste in Consumer Societies.* New York: Routledge.

Bell, David, and Gil Valentine. 1997. *Consuming Geographies: We Are Where We Eat.* London: Routledge.

Benson, Susan Porter. 1986. *Counter Cultures: Saleswomen, Managers and Customers in American Department Stores, 1890–1940.* Urbana: University of Illinois Press.

Berger, Arthur Asa. 2000. *Ads, Fads, and Consumer Culture: Advertising's Impact on American Character and Society.* Lanham, MD: Rowman & Littlefield.

Bernstein, Eldon, and Fred Carstensen. 1996. "Rising to the Occasion: Lender's Bagels and the Frozen Food Revolution, 1927–1985." *Business and Economic History* 25 (1): 165–175.

Biggs, Lindy. 1996. *The Rational Factory: Architecture, Technology, and Work in America's Age of Mass Production.* Baltimore, MD: Johns Hopkins University Press.

Bilstein, Roger E. 1984. *Flight in America 1900–1983.* Baltimore, MD: Johns Hopkins University Press.

Blaszczyk, Regina Lee. 2000. *Imagining Consumers: Design and Innovation From Wedgwood to Corning.* Baltimore, MD: Johns Hopkins University Press.

Borgmann, Albert. 1984. *Technology and the Character of Contemporary Life.* Chicago: University of Chicago Press.

Bowden, Sue, and Avner Offer. 1994. "Household Appliances and the Use of Time: The United States and Britain since the 1920s." *Economic History Review* 47 (4): 725–748.

Brandon, Ruth. 1977. *A Capitalist Romance: Singer and the Sewing Machine*. New York: J. P. Lippincott.

Braverman, Harry. 1974. *Labor and Monopoly Capital: The Degradation of Work in the Twentieth Century*. New York: Monthly Review Press.

Breen, T. H. 2004. *The Marketplace of Revolution: How Consumer Politics Shaped American Independence*. New York: Oxford University Press.

Brewer, Priscilla J. 2000. *From Fireplace to Cookstove: Technology and the Domestic Ideal in America*. Syracuse, NY: Syracuse University Press.

Bronner, Simon J., ed. 1989. *Consuming Visions: Accumulation and Display of Goods in America, 1880–1920*. New York: W. W. Norton.

Brooks, J. 1981. *Showing Off in America: From Conspicuous Consumption to Parody Display*. Boston: Little, Brown.

Burman, Barbara, ed. 1999. *The Culture of Sewing: Gender, Consumption and Home Dressmaking*. Oxford, UK: Berg.

Butsch, Richard, ed. 1990. *For Fun and Profit: The Transformation of Leisure into Consumption*. Philadelphia, PA: Temple University Press.

Calder, Lendol G. 1999. *Financing the American Dream: A Cultural History of Consumer Credit*. Princeton, NJ: Princeton University Press.

Campbell, Colin. 1987. *The Romantic Ethic and the Spirit of Modern Consumerism*. London: Basil Blackwell.

Carrier, James G. 1994. *Gifts and Commodities: Exchange and Western Capitalism since 1700*. London: Routledge.

Carrier, James G., ed. 1997. *Meanings of the Market: The Free Market in Western Culture*. Oxford, UK: Berg.

Carson, Gerald. 1965. *The Old Country Store*. New York: E. P. Dutton.

Caskey, J. P., and B. Zikmond. 1994. *Fringe Banking: Check-Cashing Outlets, Pawnshops, and the Poor*. New York: Russell Sage Foundation.

Clark, Thomas. 1964. *Pills, Petticoats, and Plows: The Southern Country Store*. Norman: University of Oklahoma Press.

Cochran, Thomas, and William Miller. 1961. *The Age of Enterprise: A Social History of Industrial America*. New York: Harper & Row.

Cohen, Lizabeth. 1996. "From Town Center to Shopping Center: The Reconfiguration of Community Marketplaces in Postwar America." *American Historical Review* 101 (2): 1050–1082.

Cohen, Lizabeth. 2003. *A Consumer's Republic: The Politics of Mass Consumption in Postwar America*. New York : Alfred A. Knopf.

Cole, Arthur H., and Harold F. Williamson. 1941. *The American Carpet Manufacturers: A History and an Analysis*. Cambridge, MA: Harvard University Press.

Cook, Daniel Thomas. 2004. *The Commodification of Childhood: The Children's Clothing Industry and the Rise of the Child Consumer*. Durham, NC: Duke University Press.

Corn, Joseph J., ed. 1986. *Imagining Tomorrow: History, Technology, and the American Future*. Cambridge, MA: MIT Press.

Cowan, Ruth Schwartz. 1983. *More Work for Mother: The Ironies of Household Technology from the Open Hearth to the Microwave*. New York: Basic Books.

Cowan, Ruth Schwartz. 1997. *A Social History of American Technology*. New York: Oxford University Press.

Cross, Gary. 1997. *Kids' Stuff: Toys and the Changing World of American Childhood*. Cambridge, MA: Harvard University Press.

Crouch, Tom D. 1983. *Eagle Aloft: Two Centuries of the Balloon in America*. Washington, DC: Smithsonian Institution Press.

Crouch, Tom D. 2002. *A Dream of Wings: Americans and the Airplane, 1875–1905*. New York: W. W. Norton.

Davies, Philip John. 2002. "The Material Culture of U.S. Elections: Artisanship, Entrepreneurship, Ephemera and Two Centuries of Trans-Atlantic Exchange." *Journal of Political Marketing* 1 (2–3): 9–24.

Davis, Pearce. 1949. *The Development of the American Glass Industry*. Cambridge, MA: Harvard University Press.

Davis, Susan G. 1997. *Spectacular Nature: Corporate Culture and the Sea World Experience*. Berkeley: University of California Press.

De Grazia, Victoria, ed. 1996. *The Sex of Things: Gender and Consumption in Historical Perspective*. Berkeley: University of California Press.

Donohue, Kathleen G. 2003. *Freedom From Want: American Liberalism and the Idea of the Consumer*. Baltimore, MD: Johns Hopkins University Press.

Evan, William M. 2004. "Voting Technology, Political Institutions, Legal Institutions and Civil Society: A Study of the Hypothesis of Cultural Lag in Reverse." *History and Technology* 20 (2): 165–183.

Ewen, Stuart. 1976. *Captains of Consciousness: Advertising and the Roots of Consumer Culture*. New York: Basic Books.

Ewen, Stuart. 1988. *All Consuming Images: The Politics of Style in Contemporary Culture*. New York: Basic Books.

Ewen, Stuart, and Elizabeth Ewen. 1982. *Channels of Desire: Mass Images and the Shaping of American Consciousness*. New York: McGraw-Hill.

Farrell, James J. 2003. *One Nation Under Goods: Malls and the Seductions of American Shopping*. Washington, DC: Smithsonian Books.

Fine, Ben, and Ellen Leopold. 1990. "Consumerism and the Industrial Revolution." *Social History* 15: 151–190.

Fitzgerald, Deborah. 2003. *Every Farm a Factory: The Industrial Ideal in American Agriculture*. New Haven, CT: Yale University Press.

Fox, Arthur H. 1957. "A Theory of Second-Hand Markets." *Economica* n.s. 24: 99–115.

Fox, Bonnie J. 1990. "Selling the Mechanized Household: 70 Years of Ads in *Ladies' Home Journal*." *Gender & Society* 4 (1): 25–40.

Fox, Richard Wightman, and T. J. Jackson Lears, eds. 1983. *The Cultures of Consumption: Critical Essays in American History, 1880–1980*. New York: Pantheon Books.

Frank, Thomas. 1998. *The Conquest of Cool: Business Culture, Counterculture, and the Rise of Hip Consumerism*. Chicago: University of Chicago Press.

Friedman, Walter A. 2004. *Birth of a Salesman: The Transformation of Selling in America*. Cambridge, MA: Harvard University Press.

Gabaccia, Donna. 1998. *We Are What We Eat: Ethnic Food and the Making of Americans*. Cambridge, MA: Harvard University Press.

Gallman, Robert E., and John Joseph Wallis, eds. 1992. *American Economic Growth and Standards of Living Before the Civil War*. Chicago: University of Chicago Press.

Garvey, Ellen Gruber. 1996. *The Adman in the Parlor: Magazines and the Gendering of Consumer Culture, 1880s–1910s*. New York: Oxford University Press.

Gibb, J. G. 1996. *The Archaeology of Wealth: Consumer Behavior in English America*. New York: Plenum Press.

Gidlow, Liette. 2004. *The Big Vote: Gender, Consumer Culture, and the Politics of Exclusion, 1890s–1920s*. Baltimore, MD: Johns Hopkins University Press.

Giedion, Siegfried. 1969 (1948). *Mechanization Takes Command: A Contribution to Anonymous History*, rpt. ed. New York: W. W. Norton.

Glickman, Lawrence. B. 1997. *A Living Wage: American Workers and the Making of Consumer Society*. Ithaca, NY: Cornell University Press.

Goetzmann, William N. 1993. "Accounting for Taste: Art and the Financial Markets over Three Centuries." *American Economic Review* 83 (5): 1370–1376.

Goffman, Erving. 1979. *Gender Advertisements*. Cambridge, MA: Harvard University Press.

Goldenberg, Joseph A. 1976. *Shipbuilding in Colonial America*. Charlottesville: University Press of Virginia, for the Maritime Museum.

Goodwyn, Barry K., Thomas J. Grennes, and Lee A. Craig. 2002. "Mechanical Refrigeration and the Integration of Perishable Commodity Markets." *Explorations in Economic History* 39 (2): 154–182.

Gordon, Robert B., and Patrick M. Malone. 1994. *The Texture of Industry: An Archaeologic View of the Industrialization of North America*. New York: Oxford University Press.

Grier, Katherine C. 1986. *The Popular Illuminator: Domestic Lighting in the Kerosene Era, 1860–1900*. Rochester, NY: Margaret Woodbury Strong Museum.

Gurstein, Rochelle. 2003. "Avant-Garde and Kitsch Revisited." *Raritan* 22 (3): 126–158.

Haites, Erik F., James Mak, and Gary M. Walton. 1975. *Western River Transportation: The Era of Early Internal Development, 1810–1860*. Baltimore, MD: Johns Hopkins University Press.

Hamilton, Shane. 2003. "The Economies and Conveniences of Modern-Day Living: Frozen Foods and Mass Marketing, 1945–1965." *Business History Review* 77 (1): 33–60.

Hanchett, Thomas W. 1996. "U.S. Tax Policy and the Shopping-Center Boom of the 1950s and 1960s." *American Historical Review* 101 (4): 1082–1110.

Hindle, Brooke, ed. 1981. *Material Culture of the Wooden Age*. Tarrytown, NY: Sleepy Hollow Press.

Hine, Thomas. 1995. *The Total Package: The Secret History and Hidden Meaning of Boxes, Bottles, Cans and Other Persuasive Containers*. Boston: Little, Brown.

Hine, Thomas. 2003. *I Want That! How We All Became Shoppers*. New York: HarperCollins Perennial.

Hirsh, Richard F. 1989. *Technology and Transformation in the American Electric Utility Industry*. Cambridge, UK: Cambridge University Press.

Horowitz, Daniel. 1985. *The Morality of Spending: Attitudes Toward the Consumer Society in America, 1875–1940*. Baltimore, MD: Johns Hopkins University Press.

Horowitz, Daniel. 2004. *The Anxieties of Affluence: Critiques of American Consumer Culture, 1939–1979*. Amherst: University of Massachusetts Press.

Horowitz, Roger, ed. 1998. *His and Hers: Gender, Consumption and Technology*. Charlottesville: University Press of Virginia.

Hounshell, David A. 1984. *From the American System to Mass Production, 1800–1932: The Development of Manufacturing Technology in the United States*. Baltimore, MD: Johns Hopkins University Press with the Eleutherian Mills-Hagley Foundation.

Hughes, Thomas P. 2004. *Human-Built World: How to Think about Technology and Culture*. Chicago: University of Chicago Press.

Hunter, Louis. 1985. *A History of Industrial Power in the United States, 1780–1930: Steam Power*. Charlottesville: University Press of Virginia for the Hagley Museum and Library.

Hunter, Louis C. 1993 (1949). *Steamboats on the Western Rivers: An Economic and Technological History*. New York: Dover.

Innes, Stephen, ed. 1988. *Work and Labor in Early America*. Chapel Hill: University of North Carolina Press.

Jackson, Kenneth T. 1996. "All the World's a Mall: Reflections on the Social and Economic Consequences of the American Shopping Center." *American Historical Review* 101 (4): 1111–1121.

Jacobson, Lisa. *Raising Consumers: Children, Childrearing, and the American Mass Market, 1890–1940*. New York: Columbia University Press.

Jaffee, David. 1986. "'A Correct Likeness': Culture and Commerce in Nineteenth-Century Rural America." In *Folk Art and Art Worlds*, ed. John Michael Vlach and Simon J. Bronner, 53–84. Ann Arbor, MI: UMI Press.

Jakle, John A. 2001. *City Lights: Illuminating the American Night*. Baltimore, MD: Johns Hopkins University Press.

Jellison, Katherine. 1988. "Women and Technology on the Great Plains, 1910–1940." *Great Plains Quarterly* 8 (3): 144–157.

Jenkins, Reese. 1975. *Images and Enterprise: Technology and the American Photographic Industry 1839 to 1925*. Baltimore, MD: Johns Hopkins University Press.

Kanigel, Robert. 1997. *The One Best Way: Frederick Winslow Taylor and the Enigma of Efficiency*. New York: Viking Press.

Kasson, John F. 1999 (1976). *Civilizing the Machine: Technology and Republican Values in America, 1776–1900*, rpt. ed. New York: Hill & Wang.

Kline, Ronald R. 2000. *Consumers in the Country: Technology and Social Change in Rural America.* Baltimore, MD: Johns Hopkins University Press.

Laird, Pamela. 2001. *Advertising Progress: American Business and the Rise of Consumer Marketing.* Baltimore, MD: Johns Hopkins University Press.

Lebergott, Stanley. 1993. *Pursuing Happiness: American Consumers in the Twentieth Century.* Princeton, NJ: Princeton University Press.

Lifshey, Earl. 1973. *The Housewares Story: A History of the American Housewares Industry.* Chicago: National Housewares Manufacturers Association.

Lohof, Bruce A. 1978. "Hamburger Stand: Industrialization and the American Fast Food Phenomenon." *Industrial Archaeology Review* [Great Britain] 2 (3): 265–276.

Long, Carolyn. 2001. *Spiritual Merchants: Religion, Magic, and Commerce.* Knoxville: University of Tennessee Press.

Lupton, Ellen, and J. Abbott Miller. 1996. *The Bathroom, the Kitchen and the Aesthetics of Waste: A Process of Elimination.* Cambridge, MA: MIT List Visual Arts Center; New York: Architectural Press.

Lury, Celia. 1996. *Consumer Culture.* New Brunswick, NJ: Rutgers University Press.

Luxenberg, Stan. 1985. *Roadside Empires: How the Chains Franchised America.* New York: Viking Penguin.

Marchand, Roland. 1986. *Advertising the American Dream: Making Way for Modernity, 1920–1940.* Berkeley: University of California Press.

Martin, Edgar W. 1942. *The Standard of Living in 1860: American Consumption Levels on the Eve of the Civil War.* Chicago: University of Chicago Press.

Matt, Susan J. 2002. *Keeping Up with the Joneses: Envy in American Consumer Society.* Philadelphia: University of Pennsylvania Press.

Mayo, James. 1993. *The American Grocery Store: The Business Evolution of an Architectural Space.* Westport, CT: Greenwood Press.

McClymer, John F. 1986. "Late Nineteenth-Century American Working Class Living Standards." *Journal of Interdisciplinary History* 17 (Autumn): 379–398.

McCusker, John J., and Russell R. Menard. 1985. *The Economy of British America, 1607–1789.* Chapel Hill: University of North Carolina Press.

McGaw, Judith. 1987. *Most Wonderful Machine: Mechanization and Social Change in Berkshire Paper Making, 1801–1885.* Princeton, NJ: Princeton University Press.

McGaw, Judith, ed. 1994. *Early American Technology: Making and Doing Things from the Colonial Era to 1850.* Chapel Hill: University of North Carolina Press.

McShane, Clay. 1995. *Down the Asphalt Path: The Automobile and the American City.* New York: Columbia University Press.

Melosi, Martin V. 1981. *Garbage in the Cities: Refuse, Reform, and the Environment, 1880–1980.* Chicago: Dorsey.

Miller, Daniel. 1987. *Material Culture and Mass Consumption.* London: Basil Blackwell.

Miller, H. Laurence, Jr. 1960. "A Note on Fox's Theory of Second-Hand Markets." *Economica* n.s. 27: 249–252.

Milner, Murray, Jr. 2004. *Freaks, Geeks, and Cool Kids: American Teenagers, Schools, and the Culture of Consumption.* New York: Routledge.

Modell, John. 1978. "Patterns of Consumption, Acculturation, and Family Income Strategy in Late-Nineteenth-Century America." In *Family and Population in Nineteenth-Century America*, ed. Tamara K. Hareven and Maris A. Vinovskis, 206–240. Princeton, NJ: Princeton University Press.

Monod, David. 1996. *Store Wars: Shopkeepers and the Culture of Mass Marketing, 1890–1939.* Toronto: University of Toronto Press.

Naim, Moises. 2005. *Illicit: How Smugglers, Traffickers and Copycats Are Hijacking the Global Economy.* New York: Doubleday.

Nelson, Christina H. 1984. *Directly from China: Export Goods for the American Market, 1784–1930.* Salem, MA: Peabody Museum of Salem.

Nickles, Shelley. 2002. "More is Better: Mass Consumption, Gender, and Class Identity in Postwar America." *American Quarterly* 54 (4): 581–622.

Nye, David E. 1990. *Electrifying America: Social Meanings of a New Technology, 1880–1940*. Cambridge, MA: MIT Press.

Nye, David E. 1997. *Consuming Power: A Social History of American Energies*. Cambridge, MA: MIT Press.

O'Barr, William. 1994. *Culture and the Ad: Exploring Otherness in the World of Advertising*. Boulder, CO: Westview Press.

Ogle, Maureen. 1992. *All the Modern Conveniences: American Household Plumbing, 1840–1890*. Baltimore, MD: Johns Hopkins University Press.

Oliver, Melvin L., and Thomas M. Shapiro. *Black Wealth, White Wealth: A New Perspective on Racial Inequality*. New York: Routledge.

Ott, Katherine, David Serlin, and Stephen Mihm. 2002. *Artificial Parts and Practical Lives: Modern Histories of Prosthetics*. New York: New York University Press.

Pearce, David. 1949. *The Development of the American Glass Industry*. Cambridge, MA: Harvard University Press.

Pendergast, Tom. 2000. *Creating the Modern Man: American Magazines and Consumer Culture, 1900–1950*. Columbia: University of Missouri Press.

Perkins, Edwin J. 1980. *The Economy of Colonial America*. New York: Columbia University Press.

Pfaffenberger, Bryan. 1992. "Social Anthropology of Technology." *Annual Review of Technology* 21: 495–516.

Pleck, Elizabeth H. 2000. *Celebrating the Family: Ethnicity, Consumer Culture, and Family Rituals*. Cambridge, MA: Harvard University Press.

Porter, Glenn, and Harold C. Livesay. 1971. *Merchants and Manufacturers: Studies in the Changing Structure of Nineteenth-Century Marketing*. Baltimore, MD: Johns Hopkins University Press.

Post, Robert C. 1996. *High Performance: The Culture and Technology of Drag Racing, 1950–1990*, rpt. ed. Baltimore, MD: Johns Hopkins University Press.

Potter, David. 1954. *A People of Plenty: Economic Abundance and the American Character*. Chicago: University of Chicago Press.

Quimby, Ian M.G., and Polly Anne Earl, eds. 1973. *Technological Innovation and the Decorative Arts*. Winterthur Conference Report. Charlottesville: University Press of Virginia.

Reichert, Tom. 2003. *The Erotic History of Advertising*. Amherst, NY: Prometheus.

Robbins, Paul, and Julie T. Sharp. 2003. "Producing and Consuming Chemicals: The Moral Economy of the American Lawn." *Economic Geography* 79 (4): 425–451.

Rutherford, Janice Williams. 2003. *Selling Mrs. Consumer: Christine Frederick and the Rise of Household Efficiency*. Athens: University of Georgia Press.

Salmon, Marylynn. 1986. *Women and the Law of Property*. Chapel Hill: University of North Carolina Press.

Samuel, Lawrence R. 2001. *Brought to You By: Postwar Television Advertising and the American Dream*. Austin: University of Texas Press.

Schiffer, Michael Brian. 1994. *Taking Charge: The Electric Automobile in America*. Washington, DC: Smithsonian Books.

Schivelbusch, Wolfgang. 1988. *Disenchanted Night: The Industrialization of Light in the Nineteenth Century*. Berkeley: University of California Press.

Schmidt, Leigh Eric. 1995. *Consumer Rites: The Buying and Selling of American Holidays*. Princeton, NJ: Princeton University Press.

Schor, Juliet. 2000. *Do Americans Shop Too Much?* Boston: Beacon Press.

Schor, Juliet B. 1999. *The Overspent American: Why We Want What We Don't Need*. New York: Harper.

Schor, Juliet B. 2004. *Born to Buy: The Commercialized Child and the New Consumer Culture*. New York: Scribner.

Schroeder, Fred E. H. 1986. "More Small Things Forgotten: Domestic Electric Plugs and Receptacles, 1881–1931." *Technology and Culture* 27 (3): 525–543.

Schudson, Michael. 1984. *Advertising, the Uneasy Persuasion: Its Dubious Impact on American Society.* New York: Basic Books.

Schumann, David W., and Esther Thorsen, eds. 1999. *Advertising and the World Wide Web.* Mahwah, NJ: Lawrence Erlbaum.

Scitovsky, Tibor. 1994. "Towards a Theory of Secondhand Markets." *Kyklos* 47: 33–52.

Scoville, Warren C. 1948. *Revolution in Glassmaking: Entrepreneurship and Technological Change in the American Industry, 1880–1920.* Cambridge, MA: Harvard University Press.

Segrave, Kerry. 2004. *Product Placement in Hollywood Films.* Jefferson, NC: McFarland.

Sellers, Charles. 1992. *The Market Revolution: Jacksonian America, 1815–1846.* New York: Oxford University Press.

Shammas, Carole. 1980. "The Domestic Environment in Early Modern England and America." *Journal of Social History* 14 (1): 3–24.

Shammas, Carole. 1990. *The Pre-Industrial Consumer in England and America.* Oxford, UK: Oxford University Press.

Simon, Linda. 2004. *Dark Light: Electricity and Anxiety from the Telegraph to the X-Ray.* New York: Harcourt.

Slaton, Amy E. 2001. *Reinforced Concrete and the Modernization of American Building, 1900–1930.* Baltimore, MD: Johns Hopkins University Press.

Smulyan, Susan. 1994. *Selling Radio: The Commercialization of American Broadcasting, 1920–1934.* Washington, DC: Smithsonian Institution Press.

Spurgeon, Anne M. 1988. "Marketing the Unmentionable: Wallace Meyer and the Introduction of Kotex." *Maryland Historian* 19 (1): 17–30.

Stage, Sarah, and Virginia Vicenti, eds. 1997. *Rethinking Home Economics: Women and the History of a Profession.* Ithaca, NY: Cornell University Press.

Stanley, Autumn. 1995. *Mothers and Daughters of Invention: Notes for a Revised History of Technology.* New Brunswick, NJ: Rutgers University Press.

Stephens, Carlene E. 1983. *Inventing Standard Time.* Washington, DC: National Museum of American History.

Stephens, Carlene, and Steven Lubar. 1986. "A Place for Public Business: The Material Culture of the Nineteenth-Century Federal Office." *Business and Economic History,* 2nd ser. 15: 165–179.

Strasser, Susan. 1982. *Never Done: A History of American Housework.* New York: Pantheon Books.

Strasser, Susan. 1989. *Satisfaction Guaranteed: The Making of the American Mass Market.* New York: Pantheon Books.

Strasser, Susan. 1999. *Waste and Want: A Social History of Trash.* New York: Metropolitan Books.

Strasser, Susan, ed. 2003. *Commodifying Everything: Relations of the Market.* New York: Routledge.

Strasser, Susan, Charles McGovern, and Matthias Judt, eds. 1988. *Getting and Spending: European and American Consumer Societies in the Twentieth Century.* Cambridge, UK: Cambridge University Press.

Tebbel, John. 1987. *Between Covers: The Rise and Transformation of Book Publishing in America.* New York: R. R. Bowker.

Tedlow, Richard S. 1990. *New and Improved: The Story of Mass Marketing in America.* Boston: Harvard Business School Press.

Temin, Peter. 1964. *Iron and Steel in Nineteenth-Century America: An Economic Inquiry.* Cambridge, MA: MIT Press.

Terry, Jennifer, and Melodie Calvert, eds. 1997. *Processed Lives: Gender and Technology.* London: Routledge.

Tierney, Thomas F. 1993. *The Value of Convenience: A Genealogy of Technical Culture.* Albany: State University of New York Press.

Tobey, Ronald C. 1996. *Technology as Freedom: The New Deal and the Electrical Mechanization of the American Home.* Berkeley: University of California Press.

Tom, Gail, Barbara Garibaldo, Yvette Zeng, and Julie Pilcher. 1998. "Consumer Demand for Counterfeit Goods." *Psychology & Marketing* 15 (5): 405–421.

Turner, E. S. 1953. *The Shocking History of Advertising.* New York: E. P. Dutton.

Van Orden, Kate, ed. 2000. *Music and the Cultures of Print*. New York: Garland Publishing.

Vinikas, Vincent. 1992. *Soft Soap, Hard Sell: American Hygiene in an Age of Advertisement*. Ames, IA: Iowa State University Press.

Walker, Lynne. 2002. "Home Making: An Architectural Perspective." *Signs* 27 (3): 823–835.

Walsh, Lorena S. 1983. "Urban Amenities and Rural Sufficiency: Living Standards and Consumer Behavior in the Colonial Chesapeake, 1643–1777." *Journal of Economic History* 43: 109–117.

Ward, Barbara McLean, ed. 1993. *Produce and Conserve, Share and Play Square: The Grocer and the Consumer on the Home-Front Battlefield during World War II*. Hanover, NH: University Press of New England.

Weil, Gordon L. 1977. *Sears, Roebuck, U.S.A.: The Great American Catalog and How It Grew*. New York: Stein & Day.

Wermiel, Sara E. 2000. *The Fireproof Building: Technology and Public Safety in the Nineteenth-Century City*. Baltimore, MD: Johns Hopkins University Press.

Williamson, Harold Francis, Arnold R. Daum, Gilbert C. Close, and Ralph L. Andreano. 1981. *The American Petroleum Industry: The Age of Illumination 1859–1899; The Age of Energy, 1899–1959*, rpt. ed. Westport, CT: Greenwood Press.

Woloson, Wendy. 2002. *Refined Tastes: Sugar, Confectionery, and Consumers in Nineteenth-Century America*. Baltimore, MD: Johns Hopkins University Press.

Wright, Helena E. 1986. "The Image Makers: The Role of the Graphic Arts in Industrialization." *Journal of the Society for Industrial Archaeology* 12 (2): 5–18.

Wright, Lawrence. 1960. *Clean and Decent: The Fascinating History of the Bathroom and the Water Closet and of Sundry Habits, Fashions, and Accessories of the Toilet, Principally in Great Britain, France, and America*. New York: Viking Press.

Wright, Richardson L. 1976 (1927). *Hawkers and Walkers in Early America*. New York: Arno Press.

Zboray, Ronald. 1996. "Books, Reading, and the World of Goods in Antebellum New England." *American Quarterly* 48 (4): 587–622.

Zelizer, Viviana A. 1994. *The Social Meaning of Money: Pin Money, Paychecks, Poor Relief, and Other Currencies*. New York: Basic Books.

Zimmerman, M. M. 1955. *The Supermarket: A Revolution in Distribution*. New York: McGraw-Hill.

Zmroczek, Christine. 1992. "Dirty Linen: Women, Class, and Washington Machines, 1920s–1960s." *Women's Studies International Forum* 15 (2): 173–185.

Collecting, Collections, Museums, Museum Studies, and Public History

Alderson, William T., and Shirley Payne Low. 1976. *Interpretation of Historic Sites*. Nashville, TN: American Association for State and Local History.

Alexander, Edward P. 1996. *Museums in Motion: An Introduction to the History and Functions of Museums*. Walnut Creek, CA: AltaMira Press.

Ames, Kenneth L., Barbara Franco, and L. Thomas Frye, eds. 1992. *Ideas and Images: Developing Interpretive History Exhibits*. Nashville, TN: American Association for State and Local History.

Anderson, Gail. 2004. *Reinventing the Museum: Historical and Contemporary Perspectives on the Paradigm Shift*. Walnut Creek, CA: AltaMira Press.

Anderson, Jay. 1991. *A Living History Reader. Volume One: Museums*. Nashville, TN: American Association of State and Local History.

Archibald, Robert R. 2004. *The New Town Square: Museums and Communities in Transition*. Walnut Creek, CA: AltaMira Press.

Asma, Stephen T. 2001. *Stuffed Animals and Pickled Heads: The Culture and Evolution of Natural History Museums*. New York: Oxford University Press.

Bal, Mieke. 1992. "Telling, Showing, Showing Off." *Critical Inquiry* 18 (3): 556–594.

Belk, Russell W. 1995. "Collecting as Luxury Consumption: Some Effects on Individuals and Households." *Journal of Economic Psychology* 16 (3): 477–490.

Belk, Russell W. 1995. *Collecting in a Consumer Society*. New York: Routledge.

Benjamin, Walter. 1968 (1931). "Unpacking My Library: A Talk About Book Collecting." In *Illuminations: Essays and Reflections*, ed. Hannah Arendt, trans. Harry Zohn, 59–68. New York: Schocken Books.

Bennett, Tony. 1995. *The Birth of the Museum: History, Theory, Politics*. London: Routledge.

Benson, Susan Porter, Stephen Brier, and Roy Rosenzweig, eds. 1986. *Presenting the Past: Essays on History and the Public*. Philadelphia: University of Pennsylvania Press.

Blatti, Jo, ed. 1987. *Past Meets Present: Essays about Historical Interpretation and Public Audiences*. Washington, DC: Smithsonian Institution Press.

Bond, Julian. 2003. "Julian Bond Responds." *Southern Cultures* 9 (1): 59.

Brigham, David R. 1995. *Public Culture in the Early Republic*. Washington, DC: Smithsonian Institution Press.

Burt, Nathaniel. 1977. *Palaces for the People: A Social History of the American Art Museum*. Boston: Little, Brown.

Casmier-Paz, Lynn. 2003. "Heritage, Not Hate? Collecting Black Memorabilia." *Southern Cultures* 9 (1): 43–58, 60–61.

Clifford, James. 1988. "On Collecting Art and Culture." In *The Predicament of Culture: Twentieth-Century Ethnography, Literature, and Art*. Cambridge, MA: Harvard University Press.

Conard, Rebecca. 2002. *Benjamin Shambaugh and the Intellectual Foundations of Public History*. Iowa City: University of Iowa Press.

Conn, Steven. 1998. *Museums and American Intellectual Life, 1876–1926*. Chicago: University of Chicago.

Cuno, James, ed. 2003. *Whose Muse? Art Museums and the Public Trust*. Princeton, NJ: Princeton University Press.

Dennett, Andrea Shulman. 1997. *Weird and Wonderful: The Dime Museum in America*. New York: New York University Press.

Dilworth, Leah, ed. 2003. *Acts of Possession: Essays on Collecting in America*. New Brunswick, NJ: Rutgers University Press.

Donnelly, Jessica Foy, ed. 2002. *Interpreting Historic House Museums*. Walnut Creek, CA: AltaMira Press.

Dubin, Steven C. 2000. *Displays of Power: Controversy in the American Museum from the Enola Gay to Sensation*. New York: New York University Press.

Edwards, Elizabeth, Ruth Phillips, and Chris Gordon, eds. 2006. *Sensible Objects: Colonialism, Museums, and Material Culture*. Oxford, UK: Berg.

Eichstedt, Jennifer L., and Stephen Small. 2002. *Representations of Slavery: Race and Ideology in Southern Plantation Museums*. Washington, DC: Smithsonian Institution Press.

Elsner, John, and Roger Cardinal, eds. 1994. *The Cultures of Collecting*. Cambridge, MA: Harvard University Press.

Fitz Gibbon, Kate, ed. 2005. *Who Owns The Past? Cultural Policy, Cultural Property, and the Law*. New Brunswick, NJ: Rutgers University Press in association with American Council for Cultural Policy.

Fleming, John E. 1994. "African-American Museums, History, and the American Ideal." *Journal of American History* 81 (3): 1020–1026.

Foote, Kenneth E. 2003 (1997). *Shadowed Ground: America's Landscapes of Violence and Tragedy*, rev. and updated ed. Austin: University of Texas Press.

Haas, Kristin. 1998. *Carried to the Wall: American Memory and the Vietnam Veterans Memorial*. Berkeley: University of California Press.

Haddow, Robert H. 1997. *Pavilions of Plenty: Exhibiting American Culture Abroad in the 1950s*. Washington, DC: Smithsonian Institution Press.

Handler, Richard, and Eric Gable. 1997. *The New History in an Old Museum: Creating the Past at Colonial Williamsburg*. Durham, NC: Duke University Press.

Haraway, Donna. 1986. "Teddy Bear Patriarchy: Taxidermy in the Garden of Eden, New York City, 1908–1936." *Social Text* 11 (Winter): 20–64.

Hayden, Dolores. 1995. *The Power of Place: Urban Landscapes as Public History*. Cambridge, MA: MIT Press.

Hooper-Greenhill, Eileen. 2001. *Museums and the Interpretation of Visual Culture*. London and New York: Routledge.

Hufbauer, Benjamin. 2005. *Presidential Temples: How Memorials and Libraries Shape Public Memory*. Lawrence: University Press of Kansas.

Jenkins, David. 1994. "Object Lessons and Ethnographic Displays: Museum Exhibitions and the Making of American Anthropology." *Comparative Studies in Society and History* 36 (2): 242–270.

Jones, Anna Laura. 1993. "Exploding Canons: The Anthropology of Museums." *Annual Review of Anthropology* 22: 201–220.

Karp, Ivan, Christine Mullen Kreamer, and Steven D. Lavine, eds. 1992. *Museums and Communities: The Politics of Public Culture.* Washington, DC: Smithsonian Institution Press.

Karp, Ivan, and Steven D. Lavine, eds. 1990. *Exhibiting Cultures: The Poetics and Politics of Museum Display.* Washington, DC: Smithsonian Institution Press.

Kirshenblatt-Gimblett, Barbara. 1998. *Destination Culture: Tourism, Museums, and Heritage.* Berkeley: University of California Press.

Kohlstedt, Sally Gregory. 1988. "Curiosities and Cabinets: Natural History Museums and Education on the Antebellum Campus." *Isis* 79 (3): 405–426.

Krill, Rosemary Troy, and Pauline K. Eversmann. 2001. *Early American Decorative Arts, 1620–1860: A Handbook for Interpreters.* Walnut Creek, CA: AltaMira.

Leon, Warren, and Roy Rosenzweig, eds. 1989. *History Museums in the United States: A Critical Assessment.* Urbana: University of Illinois Press.

Lewis, Catherine M. 2005. *The Changing Face of Public History: The Chicago Historical Society and the Transformation of an American Museum.* DeKalb: Northern Illinois University Press.

Linenthal, Edward Tabor. 1991. *Sacred Ground: Americans and Their Battlefields.* Urbana: University of Illinois Press.

Macleod, S. 2005. *Reshaping Museum Space: Architecture, Designs, Exhibitions.* London: Routledge.

Marstine, Janet, ed. 2005. *New Museum Theory and Practice: An Introduction.* London: Routledge.

Messenger, Phyllis Mauch. 1989. *The Ethics of Collecting Cultural Property: Whose Culture? Whose Property?* Albuquerque: University of New Mexico Press.

Mires, Charlene. 2002. *Independence Hall in American Memory.* Philadelphia: University of Pennsylvania Press.

Mitchell, Katharyne. 2003. "Monuments, Memorials, and the Politics of Memory." *Urban Geography* 24 (July): 442–459.

Montgomery, Elvin. 2001. *Collecting African American History: A Celebration of America's Black Heritage through Documents, Artifacts, and Collectibles.* New York: Stewart, Tabori & Chang.

Muensterberger, Werner. 1994. *Collecting, An Unruly Passion: Psychological Perspectives.* Princeton, NJ: Princeton University Press.

Myrone, Martin, and Lucy Peltz, eds. 1999. *Producing the Past: Aspects of Antiquarian Culture and Practice, 1700–1850.* Brookfield, VT: Ashgate.

Orosz, Joel J. 1990. *Curators and Culture: The Museum Movement in America, 1740–1870.* Tuscaloosa: University of Alabama Press.

Place, Linna Funk, et al. 1974. "The Object as Subject: The Role of Museums and Material Culture Collections in American Studies." *American Quarterly* 26: 281–294.

Purcell, Rosamund, and Stephen Jay Gould. 1992. *Finders, Keepers: Treasures and Oddities of Natural History.* New York: W. W. Norton.

Smith, Charlotte. 2002. "Civic Consciousness and House Museums: The Instructional Role of Interpretive Narratives." *Australasian Journal of American Studies* 21 (July): 74–88.

Stocking, George W., ed. 1985. *Objects and Others: Essays on Museums and Material Culture.* Madison: University of Wisconsin Press.

Sullivan, Lynne P., and S. Terry Childs. 2003. *Creating Archaeological Collections: From the Field to the Repository.* Walnut Creek, CA: AltaMira.

Wallis, Brian. 1997. "A Forum, Not a Temple: Notes on the Return of Iconography to the Museum." *American Literary History* 9 (3): 617–623.

Wallace, Mike. 1996. *Mickey Mouse History and Other Essays on American Memory.* Philadelphia, PA: Temple University Press.

Weil, Stephen E. 2002. *Making Museums Matter.* Washington, DC: Smithsonian Institution Press.

West, Patricia. 1999. *Domesticating History: The Political Origins of America's House Museums.* Washington, DC: Smithsonian Institution Press.

Wright, Helene E. 2004. "Print Collecting in the Gilded Age." *Imprint* 29 (1): 2–13.

Zimmerman, Ellen K. 2005. "Are Indians History? A Critical Review of Native American Museum Exhibits." *New England Journal of History* 62 (Fall): 14–39.

Historic Preservation and Materials Conservation

Alanen, Arnold R., and Robert Z. Melnick. 2000. *Preserving Cultural Landscapes in America.* Foreword by Dolores Hayden. Baltimore, MD: Johns Hopkins University Press.

Allen, Keith R., and Christian F. Ostermann. 2004. "Interpreting the Physical Legacy of the Cold War: A Conference Report." *Perspectives: American Historical Association Newsletter* 42 (6): 59–62.

Barthel, Diane. 1996. *Historic Preservation: Collective Memory and Historical Identity.* New Brunswick, NJ: Rutgers University Press.

Binetti, Timothy L. 2005. "Painting the Town Red, but Only Red! How Historic Preservation Ordinances Function as a Governmental Guise for the Censorship of the Arts." *Journal of Arts Management, Law, and Society* 34 (4): 262–284.

Birnbaum, Charles A., and Mary V. Hughes. 2005. *Design with Culture: Claiming America's Landscape Heritage.* Charlottesville: University Press of Virginia.

Bluestone, Daniel. 1999. "Academics in Tennis Shoes: Historic Preservation and the Academy." *Journal of the Society of Architectural Historians* 58 (3): 200–207.

Burns, John A., and the staff of the Historic American Buildings Survey, Historic American Engineering Record, and Historic American Landscapes Survey, National Park Service, U.S. Department of the Interior. 2004. *Recording Historic Structures,* 2nd ed. Hoboken, NJ: John Wiley & Sons.

Cullingworth, J. Barry. 1992. "Historic Preservation in the U.S.: From Landmarks to Planning Perspectives." *Planning Perspectives* 7 (1): 65–79.

DeOliver, Miguel. 1996. "Historical Preservation and Identity: The Alamo and the Production of a Consumer Landscape." *Antipode* 28 (1): 1–23.

Department of the Interior. 2004. *The Preservation of Historic Architecture: The United States Government's Official Guidelines for Preserving Historic Homes.* Guilford, CT: Lyons Press.

Dubrow, Gail, and Jennifer B. Goodman, eds. 2002. *Restoring Women's History through Historic Preservation.* Baltimore, MD: Johns Hopkins University Press.

Dubrow, Gail, and Donna Graves. 2004. *Sento at Sixth and Main: Preserving Landmarks of Japanese American History.* Washington, DC: Smithsonian Books.

Dunkerly, Robert M. 2002. "'Ritual Grounds of Reunion and Celebration': A History of Battlefield Preservation." *Journal of America's Military Past* 28 (3): 40–51.

Fitch, James Marston. 1990. *Historic Preservation: Curatorial Management of the Built World.* Charlottesville: University of Virginia Press.

Fletcher, Patsy M. 1996. "Historic Preservation and the African-American Community." *Afro-Americans in New York Life and History* 20 (2): 93–105.

Frank, Karolyn, and Patricia Peterson. 2002. *Historic Preservation in the USA.* New York: Springer.

Gulliford, Andrew. 2000. *Sacred Objects and Sacred Places: Preserving Tribal Traditions.* Boulder: University Press of Colorado.

Holleran, Michael. 1998. *Boston's Changeful Times: Origins and Preservation and Planning in America.* Baltimore, MD: Johns Hopkins University Press.

Hosmer, Charles B., Jr. 1981. *Preservation Comes of Age: From Williamsburg to the National Trust, 1926–1949.* Charlottesville: University Press of Virginia.

Hufford, Mary. 1994. *Conserving Culture: A New Discourse on Heritage.* Urbana: University of Illinois Press.

Jameson, John H., Jr. 2003. *The Reconstructed Past: Reconstructions in the Public Interpretation of Archaeology and History.* Walnut Creek, CA: AltaMira.

Jester, Thomas C., ed. 1995. *Twentieth-Century Building Materials: History and Conservation.* New York: McGraw-Hill.

King, Thomas F. 2002. *Thinking about Cultural Resource Management: Essays from the Edge.* Walnut Creek, CA : AltaMira Press.

Lindgren, James M. 1993. *Preserving the Old Dominion: Historic Preservation and Virginia Traditionalism.* Charlottesville: University Press of Virginia.

Lindgren, James M. 1995. *Preserving Historic New England: Preservation, Progressivism, and the Remaking of Memory.* New York: Oxford University Press.

Lockwood, Charles. 2003 (1972). *Bricks and Brownstone: The New York Row House, 1783–1929.* Rev. and updated ed. New York: Rizzoli International Publications.

Longstreth, Richard. 1999. "Architectural History and the Practice of Historic Preservation in the United States." *Journal of the Society of Architectural Historians* 58 (3): 326–333.

Martine, Jay C. 2004. "Beyond the Brow: Researching and Restoring Historic Ships." *Nautical Research Journal* 49 (1): 44–50.

Miller, Page Putnam. 1992. *Reclaiming the Past: Landmarks of Women's History.* Bloomington: Indiana University Press.

Minteer, Ben A., and Robert E. Manning, eds. 2003. *Reconstructing Conservation: Finding Common Ground.* Washington, DC: Island Press.

Moss, Roger W. 1981. *Century of Color: Exterior Decoration for American Buildings, 1820–1920.* Watkins Glen, NY: American Life Foundation.

Moss, Roger W., ed. 1994. *Paint in America: The Color of Historic Buildings.* Washington, DC: Preservation Press, National Trust for Historic Preservation.

Murtagh, William J. 1997. *Keeping Time: The History and Theory of Preservation in America,* rev. ed. New York: John Wiley & Sons.

Myers, Denys Peter. 1978. *Gaslighting in America: A Guide for Historic Preservation.* Washington, DC: Department of the Interior.

Nylander, Jane C. 1983. *Fabrics for Historic Buildings: A Guide to Selecting Reproduction Fabrics,* 3rd ed. Washington, DC: Preservation Press.

Odegaard, Nancy. 1995. "Artists' Intent: Material Culture Studies and Conservation." *Journal of the American Institute for Conservation* 34 (3): 187–193.

Pablo, Marcia. 2001. "Preservation as Perpetuation." *American Indian Quarterly* 25 (1): 18–20.

Page, Max, and Randall Mason, eds. 2003. *Giving Preservation a History: Histories of Historic Preservation in the United States.* New York: Routledge.

Seale, William. 1979. *Recreating the Historic House Interior.* Nashville, TN: American Association for State and Local History.

Sellars, Richard West. 1999. *Preserving Nature in the National Parks: A History.* New Haven, CT: Yale University Press.

Stapp, Carol B., and Kenneth C. Turino. 2004. "Does America Need Another House Museum?" *History News* 59 (2): 7–11.

Stipe, Robert E. 2004. *A Richer Heritage: Historic Preservation in the Twenty-First Century.* Chapel Hill: University of North Carolina Press.

Tschabrun, Susan. 2003. "Off the Wall and Into a Drawer: Managing a Research Collection of Political Posters." *American Archivist* 66 (2): 303–324.

Tyler, Norman. 1999. *Historic Preservation: An Introduction to Its History, Principles, and Practice,* 2nd ed. New York: W. W. Norton.

Waid, Jack. 2004. "Touch and Go in Uniforms in the Past." *Air Power History* 51 (1): 44–47.

Wanstein, Robert A., and Larry Booth. 1977. *Collection, Use, and Care of Historical Photographs.* Nashville, TN: American Association for State and Local History.

Winkler, Gail Caskey, and Roger W. Moss. 1986. *Victorian Interior Decoration: American Interiors 1830–1900.* New York: Henry Holt.

Index

About the Editors

Helen Sheumaker is a faculty member at Miami University of Ohio in the program in American Studies and serves as coordinator of museum education for the William Holmes McGuffey Museum of Miami University. She holds a Ph.D. in American studies from the University of Kansas. Her publications include the book *Love Entwined: The Curious History of Hair Work* (University of Pennsylvania Press, 2007) and articles on nineteenth-century sentimental consumerism and human hair work in *Commodifying Everything,* edited by Susan Strasser (Routledge, 2003), and in *Fashion Theory: The Journal of Body, Culture, and Dress* (1 [4]). She has received grants and fellowships from the Smithsonian Institution, Winterthur Museum, and Virginia Historical Society. Dr. Sheumaker has received grants from the American Studies Association, Minnesota Humanities Council, and Ohio Humanities Council to develop Web sites presenting student-created exhibits on community and local history.

Shirley Teresa Wajda teaches in the department of history at Kent State University, Kent, Ohio. She also serves as coordinator of the American Studies program. She received her doctorate in American civilization with a specialization in American material culture studies from the University of Pennsylvania. She has published in scholarly journals, essay collections, and exhibition catalogues on Martha Stewart, children's cabinets of curiosities, women philanthropists, and portraiture and photography. In 2001 she co-curated the exhibition "Designing Domesticity: Decorating the American Home since 1876" at the Kent State University Museum. Her current research project explores house building, housewares, and housekeeping in Depression-era America.